ORIGINAL NATURE

Also by the First Zen Institute:

The Zen Eye

Zen Pivots

Holding the Lotus to the Rock

Cat's Yawn

ORIGINAL NATURE

ZEN COMMENTS ON THE SIXTH PATRIARCH'S PLATFORM SUTRA

Translation And Commentary

By

SOKEI-AN SASAKI

Edited by

MARY FARKAS, ROBERT LOPEZ, PETER HASKEL

www.firstzen.org

First Zen Institute of America
New York

iUniverse, Inc.
Bloomington

ORIGINAL NATURE
Zen comments on the Sixth Patriarch's Platform Sutra

iUniverse books may be ordered through booksellers or by contacting:

iUniverse
1663 Liberty Drive
Bloomington, IN 47403
www.iuniverse.com
1-800-Authors (1-800-288-4677)

Because of the dynamic nature of the Internet, any web addresses or links contained in this book may have changed since publication and may no longer be valid. The views expressed in this work are solely those of the author and do not necessarily reflect the views of the publisher, and the publisher hereby disclaims any responsibility for them.

Any people depicted in stock imagery provided by Thinkstock are models, and such images are being used for illustrative purposes only.
Certain stock imagery © Thinkstock.

Cover art, The Sixth Patriarch by Chih-weng (D. 1263) by permission of Dai Tokyu Kinen Bunko.

ISBN: 978-1-4620-5317-9 (sc)
ISBN: 978-1-4620-5324-7 (ebk)

Printed in the United States of America

iUniverse rev. date: 05/21/2012

In the Memory of

Edna Kenton & **Mary Farkas**

ACKNOWLEDGMENTS

In addition to the notetakers mentioned in the introduction who were present at Sokei-an's talks, many others subsequently assisted in the completion of this manuscript. Mary Farkas inherited these cherished collections over the years and oversaw the transcription and collation of the various versions. The results were then published in the Institute's periodical, *Zen Notes*. Mary was helped at times by various dedicated individuals, among them Vanessa Coward, Francis Bahi, and Sandy Hackney. Preparation of the final manuscript for publication was done under the auspices of the Institute's publication committee, consisting of Bob Lopez, Peter Haskel, Michael Hotz, Ian Chandler, and Peeter Lamp, current editor of *Zen Notes*. Bob Lopez completed the bulk of the editorial work in preparing the manuscript for publication. Peter Haskel and John Storm edited the final draft. Peeter Lamp lent his considerable talent to the cover art, layout and computer-related aspects of the project. Michael Hotz, president of the Institute, coordinated the overall process.

Over the past seventy-five years, generations of American Zen students gave their time rescuing this manuscript. In return they gained some insight into the early Chinese Zen that Sokei-an felt would create a suitable foundation to accompany the transmission of Zen to America. Sokei-an spoke these commentaries and labored over his translations not just for the benefit of those who were present in the 1930's, but, as he put it, "to those future beings." We are grateful for these efforts and pass the discovery of 'original nature' on to you.

CONTENTS

I only transmit to you the law of seeing original nature,
Revealing myself in the world to destroy false ideas.

The Sixth Patriarch Hui-neng

I am of the Zen sect. My special mission is to train students of Buddhism by the Zen method. Nowadays, there are many types of Zen teachers. One type, for example, teaches Zen through philosophical discourse; another through so-called meditation; and still another directly from soul to soul. My way of teaching is the direct transmission of Zen from soul to soul.

Sokei-an

BY WAY OF AN INTRODUCTION
by Robert Lopez

Had she lived, Mary Farkas would have taken on the task of writing this introduction to Sokei-an's talks on the Sixth Patriarch's *Platform Sutra*. Mary, who passed away in June 1992, left it to us at the First Zen Institute to complete the work she began in 1938 when she became, as Sokei-an put it, a pillar of his temple. That temple was the Buddhist Society of America, now the First Zen Institute of America, founded in 1930 in New York City by Sokei-an.

Sokei-an translated and commented on the Sixth Patriarch's *Platform Sutra* for his American Zen students in 190 lectures, delivered between July 1935 and June 1939. The sutra, which purports to record the sermons of the Zen teacher Hui-neng (673-18), is an important scripture of early Zen Buddhism in China. Such subjects as "seeing into one's own original nature," "no thought," and "formlessness" still lie at the heart of this unique religion we call Zen.

In the weeks before Mary's death. many of us at the Institute spent long hours in the "abbot's" quarters sitting beside her on the wooden palanquin she called her bed. During one evening's conversation about the publication of Sokei-an's commentary, Mary turned to me excitedly, and said; "You know, don't you, we are presenting not only the sutra of the Sixth Patriarch but the sutra of Sokei-an to present the teaching of Sokei-an to the world."

One need only turn the pages of Sokei-an's magnificent translation and commentary to appreciate Mary's splendid notion. "It's all here," she would say, and her face would beam with an extraordinary happiness as she perused her teacher's commentary. Nevertheless, Mary did not complete an introduction for this volume, so we must do without it, and to my sorrow, without her.

As Mary grew increasingly aware of her age, she became preoccupied with insuring that her work at the Institute would be carried on by its members; and, as I had assisted her for several years preparing the Institute's periodical, *Zen Notes,* editing the Sixth Patriarch manuscript, and compiling the first book of Sokei-an's talks, *The Zen Eye (*New York: Weatherhill, 1993), she asked me to continue with the effort she had begun so many decades before, that of getting Sokei-an into print. So, in accordance with her wishes, I have taken it upon myself to write this introduction.

Sokei-an Shigetsu Sasaki was born in the old Japanese province of Sanuki, on March 10, 1882, the son of a samurai named Tsunamichi Sasaki. Once a retainer of the Takamatsu clan, Tsunamichi became a successful Shinto scholar, teacher, and "missionary" during the Meiji period (1868-1912). Tsunamichi and his wife, Kitako Kubota, named their son Yeita. Yeita, however, was not the biological son of Kitako. His actual mother was said to be a concubine named Chiyoko. Why Tsunamichi and Kitako secured Chiyoko to bear them a son sired by Tsunamichi is not clear, but Sokei-an would remain their only child.

Sokei-an attended the usual primary and middle schools. After his father's death in 1897, Sokei-an went to Yokohama and apprenticed himself to a craftsman who specialized in exterior temple carvings. In 1898, Sokei-an walked through what he called the "Japanese Alps," supporting himself by putting into service the tools he had used as an apprentice. Traveling from one temple to another asking for restoration work, he earned about thirty-five cents a day. Later that year, Sokei-an returned to Tokyo and his widowed mother.

In 1899 Sokei-an entered the Imperial Academy of Art in Tokyo where he studied sculpture under the famous artist Takamura Koun (1852-1934). In the evenings and on holidays, Sokei-an worked in a post office. In 1903, Sokei-an had begun to study with the Zen master Sokatsu Shaku (1870-1954) at Ryomo Kyokai, or Society for the Abandonment of Subjectivity and Objectivity, whose headquarters was in Nippori on the outskirts of Tokyo. The Ryomo Kyokai was founded in 1875 by the celebrated Rinzai Zen master Imakita Kosen (1816-1892) for the establishment and practice of "lay" Zen. Sokatsu had been appointed head of Ryomo Kyokai by Kosen's famous senior heir and student Soyen Shaku (1859-1919) following Sokatsu's return from a pilgrimage in South Asia. Sokei-an describes what it was like for students at Ryomo-an.

> . . . At the time, the disciples of Sokatsu Shaku were, for the most part, university students and young doctors, with a sprinkling of members of the nobility. The farmhouses of Nippori village were favorite lodging places for the university students who came from all parts of Japan. The village itself was quiet but not too far from the city universities, and the households of the farmers afforded both pleasant and inexpensive living.
>
> In rain and snow, or in fine weather, at six o'clock in the morning we students were assembled waiting for the gate of Ryomo-an to open. Quietly, we would enter the temple and, sitting together in the big room which served as our zendo, we would practice meditation after the fashion of the sodo or monastery monks. At seven o'clock sanzen, catechism, began. One by one we would enter our teacher's room to answer the koan, or zen question, which he had previously given to each of us. After sanzen, we would quietly leave the temple, returning home for breakfast and then on to to our nine o'clock classes at school. Sunday passed as other days, except that our Roshi, our Zen teacher, gave a lecture, or teisho, which we were all expected to attend.[1] . . .

Soyen Shaku, abbot of Engakuji in Kamakura, was well known for having visited the United States in 1893 as part of a delegation of Buddhists to the World Parliament of Religions in Chicago. When a friend of Sokei-an's, a sculptor named Unkyo Goto, introduced him to Soyen, Sokei-an was taken aback:

> . . . The first moment of this interview, the Abbot's two shining eyes pierced my mind through and through. I stood in silence, aghast! The Abbot questioned me about what I wished to become. I replied, "I am studying art." "What art are you studying? "I am learning how to carve Buddhist statues."" "Who is your teacher?" "Koun Takamura." He looked into my eyes again and said, "Carve a Buddha statue for me when you become a famous artist." And he gave us tea and cakes.[2] . . .

Later, Sokatsu asked Sokei-an to carve a him a buddha. But when Sokei-an brought it to him, Sokatsu threw it out his window into a pond. Sokei-an later said, "*It seemed unkind, but it was not. He meant me to carve the Buddha in myself.*"

In April 1905, he graduated from the Academy of Art and was immediately drafted into the Japanese Imperial Army. Serving as a corporal in the transportation corps during the Russo-Japanese War (1904-1905), he drove a dynamite truck on the Manchurian front, an experience he would frequently refer to in his commentaries. Before his discharge, Sokei-an started a theater for the soldiers. He not only painted scenery and wrote plays; he acted in the productions as well. In 1906 he was demobilized, and a few months later found himself following his Zen teacher to America.

Having recently married one of the Zen students at Ryomo Kyokai at his teacher's urging, Sokei-an arrived in the United States on September 8, 1906 with his wife, Tome, Sokatsu, and a group of students Sokatsu hoped would form the nucleus of a Zen community on a small parcel of land he had purchased in Hayward, California. Sokatsu expected his community of students to cultivate the land and become self-sufficient. But when their first crop failed, Sokei-an said the neighboring farmers made fun of their produce. Sokei-an confronted Sokatsu on the practicality of using "monks, artists, and philosophers" in such an undertaking. An argument ensued and Sokei-an left. After it became clear the Hayward settlement would not succeed, Sokatsu opened a Zen center on Sutter Street in San Francisco. Sokei-an was already in the city studying at the California Institute of Art with Richard Partington, a well known portrait painter. But Sokatsu's venture in San Francisco faltered as well, and in 1910 he returned to Japan with his disciples. Sokei-an remained. He later recalled his feelings about Sokatsu's departure:

> . . . *When I lost my teacher (he went back to Japan), I was left alone in this country. I had no one to follow, and I began to meditate upon the five skandhas. Samsara—I could not understand it! Then one day I took my dog to the beach: he barked at the waves as they rolled in on the beautiful ocean strand. I realized that all this was reflected in the mind of my dog; I felt it in the dog's samsara and expressed it. I meditated upon samsara for many months. I watched the autumn foliage leave the trees. One leaf on a treetop waved to me like a hand—"I am going away, I am going away. Goodbye, winter has come!" Samsara.[3] . . .*

That year a son, Shintaro, was born to Tome and Sokei-an. A daughter, Seiko, followed two years later. Sokei-an supported his family by repairing art with the woodcarving tools he had cherished since age fifteen. In 1916 Tome, pregnant with a second daughter, who would be named Shihiko, returned to Japan with Shintaro and Seiko. Neither Tome nor Shihiko would ever return to the United States. Sokei-an missed his family and would see the face of his little boy behind the top of every bush. Following his family's departure, Sokei-an decided to leave San Francisco with the aim of seeing the United States.

> . . . *Alone in America, I conceived the idea of going about the United States on foot. In February 1911, I crossed the Shasta Mountains through the snow into Oregon. On the hillside of the Rogue River Valley was the farm of an old friend. He asked me to stay with him for a while. Summer came with the month of May. I began again my practice of meditation. Every evening I used to walk along the riverbed to a rock chiseled by the current during thousands of years. Upon its flat surface I would practice meditation through the night, my dog at my side protecting me from the snakes. The rock is still there.*
>
> *For several years I led a wandering life, finally reaching the city of New York. My carving tools, cherished from the age of fifteen, provided me with a hand-to-mouth livelihood. One day all of a sudden, I realized that I must see my teacher. I packed up my things and in October, 1919, left New York.[4] . . .*

A more vivid account of the circumstances of Sokei-an's departure for Japan was offered by his second wife, Ruth Fuller Sasaki.[5]

> *Sokei-an went to New York and lived in Greenwich Village and got to know some of the poets of those days. He knew Maxwell Bodenheim, with whom he translated poems for the* Little Review. *Another person he knew was [Aleister] Crowley. And while his interest in Zen kept on, during this period he was finding out a lot about life, And then in 1919, on an awfully, awfully hot day in July he was walking down the street and suddenly in the street he saw the carcass of a dead horse, and something happened to him psychologically and he went straight home to his rooms and packed up his things and got a ticket for Japan and went back to Sokatsu.*[6]

On March 28, 1922, after an intense period of Zen study, Sokatsu granted Sokei-an *inka.* a Zen master's seal of approval authenticating a student's experience of realization. Returning to the United States in September 1922, Sokei-an once again settled in New York City, resuming his art restoration work and his literary efforts. Sokei-an wrote and published four volumes of essays on his experiences with the character of Americans. These volumes had tittles like, *America a Land Troubled by Money and Women.* During this second stay in New York, he began to give lectures on Buddhism at the invitation of the Orientalia bookstore, on East 58th Street opposite the Plaza Hotel. Four years later, summoned by Sokatsu, Sokei-an returned to Japan and resumed his Zen study. Meanwhile, a committee of American and Japanese Buddhists had sent a letter to Sokatsu formally requesting that Sokei-an be appointed teacher for their group in New York.

> *We know the reputation of Shigetsu Sasaki Koji who once taught here and inspired enthusiasm among Japanese as well as American Buddhists, who were deeply impressed with his splendid teachings. His vast knowledge of English, Sanskrit, Chinese, and Japanese, coupled with his remarkable understanding of social conditions in this county, fit him for a return here in this capacity. May we then urge his visit to this country even if only for a brief period, say, six or eight months, so that we could continue our study of Dharma with his invaluable aid?*[7]

In his reply to the New York group in May 1928, Sokatsu wrote: "Shigetsu Koji will come to you not only as one of the officials of our associated temples, but also in the capacity of Reverend, and assume the responsibilities of opening the American Branch of the Ryomo Society." In July 1928 Sokei-an received formal certification as a teacher and missionary to the United States for the Ryomo Society. In August, when Sokei-an arrived in New York, the committee sent an ecstatic letter to Sokatsu thanking him and informing him of Sokei-an's arrival. But the New York group did not live up to its promise. Their interest had so seriously waned that after a short time Sokei-an just disappeared. Now and then, he said, he "busied himself preaching the Dharma in various quarters."

> *When [Sokei-an] went back again to New York in 1928. [Ruth Sasaki noted,] he felt he was completely alone with nothing but his Zen. His teacher had told him that now his life was to be devoted to teaching Zen and no more to earning his living by some other manner and toying with Zen on the side, and so at first he didn't know quite what to do. He didn't have any group to go to. He was more or less alone. He had a commission from some magazine or newspaper . . . to write a series of articles on the various foreign people who lived in New York City and made up its population. So instead of going back to Greenwich Village and picking up that type of friend and acquaintance again he lived for two or three months apiece with an Italian family, a Portuguese*

family, and eventually a Negro family. I don't know how many others, but the Negro family was the last, and then he was forced to do something to eat and he went to Mr. Mataichi Miya, of the Yamanaka Company, for antique furniture. Whether he had known him previously, or how he got to know him I don't exactly know, but at any rate, Mr. Miya was very interested in Zen and had studied Zen previously, and so he gave Sokei-an $500 and went around and hunted for a place for him to live and to begin to give his lectures." [8]

At some time, after he received his appointment from the Ryomo Society, Sokei-an decided that if he was to make any headway with Americans, it was essential he become a priest. He, therefore, arranged to become a disciple of Master Aono Futetsu, abbot of Manmanji, a branch of the famous headquarters temple Daitokuji. On March 15, 1933, Sokei-an formally received the precepts and the religious name Soshin and moved up through the ranks at Daltokuji. All of this, through a complex but accepted procedure, was carried out while Sokei-an remained in New York.

Sokei-an's ordination as a priest very much displeased Sokatsu. Sokatsu would have preferred that Sokei-an remain a lay teacher. Indeed, Kosen and Sokatsu's original intention in creating and maintaining the Ryomo Society had been to establish a lineage based squarely on lay practice and represented by lay teachers. On February 15, 1930, with the support of his many Japanese and American friends, Sokei-an finally opened the Buddhist Society of America at 63 West 70th Street, situated a block from one of his favorite New York City locales, Central Park. From 1929 until September 1941, 63 West 70th Street not only served as the headquarters of the Buddhist Society of America but as Sokei-an's place of residence.[9] On December 7th, 1941, the day of the Japanese attack on Pearl Harbor, the Buddhist Society moved into its new quarters at Ruth Fuller's home at 124 East 65th Street. As Ruth recalled, disaster loomed on the horizon for the Institute, and for Sokei-an:

> *. . . From that time on, of course for months we didn't know it, but there were two FBI people under the present apartment verandah twenty-four hours a day. Mr. Sasaki was interviewed many times by the FBI, and so was I; but the meetings were permitted to be continued until June. On the 15th of June, 1942, he gave his last talk; and the next day he was taken and was interned.*[10] *. . .*

After 36 years in the United States, Sokei-an was arrested as an enemy alien and sent to Ellis Island, New York. In October 1942, he was transferred to Fort Meade, an internment camp near Baltimore, Maryland. Sokei-an was shocked by the actions of his adopted country. Many of the letters he sent from Ellis Island are heartbreaking; others are funny. In a 1942 letter to Ruth Everett, Sokei-an observed, "The Island is shrouded in drizzling rain. Avalokitesvara weeps over me today . . . . I am waiting for Alice in the wonderland to come."

After spending close to a year in the Maryland internment camp, Sokei-an was finally released by the government in August 1943 following a vigorous campaign mounted on his behalf by several of his American students. Sokei-an returned to Manhattan, and the following year he traveled with Ruth Everett to Little Rock, Arkansas, to obtain a divorce from his first wife, Tome, and to marry Ruth. Sokei-an's arrest effectively ended his "formal" teaching career, but he would continue to give *sanzen* until his death twenty-one months later. On May 17, 1945, he died from a variety of complications due to high blood pressure, passing away in his apartment on 65th Street surrounded by his wife and friends. Shortly before his death, Sokei-an made a request of Mary Farkas, who wrote:

When Sokei-an overstayed his leave in this world according to his own calculations, that is, outlived the day he predicted for his own death, he asked me, somewhat jokingly, to give him a new name, as he said this was the custom. I racked my mind for a name for this great and wonderful person who was my teacher, warm and close as a member of my family from one point of view, remote as the final nirvana he was about to enter from another. Only one name came to my mind: "Tigerheart." He accepted this as quite appropriate, and a few weeks later he was gone.[1]

When Sokei-an sat before his Zen students in his Manhattan studio in the summer of 1935, he was giving the first English commentary on one of Buddhism's most popular and enduring works of religious literature. In the remarks with which he introduced the celebrated fourth chapter of the Sixth Patriarch's *Sutra*, "Samadhi and Prajna," Sokei-an expressed his astonishment and delight that the words of the Sixth Patriarch were being presented in America.

I think the Sixth Patriarch never dreamed his record, and especially this chapter, would be explained to Westerners in New York. Reading this chapter, I feel that I am in a valley between huge mountains, and that the ancient simpleminded woodcutters, fishermen, monks, and nuns who are living in these mountains have come to the place where they always make their gatherings, and that I am one of them now.

In fact, it is a wonder that we have this record today. It is surely a testimony to the affection Sokei-an's students had for him that they preserved so accurately and conscientiously this work, which took four years for Sokei-an to complete, and which has taken nearly fifty years to find its way into our own hands. In a 1941 letter to a friend, Sokei-an described the difficulty of transmitting Buddhism to Americans:

In New York, my work is somewhat taking root in the mind of several Americans. I am encouraged. As we say, it is like transplanting the lotus to the stones. This means that Buddhism is a slow-growing religion and hard to take root in peoples' minds. Of course, Buddhism is not a weed. It is a huge tree. It is very slow to take root and very slow to grow. The Buddhism which is carried into this country, especially among Japanese, I do not consider to be a religion for Americans. But the Buddhism which touches the American mind is that which teaches simplicity, without any Amida Buddha or any personage to be worshipped.[12]

Few of Sokei-an's talks were ever written out by him. For Mary Farkas, his impromptu, extemporaneous talks "transcended the spoken word." She recalled her first meeting with him at the Buddhist Society:

. . . One evening it happened to be June 22, 1938, I entered a room at the main floor front of 63 West 70th Street, New York City . . . . Promptly at 8:30 a lady with large brimming eyes reminiscent of a character in Swann's Way . . . took a position at the reading desk and announced that Samanna Sokei-an Sasaki . . . would read a translation he had made from the Sutra of the Sixth Patriarch of Zen in China and comment upon it. Thereupon a rather large Japanese, robed as a priest, entered through a pair of sutra-papered doors at the north end of the room and performed a brief ceremony that included the burning of incense and chanting. At its conclusion, he seated himself at a reading desk on which were, in addition to his manuscript written in red Chinese characters, a ceremonial

fly whisk, a crystal glass, and a curious scepterlike object with an involute top. We then observed a period of silence, during which he sat before us like an image on a mountaintop. To tell the truth, it was more like a mountain, if a man may be said to be like a mountain, in huge immobility.[13]

Sokei-an never intended to work over his hundreds of talks, lectures, and commentaries. In his commentary on the closing chapter of the Sixth Patriarch's *Sutra* Sokei-an says, "I hope after my death someone will publish this translation in a book for future Zen students." He wanted his American students to create his "record," much as the Zen records of past masters were created by their disciples. Although early models of the tape recorder were available in the thirties and forties, Sokei-an's students did not use them. Every lecture he gave of which a record remains was recorded by one or more of his students who were present. The notes were typed, and then typed once again, one under the other, very much like the text of a chorale or cantata, so that they would all coalesce into a seamless record of the evening's presentation, recreating Sokei-an's voice through a sort of common consent.

In the early forties, however, at the behest of Ruth Fuller Everett, Sokei-an did begin to write out a commentary on the *Record of Lin-chi* and in 1940-41 he composed articles for his newsletter, *Cat's Yawn*, dealing with the history of his lineage and the particulars of Zen training. Besides the lectures he gave at the Buddhist Society, Sokei-an also spoke at other religious organizations in the Boston and New York City area, including some black churches in Harlem.

In the early thirties, two of Sokei-an's longtime Zen students, Audrey Kepner and Edna Kenton, were the principal note takers. Edna, whom Sokei-an said he "used like an old shoe," was a playwright and author, as well as the Buddhist Society's archivist, historian, and treasurer. Audrey Kepner, the recording secretary of the society, was a retired high school history teacher who helped Sokei-an with his English and assisted him with his first major translation.[14] Audrey began studying with Sokei-an in 1930, Edna in 1933. Mary Farkas, sometime after her own arrival in 1938, joined the groups that met to compile and edit Sokei-an's lectures. Other note takers included George Fowler, Jan Welsh, Frieda Stern, Winifred Bartlett, and beginning in 1939, Ruth Fuller and Mary Farkas. These notes are available in the Institute's archives. It was from these edited versions that Mary prepared the final form of Sokei-an's lectures for *Zen Notes*. Mary wrote about this process in response to a query about how she assembled a Sokei-an article.

> *... The notes were taken by a writer, Edna Kenton, and a school teacher, Audrey Kepner, whose major interest was comparative philosophy and religion. Their accuracy is judged three ways: by each other; by the facts ascertainable elsewhere; by agreement with statements made by Sokei-an on other occasions.*
>
> *Our first step is to try to find out what Sokei-an said. After a collation sheet is made, in this case from two persons, sometimes from more, a rough draft is made . . . . It should be Sokei-an's actual words, as nearly as possible. His English was, of course, not English, but reading his actual words, as he habitually used them, in many different cases, gives a clearer sense of what he had in mind than a completely polished version of what anyone else believes he meant. It is therefore his sense I try to find, not just a sense. This can only be determined by acquaintance with his thinking.*[15]

When Edna Kenton died in 1954 at the age of 78, Mary Farkas inherited the mantle of Sokei-an's "editor." Edna had doggedly safeguarded his lectures from the beginning of his career at 70th Street, and was a principal note taker for the Sixth Patriarch's *Sutra*. But it was Mary who seized the opportunity of rescuing Sokei-an from his students' notebooks and began publishing the edited articles in *Zen Notes*. That is why Mary shares the dedication with Edna, Sokei-an's "Iron Mortar," his name for his cherished student and friend.

We have retained the original format in which the translation was read and then lines of the text were repeated as Sokei-an gave his commentary. Sokei-an's individual lectures have been marked off by a lotus icon, a design derived from the master's personal copy of the Taisho Tripitaka. This format keeps the work in its original context. It was never a book, but a rolling introduction to Zen for new people who came, as well as the ongoing story of the Sixth Patriarch.

Sokei-an was intensely attracted to the Sixth Patriarch's *Sutra* and as a Zen student would carry it with him everywhere he went. Indeed, his special affection for the text played an important role in the acquisition of his name. In 1932, in a reply to a letter from the American Buddhist Dwight Goddard, Sokei-an explains the origin of his religious names, Shigetsu and Sokei-an.

> *To come to your question about "Anja* Shigetsu." Anja *means the laborer in the temple, one who polishes the rice, or picks up the kindling wood from the mountain, or brings water from the pool, or does all the hard labor for the monks. He is not of the same rank as a monk but lives in the temple community, observing the same commandments as does the novice.*
>
> *The Sixth Patriarch of China was an* anja. *We call him Lu* Anja *because his lay name was Lu. He Succeeded to the torch of Zen from the Fifth Patriarch and went to the southern part of China. While he was concealing his effulgence, he still called himself Lu* Anja. *I was also in the temple of my teacher. I was born a samurai. My father became a Shinto priest after the old form of feudal government in Japan passed away. At the time of his death. I was fifteen years of age. At the age of twenty years, I became a disciple of my teacher, leaving to my mother my father's scanty property, but I did not shave my head, being accepted in the temple as an* anja. *Until I was ordained as a Zen master, I was an* anja, *so I called myself* Anja Shigetsu. *Shigetsu is the name my teacher gave me as a Zen novice. "Shi* is to point out with [the] finger; "getsu" *means moon. "To point out the moon" means a sutra, because a sutra points out the moon of the soul, but no one sees a moon but sees a finger, just as when pointing out food to a dog, he sees not the food but your finger. I was taking the philosophy of Buddhism very seriously but did not know the moon of the soul to which the philosophy was pointing, so my teacher called me "moon pointer who does not know to what he is pointing." When I was ordained, he said, "After all, that blind finger was a moon."*
>
> *"Sokei-an" is the name of my hermitage that I am supposed to have—given by my teacher to me as an ordained one. "An" means hermitage. "Sokei" is the Japanese pronunciation of "Ts'ao-ch'i," the Chinese name of a place in which the Sixth Patriarch of China was living. There are not many* anjas *who have become ordained Zen masters, [though] there were several in the lineage of the Zen torch bearers. But an* anja *like myself, holding the reflection of the moon, ordained as Zen master and striving not to lose it, is an omen of the decline of Zen in the Orient, alas!*

Sokei-an's intention to personally introduce his students to the tenets of the Buddhist "canon," as he called it, through his weekly meetings made it imperative that he translate the selected materials himself. This he did from his complete edition of the Taisho Tripitaka, the multi-volume collection of Buddhist texts in Chinese that had been recently published in Japan and was donated to the Buddhist Society in 1930 by Sokei-an's admirer and friend Kazuo Kawazuchi.

Sokei-an's translations and commentaries provided his American students with an authentic context for their faith as Buddhists; and his *sanzen*, the "face-to-face," or "mind-to-mind" encounter between master and student, provided them with the core of Zen itself, the perspective of what he called their "original aspect."

Sokei-an spoke in a natural manner, free of pretension, ostentation, or artifice. He learned his English in the farmlands and cities of the West and the apartments of Harlem and Greenwich Village in the East. He told his students that he was "from Missouri" and had to be *shown* the answers to the koans he assigned them. Sokei-an's talks are filled with the intimate details of his life in America and Japan. He comments upon the triumphs and frailties of human nature in a profusion of anecdotes and tall tales of every variety. His examples, drawn from his own experiences with his family, friends, students, and teachers, as well as the turbaned gurus of his day, are told in a voice that is remarkably perceptive and delightfully frank.

Sokei-an's talks can be understood by anyone. They require no special training or education. You needn't know much about Buddhism or Zen to ride the wave of his commentary. Speaking from the platform of the Sixth Patriarch, Sokei-an expresses his inmost nature without restraint or reservation. "For Zen students," he said, "the conclusion of Zen is daily life, and it is not so easy to come to this. Then there is one more stage, art; the art of life."

[1] For a full-length biography of Sokei-an, readers should consult *Holding the Lotus to the Rock, The Autobiography of America's First Zen Master* (New York:Four Walls Eight Windows, 2002).

[2] *Cat's Yawn*, (New York: The First Zen Institute of America, 1947). 1, p.19; Ibid., p.3.

[3] Unpublished commentary on the *Sutra of Perfect Awakening*, November 1. 1939.

[4] *Cat's Yawn*, p.23.

[5] Sokei-an and Ruth Fuller Everett were married in 1944. In 1958 Ruth Sasaki was appointed Priest of the Rinzai Zen Temple Ryosen-an at Daitokuji in Kyoto. At Ryosen-an she was given permission to open the First Zen Institute of America in Japan for westerners who wished to study Zen.

[6] *Wind Bell* (Zen Center of San Francisco), "Excerpts from 'Our Lineage,' by Shigetsu Sasaki Roshi, with comments by Ruth Fuller Sasaki and Gary Snyder. Volume VIII, Number 102 (Fall 1969), p.13. The "excerpts" of the title were taken from *Cat's Yawn*.

[7] *Zen Notes*, Volume XXVII, Number 7 (July 1981).

[8] *Wind Bell*, p.14.

[9] See Mary Farkas's introduction and appendix in *The Zen Eye* for more details on Sokei-an and the Buddhist Society during the thirties and forties.

[10] *Wind Bell*, p.15.

[11] Unpublished notes on Sokei-an by Mary Farkas.

[12] Letter to a Mrs. Wills dated February 10, 1941.

[13] Unpublished notes on Sokei-an by Mary Farkas.

[14] *Ananda and MahaKasyapa. From the Chinese Version of the Sutras of Buddhism.* Sokei-an Sasaki. trans. (New York: C.M. Neumann, 1931).

[15] Letter dated February 15, 1961.

A NOTE ON THE TRANSLATION
by Peter Haskel

The *Sixth Patriarch's Platform Sutra* is probably the most celebrated of Zen (C. Ch'an) classics. It is the only record of a Zen master that bears the title of sutra, a designation usually reserved for works purporting to record the words of the Buddha himself, and the only sutra with a distinctly Chinese (rather than Indian) setting. In addition, the heroic image of the Sixth Patriarch presented in the *Platform Sutra* has in many ways been central to the development of the Zen school over the centuries, and is likely to remain so as long as the Zen tradition itself continues. Yet, in reality, we know little or nothing of the actual Sixth Patriarch or of the origin of the work that bears his name.

The Sixth Patriarch's *Platform Sutra* claims to record the biography and teachings of the Zen master Hui-neng (683-713), an illiterate peddler of brushwood who joins the assembly of the Fifth Zen Patriarch, Hung-jen (601-674), ultimately succeeds to his teachings, and becomes the founder of the "Southern School" of Zen. The historical record, however, remains scant and inconclusive, providing little support for the events and views found in the text. Indeed, despite considerable scholarly research and debate, virtually nothing can be said with certainty about either the historical Hui-neng or the character of his teaching.

Chinese, Japanese, and Western scholars generally agree that the original form of the text was set down during the late Tang dynasty, probably in the late eighth or early ninth centuries. But the identity of the sutra's original author(s) or compiler(s), their backgrounds and motivations, are unclear. In searching for clues, certain scholars have focused on the school of Hui-neng's Dharma heir Ho-tse Shen hui (670-762), whose recorded sermons bear a marked resemblance to the teachings attributed to the Sixth Patriarch in the *Platform Sutra*, suggesting that the Sixth Patriarch's record as we have it may be largely the creation of Shen-hui and his followers, an attempt to enhance their standing among the Zen schools of the day by acclaiming Hui-neng the sole legitimate successor to the patriarchate. Others have recently sought to establish the sutra's origins in the Niu-t'ou, or Ox-Head school, a school of Zen active in southern China during the late Tang, arguing that the teachings that form the core of the *Platform Sutra* are the product of this school and originally bore no relationship whatever to Hui-neng, having been simply appropriated to him by Shen-hui's followers, who then revised and expanded the text, adding their own material.

While Sokei-an, working in the mid 1930's, was cognizant of certain aspects of the debate surrounding the origins of the *Platform Sutra*, his relation to the sutra and to the Sixth Patriarch was clearly that of a Zen teacher, not a historian, and the truths that concerned him in approaching the text were religious rather than factual in nature. Sokei-an's was not the first English translation of the sutra. It was preceded by the 1930 translation of the Chinese scholar Wong Mou-lam,[1] and has been joined since by a number of other translations. However, Sokei-an's was the first and to my knowledge remains the only complete translation of, and commentary on, the sutra to be directly presented in a Western language by an authenticated Asian Zen master (a master being the only person authorized within the Zen school to comment on a Zen text). This project, in turn, formed part of Sokei-an's broader program in introducing Zen to America. As the first Rinzai master to settle permanently in the United States, Sokei-an wished to give his American students access to the original Tang Zen texts, which, he believed, embodied the roots of the Zen experience itself. By contrast, in his talks Sokei-an never expressed the slightest interest in the works of Japanese Zen teachers, medieval or modern, but focused on the records of Zen's Chinese founders, such as his namesake, the Sixth Patriarch Hui-neng, the central figure of the *Platform Sutra*.

Sokei-an based his translation on the *Liu-tsu ta-shih fa-pao t' an-ching* (*The Sixth Patriarch's Treasure of Dharma Platform Sutra*) sometimes referred to as the "Yuan" or "Ming" text. The 1291 work was compiled on the basis of several earlier manuscripts by the Yuan-dynasty monk Tsung-pao (n.d.) and later included in the Ming Tripitaka, a compendium of Buddhist scriptures in Chinese published in the early fifteenth century. Sokei-an translated only the ten sections that form the body of the work, eliminating the various introductory materials and epilogues.[2]

An earlier, shorter text of the *Platform Sutra*, apparently dating from the late Tang dynasty, was discovered in 1900 in a cave at Tun-huang, in China's Kansu province. The Tun-huang version of the sutra is about half the length of the Yuan text, and there are certain differences in the materials included in each version and in the overall ordering of the contents. Nevertheless, both texts are very close, and there are few if any marked differences between the teachings conveyed in each.[3]

The Tun-huang manuscript was included in the Taisho Tripitaka, the noted compendium of Buddhist scriptures in Chinese published in Japan between 1924 and 1934, and was thus available to Sokei-an. But although he was aware of the Tun-huang text, which had generated considerable excitement among scholars of Chinese Buddhism, in his lectures Sokei-an chose to rely on the Yuan version, which was probably more familiar to him. This was the text commonly consulted in Japanese Zen temples since at least the Tokugawa period (1600-1867), and is likely to have been the version of the sutra that Sokei-an studied during his own Zen training. Sokei-an's choice of the later edition may also have been influenced by the fact that it contains certain celebrated passages not included in the Tun-huang text. The two most obvious examples are the phrase "From the beginning not a thing exists," which Hui-neng recites in response to the poem of the senior monk Shen-hsiu; and the question, "Thinking of neither good nor evil, at that moment, what is your original appearance?" which Hui-neng puts to the monk Hui-ming, who pursues him from the Fifth Patriarch's temple. The first of these is among the standard "capping phrases" (*agyo*, or *jakugo*) employed in koan study in Japanese Zen temples; the second is itself a koan, one particularly favored by Sokei-an.

Unlike his commentary on the *Platform Sutra*, which was delivered impromptu in English and recorded by members of his audience, Sokei-an's translation of the text was composed by him beforehand and written out, with assistance on wording from his American students. In preparing his lectures, Sokei-an's method was to go through the original text on which he was speaking, writing out the Chinese characters for each line and placing his proposed English translation directly beneath. Although Sokei-an was trained in classical Chinese since childhood and had labored over the complexities of translation in preparing his weekly talks on the *Platform Sutra*, his perspective was always that of a Zen master rather than a linguist. His aim was to present the Sixth Patriarch's essential teaching, as he saw it, rather than a scholarly translation that hewed to the text in every detail.

By December 1941 the text of Sokei-an's translation of the *Platform Sutra* had been separately typed and bound. A memo prefacing the surviving typescript states that it represents an uncorrected version, and warns against letting anyone have access to it without Sokei-an's permission—indicating that though the process of editing may already have begun in Sokei-an's lifetime, he regarded the task as incomplete.

After Sokei-an's death, the work of editing the sutra notes was taken up by his student Mary Farkas, director of the First Zen Institute of America, the organization Sokei-an had founded in New York

City. From 1975 till her death in 1992, Mary presented Sokei-an's Sixth Patriarch lectures in *Zen Notes*, and gradually began to prepare the full manuscript for publication with the assistance of Bob Lopez. Bob labored assiduously to annotate the translation. But due to to the extreme length of Sokei-an's commentary, which is, after all, the heart of the book (and which, along with the glossary, explains many of the references), the Institute's publications committee decided to drop most of the footnotes, though they remain available in the FZI archives.

At Mary's request, she and I went through the translation portion together, line by line, as Sokei-an had done, comparing it with the Chinese of Tsung-pao's original text, a task in which we were assisted by a grant from the Numata Foundation. In editing the translation, we sought in part to use the Chinese original to clarify certain of Sokei-an's less precise renderings, many of which had apparently been suggested by his American students. But by and large our effort was simply aimed at enhancing the peculiar force implicit in Sokei-an's understanding of this remarkable Zen text. It is my hope that we may have succeeded, to at least some extent, and that Sokei-an would have appreciated our attempts to "polish the mirror" he left behind.

New York City
Summer 2011

A PRELIMINARY NOTE
by Mary Farkas

I hope you will read the Sixth Patriarchs message we have presented to you all ears and all eyes. I have personally gone to a great deal of effort to pass such messages on to you accurately. I hope you will keep your copies so you can refer to them later, as many are of a nature that call for reading many more than one time. Please do not think that Sokei-an's talks on the Sixth Patriarch's *Platform Sutra* are for scholars, philologists, historians, or religious people of a superstitious bent; they are for practicing students. Also, please do not think that by sticking to the (probably almost entirely fictitious) events described, or by memorizing definitions of terms or doctrines, or even answering the koans, that you will have obtained the great teaching. How, then, can we use printed matter like this to get to know Sokei-an and the Sixth Patriarch, and see with the same eyes and join hands with not only them but all the masters of the past and future?

For more than a quarter of a century, I have been collecting the scattered beads dropped by Sokei-an and stringing them together into a rosary as a testimony of faith that can be passed on to the sentient beings of the future world. I do not know as yet how many beads it has, or when all are matched, cleaned, polished, and strung, what form it will take. Though the individual beads have been presented singly, in each the whole string may be glimpsed. Carrying my metaphor a bit further, it is my idea that by getting to know any Zen master, even through *one* of his words, you are on a direct line with the whole lineage. Just as really getting any koan you are strung on the string yourself, as on Mumon's skewer that caught Tenryu, Gutei, and the fingerless boy.[4]

The masters, not unmindful of the needs of students, devised various methods of contacting them, of getting them on the line, of catching them on the straight hook. The most intimate, direct and electrical contact we can have is *sanzen*, the meeting in Zen with a living master. A master even present in the too, too solid flesh, is somewhat mythical, as well. So to know him isn't any easier than for a wise father to know his own son, or a man his wife, or a person oneself. How do we get to know the masters of the three worlds of past, present and future? How do we relate to them present, or absent? The Sixth Patriarch, in order to initiate relations with them, gave his audience a Zen talk from the altar platform.

A student is supposed to realize the first word. What was the Sixth Patriarch's first word? Before the Sixth Patriarch's first talk about himself, before he said anything aloud, he manifested silence. You may also have noticed that in the description of the Buddha's transmission of Zen, he, too, first manifested silence. When Sokei-an was alive, *sanzen* always began with silence, as did his talks. When you offer incense to Buddha, it is an opportunity for you to manifest this silence—your mini-*samadhi* in that single-minded act. How can it be said more clearly? In the West there is a saying, A word to the wise is sufficient. I'd like to emphasize that word to the wise. It is the wisdom of the bodhisattva, always there to be contacted. So the kind of words we must strive to present are those that can act toward that wisdom-being, like the shadow of the whip is to the good horse (student) who is plodding along at the moment.

Only human beings can get this sort of message. Our particular medium is language, isn't it? Of course, gestures may also convey the message. Tenryu's finger, which was enough for Gutei's whole life, is famous in the Zen world. Spoken or unspoken, a message is conveyed, communication takes place. One way is by hearing. For twenty years now, I have been bringing you the words I heard from my masters. These words are for you. Take the advice of the Sixth Patriarch when you have the opportunity to hear the words of a master: Whoever may be listening to this teaching. I pray you to purify your mind first, and after you have listened, clear your doubts.

THE GREAT SIXTH PATRIARCH'S SUTRA OF THE
TREASURE OF BUDDHISM FROM THE EARTHEN ALTAR

Edited by Tsung-pao
Heir of the Patriarch and Abbot of Ch'an Temple Kuang-hsiao built as a Testimony of Gratitude
for the Wind and the Banner

CHAPTER I

THE AUTOBIOGRAPHY

When the Great Master reached Pao-lin Temple, Wei Ch'u, prefect of Shao-chou, together with other local officials, went to the mountain to implore the Master to give the teaching at the hall of Ta-fan Temple within the walls of the town. The Master ascended the high seat. The Prefect and some thirty local officials, more than thirty Confucian scholars, and over a thousand monks, nuns, and lay people all bowed and entreated him to impart his teaching of the Dharma. The Great Master addressed the assembly:

"Good friends, the intrinsic nature of wisdom is originally pure in itself. We have only to use it to become Buddha directly. Give heed for a time while I tell you how I, Hui-neng, finally attained the Dharma:

"My father was a native of Fan-yang. Later he was relegated to an inferior post and banished to Ling-nan, becoming a commoner in Hsin-chou. I was unfortunate. My father died early, and my mother was left alone with me. We moved to Nan-hai, where we were distressed by poverty so great that it drove me to peddle brushwood for fuel in the marketplace. One day a customer asked me to deliver some brushwood to his dwelling. I went there and received payment. When I came out of the gate, I noticed a man reciting a Buddhist sutra. As I heard the words of the sutra, my mind suddenly opened. I questioned him: 'What is the name of that sutra you were reciting?' He said: 'It is the Diamond Sutra.' *I questioned him again: 'Where did you come from, and where did you find that sutra?' He said: 'I have come from Eastern Ch'an Temple in the district of Huang-mei in Ch'i-chou. In this temple, the Fifth Patriarch, Hung-jen, is in charge of the instruction of the monks, who number more than one thousand. I went there, paid my homage to him and heard this sutra. The Patriarch always advises monks and lay people to just observe this* Diamond Sutra, *since one who follows this will discover his essential nature and become a buddha directly.'*

"I, Hui-neng, had the good fortune to be informed of this. It may be that I had some tie of causality with this sutra from a past incarnation. Then, too, a stranger gave me ten taels in silver, which allowed me to provide for the needs of my old mother, and suggested that I go to Huang-mei to pay homage to the Fifth Patriarch. I, therefore, furnished my mother with all she might need in my absence and left. I journeyed about thirty days and finally reached Huang-mei, where I paid homage to the Fifth Patriarch.

"The Patriarch questioned me: 'Where have you come from and what do you want?'

"I replied: 'I am a commoner from Hsin-chou in Ling-nan. I have come this long way to pay homage to the Master. I want nothing but to become a buddha.'

"The Patriarch said: 'You are from Ling-nan. That means you are a savage! How can you become a buddha?'

"I said: 'To be a native of the South or of the North is natural to a man, but there is neither North nor South in the nature of Buddha. The flesh of a savage is not the flesh of an abbot, but how can my buddha-nature be discriminated from yours?'

"The Fifth Patriarch wished to talk further with me, but seeing that the other monks were there, he then ordered me to do some work along with the rest of the assembly.

"I said: 'I would like to say to the Abbot that wisdom is always growing from my own mind. When one does not stray from one's own nature, one finds the 'field of merit.' I wonder what labor you ask of me.'

"The Patriarch said: 'This savage is too smart! Not another word! Get to work!' I retired and went to the rear of the temple. A lay brother was there who told me to split firewood and pound rice with the rice pestle. This I did for more than eight months.

"One day, unexpectedly, the Patriarch came to see me and said: 'I thought that your view was acceptable, but I feared that some ill-natured persons might do you harm. That was the reason I did not talk further with you then. Did you perceive that?'

"I replied: 'I understood my master's mind. That is why I have never gone to the front of the temple—to keep people from realizing the situation.'

"One day the Patriarch summoned all the disciples and said: 'I have brought you all here to tell you that the question of life and death is the greatest problem of human life. All day long you are seeking the 'field of merit' instead of deliverance from the bitter sea of life and death. If you are deluded about your self-nature, merit is useless to save you. Go and look into your own wisdom. With your original wisdom [prajna], each one of you make a gatha and present it to me. If you have realized the great principle of Buddhism, I shall transmit the robe and the Dharma to you and ordain you as the Sixth Patriarch. This is urgent. Go at once! Do not delay! If you deliberate, it will be useless. One who realizes his own nature sees it instantly. If you are able to do this, you will realize it even in battle under slashing swords.'

"Following the Master's instructions, all the monks retired. Discussing the matter among themselves, they said: 'It is unnecessary for all of us to clear our minds and try to make gathas. What merit can we expect merely from making them and presenting them to the Master? The head monk Shen-hsiu is virtually our instructor. He is certain to succeed. Why should we make gathas, exhausting our minds to no purpose?'

"Hearing this, the rest of the monks also gave up the endeavor. They said: 'We shall rely on our teacher Shen-hsiu and not trouble ourselves to make gathas.'

"Shen-hsiu thought: 'The reason the monks are not presenting their gathas is that I am their instructor. I must therefore make a gatha and offer it to the Abbot. If I do not offer a gatha, how can he see whether my understanding is shallow or deep? If in offering a gatha I desire only the Dharma, my purpose is good; but if I seek the honor of becoming Patriarch, my purpose is bad. It is just as though one with a common mind tried to usurp the position of a sage. Yet, if I do not present my gatha, I cannot obtain the Dharma. How very difficult this is!'

"Leading to the hall of the Fifth Patriarch were three corridors. It was intended that the court artist Lu-chen would be invited to paint on the walls a mandala suggested by the Lankavatara Sutra as well as the genealogical tables of the Five Patriarchs, so that tradition would be venerated and transmitted.

"Shen-hsiu, having composed a gatha, came several times to the front of the hall to offer it to the Patriarch. But each time his mind became so confused that his whole body was drenched with sweat and he could not present his gatha. After four days had passed and he had made the attempt more than thirteen times, he had still failed in his purpose. He then asked himself what he should do.

"'It is better,' he thought, 'that I write [my gatha] on the wall of the corridor. If the Abbot sees and approves it, I shall come forward, and bowing down, tell him that I am its author. If it does not meet with his approval, then my years in this temple, accepting everyone's reverence, are of no significance for my practice of Buddhism.'

"That midnight, without letting anyone know, he took a light and wrote his gatha *upon the wall of the southern corridor. The* gatha *said:*

'This body is a tree of wisdom
This mind, a clear mirror
Wipe it diligently always
Let it gather no dust'

"After he had completed writing his gatha, *Shen-hsiu went back to his cell without having been discovered by anyone. He debated in his mind: 'Tomorrow the Fifth Patriarch will see my* gatha, *and if he is pleased, it will signify that I have an affinity with Buddhism. If, however, it does not meet with his approval, I must realize that my delusions from the past are very deep and that, obstructed by them, I am unable to obtain the Dharma. It is impossible for me to fathom my teacher's mind.'*

"Occupied with such thoughts, he tossed anxiously in his cell until dawn.

"The Fifth Patriarch knew that Shen-hsiu had not entered the gate or found his true nature. In the early morning, he summoned the court painter Lu to do the proposed painting on the corridor wall. Suddenly discovering the gatha, *the Patriarch told him: 'It is unnecessary to paint anything on this wall. I am grateful to you for having come such a distance. In the* Diamond Sutra *it is said that all that has form is false. I shall keep this* gatha *here for people to recite. One whose practice is in accordance with this* gatha *will acquire great merit and can keep himself from falling into evil ways. Let my disciples bow and burn incense to this* gatha. *Those who recite it will find the realization of their true nature.'*

"All the disciples read the gatha *of Shen-hsiu and expressed their admiration for it. At midnight, the Patriarch summoned Shen-hsiu to his quarters and questioned him: 'Did you write that* gatha?' *Shen-hsiu replied: 'Yes, it was I who wrote it; but I dare not aspire to the position of patriarch. My hope was that out of compassion you might ascertain whether or not I have some slight knowledge of Buddhism.'*

"The Patriarch said: 'If it is your gatha, *you have not yet seen your original nature; you have reached the outer gate but not yet entered. Your understanding indicates that though you have sought supreme enlightenment, you have not yet attained it. Supreme enlightenment should be attained instantaneously. When you find your original mind and see your original nature, you will realize that it has never been created and will never be destroyed. At all times, at every moment, you see it. Then no barriers remain between things, one truth is the truth for all, each thing in the world is just as it should be, and the mind's self-awareness is the nature of Reality. One who understands this has understood the supreme enlightenment of self-nature. You had better return to your cell. Ponder this for one or two days, then write another* gatha *and bring it to me. If I see that you have entered the gate, I shall transmit the robe and Dharma to you.'*

"Shen-hsiu made a bow and retired. Several days passed, but he did not succeed in writing another gatha. *His mind became confused and uneasy as though he were in a dream. He felt uncomfortable whether he sat or walked.*

"After several days had passed, a novice went by the mill reciting Shen-hsiu's gatha. *When I heard it, I knew at once that whoever had made this* gatha *had not yet seen his original nature. For, though I had received no instructions from anyone, I already understood the main principle of Buddhism. Finally, I questioned the novice: 'What is the* gatha *you were reciting?'*

"The boy replied: 'Oh, you savage! Don't you know the word of the Master? He said that life and death is the greatest problem of human existence. He wishes to transmit his robe and Dharma, and has ordered

his disciples to compose gathas *and bring them to him. If he finds that anyone has understood the main principle of Buddhism, he will transmit to him his robe and Dharma and make him the Sixth Patriarch. The head monk Shen-hsiu wrote a* gatha *on formlessness on the wall of the south corridor. The Master commanded all of us to recite it, saying that one whose practice is in accord with this* gatha *can keep from falling into evil ways and receive great benefit.'*

"I said: 'I should like to read that gatha in order to establish some affinity with Buddhism in a future incarnation. Honorable one, I have been here treading this pestle for more than eight months and have not yet been to the front of the temple. I hope that you will lead me there and allow me to bow before the gatha.'

"The boy led me there and let me bow before the gatha. I said: 'I am an unlettered man. Please, honorable one, read it to me.'

"An official of Chiang-chou whose name was Ch'ang-jih-yung happened to be there and read the verse aloud. When I heard it, I said: 'I too have made a gatha. Oh officer, please write it down for me.'

"The official said: 'What! You, too, have made a gatha? That is odd.'

"I replied: 'He who would study supreme enlightenment should not slight a beginner. The lowest of men may have the highest wisdom, and the highest of men may have wisdom that is unawakened. If you slight anyone, you will commit immeasurable offence.'

"The officer said: 'Just recite your gatha, and I shall write it down for you. But if you obtain the Dharma, you must save me first. Do not forget my request!'

"I recited this gatha:

> 'Wisdom is not a tree
> The mirror is not a mirror
> From the beginning
> Is there anything to gather dust?'

"When the gatha was written, the monks were astonished. There was not one who did not stand aghast looking at it. They talked among themselves: 'How remarkable! Surely one cannot judge a man by his appearance! Why did we hard press that living bodhisattva for so long?'

"The Fifth Patriarch saw the amazed crowd, and fearing someone might do me an injury, he rubbed out the gatha with his shoe. He said: 'This, too, is a gatha made by one who has not seen his original nature.' Everyone accepted his word.

"The next day, the Fifth Patriarch came secretly into the mill and saw me pounding rice, a big stone around my waist. The Patriarch said: 'One who seeks true law forgets himself for the law, and it must be thus.' Then the Patriarch questioned me: 'Has the rice been polished?'

"I answered: 'It was polished long ago, but it has not yet been sifted.'

"The Patriarch struck the mortar three times with his staff and went out. I understood the meaning of the Patriarch, and when the temple drum had boomed three times, I entered his room. The Patriarch used his monk's stole as a screen in order that no one might see us, and expounded the Diamond Sutra for me. When he came to the line that says, 'Depending upon nothing, you must manifest your mind,' I was instantly enlightened. I thought: 'The manifold phenomena of the universe are not separate from my original nature!' Then I told the Patriarch: 'It was beyond my expectation that my own nature is originally pure, originally everlasting, originally perfect, originally unshakable, and that all things arise from it.'

"The Patriarch saw that I had realized original nature, and told me: 'If you are unaware of your real mind, learning Buddhism will not benefit you. If you are aware of your own mind and see your original nature, you are to be honored with the names Master, Teacher of Devas, or Buddha.'

"It was midnight when I received the Dharma. No one knew.

"Transmitting the sudden teachings as well as the robe and bowl, the Patriarch said to me: 'I appoint you the Sixth Patriarch. Guard this teaching. Save sentient beings far and wide. Promulgate this in the future, and do not let it expire. Listen to my gatha:

'Sentient beings come and sow seeds
From the soil fruits are begotten
Insentient beings beget nothing
Having no seeds and no nature'

"The Patriarch continued: 'When Bodhidharma first came to this land, no one believed in his teaching. That is why he handed down this robe as a symbol of faith, to be passed on from generation to generation. But the Dharma should be transmitted from mind to mind, and each should apprehend it through his own realization. From the remote past, the original body or substance has been transmitted from buddha to buddha, and every patriarch has secretly inherited the original mind. The robe will become a cause of strife. Keep it in your generation. Do not hand it down. If you hand down the robe, your life will be as precarious as if it were hanging by a thread. Leave quickly! I fear someone may do you injury.'

"Reverently I questioned the Patriarch: 'Where should I go?'

"The Patriarch told me: 'Stay at Huai; hide at Hui.'

"It was midnight. Accepting the robe and the bowl, I said: 'I am from the south. I do not know the mountain passes or how to make my way to the river.'

"The Patriarch answered: 'Do not worry. I myself will show you the way.' He conducted me to the river station at Chiu-chiang. There he took me with him in a boat and took the scull and worked it himself.

"I said: 'Your reverence, pray be seated! Your disciple will scull the boat.'

"The Patriarch replied: 'To ferry you over the river is my service.'

"I said: 'While I was astray, you ferried me [across the river], but now that I have awakened, I shall ferry myself. The word "to ferry" is the same, but its uses are different. I was born in such an out-of-the-way land, speaking this rustic tongue with its odd sound. But now, I have received your Dharma and am enlightened. Turning to my original nature for guidance, I shall ferry myself.'

"The Patriarch answered: 'Well said! Well said! In time, Buddhism will be widely spread by you. Three years after your departure, I shall be dead. It is better for you to leave me now. Try to keep to the south. Do not give your teaching too soon. Buddhism may suffer persecution.'

"I took my leave of the Fifth Patriarch and set off southward. After some months I reached the Ta-yu Mountains. Several hundred monks had pursued me in order to seize the robe and bowl. Among them was one whose family name was Chen and whose monk's name was Hui-ming. Once he had been a commander of the fourth order. His nature was irascible, but he was an ardent student. He came ahead of the others and was about to overtake me.

"I flung the robe and bowl upon a rock, saying: 'The robe is the symbol of faith. No one can take it by force.' I then concealed myself in the bushes.

"Hui-ming arrived at the rock intending to take the robe and bowl, but he was unable to move them. He cried aloud, 'Oh, lay brother, I came for the Dharma, not the robe!' Then I came out and sat down on the rock. Hui-ming bowed and said: 'I beg you to expound the Dharma for me.'

"I answered: 'Since you came for the Dharma, disregard all that has transpired, do not entertain even a single thought, and then I will speak of the Dharma for you.'

"Ming remained silent for a time. Then I said: 'Thinking of neither good nor evil, at that moment, what is your original appearance?'

"Upon these words, Hui-ming was enlightened.

"Hui-ming again questioned me: 'Is there another, secret truth besides that which you have told me?'

"I answered: 'What I told you was not secret. If you look into your own consciousness, you will find the secret within yourself.'

"Hui-ming said: 'Although, I was studying at Huang-mei, I did not recognize my original appearance. Now, having been instructed by you, I feel as one who drinks water and knows for himself whether it is hot or cold. Oh, lay brother, you are now my master.'

"I replied: 'If this is your true conviction, your master is the one at Huang-mei, just as mine is. Guard your own enlightenment!' Then Hui-ming asked: 'From here, where shall I go?'

"I told him: 'When you come to Yuan, stop there; when you come to Meng, stay there.' Hui-ming made a bow and departed.

"Sometime after that, I reached Ts'ao-ch'i. Again pursued by adversaries, I took refuge in Ssu-hui, where, covering my trail among a group of hunters, I passed about fifteen years. When the occasion arose, I would give the hunters some appropriate teaching. They had me watch the hunter's noose, but whenever I found a creature trapped, I released it. At mealtimes, I cooked my greens in the pot of meat. If anyone questioned me, I said: 'I like to eat greens cooked with meat.'

"One day I thought: 'The time to spread my dharma has come. I cannot remain hidden forever.' Accordingly, I went to the Fa-hsing Temple at Kwang-chou, where I met Dharma Master Yin-tsung, who chanced to be lecturing on the Nirvana Sutra.

"On that day, the banner of the temple was moving in the wind. One monk declared: 'The wind is moving.' Another monk declared: 'The banner is moving.' The debate was endless. Approaching them, I said: 'Neither the wind nor the banner is moving. Your minds are moving.' The monks were all astonished.

"Yin-tsung asked me to take the seat of honor and questioned me about the secrets of Buddhism.

"When Yin-tsung realized that my answers were concise, sound, and did not rely on the words of the scriptures, he said: 'Lay brother, I am convinced that you are an unusual man. For a long time it has been reported that the robe and canon of Huang-mei had been carried to the south. Are you not the one to whom they have been transmitted?'

"I answered: 'Yes, unworthy though I am.' Thereupon Yin-tsung made a bow and begged me to show his followers the robe and bowl that had been transmitted to me. Then Yin-tsung asked: 'When the Fifth Patriarch transmitted the doctrine to you, what did he teach?'

"I answered: He did not teach anything. He only spoke about seeing into one's own intrinsic nature. He did not speak of meditation or deliverance.'

"Yin-tsung asked: 'Why did he not speak of meditation or deliverance?'

"I said: 'Because that is the teaching of duality and not Buddhism, which is the teaching of non-duality.'

"Yin-tsung asked: 'What is the Buddhism that teaches non-duality?'

"I said: 'The Nirvana Sutra, *on which you are lecturing, elucidates buddha-nature. This is the Buddhist teaching of non-duality. Thus, in that sutra it is said that Kao-kuei-te-wang Bodhisattva asked the Buddha: "Does one who has violated the four grave prohibitions, committed the five nefarious crimes, or is a heretic born beyond redemption destroy the excellent roots of buddha-nature?" The Buddha answered him: "There are two kinds of excellent roots, one perpetual, the other mutable. Buddha-nature, however, is neither perpetual nor mutable, it cannot be destroyed; therefore, it is called non-dual. There are good roots and evil roots, but buddha-nature is neither good nor evil, and therefore it is called non-dual. An unenlightened man takes the view that the five shadows of mind [the five skandhas] are different from the sensible exterior [the eighteen* dhatus]; *but an enlightened man realizes that in their essential nature, these are not two separate existences. This non-dual nature is buddha-nature.'*

"*Yin-tsung, listening to this address, was delighted, and joining his palms, said: 'My humble commentary on this sutra was as worthless as a pile of logs, while your discourse is like pure gold.' Thereupon, he shaved my head and entreated me to become his teacher.*

"*So under the Bodhi tree in Ts'ao-ch'i, I opened the gate of the teaching of the Eastern Mountain. Since receiving that teaching, there is no difficulty I have not undergone, and many times my life has hung by a thread. That today I am holding this meeting with you, the prefect and his staff, the monks, nuns and laymen, surely indicates a recurring relation among us through many* kalpas, *and the cultivation of meritorious roots common to us all, a result of making offerings to the buddhas in past lives. Otherwise, we could not have heard this teaching of sudden enlightenment that is the cause of attaining the Dharma. The teaching is that transmitted by previous patriarchs. It is not my own idea. Those of you who wish to hear this teaching of the patriarchs must first purify your minds, and after listening, clear away your doubts. Then you will be no different from the patriarchs of old.*"

Having heard this teaching, the multitude retired in great joy, bowing low.

SOKEI-AN SAYS:

This is the first Zen record of the Zen sect, dating from the early period of the T'ang dynasty in China, the end of the eighth century. (The last few years I have been giving commentary on *The Record of Lin-chi*, translating it from the Chinese into English. I think this translation will also take about three years.) And now I shall give my humble commentary . . .

All sects of Buddhism derive from the Buddhism of the Buddha, from primitive Buddhism. So all sects of Buddhism bow down to the Buddha as the original teacher, but we do not call the Buddha the first patriarch. His disciple Mahakashyapa is the first patriarch, and Ananda is the second. Somehow there were twenty-eight patriarchs handing down Buddhism—the soul of Buddhism—from generation to generation.

Why do we call Hui-neng the Sixth Patriarch? Because he is the Sixth Patriarch of the Zen sect in China. Bodhidharma was the twenty-eighth patriarch in India and the first patriarch of Zen in China. When he came to China, the Hindu monks already there did not accept him as patriarch. The monks previously in China were Buddhist sophists and philosophers, and they did not agree with him. Bodhidharma paid no attention to them. He just stayed in the holy temple of Shao-lin on a high mountain for about nine years and died there. The second patriarch was Hui-ko; the third was Seng-tsan; the fourth, Tao-hsin; the fifth, Hung-jen; and the sixth, Hui-neng. His disciples called their master's Buddhism "Ch'an," [in Japanese pronounced "Zen."] Before him, no one called this sect the Zen sect. It was only some peculiar kind of

Buddhism and did not form any particular sect till that day. Sometimes they called this sect the Yoga sect because it came from India. Sometimes they called it the Lanka sect because it was of this school of Yoga before Bodhidharma reached China. It was also in Ceylon, Java, and Sumatra before Bodhidharma. Bodhidharma called it the Buddha-mind sect.

The transmission stories of the Zen teachers were written down in this record. I shall trace them and give my commentary on them later, so I shall not speak more about this now.

The Great Sixth Patriarch's Sutra of the Treasure of Buddhism from the Earthen Altar. Each point of Buddhism that came from the Buddha's lips was called a jewel, so the teachings of Buddhism, the Dharma, were called a "treasure."

When the visitors reached Pao-lin, the temple was so small the Master could not receive them all. Therefore, his adherents made an altar of earth with a high platform on the raised ground; and for seven days Hui-neng gave these lectures from that platform—gave the "Treasure of Buddhism from the Earthen Altar." I translated it as "Treasure of Buddhism," but it should really be "Treasure of Dharma."

Edited by Tsung-pao Heir of the Patriarch and Abbot of Ch'an Temple Kuang-chou: According to my study, Tsung-pao was not a direct successor to the Sixth Patriarch; he was a distant successor. This record was probably his teacher's, so he edited and published it. The writer of the record had kept a notebook or memorandum of the patriarch's lectures. This record was somehow edited from that notebook.

There are about three versions of the Sixth Patriarch's "Sutra." These differ a little. There is this version I am translating and another which was recently excavated from Tun-huang after being covered with sand for about a thousand years. Everyone has been comparing the newly discovered one with this version edited by Tsung-pao. We find that some parts are different, but the backbone is exactly the same. Another one was found in the old library of Kôshô-ji in Japan, concealed in a pile of sutras for about eight hundred years. Now it has come to light and has been studied comparatively with other records. It also differs a little, but the fundamental parts are exactly the same.

Why do these records vary in detail? Because they come from the notes of different monks who recorded them from the patriarch's lectures—as you are now recording my lectures. And if yours are published, there will be differences.

Why did I pick this version? I selected it because it is the most complete and was recorded by a more intellectual monk. Others were recorded by monks who were not scholars, while this one has some scholastic merit.

Built as a Testimony of Gratitude for the Wind and the Banner. I think you know about the "Wind and the Banner." Once the Sixth Patriarch, who was concealing himself in a little temple, was sweeping the ground with a bamboo broom. Two monks were arguing with each other about a waving flag. One monk, pointing to it, said, "The flag is waving." The other said, "The wind is waving."

This is a very deep question. When you go to the beach, you see the waves traveling from shore to shore. You say, "The waves are traveling." Another says, "The waves are not traveling." You throw your hat, it stays in one place. You say, "But the foam of the wave is traveling!" The other says, "The water is not traveling, but the foam is!" You argue and argue and never find out what is really traveling.

One monk said, "The flag is waving." The other said, "The wind is waving." The Sixth Patriarch heard this. It was so interesting, he forgot his disguise as a laborer. Holding his bamboo broom in his hand, he entered the garden and said: "Neither the flag nor the wind is waving. Your minds are waving."

The abbot of the temple heard this from within. When he heard the words of the Patriarch—a workman in the temple—the hair on his body rose: "Oh, this is not a mere laborer! I heard that the heir of the Fifth Patriarch, after having received the torch from him, has been in hiding for the last fifteen years. Maybe this is the patriarch!"

Thus, the Sixth Patriarch Hui-neng was discovered. "The Wind and the Banner" was the second of the koans that he gave to others. By this koan he opened their eyes, so they would find the essential unity of the universe.

When the Great Master reached Pao-lin Temple, Wei Ch'u, prefect of Shao-chou, together with other local officials, went to the mountain to implore the Master to give the teaching at the hall of Ta-fan Temple within the walls of the town. The Master ascended the high seat. The prefect and some thirty local officials, more than thirty Confucian scholars, and over a thousand monks, nuns, and lay people all bowed and entreated him to impart his teaching of the Dharma. The Great Master addressed the assembly: "Good friends, the intrinsic nature of wisdom is originally pure in itself."

SOKEI-AN SAYS:

This "pure" has nothing to do with sin or no sin. It means pure existence, essential existence. In Buddhism, we do not express our faith in the same way as Westerners. We do not say that God gives us salvation. We say intrinsic wisdom is our nature. I do not explain what that wisdom is, but it is not what you get by education. This is the intrinsic wisdom that enshrines in every soul. Sometimes it is sleeping, as the soul of a tree or an insect or some human beings.

You have intrinsic wisdom, but you do not know it because you are looking for it outside. You use the physical eye, or you think it is not enough and use a magnifying glass. God gives you wisdom, but you do not use it. You entirely forget this intrinsic wisdom that is within you. You say "intrinsic wisdom," but it's like standing in water up to your chin and crying, "Give me water!" You are God's child. You have God inside yourself, only you do not know it. But something awakens you, gives you a hint—"Awake, my child, awake!" It is no God from the outside, but your own intrinsic wisdom that awakens you. I hope you awaken in this lifetime.

"We have only to use it to become Buddha directly." Who is Buddha? The Buddha is within you, and if you awaken, you will find the Buddha within yourself. You are Buddha.

"Good friends, give heed for a time while I tell you how I, Hui-neng, finally attained the Dharma."—"How I grasped it, not reading or listening but attained it myself."

"My father was a native of Fan-yang. Later he was relegated to an inferior post and banished to Ling-nan, becoming a commoner in Hsin-chou." He was dismissed from his position as head of the prefecture for some political reason. So the Sixth Patriarch was not the child of a Canton peasant. He was born with the blood of an intellectual type of man.

"I was unfortunate. My father died early, and my mother was left alone with me." The man of today does not feel so unfortunate, though he is born in the house of a slave. For the social order today is not so strict as in ancient times, especially here in America. Here, the child of a shoeshiner can become president of the United States—not a big possibility, but the law of the land does not prohibit it. In those days, in China or Japan, it was impossible for a child of inferior birth to become an official of the government. Even today there is such a tendency. If a man loses his social standing and becomes a "mere" farmer, he is very unfortunate. A family, to regain its former position, will struggle through five or six generations.

"We moved to Nan-hai, where we were distressed by poverty so great that it drove me to peddle brushwood for fuel in the marketplace." I do not see this kind of wood in America. This brushwood comes from a tree that looks like an elm. It is cut into sticks of the same length, made up into bundles, and tied with a rope. When you see the Sixth Patriarch's picture, you will see such a bundle. In his picture he is shouting, "Buy brushwood!"

"One day a customer asked me to deliver some brushwood to his dwelling. I went there and received payment. When I came out of the gate, I noticed a man reciting a Buddhist sutra. As I heard the words of the sutra my mind suddenly opened." When Japanese monks speak about the Sixth Patriarch, they speak mysteriously about this part. According to one version, Hui-neng was born of poor parents and did not have the opportunity of educating himself—he picked up the language as best he could. He was not a gay child but was depressed and quiet. Usually, his mother found him sitting on a stone quietly meditating upon something quite unknown to her. Sometimes he would just stand in the garden and gaze up at the trees. When he was twenty-three or—four, he bore firewood on his shoulders to help his mother. One day an unknown man appeared and stood before him, asked to have some kindling wood delivered to his dwelling, and disappeared. Hui-neng looked around, but the man seemed to have vanished like smoke. He went to the address and saw a man standing under the eaves. The man said, "I have been waiting for you a long time." There was no shortcut to this place, but Hui-neng had come in haste and did not understand why the man had said this. Hui-neng said, "I am very sorry," and handed the wood to the man. He received it as lightly as though it were a bundle of paper. Then he vanished. Hui-neng thought this was strange. Looking into his palm, he saw the money—almost enough to support himself for four or five years. "What is this?" he said," It must be a mistake!" Then he went out of the gate and saw a man standing there reciting a Buddhist sutra. He felt drawn into it and stood there listening.

This is the way Japanese monks speak about this part. It's not exactly like the actual record, but there is a shade of meaning that suggests an unknown power pulled the young man into enlightenment. It's as if this enlightenment was not his first, that he had had many incarnations of enlightenment.

This type of thought is by no means new in Buddhism. In the *Jataka Tales*, it is stated that the Buddha was a bodhisattva through many incarnations, until finally, under the Bodhi Tree, he opened the final eye of enlightenment and attained buddhahood. In Zen study, one observes a koan and comes to understanding; but this is different, something is attained like a flash of lightning, and the volume of enlightenment is greater. One has attained through many incarnations, has forgotten his former enlightenment, and is born again. Such a child has a tendency to meditate, to introspect. Then someday—suddenly—"Oh!" He finds enlightenment. But we must not be deceived by the enlightenment attained by someone who after a long struggle suddenly attains, when it may merely be like a firecracker set off by a child on the Fourth of July—Pft!—and that is all. It is enlightenment, but in a couple of days he has forgotten it.

Of course, passing through koans like a blind man stepping on dog-dung does not make a miracle. To pass one koan and forget about it doesn't mean anything at all. It's like nailing spikes into ashes. The spike will go in, but it will not stay there. There are many students of this type in Japan and elsewhere. I hope some day, by some koan, you will come truly to your own realization—come face to face with real enlightenment.

"I questioned him: 'What is the name of that sutra you were reciting?' He said: 'It is the Diamond Sutra.'" The *Diamond Sutra* in Sanskrit is the *Vajracchedika-sutra*, the "sutra of diamond wisdom." With this transcendent wisdom, you reach the other shore.

The monks speak mysteriously about this also. This man is said to be Avalokiteshvara appearing in human form to lead Hui-neng to enlightenment, not a real man. The monks say the man answered: "I got this from the Fifth Patriarch, Hung-jen. You must go there to his temple and meet him."

When you read the *Diamond Sutra*, you will read these characters: "Depending upon nothing, you must find your own mind." It is not easy. Each one tries to depend upon something. We depend on Buddha, prayer, science, philosophy, or Christ for enlightenment, like an old man who must depend upon his cane. You depend upon methods, words, thoughts, symbols, logic—there must be something. When you say, "I have attained," it is some image, not true enlightenment.

Hui-neng listened as the man recited the sutra, and when he came to these words, "Depending upon nothing, you must find your mind," he felt as if his hair stood in the air—"Oh!" His enlightenment came suddenly.

Such an experience does not come through some Hindu who pinches your nose and says: "Do you see a light, a green light? You are enlightened!" and you pay him twenty-five dollars. No, you must be alert at every moment, always keep yourself awake; then you will be ready. If your mind is always asleep, when the moment comes, you will miss it. But when you are ready, suddenly, by some contact, it comes.

One monk was always sweeping the garden. One day a pebble from his broom struck a bamboo tree, and at the sound—"Ah!"—he suddenly entered into absolute wisdom. It had been a long struggle.

Another monk had been meditating day and night. One morning the gong of the temple resounded through the air. He felt as if that sound had come from the bottom of his mind. Suddenly, he realized that the whole universe was within him. His mind jumped out from the universe. Such a moment has nothing to do with the brain.

"Depending upon nothing, you must find your own mind." When you observe Hui-neng's koans, you will observe this one. I hope you will attain as he attained.

"I questioned him again: 'Where did you come from, and where did you find that sutra?'" Hui-neng was very eager.

He said: 'I have come from Eastern Ch'an Temple in the district of Huang-mei in Ch'i-chou. In this temple, the Fifth Patriarch, Hung-jen, is in charge of the instruction of the monks, who number more than one thousand.'" The Fifth Patriarch was quite famous. He was Hung-jen, a Zen master. His temple, on Yellow Plum Mountain, was a big temple, and he was in charge of the instruction of his more than one thousand disciples. In Japan the temples are not so large. Daitoku-ji has about three hundred monks; Nanzen-ji, about three hundred. No temple in Japan has a thousand monks, but in China, in the T'ang dynasty, there was an army of monks.

"'I went there, paid my homage to him and heard this sutra. The patriarch always advises monks and lay people to just observe this Diamond Sutra'": It is not necessary to observe any other sutra. As a Buddhist, you must *observe* the *Diamond Sutra*; however, it is not necessary to *read* it. In Zen, there are three koans that cover it. If you pass through these three koans, you will know what the *Diamond Sutra* is. Hui-neng's enlightenment came from this sutra. These three koans are on the same three points the Fifth Patriarch gave to Hui-neng in his commentary before he appointed him the Sixth Patriarch. These are the koans you must pass. The three koans or points are:

1) Depending upon nothing, you must manifest your mind.
2) Buddha and his enlightenment come from this sutra.

3) If you try to see *Tathagatha* with your eye, or if you try to hear Tathagata with your ear, your practice is wrong.

We are still observing these three important points, called the "three eyes." Such great koans give you the foundation of mind. I hope that someday, by some koan, you will come truly to your own realization, face to face with this enlightenment.

"*. . . Since one who follows it will discover his essential nature*": What is essential nature? Where is your essential nature? Of course human nature is essential nature, but underlying human nature is animal nature. Is animal nature your real nature? Underlying animal nature is vegetable nature. Is that your essential nature?

When I came to this country, all the teachers here were talking about "higher" and "higher" nature. Of course that would be the New York style of speech because the skyscrapers here are getting higher and higher. The Equity Building is higher than the Metropolitan Tower, and the Woolworth Building is still higher, and now there is the Empire State. In Buddhism, we do not say "higher," we say "deeper." We do not seek the future, we return to the past. We do not try to take the brain out and throw it into the sky. We go deeper and deeper into the heart, not higher and higher. We dig into our own mind. We dig our heart deep so as to find the true nature that has been covered by the dust of habit and education.

"*. . . And become a buddha directly.*" The patriarch said he will himself become a buddha. What is Buddha, after all? He was a human being, but he attained buddhahood. So we, too, will attain buddhahood. Everyone will attain buddhahood.

"*I, Hui-neng, had the good fortune to be informed of this.*" This is a very short line, but it states the Oriental attitude. He listened, and he heard this. We have been informed many times, but the information that would be very valuable does not enter our ears. The train-time to Coney Island you can remember, yes. But that which is your good fortune to hear, you do not hear, and you are not informed of it. Hui-neng had the good fortune to be informed of it, and he said, "I thank you very much." He was so grateful. When he heard it, it really entered his heart.

Someone in Alaska was informed that there was an old mine which an old man had dug unsuccessfully until he died. Another man came and dug for another ten years and died there as well. A fourth man came along and heard of the other two. Finally, this man dug out the channel of gold, and in his excitement, he became crazy and committed suicide.

In the Zen school, this spiritual gold mine is found. The channel is already dug; you must only inform yourself of the way there. This channel of Great Spirit was struck by Shakyamuni Buddha twenty-five-hundred years ago, and the gold still comes out, an endless channel of spiritual gold.

Maybe we were there, twenty-five-hundred years ago, and our minds still remember. So when Hui-neng heard that line, he suddenly found his soul and said:

"*It may be that I had some tie of causality with this sutra from a past incarnation.*" This idea of reincarnation reaches into our human life. When I entered the monastery, I never dreamed I would come out as a Zen master. And when I first came to America in 1906, to San Francisco, I never dreamed I would come to America and finally teach Buddhism in English.

When I came to New York about eighteen years ago, my intention was to see the works of Rodin and to study modern sculpture. I went to Central Park and sat on a bench—I remember that clearly. But it was not in my mind to stay. Yet, I must now think there was some previous relation, so that now we are together, and I lecture Buddhism to you.

"Then, too, a stranger gave me ten taels in silver, which allowed me to provide for the needs of my old mother, and suggested that I go to Huang-mei to pay homage to the Fifth Patriarch. I, therefore, furnished my mother with all she might need in my absence, and then left." In China, old men and women are greatly respected. If a child falls on the street, no one pays any attention to it. But if an old man or woman falls on the street, everyone runs to pick them up. The child has done nothing for the people of the world, so there is no reward to accept. But the old person has done enough for the people of the world to accept the reward. To accept the reward is their privilege. According to filial piety, if any young man deserts his old mother, he will not be accepted as a member of the village when he returns. An old country like China has its golden age in the past, so all look back and the future is of no importance. If there was nothing done in the past, what can they expect in the future?

This boy was eager to go and meet the Fifth Patriarch, but his old mother was a drawback to him, so he was unable to go. Fortunately he was given the money—ten taels—ten large silver pieces that could provide for all his mother's needs in his absence. Therefore he had the opportunity to go to Huang-mei to pay homage to the Fifth Patriarch.

Hui-neng's home was where Canton is today, in Hsin-chou in the southern part of the state of Canton. Today, Canton is a famous city; but in the period of the T'ang dynasty, it was just a village, and aborigines were living there. Some of the southwestern part of China is still a country of savages. The English are trying to occupy that area because of the gold mines there. It is very hot, with huge jungles where no man would ever put a foot. Today, Canton is a sublime city, but in the T'ang dynasty, it was a savage land.

So Hui-neng departed from that savage land, passed through the mountain range of mainland China to the north, and sailed across the great river where on the other shore was Huang-mei—Yellow Plum. Many yellow plums were there on Yellow Plum Mountain. By foot, the journey took about one month.

"I journeyed about thirty days and finally reached Huang-mei, where I paid homage to the Fifth Patriarch." In the morning, as was the custom, the Fifth Patriarch would go to the main temple to receive anyone who had come. Hui-neng was not a monk, so he paid homage with the multitude. Standing there with many people behind him, he took the opportunity to make a conversation with the Fifth Patriarch while paying his homage.

To pay homage is not to shake hands, but to kneel down with the forehead touching the ground. In India, the visitor embraces the feet of the master and touches them with his forehead, but in China the visitor cups his hands before the master's feet and raises them up. Today, we do the same thing in Japan when we take *sanzen*. In China, from ancient days, this gesture has meant to hold up [raise] the teacher's feet.

"The patriarch questioned me: 'Where have you come from, and what do you want?'" From what direction? There are manifold directions. From what direction do you come?

The question is simple; the meaning is deep—the usual questions. One must expect this when paying homage.

"I replied: 'I am a commoner from Hsin-chou in Ling-nan. I have come this long way to pay homage to the Master. I want nothing but to become a buddha.'" Certainly he stated something! He had some nerve to say such big words! Of course, when he heard that line recited by the stranger—"Depending upon nothing, find your own mind"—he opened the eye of his mind. He already had some enlightenment to say, "I came to see if my buddha-nature is true or not."

The Sixth Patriarch was very modest: "I am a commoner of Hsin-chou." He did not say he was the son of an official. He said he was a "commoner." "I have come this long way (one month's journey, walking day and night through mountains and rivers) to pay homage to the Master. I ask nothing but to become a buddha, to realize the buddha within myself."

An honest, sincere student. When he heard the words, he could not wait, but crossed over mountains and rivers changing many straw sandals, sleeping in fields and on mountains, and finally reaching Huang-mei. "I desire to attain buddhahood!" In this, it is already implied that he will attain to the place of the Sixth Patriarch. There is no doubt that upon this word, the Fifth Patriarch looked at him.

"The patriarch said: 'You are from Ling-nan. That means you are a savage! How can you become a buddha?'" A test for him! In a Japanese temple, when a young boy wishes to study Zen, begs to study, the master tests him this way to find out what his nature is. "Look at my face!"—bang! If the boy says, "You hit me!" and runs out, foolish boy. It's a test. The master finds his nature immediately. There is a saying: "Pure gold must be tested by fire; green jade must be tested by stone." This means: "You are a savage. How can you realize buddhahood within you? Go away! No good! Go away!" Maybe this is the old style, but it is good to test the true one.

In my day, when a boy became twenty or so, he had to go to the army, to a regiment. The officer would slap his face. Of course, this is very rude, but there is something in it that is very warm.

"I said: 'To be a native of the South or of the North is natural to a man, but there is neither North nor South in the nature of buddha. The flesh of a savage is not the flesh of an abbot; but how can my buddha-nature be discriminated from yours?'" I think it's not necessary to give a commentary on these lines. It's stated clearly.

I felt racial discrimination quite strongly when I was in California, where the Japanese were discriminated against. Once I tried to get on a trolley car and ran after it, but it would not stop. Then I waited and waved, but the car would not stop for me. I looked around a corner where two ladies were waiting. They got on and I hurried after them, but the car did not wait. It was uncomfortable. I do not particularly blame Americans. Race prejudice exists everywhere. But there is no race prejudice in Buddhism. At such times, I always recalled this line and would say, "The flesh of a Japanese is not the flesh of an American; but how can my buddha-nature be distinguished from his?" I think in another century this feeling will not exist anymore. I myself felt it quite strongly when I was twelve years old. I went to a seaport and saw a white sailor for the first time, and the sight was very strange.

"The Fifth Patriarch wished to talk further with me, but seeing that the other monks were there, he then ordered me to do some work along with the rest of the assembly." Any student or monk who goes to a strange temple, a temple where he does not belong, from the first day must undertake some manual labor with the other monks or lay brothers.

Today in Japan the monks are rich and protected by the government; and, as they are participating in politics, they are protected by the dictator. Meanwhile they are not studying anything. They have been sleeping for four hundred years, and they do not know the meaning of the sutras. But those early monks in China were producing their own food by manual labor and supporting themselves by their own work. In their spare time they were studying Buddhism or meditating. That is the true attitude of a monk's life.

In accordance with the rule of the temple, the patriarch ordered Hui-neng to do some manual labor with the multitude. It meant that the Fifth Patriarch would keep him in his temple, and that he would be accepted as a member.

"I said: 'I would like to say to the Abbot that'": If he were a real monk, he would not say this. A monk would say, "Yes, my master," when the patriarch said, "Do some manual labor." But Hui-neng was not familiar with the rule and tried to say something.

"'*Wisdom is always growing from my own mind.*'" The wisdom that grows from your own mind is not the *informed* knowledge that grows from your intellect. In Buddhism, this wisdom is *intrinsic*. It is the Knower.

It is strange that we have this wisdom while the vegetables in the vegetable kingdom do not. Of course they have it, but it is in dormancy, it is sleeping. When you cut a branch, the vegetable does not feel pain, but if you cut a branch of a human body, how it feels! Not only that, but you are gathering thoughts, you are thinking something. What is that thinker? It is wisdom. In what part of your body is it? Where is this function and the root of this function? You say, "In the brain!" What part of the brain? Where is the throne of this wisdom?

This wisdom is buddha of course. You know that wisdom is in you, but you do not localize it. How do you see if you cannot localize your eyes? I can see the sky, and it is blue. The flower is red; the grass is green; but what *does* this? It is curious to me. I do not know. Some function that is unknown to me is in me, and it sees, but I cannot localize it. Your wisdom thinks, your wisdom knows, and your wisdom gathers thoughts. Your wisdom reasons, but if you never see wisdom, you never clearly localize it.

I had my own experience before I found the real figure of my wisdom. All those many, many years, I was nothing but intoxicated. My wisdom acted, but it did not act accurately.

In the Zen school, there are three gates: First we find the universal position of our self; second, we localize wisdom; third, we realize or prove nirvana. In the realizing of these three great gates, there are intervals. Though you pass a koan once a day, there are intervals. Usually it takes six or seven years.

When you find nirvana, then nirvana enters you. After six or seven years you say, "Oh, this way!" Suddenly you find the eye of the mind, and with this eye you can look at pure, clear nirvana—emptiness. No mind center can observe this nirvana. The only eye that can see nirvana is the eye of wisdom. If you find this, in one or two years, you will find the eye of nirvana. Then slowly you can free yourself from all bondage. About ten years after finding nirvana, you will find your own salvation.

True religious experience takes time. You sow the seed of a peach or a chestnut tree, and it is three years before it bears fruit. You sow the seed of a persimmon and wait for eight years. For attaining Buddhist experience, you must wait thirty years—quite a long time. Wise man or idiot, when you enter into the way of religion, you must wait about thirty years. You must enter from a true gate. Otherwise in thirty years, you have nothing. "Please, God, do not let Abyssinia and Italy fight!" This is asking too much. This is not religion at all. When you have true religion, you do not need to supplicate.

"'*When one does not stray from one's own nature, one finds the 'field of merit.'*'" Like water springing ever and ever from the well of our soul. This "field of merit" is not the fortune of old oil wells or gold mines. It is the true understanding of human life. Why do we have to labor? Why do we have to work? Someone lives to seventy or eighty years, then dies. He has never asked himself why he has to work, why he has to labor. Someone wakes up at midnight and asks himself: "Why do I have to live?" Perhaps he cannot answer. This is the life of an animal.

Understanding is the field of merit, and this field of merit lies within my own nature.

"'*I wonder what labor you ask of me.*'"—"I am always laboring to dig out my wisdom."

"*The patriarch said: 'This savage is too smart! Not another word! Get to work!*'" Very kind! To speak is not religion. Where he works, there is religion. In American slang: "You're too fresh! Go! Get to work!"

"*I retired and went to the rear of the temple. A lay brother was there who told me to split firewood and pound rice with the rice pestle. This I did for more than eight months.*" I think I once told you about the pestle and mortar. The mortar was a very big stone, and the pestle was made of heavy wood with a very long shaft. Two crosspieces were balanced with stones, and when you stepped down, the stone crashed down.

The Sixth Patriarch was treading on this shaft every day. As he was a small man, his weight was not enough to press the pestle down, so he carried a large stone around his waist. (When I was eight or nine years old, it was my work to help harvest rice for one hour after I came home from school every day.) The Sixth Patriarch spent eight months doing this, eight months of hard work, and he did not say a word. He spoke no doctrine, no philosophy. It shows that he was true material for true religion.

"One day, unexpectedly, the patriarch came to see me and said: 'I thought that your view was acceptable, but I feared that some ill-natured persons might do you harm. That was the reason I did not talk further with you then. Did you perceive that?'"—"I understand your viewpoint. It wasn't so bad, but I didn't speak to you then because we were surrounded by many monks who might harm you. There are many jealous and envious monks."

This part is very strange. The Fifth Patriarch came into the barn and explained. In the newly discovered record at Tun-huang, this part is not written. Perhaps someone inserted it to show admiration for the Sixth Patriarch. The excavated sutra was found in a cave temple outside the western border of China, near Tibet. Shifting sands had gradually covered the temples, which were cut into the wall of a mountain. The French and Russians wanted to find something and discovered *The Sixth Patriarch's Record* covered by sand and concealed from the eyes of students for about a thousand years. Today we open and compare. In places it is very different and very interesting.

"I replied: 'I understood my Master's mind. That is why I have never gone to the front of the temple—to keep people from realizing the situation.'" I think this part is not necessary. I believe the Sixth Patriarch's not going to the front part of the temple was not to conceal the situation between himself and the Fifth Patriarch. I think this is a rather farfetched explanation. The Sixth Patriarch was not a man who planned something ahead of time. He was an honest student. It was simply that he had no business in the front part of the temple. He was so busy with his own thoughts that eight months passed like a dream. He never tried to meet the Fifth Patriarch. For eight months nothing existed in his mind, not even his work. He was in *samadhi*. He was just pounding and concentrating into his own wisdom.

This part is really negligible, but it was in the sutra I was translating, so I keep it exactly as it was written.

One day the patriarch summoned all the disciples and said: "I have brought you all here to tell you that the question of life and death is the greatest problem of human life. All day long, you are seeking the "field of merit" instead of deliverance from the bitter sea of life and death. If you are deluded about your self-nature, merit is useless to save you."

SOKEI-AN SAYS:

There is no other question in the world. All questions are really about life and death. In misfortune you will be confounded because it means death to you. When you find a nickel on the street, you will be delighted because it means life to you. More or less all questions are connected with your life and death, and while you are talking about it, your life will come to an end. You cannot say in this last moment, "Wait a little because I must settle my questions!" Before you can define what life and death are, you must close your eyes and give up breathing and say goodbye.

Of course, if you do not care about this, you cannot say anything about it. But if you have wisdom, this wisdom will not permit you to die in ignorance. You have a stomach: if you try to die by not eating food, your stomach will not permit you; if you do not fill your stomach, it will complain until you feed it. You have a brain: if you do not fill your brain with mental food, *it* will complain. You are quite faithful to your stomach, but you are very unfaithful to your brain. Of course the stomach is first, but if you fill your brain with mental pabulum, your brain will degenerate, and you will become a *preta*, a hungry ghost. You will be in a state of everlasting hunger. You will have that starved look.

Perhaps it is your habit to eat so as to reduce your body, but you do not need to reduce your brain. When you look at someone who does not feed his brain, he looks so cheap; and when he speaks, he is a *preta*, a hungry monster. Though he goes about with his head up and a big cigar in his mouth, we do not call him a gentleman because he does not feed his brain. Though he has money, we do not call him rich because he seeks no deliverance, no emancipation from his sea of agony—life and death. He will die in this sea of agony like a cat and drop into the gutter.

"Go, look into your own wisdom." Go back home and meditate, and look into your own wisdom.

When you are told about wisdom, you do not need to open and look into books, or listen to anyone. Go back home and meditate on your own wisdom. Wisdom is in you, not in books. Use it!

*"With your original wisdom [*prajna*]...":* This is your own original *prajna*-nature, your transcendental wisdom. When we understand everything at once, without thinking or speaking, it is *prajna*-wisdom. If we say life and death are all one, this is the usual wisdom; it is not *prajna*. *Prajna* is different. It is not to be expressed in words. When you have this wisdom, you will look at a friend who also has it, and you will both understand. We do not need to say a word. But if you have no *prajna*, though you meet one who has it, you will not know, will not understand. It *is* strange.

Once a gentleman came here saying he came from China. He said he had a monastery in China and was going to start one here. I asked him, "How do you teach?" He said, "Oh, by lecture and meditation." He was not a Zen man. I forget his name, it was a very long one. If he had Zen, and I had asked him, "How do you teach Zen?" he would have looked at me and there would be no need of a word.

If a student under Rinzai came here and I asked him, "How do you teach Zen?" his hand would be very quick. You cannot fool a Zen teacher.

"Each one of you make a gatha *and present it to me."* A *gatha* is a little formal poem of four lines. There is a *gatha* that was some student's answer to the koan:

> *Throughout the three worlds*
> *There is nothing,*
> *No entity.*
> *Where do you find your soul?*

This was his answer:

> *The white cloud is my canopy*
> *The running stream is my heart*

I play a tune or two
But no one can hear them
After the rain
The pool of midnight is bottomless

You must understand that this *is not* the answer to the koan, but the articulation of his answer *already* made. First there must be the *manifestation* of the answer. My translation is not beautiful, but the poem is very beautiful. The answer is hidden, but the student of Zen can see it.

When you pass a koan, the teacher may say, "All right," and then says, "To this there was such-and-such an answer:

The white cloud is my canopy
The running stream is my heart
I play a tune or two
But no one can hear them
After the rain
The pool of midnight is bottomless

"I" play. This is a very big "I!" No one has an ear to hear this.

"'If you have realized the great principle of Buddhism, I shall transmit the robe and the Dharma to you and ordain you as the Sixth Patriarch.'" When Bodhidharma came from India to China, he transmitted his canon to the Second Patriarch, Hui-k'o. He said: "I have transmitted my Dharma, which is sealed by my mind. Besides this, I shall transmit these four volumes of the *Lankavatara Sutra.*"

This was not such an old sutra, but the Zen school was relying upon it. The Fifth Patriarch, however, recommended the *Diamond Sutra.* Our view today is that the true Zen school does not rely upon any sutra. The sutra of the Zen school is *this* living mind, *this* living body. Without this living body, there is no sutra.

The pedigree of the line from Shakyamuni Buddha today somehow still exists. There are two different streams in the pedigree, but the two finally met in Japan about four generations ago. So now there is just one column. If a teacher has no pedigree, we do not accept his authority. We ask him: "What is your pedigree? What master have you succeeded to in Zen?" Of course, we do not care about a written pedigree when we have faith in our Dharma. But in the Zen school, pedigrees are very important. In other schools, pedigrees are not so important.

In the Zen school, there is this transmission from mind to mind, face to face, not writing or speaking, so the teacher is very important. If the teacher is no good, then all his disciples are of no significance. In all other schools, the monk kneels down before wooden and painted images. In the Zen school, the monk kneels down only to the *roshi*, the symbol of the Three Treasures—Buddha, Dharma, Sangha. So when you come to the Zen room, you are saluting not the teacher but the Three Treasures in the mind of the teacher. You join hands and bow, not to human flesh, but to the principle within you.

In ordinary life, ancestry and parentage play an important part. But in the Zen school, if he has the Dharma, we do not care if a man comes from the house of a king or the house of a criminal.

Until you understand Zen, you will not understand the principle of transmitting the Dharma from heart to heart, mind to mind. When you enter the Zen school, you will realize the significance of the tradition of transmission. And when you have finished your Zen, the teacher will transmit the robe—"This is my robe from my teacher who had it from his through three generations"—and the canon. This means *all* the canon. We remember in our heart, but there is also a written part. We believe the canon is from the Buddha.

Sometimes when the teacher talks like this, the student thinks, "Well, I will steal it!" He goes into the teacher's room and opens the teacher's big chest. These are foolish students. Before a student knows anything, he may have such a foolish idea. He doesn't realize this would blind him forever. If a true student were to find it on the floor, he would turn his face away. It's too soon for him to know. In that moment, the eye of the mind can become blind. Such a student would never attain *dharmakaya*. Foolishness!

"'*This is urgent. Go at once! Do not delay! If you deliberate, it will be useless. One who realizes his own nature sees it instantly. If you are able to do this, you will realize it even in battle under slashing swords.*'" If you deliberate upon this *prajna*-wisdom, you cannot put it to use. If you think, "Well, what can *prajna* be? I will see my friend and ask," or "I will close my eyes and meditate upon it," this is no good. It is like putting a candle in an icebox and not using it. You must put it in a candle-stick and use it. Of course, if you have not yet found it, you cannot use it.

In the first koan, you will find the great universe. Then, sometime after that, suddenly, you will come to *prajna*. It is the first experience. But if you once come to *prajna*, you will find it again. You may pass through many koans, but still not find your wisdom. A wise student will find it in the first koan.

Look at it! How do you look at *prajna*? When I speak of this, you must look at it instantly! How do you do it?

In Zen, you know, we do not talk about God or Buddha—we ask you: "Where is God? Show Him to me." Well, it's impossible to show you God! God! Where? Show me the invisible! In Zen, we talk about *realization, manifestation*. There are many things to talk about, but if I do, I am not very kind.

If you attain it, it is not invisible. I ask you to show me. You say it is invisible. Humph! You will find it everywhere. You will find it on the tip of your toe. You will find it on top of your head. At midnight or in the morning, you will find it and see it.

"*Following the Master's instructions, all the monks retired. Discussing the matter among themselves, they said: 'It is unnecessary for all of us to clear our minds and try to make* gathas. *What merit can we expect merely from making them and presenting them to the Master? The head monk Shen-hsiu is virtually our instructor. He is certain to succeed. Why should we make* gathas, *exhausting our minds to no purpose?' Hearing this, the rest of the monks also gave up the endeavor. They said: 'We shall rely on our teacher Shen-hsiu and not trouble ourselves to make* gathas.'"

SOKEI-AN SAYS:

Fifteen hundred monks discussed this matter. In this corner was one group; in another corner was another group; and here and there others, saying: "It's unnecessary for us to clear our minds and compose *gathas*."

To "clear the mind" means, in meditation, to exterminate all mind-stuff. We do not need names, but to talk about something we need names. If you ask me, "What is this?" I say, "A glass of water." But for my own self, I do not need to question or answer—*this is this*. A word is like a ferry boat to carry meaning to the *other* one. If you ask me, "What is your name?" I say, "Sasaki"; but to me, my name is useless. In the Zen school, we do not need names at all, nor do we use symbols. A name is a type of symbol, like the symbols of algebra or chemistry: x,y,z. It's as if a doctor were to say: "Go back home and swallow a, b, and c," and you go back home and tear out the "a," "b," and "c" pages from the dictionary and eat them. This will not cure you; you must take the medicine itself. It is like philosophy: you can read the philosophy of reality, but you will not know reality. If I should ask you, "What is reality?" you would not know what to say. Reality is a big name in philosophy and religion; it's the conclusion of both. But no one knows how to answer the question: "What is reality?"

To clear the mind, you put strength into your meditation. You go into water or fire without disturbing yourself with useless mind-stuff. Mind-stuff is an instrument used to express something, like the silverware on the dinner table. After dinner you do not need such things. You clear the table and put the silver away. In the Zen school we despise anyone who when alone talks to himself. We use words in conversation, but when the conversation is over, we put these words out of our minds. You must clear the mind so that you can grasp something that is not in words, something you can prove, something you can realize. You will get nowhere in talking, brain-introspecting, or recalling incidents. You will not see the clear sky of Reality. But clearing the mind, you make room for something. If you talk to yourself—"I owe Mr. Brown five dollars from five years ago," or "I borrowed a pound of sugar from my neighbor"—it is no good. When you brush these clouds from your mind, you will see the full moon of truth. This is the truth that shines alone in the universe. In the orient, the moon is the symbol of this truth of the mind. It is not the symbol of love. And sometimes we do not need this moon at all; we smash it to see the clear sky. When I talk with someone, I use names like "moon" and "sky," but to myself, I use no names.

Before you make a *gatha*, you must realize the real state, and *then* put that experience into a *gatha*. If you are going to talk about New York, you must come to New York. Then you can go back and talk about it. In the Zen school, we do not permit talk about anything we have not experienced. To make a *gatha*, you must go back to your room and clear your mind.

Hung-jen's monks asked themselves: "What merit can we expect merely from taking our *gathas* and presenting them to the master?" These monks were no good. They were blind monks! There are many blind monks in Buddhism. They have the two eyes they got from their mothers, but they have no eye of the mind, so they cannot see the benefit they would get from clearing their minds.

The head monk, Shen-hsiu, was one of the great monks of that day. Everyone thought he would be the Sixth Patriarch, until the true Sixth Patriarch (according to this record) appeared. Shen-hsiu was a good man and a real scholar, the true scholar type. He read many sutras and was a student of the *Abhidharma*. He gained his knowledge from systematic Buddhist philosophy, in contrast to Hui-neng, who was just a common man who sold kindling wood in the streets of Canton. Hung-jen was very old, so he had given his position as instructor to Shen-hsiu without appointing him. So the monks thought: "Though we make *gathas*, exhausting our minds, we will not be able to beat Shen-hsiu anyway. He will make a *gatha* and become the Sixth Patriarch no matter what we do, so we need not make the effort."

They all gave up. One dog bays at the moon and thousands of dogs bay. Though there is no moon in the sky, if one dog bays, all the dogs of the town follow its example. In the same way, when one blind monk says something, all the others follow the common mind because they have no guiding principle to stand upon. It's as though someone were to say: "I'm enlightened! Someone pinched my nose, and I saw a green light! And all I paid was twenty-five dollars!"

In every generation, there is always one lodestone, and we rely upon him. After the Buddha's death there was Mahakashyapa, then Ananda. It's fortunate when everyone relies upon a Zen master who has been ordained by a teacher, a recognized torch holder. When the torch holder is designated, everyone can rely upon him with assurance.

In our meditation, we may reach a place we cannot speak about to just anyone: "I feel this and I think this, but no one would know what I am talking about." Our understanding is clear to us, but we may not know anyone who can approve it. So we search out someone who has the experience to approve it for us. We may go to this one and manifest our experience. If our experience is real, the teacher will say: "That is right. I, too, proved it the same way."

My teacher proved it for me, as he had it proved by his teacher; and with his teacher's teacher, it was the same. There is not much talk. The teacher will look at it and say, "That is all right." It is not imagination, not words. In the same way an antique dealer might go to a jeweller carrying a valuable object. He goes to an authority for assurance. The jeweller looks at it. It is true or it is false, and that is all. Show it to me, prove it to me, and if it is wrong, I will say, "No."

This is Zen. Everyone recognizes this in China, Japan, and Central Asia. I hope America will recognize it, too. This is not a notion we create in our minds and talk about. We prove it to one another but rely only on one who has the torch. There might be one who has a candle, but if there is no light, it is no good.

"Shen-hsiu, thought: 'The reason the monks are not presenting their gathas *is that I am their instructor. I must therefore make a* gatha *and offer it to the abbot. If I do not offer a* gatha, *how can he see whether my understanding is shallow or deep? If in offering a* gatha *I desire only the Dharma, my purpose is good. But if I seek the honor of becoming patriarch, my purpose is bad. It is just as though one with a common mind tried to usurp the position of a sage. Yet, if I do not present my* gatha, *I cannot obtain the Dharma. How very difficult this is!'"*

(Sokei-an comments: This is poor, the most miserable part. It proves that Shen-hsiu was blind. When a master looks at a student, he knows without listening to his *gatha* whether he is deep or shallow. But Shen-hsiu was blind and could not see this. We can see a vegetable, but the vegetable cannot see us. To see something, you must have an eye. Without it, though you meet an enlightened one on the street, you will not realize it, you will miss him. But Shen-hsiu was a true monk, honest, and very modest.)

"Leading to the hall of the Fifth Patriarch were three corridors. It was intended that the court artist Lu-chen would be invited to paint on the walls a mandala suggested by the Lankavatara Sutra *as well as the genealogical tables of the Five Patriarchs, so that tradition would be venerated and transmitted.*

"Shen-hsiu, having composed a gatha, *came several times to the front of the hall to offer it to the patriarch. But each time his mind became so confused that his whole body was drenched with sweat and he could not present his* gatha. *After four days had passed and he had made the attempt more than thirteen times, he had still failed in his purpose. He then asked himself what he should do.*

"'It is better,' he thought, 'that I write [my gatha] *on the wall of the corridor. If the Abbot sees and approves it, I shall come forward, and bowing down, tell him that I am its author. If it does not meet with his approval, then my years in this temple, accepting everyone's reverence, are of no significance for my practice of Buddhism.'*

"That midnight, without letting anyone know, he took a light and wrote his gatha *upon the wall of the southern corridor. The* gatha *said:*

> *'This body is a tree of wisdom*
> *This mind, a clear mirror*
> *Wipe it diligently always*
> *Let it gather no dust*

SOKEI-AN SAYS:

"'This body is a tree of wisdom'": The Buddha was enlightened after six years under the Bodhi Tree in India. The offspring of that tree was carried to Ceylon, where its offspring exists to this day. About ten years ago, too much wine was poured on its roots as a sacrifice, so, as the tree was dying, the English put a fence around it and forbade the pouring of any more wine.

The Bodhi Tree was a real tree of the vegetable kingdom, but "this body" is not vegetable. What is the meaning of "this body"? *This body* is a tree of wisdom—*This is That!* Some scientists would say it is electron, proton, quantum. An English scholar would say something else. But in the Zen school, *this body* is the four elements: earth, water, fire, air. *This* is body.

"'This mind, a bright mirror'": The soul is like a clear mirror. And, of course, this mirror is not made of iron or glass. It is the mirror on which all is reflected—soul-consciousness. The five shadows of mind are written in this mirror. Covering it, the five shadows are the constituents of this mirror. This mirror is intrinsically pure and made of sky. This mirror is infinite.

"'Wipe it diligently always'": Wipe it diligently hour by hour. Wipe it as you would a diamond. You have this diamond consciousness, this mirror made of infinite sky, so wipe it always.

"'Let it gather no dust'": Dust is mind-stuff. Clean it of mind-dust, the turmoil of mind padding, which is of no use and causes harm. The human being lives in this turmoil of dust from morning to evening, driven continually by this master. Your mind should be an instrument for your own use. But instead, driven by mind-stuff, it runs to the South, to the East River, to Peekskill, to Staten Island. You are used by your own servant whom you cannot use.

Shen-hsiu's point of view, "Let it gather no dust"—keeping mind-stuff off the surface of this consciousness—is his final conception. Later, the Sixth Patriarch thought that Shen-hsiu had not entered the gate of true Buddhism. From the view of true Buddhism, Shen-hsiu's way of thinking is not the true Law [Dharma]. But many Buddhists take his attitude, and all come to it at one time or another. To say that through this gate one will enter true Buddhism is not bad, but it is far from the highest aspect of Buddhism.

Most religious teachers take such a view of the human mind. Shintoism is like this and also Christianity. Keep your mind pure and your body clean. This attitude is not bad, but the view does not penetrate. There is more to think about. There are more worlds to enter. This is not the end of religion, not real salvation. In religion, there is true salvation.

"After he had completed writing his gatha, *Shen-hsiu went back to his cell without having been discovered by anyone. He debated in his mind: 'Tomorrow the Fifth Patriarch will see my* gatha, *and if he is pleased, it will signify that I have an affinity with Buddhism.*

In Buddhism, as in all the Orient, we think that we meet in this incarnation and love because we had an affinity in some past incarnation. Parents and children are thought to be the first meeting in such a chain. Perhaps in our next incarnation, with this past affinity, our bodies will incarnate into different sexes. Then, when we meet each other, an unconscious affinity will drive us to love and to become man and wife. In daily speech, we often speak like this. When a young man tries to make access to a young lady, taking refuge under a tree during a shower, he might say, "Well, young lady, we must have had some affinity in a previous incarnation since we are now under this tree together." Or when he takes leave of her, for instance, he might say, "Farewell, we shall meet in another incarnation." I am sure the Buddha would never have thought the doctrine of reincarnation would be used for making access to young ladies!

In Japan, when strangers drink from the same stream, one may say it is because they must have had some previous affinity. Of course, when the people are dying from a plague on both sides of a stream, there is certainly some affinity from drinking the same water. If a moth enters this candlelight, and you try to kill it, someone might say, "No, it may be the spirit of your grandmother!" It's quite poetical, perhaps religious, but it's also ridiculous. If my uncle reincarnates into a fly, I will kill it at once in order to emancipate him from that terrible body. Once a novice was eating fish and his superior screamed at him. The novice answered: "The soul of the universe is in that fish, and I eat it so that it may function in me."

Though we meet on a train or on a street corner, our unconscious affinity will make us greet one another as friends, and we will associate as master and servant or as teacher and disciple. In this record, the Sixth Patriarch remarks that, "There must have been a recurring relation between us through many *kalpas*." This is the usual Buddhist style, the usual talk in a Buddhist land.

If, however, it does not meet with his approval, I must realize that my delusions from the past are very deep and that, obstructed by them, I am unable to obtain the Dharma. It is impossible for me to fathom my teacher's mind! Occupied with such thoughts, he tossed anxiously in his cell until dawn." From a past life, I carry some delusion, not only from one incarnation, but perhaps from seven or eight incarnations. That is, one is deluded over and over again. Sometimes, a pupil in the temple after ten or fifteen years of hearing something over and over again still does not understand because he is so deluded. A monk will encourage such a boy: "I think you will not be able to understand it in this incarnation, but in the next." Very nice encouragement! Such a boy will take these words very seriously and study for the next incarnation. Another line relates to this same idea: Later, the Sixth Patriarch says, "I should like to read that *gatha* in order to establish some affinity with Buddhism for a future incarnation." This is Buddhist sentimentality, but it is quite optimistic. The idea is that man's life is not centered in this life only, he will have a future life. So if he cannot obtain enlightenment in this life, he will attain it in the next. If not in the next, he will incarnate seven times in the human shape and will attain enlightenment at last.

In Tibet, an ignorant person who cannot read sutras goes to the temple, listens to quantities of sutras, bears them on his back, goes up and down the mountains, and walks around a great *stupa* seven times; then dumps these sutras and gets more, over and over again. Such a person is trying to establish an affinity with Buddhism for future incarnations. "Though I cannot read these sutras, in some future incarnation I will, but I must make some relation now."

Poor Japanese novices who come from a farmer's family, though their brain is incapable of understanding the highest philosophy of Buddhism, will read the sutras anyway to establish an affinity with Buddhism. Of course, among them are some who can read sutras, understand the meaning and grasp the core of it. Naturally, they are venerated by the other monks. Or there might be some old country man who was born in a far-away land, who never had the opportunity to meet an enlightened teacher, or to stay in a temple where the true teaching prevailed. At eighty years of age, after having worked all his life long, he has ceased his labor in the foreign land. Now, before his death, he says, "I will go just once to a temple to establish some affinity with Buddhism for a future life." And from perhaps eight hundred miles away, the old man, supporting himself with a cane, takes this long walk. Begging for food, he comes to the headquarters temple where he will join the lecture to which all the monk's are listening. With an ear like a paper screen, he just listens to the sound, not understanding the meaning but listening with intensity in order to establish a future relationship. In ancient days, Japanese monks would go to China or India. Some would return, the rest having died on the way.

"The Fifth Patriarch knew that Shen-hsiu had not entered the gate or found his true nature. In the early morning, he summoned the court painter Lu to do the proposed painting on the corridor wall. Suddenly discovering the gatha, *the patriarch told him: 'It is unnecessary to paint anything on this wall. I am grateful to you for having come such a distance. In the* Diamond Sutra *it is said that all that has form is false. I shall keep this* gatha *here for people to recite. One whose practice is in accordance with this* gatha *will acquire great merit and can keep himself from falling into evil ways. Let my disciples bow and burn incense to this* gatha. *Those who recite it will find the realization of their true nature.'"* It is true. Anyone who takes this *Hinayana* attitude will never fall into evil ways. Sometimes when people try to take the Mahayana attitude, they fall into hell. In Mahayana Buddhism, you jump from the frying pan into the fire unless you thoroughly understand the Hinayana attitude. The practice of Mahayana is dangerous without the understanding of Hinayana Buddhism. One cannot exist without the other. There is no Hinayana without Mahayana. They are like the two wings of a bird or the two wheels of a cart. To be a true Buddhist, you must understand both.

"All the disciples read the gatha *of Shen-hsiu and expressed their admiration for it. At midnight, the patriarch summoned Shen-hsiu to his quarters and questioned him: 'Did you write that* gatha?' *Shen-hsiu replied: 'Yes, it was I who wrote it. But I dare not aspire to the position of patriarch. My hope was that out of compassion you might ascertain whether or not I have some slight knowledge of Buddhism.' The patriarch said: 'If it is your* gatha, *you have not yet seen your original nature'"*

SOKEI-AN SAYS:

It is like your experience in preparing to offer an answer to your teacher in *sanzen*. In your mind you feel that your answer is tangible, but you cannot express it. You feel that you understand. But in the presence of the teacher, you cannot manifest it. You can talk about it, but you cannot grasp it with the true faith of your mind. It is like scratching your shoe when your foot itches. The *gatha* Shen-hsiu had written on the wall in the middle of the night was exactly like that.

> *This body is a tree of wisdom*
> *This mind, a clear mirror*
> *Wipe it diligently always*
> *Let it gather no dust*

To say that this body is a tree of wisdom is true. To say that this soul, this consciousness, is a mirror is also true. But to say, "Wipe it diligently always / let it gather no dust" is not quite Buddhism. Many religions take this attitude of keeping your soul clean. It is an idea created by a human being. But observe nature!

No pine tree takes this attitude, nor does the willow. Yet all religions must take this attitude as the first step in attainment. Without it, you cannot enter the gate. So all Buddhist monks take that attitude. Without passing through that gate, you cannot take the real attitude. Some adopt a false attitude: "I do not care if my soul collects dirt, I do as I will. After all, there is no dust, no mirror. I'll take it easy and drink wine, for there is no mirror, no soul, nothing!" Many think that this is Mahayana Buddhism, that this is freedom.

There is no way to prevent anyone from having that thought, but I know its consequences. You can accomplish your desire, but you will have to pay for it. So you think, "All right"; but if you chop off a policeman's head, you will have to pay the consequences! Desire must take a balance [balancing the gong-stick on a finger]. Desire and outcome; outcome and desire. You must always watch the balance.

Of course the Buddha taught the Middle Way—"to take a balance." This was also one of the important teachings of Confucius. It is interesting to know Confucius' own confession about this: "For forty years, I have been thinking about this Mean and practicing how to attain it. But whatever I have done, I realize that I have never accomplished this." Confucius created his theory of the Middle Way and practiced it, but he confessed that in forty years of practice, no deed of his perfectly realized the Middle Way. Well, he confessed; but if you observe his attitude very carefully, you will see that he manifested the Middle Way, for, without anxiety, he lived in this balanced state of mind. Of course, his state of mind was different from ours. Our state is lunatic. The greatness of Confucius is understandable when we read such wonderful words.

So you have to show the Middle Way itself, not this diagram I am showing you with my stick. This is not the real Middle Way. When you find it, you will be able to live and to sleep comfortably. If you take Shen-hsiu's attitude of "no dust," you cannot attain. To wipe the mirror every day is not a natural act. To live the natural way is very hard.

"You have reached the outer gate but not yet entered." Many religious teachers talk about religion but have never entered. It is like someone standing outside a restaurant. He smells the beefsteak being broiled, never having eaten it.

I think you know the story of the fish restaurant in Japan. Japanese fried fish has a very delicious smell. A poor student was standing outside the fish restaurant eating a poor lunch of bread while smelling the delicious fish. The owner of the restaurant came out and said: "Young man, you are smelling my food, and yet you never pay me a penny for it. You must pay for this delicious smell!" The student took a small coin from his pocket, threw it on the floor and said: "Certainly, I will pay. Please take this sound. For the smell of your food, I pay with the sound of this money." Sound pays for smell, neither has any substance. Some teachers, never having entered the gate, have not experienced what they are teaching. We do not waste time like that. Names are only symbols. We have to grasp Reality. Do not waste your time!

Finally, Hung-jen told Shen-hsiu:

"'Your understanding indicates that though you have sought supreme enlightenment, you have not yet attained it. Supreme enlightenment should be attained instantaneously. When you find your original mind and see your original nature, you will realize that it has never been created and will never be destroyed. At all times, at every moment, you see it.'" Too much! Too many words are written here. It's as if you're selling water by the riverside where there is plenty of water already. No one wants to buy it.

When the teacher says the first word, you must grasp it. There is no time for thinking—"Before father and mother, what was your original aspect?" You must grasp it immediately! Do not carry it around with you for two or three years. Grasp it, and manifest it. At all times, at every moment, you will see it. You do not think or feel something. *You actually see it.* Like the disciple who touched the wounds of Christ and cried, "I believe!" He *saw* it. *See* the seamless tower that Indra built, and you will believe.

This word "see" is a very important word in the Zen school. When you say "Oneness" or "Eternity," the teacher will say: "Show it to me!" You can see it always, and it never disappears. It is as clear as the tip of your nose.

I think all this philosophy has very little value in Zen. Probably these lines were written by a monk during some lecture, and later the writings on the margin were carried into the main sentence to make this kind of a mess.

"*Then no barriers remain among things, one truth is the truth for all, each thing in the world is just as it should be, and the mind's self-awareness is the nature of Reality.*" The mind knows of that awareness. It is the nature of Reality. In other words, this feeling is the feeling of God. The awareness of God and the awareness of human beings are not two different awarenesses.

"*One who understands this has understood the supreme enlightenment of self-nature.*" I would not give a penny for this line. It is not the Fifth Patriarch's. All that philosophizing! Although we sometimes speak such nonsense to teach young monks.

"'*You had better return to your cell. Ponder this for one or two days, then write another* gatha *and bring it to me. If I see that you have entered the gate, I shall transmit the robe and Dharma to you.' Shen-hsiu made a bow and retired. Several days passed, but he did not succeed in writing another* gatha*. His mind became confused and uneasy as though he were in a dream. He felt uncomfortable whether he sat or walked.*" The Fifth Patriarch seemed to encourage Shen-hsiu, but his tone of voice showed desperation. Shen-hsiu had been staying in the temple for years, yet he had not entered the gate. How could he make a *gatha* and enter the gate in a couple of days?

Shen-hsiu returned to his cell and tried to meditate upon a new *gatha*. He had forgotten his standpoint of Zen: had become an artist and was not a Zen monk any more. When one tries to "make" something, he forgets his own standpoint.

In my own case, I studied art for years, but I gave it up because an artist is making something besides his own daily life. His daily life is no longer true. He must express more than the ordinary person, must "make" something extra. This annoyed me a great deal. I like to take a real attitude. When I walk, sleep, eat, talk—every moment is religion to me. I do not like to copy anything. I see a mountain, a woman, a tree, that is enough. Why should I make a portrait?

Somehow art and the attitude of the artist is not the true thing. Art is a branch of the true thing. There is a distinction between the artist and the religious person. A man may be a wonderful actor, but when he shouts "O-O-O-H!" on the stage, it is not real to him, not his own. But when I shout "O-O-O-H!" in my room, it is real to me and not a copy. Some artists will take exception to this view, but that is the reason I gave up art. I have my own face; I do not need to make a portrait. And I have my own world; I do not need to make a copy of it. I do not wish to lead a double life. I am trying to be simple. I do not mean to discourage other artists, but this is my attitude.

When Shen-hsiu tried to express himself in a *gatha*, he entered into a different channel. Why make an effort to express oneself? If he had understood Zen, he would have expressed himself spontaneously, and that would have been a beautiful *gatha*. His attitude was not that of a Zen monk, so he could not make a new *gatha*. His mind became blank and uneasy. He had no word to say. If there is any thought in the mind, it is not Zen. There is no word to utter. So when he tried to "make" something, his mind became blank and uneasy. This is the sickness of Zen monks.

It was as though he were in a dream. He was swimming in the air. Many people are like that. From morning to evening they are living in thoughts that are not real. All words are thoughts and not real.

The Ethiopians are fighting the Italians, the Italians are fighting the English, and the League of Nations is talking, talking, talking—all words. The modern tendency is to discuss everything. When Japan tried to take Manchuria and the whole world was against it, they could not say a real word—"We want that land, and we are going to get it!" Nor could they say, "We need this land because we are overpopulated." Instead, they had to say, "We have no intention of taking their land," and then they went ahead and took it! This is the diplomacy of today: cover things with thoughts and believe these thoughts. It is just living in a dream. Their feet are not on the ground.

"After several days passed, a novice went by the mill reciting Shen-hsiu's gatha*.—'This body is a tree of wisdom / This mind, a clear mirror / Wipe it diligently always / Let it gather no dust.*

"When I heard it, I knew at once that whoever had made this gatha *had not yet seen his original nature."*

SOKEI-AN SAYS:

He had not entered the gate of Buddhism. The body is a tree of wisdom, that is to say: This body is not flesh, it has no material existence. It is just a vision. The real existence of the body is intrinsic wisdom. The soul is the mirror of consciousness. It is perfect, but we forget this because it is covered with dust—delusion—so we must find this delusion and destroy it. We do not care about this material world. We must wipe the mirror (soul) clean and find that true mirror of consciousness.

Such transcendentalism is not true Buddhism, it is Hinayana. But a good Hinayanaist does not believe this. There is no such monster in a true human being. Even a dog or a cat does not take such an attitude. Only foolish human beings take it. Especially in this country where Buddhism is not really taught.

Shen-hsiu's attitude was good, but it is not true Buddhism. When you enter true Buddhism and experience the seamless tower with your living flesh, you will know that matter and spirit are relative. If we refuse matter, we must also refuse spirit.

"For, though I had received no instructions from anyone, I already understood the main principle of Buddhism." Hui-neng had no instruction from any monk or teacher. He had heard one line from the *Diamond Sutra*: "Depending upon nothing, find your actual soul!" When he heard this, he was suddenly enlightened. Then he entered the temple of the Fifth Patriarch, and for eight months, he was pounding rice. He never heard one word of Buddhism. Yet, when he heard the *gatha* of Shen-hsiu, he said: "It is not true!"

"Finally I questioned the novice: 'What is the gatha *you were reciting?' The boy replied: 'Oh, you savage! Don't you know the word of the master? He said that life and death is the greatest problem of human existence. He wishes to transmit his robe and Dharma, and has ordered his disciples to compose* gathas *and bring them to him. If he finds that anyone has understood the main principle of Buddhism, he will transmit to him his robe and Dharma and make him the Sixth Patriarch. The head monk Shen-hsiu wrote a* gatha *on formlessness on the wall of the south corridor. The Master commanded all of us to recite it, saying that one whose practice is in accord with this* gatha *can keep from falling into evil ways and receive great benefit.'"* The master did not say one will get great emancipation and find freedom. He said, "In everyday life, one can save oneself from falling into evil ways." Hmm! A true Zen student will not apply the measure of good and bad. True existence is neither good nor bad.

I am not at all certain this *gatha* was made by Shen-hsiu. I will explain later how this whole record was made. When we come into what looks like the true record of the Sixth Patriarch, you will feel that this part is just dramatization. But to understand Zen, it is not bad to begin with this part. From it, you will understand the mind of the Zen student of that day.

"I said: 'I should like to read that gatha *in order to establish some affinity with Buddhism in a future incarnation. Honorable one, I have been here treading this pestle for more than eight months and have not yet been to the front of the temple. I hope that you will lead me there and allow me to bow before the* gatha.'" Even today, if you go to China, you will see these former *gathas* written on the wall. The monks go there and burn incense, bow down and read them. And while they are reading them, thousands of tourists come from America and take pictures of them. They will ask about the light, "How long has it been burning?" A monk will answer, "Three thousand years." Some tourist will say, "Oh!" and blow it out. From the Oriental standpoint, they are just barbarians, but I hope this is just a story.

"The boy led me there and let me bow before the gatha. *I said: 'I am an unlettered man. Please, my honorable one, read it to me.'"* The boy must have been seventeen or eighteen years old, yet Hui-neng said, "My honorable one"!

"An official of Chiang-chou whose name was Ch'ang Jih-yung happened to be there and read the verse aloud. When I heard it, I said: 'I too have made a gatha. Oh officer, please write it down for me.' The official said: 'What! You, too, have made a gatha? *That is odd.'"* Poor fellow! The magistrate, as in Rome, is the censor of morality. He investigates the population and its culture. He goes around the state about twice a year and is like an educational monitor and is head of the bureau of police. The officer in attendance upon the magistrate follows him as a guard. This was the officer in attendance upon the magistrate. This officer was visiting the temple of the Fifth Patriarch, and he was in the south corridor looking at Shen-hsiu's *gatha*. He had heard the conversation between the novice and the manual laborer, so he read the *gatha* aloud for him. And when Hui-neng heard it, he said, "At last!" He had been holding back, but finally became impatient.

"I replied: 'He who would study supreme enlightenment should not slight a beginner. The lowest of men may have the highest wisdom, and the highest of men may have wisdom that is unawakened. If you slight anyone, you will commit immeasurable offence.' The officer said: 'Just recite your gatha, *and I shall write it down for you. But if you obtain the Dharma, you must save me first. Do not forget my request!'"* That is, if you attain enlightenment, and if your enlightenment is recognized by the Fifth Patriarch, and if you succeed in becoming the heir of the Fifth Patriarch, you must save me first with your enlightened power.

"I recited this gatha:

> *'Wisdom is not a tree*
> *The mirror is not a mirror*
> *From the beginning*
> *Is there anything to gather dust?'*

"'Wisdom is not a tree'": Where is wisdom? It has no shape. It is not mind-stuff. It is not a dream. Wisdom is not a moonbeam, not electricity. Wisdom has no home, no place where it can stay.

"'The mirror is not a mirror'": This consciousness is not a mirror. This consciousness that we have is like a mirror, but is there any shape to consciousness?

"'From the beginning'": Before father and mother, or before the creation of the world.

"Is there anything to gather dust?" There is nothing—no thing. So there is no place where dust can gather. I would say, "Is there any dust?" If you really understand this, your study of Zen is over.

When I finished my Zen, when my teacher sealed my diploma and gave it to me, he said: "Your Zen is over." I knew I had finished it, and I came back to my own quarters and I thought, "This is the end. At the end of twenty years, what is this after all?" I could not understand. "Of course this must be Zen, but what is this under heaven and on the earth?" I made a poem—

> *I was looking for my own house.*
> *Many times I came to the gate,*
> *But I forgot my own house;*
> *I did not go into it.*
> *And after long, long travelling*
> *I returned to my own house.*
> *I realized that my furniture, my books*
> *And everything that belonged to me were there,*
> *Just as they were there when I left*

When I made this poem, I recalled an old man's poem. After many, many years he returned to his home on the Yangtze River. His wife and his two children had died, but everything was still there! Everything was in the kitchen. The chickens were still in the garden, and the rats were still in the house. Nothing had really happened in those many, many years. But his fingers told him that the wrinkles on his cheek had become deeper. That was the poem.

For a little while, I did not realize that this was, for me, complete emancipation. There is some danger for a little while after you have finished Zen. You can take a religion like Christianity or Mohammedanism, but this is very hard to take. However, in this Zen, you will find yourself.

"When the gatha *was written, the monks were astonished. There was not one who did not stand aghast looking at it. They talked among themselves: 'How remarkable! Surely one cannot judge a man by his appearance! Why did we hard press that living bodhisattva for so long?'"* What did he say after all? One need not wipe dust from one's soul. There is no soul, and there is no dust. But Shen-hsiu's *trikaya*—"This body is a tree of wisdom / This mind, a clear mirror / Wipe it diligently always / Let it gather no dust"—means you must keep your soul clean and keep your wisdom free. Do not let it gather dust. You must wipe it always. Do not gather dust; do not commit any sin; and do not think any impure thoughts—that was Shen-hsiu's *gatha*. It expresses the usual Hinayana attitude, the attitude taken by all the religions of the world.

In my own country, there is a religion called Shinto—"The Way of Gods." In the deepest part of the Shinto shrine is the place of the Kami, the god, and in that place is a mirror made of iron. The mirror in the shrine of the Imperial household is octagonal, which is the symbol of the soul. When the priest nears this mirror, he covers his mouth with a triangular-shaped piece of paper in fear that his breath might mark the mirror, defiling it, as a Turkish woman covers her mouth with a veil. In ancient Egyptian pictures, the priest also covers his mouth with a cloth or paper. Once the mirror is carried to the sanctuary, no one will touch it for two or three hundred years. Finally it gathers dust and rust; it becomes red, then green. No one will touch it because it is a sacred object. But actually, Shinto teaches that the mirror is our own soul in which God enshrines, so we must take away the dust and keep it always pure. Shen-hsiu's Buddhism is the same as Shintoism—always keep your soul clean and free from impurity. It proves that religion is based on a consciousness that always exists and cannot be destroyed.

The Buddha's Buddhism does not take such an attitude. The Buddha thought that consciousness is in this existing world and has no place of existence elsewhere. No one created this consciousness. When something comes from the outside of consciousness, this consciousness reflects it as a mirror would. But when all objective existence disappears, consciousness also disappears. When you sleep deeply, it disappears. When you dream, consciousness is there, faintly. You cannot prove this consciousness in sleep. If you say it is dormant or latent consciousness, yes, but it is unconscious. You cannot call it "unconsciousness-consciousness."

Consciousness is *here*. The Buddhist does not believe it is mind or in any one part of the body. We believe that every particle of the body—the whole construction of the nervous system and all nerve centers, all of *this* body—everything—is consciousness. Do not ask me what consciousness is; everything is consciousness. And when I ask you, "What is consciousness?" do not shut your eyes. Open your eyes and look at me! That is the answer. It is just your imagination that you must keep consciousness clean. When all is consciousness, how can you keep it clean? Do you wash your body twenty-four hours a day? The Shintoist does. He washes his hands about fifty times a day. I observed my father doing this. Before he would speak, he would go into the kitchen and wash his mouth. Before eating, he washed his hands. Before going to the shrine he washed his whole body. Once every year he would go into the shrine and blow, and all his sins would be blown away. Then he would wipe his body with a paper shaped like a man. By morning, all the sins of the people in the village were gone. Shinto is a very good religion, very convenient, too! In ancient days the Shinto priest would take a man to the river, wash him, and bring him out all clean, all pure. To clean your soul with water is common, old-type religion. Christianity has it, too. But the Shinto priest actually washes his body thinking he is washing consciousness.

Hui-neng's religion is quite different. He thinks wisdom is not a tree, it has no shape; and consciousness is not a mirror, having no place and no one to create this consciousness. Originally, there was nothing to gather dust. What can gather dust? And when there is no dust, what are you talking about? Hui-neng had no need to wipe diligently, he had no fear of gathering dust. So the monks thought: "He is no common laborer!"

SOKEI-AN SAYS:

"The Fifth Patriarch saw the amazed crowd, and fearing someone might do me an injury, he rubbed out the gatha *with his shoe. He said: 'This, too, is a* gatha *made by one who has not seen his original nature.'"* Original nature is the nature of Universal Being. The nature that appears here in myself is human nature, but it is also universal nature. And when you find it out, it is buddha-nature.

"Everyone accepted his word." "Yes, I thought so too." It is easy to fool anyone. It is no good to follow like a blind mule. Such people are led by the nose because their souls are blind, and they cannot choose their own direction. Such a one is not living his own life, he is not talking in his own words. So, actually, he is not living; he is a ghost, and that is all.

"The next day, the Fifth Patriarch came secretly into the mill and saw me pounding rice, a big stone around my waist." Hui-neng was a small man. The shaft was so big that the weight of his body was unable to push it down with his foot. So he fastened a big stone to his waist. This is how he pounded the rice in

the huge mortar. After writing the *gatha* on the wall, he immediately went back to the mill and kept on working. The patriarch came in and looked at him.

"The patriarch said: 'One who seeks true law forgets himself for the law, and it must be thus.'" This line is an old saying in Buddhism.

"Then the patriarch questioned me:" The patriarch came near the mortar, sifted the rice through his hands and asked:

"'Has the rice been polished?' I answered: 'It was polished long ago, but it has not yet been sifted.'" The conversation is plain, isn't it? There is no display of thoughts or entanglements of philosophy. "Has the rice been polished?" "Yes, my Master, but it has not yet been sifted." Sift the rice and all the dust comes down, and the pure polished rice is there. They are not speaking of rice, you know. It is like saying, "Do you really grasp Buddhism?" "Yes, my Master, I polished the rice a long time ago, but no one has acknowledged it. You haven't tested my knowledge."

"The patriarch struck the mortar three times with his staff and went out." Perhaps there was somebody listening to the conversation between the two of them. So no one could understand what they were talking about when the patriarch struck the mortar three times and looked at Hui-neng.

"I understood the mind of the patriarch, and when the temple drum had boomed three times, I entered his room. The patriarch used his monk's stole as a screen in order that no one might see us, and expounded the Diamond Sutra *for me."* As I have said, there are three important parts, or points, in the *Diamond Sutra*:

1) Depending upon nothing, manifest your mind.
2) Buddha and his highest enlightenment come from this sutra.
3) If you try to see Tathagata with your eye, or if you try to hear Tathagata with your ear, your practice is wrong.

These are the important points in this sutra. As in Hui-neng's time, we are still observing these three important points. We say they are the "three eyes" in the *Diamond Sutra*.

"When he came to the line that says, 'Depending upon nothing, you must manifest your mind,' I was instantly enlightened." I knew it a long time ago!" Hui-neng understood the mind of the patriarch.

"I thought: 'The manifold phenomena of the universe are not separate from my original nature!'" This is the standpoint of Zen. While other students of religion try to see the law of the universe on the outside, through phenomenal existence, the Zen student tries to find it within himself.

If you wish to understand the laws of reincarnation, observe the reincarnation of your own mind. Each mind is an element of Being and will tell you how it reincarnates. When we observe all those laws of the universe within us—when we study koans—we are really observing these universal laws. In the higher study of koans, you will find many laws in different systems. If you understand the law within yourself, you will understand the law of the universe. This was the Buddha's attitude. Of course, this is an endless study.

"Then I told the patriarch:" In those days, Zen was very immature in expression; the students were struggling to express their understanding. There is no fixed way of expression. Since then we have invented many ways of expressing the understanding between master and pupil. In those days, it was expressed in daily action. Of course, today, Zen is like pool swimming, not ocean swimming. Students come here for five or six years and study Zen as they would mathematics, seeing only its shadow in daily life. But a humorous nature is common to all Zen students, and they are optimistic.

"'It was beyond my expectation that my own nature is originally pure, originally everlasting, originally perfect, originally unshakable, and that all things arise from it.'" These were the first words truly uttered by the Sixth Patriarch to the Fifth Patriarch. Usually it is the conception of man that his own nature is low to begin with. You must educate, punish, train it, bring it gradually to a higher stage, then higher and higher until it finally becomes God. This is the way man thinks, the usual attitude. But Hui-neng's attitude was different. He considered man's original nature to be pure, and believed one had only to find it. If we find it, we do not have to do anything more. So the Zen attitude is to dig down rather than pile up.

When I came to this country, I observed many things about the buildings. For instance, you paint your houses each year, first one color and then another. When a house is fifty years old, how thick the layers of paint must be! If you go to Japan, you will see houses of natural wood. If paint gets on them, we scrape it off.

Zen purity is different from the usual idea of purity. The principle of purity in Zen has nothing to do with a moral conception, nothing to do with ethics. When you enter Zen, by going through the koan, "Before father and mother, what was your original aspect?" you will attain this pureness. You annihilate all those ideas about matter, spirit, time, space—all those relative thoughts—and you attain original purity, the absolute.

When I first went into *sanzen* with this koan, my answer was "Absolute!" My teacher said, "No such thing as 'Absolute.'" I went out and cried. The next day I said: "It is like color that has no color." My teacher said: "We do not deal in likenesses or analogies. Bring me the thing itself." And he again drove me out from his room. I was fairly dumbfounded. This is the way we begin to attain pureness.

When you attain this pureness, then you know it is "originally everlasting." You are sitting alone on top of the universe, alone in meditation through all the *kalpas*, and you realize that one moment is a million years. Of course this physical body is ephemeral, changeable; but as Reality, it exists forever.

When I was in Seattle, Washington, a gentleman asked me about Buddha. I said, "Buddha is omnipresent." "Oh, is that so? Is Buddha the same in India as in America?" I looked at him, puzzled. "He is omnipresent." My idea of omnipresent was different from his. Once I met an omnipresent cat in Washington Square, then on a doorstep. I went to a restaurant—he was there. I went to a cigarette store, and he was there, too!

Nothing is less and nothing is more. You die, nothing disappears from this world. You are born, nothing is added. It is always perfect, "originally perfect" and "originally unshakable"—originally unchangeable.

Nothing is changeable, nothing is shakable. The moon in the sky is so quiet, even the hurricane cannot blow it away. Consciousness—existence—is so deep, so quiet and unshakable. Your mood is changeable, but consciousness exists and is unchangeable. And all entities, all thoughts and all philosophies come out of it, like a frog begetting tadpoles—many from one. These were the words that burst from Hui-neng's mouth.

"The patriarch saw that I had realized original nature": When the Sixth Patriarch uttered these words, the Fifth Patriarch looked at him. In the sanctuary, when a student offers his answer to the master, the master observes his attitude, the way he expresses his answer. He looks at his mood, his decision. The word you use in the Zen room is negligible. What is important is the way you express it. The master is always watching the mood—like a boxing blow, a soft punch is no good. So when you understand the knack of Zen, your attitude is different. You will use this attitude in your daily life.

The patriarch acknowledged Hui-neng's attainment. It is easy to observe another's understanding when he really grasps it. When you are studying koans and then visit some friend who has studied philosophy, Theosophy, or New Thought, you will feel that all is just talk. It is easy after you get into Zen.

Before you enter, you will hear the teachers just speaking something; but once you enter Zen, you will have a standard by which to measure the teacher.

"And told me: 'If you are unaware of your real mind, learning Buddhism will not benefit you.'" Sometimes you grasp it through the first koan. Or perhaps, you will study Zen for a year or two, try one gate, then another gate until you enter. Without this, your study of Buddhism is nothing.

If you go to a restaurant, even if you read the whole menu but do not eat, you will come away hungry. Though you read the label on the medicine bottle, it will not cure you. So if you read the sutras, you are just reading sutras and do not get anywhere.

"'If you are aware of your own mind and see your original nature, you are to be honored with the names Master, Teacher of Devas, or Buddha.'" But do not overestimate yourself if you have passed two or three koans, and think: "Now I am a teacher."

"It was midnight when I received the Dharma. No one knew." Heart to heart, that is all. The master's acknowledgment is just: "That is right."

My acknowledgment is not that of Sokei-an. It is three thousand buddhas and bodhisattvas that give you acknowledgment, because my acknowledgment is my teacher's acknowledgment. It is Mahakashyapa's acknowledgment from the Buddha. So you must respect the acknowledgment of a Zen master. You will prove your own understanding when you have passed your koan. This is called "receiving the canon."

"Transmitting the sudden teachings as well as the robe and bowl, the patriarch said to me: 'I appoint you the Sixth Patriarch. Guard this teaching. Save sentient beings far and wide. Promulgate this in the future, and do not let it expire.'" The transmission of Zen is clearly written here.

Every Zen master, when he transmits the Dharma to his disciple, utters these words: "Guard this." It is like a flame that you guard under your sleeve—"You will save sentient beings far and wide, never let it expire." Once it expires, there is no more teaching. You cannot find it in a book, you cannot find it in writing. When the flame expires, that is the end of the Buddha's teaching. So if you have not had your teacher's acknowledgment, you may always have a doubt.

Next we will read the Fifth Patriarch's *gatha.*

"'Listen to my gatha*:*

> *'Sentient beings come and sow seeds*
> *From the soil fruits are begotten*
> *Insentient beings beget nothing*
> *Having no seeds and no nature'*

"'Sentient beings come and sow seeds": A sentient being is a man. But particularly, it means a man who has a soul. I think you will understand through these lectures how Zen was transmitted from generation to generation. We are still keeping the same means to transmit Zen. A "seed" of this esoteric teaching implies the transmission of Zen from India to China by Bodhidharma.

"From the soil fruits are begotten'": I have heard many times of esoteric teachings in New York, but it seems to me that what they call esoteric is not esoteric. They do not know what they are talking about. There is nothing transmitted esoterically. When they speak about everything, how can they call it esoteric? The true esoteric teaching cannot be spoken. We cannot make anyone understand by talking about it. If anyone wants to understand, he must practice as we practice to attain it.

In the Fifth Patriarch's time, this seed begat the fruit. Just one seed begat the fruit of the Sixth Patriarch and his disciples.

"'Insentient beings beget nothing / Having no seeds and no nature.'" Many people are afraid of the thought of emptiness because they have the wrong idea. In Buddhism, Emptiness is not empty. So when they rid themselves of that funny idea, then real emptiness will come. It is the real emptiness of the sentient universe. There is no universe without a soul. If any teaching has entire annihilation as the goal of practice, such a tendency is not Buddha's Buddhism.

Usually Buddhism is misunderstood by ordinary people. If the annihilation of sentient life is the aim of Buddhism, why must we practice to attain? Why not jump off some corner of a cliff? Someone may well ask: "If there is such a Buddhism, what good is it to human life?"

The founder of the Pure Land sect in China, Hui-yuan, in his zealous desire to go to the Pure Land committed suicide because he hated sentient life. This is not the Buddha's idea; it is just a notion. Hui-yuan's idea of a pure land was just childish and picturesque, not the real Pure Land. The Zen master Hakuin said in his chant of Zen: "This is the land of the Lotus / And this very body is Buddha." This world is the Pure Land and this body is the body of Buddha. This soul is buddha-nature. If you know it, you will discover it in yourself. Though you do not know it, you have it always. Known or not, this is the Pure Land. This body is Buddha, and this soul is Tathagata.

Believe it or not, every sinner is already saved. Although he is in the agony of delusion, originally he is saved. Though a baby never knows its mother, the mother is always there. The sinner or soul struggles in his own delusion, but he is originally saved. There is some such doctrine in Christianity, too. But if you know it yourself, you can save others as well as yourself. If you see your mother's face, you can not only receive her love, but you can love her and so manifest the original nature of universal being. But if you have the notion that there is an "impure" land and that there is a "pure" land somewhere else, and that you must go there, and that this existence must be wiped away, you will abandon this life and commit suicide. And when you see your consciousness disappear, you will feel that your consciousness is lost, and you will hold the edge of the bed, and scream, "I have not found the Pure Land!" You had thought that Amitabha would come with his angels to save you. But now you cry: "My consciousness is going as a light that vanishes! I cannot see or hear! Who can help me?" It's your mistake. If anyone teaches you such Buddhism, it is not Buddhism. It's just a ten-cent novel.

We must appreciate our own capacity of mind that enables us to understand this high type of teaching. The Fifth Patriarch spoke out here in order to avoid the mistakes of future disciples.

"The patriarch continued: 'When Bodhidharma came to this land, no one believed in his teaching. That is why he handed down this robe as a symbol of faith, to be passed on from generation to generation. But the Dharma should be transmitted from mind to mind, and each should apprehend it through his own realization.'" Bodhidharma? What is he talking about? Bodhidharma did not say a thing. He just sat before a wall. The Chinese thought him a lunatic. No one believed in his teaching.

There is a famous story about an Indian teacher who was on his way to China when a typhoon neared the ship. The Indian teacher cast all his sutras into the sea and saved himself and his disciple, an eighteen-year-old boy. Barely escaping the typhoon, they drifted to Japan. Thinking to reach China, they arrived in Kyoto. Fortunately, Buddhism was already known in Japan. It was the golden age of Japanese Buddhism. The one little sutra he had saved, he showed to the Japanese monks. They immediately understood that he was an Indian sage. No one understood Sanskrit, but he showed them the signs of the Shingon sect with his hands, fingers, and body. They understood that he was of the Shingon School, but could not understand his real teaching. So he thought, "My coming here is too soon. They are too immature." Then he made a copper jar, put the sutra in it, and buried the jar. After that he went to China. Years later, many hundreds of years, Kobo Daishi excavated this sutra. Opening it, he was able to read it. However, as his desire was great, he went to China in order to learn about it. Real Shingon was then carried to Japan by Kobo Daishi.

Bodhidharma also came to China too early. No one understood him, but he handed down Buddha's robe. It went down to the Fifth Patriarch, and from him to the Sixth Patriarch as proof of their faith. In the same way, my robe came from my teacher as a testimony of my faith, also the canon. The canon should be transmitted from mind to mind, and each should apprehend it through his own realization. We receive the robe by faith, but the canon we cannot receive by faith. We must receive the canon by intuition. In Christianity, if you have faith, you are saved. But in Buddhism, faith is not enough. Blind faith does not amount to much in Buddhism. You must have understanding. You must open the eye of your mind and meet Reality. I cannot tell you to do this or do that; you must not expect that of any teacher. If you have an idea that if you hang about long enough Sokei-an will teach you something, you are mistaken. But if you are sleeping, I will shout to wake you up!

"*From the remote past, the original body or substance has been transmitted from buddha to buddha*": This "original body" is the body of this whole universal existence You will attain it when you pass the first koan—not the theory, but the *original body*.

"*And every patriarch has secretly inherited the original mind.*" Original body and original mind are the same thing. Buddhism is not dualistic, so we do not speak of body *and* mind. Nothing is secret about it, but it is naturally secret.

"*The robe will become the cause of strife.*" Everyone wishes to have this robe, and if it just *exists*, everyone wants it and is jealous of its possessor. Humans are awfully funny beings!

"*Keep it in your generation. Do not hand it down. If you hand down the robe, your life will be as precarious as if it were hanging by a thread. Leave quickly! I fear someone may do you injury.*" There is no particular formula, no particular type of answer. All answers are created by the student. If his answer meets the answer that has been handed down, the teacher will say: "Your answer is all right, but the best answer we know was like this . . ." So you will compare your answer with the old type of answer, and you will see that it is not so different. Do not think that there is one particular answer. If what is handed down is a formula, it will not exist a long time.

"*Reverently I questioned the patriarch: 'Where should I go?' The patriarch said: 'Stay at Huai; hide at Hui.' It was midnight. Accepting the robe and the bowl, I said: 'I am from the south. I do not know the mountain passes or how to make my way to the river.' The patriarch answered: 'Do not worry. I myself will show you the way.' He conducted me to the river station at Chiu-chang. There he took me with him in a boat, and took the scull and worked it himself.*"

SOKEI-AN SAYS:

It was midnight when Hui-neng received from the Fifth Patriarch the canon and the robe handed down from Shakyamuni, generation to generation. When you become an ordained monk, the teacher will fasten the robe around your neck and put the bowl in your hand. It means that in this lifetime, you will not forsake him.

Once I was asked by a Woolworth's building manager to bear witness for him in court, to testify against the attorney of the customs house. He wanted me to prove that incense was for religious use so as to avoid paying customs duty. The attorney asked me, "What is your profession?" I said, "*Bhikshu.*" He asked: "What is bhikshu?" I answered, "In your language, it means 'mendicant.'" "What! Mendicant?" I thought for a moment he would send me back to Japan because beggars are not allowed in America! "Oh, yes," I said, "people pay respect to mendicants in Japan." He said, "They pay respect to beggarmen?" I answered, "It's different from beggars selling pencils in the subway. We often come from rich families. We may be sons of rich men, but it's the custom to beg for alms for the sake of Buddha." He said, "It seems to me that you are crazy." I said, "And it seems to me that *you* are crazy." He was very angry.

The Fifth Patriarch had handed down the canon to Hui-neng, soul to soul. It is not a theory, a doctrine, or a hypothesis. In Christianity you receive your education from a teacher, or from a theological seminary, but in the Zen school, there is no education to give. All the teacher does is take everything from you—all notions, all ideas, and all those philosophies and what-not that you are entertaining in your brain. He will strip them all away. The master will not give you anything but the transmission of true Buddhism. Before you are stripped of everything, you cannot understand this teaching. But when your body and mind are empty and pure as the sky, the master will hand down to you the canon that is empty—"If you try to see Tathagata with your eye, to hear Tathagata with your ear, there is error in your practice." With such a koan, you will receive this empty torch. *That* is the canon of Zen, of real Buddhism. ("Canon" is the English word I use here provisionally instead of "Dharma," because Dharma in Sanskrit is not exactly what is meant here. Do not think this canon is some doctrine; it is true Dharma.)

Besides receiving the canon, Hui-neng received the robe and the bowl, though he had been pounding rice as an *anja*, a laborer in the temple, for eight months in the mill-house of the Fifth Patriarch. Now he was pronounced the "Sixth Patriarch" and handed down the canon and the robe of Buddha. The canon was the testimony of his attainment in Buddhism. Later, in the southern part of the country, he would have his head shaved, put on the robe, and become a monk. But at this time, he was a layman.

In the Zen school, the torch is not always handed down to a monk. Sometimes it is to a nobleman or a gentleman. However, if the gentleman's head is solid ivory so that he cannot receive the canon, it will be handed down to a butcher or a wood chopper—if he can open the eye of the mind and has the capacity, as an enlightened soul, to receive it.

To the true Buddhist eye, the priest who just wears rich robes and jewels and a rosary while chanting the sutras is nothing but a puppet. Whatever he says, he is merely parroting like a bird. There are many such beings in the world. They are talking about Reality, but when we ask them what Reality really is, they speak mere words. Then, to explain these words, they speak one hundred more, and to explain these one hundred words, they will speak one thousand. Just words!

If we ask them, "Without speaking a word, show me your Reality," and they do not know what to do, it proves that they do not know true Reality. They have not seen it. They have *heard* that there is Reality, but they have not experienced it. How can they be religious teachers?

The Fifth Patriarch took Hui-neng in a boat, and he himself took the scull and worked it. It was almost dawn in the popular picture of this scene. The eastern sky is brightening, and in the wide water between cliffs, there is a small boat. Hui-neng holds the robe and the bowl in his arms, and at the end of the boat, the Fifth Patriarch stands holding a single oar.

"I said: 'Your reverence, pray be seated. Your disciple will scull the boat.' The patriarch replied: 'To ferry you over the river is my service.'" To ferry you over the river of delusion, to the shore of enlightenment, is the meaning of his words.

"I said: 'While I was astray, you ferried me [across the river], but now that I have awakened, I shall ferry myself. The word "to ferry" is the same, but its uses are different. I was born in such an out-of-the-way land, speaking this rustic tongue with its odd sound.'" In China the people from different areas speak their own vernacular and do not understand one another. Here, in Chinatown, it is the same—like a Texan who goes to London. Once a Second Avenue man went to Japan and was asked: "What nationality are you?" "I'm an American." I am sure Hui-neng spoke very bad Chinese. But in Zen, no one cares about one's way of speaking. It has no importance.

"'But now, I have received your Dharma and am enlightened. Turning to my original nature for guidance, I shall ferry myself.'" We naturally have intrinsic wisdom, but it is painted over with acquired wisdom. Whatever notions we get from books, from lectures, from Christianity, from Confucius, or from Christian Science, entirely blinds the real eye of your mind. With Christianity, you put a veil over it. With Hinduism, you put a bandage on it. With Theosophy, you put a whole cushion over it. How can you see anything? Return to your own original nature. It is the only way to enlighten yourself. You do not need any "isms." Go back home, sit down on a cushion and meditate. Do not meditate on any thoughts. Just open your own consciousness and do not go into a dream!

In Seattle, someone asked me: "Sokei-an, you have finished your koans, but you are still meditating. On what do you meditate?" I said: "I am like a soldier at attention. I am meditating on my soul." I am watching my awareness of my soul, so that dreams will not take away my attention. I am watching in awareness, and I do not speak or act absentmindedly. I am always on the alert, at attention. I struggled for many years before I gave myself entirely over. During that time there was a state between pseudo-meditation and true awareness. I was struggling even after I finished my koans. I am still practicing this true awareness.

"The patriarch answered: 'Well said, well said! In time this Buddhism will be widely spread by you.'" Three years after the departure of the Fifth Patriarch, that is, after his death, and about twelve years later, the Sixth Patriarch was discovered in hiding. There was talk among the monks of the temple where he was staying. He was sweeping the garden walk with a bamboo broom, when two monks were arguing about a flag. One said, "The wind is moving," and the other said, "No, the flag is moving." Hearing this, Hui-neng said, "Neither the flag nor the wind is moving. Your minds are moving." The Sixth Patriarch said neither flag nor wind, but Mind is moving.

A story is told of a monk of my temple, Daitokuji, who had been living among beggars for many years and was terribly in need of a new robe. Only one nun knew his face, so she asked a gentleman to give her a new robe for this monk. She took him the robe and asked him to put it on and to throw the old one away. "Later, you will be the patriarch of Daitokuji," she told him, "and I have found my roshi this robe. Please put it on." "Ah, thank you," he said. "Go away, and I will put it on." The nun went away. From a bridge, where she could look back, she saw him carefully picking small things off the old robe and placing them on the new one. They were his cooties! After the death of the nun, there was no one who knew the monk; he had disappeared. After many years, a patriarch tried to find him, saying, "I have only one disciple to succeed to my Dharma. Please find him!" Someone said that he was a crippled beggar who liked musk melons. So this patriarch gave a party for crippled beggars, with musk melons to be given away. One came limping and stood behind the others. The young monk who was giving out the musk melons said to this beggar, "Come here and take this musk melon without using your feet." "No," said the beggar, "you give me the musk-melon without using your hand." "Ah," said the monk, "this is the patriarch!"[5]

This is a particular type of Zen. There are many such stories. I was hiding myself here in this city for about ten years before Mr. Miya found me. I was associating with him for three years before he said, "I hear you are a Buddhist monk." I said, "No, I am not a monk."

One must wait for some time to be discovered. It is shameful, to a monk, if he says, "I am a monk." And it is a greater shame to say, "I am a Zen master." He has to wait until someone discovers him.

"'Three years after your departure, I shall be dead. It is better for you to leave now.'" The Fifth Patriarch had told Hui-neng: "Go away quickly! I fear someone will do you an injury." In a place like a Buddhist temple, there are many commoners, just laymen-hearted monks. So there will always be some who are jealous, who will injure the one who has received the canon, the torch of Buddhism handed down from generation to generation. This happens even today.

After transmitting his canon to Hui-neng, the Fifth Patriarch had unloaded his heavy burden. He could now die, having transmitted the canon. All Zen masters have an obligation to previous masters; it is an unhappy death for a Zen master not to have left an heir.

"Though you stay with me, there are not many days left to us. It is better for you to leave me now." It will be the same for you even though you stay with me. When *you* have the canon, you have grasped the cardinal principle of Buddhism.

When a Zen master has made an heir, he lets him go, far away. He is like the tiger or the lion that lets its child go. He does not depend upon him—"Oh my disciple, I am hungry. Send back some potatoes you get from the laymen." No, it is the end of their relationship—"Go! Farewell!" There is no more communication between them. It is like the mother lion that drops her cub off the cliff, hoping it will be all right. This is the tradition of the Zen school. But the Zen master does not give his permission before the disciple is mature and fully understands the teaching.

"'Try to keep to the south.'" Do not go astray. Whatever difficulties you encounter, do not change your mind. Just go to the place with which you have some relationship.

"'Do not give your teaching too soon.'" No Zen heir will give the teaching as soon as he has received the canon. When he accepts the canon from his teacher, he is like an infant who has just been given birth to by his mother, so it is too soon for him to give the teaching. As a monk, he may be old, but as a Zen master he is a child. He must wait for a long time, usually about eight to ten years. Even though he finishes his study of koans, the master does not appoint him a Zen master immediately. There is no koan to study, as he has finished his Zen; but he does not take the position of teacher. He must wait before he slowly begins to teach.

I finished my koan study one year before the great earthquake of Tokyo [September 1, 1923]. Before that time, I had come to America and spent about four years. Then I went back to Japan and remained two years there. Then my teacher appointed me Zen master. Six years after finishing my study, I returned to America. The first year I spent roaming around. About seven years after finishing, I began to teach Zen.

The Sixth Patriarch waited for fifteen years before he began to teach. Many Zen masters wait for a longer time. Usually, they will not start teaching until someone finds them out, so they hide themselves living in obscurity. The more they are hidden, the more effort people must make to discover them. Precious things are always hidden; they are never exposed on a streetcorner. If you have a diamond, you will not leave it on the corner of your desk; you will certainly keep it somewhere so that a stranger cannot find it. Only true things try to hide themselves. It is natural. Only imposters come around with brass bands—"Here I am!" The true one waits until someone recognizes him. But in today's civilization, what is true in human life is never found.

"*Buddhism may suffer persecution.*" All true things have always been persecuted.

"*I took my leave of the Fifth Patriarch and set out southward. After some months I reached the Ta-yu Mountains.*" Farewell! Goodbye, my teacher. I am grateful to you for your teaching. Now, farewell. If we are to have further relations, I shall see you again.

In Shakyamuni's day when a disciple would go far away, the teacher would put his hand on his head, saying, "May all be well." In Shingon, there is the same hand on the head. It is in Christianity also, but it came from Buddhism. In India, I have heard that the pupils in affectionate moments pat the head of the teacher as well.

When the Fifth Patriarch went back to his temple sculling the boat, he arrived about noontime. He went to his own quarters and did not come out for four or five days. He did not give the usual teaching in the central hall, so the monks were worried. His attendant asked him, "Are you ill?" "No," he said, "but my canon is gone." "What?! It's gone?!" (Blind monks think the canon is something material.) "Who took it?!" "Oh, that rice-pounder in the mill. He took my canon and ran away to the south." "Oh! We cannot permit that!" The Fifth Patriarch was laughing at them, thinking Hui-neng was safely gone. But those crazy monks did not stop running after him for two months. Finally they overtook him on the top of a mountain. But not all went up, only a few. Some looked for him at the foot of the mountain or in the village.

A number of monks went running after him to take away the robe and bowl. Foolish monks! There are still such foolish ones. Sometimes, when the teacher has the canon, the pupils try to trap him and take the canon away. Or they will open the teacher's trunk and try to copy something that the teacher put there, but they find nothing. In ancient days, such a one was hung upon a big gong, and the monks struck him with the clapper and squashed him.

"*Several hundred monks had pursued me in order to seize the robe and bowl. Among them was one whose family name was Chen and whose monk's name was Hui-ming. Once he had been a commander of the fourth order. His nature was irascible, but he was an ardent student.*" There was no *sanzen* in those days. He had been practicing meditation and reading sutras since he was a young man. Now he was about sixty years old, yet could grasp nothing. Then someone came from the country and for eight months pounded rice, then took away the robe and the canon! With a quick temper he ran after him. But he was a good-natured and honest student.

"*He came ahead of the others and was about to overtake me.*" He was ahead of the crowd and overtook Hui-neng. Hui-neng saw him and knew his hot temper.

"*I flung the robe and bowl upon a rock*": This was not a road stone on the mountain; it was a huge flat boulder about the size of a room.

"*. . . Saying: 'The robe is the symbol of faith. No one can take it by force.'*" Taking the robe does not make one a monk. To buy a robe in Japan and put it on cannot make one a master. There are blind monks everywhere. They have the robe, but no canon in their minds.

A true monk must possess the canon even though he was ordained and given the robe and bowl. You can get the canon by the acknowledgment of the three thousand buddhas and bodhisattvas, then the teacher ordains you. But it is the *rakshas*, *devas*, and *nagas* that must ordain you as Zen master. There are many Zen masters acknowledged by teachers, but the pupils do not accept them as masters. The teacher will give you the canon but will not support you.

The canon cannot be taken by force. Hui-neng knew this and protected himself. *This body* is the shrine of Consciousness.

"I then hid myself behind a thicket. Hui-ming reached the spot, intending to take the robe and bowl, but he was unable to move them." "Oh, the robe and the bowl! They do not belong to him! I will take them back!" The monk came and attempted to lift them, but they were as heavy as a mountain.

"He cried aloud, 'Oh, lay brother, I came for the Dharma, not the robe.' The robe remained motionless. Though hot-tempered, he was a monk, so when he faced the robe that had been handed down from the Buddha and touched it with his hand, the pang of conscience would not permit him to lift it. This is a koan: "The robe and bowl are as heavy as Mount Huang-mei. Chen cannot lift them."

"Then I came out and sat down on the rock. Hui-ming bowed": When anyone who has a true heart really meets things that are true, he must bow down. This is the beautiful aspect of Buddhism. Though he is only a child of three, if he has the truth, I shall bow down before him. If a man is seventy years old, yet has no truth, I shall teach him. Such is the Buddhist attitude. Hui-neng is a mean rice-pounder, but he has the truth. Chen was a commander and then a monk, but he bowed down.

". . . And said: 'I beg you to expound the Dharma for me.'"—"Please give me some hint, for mercy's sake! I have been studying twenty years but can see no light in the darkness. Before you go away, give me some hint so I may enlighten myself!"

"I answered: 'Since you came for the Dharma, disregard all that has transpired'": Jealousy or any feeling of superiority or inferiority—all those worldly habits.

"'Do not entertain even a single thought, and then I will speak of the Dharma for you.'": To receive the Dharma from any teacher, all those preconceived notions must be thrown away—Hinduism, Theosophy, etc.

"Ming remained silent for a time. Then I said: 'Thinking of neither good nor evil, at that moment, what is your original appearance?'" This is a famous koan. All of you observe this koan when you enter the Zen school. (In another Sixth Patriarch's "Sutra," it is written: "Before father and mother"—beyond past, present and future—"what is your original appearance?")

"Good" and "evil" are dualistic thoughts, relative thoughts. These words signify all phenomenal relations: black and white, zero and one, day and night, spirit and matter, time and space, phenomena and noumena, absolute and relative. All is relative. To make a conception of the absolute, you must think of the relative. Without a conception of the absolute, you cannot prove the relative. Without zero, you cannot think of one. Zero is not absolute, and one is not absolute. Your mind cannot but form a relative basis. It is not absolute.

When you think nothing, then your brain is empty—transparent. You get this state of consciousness by meditation. When anyone asks you, in that moment, what is your original aspect?—*This is That!*

It is easy to attain enlightenment. By meditation, clean up your mind, and then come to see me in the *sanzen* room.

So in the beginning, Hui-neng destroyed all those relative observations that are really the notions that you entertain in your mind. They have nothing to do with Reality. You get a menu at Delmonico's restaurant and you talk about it, but you never eat. You talk about the prescription from your doctor, but you do not take the medicine. Get into Reality, immediately, without vibrating the skin of your lips! If I were really manifesting Zen, I would not give these lectures.

So when you are thinking neither good nor evil, what is your original appearance? If you really grasp the point of what is "good nor evil," you do not need to struggle to find your original appearance. But your five senses bother you, and you do not attain realization. Hui-ming was a good student, though he was quick-tempered.

"Upon these words, Hui-ming was enlightened." In Japanese, *satori.* In Chinese, *wu.* In that moment, this man was washed in sweat. Precious moment! His twenty years' study of Zen was repaid.

I fear your conception of enlightenment is different from ours.

"Hui-ming again questioned me: 'Is there another, secret truth besides that which you have told me?'" This line says that though he grasped Zen, he was still attached to the shell of a previous nature. It's as if a chicken were to come from the eggshell and look back at the shell once more. He has to look at the "truth" once more. There is no esoteric, "secret" truth. And when you enter, you do not need to think of the "truth" anymore. Throw it into the middle of the Pacific Ocean and forget about it.

"I answered: 'What I told you was not secret.'" It is true; the "truth" of Hui-neng was not secret, but the understanding that flashed into Hui-ming's mind was secret. I do not like to use the word "flashed" because it is so ephemeral. Enlightenment is not ephemeral. Once you grasp it, it's just like your own hand; you cannot throw it away—"You know, I once went to a Zen master and grasped it, but now it is so vague." If you feel so, it is not enlightenment. Enlightenment is just like this [slapping his body], just like heaven and earth. It's as if some philosopher would tell you that all this phenomena is nothing—that all this we are observing is empty. You do not need to believe a word of it—just give him a black eye and make him understand! When Rinzai was asked, "What is Buddha?" he just gave the questioner a blow of his staff. That was answer enough. And Jôshû, another Zen student who could not be caught by these hypotheses, kicked a stone.

"'If you look into your own consciousness, you will find the secret within yourself.'" It is not a simple secret, but a detail of it. When you look deep into your own consciousness, all law is there. All the pores of your body are the eye of consciousness, so you will observe this consciousness in detail. The secret is of as fine a texture as the fiber that makes your skin. So observe it in meditation.

"Hui-ming said: 'Although, I was studying at Huang-mei, I did not recognize my original appearance.'" The old Zen monks try to hide the secret. He did not say "original consciousness" or "original mind," but "original appearance." What is "original appearance?" Endless chaos that has no time, no space. This is original appearance. So you believe your original appearance is just empty sky—no body, no feet, no head or hands. Such has never been in the universe!

"Now, having been instructed by you, I feel as one who drinks water and knows for himself whether it is hot or cold." Just that. When you are an infant, you do not have this awareness. You drink your mother's milk without knowing.

Enlightenment is not a dream, it is not contemplation or philosophy. If you are really aware of your own existence, you can be happy, be plain, be bright. Yes. One who is enlightened is different from others because others are not aware of their original appearance. It is awareness that makes this distinction. Awareness is a very important word in Buddhism. The knower is Buddha, the awakened one. This awareness is called *bodhi*—to awaken.

You may live for seventy or eighty years, but you are always sleeping. Your eyes are open, and you look at the blue sky, but you are snoring.

"'O lay brother, you are now my master.'"—"I was in Huang-mei for many years, but I did not recognize my true nature. Now all is bright."

"I replied: 'If this is your true conviction, your master is the one at Huang-mei, just as mine is.'"—"The Fifth Patriarch is your master. I have nothing to do with you. All the knowledge I have is from him, so you are also enlightened by him. He is your teacher, as he is mine."

"'Guard your own enlightenment.'" This is the word always given as you leave the temple. Do not guard a book. If I did not have the key of Buddhism, I would think those words to be a castle of secrets.

"Then Hui-ming asked: 'From here, where shall I go?'" This, too, is a deep question. It has several meanings. From this point where do you go? Many people are enlightened in a desert or the woods and think that this is the end; but it is only the beginning. You can easily go astray. So where do you go from here?

"I told him: 'When you come to Yuan, stop; when you come to Meng, stay.'" This is as though he were repeating the words given to him by the Fifth Patriarch. Do you remember?

"Hui-ming made a bow and departed." The transmission of Zen is like this. He was awakened twenty minutes ago, and now he is a disciple of Hui-neng. If you are not disposed to endeavor in your meditation or in *sanzen*, you will not come to this enlightenment. Enlightenment will not come when you are sleeping. Endeavor!

"Sometime after that, I reached Ts'ao-ch'i. Again pursued by adversaries, I took refuge in Ssu-hui, where, covering my trail among a group of hunters, I passed about fifteen years. When the occasion arose, I would give the hunters some appropriate teaching. They had me watch the hunter's noose, but whenever I found a creature trapped, I released it. At mealtimes, I cooked my greens in the pot of meat. If anyone questioned me, I said: 'I like to eat greens cooked with meat.'

"One day I thought: 'The time to spread my dharma has come. I cannot remain hidden forever.' Accordingly, I went to the Fa-hsing Temple at Kwang-chou, where I met Dharma Master Yin-tsung, who chanced to be lecturing on the Nirvana Sutra.

"On that day, the banner of the temple was moving in the wind. One monk declared: 'The wind is moving.' Another monk declared: 'The banner is moving.' The debate was endless. Approaching them, I said: 'Neither the wind nor the banner is moving. Your minds are moving.' The monks were all astonished.

SOKEI-AN SAYS:

"Sometime after that, I reached Ts'ao-ch'i. Again pursued by adversaries, I took refuge in Ssu-hui." Ssu-hui was a barbaric district deep in the mountains of China. A different race lived there. Hui-neng took refuge in its forest. This was according to the directions given to him by the Fifth Patriarch: "When you come to Huai, halt; when you come to Hui, hide."

". . . Where, covering my trail among a group of hunters": Often a monk hides his trail among fishermen or hunters when he is pursued by an enemy.

"I passed about fifteen years": "Well, he has given up his intention to become a monk. We do not need to pay any attention to him." So Hui-neng went into the deep forest and lived with hunters who were killing the fox, catching the muskrat, and snaring the tiger. Perhaps one of his pursuers said: "Well, he got married to a girl of the tribe, and gave up the idea of becoming the Sixth Patriarch. Let us go back to our own country and build up our own patriarch. It will be nice." So all his adversaries went back. Jealousy is the real enemy of the human race. Fifteen years is a long time.

"When the occasion arose, I would give the hunters some appropriate teaching." "Appropriate teaching" is very interesting to an audience; the one that receives it does not think it is Buddhism. I have written nine or ten volumes of teaching, but everyone thinks them naughty stories. I am now writing for a Seattle

paper in the vernacular, and the same in New York. They think it is nonsense. If I wrote about Buddhism, they would not read it.[6]

"They had me watch the hunter's noose, but whenever I found a creature trapped, I released it." This kind of watchman is no good for hunters. "Oh, poor fox, I will let you go!" No good. "Oh poor rabbit." Oh, poor fish!" I do not believe this story. If I were the Sixth Patriarch with those hunters, it would be entirely different.

"At mealtimes, I cooked my greens in the pot of meat. If anyone questioned me, I said: 'I like to eat greens cooked with meat.'" A nice excuse to make! A Chinese monk came to this city, and when anyone offered him soup, he would ask: "Is this the juice of a chicken?" If the answer was no, he would take it. If yes, he said, "Take it away!" When a Japanese monk came here, there was a professor who blamed him because he was eating raw fish—"Oh, monks are cannibals!"

Though you do not eat meat of any kind, nor kill any insects all your life long, if you do not attain enlightenment, there is no merit. Your duty is to be enlightened, not to refrain from eating meat.

Of course, to refrain from eating meat is to show compassion towards all creatures.

Why doesn't a monk blow out a candle flame with his breath? Because he might blow some little, invisible, insect into the fire and kill it. So he always uses his hand. There is something beautiful in this. A Japanese gentleman living in Inwood, New York, sent for the sanitary inspector because he was cultivating cockroaches in his kitchen. Well, so was I last winter! It is very interesting to hear about these old commandments, but they are not useful in this present life. In the old days, they had value. In modern times, they create a nuisance.

In Japan, when the guest departs, the host goes out before him, throwing stones out of the road so that his carriage may go smoother. These days, with the automobile, this custom is very uncomfortable.

"One day I thought: 'The time to spread my dharma has come. I cannot remain hidden forever.'" The time must come, and one must grow with the times. If one does not know this, he can do nothing. A foolish teacher might come to the city and spend twenty thousand dollars for a building to which no one would come. And then he would fail because his expenses were too heavy. One must know the time to spend and to accept help. In the beginning, you are setting the net and cooking your food—one year, two, three. Then one by one, people will feel the light even though you muffle it in yourself.

I have a favorite grocery man. At first he greeted me: "Hello, Charley." After a year he said, "Mr. Charley." The next year it was "Reverend." And now he calls me "Doctor." He has completely dropped the "Charley." It is quite funny.

The hunters began to feel uncomfortable keeping Hui-neng with them: "Please go," they said. "If anything happens to you, we will come." It was the same when I had a gangster friend in New York. One time he told me: "If you get into trouble, call on me, and I will help you with my gang." In the same way, the hunters told Hui-neng: "Go back to Canton and do your work." After fifteen years, certainly, the hunters recognized him for the man he was.

"Accordingly, I went to Fa-hsing Temple at Kwang-chou, where I met Dharma Master Yin-tsung, who chanced to be lecturing on the Nirvana Sutra.*"* Any monk who can give a lecture on the *Nirvana Sutra* is a hundred-percent monk. Hui-neng went there as a laborer. He wore a robe with short sleeves and tied his skirts to his legs. Holding his arms under his sleeves, he called out: "O-O-OH!" which is a signal: "I'm a laborer! I've come to serve the temple! Is there any work for me?!" A monk came out and said: "Go to the kitchen, then go to the mill!" And after the lecture, he would sweep the garden with a bamboo broom.

A novice will come to the temple and sit on the ground all day long and all evening. Then someone will say, "Why did you come here?" "I came to see the Master." "Well, come in and someone will introduce you." Sometimes the master's attendant will come—"What do you wish? How many days have you been here?" Then he will introduce him to the master, and the master will tell him to stay or go. This custom exists today in China and Japan. The monks wanting to see the new master may sit for three days, while the monks are watching to see what kind of student he is. If they do not like his looks, they will drive him out. The Orient is a bad place for young men.

"On that day the banner of the temple was moving in the wind. One monk said, 'The wind is moving.' Another monk said, 'The banner is moving.' The debate was endless." The banner is material and the wind is spirit. That was the point of the debate. Today, scientists are still trying to compare matter and spirit. They have not finished their work yet.

"Approaching them, I said: 'Neither the wind nor the banner is moving. Your minds are moving.' The monks were all astonished." Now the Sixth Patriarch showed his metal. They were good monks, and somehow they understood him. They began to question themselves: "Who is this? Today, we have a strange *anja* who never said a word before."

"Neither the wind nor the banner is moving. Your minds are moving." This is one of the famous koans. If you really find the nature of the *alaya*-consciousness, you will get out of this limited body and enter the boundless one.

"Yin-tsung asked me to take the seat of honor and questioned me about the secrets of Buddhism.

"When Yin-tsung realized that my answers were concise, sound, and did not rely on the words of the scriptures, he said: 'Lay brother, I am convinced that you are an unusual man. For a long time it has been reported that the robe and canon of Huang-mei had been carried to the south. Are you not the one to whom they have been transmitted?'

"I answered: 'Yes, unworthy though I am.' Thereupon Yin-tsung made a bow and begged me to show his followers the robe and bowl that had been transmitted to me. Then Yin-tsung asked: 'When the Fifth Patriarch transmitted the doctrine to you, what did he teach?'

"I answered: He did not teach anything. He only spoke about seeing into one's own intrinsic nature. He did not speak of meditation or deliverance.'

"Yin-tsung asked: 'Why did he not speak of meditation or deliverance?'

"I said: 'Because that is the teaching of duality and not Buddhism, which is the teaching of non-duality.'

"Yin-tsung asked: 'What is the Buddhism that teaches non-duality?'

"I said: 'The Nirvana Sutra, on which you are lecturing, elucidates buddha-nature. This is the Buddhist teaching of non-duality.

SOKEI-AN SAYS:

"Yin-tsung asked me to take the seat of honor and questioned me about the secrets of Buddhism." Yin-tsung asked Hui-neng to take the seat of honor and interpret Buddhism. It is written that Yin-tsung asked about all the important points in Buddhism: the three bodies, the five shadows, and the alaya-consciousness—how our consciousness appears. Usually, a teacher will answer with words written in the sutras. For instance: "What is Dharma?"—"Dharma was created from the beginning and lasts to

the endless end. Though you have eyes, you cannot see it. It is ungraspable. No one can demonstrate the Dharma." In such a way, teachers repeat the words written in the sutras.

In ancient days, there was a monk giving a lecture on *dharmakaya*, talking about it in the usual way. A Zen monk was listening, and he laughed. The monk came down from the altar: "You laughed at my lecture. What was wrong?" The Zen monk said: "You were *talking* about *dharmakaya*, but you cannot *prove* it." The monk stopped giving lectures and was converted to the Zen school. Such a lecture is like parrot talk. I do not appreciate it.

"When Yin-tsung realized that my answers were concise, sound, and did not rely on the words of the scriptures . . .": Hui-neng always answered concisely. When someone asked "What is Dharma?" he would say: "THIS!"—extending his arms. "What are the five shadows?" "Lost in a fog." "What are the Three Bodies?" Hui-neng slapped his head and popped out his tongue.

"He said: 'Lay brother, I am convinced that you are an unusual man. For a long time it has been reported that the robe and canon of Huang-mei had been carried to the south. Are you not the one to whom they have been transmitted?' I answered: 'Yes, unworthy though I am.'" In Chinese, this is said in two words, meaning: "I could hardly say that I am the one." Those ancient Zen masters' attitudes were different from today. Now they come ringing a bell, "I am a Zen master from Tibet," and they open a school in New York. But Hui-neng was hiding for fifteen years. The great man's attitude is different.

"Thereupon Yin-tsung made a bow and begged me to show his followers the robe and the bowl that had been transmitted to me."—"Oh, this is the Sixth Patriarch!" The Chinese are wonderful. The Japanese have imitated them, but all of it was really born from the Chinese heart.

When I was in Seattle, Washington, a Chinese gentleman came into my backyard catching crickets. "Please let me into your yard. I like having a cricket in a cage to enjoy its singing." He will put it on a pillow while he sleeps. There is something lovely and poetical in the Chinese heart. They will work hard all day and night; and just for a couple of minutes, they will enjoy listening to the chirping of a cricket.

Then Hui-neng asked a novice to get a knapsack from his living quarters. The novice brought the knapsack (it looks like a potato bag) and opened it, handing out the robe and the bowl. All the monks prostrated themselves.

"Then Yin-tsung asked: 'When the Fifth Patriarch transmitted the doctrine to you, what did he teach?' I answered: 'He did not teach anything. He only spoke about seeing into one's own intrinsic nature. He did not speak of meditation or deliverance.'" That is a true answer!

Yin-tsung asked: 'Why did he not speak of meditation or deliverance?' I said: 'Because that is the teaching of duality and not Buddhism, which is the teaching of non-duality.'" Hear that! Hui-neng said that meditation and deliverance are not Buddhism. Meditation is not deliverance, and deliverance is not meditation. Wooden men dance, and stone women sing, but that is not deliverance. When you prove yourself in the koan, "Before father and mother," it is not dualistic. When we are emancipated, we are meditating, we are "depending upon nothing." How do you manifest this?

"Yin-tsung asked: 'What is the Buddhism that teaches in one way only?' "I said: 'The Nirvana Sutra, *on which you are lecturing, elucidates buddha-nature. This is the Buddhist teaching of non-duality."* Such a foolish question! A frog opens its mouth and shows its tongue. Yin-tsung was lecturing on Buddhism, but he did not know it. Hui-neng heard his words while he was scraping the yard. He then proved the Buddhism that teaches in only one way.

Hui-neng is saying that Buddhism is the single way. If there is dualism, it is not Buddhism. To practice meditation and to desire emancipation are opposites. By practicing meditation, we cannot find emancipation. In the friction of life there is no meditation. So if you attach to the formula of meditation or to the notion of freedom, you will not be able to grasp both meditation and freedom. Buddhism is always the single way. When you have grasped real understanding, passing through the koan, "Before father and mother, what is your intrinsic nature?" you will realize meditation, tranquillity, and emancipation all at the same time, and all at once.

'Thus, in that sutra it is said that Kao-kuei-te-wang Bodhisattva asked the Buddha: "Does one who has violated the four grave prohibitions, committed the five nefarious crimes, or is a heretic born beyond redemption destroy the excellent roots of buddha-nature?" The Buddha answered him: "There are two kinds of excellent roots, one perpetual, the other mutable. Buddha-nature, however, is neither perpetual nor mutable, it cannot be destroyed; therefore, it is called non-dual. There are good roots and evil roots, but buddha-nature is neither good nor evil, and therefore it is called non-dual. An unenlightened man takes the view that the five shadows of mind [the five* skandhas] are different from the sensible exterior [the eighteen dhatus]; but an enlightened man realizes that in their essential nature, these are not two separate existences. This non-dual nature is buddha-nature.'

"Yin-tsung, listening to this address, was delighted, and joining his palms, said: 'My humble commentary on this sutra was as worthless as a pile of logs, while your discourse is like pure gold.' Thereupon, he shaved my head and entreated me to become his teacher."

SOKEI-AN SAYS:

"'Thus, in that sutra it is said that Kao-kuei-te-wang Bodhisattva asked the Buddha: "Does one who has violated the four grave prohibitions, committed the five nefarious crimes . . . '": Here Hui-neng brings up a passage from the lecture that had been given by Yin-tsung in which a bodhisattva questioned the Buddha about the four grave prohibitions. The four grave prohibitions are the four great Hindu commandments: 1) Not to kill a human being; 2) Not to steal; 3) Not to violate a woman; 4) Not to lie (particularly not to say one is enlightened when one is not).

Anyone who violates these four commandments cannot stay in the sangha; he must be disrobed. For instance, if a monk on his way through the woods meets the daughter of a villager or a nun and violates her, he cannot stay in the sangha. Of course, there are difficulties in judging. For example, a monk thought he had killed a man and then discovered it was only a table that he had struck. Another cut something, thinking it was a table, and killed a man as a result. How would you judge these? There are many similar situations, so it is certainly not simple if you study such cases carefully. One monk stole something that he thought belonged to a certain man, and later found out that it belonged to no one.

The worst crimes in the Buddhist sangha, the five nefarious crimes, are: 1) To kill your father; 2) To kill your mother; 3) To shed the blood of a buddha; 4) To kill a bodhisattva; 5) To destroy the sangha (whether you are living in a lay family or in the sangha). For instance, a nun tried to destroy the sangha. One day while the Buddha was giving a lecture, she entered holding a nut bowl under her robe and said, "Buddha, what have you done to my stomach?" The Buddha said: "No one knows about this but you and me; we know." And she said, "Why, of course, we know." The wind came and fluttered her garments, and as she tried to cover her legs, the nut bowl dropped down and rolled on the ground. Everyone laughed, and then the earth rose and swallowed her. That is the story. Nuns are a great difficulty.

"' . . . Or is a heretic born beyond redemption destroy the excellent roots of buddha-nature?'" This word "root" is one of the technical terms of Buddhism. If you had no root of faith in your mind, then your mind is a non-conductor of religion, as glass or china is a non-conductor of electricity. So religion cannot enter such a heart, and you cannot attain nirvana. To have "no root" means "one with no faith, no truth, no conscience in his consciousness."

"The Buddha answered him: 'There are two kinds of excellent roots, one perpetual, the other mutable.'" The "excellent roots" of buddha-nature refers to deep consciousness (alaya-consciousness) and present consciousness.

"'Buddha-nature, however, is neither perpetual nor mutable, it cannot be destroyed; therefore, it is called non-dual.'" One who has committed a nefarious crime can come to the end of his life and realize that his crime has been expiated when he understands that his consciousness, even though that consciousness carries his crime, will not be punished in his buddha-nature. This part is analogous to Christianity. The Christ bore all the crimes of sentient beings. Christ *is* consciousness, a symbol of perfect consciousness. So the one who committed felonious crimes, but who practiced and became a bodhisattva, did not have two different natures.

"'There are good roots and evil roots, but buddha-nature is neither good nor evil, and therefore it is called non-dual.'" When you enter Zen, when you "think neither good nor evil," what is your intrinsic nature? When the Sixth Patriarch said this to the monk on the mountain top, the monk immediately enlightened himself. "Good nor evil" is the symbol of all the opposites. When you are enlightened, you realize that you are neither a good man nor an evil one.

"An unenlightened man takes the view that the five shadows of mind [the five skandhas*] are different from the sensible exterior [the eighteen* dhatus*]'":* The "five shadows of mind" are the "scales of consciousness." They are not different from the seven colors of the rainbow, or the seven sounds, or the five senses, or the two-hundred-fifty scents. You cannot divide the outside from consciousness, nor consciousness from the outside. The wise understand that their nature is non-dual.

"'But an enlightened man realizes that in their essential nature, these are not two separate existences.' This non-dual nature is buddha-nature." I hope all the members of my sangha know this.

"Yin-tsung, listening to this address, was delighted, and joining his palms, said: 'My humble commentary on this sutra was as worthless as a pile of logs, while your discourse is like pure gold.' Thereupon, he shaved my head and entreated me to become his teacher." Hui-neng was an anja, even though he was the heir of the Fifth Patriarch. (As I was a *koji*, a lay pratitioner, for a long time.) But when the time came, he asked an old monk to shave his head, and he became a member of the Buddha's sangha.

When his head was shaved, he was no longer the disciple of a teacher but a disciple of Buddha. If one is enlightened, he is the heir of Dharma.

"So under the Bodhi tree in Ts'ao-ch'i, I opened the gate of the teaching of the Eastern Mountain. Since receiving that teaching, there is no difficulty I have not undergone, and many times my life has hung by a thread. That today I am holding this meeting with you, the prefect and his staff, the monks, nuns and laymen, surely indicates a recurring relation among us through many kalpas, and the cultivation of meritorious roots common to us all, a result of making offerings to the buddhas in past lives. Otherwise, we could not have heard this teaching of sudden enlightenment that is the cause of attaining the Dharma. The

teaching is that transmitted by previous patriarchs. It is not my own idea. Those of you who wish to hear this teaching of the patriarchs must first purify your minds, and after listening, clear away your doubts. Then you will be no different from the patriarchs of old."

Having heard this teaching, the multitude retired in great joy, bowing low.

SOKEI-AN SAYS:

"So under the Bodhi tree in Ts'ao-ch'i, I opened the gate of the teaching of the Eastern Mountain. Since receiving that teaching, there is no difficulty I have not undergone, and many times my life has hung by a thread. That today I am holding this meeting with you, the prefect and his staff, the monks, nuns and laymen, surely indicates a recurring relation among us through many kalpas, and the cultivation of meritorious roots common to us all as a result of making offerings to the buddhas in past lives. Otherwise, we could not have heard this teaching of sudden enlightenment that is the cause of attaining the Dharma. This teaching is that of the Sixth Patriarch. He emphasized the idea of sudden enlightenment. But we do not think this record was written by him; it disparages the Northern School. I have carefully read the records of the Northern School, and if I live a little longer, I shall translate these records. It would be very good for Westerners.

The teaching is that transmitted by previous patriarchs. It is not my own idea. This is a very important line. Certainly all Zen masters from generation to generation must pound this into the brains of their pupils. The Buddha's teaching passed from India to China to Japan. Altogether, from the Buddha to my teacher, one hundred eight generations transmitted the teaching as this water is passed from jug to glass and so on. We say, "transmitted from torch to torch."

Today, we transmit this by *sanzen*, face to face. There is no Zen by correspondence. It is face to face, eye to eye, and soul to soul. So the Zen master is very important. The Zen master is the main pillar of the Zen School, and all abbots, those who make contact with lay families, must kneel down to the Zen master, even though he lives in a hut on a hillside. He may be a monk, a layman, anybody.

The masters of Zen are those to whom the teaching of previous sages have been transmitted. No one creates a new Zen understanding by his own wit. And all who attain will look at each other and understand just by this looking. Any gesture and they understand. There is no fooling in the Zen School. All is transmitted. If anyone says, "I am reading Zen," he cannot know anything about it.

Those of you who wish to hear this teaching of the patriarchs must first purify your minds": To come here and listen to Zen, wash your brain first, and do not try to interpret Zen by your previous notions. To those who study by some arcane school or by philosophy, by Theosophy, or psychoanalysis, I will emphasize this: please do not try to interpret my teaching with it. Make your brain clean, a sheet of white paper. I will do this when I go to *them*. Why come to a Buddhist school if you mean to interpret Buddhism by what you have previously studied? Stay in your own school. Come here as you would go to a hot spring—take off your clothes and get in.

"And after listening, clear away your doubts." And do not ask me questions to hide your ignorance, or to appear bright.

"Then you will be no different from the patriarchs of old." If someone has done this, though he is three years old, I will bow to him. And if not, though he is eighty years old, I will teach him. It is hard to bow down to a three-year-old child. I could not answer Mr. Blake, who said: "Come with me and kneel down before Father Divine!"

Having heard this teaching, the multitude retired in great joy, bowing low.

CHAPTER II

PRAJNAPARAMITA

The next day, entreated by Prefect Wei, the Master ascended the high seat and spoke to the multitude: "All of you, clear your minds and concentrate on mahaprajnaparamita."

*He continued: "Good friends, man innately possesses awakening-wisdom (*prajna*), but because of his delusions he cannot realize it and must ask one who is wise to lead him to see his own original nature. You should know that the buddha-nature of the ignorant is intrinsically no different from that of the wise. However, the ignorant one is deluded, and the wise one is enlightened.*

"Now I am going to speak to you about mahaprajnaparamita *and bring each of you to wisdom. Listen to me with undivided attention. I am speaking about this for you.*

"Good friends, the man of the world continually speaks of wisdom with his mouth but never knows the wisdom of his own nature. It is like someone who speaks of food he has never eaten. Such a person only speaks of emptiness. Through an aeon of time he will never find his intrinsic nature. What good is that?

"Good friends, mahaprajnaparamita *is a Sanskrit word. It means that carried by the highest wisdom, one reaches another shore. You must practice this with the mind. You cannot realize it by reciting words with the lips. Even if you recite the words with your lips, if you do not practice with your mind, it is like a mirage, a phantom, a dewdrop, or a flash of lightning. When you recite it with your lips and practice it with your mind, mind and lips will be in harmony. Your intrinsic nature is Buddha; there is no Buddha apart from your own nature.*

"What is 'maha'? 'Maha' means 'great,' that mind which is vast, like the sky, without boundary. It has no form—round or square, large or small. It has no color—green, yellow, red or white. It has no position—above or below; it is neither long nor short. It is neither anger nor joy, right nor wrong, good nor evil, beginning nor end. All the Buddha's dominions are as empty as the sky. The marvelous nature of people in the world is originally empty. There is no tangible manifestation within it. Such is the absolute emptiness of your intrinsic nature."

SOKEI-AN SAYS:

In the early period of Zen, this record was left by the Sixth Patriarch and his disciples. In it, the foundation and structure of Zen was written clearly, as clearly as you see your own palm. If you can penetrate the meaning of these words, you do not need to take *sanzen*. Certainly you can attain Zen immediately. But, as Lin-chi said, the trouble with students is simply that they have no self-reliance. They are seeking in external words.

The Sixth Patriarch did not speak differently from other Zen masters of ancient times or today. Zen students always speak the same way because their attainment is the same.

The next day, entreated by Prefect Wei, the Master ascended the high seat and spoke to the multitude: Because the Sixth Patriarch was a small man and the multitude could not see him, he was entreated to take a high seat that was made of earth. Then he said:

"All of you, clear your minds and concentrate on mahaprajnaparamita." To clear your mind to listen to a Buddhist teacher, you must not keep any previous notion in your mind. If you are studying philosophy, you must put it aside for a while. If you are studying any cult, lay it on the shelf. Listen with pure-mind, and do not measure what you hear by your preconceived notions. Do not think about something else. Concentrate upon the topic of the master's lecture.

He continued: "Good friends": There were many Taoist scholars, and also ordinary people. In this country, he would say, "Ladies and Gentlemen."

*"Man innately possesses awakening-wisdom (*prajna*), but because of his delusions he cannot realize it."* Among the ranks of consciousness, awakening-wisdom (*prajna*) is the highest. With it, you can see nirvana. With no other consciousness can you see nirvana. You can really perceive nirvana only with awakening-wisdom. Isn't it strange that you cannot see nirvana with this eye consciousness, nor with this ear consciousness, nor with thoughts, nor with philosophy or logic? Nor can you see nirvana with feeling, belief, or dreams. You cannot see it with sleeping consciousness. You can see it only with awakening-wisdom consciousness. When you really find this, your study of Buddhism is over.

The word "wisdom," in English usage, denotes that activity with which people discern something intellectually, that is, judge something. It means to be educated and wise. But in Chinese, wisdom is *intrinsic* wisdom, the wisdom common to all sentient beings, and not only human beings but insects, plants, and all that has life.

It is odd to think of wisdom in insects and plants, but here is an instance of this unconscious wisdom: In darkness, ivy will search with its long tendrils for the sun's rays, will push out from a crack in the wall, and finally, through a small gap in the building, feel the sunshine in its tiny green palm. In pictures of a town in Switzerland that someone showed me, I saw ivy that was a thousand years old and very beautiful. Even ivy has this wisdom. Perhaps in English you would call it "instinct." In Chinese, the word stands for both instinctive and intuitive. But I translate it as wisdom, after English scholars and also Dr. [D.T.] Suzuki of Japan. This is the wisdom spoken about by the Sixth Patriarch.

I was very stupid, but I found this wisdom when I was forty-two or—three years old. Then the rest of my study of Buddhism was very quick. Before that, I was in emptiness. I really do not know how I managed myself in that empty stage through six or seven years—not only in meditation but in practical daily life. I just took, so to speak, a relaxed attitude, like a willow tree swaying according to the wind. I was like a cloud in the sky swept along by the wind and loitering about the moon. I think I was a brave man to keep that state for seven years, empty of all desire, all purpose, everything.

One day a friend visited me and spoke about something. When he went away, I conceived a question: "I have emptied out everything from my mind. From where does this awareness come, this awareness that I am existing now at this moment and that I know my existence here?" It was a great question, and I took that question into myself. I was really born in that question. And then—"Ah!" It was something like this—as if I had turned a cone-shaped flower inside out. "Why, this is wisdom!" And from the center of wisdom, suddenly I saw entire existence.

Really I finished Buddhism then. I went back to Japan and observed some more koans with my teacher. Face to face, I proved that my experience was not erroneous, that it was all right. Of course I had been studying Zen and taking koans since I was twenty years old. But the real enlightenment comes in its season, and then all those koans you have observed blaze like fire, and you really understand what you have been doing. I have clearly stated my experience—how I attained wisdom—and you think you understand. But some day, I promise, you will come to it and know that Sokei-an did not speak a lie.

We possess this awakening-wisdom as ivy possesses the nature to stretch out its tendrils toward the light. But most men do not care about their awakening. They are busy pursuing money, women, or something. They never heard that they could awake. They do not understand awakening. Some of these men question their mind: "What is *this*?" [striking self]. If they do not know what *this* is, they do not know what to do. They are dishonest and careless. They feel that whether or not they commit errors is not their responsibility. If you are really honest, you cannot do things you do not understand. Buddhism gives you the knowledge of what *this* is.

Christianity is a religion that tells you what to do—do this or do that actively; save your neighbor; change a bad situation. The Buddhist takes a different attitude: "What is this gong?" "What is this self?" "What is heaven?" If you understand what *this* is, then you will know what to do. A stranger comes to New York and wants to go somewhere on Lexington Avenue. But he does not know how to get there, so he buys a map, and there is a summary of New York: Fifth Avenue, Madison Avenue, Park Avenue, Lexington Avenue. Now he knows how to get there. It is not necessary to ask what to do. If you know what *this* is, then what to do naturally comes to mind. When you are sick and do not know what to do—since you do not know what your body is—you go to a doctor. He knows what it is and what to do. People are very careless. They do not care about knowing. They are muffled with delusion, so they never realize the wisdom of awakening that is within them.

"*. . . And must ask one who is wise to lead him to see his own original nature.*" The "wise" one is Shakyamuni Buddha. There are many wise ones. Guided by them, you will find your original nature.

When you come to a Zen temple to study Zen, you give away your speaking mind, and in profound silence, suddenly, on a sharp pinpoint, you find the whole universe within yourself. Without giving any explanation at all, you realize the value of it. All other teachings, all those explanations that are given to you, just give you more words, more to explain, and more to think about.

A Zen master takes a different attitude. Zen strips you of everything—all those preconceived notions; all that you studied; all words. Then you find yourself. Suddenly you realize, "Ah . . . *This is It*." And you don't take a dramatic attitude, but just a quiet "Ah . . . *This is It*."

However, you need guidance from one who has experienced it. For spoken experiences, you need no teacher. You can study them anywhere—in the bathtub, in bed. But for Zen, you really need a teacher to receive what was handed down from generation to generation.

"*You should know that the buddha-nature of the ignorant is intrinsically no different from that of the wise. However, the ignorant one is deluded, and the wise one is enlightened.*" The enlightened one so intimately finds buddha-nature in himself that there is no one anymore. You realize that buddha-nature exists only in yourself. This is so clear to you that from morning to evening you are always buddha-nature. Of course, there is much dust in it, but you clean it day by day. You find the gold, and see it clearly, for there is much impurity in it. You must put the gold into the fire, refine it, and beat it with a hammer to make it pure. Buddha-nature is like that. When you find buddha-nature in yourself, it is crude. It must be shaped and refined. A good teacher is a harsh teacher who takes off all pride and selfishness. There will be turmoil for five or six years. It is hard to find such a teacher. He does not care whether the disciples come or go, or whether they will starve tomorrow. He snarls at them and many go away. I do not blame the teacher. I blame the disciples. I wish I could be a teacher like that!

"Now I am going to speak to you about mahaprajnaparamita *and bring each of you to wisdom."* The Sixth Patriarch speaks too much. If he were Lin-chi, he would not repeat himself so many times. He would spit—grrrrh!

I am sure this was not spoken by the Sixth Patriarch, but the writer assumes this. Perhaps the patriarch said two or three words.

"Listen to me with undivided attention. I am speaking about this for you." This is the usual monk's attitude. Speaking is not the business of the Zen master.

"Good friends, the man of the world continually speaks of wisdom with his mouth but never knows the wisdom of his own nature." It is usually the case when someone is always talking about God day and night. Like a drunken man, he does not know what he is talking about. It is terrible to build a great cathedral, make a wonderful two-hundred-fifty-pipe organ, and sing "Ah-h-h!" but not to know what the singing is about.

"It is like someone who speaks of food he has never eaten." He says he has studied this and that, or written and read this and that book. Yet look at him: His mind and his personality are just like anyone else's. He speaks of taste, but he has never eaten. He speaks of food, but he has not nourished his own body and soul. I do not like that attitude.

"Such a person only speaks of emptiness. Through an aeon of time he will never find his intrinsic nature. What good is that?" Perhaps he has been speaking of Buddhism for eighty years; then, by some good fortune, at the end of his life he finds a Zen master and goes to study Zen. The Zen master gives him the koan: "Before father and mother . . ." Though he has been talking Buddhism for eighty years, he cannot pass his koan, so he dies with it.

Once I met an old man and gave him this koan. He said: "It has no meaning, but if you ask me what was before father and mother, I will tell you." And he knelt down to an image. I told him he was wrong, and he said: "I'm all right." I did not say yes or no. He was just worshipping a wooden image. What merit would it be to him?

"Good friends, mahaprajnaparamita *is a Sanskrit word. It means that carried by the highest wisdom, one reaches another shore."* "Another shore," *paramita*, means nirvana. The Sixth Patriarch did not say nirvana, but it can be understood from what he says at the end of his discourse.

"You must practice this with the mind. You cannot realize it by reciting words with the lips." Saying a million words, singing hymns, or ringing bells from the top of a tower may amuse the devas in the sky, but will not cure your hunger for truth. Practice is not dramatization. It means meditation or taking *sanzen*.

Monks begin their practice by analyzing the mind according to the theory of the five shadows, or skandhas. Skandhas means "piled up." First, you define outer existence. Look at it, observe it with your five senses, and if your five senses are not good enough, use a powerful microscope and analyze it into protons, electrons, and so forth.

Scientists think they have found Reality this way, but from our standpoint it is just phenomena. We call it rupa, the first of the five shadows. However small it may be—so small a microscope is unable to see it—if it is matter, it is still rupa and belongs to the five senses.

The second shadow is vedana—perception, sense-perception, which includes all feelings, pleasant and painful, agreeable and disagreeable, hunger or itching.

Next you have to solve, or as we say, annihilate the third of the five shadows, samjna. You cannot destroy samjna as you would a spoilt tomato in your garbage pail. But gradually you annihilate it starting from the corners with philosophical analysis. The brain has this logical faculty, and to solve questions is within the scope of the third of the five shadows. Your work in *sanzen* is the cleaning up of this area. As you are experiencing getting into *samadhi* or meditation, sometimes a question flashes through your mind. Then the whole world, the whole universe becomes one great doubt, and you cannot enter nothingness. Your mind is filled with a question. The brain's chief work is to painstakingly solve this question. It may take a long time—years—to observe this mental activity, solve the question, and drive this question into emptiness, as the wind drives the clouds out of the sky. This is a big job, but you must succeed in it.

The next practice is to solve the fourth of the five shadows, samskara. In the Buddha's time, samskara was not spoken about. Later, monks divided this fourth shadow in two, as though there were a shelf separating the two parts. Above the shelf are thoughts, the area of thinking. Under the shelf is what you might call the subconscious. It is, however, somewhat conscious mind-stuff. I think all Buddhist monks and laymen must spend a lifetime, day and night, annihilating this shadow. Even in sleep, they keep an eye on this mind-stuff. Emotions like laughing, crying, joy, and anger are samskara. Reason cannot reach there, but it is the foundation of your thoughts. If you clean up samskara, you can be called a sage. Your mind will become clear as crystal. There will be no cloud or mist between your eye and consciousness. You will have clear perception. Nothing will distort or disturb your observation. But nothing can clean this up except meditation, so meditation takes the largest part of Buddhist practice.

The fifth shadow is consciousness, vijnana. Sages struggle to annihilate the seeds in the deepest consciousness, the alayavijnana. This is a little too much. Even the Buddha could not annihilate the seeds accumulated through many eons in the alaya-consciousness. Some make great opposition to this kind of theory, saying that the nature of meditation is not such an abstract system. When you practice by this system, starting from the outside to the center of consciousness, it is Hinayana. Returning from the deepest consciousness to this conscious state is Mahayana.

The complete experience of meditation, however, is not on a "plane." Perhaps it could be called "cubic." When you go from the outside to the inmost reality, at the same time you are going from the innermost to the outermost. Going up and coming down are at the same time. You will realize what I am talking about when you take *sanzen*. Your answer to the first koan, "Before father and mother, what is your original aspect?" proves this. If you annihilate all outer existence and close your eyes in mute silence when you come into my room for *sanzen*, I say, "No." But when you are in Emptiness and manifest the whole phenomenal world, manifest the minus and the plus—the whole universe all in the same moment—I say, "Yes."

In China, two monks were disputing, looking at the water draining in a tub. One said: "The water is circling to the center." The other said: "No, the water is circling from the center to the outside." A third monk, who was watching said: "It is neither converging to nor diverging from the center. Both are happening at once, circling at once." "How do you prove it?" asked the first monk. "I will prove it to you," said the third, and gave him a terrific smack in the eye—"Ka-a-a!" Then the first monk understood. Centrifugal and centripetal at the same moment are just one direction, not two. You cannot express such things by words; you have to experience them.

I hope you who are taking *sanzen* understand this. This final attitude is true Mahayana, true nothingness—not coming up from the bottom or going down from the top, but all at the same time. A monk asked Lin-chi: "What is Buddhism?" Lin-chi answered: "Ka-a-a!" That is all. There are 5,048 volumes of sutras to explain Buddhism, but Lin-chi answered in one shout.

You must understand. Zen takes a the cubic attitude—going up and coming down occur at the same time. When you are stretching out your arm, it is already coming back. And when you are coming back, you are already going. When you are stopping the hurricane, it is blowing. But I shall not talk more about this important point of Zen. I think you understand.

"Even if you recite the words with your lips, if you do not practice with your mind, it is like a mirage, a phantom, a dewdrop, or a flash of lightning. When you recite it with your lips and practice it in your mind, mind and lips will be in harmony." When you speak about Reality with your lips—la, la, la—you must know what it means. When you say, "I am taking a pill from a pillbox," you must know what you are doing; it is not a mere pill. And when you are taking communion, the conversion of the wine into blood and the bread into the flesh of Christ, you must know what you are really doing, you must know what you are practicing. Otherwise, it has no value.

Why do you join your hands before eating? Because it is religion. Not knowing the meaning of transubstantiation, you just eat. If human life is as shallow as the water on a plate, there is not much delight in it—from morning to evening, just running around. It's a pretty kettle of fish! But almost all people take life in such a poor way. No wonder they do not enjoy it and have to acquire money and fame or something besides life itself.

Your intrinsic nature is Buddha; there is no Buddha apart from your own nature." This is simply expressed, yet it covers all. When you stand up and put your arms on your breast, when you enter the universe and the universe enters you, that is Buddha.

"What is 'maha'? 'Maha' means 'great,' that mind which is vast, like the sky, without boundary." The Sixth Patriarch is here explaining the part of Buddhism that is called "maha"—simply, big, or great, as in maharajah. But in Buddhism it is a little different. It means something that is immeasurable. Has the soul a size? If the soul has no size, then the universe has no size.

"It has no form—round or square, large or small. It has no color—green, yellow, red, or white. It has no position—above or below; it is neither long nor short. It is neither anger nor joy, right nor wrong, good nor evil, beginning nor end." There is no alpha, no omega. There is nothing. So the true attitude of your mind must be empty—empty but shining. Shining, but there is no illumination.

"All the Buddha's dominions are as empty as the sky." Buddha's domain does not exist in the outer world. Each one of you is Buddha's domain—all empty as the sky. That is the attitude of Buddhism.

"The marvelous nature of people in the world is originally empty." My teacher said: "It's as clean and empty as your ass washed in a river." This is the best attitude. In Christianity, you would say, "He has a clean heart." We would say, "He has a clean ass." But if you try to be clean, you are not; and if you try to dramatize this cleanness, you are a failure. Dramatization is no good for Buddhism. Though you hold up your hands and try to look like a sage, it is only a "moving picture." You think a sage should look august. But sagehood is not in one's outer look; it is in one's heart. Take Hotei, who just laughs, with his fat belly and hairs all around his belly button. To you, he does not look like a sage, but he is a sage at heart.

"There is no tangible manifestation within it. Such is the absolute emptiness of your intrinsic nature." These are very important lines. If you recite these lines every day, I think you will understand Zen very quickly. This is the Buddhist attitude.

When I met my teacher forty years ago, his attitude was quite soft. That was his emptiness at the time. But later, when he became a mature Zen master, his nothingness became ferocious. At first he was in dramatic nothingness. For instance, when someone came to make a donation, he would say: "Yes, thank you, thank you very much." But later he would say: "What is this? What is it for? Five hundred dollars? Take it back, and give me two thousand!" Now his nothingness is different. It is hard to understand this nothingness. Studying nothingness is the one thing in the universe that is very interesting. What is nothingness?

Christian teachers are always accusing Buddhists: "Oh, Buddhism is empty, negative, pessimistic. There is no happiness in it. Look at India today! That is nothingness! And how miserable the people are!"

Of course, they have not been to Japan. Someday if I have the opportunity, I'd like to teach them what nothingness really is.

"Good friends, when you hear me speaking of emptiness, do not become attached to it. Do not become attached to emptiness, whatever you do. Sitting still with your mind vacant, you will become attached to notional emptiness.

"Good friends, the boundless emptiness of the sky embraces the ten thousand things of every shape and form: the sun, moon, and stars, mountains, rivers and earth, springs and rivulets, bushes and trees, bad people and good, good teachings and bad, heavens and hells, the great oceans and Mount Sumeru. All these exist in the emptiness of space. The emptiness of people's original nature is just like this.

"Good friends, your original nature, too, embraces everything. To this the word 'maha' applies. For within your own nature, all entities exist."

SOKEI-AN SAYS:

The Sixth Patriarch is talking about finding your original nature. It is the answer to the first koan we use: "Before father and mother, what is your original nature?"—if you say it in words.

"Good friends, when you hear me speaking of emptiness, do not become attached to it. Do not become attached to emptiness, whatever you do." You think your original nature is empty, as the universe is empty before creation, or as the whole cosmos is empty after a total disaster—you think there would be nothing. But nothing appears from something. If something does appear, nothing was not empty. Before creation, there is emptiness. How do the "ten thousand things" come from this emptiness? That they do come from it proves that it isn't really empty. When you just close your eyes, stop the motion of your mind, and squeeze your stomach muscles thinking it is empty, that is just your notion. There is no such emptiness. If you become attached to this kind of emptiness, you are a fox in a cave; you are meditating in darkness. You may think you are holy, but you are more like a tadpole in a deep well.

First of all, to be a Zen student, a true Buddhist, you must give up any notion you have of emptiness. Many disciples of the Buddha, from generation to generation, have fallen into the pit of notional emptiness. If you do so, you are just like any superstitious person, for if you take that notion as true emptiness, your religion is superstition. So you must realize, when you have received the koan "Before father and mother, what is your original aspect," and you come to me saying, "There is nothing" or clench your teeth, put your hands on your lap, and say nothing, it is just a notion. When you show the true manifestation of emptiness, I will agree with your answer. But until you do, I'll ring the bell.[7] The notion of emptiness is always around, and everyone will step into it at least once. It is very seldom one jumps over and suddenly comes to the manifestation of true emptiness. Those who do are good students.

"Sitting still with your mind vacant, you will become attached to notional emptiness." Notional emptiness is a kind of agnostic emptiness. The so-called agnostic, because he falls into the notion of

emptiness, does not see the source of the universe. Those who think religion is "nothing" also fall into this notional emptiness. It is a negative, a passive emptiness. It is a senseless emptiness.

Many monks fall into this and do not get out of it all their lifetime, and they look it. Their long faces show they are in that notion. They pinch their mouths, or they are always smiling—two sides of the same thing, one negative, the other positive. It's as bad as that.

"Good friends, the boundless emptiness of the sky embraces the 'ten thousand things' of every shape and form: the sun, moon and stars, mountains, rivers and earth, springs and rivulets, bushes and trees, bad people and good, good teachings and bad, heavens and hells, the great oceans and Mt. Sumeru. All these exist in the emptiness of space." All phenomena. You don't need to hide away nor brush away nor annihilate anything. You will prove that inside is empty and that outside is empty. Both inside and outside are empty at that moment.

The word "emptiness" is deceptive. People think it is zero. But it is neither zero nor one. Or they think it is mystical and secret. But there is no secret in Zen. Emptiness is like the inside of a kaleidoscope. All phenomena are revealed at once in this kaleidoscopic universe. That is emptiness. You do not need to close your eyes, nor pinch your lips, nor squeeze your stomach muscles. With this kaleidoscopic universe—this entire manifestation—you prove emptiness. Having given up notional emptiness, you come to true emptiness. If you really want to know what Buddhism is, you certainly must grasp this point.

"The emptiness of people's original nature is just like this." Emptiness is *this*, the whole universe. It is like the sky, it embraces everything. Now do not close your eyes and say, "Emptiness! Emptiness!" Just take the "Emptiness" away and be empty. Mind is like a baby just born from his mother's womb—everything is in him. His mind is like the sky that has everything in it.

That is our mind's attitude in everyday life. In the clear sky, little white clouds occupy space. We know our mind is like the sky. We do not need to brush the clouds away, but when the time comes, the clouds will disappear.

"Good friends, your original nature, too, embraces everything. To this the word 'maha' applies. For within your own nature, all entities exist." Everything you can see—animals, flowers and weeds—is in your consciousness. When you cast your horoscope, there are twelve zodiacal signs. Why only twelve? Look at all the animals in the world! Look how many there are—kangaroos, birds, fish! And the plants! How many trees and weeds! They are all elements, all included in your consciousness. Your nature includes everything. Why limit it to twelve?

When you prove the first koan, everything is there at once—all empty. You can show this without saying a word. That is the entrance to Buddhism. It is the end of philosophy and the beginning of Zen.

The Sixth Patriarch's record is very simple. It is one of the oldest records. Before it, there were two or three others. But here, everything is explained so simply that a child could understand it.

"Witnessing good or evil acts without being affected or becoming interested or involved, your mind is boundless as the sky. This attitude is called 'great,' 'maha.'

"Good friends, the unenlightened mouth words about it; the enlightened practice it with the mind. There are also some ignorant people who sit still in meditation, emptying their minds, rejecting all thought and calling this 'maha.' Do not talk with such people; their view is wrong.

"Good friends, the magnitude of mind is boundless. It pervades the universe. Use it and it clearly reveals its intrinsic adaptability; put it to work and you will come to know the unity of all existence. All is one, one is all. Going and coming is your prerogative. There is no hindrance throughout the sphere of mind. This is what is called 'prajna.'"

SOKEI-AN SAYS:

When I read this, I realize that the whole theory of the Zen school was told in *The Record of the Sixth Patriarch*. As spoken, Zen was then completed. At this time, we do not really need to speak about Zen; our Zen is merely practice. No wonder that after this patriarch, there are not many who speak of Zen! Lin-chi left only one pamphlet. Huang-po also left but one very thin pamphlet. Several other Zen masters left memoranda. Almost all Zen experience was expressed in the form of poetry. In Japan there were not many Zen masters who left descriptive writings. Throughout Zen history, when Zen students were writing something, it was a mark of Zen decadence. When Zen students are not paying much attention to the records, Zen flourishes.

You must understand that speaking of Zen is useless. In Zen experience, we ask you: "What is *this*?" You say: "A glass of water." But this answer is not the same as that you give in daily life. It is the same word, but when you say it, it is just a name. When we really say, "A glass of water," fathomless depths exist within the word. Even though we are penniless, our life is very rich. For at every moment, our life pervades the universe. You must understand the joy of it.

"Witnessing good or evil acts without being affected or becoming interested or involved, your mind is boundless as the sky." When you see people who are doing good or evil, of course you will like them or dislike them.

There was a Japanese gentleman in San Francisco who was the owner of a Japanese-American bank, the only bank for Japanese immigrants on the Pacific coast. All the Japanese farmers working there kept their money in that bank. One day, all of a sudden, the bank closed. They stopped paying anything and announced bankruptcy. Many farmers committed suicide or became insane. It was a real tragedy. I lost about eighty dollars. Everybody was talking very badly about him at that time, but today they speak of him as a god. With the money, he had bought land they called the Imperial Land. It was just a big desert where nothing would grow. But after the land bill was passed, all the Japanese streamed into that "imperial land" and cultivated the sand, making fields of vegetables. Soon they were supplying greens to a large area of Southern California. His bad deed turned out to be a good deed. Good and bad are always like this. There is no permanent goodness and no permanent badness. For the time being, a certain deed is bad, but in time, it will be good and vice versa.

"This attitude is called 'great,' 'maha.'" A really great man, whether he sees a criminal or a sage, does not change his attitude. Though I could not practice it, I was always told by an old monk: "If you wish to win the struggle of existence, there is only one way, and that is maha." Here in America, I have seen—many times—an American woman slap a man's face, and the man say, "I am very sorry, I think you hurt your hand." And when she slaps him again, he smiles. Perhaps this is some type of maha—if he takes that attitude toward everything. I was trying to practice this for a little while; however, I don't like dramatization. If it does not come from my own heart, I will not do it.

"Good friends, the unenlightened mouth words about it; the enlightened practice it with the mind." There are different types of maha. George Washington practiced one type, Lincoln another. Missolini,

though in the movie houses everyone is hissing him today, is a type of maha. Christ was a type of maha, and the Buddha was another type.

"There are also some ignorant people who sit still in meditation, emptying their minds, rejecting all thought and calling this 'maha.' Do not talk with such people; their view is wrong." Like some priests who are very bad in this respect. They absent-mindedly meditate like a doll looking at the sky. In a thousand years, they will gain nothing. If you meet one who calls himself a Zen student, be very careful. If he has this type of understanding, he is not your friend.

In the past I was asked several questions by my own students: "What is the good of it, rejecting everything to meditate upon nothing? I feel I am reverting, going back to the savage." That question has a value, but I cannot explain it until the student comes to a certain point in his own understanding of Zen. Of course, Zen does not refuse knowledge. But we simply cannot make anyone understand this if he does not practice meditation. So there is no use in speaking about it.

"Good friends, the magnitude of mind is boundless. It pervades the universe." It is effulgent, boundless, and pervades the entire universe. When you pass the first koan, you will understand this.

For days after I passed my koan, I felt that I was in the sky. My heart was beating for joy and I could hardly sleep. It was really a sudden enlightenment. If you have not had such an experience, you must wait for it in the future. It is not all of Zen; it is just the entrance. But day by day, moment by moment . . .

"Use it and it clearly reveals its intrinsic adaptability; put it to work and you come to know the unity of all existence." When you understand the unity between *this* and *that*, you and me—the entire world as just one mind working according to the same law of adaptability—you understand this law of unity. We also clearly understand the law of society, the law of the human being and of nature—the law of everything. The same law works in the human heart as in trees, weeds, and so forth. When I was studying painting, I understood clearly that the same law was working in the human being as in the leaf of a tree.

Sometimes this intrinsic adaptability of soul does not work too well. You have to dig it out by practice and use it. This is really the Buddha's teaching. This is the soul whispering, the voice of the soul. You will probably call it conscience, and you will listen to it. But it is very hard to take that order—"You must not eat any more sausage!" "Well, I think I will eat half a one."

In Manchuria I watched the women at the train as the soldiers were leaving. The train must go, but many embraces delayed its leaving. I have seen that miserable attachment in the battlefield, in the moment of life and death. Happily, the Japanese army did not carry women along with it. If it had, it would have been the same agony, the sadness of the human being. We know the law, but we cannot obey it. Some old monk would say laughingly, "Perhaps, after all, it's adaptability." I agree. Adaptability, after all, is not as cold as ice.

"All is one, one is all. Going and coming is your prerogative. There is no hindrance throughout the sphere of mind. This is what is called 'prajna.'" Of course, this can be seen by the clear understanding of human life. Often we just blindly struggle, feel agony, and know nothing, so we ask, "What is *this*?" But when we clearly understand this law, we know.

Sokei-an in New York, giving lectures in this terrible language, is the position he must accept. All must accept their position. It did not happen yesterday or today. According to Buddhism, it is just part of your karma.

"Good friends, complete prajna *springs from your own nature. It does not come from the outside. Make no mistake! This is the natural functioning of true nature. All truth is one truth. Behold the magnitude of your own mind! Do not be disturbed by trivialities. Do not speak of emptiness all day long without exercising it in your mind. Do not be like someone who is in reality a commoner but calls himself a king. If you are of that ilk, you are not my disciple.*

*"Good friends, what is that which is called '*prajna?*' As expressed in Chinese,* prajna *denotes wisdom. In all places and at all times, in every pulse of your mind, if you are not foolish but always act according to wisdom, you are practicing* prajna. *In a moment of your foolish mind,* prajna *ceases to exist; in a moment of your wise mind,* prajna *arises. The man of the world is deluded by his own ignorance. He speaks of* prajna, *but not seeing* prajna, *his mind is perpetually stupid. Yet he asserts that he practices* prajna. *At every moment he speaks of emptiness, but he is unaware of true emptiness.* Prajna *is no formula; the mind that exhibits wisdom is* prajna. *If you understand this, that is* prajna *wisdom."*

SOKEI-AN SAYS:

You know that frequently I suspect this record. Many lines were inserted between the lines at a later time, or someone just wrote the lines as memoranda—perhaps the commentary of a teacher or of a copyist who wrote every line as though the Sixth Patriarch had spoken it. Compared with later Zen records, this is a very primitive description, not written by a man of letters.

If we read the records of the Northern School, we find the perfect usage of Chinese idiom and perfect expression. I think the Sixth Patriarch's speech was still more primitive than these records. Some Chinese scholar said this record was written by his disciples. Dr. Suzuki does not agree with him, but I do. Someday I will speak about this. According to the nature of this type of record, it develops and grows through the ages.

"Good friends": "Good friends" is a good translation. It is not necessary to call the audience "scholars." They were not scholars, but good men of good wisdom.

"Complete prajna *springs from your own nature. It does not come from the outside."* "Complete *prajna*" is a Chinese translation of the Sanskrit word *sarvajna. Sarvajna* and *prajna* are almost the same thing. Both are "one-wisdom," with all seeds in it; one seed contains all seeds.

To make a smooth sentence in Chinese, it was repeated: *own* nature, *own* soul, *own* consciousness. "Own nature" means your intrinsic nature, not your temperamental nature. If you pass the first koan, you will realize this. If you have not realized it, you must do so. *Prajna* springs from your own soul or consciousness. Your own nature does not come from the outside—from trees or images, from cathedrals or wonderful sermons.

"Make no mistake! This is the natural functioning of true nature." You use your mind to read sutras, or to invoke God with prayers, or to sing loudly to the thunderous voice of the pipe-organ. It is beautiful to hear the choir in the magnificent Mormon church of Utah, but all these are trivial uses of the mind. The "natural functioning of true nature" as you practice it every day is the conclusion of Buddhism, the Buddha's Buddhism. Buddhism teaches what *is*, not what to *do*. Throughout the 5,048 volumes of the sutras, there is only one line that tells you what to do. It is this: "Act according to circumstances." That is the end, the conclusion of religion. The rest is developed from religion. In all lines of life—in law, art, politics, or science—"Act according to circumstances" is the terminal. So singing aloud, observing rituals that were in use thousands of years ago, may not be called the "functioning of true nature." Do not attach this name to such things.

"*All truth is one truth.*" This line is not necessary in this place, but such a line can be used anywhere in a Zen record, so it is put in again here.

"*Behold the magnitude of your own mind!*" Here "magnitude" is the "body" of mind. I translate it as magnitude—size. But it is the size of light, heat, or such things. "Behold the magnitude of your own mind!" This is important in human life, an important koan. It is the search for your own soul.

"*Do not be disturbed by trivialities.*" "Trivialities" here means almsgiving, or giving lectures, or attending meetings. Such things are trivialities. It is also trivial to take conflicts with friends too seriously and to become disturbed. When I was living in the temple, I did not listen to back talk or gossip for many years. I cared only to enlighten myself. I did not pay attention to my teacher's criticism or to the criticism of my friends. I simply went to *sanzen*, with an answer or without.

"*Do not speak of emptiness all day long without exercising it in your mind. Do not be like someone who is in reality a commoner but calls himself a king. If you are of that ilk, you are not my disciple.*" "Do not speak of emptiness" means: Do not speak about the philosophy of Buddhism. Philosophy does not enlighten. It is like the blocks of wood with which children play, the ABC's that you build up, tear down, pile up again, and destroy again. It is just a structure built with your own mind-stuff. All that is visible, the outside, is the delusion of your mind, and your moods are ripples of samskara, just like waves or clouds that have no true existence. All is mutable. All are but waves of the sea. If you talk about nothingness, then you know nothing about it. It is like the commoner who calls himself a king. "If you are of that ilk, you are not my disciple." Go to some university of Buddhism, but do not come to my Zen temple.

"*Good friends, what is that which is called* 'prajna?' *As expressed in Chinese,* prajna *denotes wisdom. In all places and at all times, in every pulse of your mind, if you are not foolish, always acting according to wisdom, you are practicing* prajna." But you cannot practice *prajna* until you find it. When you find it, you will know how to act according to circumstances. But if you are lazy, though you have found it, you cannot carry out its indications. You must be deadly honest with your *prajna*; then you will know how to carry out its mission. But you must have real *prajna*, you know. You must not mistake your previous conceptions, the remarks and conceptions of others or a line or two from the Bible, for the ruler of your mind, and use them to correct your thoughts or to limit your actions. You may think it is *prajna* when it is not. To find *prajna*, you must have a naked soul. It is very hard to find, very hard.

"*In a moment of your unwise mind,* prajna *ceases to exist; in a moment of your wise mind,* prajna *arises.*" "Unwise mind," that is, the mind that you believe to be true but is not. You have heard: "If someone hits you, turn the other cheek." But that doesn't apply to all circumstances. If he goes on and on hitting you, how long do you let him? According to the circumstances in which Jesus said it, it had value; but in other circumstances it does not apply. It was a shining, wonderful teaching, but sometimes such words can become a real obstacle. "Obey your father" is also a wise teaching. But what if your father is evil: how can you obey him?

"*The man of the world is deluded by his own ignorance. He speaks of* prajna, *but not seeing* prajna, *his mind is perpetually stupid. Yet he asserts that he practices* prajna. *At every moment he speaks of emptiness, but he is unaware of true emptiness.*" Such people speak of emptiness, but they cannot show it. In a Zen temple, if someone asks me, "What is emptiness?" I will say, "Come here, I will teach you what emptiness is."

"*Prajna is no formula; the mind that exhibits wisdom is* prajna." Now I would have to say to the Sixth Patriarch: "Enough! Though it is a nice pie, I have already eaten three or four pieces!"

"*If you understand this, that is* prajna *wisdom.*" Too much repetition. I have faithfully translated every line, so do not blame me. It was recorded in this style.

"What does 'paramita' mean? This is an Indian word which, expressed in Chinese, denotes 'to have reached the other shore.' One who understands its significance transcends life and death. When you attach to outer existence, life and death arises, as when water has waves. That is called, 'this shore.' When one transcends outer existence, then there is no life and death, as when water flows freely. That is called the 'other shore.' This is expressed by the term 'paramita.'

"Good friends, the deluded one recites this with his mouth, but, as he does so, he harbors ill and erroneous thoughts. But if one practices this paramita *moment by moment of mind activity, he will find himself in his true nature. He who becomes aware of this will apprehend* prajna-*dharma. And he will be practicing* prajna*. He who does not practice this is an ordinary man. However, if he practices this for even a moment of mind, he himself will be Buddha. Thus, even an ordinary man is Buddha, and delusion is* bodhi*. In his former delusion, he was an ordinary man, but in his awakening a moment later, he is Buddha. His former thoughts adhering to the outside were delusions, but his later thoughts transcending it are* bodhi*."*

SOKEI-AN SAYS:

Here the patriarch explains *"paramita"* as he explained *"maha"* earlier.

"What does 'paramita' *mean? This is an Indian word which, expressed in Chinese, denotes 'to have reached the other shore* [nirvana]'. *One who understands its significance transcends life and death* [samsara]." The meaning of reaching the other shore in Chinese is "will get free from," "will be delivered," or "relieved." But in English, "will transcend life and death."

"When you attach to outer existence, life and death arises, as when water has waves. That is called 'this shore.'" If you adhere to outer existence (externals or circumstances) instead of transcending it, it is another burden you have to carry on your back. "Outer existence" here means not only the outside, the phenomenal world, but also inner thoughts, the three worlds and the three bodies—all those states described by Buddhist terms. If you objectify samsara, the endless circling wheel of transmigration from one existence to another, and nirvana (extinction), you experience agony. Attachment begets life and death.

Just as waves pertain to the nature of water and are essential to water, you cannot see water without waves. Life and death, samsara and nirvana, like waves and water, are inseparable. If you try to brush away the waves to get to the water, the waves are water. In the practice of true meditation, you will understand this. Trying to annihilate mind-stuff in meditation, you will find that the true activity of mind always has this mind-stuff; but one foolishly keeps trying to brush it aside to get the true element of mind. Then what do you do with this mind-stuff? There are many koans to help you: "If you call this a spade, you oppose Reality. If you do not call this a spade, you go contrary to convention. So what do you call this, and how do you understand these two opposing aspects?"

"When one transcends outer existence": When you hear this, you think that you have to jump out of this world into the chaos of the fathomless. There is no such world, so do not entertain such a fantasy. You transcend the outer world by your attitude of mind. Then samsara and nirvana cease to exist.

"Then there is no life and death, as when water flows freely." When you transcend life and death, you will observe that you will be one with that perpetual flowing, from beginningless beginning to endless end.

"That is called the 'other shore.' This is expressed by the term 'paramita.'" Here is conceived the idea of "reaching the other shore"—paramita. When you leave *this* shore, naturally you come to some idea of

another shore. But there is no need to jump into the fathomless, nor to fly into the sky. In your chair or standing, you can reach the other shore.

Just here is the difference between Hinayana and Mahayana Buddhism. Hinayana would say that to enter the transcendental life, you must become a recluse. But Mahayana says: "Sitting in your chair or standing on your feet you can reach the other shore." As a koan says: "Without walking a step from this room, stand upon the Himalaya Mountain," or, "In the flesh, step into the stone pillar." You must understand the deep meaning of this. In koans such as these there is paramita. But paramita is not this shore or the other shore. So what is this paramita?

"Good friends, the deluded one recites this with his mouth, but, as he does so, he harbors ill and erroneous thoughts. But if one practices this paramita moment by moment of mind activity, he will find himself in his true nature." This means he will enter the gate of Zen. When you pass the koan "Before father and mother, what were you? What was your original nature?" you will find the true nature within yourself. In that moment, you are practicing paramita in your mind. In that moment—not jumping into the fathomless, not jumping into the sky—you reach paramita. Otherwise, Buddhism is nothing but parroting—"Say Papa! Say Momma!"

As I was walking in the street in Tokyo, there was a parrot that said, "Hello, hello!" It was an American parrot, and no one understood the meaning of its "Hello!" I answered, "Hello, dear!" But the parrot didn't understand. You talk about paramita in the same way. Without the study of Zen, you will never know its meaning.

"He who becomes aware of this will apprehend prajna-dharma. *And he will be practicing* prajna." What is *prajna* practice? You must understand this. When you pass the koan: "The *dharmakaya*—the boundless body of omnipresence—eats food; the food eats *dharmakaya*. How does the food eat *dharmakaya*?" that is really *prajna* practice.

"He who does not practice this is an ordinary man." Even if he shaves his head clean, wears a robe of gold, carries beads in his fingers, and takes the attitude of a monk, he is still a man of the world, though everyone thinks he is a sage and gives him donations. He makes a fool out of you, and you do not know it.

"However, if he practices this for even a moment of mind, he himself will be Buddha." Even a moment. Just a moment before attaining that true answer, he is a mere man of the world, but all of a sudden he turns the corner of the universe and sees the entire body of Buddha. You will attain buddha-nature, and not only buddha-nature, but Buddha's appearance as well. In one moment, a man of the world becomes Buddha!

"Thus, even an ordinary man is Buddha, and delusion is bodhi. *In his former delusion, he was an ordinary man, but in his awakening a moment later, he is Buddha. His former thoughts adhering to the outside were delusions, but his later thoughts transcending it are* bodhi." This is different from other teachings. Here, there is no process of becoming. When you talk about becoming, it is just as water becomes steam, but there is no changing. A man of the world may be selling potatoes or carrying ice from door to door, but he is originally a buddha. Delusion is therefore *bodhi*—awakening. There are no special thoughts called *bodhi*. Your delusion is *bodhi*. The word of delusion you were speaking yesterday—delusion is today a word of wisdom. "Good morning, how do you do!" has a different sound. In his former delusion, he was an ordinary man, but in the awakening of a moment later, he is Buddha. The former thoughts adhering to the outside were delusion. Just a second before, you were talking like a drunken man: "O beautiful moooon . . . !" When you are enlightened, all becomes buddha-dharma.

"Good friends, mahaprajnaparamita *is the most sacred, exalted, and important principle. It occupies no position, neither comes nor goes. Nevertheless, all the buddhas of the three worlds come forth from it. Practice this great wisdom to destroy the afflicting stuffs of the five shadows of mind. If you practice this, you will without doubt attain buddhahood, and your greed, anger, and ignorance will be changed into the precepts, meditation, and wisdom.*

Good friends, according to our teaching, the 84,000 wisdoms come forth from one prajna. *Why is this? Because man in the world has 84,000 afflictions. But if he avoids them, he can find wisdom everlasting, without being separated from his original nature. He who awakens to this will attain the mind not occupied with stuff, not haunted by thoughts, not attached to things. So he will not entertain delusions. Using his intrinsic nature, which is* bhutatathata, *contemplating with* prajna *wisdom, he is neither attached to nor detached from existence. In other words, he sees his true nature and realizes buddhahood."*

SOKEI-AN SAYS:

In Buddhism, there are six *paramitas,* ways "to reach the other shore," nirvana: by giving, by observing commandments, by forbearance (patience), by making effort, by practicing meditation, and by attaining wisdom by meditation.

"Good friends, mahaprajnaparamita *is the most sacred, exalted, and important principle."* The sixth *paramita* is *prajnaparamita*—attaining wisdom by practicing meditation, and then using this wisdom as a vehicle to reach the other shore. Among the paramitas, *mahaprajnaparamita* is the most sacred and important. Anyone who tries to reach nirvana with another *paramita* occasionally harbors doubt and does not make the crossing. But one who attains the sixth *paramita* will find no failure.

"It occupies no position": When an object stands somewhere, it occupies a position. When you stand upon the floor, you occupy a point. When you think something, it occupies a position in your brain. When you are thinking *a,* you cannot think *b,* and vice versa. So thought occupies a position, not a geometrical one, but a mental position. *Mahaprajnaparamita,* however, occupies no mental position.

"Neither comes nor goes." If you have a position out of which you go and into which you come, it is not *mahaprajnaparamita,* for *mahaprajnaparamita* has no position. Strange, isn't it? I hope you will understand this and will find this paramita. In Zen, if you stand or shout, if you say "Ah-h-h," it occupies a position. This is secondary understanding, it is not *prajna.* These lines are very clear in denoting this true point of Zen. If you understand the point denoted here, you have found it.

"Nevertheless, all the buddhas of the three worlds come forth from it." It is said, "All these buddhas come forth from the *Diamond Sutra."* This is a koan to which you must make answer. Here, "all the buddhas" are the same Buddha, the highest wisdom. Buddha came from this diamond-wisdom. What is diamond-wisdom? You must practice to answer.

"Practice this great wisdom to destroy the afflicting stuffs of the five shadows of mind." I hope you will practice this great diamond-wisdom. It is a thunderous wisdom. With this wisdom you destroy the five layers of tenacious mind-stuff, the conflicting stuff of the five consecutive shadows of mind. But this is only a symbol. You must find the true thunderbolt in yourself and destroy the world of "seeming."

The mind is like the five roofs of a pagoda heaped one upon the other. The first, at the base, is vijnana, the consciousness of all sentient beings. The second is samskara, natural consciousness. Chickens hop out of the shell at exactly the right time. How does the hen know the time to break the shell? The chick will not come out of the shell before the hen breaks it, and the hen will not break the shell before the right time. It is the same with the Zen master and student: the master watches the student and sees exactly the time to break the shell and pull him out. Telling the answer to a pupil is the same as killing a chick. How do animals know the time? If you are using your body without purpose, you will know the exact time. If you are using your body for your own purpose, you will never know the exact time. But if you it without purpose, you will find samskara.

Above this is the consciousness with intention (samjna), and then sense-perception (vedana) and all objective existence (rupa). These are the five shadows of mind. This mind-stuff is added, like cotton in a pillow, and it afflicts you. You must destroy it with the thunderbolt of wisdom.

"If you practice this, you will without doubt attain buddhahood": If you ventilate your mind and take all that stuffing out, without a doubt you will attain buddhahood. This natural consciousness and universal consciousness will make unity without any stuffing between them. With this consciousness, you will attain universal consciousness, and then buddhahood.

But in your consciousness are the tenacious cockroach thoughts you must exterminate with koans. For it is with the power of the koan that you annihilate conflict. If you go to China or Manchuria, you will see beggars taking sunbaths and annihilating their cooties in such a way. It is the same with your thoughts: You destroy all the questions of your mind by meditating. In the beginning, you cannot do it, questions arise. But eventually, as you practice meditation, all these consciousnesses just become one consciousness.

When you push through the bottom of the bucket with your foot, you attain buddhahood. An old Zen master said: "Carry the moonprint in the bucket without a bottom." How can you carry the moonprint without water? How will the moonprint reflect? With your bottomless mind, you carry the moonprint of consciousness.

"And your greed, anger, and ignorance will be changed into the precepts, meditation, and wisdom." Greed, anger, and ignorance are the three poisonous elements. Every man has them. In ancient translations, these were written as "passion, anger, and ignorance," as if they meant the desire for sex, the desire for possession, and ignorance. These were the three poisonous elements. All sentient beings live to accomplish these three elemental desires. But ignorance will change to wisdom and anger to meditation. They are not different elements but come from the same element.

"Good friends, according to our teaching, the 84,000 wisdoms come forth from one prajna. *Why is this? Because man in the world has 84,000 afflictions; but if he avoids them, he can find wisdom everlasting, without being separated from his original nature."* Eighty-four thousand is not a particular number, you might also say a million or a billion.

Everyone has the 84,000 afflictions. Eighty-four thousand is a symbol of human nature. Take, for instance, the washerwoman working in the hot steam of a laundry: she cries and laughs and is excited and jealous all day long—she is continually disturbed. But the sage meditates all day long and tries to find the cause of things. The sage and the washerwoman have the same human nature; but one will get wisdom and the other will gets afflictions.

"He who awakens to this will attain the mind not occupied with stuff, not haunted by thoughts, not attached to things. So he will not entertain delusions." Buddha's mind and the washerwoman's mind are the same. The Buddha used the 84,000 elemental thoughts that come from *prajna* to attain wisdom. The washerwomen uses them, too, to entertain delusions in terrible turmoil.

"Using his intrinsic nature, which is bhutatathata*":* Your intrinsic nature was found when you passed the first koan: "Before father and mother, what were you? What was your intrinsic nature?" *Bhutatathata* is the revelation of self-evident truth.

66

Bhutatathata is a Sanskrit word, a famous term in Buddhism. The Japanese translate it as *shinnyo*, "truth which is as it is." The word certainly cannot express this. *Bhuta*, in English, is "be"; *tathata* is "that." The nearest to a literal translation would be: "*This is That.*"

To speak of reality according to Western philosophy, one tries to prove it abstractly, so it is a metaphysical thought. Reality cannot be demonstrated; it is beyond experiencing with our five senses. What the five senses can feel or see is phenomena, it is not real existence. Things that exist here are a vision manifested upon the retina of our eyes, and we cannot describe what that reality is. So the reality of this gong cannot be demonstrated. No one can know what this gong is, really. As a vision that appears on the eye, we see *this*, and, as a feeling on the fingertips, we feel *this*. And as sound that appears on our eardrum, we hear *this*. What really takes place? The real condition or state of *this* is unknown, but it really exists and is called "reality," in philosophical terms. But Reality—what *we* call Reality—has no philosophical sense. Please do not mix up the two—the "real" and Reality. Reality is what I am talking about; the real is pure metaphysics, purely theoretical, the logical conclusion, not the physical conclusion. People usually mix all this up.

The Western way of thinking of reality is abstract because the Western mind takes the dualistic attitude of matter and spirit, but it is not the Oriental way. In the Oriental conception, no line is drawn between metaphysical reality and physical actuality. To the Buddhist, whatever this gong is, appears on our retina as *this*. So, why talk metaphysics? Settle it at once! What *this is,* is the Oriental way. *This* is called neither spirit nor matter. We call *this*, suchness, bhutatathata.

You must realize *this* with your enlightenment. You cannot think or talk of it. In your meditation, it must come forth as lotus buds burst open—from the center. We say that your lotus bud of the mind has suddenly opened. The lotus was in the earth; it came up through the water and into the air. Under the sunlight, it opens with the heat. It passes through the three stages of earth, water, and air. Earth is this physical world; water is the world of thoughts; air is the world of emptiness. Under the sun of wisdom, *prajna*, the lotus bud will open suddenly.

When you go home, sit down and put your strength in your abdomen. Set your mind free with meditation. Sit upon the universe, and keep sitting until the barrier that is between you and the universe is annihilated. Sit upon silence. If you are thinking what or why, in one hundred years, you will not enter into Zen.

"*. . . Contemplating with* prajna *wisdom*": That is, you become one with this or that. You contemplate or practice to become one with the state of *samadhi*. When you are doing something, do not think of anything else. When you are saying "Ah," you must be "Ah." This kind of practice is not in the Western world, but it is the main teaching of the Orient.

"*. . . He is neither attached to nor detached from existence.*" Using your intrinsic nature and practicing your contemplation of true wisdom, you are neither attached to nor detached from the existence of the world. Neither to attach *to* nor to detach *from* are the true attitude. When you sit upon the universe and make unity with your body, mind, and senses all at once, this attitude is not attachment "to" nor detachment "from" existence; it is neither physical nor mental. If you are a Zen student, remember my words.

"*In other words, he sees his true nature and realizes buddhahood.*" It is very difficult to find your buddha-nature and achieve buddha-dharma. But when you have done so, it looks so easy you cannot understand why you made such a struggle.

"*Good friends, if you desire to enter the most profound* dharmadhatu *and the contemplation of* prajna, *you must exercise* prajna *practice and uphold and recite the* Diamond Sutra. *Then you will be able to see your true nature. You should realize that the merits of the sutra are immeasurable and boundless, but as these are clearly praised in the text, I need not enumerate them here.*

"*This gate of dharma is the highest vehicle, told for those of great wisdom and superior endowment. Men of lesser wisdom or endowment would have doubt if they should hear this teaching. Why is this? It is as when the great dragon brings rain upon Jambudvipa, citadels and villages will be set adrift like the drifting leaves of the jujube tree; but when it brings rain upon the great sea, the waters will neither increase nor decrease.*"

The Sixth Patriarch is repeating again, so I am reciting it this way.

"*Good friends, if you desire to enter the most profound and the contemplation of* prajna, *you must exercise* prajna *practice*": The word "profound" makes trouble here because it suggests something like a deep well. There isn't any deep well. The deepest well is on the carpet, here at this moment. Stay away from that sickness, that habit of picturing everything.

A foolish woman came here many times last year and said: "I am in a deep green light." I told her: "The deep green light is in your eyelid." If she had not been a woman, I would have given her a black eye. Finally I drove her out of my house. I do not like lunatics.

But the patriarch's words—"most profound *dharmadhatu*"—give such an impression. Good gracious! If Lin-chi came here, he would tear up the paper and throw it in the river, and I would not blame him.

"*. . . And uphold and recite the* Diamond Sutra. *Then you will be able to see your true nature.*" There are many monks in China and Japan who recite sutras from morning to evening. Why would anyone want to recite constantly? Enlightenment is no such thing. This is like a Hindu priest pinching Miss Kepner's nose and asking, "Do you see a green light?" and Miss Kepner saying, "Yes." And suddenly, she would be enlightened. And she only paid thirty-five dollars for that enlightenment!

Someone put in this line, and it was carried down to us, so I must warn you not to be involved with such lines.

"*You should realize that the merits of the sutra are immeasurable and boundless, but as these are clearly praised in the text, I need not enumerate them here.*" This is true when you can digest the meaning; but to recite it constantly?

Many people think this is true Buddhism, and that is why they say Zen monks are agnostic. To such people, we are demons because we have strong will power and will go to places and snatch the sutras away. These people are foolish, of course.

If you think Buddhism is such a thing, you will hate it. This is the way true Buddhism perishes.

"*This gate of dharma is the highest vehicle.*" "This gate of dharma" means *this* wisdom or heart. When you are sleeping there is no wisdom; it is there, but it is dormant. When you are in a very early stage, it is sleeping. And when you come into the animal stage, it is like a dream. The dreamer has forgotten to eat and goes hungry. He looks for food but there is none. He goes home, goes to sleep, opens his eye, then goes back to sleep. This condition proves that he is dreaming. His *prajna* is weak. And then he becomes a man. Gradually, through many incarnations, he finally grasps *prajna*. It shows in him; it rules his conduct. Of course, the "gate of dharma is the highest vehicle." Without it, we are just sleeping animals.

"*Told for those of great wisdom and superior endowment. Men of lesser wisdom or endowment would have doubt if they should hear this teaching.*" You do not need to sit from morning to evening. In a moment of snapping your fingers, you will be suddenly enlightened and will obtain *prajna*. But if I give such a teaching to lunatics, they will have doubt.

"Why is this? It is as when the great dragon brings rain upon Jambudvipa, citadels and villages will be adrift like the drifting leaves of the jujube tree. But when it brings rain upon the great sea, the waters will neither increase nor decrease." This refers to a passage in the *Lotus Sutra*. You know, the Sixth Patriarch had never read this sutra. Much later a student came and said that he had been reading it for eighteen years. "I have never read it. Please recite it," said the Sixth Patriarch. So the student recited it from beginning to end. The patriarch listened and picked up a word or two.

If such a great teaching comes to men of small knowledge, they will believe it. But if such a teaching comes to men of great knowledge, they will swallow it and understand it. So these highest teachings, like Zen, are also for people with the best endowment and highest wisdom. To men of small knowledge and no endowment, Zen can be rather a menace. The teacher will not give a great deal. In the Zen room, I shout to wake you up. But perhaps you will feel insulted and become discouraged.

"When men of the great vehicle, the highest vehicle, hear the teaching of the Diamond Sutra, *their minds will be opened and they will realize enlightenment. Then they will understand that the wisdom of* prajna *is inherent in their original nature, and employing their own wisdom, they will always introspect their own prajna, so that they have no need of words and letters. It is said, for example, that rainwater does not originate from heaven. It is a dragon who carries the water up to heaven and makes it rain, refreshing all living beings, plants, and all sentient and insentient things. Then the rivers and streams bring the waters back to the great sea, and the waters assemble once again to form the oneness of the ocean. The* prajna *wisdom inherent in the original nature of all sentient beings is like this."*

SOKEI-AN SAYS:

I am translating this record from the Chinese into English. Tonight the Sixth Patriarch is again speaking about *prajna*, intrinsic wisdom.

"When men of the great vehicle, the highest vehicle hear the teaching of the Diamond Sutra, *their minds will be opened and they will realize enlightenment."* The "great vehicle, the highest vehicle" is Mahayana Buddhism. Hinayana Buddhism is the based on the concept of nirvana. It is the ascending process from this physical world to spiritual enlightenment, from the everyday, familiar world to the transcendental world, from the foot of the mountain to the mountaintop. Here we must be recluses—once in a lifetime we must take an aloof attitude and live in a cave. But the process we call Mahayana Buddhism is from enlightenment to the actualization of this enlightenment, from the top of the mountain to the foot, where one descends to mingle again with the familiar world in order to promulgate the teaching. The mountain monk comes down to the village, down to compassion and sympathy with human emotions. He will see his father, mother, sisters, and brothers once more. As a theory, this has some value, but as practice, it has very little—it is just dramatic names. In real Buddhism, both attitudes occur, simultaneously, as part of daily life.

In the *Diamond Sutra*, the *Vajracchika-prajnaparamita Sutra*, the "Diamond-Cutter Sutra" made in India about five hundred years after the Buddha's death, there is a part that teaches about diamond-consciousness. Metaphorically, the diamond is the hardest stone in the world, and no one can destroy it; so this consciousness of ours is the hardest among substances, and even death cannot destroy it. We call this the *"vajra* (diamond) *prajna* (wisdom) *paramita* (to reach the other shore)" teaching. If you hear the teaching of *vajraprajnaparamita,* this diamond-consciousness, you will reach the other shore, enlightenment.

What the Sixth Patriarch is referring to here is not the *Diamond Sutra* that carries the teaching written on paper. The Sixth Patriarch is emphasizing the living sutra, the sutra that is not made of paper but is written on our hearts. All law is written on this sutra, our heart. And all races of the world can read this without a word. The Sixth Patriarch is not referring to printed characters. He means the "One Living Diamond Sword." How can one attain this? How do you read this? Do you put on your eyeglasses and turn on the light? You must read this by meditation.

It is truly so. You cannot open your mind from the outside. You must go inside to grasp the principle of this everlasting diamond-consciousness. Even the fire at the end of the universe cannot destroy it.

I think you have all heard the story of the conflagration at the end of the kalpa when after aeons of time the whole universe will be burned to ashes, and the ashes will be dissolved into the elemental ether, and nothing will exist throughout the world. It will become absolutely empty, not void-space but really elemental space, and from this emptiness the whole universe will be recreated.

This is, of course, an allegory of the state of consciousness in meditation. When you are in meditation, the active part of your consciousness enters into emptiness, and from that emptiness your activity comes once more. It is like sleep. In sleep you are annihilated, and in awakening you will come out once more. You must grasp that principle by meditation.

"Then they will understand that the wisdom of prajna *is inherent in their original nature, and employing their own wisdom, they will always introspect their own* prajna, *so that they have no need of words and letters."* This *Diamond Sutra* cannot be found from the outside because it is inherent in original nature. When this diamond-consciousness is active, we call it wisdom, *prajna.* You are using it at every moment, to sneeze, to scratch your head. It is not necessary to employ this consciousness. Original nature is always active in you. It is always acting with your activity—unconsciously. To contemplate or to introspect this wisdom is a natural process, a natural activity. Just as the ivy seeks the sunlight, intrinsic wisdom finds the truth within you. So you need not purposely quiet yourself in meditation. When you think something, your original nature naturally takes the attitude of meditation.

Of course, the best attitude in meditation is seen in the figures of Buddha—quiet. In profound stillness, he thinks. It's much better than lying down on a couch or supporting your head on your hand like Rodin's thinker. When I came to this country, I went to the Metropolitan Museum and saw that thinker. It was disgusting to me. I respect the value of the sculpture, but I do not grant anything to such an attitude of contemplation.

To introspect wisdom is a natural process. To study wisdom, use wisdom. By contemplation, by introspection, you must study this yourself. You can make a good analysis by yourself, without any words of explanation. You do not need a knife to operate on the brain. Just feel it immediately. Philosophy is entirely useless for attaining real wisdom.

"It is said, for example, that rainwater does not originate from heaven. It is a dragon who carries the water up to heaven and makes it rain, refreshing all living beings, plants, and all sentient and insentient things. Then the rivers and streams bring the waters back to the great sea and the waters assemble once again to form the oneness of the ocean. The prajna *wisdom inherent in the original nature of all sentient beings is like this."* These are famous metaphors from the *Lotus Sutra.* They are not of much value, but I will give you a little explanation. Some scholar translated this omitting the dragon. It is true that it is not scientific, but when I translate it, I keep it as written.

In ancient China, they thought that rainwater did not originally come from heaven, that the tornado was a dragon carrying water up to heaven, which later showered the water on the earth. Occasionally, in China, live fish rained from heaven. The Chinese thought that a dragon had swallowed the fish alive and carried them through heaven, from where they rained down. The dragon is a metaphor for your consciousness. Your consciousness was once in the ocean of consciousness; then this consciousness was distributed or bestowed upon each individual; and now, you act, you speak, you listen to me with this consciousness. Just so, all plants are moistened by rain water. No one is ever separated from the ocean of consciousness.

This is different from the Christian idea of the soul. At death, the individual Christian hides somewhere in a cave until judgment day. The Buddhist believes that as soon as we die, we return to the ocean of consciousness.

"Good friends, when a man of small endowment hears of this teaching of sudden enlightenment, he is like a plant that has shallow roots. When it is washed by a great rain, it falls to the ground and cannot rise again. Yet, the man of small endowment inherently has the wisdom of prajna, *as does the man of great endowment. Why doesn't he open his mind and become enlightened when he hears the Dharma? Because his mind is heavily shrouded by his erroneous views. His agony is deeply rooted. It is like a great cloud covering the sun: the sun cannot shine until the wind blows the cloud away.*

"In prajna *wisdom there is neither great nor small. But because the minds of sentient beings differ in being either enlightened or deluded, those whose minds are deluded search outside, trying to find Buddha by performing religious practices. They have not yet awakened to their own nature, so they are men of small endowment. If they open their eyes to the teaching of sudden enlightenment, they will be unable to direct their practice outside; and since they will always manifest the true view inside their minds, their minds can never be stained by the dust of afflicting* klesha. *This is what is called seeing one's own nature.*

"Good friends, if you attain this, you stay neither inside nor outside; to come or to go is your privilege. Free from attachment, your mind penetrates without hindrance. When you perform this practice, it is not different from that which is written in the prajna *sutras."*

SOKEI-AN SAYS:

According to original Buddhism, the Hinayana, men would be enlightened by practicing the Four Noble Truths and its Eightfold Golden Path, the twelve *nidanas*, and the four *dhyanas* for many, many years. Or, like Shakyamuni, they would become enlightened after many repeated incarnations. But Hui-neng's Buddhism was different. He said that man is originally enlightened but that he must discover it for himself. At any moment he may be enlightened. This is the teaching of sudden enlightenment. One morning he is just a common man, and in the evening he is an enlightened one.

"Good friends, when a man of small endowment hears of this teaching of sudden enlightenment, he is like a plant that has shallow roots. When it is washed by a great rain, it falls to the ground and cannot rise again." When he hears this teaching of sudden enlightenment, he is rooted out and thrown on the roadside to dry and die there. He cannot take such a drastic teaching.

When Te-shan, a great T'ien-t'ai monk, heard of the school in Southern China that taught sudden enlightenment, he was furious. "One who is enlightened after practicing Buddhism for many kalpas, that I can understand, but how can one be enlightened as soon as one hears the Dharma? I will go down there and break their necks!" And Te-shan went down in great wrath, bearing his volumes of commentaries on the *Diamond Sutra*. After a long journey to Southern China, he arrived at a tea hut and found an old woman there serving tea to travelers. She asked him: "What are those big books on your back?" Te-shan answered with a grand air, "These are my commentaries on the *Diamond Sutra*." The old woman said: "I will make a bargain with you. If you can answer a question, I will give you tea for nothing. If you cannot answer, please go elsewhere." Te-shan said, "Ask any question, and I will answer." Then the old woman asked: "It is written in the *Diamond Sutra*: 'The past mind is impossible to grasp; the present mind is impossible to grasp; the future mind is impossible to grasp. What mind do you immediately grasp?'" Te-shan could not make an answer, so the old woman drove him out. Then Te-shan thought, "In Southern China even an old woman by the roadside knows Buddhism!" This was the beginning of his taking his hat off to Zen. He was a monk, so of course he did not have a hat on his head, but he was a man of great endowment. If a man of small endowment heard such a thing, he would not believe in Buddhism, or perhaps, anything else. He would probably go to Father Divine or something like that.

"Yet, the man of small endowment inherently has the wisdom of prajna, *as does the man of great endowment. Why doesn't he open his mind and become enlightened when he hears the Dharma? Because his mind is heavily shrouded by his erroneous views. His agony is deeply rooted."* I feel it when I meet a student who is struggling to take off his shroud.

"It is like a great cloud covering the sun: the sun cannot shine until the wind blows the cloud away." Even though he has *prajna* nature in himself, his erroneous view—his ignorance—shrouds his soul. And besides, his afflictions, his daily life, worry him, give him fear and distress, so that he cannot see and take the true Dharma into his mind.

When I went to Boston, I met someone who said, "I cannot see any value in this Buddhist view." I said: "Buddhism has existed for 2,400 years in India and 500 years in Japan, so it must have some value in it. But if you think not, please go away."

"In prajna *wisdom there is neither great nor small. But because the minds of sentient beings differ in being either enlightened or deluded, those whose minds are deluded search outside, trying to find buddha by performing religious practices."* It is like comparing a lamp that has a big candle power with a lamp that has a small candle power. One has a great light, the other a small light, but both come from the same electricity. The nature of *prajna* is just the same, but blind men cannot see their own *prajna*-mind in themselves. They are deluded by many things. They must use a microscope or find something from books, or use the terminology of philosophy, or sing the hymns of Father Divine.

Hakuin said it is like swimming in water or standing in water up to your neck. You are calling for the water that is one inch below your throat. Where does Buddha live? Buddha is between your eyebrows, on your fingertip, on the tip of your nose. But you cannot find this Buddha. Sometimes you go to Ceylon to seek Buddha, or even to Tibet. You forget the Buddha that is living on the tip of your nose. This is the Sixth Patriarch's type of teaching.

"They have not awakened yet to their own nature, so they are men of small endowment." Men of small endowment before they find out the truth about the universe do not clean up their preconceived notions. Being deluded by these previous notions, practicing this and that, they cannot find the truth. They cannot find the Buddha. The previous notions they had, without making any particular study of them, give them deluded conclusions.

Almost all human beings accept what they are told when they are children. Without correcting these notions, or carefully observing them once more, we use them as a rule or measure to judge all occasions and occurrences, all things that happen to us. The Buddha said this is because we begin our lives from unconsciousness and ignorance, not knowing the truth.

Now, suppose a child heard that a man with a certain type of jaw has a nature as ferocious as a tiger, and is told not to associate with him. When the child grows up, he will dislike all men with such a jaw. These men may be good, but to the one who was the child, they will be ferocious.

If you take a dualistic view in judging the world, everything will be in two separate conditions—good and bad, etc. From this dualistic viewpoint, you cannot do anything, for you think *not* doing anything is good because it does not do anyone harm. But the Buddha did not teach such a dualistic viewpoint in his precepts. If you study his words and his commandments very carefully, you will understand this. Those with such a viewpoint have not awakened to their own nature, and they are not living in it. They are living in notions traditional to the human mind.

Those who hold traditional notions must awaken to their own natures before they accept them as truth. Before you can taste soup, you must wash your nicotined tongue.

"If they open their eyes to the teaching of sudden enlightenment, they will be unable to direct their practice outside, and since they will always manifest the true view inside their minds, their minds can never be stained by the dust of afflicting klesha. This is what is called seeing one's own nature." This teaching of sudden enlightenment dates from the Buddha's time, but according to the sutras, Buddhism was the practice of gradual enlightenment. They were practicing the twelve nidanas from the end to the beginning and from the beginning to the end in order to attain enlightenment.

Why do we have old age and death? Because we have this living body. Why do we have this living body? Because we possess it. Why do we have this possession? Because we have accepted it and we keep it. Why have we accepted it and why do we keep it? Because we have desire. In such a way, we trace back to the beginning of our consciousness, which is in darkness—the unconscious, *avidya*, fundamental darkness. So we understand the beginning of life, and we observe this darkness, this unconsciousness, consciously. Then we destroy this darkness, open our eye to *prajna* and attain enlightenment.

According to the old sutras, this was the way the Buddha attained enlightenment. This is the way of gradual enlightenment as told in the sutras. But the teaching of sudden enlightenment is entirely different. We do not need to observe the twelve nidanas from top to bottom or from bottom to top. Once when a Chinese monk was sweeping the ground, he picked up a pebble with his broom and threw it out of the garden. Hearing the sound as it struck a bamboo tree, he opened his eye—"Ah!" At that moment, he was enlightened. "How different from that in which I was just a moment ago!" Enlightenment is such a thing.

When I passed the first koan, for three days I felt I was walking on air. Going to art school through the park in the morning, I felt that everyone coming my way was myself. All were myself. There was no time and no space. Time and space were endless. There was just one enormous *BEING*, walking and thinking. I felt I would stay in that condition all my lifetime. Now I have forgotten which world I really lived in before that moment—it is in oblivion—but I faintly felt that I was in a terrible mess of confusion and fear.

Perhaps I was foolish when very young. I started to study art, to copy famous pieces of ancient artists, to study from nature. But when I conceived the question, "What is life for, after all? And why am I studying art?" the value of everything disappeared. I could not work; it was meaningless. I could not live so. Today, tomorrow, I could not study art meaninglessly. There must be meaning—must be something. I go to school and bow to the teacher—what for? I bow to my mother—what for? To build a house upon the ground, you must lay some foundation. Without a foundation, what building can you build? You must build your life upon some foundation.

My doubt came when I was nineteen years old. I thought that it must be the same with everyone, that everyone must pass through that agony. But now I know it is not so at all. Others do not care about such things. They do not care if life has meaning or no meaning. They work because they must have money to eat, must eat to live, must live to work, must work to make money to eat! I could not look at life in such a way, live in such a way. Therefore, I lived fighting against agony. I passed many mental crises. But, passing through, I always came back to my true view. I kept myself calm, and I realized that all that was going on in my mind was nothing but klesha, mental affliction. I was determined not to believe what was going on in my mind, but I watched it as I would watch a hurricane going through the sky, and I passed through that crisis. I really found my foundation of mind by practicing this Zen, so I am trying to give it to my beloved friends.

"Good friends, if you attain this, you must stay neither inside nor outside; to come or to go is your privilege." Everyone thinks that in meditation you stay inside your mind, and that when you open your eye and look at phenomena, your mind is outside of your body. Really, there is no inside or outside. If you attain this, temporarily you can come inside or go outside. It is your privilege. If you wish to go out, you go out; if you wish to come in, you come in. But if you study some queer religion, you will be taught that you must not go outside.

"Free from attachment, your mind penetrates without hindrance." Free from all attachment—attachment to each *nidana*, each *skandha*, each *dhatu*. You attach to your desire or, if not, then you attach to your mental idea. If neither, then you attach to the world of formlessness—endless space and endless time. Some scholars speak about these three attachments—to desire, form, and formlessness.

In Buddhism, meditation is not an aim. It is a method, a contrivance to attain something. Meditation is not the terminus. But to those who attach to formlessness, meditation is an aim. Their belief is that nothing exists in this world, that all this phenomena is not Reality. Their reality is dualistic. In Buddhism, all this phenomena *is* Reality.

Those who take the dualistic view always drop into hedonism—"Eat, drink, and be merry, for tomorrow you die! Now, at this moment, I will satisfy my idea of pleasure." They think they can do anything in the phenomenal world.

This is the scholar's idea of attaching to formlessness—*arupadhatu*. It is just one type of teaching, one type of explanation—a little different, but quite interesting. Or you may attach to the five *skandhas*, or to any point of the twelve *nidanas*. Speaking about it and thinking about it from that point of view, you go back to practice with the true view of what lies inside your mind.

The Buddha talked about the "true view" in the Eightfold Golden Path. Open the *Record of Lin-chi* and read: "Scholars today must have true understanding." Your *sanzen* is a practice to find and to keep this true view. The true view is the life of a Buddhist. From that view, you live your daily life. Of course, the Buddhist is not dualistic, so there is no good and bad. So, from the true view, how do you act in daily life?

There is so much misunderstanding, we cannot talk much about this true view. It is better not to speak about the non-dualistic outlook of the Buddhist, or you will be considered evil. But we have a true view, and according to this view, we make our life. So it is quite important that we understand that attitude.

"When you perform this practice, it is not different from that which is written in the prajna *sutras."* You do not need to read those sutras if you open the true eye and find the true realization. *Prajnaparamita* is written in your mind and body.

Now, war is bad, and killing men is bad, so how do you act on the battlefield in accordance with this good/bad idea? It is good practice.

On the battlefield, you say, "Oh, my dear friend, I cannot kill you." And he says, "Please kill me!" Dying, he says, "I'm dying, but I'm sinless." Will you let the other kill you to remain sinless? He does not wish to commit the crime himself, but lets his dear friend, the enemy, commit the crime, thinking he himself is sinless and not committing any crime. How can he say that? Certainly, if you have a dualistic attitude on the battlefield, you cannot do anything. You will stand in the fire of delusion, and you will leave your body in a great question mark, and all these problems of conduct will be taken up.

It is like Te-shan when he shouted to his disciples. With his angry face and his six-foot long oak-tree stick, he said: "Whether you answer or you do not answer, I will crush you with this stick. Quick! Answer!"

Well, what do you say? You must observe this koan someday. Under that six-foot stick, you will pass that koan and open your eye to the law of Buddhism.

"Good friends, all the sutras, words and letters, all the great and small vehicles, and the twelve divisions of the scriptures [8] are attempts at adjusting those teachings to people's various tendencies of mind. They are founded in accordance with the nature of wisdom. If there had never been a man on earth, these millions of laws would never have existed. Thus you see that all laws were originally initiated by man and that all scriptures vary in doctrine according to the author.

"Among mankind there are those who are wise and those who are foolish. The foolish are small men, and the wise are great men. The foolish ask the teaching of the wise. The wise give the teaching, explaining it to the foolish. But when the foolish open their minds and are suddenly enlightened, they differ not a whit from the wise."

"Good friends, without enlightenment, a buddha would not differ from a sentient being; and a sentient being who is enlightened in one moment of mind does not differ from a buddha. Know therefore that all laws exist within your mind. Why not instantly discover the original nature of bhutatathata in your own mind. It is said in the Sutra of the Bodhisattva Commandments: 'Our intrinsic nature is originally pure. When we know our own mind and see our original nature, all attain buddhahood.' It is said in the Vimalakirti Sutra: 'If at this very moment you open your mind, its original clarity instantly appears.'"

SOKEI-AN SAYS:

This evening, I am speaking about my own sect of Buddhism, called Zen. Everyone thinks that Zen is a religion of China, but Zen is the real principle of the Buddha himself, handed down from generation to generation. The twenty-eighth [Indian] patriarch, whose name was Bodhidharma, brought this religion to China, and then about two hundred years later, it came from China to Japan. This sect was accepted by Japan, and it became dominant. It is still quite dominant among the intelligentsia. To understand art or politics or diplomacy in Japan—to understand anything—you must understand Zen.

I am translating the record of the Sixth Patriarch of China, whose name was Hui-neng. He is speaking, as written here, from an earthen platform to Prefect Wei of Shao-chou and five hundred monks, nuns, Taoists, and Confucianists. In this passage, he is speaking about self-enlightenment—not about enlightenment by any God or gods, demons or any outside agency, but about how a man enlightens himself by his own exertion.

"Good friends, all the sutras, words and letters, all the great and small vehicles, and the twelve divisions of the scriptures are attempts at adjusting those teachings to people's various tendencies of mind." We could say that one hundred years after the Buddha's death his teachings were forming into divisions. It was not a mushroom growth but a development. These divisions are the seeds of the Buddhist teaching.

"They are founded in accordance with the nature of wisdom. If there had never been a man on earth, these millions of laws would never have existed. Thus you see that all laws were originally initiated by man and that all scriptures vary in doctrine according to the author." Nagarjuna, Asanga, and Vasubandhu all wrote and taught their own views about Buddhism; and in the Buddha's time, Shariputra's teaching and that of Maudgalyayana also adopted different viewpoints. Standing on different points of view, they talked about the world that they observed.

This is an important point in Buddhism. So you must understand that, objectively, there is no particular world. The world that we observe is our own world—my world is not exactly the same as yours. Reality has no particular shape, sound, taste, smell, distance, time, or space. These are our sense-perceptions, our subjective existence. You must understand this: Objectively, there is no fixed existence. The eye of a fly crystallizes the outside world like a net, a rainbow net in which there are more colors than we could ever put a name to. There is no particular form. Your cat does not see your face as you see it in the mirror. But we cannot say, "Poor cat, you cannot see as we see," because the cat would say the same thing to us. When I give you the koan, "Before father and mother . . .," if you take any particular view of this, it is not a true view. From no-view you can truly observe the world and the world of insects, fish, and cats. But as our world is the nearest world to us, we decide to live in this world as human beings and not as cats and dogs, horses and flies.

Buddha's world is different from our world, and our world is also different from that of the man who is living in the *naraka* or *preta* stages. So we cannot say, "My world is right and yours is wrong." The Buddha's view was no-view, and that is the true view. There are those who decide to live in the transcendental world, denying this world, and jump off a cliff and commit suicide. And there are those who try to exist in an absolutely material world—"Even if I sell my daughter, I commit no crime." Of all views, you know, it is this view that is the most dangerous one.

The Buddha's view is to take no-view, and we are trying to make Buddha's view our own. Through each koan you are approximating the Buddha's view. For instance: Is one who is enlightened subject to cause and effect or not? According to one view, one who is enlightened is not subject to cause and effect. Another view holds that an enlightened one is not bothered by causation. These are the two views: one is materialistic and subject to causation; the other is free from causation. But with either view, there is suffering. So you must not take either view, but one that is adapted to both. Finally, you will cremate both views and will hold no-view.

"Among mankind there are those who are wise and those who are foolish. The foolish are small men, and the wise are great men. The foolish ask the teaching of the wise. The wise give the teaching, explaining it to the foolish. But when the foolish open their minds and are suddenly enlightened, they differ not a whit from the wise." That is, the foolish suddenly see true existence.

You cannot see true existence from different types of view. You must slough off all views. You cannot see the world from the fly's standpoint, nor from the cat's, the fish's, nor the horse's. So destroy all views, and you will swallow your breath and not utter a word. This is enlightenment. Even Buddha cannot say a word to express it. The cat will "Meow!" but Buddha does not say a word because he has the true view.

Enlightenment destroys all views and sees real existence. Before father and mother, what were you? If you see that . . . but perhaps you will *not* see it for thirty years.

"*Good friends, without enlightenment, a buddha would not differ from a sentient being; and a sentient being who is enlightened in one moment of mind does not differ from a buddha.*" The word enlightenment is used many times. This word is not so easy to explain. Enlightenment is an English word that I do not like to use, but there is no other word. However, please do not think it is a light in your brain, or electricity, or anything mysterious like spiritual television. I think it is not necessary to repeat this so many times for my own pupils, but for strangers, perhaps it is best to describe it once more.

Under the Bodhi Tree, after six years of meditation, the Buddha enlightened himself and called his enlightenment the "Middle Way." It is not the way of materialism or the way of metaphysical reality. Metaphysical reality is a term that is frequently used in Western philosophy, so I let it stand.

Tonight, I shall not explain this metaphysical reality, but to my own pupils I will repeat that Reality is not that which we can see, touch, taste, or think. So when I say, "Absolute Reality," please do not think that I am talking about any such thing. Oriental "Reality" is different.

Usually human beings take two different attitudes: One thinks there is nothing spiritual in the world, that there is only the material, the realistic world. (Please do not mix up "Reality" and "realistic," they are two entirely different words. And do not think that Western reality is the same as Buddhist Reality.) Materialistic people are quite egoistic. They think it is the end when they physically die, that there is no hereafter. "So what can I do in this life? I can eat, sleep, and make money, and I can go anywhere I want—tomorrow Florida!" That is the meaning of the material life. Eat plenty and marry a beautiful woman, a Greek goddess. There is no reward or punishment after death. That is the materialistic attitude, and it is the logical tendency of modern life. This side is one extreme—to escape from agony and go down into material existence.

The other side is transcendental spiritualism, or abstract reality. Those who believe in transcendental spirituality think that Reality is something that exists outside our five senses. They think that pure spiritual power reaches there, that man, with his physical body can never reach there. So in order to succeed, you must torture this physical body: practice mortification, eat only one grain of rice a day, stand in water all day long, sleep in nettles, take out your eye, break your eardrum, etc. You must hate and abominate this existing physical body so that you may realize Absolute Reality—God. This is the other side of human life. Don't speak a word, don't see anything, just meditate in a dark cave. The one who practices this way of living is already a skeleton. His living is just a preparation for committing suicide. Outside of this world, he hopes to find the "Land of Pure Fire," or something like that.

We can divide the human mind into these two baskets. If it doesn't incline to one side, it will incline to the other. These concepts were existing in the Buddha's time and are still existing today. But the Buddha cast away these two viewpoints and found his Middle Way. Matter and spirit are not two different existences. They are two different names for one thing. If you have no physical body, you cannot prove the spiritual side. If you have no spiritual side, you cannot see the physical body. They are two sides of one existence, and we must observe both from one standpoint. This one standpoint is called the Middle Way. It is the Buddha's way.

Nothing exists alone. It's like a rainbow. No green light exists alone, but only between blue and yellow. Purple exists only between blue and red. All colors exist entirely in relatedness. If there is no blue, there is no red; if there is no red, there is no blue. The Buddha said: "If *this* does not exist, *that* does not exist. If *that* does not exist, *this* exists. If there were only one existence, then this one existence would not exist."

When you go to Japan, you can see fish swimming in the hot springs. These fish have never known heat because they have never known cold water. So hot water does not exist for them. Fish in the sea do not know salt water because they have never known fresh water. If we had no physical body, there would be no abstract consciousness. The two prove one another. If there is no abstract consciousness, how can we prove our physical body? They exist together.

Some say this physical body is a burden; and as long as we live, we cannot go to heaven. This is not a Buddhist conception. If we have no physical body, how can we know heaven? Buddhism does not take such an attitude. Everything exists relatively, and, therefore, we stand upon relative existence. This world does not exist for me alone. I exist for the world, for the sake of human beings. That is the true attitude. Consider the boss of a big factory. He looks at the workers and he makes a sweatshop out of them. That man thinks the whole factory exists for him. The true view is that he is a workman for the sake of all the workers. If the other workers did not exist, he would not exist. You must understand this principle.

Whoever understands the relativity of existence will say: "I am not existing for myself, but I exist for others and for the country." This is selflessness, non-ego. It is the Middle Way.

If the fruit of the tree should think that the treetrunk, branches and leaves exist for it, what would the treetrunk, branches and leaves say to this? The fruit is important for seed, but it cannot exist without the whole tree. If you really understand the Middle Way, you are Buddha.

"Know therefore that all laws exist within your mind. Why not instantly discover the original nature of bhutatathata *in your own mind? It is said in the* Sutra of the Bodhisattva Commandments*"*: Bodhisattvas are those who can take the monk or lay life. So statesmen, dictators, generals, rajahs, and prime ministers can become bodhisattvas. They may be lay people, but they are real bodhisattvas. Bodhisattvas love all people and take the salvation of others as their duty. From the Buddha's standpoint, Christ was one of the great bodhisattvas.

"'Our intrinsic nature is originally pure.'" This "pure" does not indicate a dualistic attitude; it does not take either of the two attitudes we have described. It is just as a baby takes milk from its mother. Without dislike or attachment, the baby's attitude is originally pure. But later some notion comes in. Perhaps the baby will grow up to think that to be born is something impure and later commit suicide or perhaps take the opposite attitude—eat, drink, and enjoy. Both attitudes are just notions and not the attitudes of a normal human being. Why hate your physical body because of a notion? And why attach to physical life because of another notion?

"'When we know our own mind and see our original nature, all attain buddhahood.' It is said in the Vimalakirti Sutra*: 'If at this very moment you open your mind, its original clarity instantly appears.'"* Do not wait for some time in the future, or try to get Reality from books, or from someone else. If you open your mind, you will find IT. That is Buddha. This is the Sixth Patriarch's Buddhism, but it is not different from the Buddha's Buddhism. The Buddha attained in such a way, and you must attain in the same way.

"Good friends! When I was in the temple of Hung-jen, I asked him one question, and upon his answer, I understood. I suddenly found the true nature of bhutatathata*. This is why I advocate this teaching and disseminate it so that you, too, will instantly realize enlightenment.*

"Every one of you, observe your own mind, and find your own original nature. If you are unable to realize it, you must ask instruction of a great teacher, one who knows the law of the highest vehicle and will

immediately point out for you the right way. A great teacher has experience from the remote past. He will lead you and initiate you into the realization of your original nature. A great teacher is the source of all good teachings."

SOKEI-AN SAYS:

"Good friends! When I was in the temple of Hung-jen, I asked him one question, and upon his answer, I understood." "I understood" means "I awakened." It is rather obscure, in accordance with this description, which of his conversations with the Fifth Patriarch Hui-neng is referring to.

"I suddenly found the true nature of bhutatathata." The Sixth Patriarch found the original nature of *bhutatathata* just as Shakyamuni found it after six years of meditation. Going through the many stages of metaphysical thought, he finally reached the state that actually exists. That is *bhutatathata*. The Buddha called it the Central Way. So Buddhism does not take a dualistic attitude. Later, we called that period of the Buddha's initiation into the true law, Buddhism.

Not only the Sixth Patriarch, but all the masters of Buddhism from generation to generation attained this awakening. While your mind is in the state of dualism—spirit and matter, time and space, black and white—you are not awakened, and you do not attain *bhutatathata*. You are caught in the cycle of life and death.

"This is why I advocate this teaching and disseminate it so that you, too, will instantly realize enlightenment." You will not need to spend kalpas of incarnations to attain enlightenment. You will attain suddenly.

Why do we call it sudden enlightenment? Because just a moment before, you were unenlightened. Suddenly you realize—"Oh, *This* is *Bhuta*! All the universe is *Bhuta*!" This is the end of philosophy and the beginning of Zen.

Compared with the views of the heretics of the Buddha's time, this is entirely different. The Yoga school believed they would find *samadhi* in deep meditation, that their souls would return to the creator of the universe, to Brahma. So to them, this actual existence—what we see, hear, etc.—did not mean anything, it was nonsense and impure. This was their teaching.

The *Sankhya* school did not place emphasis on the practice of meditation. They believed that somehow by philosophical observation, they would find something that is eternal, and could reach a state higher than Brahma. That school also paid no attention to this existence and took the abstract attitude. This was the usual Hindu thought of that time.

The Buddha's attitude came from an entirely different standpoint. He did not separate matter and spirit; he did not find it necessary to ascend to Brahma. He found all that he wanted here before him. Through calm meditation, everything was within his reach in this actual existence. It was remarkable that the Buddha found that truth at such a time—2,500 years ago!

Today we still find some who have the heretical attitude: "Oh, I will ascend higher and higher!" They have the Buddha climbing stairs to heaven—like climbing a skyscraper in New York! The Buddha did not have the old notions. He found the truth from his own consciousness.

The religion of reaching up, up, up to the spiritual and despising the material is a menace. Why don't they just commit suicide right away? It's a menace to human beings to teach inactive meditation. Naturally, to such people, this active life does not mean anything. Stupid, unenlightened monks brought Buddhism to this state in India, and as a result, Buddhism was wiped out in that land. In China and Japan there are crazy monks, too. They never read the sutras, never have instruction from a teacher. They just have their own crazy notions, put robes on their shoulders and call themselves monks. I am not introducing this Buddhism into America.

The Sixth Patriarch had no such Buddhism. He had his feet on the earth.

"Every one of you, observe your own mind, and find your own original nature." It is not necessary to observe *brahmacariya* or Avalokiteshvara. Just observe your own mind, constituted of the five shadows of mind—rupa, vedana, samjna, samskara and vijnana. When you observe your own mind and find your original nature, so-called *brahmacariya* and Avalokiteshvara will be there.

"If you are unable to realize it, you must ask instruction of a great teacher, one who knows the law of the highest vehicle and will immediately point out for you the right way." Not the way to go to heaven or the way to torture your true physical body. The true teacher will tell you that you will find everything in your own mind.

When I say, "Before father and mother . . .," you immediately get an idea of time. You think of the material construction of creation. You think that something was created from nothing. How could something be created from zero? If there is "One" it must always have existed from the beginning to the end. If you forget your five senses, you will go back to the original state. Creation is not in the remote past. It is in the present.

"A great teacher has experience from the remote past. He will lead you and initiate you into the realization of your original nature." In the Sixth Patriarch's record, "nature" does not mean good, bad, or quick-tempered nature. It means the original soul, the universal soul.

The universal soul is the original nature of all sentient beings. According to the Buddhist idea, the "great teacher" is not a teacher for the first time on earth. He has been a Buddhist many times and a teacher many times. There is some idea of the unconscious here. Today we have an entirely different idea of the unconscious, but that which was hypothetical in Buddhism perhaps has some value even today.

"A great teacher is the source of all good teachings." This last line does not mean anything. Perhaps some blind monk put it here. We cannot be sure which are really the lines of the Sixth Patriarch. Of course, this record was composed by his disciples after his death. Even Lin-chi's record was not written by himself, but by this disciples. When I die, my record will not be written by me, but by my disciples, and it will not be my lecture. The real record of a Zen master cannot be made from any pedantic standpoint.

This is a Zen record, but true Buddhism is not different from Zen. Many sects of Buddhism take different attitudes. Later, Buddhism was separated into many different sects, and some of those sects are not Buddhism at all. Even the sects in India and Ceylon are not exactly the same as the Buddha's Buddhism.

The sutras are true sutras, but the monks are not enlightened. The monks of today keep the corpse of Buddhism but not its vital force.

"The buddhas of the three worlds and the twelve divisions of the canon are originally inherent in human nature. If you are unable to enlighten yourself, you must seek instruction from a teacher and then you will understand. But if you are able to do it by yourself, you have no need of help from the outside. If you insist that one must have a good teacher in order to free oneself, your view is incorrect. Why? Because self-enlightening wisdom is in your own mind. If delusions, wrong notions, and inverted views arise, even the instruction of a good teacher cannot free you. But if you contemplate with real wisdom (prajna), in one moment those wrong notions will cease to exist. Finding your original nature, at the first realization, you reach the enlightened state of buddhahood."

SOKEI-AN SAYS:

The Sixth Patriarch kindly repeats his true view. True view is one item of the Eightfold Noble Path. From the Buddha's time until today, if a Buddhist does not have the true view, he is not a disciple of Shakyamuni Buddha. But in this decadent period of Buddhism, there are many Buddhists adherents who have no true view. Therefore, the Sixth Patriarch repeated many times the importance of this true view. As you remember, Zen Master Lin-chi also spoke repeatedly of the necessity of obtaining the true Zen standpoint.

"The buddhas of the three worlds": The "three worlds" are the past, present, and future. There were many buddhas in the past. The present buddha is Shakyamuni. The future buddha is Maitreya. Buddhists are expecting him in some future kalpa to appear in this *sarvaloka*, that is, this world conceived and visualized by human beings.

We think all worlds belong to human beings; but to the Buddhist this view is erroneous. We observe the world we can conceive in our mind and visualize with our five senses. The Buddha called that world *sarvaloka*. We think that is all; and in this world, we will struggle. When we come from our mother's bosom, we open our eyes and cry aloud. We gaze at this curious world of color and recognize the three-dimensional world. Then we conceive the meaning of this phenomena, make many suppositions and metaphysical conceptions. At last, we close our eyes and die. It is a very small and limited life. We feel that there are many inconceivable worlds surrounding us.

The old Indian scriptures usually include seven buddhas of the past, of whom the most frequently mentioned are Kashyapa Buddha, Kanakamuni Buddha, and Vipasyin Buddha. "Buddha," as a title, means an enlightened teacher. In the case of Shakyamuni Buddha, it means the sage of the Shakya tribe. In an abstract sense, "Buddha" means the awakened knower of the universe.

". . . And the twelve divisions of the canon are originally inherent in human nature." In the third generation, the followers of the Buddha prepared the sutras of primitive, or radical, Buddhism. Nine divisions included the teachings given orally by the Buddha, which were repeated by his disciples, and later three more divisions were added. These twelve divisions comprise the Mahayana canon.

The teachings we have now are the "molded" teachings of Shakyamuni, that is, prepared and arranged in the particular forms selected at the time of their composition. It is the same as putting ice cream into a mold, or making gelatin pudding by molding it into a form from a particular utensil you buy in a shop—perhaps shaped like a flower or a triangle. In the same way, the Buddha's original teachings were cast into molds. And generation to generation we are transmitting these.

As I was telling you recently, the four Buddhist terms—mutability, agony, non-ego, emptiness—are also four molds. You have heard these terms many times. All the world is mutable; therefore we feel agony because nothing goes according to our desire. But who feels the agony really? Since all is in relative existence, all exists relatively—our minds, our bodies are one. There is no separate soul, so we do not exist separately; we are non-ego. Really, no one is feeling agony. Agony is feeling agony. Nothing is really suffering. In such a way, in such molds, Buddha's actual teaching was handed down. So you cannot get true Buddhism from these teachings. You get the five *skandhas*, the *trikaya*, the twelve nidanas, the four noble truths, and all those others—all molds. That is the Buddhism that was handed down by Ananda—exoteric Buddhism. The Buddhists did not want to spill out the teaching all over to disappear, so they put it into molds.

But the Buddhism that was actually transmitted was not put into any mold, any word or diagram or symbol. It was handed down from soul to soul, mind to mind, from Mahakashyapa on. This is Zen. This, according to the tradition, was handed down to the Sixth Patriarch from the Fifth Patriarch, from the

Fourth, Third, and Second Patriarch, who received it from Bodhidharma, who was the Twenty-Eighth Patriarch of India and the first of China. This was the esoteric transmission. So if you really wish to understand Buddhism, you must understand both the exoteric and the esoteric. This is not written here, of course. It is just as going to a restaurant and reading the menu is not the same as eating. Or like having a prescription your doctor gives you and not filling it—if you do not have it filled, it is just a prescription.

All the writings are in your heart. They are inherent, the intrinsic law of your nature. You cannot find them anywhere outside yourself.

"If you are unable to enlighten yourself, you must seek instruction from a teacher and then you will understand. But if you are able to do it by yourself, you have no need of help from the outside." If you are unable to enlighten yourself through your own effort, you should seek help from a good teacher. A good teacher is one who has experience. The Sixth Patriarch is not saying, "Get it from me." He is saying, "Get help from someone who has received the transmission from someone who received it from this true line of descent from the Buddha."

The Buddha's Buddhism was built on a particular ground, a particular foundation. The Buddha built this religion upon *this* mind, *this* consciousness, *this* child of God. Sometimes you call it body, sometimes you call it God or demon. We do not use any name for it, really. We say, *This is That*, or just *That*. That is all. Your body is not bounded by the surface of your skin, you know. The sun and moon are your body. The oceans and rivers are your body. The whole universe is your body.

Buddhists take a peculiar attitude compared with other religious groups. A Buddhist does not join his hands and look up into the sky and say, "Lord, Lord!" His Lord is in himself. He closes his eyes and puts his hands in his lap and looks inward. The mystery is really your soul, your mind. So the Buddhist clasps his hands and finds the law in himself and sees God face to face. But this God is not the god that has six legs, six faces, and six hands. When you meet God face to face, you understand who he is. You do not need to look for wisdom in any corner of the universe. You cannot get it in a library.

"If you insist that one must have a good teacher in order to free oneself, your view is incorrect." Shakyamuni went to seek it among the ascetics meditating in the woods of India. He visited Alara Kalama. He found that Alara Kalama's viewpoint ended in meditation, so this actual world was not important to him. He thought that when he was meditating, he was with God, but that to awake to life in *this* world was not to be with God.

The Buddha did not agree with this view, so he went to another ascetic whose name was Uddaka Ramaputta. It seems Uddaka's view was not too different from Alara's. His particular attitude was not to make an effort to think anything. He took the attitude that his soul was not his soul, his thoughts were not his thoughts, that everything was done not by him but by Nature, so to think that something himself would be erroneous. The thing to do was to lie down in the shadow of the trees and dream—let Nature do the thinking. When you are hungry, someone will bring you food. One could not do this in Alaska!

Well, the Buddha did not agree with Uddaka's view, either, but found his own position and stayed with it. So the two teachers of the Buddha really gave him nothing. He attained his own position. The thing he wanted to attain he did not find outside himself, nor in metaphysical reality, nor in the force of nature, nor in the weeds of the ground, but in *this* existence [indicates self]. You despise this body because you perceive it with your sense organs and attach to consciousness, or vice-versa. You must take the central view. The central view is the true view. Usually we observe in two ways only: either we observe from the spiritual or from the physical point of view. I cannot speak more of this now. Sometime I will.

"Why? Because self-enlightening wisdom is in your own mind." Shakyamuni Buddha attained enlightenment by himself; and the Sixth Patriarch also attained enlightenment upon hearing one word from the Fifth Patriarch, for he had already found the true view in himself and had understood. If one meets another who has the true view, when they look at one another, each knows the other is enlightened. Fire shines and is always the same fire. Thus it is transmitted.

"If delusions, wrong notions, and inverted views arise, even the instruction of a good teacher cannot free you." If delusions, wrong notions, and inverted views arise in your mind, you must conquer them yourself. The notions you entertain entertain you, so you cannot divorce them very quickly. Even though you feel suffering, and you know it is your delusion, you live with it.

"But if you contemplate with real wisdom (prajna*), in one moment those wrong notions will cease to exist. Finding your original nature, at the first realization, you reach the enlightened state of buddhahood."* You have this real wisdom as you have your own eyes. In one moment those wrong notions—everything—will cease to exist, but it is not so easy. Really, in that moment, you cannot depend upon anything save *this* [indicates self]. But we do not call *this* "physical body." There is one consciousness that could be compared to your wrist, and this consciousness develops into five consciousnesses, or shadows of consciousness: *rupa, vedana, samjna, samskara, vijnana*—the five *skandhas*. *This* consciousness, *this* mind movement, *this* active mind you think is yours, is not yours. While you are sleeping it digests your food. There is nothing after all that you can call yourself. All is the great universal consciousness—Non-Ego.

This is original nature. You do not need to find it. In the kitchen, down in the cellar, in the attic, wherever you are, wherever you go, you are always carrying *this*. But when you become aware of it, it is as though you had found it.

"Good friends, if you, with your own wisdom, contemplate penetratingly within and without, you can recognize your original mind. Recognizing your original mind is original emancipation. The attainment of original emancipation is prajna-samadhi, *which is none other than no-thought.*

"What is meant by no-thought? When you see all things, if your mind is not attached to any of them, this is no-thought. When your mind functions, it will pervade all places, yet will not be attached to anything. Purify your original mind, and let the six consciousnesses go out of the six gates unstained by the fields of dust, freely coming and going, functioning without obstruction. This is emancipation at will in prajna-samadhi *and is called the practice of no-thought. If you imagine no-thought signifies that one should not think anything in a hundred situations and cut off all thoughts, this is called 'being in the custody of one's own conception,' and a 'biased view.'*

"Good friends, those who realize the teaching of no-thought will penetrate all the myriad teachings. They will reveal the realms of all the buddhas and attain the stage of buddhahood."

SOKEI-AN SAYS:

The Sixth Patriarch is speaking about the importance of the principle of "inattentiveness," no-thought, which is famous in Buddhism as the daily attitude of the practical mind in Buddhist life, a principle badly understood by those outside of Buddhism.

"Good friends, if you, with your own wisdom, contemplate penetratingly within and without, you can recognize your original mind." This original mind is the usual term in the religion of the Sixth

Patriarch. It describes the intrinsic nature of man. Sometimes I use "soul" to denote the most profound consciousness, sometimes "mind" and then sometimes "brain." So the one word "mind" can be translated "soul," "consciousness," "heart," "brain," or "mind."

The Sixth Patriarch spoke of original mind or original soul, but do not take this soul as the usual superstition of Western people, as a thing kept somewhere in the body, which, after death, will take an independent attitude and wander through the sky, or hide behind some rocks until the final day of judgment. When you have studied Buddhism for five or six years, you will realize that Buddhism is based upon this entity that has a physical body consisting of the first *skandah*, *rupa*, the four great elements—earth, fire, water, air—and a mental body consisting of the other four skandhas—*vedana, samjna, samskara, vijnana*. In the four physical and four mental elements, the whole unity of the universe is completed.

We do not look for God outside of our body. He is within us. We believe that this physical body is the shrine of consciousness, but we do not take the old attitude of the pre-Brahmanic faith. They believed that the physical body is the center of life, so they made the cow a symbol of the sexual life and worshipped its image. Such an attitude naturally falls into sex worship, as the Freudian school thinks sex is the center of human life. The other extreme is the mortification of the physical body. Therefore, daily life means nothing to them, just as moral values mean nothing to the worshipper of sex. It is the usual way of human beings.

We Buddhists find a center, not in a God that is outside our body or in the sex that is common to all nature—animals, trees, and weeds. We find a different consciousness in ourselves. We find this present consciousness. Of course, the Buddhist includes the deeper phases of consciousness—alayavijnana and *klista-manas*-consciousness. But the actual foundation of the Buddha's Buddhism is this *present* consciousness, that which we are using every day. This is not a sleeping consciousness in the hand of nature, nor is it abstract like God. Our everyday consciousness is our own seat on which we are resting. In later Buddhism, this consciousness came to be called Avalokiteshvara.

Avalokiteshvara symbolizes our own seat. He is our "personal God" because he is God in person. Our "personal God" idea is that God is in this practical person. So our practical consciousness, Avalokiteshvara, is the foundation of our daily life. Avalokiteshvara has one thousand arms and legs, one thousand hands, one thousand eyes. In his hands are one thousand different instruments with which he does everything.

When a Japanese child once looked at a crucifix and saw Christ on the cross, he asked: "Why has this Avalokiteshvara only four arms?" The child saw the cross as arms. Avalokiteshvara, in Japanese Buddhism, takes the position of Christ in Christianity. So from this standpoint, Buddhism and Christianity are not two different religions.

"Recognizing your original mind is original emancipation." Not alaya or manas consciousness, but this present consciousness. You need not go deeper because it is bottomless. That is all. Why do you have to worry about it? For what are you seeking? You are trying to hunt out God in the sky and to find the devil in hell. This is because you do not know your original soul. Do not look for God anywhere outside of yourself. From this viewpoint, Avalokiteshvara and Christ are the same, and Buddhism meets Christianity.

"The attainment of original emancipation is prajna-samadhi*":* You do not need to seek God in heaven or worship stone images or painted images on a wall. Our daily life from morning to evening is transubstantiation. When we stand with hands clasped across our breast, it is our symbol of this transubstantiation. The Triune Body, *trikaya,—dharmakaya, sambhogakaya, nirmanakaya*—is revealed upon this flesh, and all laws are written in our mind and body. Following this view, all people are originally

84

related, and we carry peace into the world and security into the family. Thus we avoid disaster, living in tranquillity and peace. *Prajna-samadhi* is concentration with wisdom in daily life.

"*. . . Which is none other than no-thought. When you see all things, if your mind is not attached to any of them, this is no-thought.*" "No-thought," in Sanskrit, is *asmrti*,[9] which means "not attaching to mind-stuff." *Smrti* means "to think," and *asmrti* means "not to think," therefore, "forgetfulness" or "inattentiveness." But these words do not indicate the real point and significance of these terms—"You shall not attach to any particular mind-stuff." It is not necessary to avoid mind-stuff, but do not cling to any particular idea.

In the practice of meditation, this is what you practice. Mind-stuff goes out and comes in. You observe it, but you do not pursue any of it. You do not refuse that which comes out of the bottom of your consciousness, nor do you pursue it as it disappears. You use it when you need it, and then let it go when you no longer need it, just as a man uses his horse when he needs it, and keeps it in the stable when he does not need it.

You are using words and mind-stuff everyday, but where do you keep these when you do not need them? Usually, blind monks explain this by saying: "Do not look at this or that face. Do not hear this or that sound." But *asmrti* means to hear all sounds at once, see everything at once. Don't give attention first to one thing and then another.

Well, psychologically, we cannot do this. Our minds are always fixed on one point at a time. Our mind shifts quickly, but for a brief moment, it is always fixed on one point at a time. So *asmirti* means that you have no selfish desire for this life, no particular attachment. You take no particular pains to hold onto anything.

It is like a seventeen-year-old girl to whom it is not important to get a husband. She goes out with a gentleman and she laughs. Her mind is not particularly attached to any one gentleman. We monks are taught this attitude by begging door to door. We ring the bell and chant—"Ho-o-o! H-o-o-! We wait one moment, and if no one comes, we move to the next door. If someone comes out and says, "Go away!" we go away. Perhaps we will also be refused at the next door, but we just go on.

When you practice to speak on the stage, at first, if you are nervous, you are not asmrti, and your voice goes high. If your mind is attached to anything other than what you have to say, you will become nervous, unable to speak naturally. When you think, "I must succeed," then you find yourself in a pretty kettle of fish! But when you are asmrti, your voice will become strong.

"*When your mind functions, it will pervade all places, yet will not be attached to anything.*" This is the second attitude, and when you take this attitude, there are no obstructions in space. It is like heat or electricity.

The third law or attitude is also *asmirti*. As the Sixth Patriarch said, "Without depending upon anything, manifest your mind."

"*Purify your original mind, and let the six consciousnesses go out of the six gates unstained by the fields of dust*": These are eye, ear, nose, tongue, touch, and mind. The six consciousnesses are really derived from one consciousness, as the five fingers are the hand. The thumb is color, the first finger is sound, the second is smell, the third is taste, the fourth is touch. The sixth sense is this present consciousness (mano-vijnana), the palm of the hand. The seventh is manas (klista-mano-vijnana), and the eighth is alayavijnana—but all are included in this present consciousness. The six fields of dust are the fields of consciousness. Color is the field of the eye, sound is the field of the ear, etc. Dust is phenomena.

"*Freely coming and going, functioning without obstruction. This is emancipation at will* in prajna-samadhi *and is called the practice of no-thought.*" This is a difficult practice, though we can speak so easily about it. I realize that in each koan you take, you stick to one little notion, like a fly in a jar of syrup. You struggle and struggle and finally come to the edge of the jar and lick the syrup off your legs. But then comes another koan and—"Good day, syrup!"

"If you imagine no-thought signifies that one should not think anything in a hundred situations and cut off all thoughts . . .": Many teachers teach that you should not think anything. If something is sad, you must not look at it; and if something is joyful, you must also not look at it. You must keep your mind blank. This is not *asmirti*. If one practices in this way, he annihilates his mind, and he is no longer a human being. It is like committing suicide. No buddha would teach such a religion.

"This is called 'being in the custody of one's own conception,' and a 'biased view.'" You are under the constraint of your own thoughts.

A young monk came to the Third Patriarch, Seng-t'san, and asked: "Please teach me how to emancipate myself." The patriarch answered: "Has anyone bound you?" "No." "Where is the rope that constrains you?" "There is no rope." "Then why do you need emancipation?" This monk, Tao-hsin, was suddenly enlightened and became the Fourth Patriarch. With your thoughts, you put yourself "into constraint," and you refuse to come out.

One school in India took the attitude of complete silence. This attitude of silence and the uselessness of words is a misconception of truth. The "Barbarian," Bodhidharma, always kept his mind in silence, but his silence was true silence.

The other extreme is the attempt to prove everything by words. To prove one word, a hundred pages are used. This is also a biased view. In Zen, you do not attach to a word nor do you keep absolute silence. The words you use must have substantial background. When you find the Zen answer, you realize that philosophical answers are no good. The words have no substance. In Zen, you put an answer into substance and manifest it. "Where do you come from?" "Where are you going?" Explained, metaphysically, there is only a dry answer with no moisture in it.

""Good friends, those who realize the teaching of no-thought will penetrate all the myriad teachings. They will reveal the realms of all the buddhas and attain the stage of buddhahood." In sports, you use asmrti. You try to win, but if you lose, you shake hands with your opponent and put it out of your mind. It is over. Buddhists take this attitude every day, at every moment, in everything. A gambler who stakes everything on one throw of the dice, loses and walks away unaffected is an example of *asmirti*.

These are the real words of the Sixth Patriarch. We do not ask everyone to accept the Buddhist view, but only those who have some affinity with Buddhism.

"Good friends, in the future, you who would inherit my Dharma should accept this teaching of sudden enlightenment and make a vow to uphold it among those who hold similar views and those who follow the same practices, just as if you were serving Buddha. Thus upholding [this teaching], you who do not depart from it throughout life will indubitably attain the rank of sage. You must, however, transmit [it] in silence, as it was transmitted in this way from former generations. You must not withhold this real Dharma. Those not holding similar views or not following the same practice are alien to Dharma and cannot receive the transmission. To do so would harm the effort of previous masters and ultimately be of no benefit. The idiot who could not comprehend it might slander this teaching and annihilate the seed of buddhas for a hundred eons and a thousand incarnations."

SOKEI-AN SAYS:

I think this part of the chapter was really spoken by the Sixth Patriarch and not put in later by students in other generations.

In this part, there is a very important element—the teaching of sudden enlightenment. Today, we call it Zen. Sudden enlightenment, Zen, is the method to reach the attainment of Shakyamuni Buddha. It is a method to get into Buddha's Buddhism. Today, in the Orient, there are many methods by which one can enter Buddhism: emotionally, by adoring the Buddha; from moment to moment, by calling the name of the Buddha; taking a vow before the symbol of a certain type of mind of the Buddha and concentrating into that vow at every moment; philosophizing the words and the meanings of the teachings and metaphysically grasping the reality; making incantations and offering prayers. The method of sudden enlightenment is different from all others. Sudden enlightenment is the Buddha's method. Without following any other method prevailing in India at that time, he invented it after six years of meditation. Bodhidharma carried it from India to China, and the Chinese upheld it, transmitting it from generation to generation. As this method came directly from the Buddha, it had to be transmitted from teacher to disciple, face to face. If this method were only described in a sutra, it would vanish.

Here in the West, several have attained enlightenment by methods that were really Zen, but they did not transmit their attainment by teaching. Therefore, their disciples could not grasp their master's enlightenment and carry it on. This method is entirely new in the West. Here, people try to find something essential to the human being, something called "God." Some have found it accidentally, but as they found it by accident, they were not aware of the method and could not use it. To them it came as a flash of lightning. They never dreamed there was a method by which Truth could be attained and transmitted.

The attainment in the West is by talking, talking, and more talking. Explaining everything, they do not get anywhere. They live in their "talk" and cannot really grasp anything. Pupils spend their time listening to their teacher's preaching. They think they will experience something in their minds that will correspond to that in their teacher's mind. It's like someone who has five thousand dollars talking to someone who does not. In the Zen method, we first give something that is substantial—"Before father and mother, what were you?" You find something by your own exertion, you grasp it, and then you have the five thousand dollars. After you have grasped it, we tell you that this is *dharmakaya*, and from that, you have a basis of understanding with which to go on. In church, when you are listening to the preacher, how can you identify your nature with what is being said? That type of teaching is wrong. They are just transmitting "talk." They are "talking" of five thousand dollars from generation to generation to those who do not have a penny. It is like trying to form an oil corporation before the oil is discovered. There are wonderful buildings, many teachers, and many volumes of scripture, but there is no substance in this kind of teaching.

"Good friends, in the future, you who would inherit my Dharma should accept this teaching of sudden enlightenment and make a vow to uphold it among those who hold similar views and those who follow the same practices, just as if you were serving Buddha." This is our heart. In *sanzen*, I am holding the treasure transmitted from the Buddha down the generations—transmitted by Bodhidharma, and transmitted by the Sixth Patriarch. I am giving it to you. You must accept it with sincerity. This is from heart to heart, not from a foreigner to an American, not from a yellow face to a white face. We are facing each other in bare truth, untouched by notions of any kind. You must render your service to this teaching as you render it to Buddha.

"Thus upholding [this teaching], you who do not depart from it throughout life will indubitably obtain the rank of sage." The "rank of sage" means bodhisattvahood.

"You must, however, transmit [it] in silence, as it was transmitted in this way from former generations." As I transmit to you, not explaining, not philosophizing, but from silence to silence. This was the method transmitted by our ancestors.

Zen in our day is much developed from the Sixth Patriarch's time. Then, there was not much intricacy, it was like a straight tree. But Zen today has many small branches and includes many things. Philosophy and nearly all the different methods of Buddhism mentioned earlier are in the Zen school of today. Poetry and art are also included. So in the transmission of Zen, we cannot exactly follow the method written here. To transmit in silence will be understood by you, but no outsider will understand it.

"You must not withhold this real Dharma." Everything from head to toe must be manifested. Nothing must be hidden. From zenith to nadir, you must conceal nothing. The outsider will say, "It's a riddle to me, a mystery." But there is no riddle and no mystery. It's as clear as your own face in the mirror. There is no clearer teaching in the world, and yet Zen is called a riddle, a mystery. People make fun of it—make a toy of Bodhidharma for children. They ridicule the teaching because they do not know the real value of it. Although we are not hiding anything in Zen, they cannot see it because they are blind.

"Those not holding similar views or not following the same practice are alien to Dharma and cannot receive the transmission." The Sixth Patriarch is saying, "He is foreign to us, a heretic, so we do not transmit our Dharma." In *sanzen*, when you come to that which is exactly what I have in my own mind, then you are not alien to me. I will transmit my Dharma to you and tell you the famous answers made by the patriarchs. But until that moment, until you reach that point, you are alien to me, and I do not transmit my Dharma.

"To do so would harm the effort of previous masters and ultimately be of no benefit." You may say: "He's cruel. He's torturing me. Why doesn't he teach me?" But if I did tell you the answer, it would not be Zen. It would be a drama, a dance, or a pantomime, and there would be no benefit to you. You must choose a real Zen teacher when you try to study Zen.

When a Zen teacher transmits his Dharma to his disciples, he makes no distinction between young and old, rich and poor. If the disciples do not comprehend, they are not given the Dharma, regardless of their circumstances.

"The idiot who could not comprehend it might slander this teaching and annihilate the seed of buddhas for a hundred eons and a thousand incarnations." It's true. If I teach pantomime Zen because I am paid for it, what will happen in the future? If you are not an idiot, you will not enjoy such a teaching. And if I am not a lunatic, I will not enjoy having such a group.

In this modern period, there is nothing much that is sacred, but this Zen method is not yet printed on any paper, and this principle of Zen is not written in any book. It is not spoken by any master or surrendered to any power of gold. We uphold this teaching as sacred, from the Buddha through the generations to our own time.

"Good friends, I have a gatha *on formlessness. Each of you should recite it. Both you who lead the family life and you who are monks, just follow this practice. But even though you learn it by heart, you will receive no benefit from the recitation unless you practice its teaching yourselves.*

"Listen to my trikaya*:*

"He who penetrates this teaching with his mind and masters the art of expressing it
Is like the sun in the sky

I only transmit to you the law of seeing original nature
Revealing myself in the world to destroy false ideas

The law is neither sudden nor gradual
Slow or quick has only to do with whether one is deluded or enlightened

The gate of seeing one's original nature
Is inaccessible to the foolish
There are a thousand ways to speak about it
But in the end, all merge into one

In the darkness of the house of suffering
You must always give birth to the sun of wisdom

When you cherish a wrong view, there is suffering
When you attain the right view, suffering is eradicated

When you do not have recourse to either view, you realize the original pureness of soul
Where nothing more remains

Bodhi is your original nature, but as soon as you give rise to thoughts
You are deluded

Yet pureness of mind resides within your erroneous mind
If your mind is not biased by any notion, the three hinderances offer no barrier

If you practice the Way
Nothing impedes you

Always recognizing your own faults
You are in conformity with the Way

All creatures have their own ways
But these do not interfere one with another

Leaving the Way to seek some other way
You will spend your whole life and never find it

Chasing about frantically all your life
Will only bring you anguish in the end

If you desire to find the true Way
Practice the truth—that is the way

If you lack the zeal to find the Way
You wander through darkness, blind to the Way

If you are truly practicing the Way
You will not see the faults of others

If you see the faults of others
You are at fault

Even though the other is wrong and you are not
Finding fault is the offense

If you eradicate the mind of accusing
You can rid yourself of your afflictions

If you are are not swayed by love or hate
You can take a rest and stretch out both legs

If you wish to teach others
You must have a method

Do not let the other entertain doubts
Then original nature will manifest itself

Buddha's Dharma is in the world
It is not realized apart from the world

If you look for bodhi *apart from the world*
It is like looking for horns on the head of a hare

'Out of the world' is a name for the right view
'In the world' is a name for the wrong view

Away with both views, right and wrong
That is the state of bodhi *itself*

This chant is the teaching of sudden enlightenment
It is also called 'The Ship of Great Dharma'

You may listen in delusion for ages
But when realization comes, it is in an instant"

Again the Master spoke: "I have now expounded the teaching of sudden enlightenment in Ta-fan Temple. I pray that upon this word, sentient beings everywhere attain buddhahood by seeing their own original nature."

When Prefect Wei-chu, his staff, and both monks and laymen heard the words of the Master, there was none who was not enlightened. They bowed all together and praised him, exclaiming: "How wonderful! Who would have expected a buddha to appear in Ling-nan!"

SOKEI-AN SAYS:

This is the end of the chapter on *prajnaparamita*. I have been translating this chant for three weeks. This chant is in a poetical form in Chinese. Every line has five syllables. It is impossible to keep this form in the English translation, so I am translating the meaning. In the future, if any student of Zen is able to translate this in poetical form, I leave it to him. Now, I shall give an explanation in accordance with these lines.

"Good friends, I have a gatha on formlessness. Each of you should recite it." This formlessness, *alakshana* in Sanskrit, is nothingness, *shunyata*. I think my students will understand the meaning of this nothingness, the usual Buddhist term frequently used in the sutras. In Buddhism there are many points of view from which to grasp it.

The most famous one is *asankhya-kalpa-shunya*, meaning "innumerable eons of time," "nothingness through endless time." *Asankhya* will come after the destruction of the whole universe. This period of nothingness follows through innumerable eons of time, and then, from that nothingness, everything will spring forth once more. So, metaphysically, that period is not nothingness, for all potential energy is conserved in it, and everything will be reborn from it. So this nothingness is not annihilated nothingness, but that period is not perceivable. We cannot think about it, we cannot see it, we cannot feel it, hear it, smell it. This is one phase of *shunyata* (emptiness), a phase that is easy to grasp, the Buddhist conception of nothingness.

And next is *asamjna-vedana-shunya*. *Vedana* means perception—to see, hear, taste, smell, and touch—in other words, the activity of our senses. *Avedana* means no perception. *Samjna* is thoughts, conceptions. *Asamjna* means no-conception. If we have no sense organs with which to perceive and no thought organs to combine these sense perceptions, then all existence is in the original state of reality and we cannot think anything about it. We give it a name, Noumenon, or Reality. It is emptiness, shunyata. But it is not annihilated nothingness. It is intangible to sense perception, and therefore unintelligible.

The third is *asmrti-shunya*, not-mindingness. We see everything in the eyes, hear in the ears, and we feel heat or cold, smoothness or coarseness, on our skin. But asmrti-shunya—"unminding," not-minding (I wonder if there is such a word in English)—is very inconvenient to translate. In the state of *asmrti-shunyata*, this existence is just like nothing. Now, when you are thinking very hard, your eardrum vibrates violently with the sound of the elevated train, but you do not hear it. When you are watching intently in the cinema, you may suddenly think: "I left my door open! Someone will come and steal my diamonds!" Your eye is open and you are looking at the screen, but you do not see it. When you are in deep meditation, you see with your eye and hear all sounds with your ear, but your mind is so quiet that what you see and hear does not exist. You are *in asmrti-shunyata*. It is not necessary to destroy everything in a *kalpa* fire; it is not necessary to tear off anything from the eye or ear. You simply do not see or hear. For you, nothing is existing.

I think you remember the story in the sutras about the thunderstorm during the Buddha's meditation. After the storm the people came and said: "What a terrible storm! It killed four oxen and two men!" The Buddha said, "I heard nothing." All the people said, "How wonderful! The Buddha was in such deep meditation that he heard no storm and knew nothing of the four oxen and two men!"

Most people will think this was deep meditation,. But the Buddha was not deaf. If you read this sutra so, you are not a Buddhist. *Asmrti-shunya* is described here. The thunderbolt roars, but the sound does not impress the mind. The Buddha hears and sees, but his mind conceives nothing. It is as when a brave warrior, fighting through a river of blood in the rain of fire, remains unmoved by the scene. He is just fighting bravely. Or perhaps you have been working intensely for five or six hours, concentrating, unconscious of the time, and conscious only of the one thing you are doing. This is different from sleeping, isn't it? In his chant, the Sixth Patriarch is talking about this kind of *asmrti-shunya*, and he calls it *alakshana*, formlessness. It is the same as *asmrti-shunya*.

The last of the tenfold commandments states that you must not destroy your mind. You must keep it always in the condition of *asmrti-shunya*; you must not destroy it. This is the foundation of all commandments. It is not so hard, you know, if you are master of your mind. But if you are taken over by such sights as the contests of beauty in Atlantic City—Miss America, Miss Boston, Miss etc.—then you are not *in asmrti-shunya*!

"Both you who lead the family life and you who are monks, just follow this practice. But even though you learn it by heart, you will receive no benefit from the recitation unless you practice its teaching yourselves." This discipline of Buddhism is the way of *asmrti-shunya*. When I join my hands, this *is asmrti-shunya*. When I bow down to Buddha, this is *asmrti-shunya*. And when I come to take *sanzen*, bowing down to the teacher, this is *asmrti-shunya*. When a cat watches a hole to catch a rat—asmrti. When the batter waits for the baseball—bang!—*asmrti*. All gather up to the center.

Do you understand Buddhist nothingness? To sleep is not nothingness. When you meet a Zen student, he is concentrated. It is very different from someone, perhaps a blonde and beautiful lady, who giggles a greeting. To me, she is not beautiful at this time.

Asmrti is the only practice that the Buddhist needs.

"Listen to my gatha:

> *"He who penetrates this teaching with his mind and masters the art of expressing it*
> *Is like the sun in the sky"*

There are many students who have really experienced this nothingness, but who cannot explain it. And there are others who can talk about it, but who have never had the experience. But one who both has it in his mind and has the knowledge to explain it is like the sun in the sky.

> *"I only transmit to you the law of seeing original nature*
> *Revealing myself in the world to destroy false ideas"*

You cannot have *asmrti-shunya* if you have any doubts of any kind, metaphysical or otherwise. If a notion comes—"What was I before I was born? Where will I go when I die?"—you cannot concentrate. If you are in the battlefield, sword on sword, point to point, your mind must have no doubt, no regret, no question. Your mind must be clear as crystal and decisive; it must not shake.

I had a friend with me in Manchuria. He was a sentinel. One day he killed a man, then he fell to the ground. We carried him to the tent and took off his clothes, thinking he was dead, but he had just fainted. He was a good man, but not a very good soldier. He was not concentrated, not in *asmrti*.

To clear out your doubts and notions, you must find your original nature. And when you carry out your true Dharma, the wrong teachings will fade away naturally.

"The law is neither sudden nor gradual
Slow or quick has only to do with whether one is deluded or enlightened"

All the teachings of the Buddha are the same. He never said: "There is sudden enlightenment and there is slow enlightenment." To the Buddha, there is just one enlightenment.

The gate of seeing one's original nature
Is inaccessible to the foolish

"Foolish" does not mean uneducated. Educated or uneducated, it's all the same. If you are honest with yourself, and if you have an honest nature, you will find your original nature. And if you have a doubt, you will not put it aside. You will think deeply, find the "because," and put an end to it. The insincere, however, though they may have a million doubts, will shrug their shoulders and refuse to think when something happens. Then they get into trouble. Their wits scatter, and they go to pieces. They are not calm. They cannot concentrate, and they cannot trust themselves. They pick up knowledge here and there, but they know nothing. If you have any doubts in your mind, you must exterminate them as you would cockroaches. You may have a thought in your mind and carry it for three or four months before you grasp it.

These days, I feel lonely, for I have no doubts in my mind. But a man who has a million doubts is like a man living with cockroaches. He may have beautiful clothes and live in ease, but he is inhabiting a house of cockroaches. How can he live so?

A man who came to see me one day kept crossing and recrossing his legs. He put his arms behind his head and looked like an imbecile. Zen develops disciplined people. They do not show rough emotions, and when they die, they do not babble. In fact, they take all of life with grace, calm, poise, and stability. Too much talking gets one into deep water, and one may never get out of it. Life is not to be explained backward and forward. It is to be lived.

"There are a thousand ways to speak about it
But in the end, all merge into one"

"There are a thousand ways," is enough to signify that there are endless ways to speak about the Buddha's Dharma. Perhaps the Sixth Patriarch means there are many teachings of the Buddha given in accordance with the capacities of the listeners. The "ways" of speaking come back into focus in the "one" consciousness that we directly experience.

There are many religions that are built upon consciousness. We have consciousness, therefore we think that there must be a greater consciousness in the universe called God. But this consciousness that we directly experience is not the climax of Buddhism. We call it *sambhogakaya*. It has two faces:

the *sambhogakaya* that is experienced by oneself, and the *sambhogakaya* that acts upon others; that is, the *sambhogakaya* that renders service to you and that which renders service to the outside. There are schools of religion that think the *sambhogakaya* that renders service to oneself is God, and that the sambhogakaya that renders service to others is God's mercy. All the schools that think *sambhogakaya* is the center of religion cannot avoid ego. After death, they have to have some place to keep the soul. If you think logically about *sambhogakaya*, it is not the conclusion of Buddhism, nor is it real existence. It is *dharmakaya* we must find, the *dharmakaya* that is truly the summit of Buddhism.

The "one" into which all the ways merge is not consciousness. What is this one?

"In the darkness of the house of suffering
You must always give birth to the sun of wisdom"

Darkness *is* the house of suffering—this world. Suffering, in Buddhism, is desire, anger, and ignorance, the three afflictions.

When I returned to Japan some years ago, a friend of mine was trying to write a scenario. Someone bought it from him and made a moving picture. I was invited to see its performance. Then I realized the tragedy of ignorance. Occasionally you see such films—badly written, with no viewpoint and no knowledge, just vulgar and abominable. You ask: "Who in the world would present such a story, spending so much money to produce it?" In this case, it made me realize the tragedy of my friend's ignorance.

Or sometimes I encounter someone who has never studied art. He spends about fifteen dollars and paints a portrait of his wife. He makes her suffer by keeping her quiet day after day. Then he asks me in, but I can't say a word. I look at the wife and then at the painting. I don't know if it's a painting of a pig or an ox—the tragedy of ignorance, one of the three great sufferings.

The other two are anger and desire. Desire is when a young man is invited to a house in some rural vicinity, is accepted as a member of the community and tries to make love to every young girl he meets. It's the first and only thought in his mind. In a couple of days, the people say to him: "You had better go back to New York. This place is too decent for you."

Perhaps in Europe it is possible to count many afflictions, but the Buddha counted these three: desire, anger, and ignorance. We are all living in these sufferings.

We need a lamp in this dark house we live in. We must give birth to our own light. We cannot wait for a light to come from the outside. With our own exertion, as our mother bore us, we must give birth to this sun, this light, to illumine our suffering. Some of those who have no capacity to find the Sun of Wisdom in their minds will be afraid—"I am in danger and in fear. Please help me!" Well, if you do not see and find the Sun of Wisdom in this world of suffering, you are certainly in ignorance.

"When you cherish a wrong view, there is suffering"

There are many wrong views, in India, Africa, and in Japan. For example, in Japan they sometimes worship the image of the phallus. If you observe everything in the world from the right view, nothing exists that is hiding its nature from your eyes. You can look at this and this and this—everything.

I made a poem a long time ago, and I showed it to a friend whom I came across in New York. He laughed at me. From his standpoint, all the poems that exist in the world are filthy stories. That is a wrong view. When a Buddhist takes no particular view, that is the best view. He washes his mind clean. He looks at everything as a baby might look at it—he does not keep anything in his mind. To find this empty mind, I struggled for twenty-five years.

When I attained *sambhogakaya*, I said: "I have found a star!" It is as the Buddha found it.

"When you attain the right view, suffering is eradicated"

When the mind is empty, suffering does not exist. It is just suffering, but it does not belong to you. When I taste sugar, it is sweet. When I drink alcohol, I am drunk and that is all. If you do not like something, you need not take it.

"When you do not have recourse to either view, you realize the original pureness of mind
Where nothing more remains"

It is true. As the Buddha said, we must have the *true* view.

One of the Eightfold Golden Paths is called "right way of living." It says that you must not do anything wrong: you must not keep animals to sell; you must not cast horoscopes; you must not make money for yourself; you must beg alms form door to door, etc. That was the Buddha's right way of living. Later, the monks decided they could accept money. This made a big split among the monks. They split into two parties. Well, of course there was no paper money at that time, so the commandment was against gold, silver, and copper. Today we can accept a check because, according to the commandment, checks are not money. Of course, what was meant was: "You shall not put any value on anything. You shall not accept money while you are preaching Dharma." Buddhism is not worth ten cents, nor is it worth a million dollars.

Though the Buddha's view was right in his own time, it is not right today. Everything happens according to condition, state, time, and place. Conditions change, right and wrong change, too.

"Bodhi is your original nature, but as soon as you give rise to thoughts
You are deluded"

Bodhi, the intrinsic wisdom that disposes you to be awakened, is your original nature. Like a pigeon that will fly 500 miles back to its nest, we have this homing instinct. With it we will find the original home of our soul.

Now take that pigeon flying home. The sparrow says, "That's not the way, this is the way." So the pigeon follows the sparrow. Then the serpent in a tree says, "Pigeon, that is not your way. Come this way." And the pigeon goes the way of the serpent and is strangled. In the same way, all those isms, all the different religious stories and philosophies, keep you from your natural orientation.

"Yet pureness of mind resides within your erroneous mind
If your mind is not biased by any notion, the three hinderances offer no barrier"

Without making errors, you cannot find pureness of soul, so all those sparrows and snakes drive you into the real course. After being driven here and there, you will come back home, as a pendulum swings to the norm and comes to rest. From this point of view, error is good. I studied philosophy and I studied junk and I found the erroneous mind. So pureness of mind resides within your erroneous mind.

On Sunday mornings, sometimes I listen to the radio. In one Sunday school, the minister was teaching the children that Christ was created by God; so, as we read in the Bible, we are superior to other races such as the Arabs and the Egyptians. It's hard on the Arabs, isn't it? Why were only Christians created by God?

With such a teaching, the children grow up biased. Perhaps it didn't mean so much in past centuries, but why must we be biased by such notions today? Many people are crucified, buried alive in such notions.

There is no salvation in religions that throw people into eternal darkness. If your mind is biased, there will be no deliverance from the three sufferings. But if your mind is not biased by any notions, your life will become free of these sufferings.

> *"If you practice the Way*
> *Nothing impedes you"*

This "Way" is the Way of Wisdom to accord with this chapter that has been discussing *prajnaparamita*—the Way of Wisdom to reach the other shore.

"Way," in Chinese, is *Tao*. But this is not the Tao that is the religion of China. This character signifies Dharma. The student must not make any mistake in thinking that Taoism is spoken of from the viewpoint of Zen. Here, Tao is the Way of Dharma. It means, therefore, to practice Buddhism—that is, not just read the Buddhist scriptures, but practice the Way with your body, lips, and mind. If you really grasp the main principle of Buddhism and manifest it with your body, even coughing, sneezing, snoring in your sleep will not hinder this.

"If you practice the way / nothing impedes you." A queer line! But from the Sixth Patriarch's standpoint it is very clear. To people who do not understand the importance of daily life in Buddhism, it is difficult to understand. To follow the religious way, they think they must go to a cave, jump off a cliff, or go diametrically opposite to the Way—perhaps, even go to Broadway nightclubs. Many take such foolish ways, thinking they are the true way. It may be the way for animals, but it is not the way for human beings. For the Buddhist, from the true standpoint, daily life, from morning to evening, from the cradle to the grave, is the way of no impediment.

> *"Always recognizing your own faults*
> *You are in conformity with the Way"*

Of course, you cannot be aware of your faults if your senses are morbid. But if you do not adhere to any notions, you will find out your faults. In the evening, perhaps you will take wine, and the next morning you will say it was too much. The Way is like a compass: the boat points this way, that way, but the point of the compass never strays from the north.

In Buddhism, to be "in conformity with the Way," you practice the "body of commandment." Of course, it is of no use to give the commandments to the inexperienced. But if you practice, you will find your original nature. And when you become quite natural, your mind will free itself from all isms, all notions. Then you will hear a small voice that will guide you. In the West, you call it "the voice of conscience." In the temple, the monk watches the novice until he hears this voice, and then gives him the commandments. The novice must practice meditation for three or four months and experience *samadhi* before he can be given a koan.

In the beginning of practice, you must relax. Take a natural position with no strain to body or mind. Let your mind go free with all those streams and dreams that haunt you, until you gradually concentrate it to the center. To pure mind. Finally, you will not let your mind wander, and you will not think anything at all. It will just be pure mind, and your body will be all muscles, tense as iron. Then you will embody yourself into the universe and embody the universe in yourself. At this time you are ready for the first koan. A student will come into my room and I will give him the koan: "Before father and mother, what were you?" The novice will concentrate himself into the koan with intense, deep *samadhi*.

There are two kinds of *samadhi*: the relaxed and dreamy state that is like sleep where you gather in all the streams of mind; and the tense state where you gather the strength of the body and mind like steel. To give a koan to people who have no experience of *samadhi* is useless. Zen is not for them. You must be able to concentrate, absorb the question by this power, not by the mind. Then you come to the teacher's room and give the answer clearly. If you are wrong, it is "No." And if you come, cross your legs and chatter, I will throw you out.

It is written in the sutras that when the Buddha's mother conceived him in her bosom, the law of commandment appeared in her mind and body. She did not like to see anything killed, and abandoned all ideas of possession. Not wishing to be bothered by property, she gave everything away. Wishing to retire to the sacred way of nature, she made her mind pure to conceive this child. The commandments were revealed in her physical and mental body. The mind must always be like this, not only on the day of conception.

> *"All creatures have their own Ways*
> *But these do not interfere one with another"*

There are many laws written in different types of minds, different species of bodies, different races, creatures, and so forth. When I go to Central Park, I always watch the pigeons and sparrows. From the view of the sparrows, the pigeons must look like elephants. Yet the pigeons do not bother them. We humans should be like that! But we cannot refrain from making trouble and interfering with each other. It's just our ignorance. We do not understand our situation in time and space. We live in a narrow present with no past and no future. In a moment of depression, we begin to struggle and fight. It's terrible. We should not look for the other's fault. We should understand our own fault of ignorance.

> *"Leaving the Way to seek some other way*
> *You will spend you whole life and never find it*
> *Chasing about frantically all your life*
> *Will only bring you anguish in the end"*

In China there is an ancient story about a rich man who habitually looked into a mirror each morning. One day he was sleepy. Looking suddenly into the mirror, he failed to see his head. Thinking it had disappeared, he jumped out into the street, ran about and shouted: "My head! Please find my head!" Finally someone said, "Your head is on your shoulders." When he returned home and quieted down, he realized that he had been looking at the back of the mirror. Well, you cannot find your head by running around the street, can you?

In Japan, if a child is lost, searchers go about beating drums and calling the child's name, and perhaps find the child. But if you go about calling your own name, will you find yourself?

You must find Buddhism within yourself and not in books. The way is written there, the way that is *you*. But you read books, go to church, go to Japan, go all over the world, yet, you do not find Buddhism. The only way to find it is to come home, sit down, and find Buddha within yourself.

If you draw a line from your mother's bosom to the tomb, this line is your living body, your pulse, the expiration and inspiration of your breath. You feed this with the four elements of earth, fire, water, and air. Without these elements, you cannot keep this life. For human beings, there is just birth, life, and death. The way of life is not to be found in books or in temples. You are keeping it by earth, fire, water, and air.

Buddhism, the way of supporting your life, is the Middle Way. It stands between mother and father, or heaven and earth. The first cry of birth is the sign of life. You remember how it was told that when the baby Buddha was born, he said, "Between heaven and earth, I am the only one to be revered." After this, whatever he spoke during his whole life was just the extension of his first words. If you do not understand, ask any baby, "What is the way of true Buddhism?" The baby will answer with the true word, "Wa-a-a!" If you do not find Buddhism in this way, you will never find it. Perhaps you will have gathered many technical terms and degrees from universities. But when you come home, you will honestly say, "I couldn't understand it." Then you go to a Zen master, and he will say:

> *"If you desire to find the true Way*
> *Practice the truth—that is the way*
> *If you lack the zeal to find the Way*
> *You wander through darkness, blind to the Way"*

The Sixth Patriarch means the Eightfold Golden Path. Right practice cannot be from any biased view but must be from the true view. You must take away all the thoughts from your mind—squash them, step on them—so your mind will be pure and not bothered by mind-stuff. This is the first period of your practicing the ascent. When you come down, you will act according to circumstances, using mind-stuff as tools.

"If someone comes and asks a man hanging by his teeth from the branch of a tree, "What is the first principle of Buddhism?" what does he say?" As you observe this koan, the bottom of the tree and top are entirely different.

The Buddha ascended the mountain to attainment. After that, he came down to the Deer Park. Buddhism always takes two standpoints at the same time. This cannot be explained. From your own experience, you will find that these are not two, but only one.

> *"If you are truly practicing the Way*
> *You will not see the faults of others*
> *If you see the faults of others*
> *You are at fault*
> *Even though the other is wrong and you are not*
> *Finding fault is the offense"*

If you are a true Buddhist, you do not spend your time talking about others' faults, carrying gossip from one corner of the city to another. You do not criticize others' opinions, or put down others' viewpoints to obstruct the promulgation of another religion. The real Buddhist is busy seeking wisdom for himself, and has no time to talk about another's faults.

One of the commandments of Mahayana Buddhism is that you should not accuse others of offences. When you accuse others, you should observe that your own ego is showing. If you have really attained non-ego, you will not be disposed to accuse others of any offense. But if you do, your criticizing is itself an offense. Also, if you make some error and ignore it, attributing the offense to another, that's your offense. Why must you pay attention to others' faults? The commandments say, "You should not offend others to please yourself." It is very interesting that we cannot refrain from censuring others.

A monk asked his teacher: "Then why did the Buddha blame all the heretics and teach that his religion was the best in the world?" This is a good question. The Buddha often said, "My teachings are the only teachings between heaven and earth; all the other teachings are wrong." "Certainly he blamed the others to please himself," said a monk. "Why did he do it?" The teacher answered, "In that moment, to the Buddha's mind, there was nothing in the world but Buddha."

Another monk asked his teacher: "It is said in the commandments that you must not abuse another for his offense. So why did Mahakashyapa abuse Ananda and drive him out of the temple?" (Mahakashyapa summed up seven offenses committed by Ananda and after the Buddha's death separated Ananda from the five hundred arhats.) The teacher answered, "In that moment, there was no one in the world in Mahakashyapa's mind but Ananda."

Do you understand this secret part of Buddhism? This is handed down from teacher to pupil, but the teacher does not ordinarily speak about this to his disciples. There is no page on which this secret teaching is described. Mahakashyapa, with great love, drove Ananda out of the temple, like the father who scolds his child, saying, "You foolish boy, why did you do it?" In that moment, the father is embodied in love for the child. There is no one in the world but the child.

"If you eradicate the mind of accusing
You can rid yourself of your afflictions"

You can destroy your afflictions and clear away obstructions. The Mahayana view is that there is no you, no me, nothing throughout the universe. So from the beginning, all those accusing minds are eradicated. Therefore, your afflictions were destroyed from the beginning and there is no obstruction.

If you reach this understanding, there is no trouble in the world, and all your sins are atoned for. They were paid for long ago, for there is no one in the universe. All the offenses that were committed by you and me were eradicated, cleared away from the beginning. But those in ignorance do not know this, so the true man within this ignorance must bear the suffering. He must bear the sin, the offenses committed in ignorance. Originally there was no sin—my sin was excused from the beginning. This commandment really says, "You shall not recognize anyone in the world to be existing."

"If you are are not swayed by love or hate
You can take a rest and stretch out both legs"

If you are not swayed by love or hate, you can lie down and take a rest—you can go to the South Sea Islands and stretch yourself out. If you have the partiality of loving and hating, nothing can go smoothly:

"I will not employ the son of my enemy"; "I need a new girl in the office. This one is coquettish, so I'll take her and not another."

You must not mistake the meaning of the words "take a rest" in this record. If you think that you can just lie down and forget about everyone, then you do not know the secret teaching.

Then there is the commandment that says, "You shall not keep anger in your mind." When you know that there is no one in the world with whom to be angry, your anger can be as pure as the thunder, and it is sacred. But if you say, "I hate him, and I love her," or "I have two girls working for me; I will kick one out to please the other," such anger is not sacred. When a soldier forces his way through a rain of fire, and dashes into the enemy's trench like an *ashura*, there is no one—no friend, no enemy, no self. It is not anger out of hate or for love. It is like a hurricane, a thunderstorm, with no human element in it. This anger is sacred. We say that you can slap Buddha's cheek three times, first one cheek, then the other, then both together, but no more than that. After that, Buddha says, "Get out!"

A Shinto priest comes to his shrine and finds a beggar sitting there in the sun, hunting cooties in his sleeve. The priest grabs him by the collar and throws him out. You find this sacred anger in the Christian Bible when Jesus went to the temple in Jerusalem and threw the money changers out.

"If you wish to teach others
You must have a method"

You cannot convince others of anything if you are not sure of yourself. Even a life insurance man cannot convince a customer unless he is sure of his own ground. But I can sometimes be easily convinced.

Once a little nun, standing by my door, didn't even have to look at me when she asked, "Please, something for the orphans?" and I was convinced. I gave her 35 cents. Or the twelve-year-old girl who came here to the door with artificial flowers—"My mother lost her job. Flowers for only ten cents!" And I paid ten cents. Awful price! Some old woman on a street corner comes up to me—she is a professional beggar—and I give her ten cents. She says, "God bless you." It has a certain dramatic value, for she has had long experience and thinks she is the best in the world. But if the monks are eating a big beefsteak dinner, how can this convince others not to eat meat?

"Do not let the other entertain doubts
Then original nature will manifest itself"

"You shall not slander the Three Treasures"—you shall not disdain or destroy the Three Treasures of Buddha, Dharma, and *Sangha*. Buddha means the universe; Dharma means the mind of the human being; *Sangha* means the community of the whole world. If you understand this commandment, you need have no doubt at all. All those buddhas that you worship—those notions, those favorites of your mind—are not the true Buddha. If you really clear out your mind, sweep out all your notions, then you will see the true Buddha, the true Dharma, the true structure of the whole world, and the true attitude of life. There will be no doubt in your mind, and you will speak bravely, without fear.

Clear your mind of all notions, all isms, and you will realize your own original nature. This will compel others to find theirs. It's a sin to stock another's brain with this and that. Show them everything clearly. Take away their notions and they will find their own original nature.

When I give you the koan "Before father and mother, what were you?" I will destroy every word that you say. Each word that you find, I will throw away. I will clear your mind, and take you back to your original nature. There you will find that which includes the Three Treasures—Buddha, Dharma, Sangha.

And finally there is the last commandment: "You shall not keep anything on the surface of the ground of your mind." The Sixth Patriarch did not speak clearly about this, but I believe this commandment was existing at his time. I am quite sure that you cannot yet understand this, but I hope you will in the future.

"Buddha's Dharma is in the world
It is not realized apart from the world"

Buddhism is in this world of human beings, not on top of the Himalaya Mountains among the clouds, or at the bottom of the sea. It is in worldly affairs—crying, fighting, enjoying, and loving, in these mundane affairs—that Buddha's Dharma dwells. It does not dwell somewhere up in heaven apart from the earth. It dwells in the knowledge of the world.

"If you look for bodhi *out of this world*
It is like looking for horns on the head of a hare"

You cannot find any because there are not any. So when the Buddhist monk takes an aloof attitude and leaves home, thinking the world is a terrible place, and saying, "To hell with it!" it's like horns on the head of a tiger. He can't really renounce the world because there is no place to go.

In the school of Transcendentalism, one goes up to the clouds and stays there, not looking down to this world anymore. But you have to come down for bacon and eggs, bread and butter. Transcendentalism must exist with people and through people if it is to exist at all. Religion cannot transcend the world. The idea of escape and emancipation is no good. For instance, how can you escape death? There is no way to escape from death, or from bread and butter.

It is like this [turns handkerchief]—positive and negative. Can you separate them? Like a sheet of paper, it is one, not two. Back and front, front and back, *samsara* and nirvana. They are just one existence, not two existences—no matter what you call it. It cannot be separated any more than the two sides of a sheet of paper can be separated. Cut it, and it still has two surfaces—front and back. Slice it again, and as often as you do, it is always two surfaces. Life and death is just the same. It is one thing. Like this handkerchief, it cannot be separated.

There is a very interesting and convenient word in Japanese to express this one thing with two surfaces. It is *soku*—"is." [The *Heart Sutra* says that] emptiness *is* phenomena, and phenomena *is* emptiness. So Buddhism is teaching you to annihilate this existence and attain nothingness. But nothingness is nothing but the back part of a sheet of paper. The Japanese fishermen say: "Under an inch of board is the bottomless abyss." Rowing in a little boat to a faraway sea, you can really feel this nothingness.

When consciousness goes, there is nothingness. When consciousness returns, everything reappears. You cannot separate entirely from this existing world when you come to know Great Emptiness. But you cannot understand this mutable existence until you have found Great Emptiness. Returning from it, you think the world, like popcorn, has just popped out from your eye.

In Zen, you see this—two surfaces. With this physical eye you cannot see the two surfaces at once; you look at this and then at that. But in Zen, *at the same moment*, you see both sides of existence. Do you understand this? Life and death are in the same moment. You do not need to separate yourself from the world when you observe the great empty universe, the great abyss.

The mysterious power of Great Emptiness is like a great ocean. It will swallow this physical world in one gulp. You are so small while you strain to hold your egotistic attitude! When you try to resist this great power, to fight this Great Emptiness, it is like a cockroach fighting against an elephant. You cannot prevail.

> *"'Out of the world' is a name for the right view*
> *'In the world' is a name for the wrong view*
> *Away with both views, right and wrong*
> *That is the state of* bodhi *itself"*

In this world, you know you have never seen that Great Emptiness. You cannot perceive it. You cannot conceive it. You cannot dream of it. All you know is the world of desire and the world of appearance. Human knowledge cannot penetrate that Emptiness. But in Zen, you will enter.

When the Buddha was dying, he gave his golden robe to Mahakashyapa, telling him to pass it on to the future Buddha, Maitreya. Mahakashyapa, holding the robe in his hands, went to the top of the Kutagir Mountain and entered into *nirodha-samadhi*, the *samadhi* of annihilation, to wait for Maitreya. Where is Mahakashyapa now?

This is a koan. When you observe such a koan, you will see Great Emptiness. For the first time after your birth, you will see it. Then, when you turn your eye to this phenomenal world, you will really enjoy it. But those who have never seen this Great Emptiness attach to this world—that is the wrong view. The true view is that you do not take any view at all—no-view. No-view is the true view. You will not stand upon *rupa* nor upon *vedana*, nor upon *samjna*, *samskara* and *vijnana*. Standing upon consciousness, you cannot take a true view. So annihilate your consciousness. Do not stand upon it. Then you will see that eternal darkness—the great abyss.

It is crazy to try to describe this darkness in words. You have to see it for yourself before you can understand it. Therefore, when you see Great Emptiness, that is the true view. But the right view and the wrong view are just two sides of a sheet of paper. In the world, out of the world—away with both! That is the state of *bodhi* itself. Now you can observe both views at the same moment.

I think you do not understand this now, but you will later, and it will be of great help in your daily life. There is a koan about this: "In the morning we fasten our eyebrows together. In the evening we associate shoulder to shoulder. What do I look like?"

> *"This chant is the teaching of sudden enlightenment*
> *It is also called 'The Ship of Great Dharma'*
> *You may listen in delusion for ages*
> *But when realization comes, it is in an instant"*

What is this sudden enlightenment? Why did the Sixth Patriarch make this point? Because in his time there were many types of meditation—practices of four or five years. In the Northern School of

Shen-hsiu, emphasis was also placed on long meditations—"Clear the mind and meditate, meditate, meditate!" Shen-hsiu, you will recall, wrote the famous *gatha*: "This body is a tree of wisdom / This mind, a clear mirror / Wipe it diligently always / Let it gather no dust." But the Sixth Patriarch did not emphasize meditation. He emphasized awareness.

In meditation, you naturally go into nothingness, and then, all of a sudden, a flash will give you awareness—"Ah, this is Emptiness!" Awareness is very important. Without it we cannot attain enlightenment. In one moment, a flash of light goes through your brain. This is called *prajna*, and it is also called *bodhi*, awakening or enlightenment. In the Sixth Patriarch's school, this awareness is the important thing.

You take *sanzen* and you make answers to many koans. The master gives you recognition, but though you have passed the koan, you may not have a real understanding because you are not *aware* of your own answer. Then, someday, all of a sudden—"Oh, this was it! Now it is clear!"

For instance, I ask you, "Where do you come from, and where do you go?" You come to my room and go back and forth, but you do not know what you are doing in this Emptiness. I say, "Are you sure?" and you cannot answer. But sometime you will become aware, and then you will know.

Without awareness there is no enlightenment. You listen to your deluded consciousness and suddenly you grasp it. Anyone can do this; even a nineteen-year-old can realize this *prajna*, this awareness. With this understanding, all of a sudden you feel that you are standing in the center of the universe. This is sudden enlightenment.

The saints of ancient days conceived of themselves as living in a desert, in Emptiness. Suddenly they attained enlightenment. In true awareness, at any moment you may hear the voice of God. But in your sleep you will miss it. It is told in the Bible that while Christ was in the Garden of Gethsemane his disciples slept. And Christ said, "Can you not watch with me for one hour?" Keep yourselves awake!

Again the Master spoke: "I have now expounded the teaching of sudden enlightenment in Ta-fan temple. I pray that upon this word, sentient beings everywhere attain buddhahood by seeing their own original nature." Upon his word!

The Sixth Patriarch gave the following koan to Ming, who was pursuing him on top of the mountain: "Before father and mother what was your original appearance?" When you pass this koan, you, too, will realize your own original nature. You can read one hundred volumes of Buddhism, but if you don't realize this true nature with your own physical body, you are not a Buddhist. Without realization, there is no Buddhism.

When Prefect Wei-chu, his staff, and both monks and laymen heard the words spoken by the Master, there was none who was not enlightened. I cannot believe that the prefect, his staff—those long-sleeved subordinates—and both monks and laymen were all enlightened by this sermon of the Sixth Patriarch. I am quite sure there were some dumb ones!

They bowed all together and praised him, exclaiming: "How wonderful! Who would have expected a buddha to appear in Ling-nan!" Ling-nan was supposed to be a country of barbarians—at least those Chinese who were living in Central China called them barbarians. Once a Zen master in Japan wrote me a letter, saying: "How difficult it must be to teach Zen to barbarians!" You must not be insulted by this.

They bowed flat to the ground, pressing their noses on the hard floor and called the Sixth Patriarch a buddha, expressing their belief in the story of Buddha's advent.

CHAPTER III

QUESTIONING

One day the Prefect Wei-chu held a great feast in honor of the Master. When the feast was over, the prefect entreated the Sixth Patriarch to take the high seat. Bowing twice, together with his staff and the others present, Wei said: "Your disciple has heard your Reverence's preaching. It is truly wonderful. However, I have a few questions. I beg you, out of your great compassion, to answer them for me."

The Master said: "If you have doubts, ask me, and I will resolve them for you."

Wei asked: "Your Reverence's teaching must be the teaching that came from Bodhidharma, is it not?"

The Master answered: "It is."

The prefect said: "Your disciple has heard that when Bodhidharma first converted the Emperor Wu of Liang, the emperor asked him: 'All my life I have built temples, ordained monks, offered alms and food. What is my merit from these deeds?' And Bodhidharma replied: 'Really, there is no merit.' Your disciple does not understand Bodhidharma's meaning. I pray your Reverence to explain it for me."

The Master said: "Really, there is no merit at all. Do not doubt the word of the long-ago sage. Wu Ti's mind was wrong. He did not know the true law. He built temples, ordained monks, and offered alms and food. This is what is called 'seeking good fortune.' Good fortune, however, is hardly what one can call merit. Merit exists in dharmakaya. *It does not consist in seeking good fortune." The Teacher continued: "Seeing your original nature is merit. Living in the attitude of same-sightedness is virtue. And when your mind's activity is unhampered from one moment to the next, so that you always see your original nature and have marvelous and spontaneous command of the mind, this is called meritorious-virtue."*

SOKEI-AN SAYS:

The title of this chapter is "Questioning" because the patron, Prefect Wei-chu, an aristocrat, is asking questions of the Sixth Patriarch. Prefect Wei-chu came from the central government of the T'ang Emperor to inspect the political and military offices. He also gathered taxes and brought them back to the central government. This was the prefect's work at that time.

One day the Prefect Wei-chu held a great feast in honor of the Master. Do not think that at this feast there were pork-chops and beefsteaks. The feasts that were given for the Master were vegetable dinners with no wine. Perhaps "feast" is not a good word here. Perhaps it should be some expression like "The Last Supper."

When the feast was over, the prefect entreated the Sixth Patriarch to take the high seat." At the end of the feast, the guests were given finger-bowls to wash their fingers and their mouths.

Bowing twice, together with his staff and the others present . . .": That is, gentlemen commoners.

Wei said: "Your disciple has heard your Reverence's preaching. It is truly wonderful. However, I have a few questions. I beg you, out of your great compassion, to answer them for me." It must have been very beautiful in the vermillion-colored temples. They weren't suffering so badly as today.

"The Master said: "If you have doubts, ask me, and I will resolve them for you." Wei asked: "Your Reverence's teaching must be the teaching that came from Bodhidharma, is it not?" The Master answered: "It is." As you know, Bodhidharma was the first patriarch of Zen in China. Zen students of today who have studied Sanskrit, Pali, and Tibetan have found no mention of him in the records, so maybe, they believe, there was no such person. I tried to find something about him among the official documents but came to the same conclusion. Of course, he is mentioned in some records, but these records are very suspicious. His name was probably inserted at some later date. When I was young, I once asked Dr. Suzuki about this, and at that time he denied the existence of Bodhidharma. But when I asked him again, in later years, he had come to the conclusion that he was an historic figure. However, he said, "The record is very slender." And according to some modern scholar, Bodhidharma arrived in China long before the record. So we're not sure.

In the legend, Bodhidharma arrived in China when he was about a hundred years old and was poisoned there. Of course, no one believed in him at that time, but he did not care about that; the time was not yet good. He tired of teaching, so he went into the Central Mountains, and there he sat for nine years. But I do not believe much of the stuff that was said about him. For example, we are told as children in Japan that Bodhidharma—known in Japan as Daruma—sprouted a root and couldn't get up from his meditation, that both his feet had rotted away!

You will find Daruma on a sign in New York—a restaurant at 1145 Sixth Avenue. Daruma is a very popular name in Japan. Often you will find him pictured like a delicate Hollywood actress. In Zen pictures, he looks fierce. When I went to Boston, someone said that I did not look at all like Bodhidharma.

The Prefect said: "Your disciple has heard that when Bodhidharma first converted the Emperor Wu of Liang, the emperor asked him: 'All my life I have built temples, ordained monks, offered alms and food.'" At that time, the emperor ordained the monks. Today, in Japan, the teacher does this, but he must have the sanction of the emperor and the Educational Board of Japan. You cannot make yourself a monk. It is different from those who say: "I'm a monk from Tibet." "And how do you teach?" "Oh, I teach by lecture and meditation." There are many fakes you know. Bodhidharma was called a fake in his time as well. I have heard it said of me: "That Sasaki is a fake!"

"'What is my merit from these deeds?'" And Bodhidharma replied: 'Really, there is no merit.'" A good answer, wasn't it? And then the Emperor asked, "What is your doctrine? Who are you?" To the second question, Bodhidharma answered: "I do not know." Then he was thrown out of the palace because he had insulted the Emperor, and he immediately went to the mountains.

A great man's attitude is different, isn't it? Bodhidharma did not flatter the emperor, nor did he say, "Your merit is wonderful!" He said, "No merit." The words he spoke then are koans today, so I cannot give any explanation. You must get it yourself.

"Your disciple does not understand Bodhidharma's meaning. I pray your Reverence to explain it for me." The Master said: "Really, there is no merit at all. Do not doubt the word of the long-ago sage." Perhaps he said this much, but the rest of the lines are quite dubious—too trivial.

"Wu Ti's mind was wrong. He did not know the true law." The emperor's attitude was erroneous. He did not know True Dharma. Gathering all his followers, the emperor was expounding on *prajnaparamita* and pretending to live like a monk. What happens to his country while he is reciting and expounding on the sutras instead of regulating the nation? If he does not care to handle the laws of his country, he has the wrong attitude and is a bad emperor. This is not the attitude of a true man.

I discovered a significant record from an old Chinese store in Chinatown that tells about an emperor's wife that was so cranky and jealous that he couldn't live with her. As he had no access to any other woman, he became quite crazy about Buddhism.

"He built temples, ordained monks and offered alms and food." This would be very good if there was no ulterior motive in his mind.

"This is what is called 'seeking good fortune.'" By dint of his effort, he thought he could bring fortune to the country. Not only the Emperor of Liang, but almost all the emperors of ancient days who served Buddhism conceived this notion in their minds. "Well, if I am very good to Buddha, and I am nice to the monks, perhaps the country will become rich, the plague will be gone, the people will be wise, there will be no war, and all of us will be protected. Yes, I will pay my devotion to Buddhism."

"Good fortune, however, is hardly what one can call merit. Merit exists in dharmakaya. *It does not consist in seeking good fortune."* Merit does not consist in devotion to fortune or service to almighty gold. This is supposed to be the Sixth Patriarch speaking, but I am not quite sure. It is has a little smell of Hinayana.

The Teacher continued: "Seeing your original nature is merit." Finding it and realizing it, as when you answer "Before your father and mother, what were you?"

"Living in the attitude of same-sightedness is virtue." If you observe all the usual phenomena—man and woman, good men and bad men, right and wrong, beauty and ugliness, high mountains and low fields—from the *dharmakaya* standpoint, the omnipresent view, and you are standing upon this view, all these appearances are changed into "same-sightedness," the same energy, the same animus. Man and woman, mountain and river, earth and sky—all differentiated appearances—are not really differentiated. From man's subjective standpoint, it can be seen through the five senses. But true existence is just one animus, one existence; there is no difference between good and bad. When you attain *dharmakaya*, in that moment, you will attain same-sightedness. And, if you attain it, you are one who is well-deserving. This same-sightedness is called the *sambhogakaya* aspect. Sometimes the Zen student thinks this is the highest standpoint and does not see this variegated world. Therefore, he cannot enter into the details of existence and act well. This is the so-called transcendental attitude. It is too high and aloof.

When I was a child, my mother made a glove for me. It had no fingers, just one big thumb. It was a mitten. Now, wearing that "same-sighted" glove, can you eat your dinner? No. And, standing aloof, can you live? If you try to stand in *sambhogakaya* and not enter into *nirmanakaya*, it is not good. So-called religious people usually stand aloof and do not see the small details of the true world. Many fall into erroneous attitudes when they return to Oneness. Our attitude is to return from Oneness to diversity. So why not open your eyes once more, see the details, see the true world? Those who return from the One, take off their glasses—"Oh! Wonderful!" The others return once more and same-sightedness is eliminated; it becomes no-sightedness. Those who return to Oneness attain *dharmakaya* and die there. They think this is Buddhism, but this is the Hinayana view.

"And when your mind's activity is unhampered from one moment to the next, so that you always see your original nature and have marvelous and spontaneous command of the mind": Now the Sixth Patriarch limits this *nirmanakaya* appearance, limits it with these details: (1) "Seeing your original nature is merit" is the *dharmakaya* standpoint. (2) "Living in the attitude of same-sightedness is virtue" is the *sambhogakaya* standpoint. (3) "When your mind's activity is unhampered from one moment to the next, so that you always see your original nature and have marvelous and spontaneous command of the mind" is the *nirmanakaya* standpoint.

"This is called meritorious-virtue." Humph, pretty cheap! If this is really the Sixth Patriarch speaking, though I took my hat off, I will put it back on and say goodbye! This is a very poor sermon—if he did really give it. It's just the usual Buddhism.

A Zen master always emphasizes *this* place. To explain Bodhidharma's "No merit" in so many words is really absurd. Perhaps the Prefect Wei was a man of commonplace mind, so the Sixth Patriarch used straw to fill up his brain. My mind is not so filled, so I will not accept this. You will observe it as a koan:

> *Emperor Wu Ti asked Bodhidharma: "What is your sacred doctrine?"*
> *Bodhidharma answered: "There is no sacred doctrine."*
> *The Emperor then asked: "Who are you, confronting me?"*
> *Bodhidharma said "I do not know."*

When you answer this koan, you will understand.

[*The Master continued:*] *"When you are modest in thought, that is merit. When you are polite in behavior, that is virtue. When you manifest all the myriad dharmas from the essential nature of your mind, that is merit. When you regain your mind's original aspect that surpasses thought, that is virtue. When you do not stray from your nature's original aspect, that is merit; and when you respond spontaneously without any self-attachment, that is virtue. If you desire to make merit, make it depending only upon* dharmakaya. *This is the real merit. One who would cultivate merit should not slight others in his mind, but respect others always. Always slighting others in your mind, you cannot forsake your own ego, and there will be no merit. So long as your own nature is false and deceitful, you cannot win virtue in any way. Because of your ego's arrogance, you will always cherish a low opinion of everything.*

"Good friends, when your mind flows without intermission, that is merit. When your mind's activity is balanced and direct, that is virtue. When you train yourself to be one with your own nature, this is merit; and when you discipline yourself, you are possessed of virtue.

"Good friends, merit must be attained though introspection of your original nature; it is not to be sought from almsgiving and offerings. So, good fortune and merit are different. It was not that Bodhidharma was wrong, but that Emperor Wu didn't grasp the truth."

SOKEI-AN SAYS:

When you read this part, it seems not so important; but it is a very interesting part, and I shall explain it for you.

"When you are modest in thought, that is merit." When you place a low estimate on yourself, the attitude of your mind is merit itself. But you must take this attitude as that of a Buddhist whose mind is like the sky, the clear sky. It is not just the usual modesty or humility. It has no dash of clouds in it. There is no idea of boasting. It is the attitude of a child, a good child, not a spoiled one.

When you reach the absolute, the origin of everything, then your consciousness (which is not really yours) obeys the universe. You need not keep any sort of pride, for you are as natural as a pine tree or a weeping willow. This is the sense in which the Sixth Patriarch speaks of "modest in thought," because anyone who has such a thought will be meritorious.

"When you are polite in behavior, that is virtue." Everyone says that the Japanese are a very polite people. Sometimes the Japanese are much too polite. I do not use polite here in this sense. The Japanese are just polite in manner and custom, not from their own minds.

When the mind is modest, your behavior will be polite. But when your mind is egoistic, your behavior will be boastful. So I am not referring to those who have polished behavior, who are polite and smiling but may be keeping something wicked in their hearts. Real politeness must come from the empty-hearted. I do not mean empty like an idiot, but empty like the sky, the clear sky. If anyone is polite in such a way, he will be virtuous.

"When you manifest all the myriad dharmas from the essential nature of your mind, that is merit." This means from your original consciousness, from your eyes, ears, nose, taste, and touch. When anyone talks about the manifestation of original nature, they do not think that eyes or ears are necessary, but just spiritual power. The real manifestation of the whole world is not such a phantom. Dharma has many meanings, but here, in this sense, it means everything—the universe with sky, clouds, color, taste—all phenomena. All you see is the shadow of your mind manifesting from your own mind. If you take off this manifestation, which was created by you yourself, there is nothing—no color, no sound, no mountain, no river.

When you go to Long Beach or Rye Beach or Atlantic Beach, any beach, you see the waves coming from the sea to the shore. You think, that is, that you are seeing it. But if someone drops a straw hat from a boat onto the waves, the waves do not carry the straw hat to the shore. Funny, isn't it? The waves come from the distance to the shore, but they do not carry the straw hat with them. That which is coming is not water, it is something else. In modern terms it is called energy. The energy of the wind dashes against the water, and it is transmuted into waves. This energy comes from the water, so it is the energy which rises, falls, and rises again. The wave is not water, but it is energy coming to the shore. It dies, and at that same moment the energy makes a sound in the air—whuf-f-f! Strange, isn't it? You can prove this.

But what is energy? You cannot see it. When I strike my gong, the sound is a vibration of air. The air does not leave the gong and jump into your ears, but it makes a wave. The sound created by your own eardrum is your own manifestation.

So all the phenomena that we see is our own production. You may call it energy—the scientists may call it electricity—but the Reality that exists is something that no one knows. It exists beyond our five senses. The Buddha said: "The whole universe is empty. There is nothing there." Of course, there was no science in his day, so he did not speak in scientific terms. But today we know that the whole universe is created by waves of energy, and if we think deeply about the speed of these waves of energy, this energy that covers everything at once, that speed is not speed. It is no-speed.

In conclusion, we say there is no speed in the absolute, only absolute stillness. I think you will now understand that all manifestations (mental and emotional) are our own production.

A small-minded man takes this as a very small world. He is angry and suspicious. He puts himself into this position. No one else has put him there. Another man, in the same condition, living in his own world of economics and morality, does it differently. In the Buddhist sense, this can be explained by a koan. But we do not need to speak of this tonight.

"Essential nature" means the untouched consciousness given by nature. This "merit," this highest achievement, is the world of Buddha. It is Buddha's production.

"When you regain your mind's original aspect that surpasses thought, that is virtue." Your original nature is covered—shrouded—and you have to unveil it. You must take off that cover. Make your mind free from all shrouding. Then it will surpass your usual suffering mind.

Once, when an old monk was dying, his disciples asked him, "How do you feel?" He said, "My sickness is running about my body, but it annoys me very little." To him, his sickness was its own business, not his business. Sickness has nothing to do with original nature, and original nature never dies.

"When you do not stray from your nature's original aspect, that is merit": This means that you are not bothered by anything outside of yourself. You stay in Reality, in the state which is not waves or light, but *truth itself*—which you then make available to your needs in daily life.

This part is very important. The Buddhist tries to attain that reality by means of all kinds of contrivances—through koans like "Before your father and mother, what were you?" through struggle, through meditation. Words mean nothing. You have to carry it out, prove it to me, and then I will agree. This is the strangest and best part of Buddhism.

"And when you respond spontaneously without any self-attachment, that is virtue." When you get this, and then come back to daily life. I will say that not making it available in daily life is the shortcoming of Buddhists. Buddhists emphasize the attainment of it, and then forget how to use it. Not making it available is also the weak point in Christianity. (I do not hear anything like this lecture from Christians.) In Christianity, the Bible is like a big cord, like the cord that anchors the Queen Mary; the lines are too big for small meanings. I have never heard the Bible interpreted in its small meanings. It is in their manifestation, drop by drop in the blood of the Western world, that I feel this Christianity.

Christianity must be a living thing. Most Christianity is dead, but you can study it in the nation's mind and activities. Christians are making this "wave" of the human mind available in a small corner. They call it Love. That is the strongest aspect of Christianity. I hope you who are Christians will understand this. Do not wait to be told by a Buddhist monk that Christianity is Love. In Buddhism, we penetrate to the top from the bottom. The Christian penetrates to the bottom from the top.

Some Christian missionaries came to Japan with a Bible in their left hand and a gun in their pockets. They gave us something, yes, but they also took something away. They thought that the Christian God had a plan before creation—Monday, Tuesday, Wednesday. This is *atman*—Ego—not the real God. The real God does not create. He is created from IT. So when you take this planning, scheming attitude, sometimes it is not love but hate. The Christian must break through to the top, and then make IT available to the bottom.

"If you desire to make merit, make it depending only upon dharmakaya." That is, the body of Reality. It wasn't created, but exists always from beginningless beginning to endless end.

"This is the real merit. One who would cultivate merit should not slight others in his mind, but respect others always." If your mind is *dharmakaya*, then the endless universe and *dharmakaya* are in everyone's heart, in everyone's nature, and you will not dislike your fellow creatures because each one has come from that Emptiness.

"Always slighting others in your mind, you cannot forsake your own ego, and there will be no merit. So long as your own nature is false and deceitful, you cannot win virtue in any way. Because of your ego's arrogance, you will always cherish a low opinion of everything." I think this part needs no explanation.

"Good friends, when your mind flows without intermission, that is merit. When your mind's activity is balanced and direct, that is virtue." This means single-mindedly. If you study art, you understand how the mind flows without intermission. Once the mind has no ulterior motive, it just flows out single-mindedly from the bottom of consciousness. It is not so easy to get into this frame of mind. In playing the piano, for instance, if your mind is clear-flowing, your fingers move rhythmically; but if you have a thought that intrudes—"I haven't enough money to pay the rent"—suddenly you are playing louder than is called for.

Single-mindedness is not the result of training, but of your attitude—how you place yourself in the human world. In other words, it is not training but guts. It is very important, this flowing without intermission.

When I first came to this country, I observed that the flower gardens were all arranged according to ideas; nothing was according to nature. The beds were arranged symmetrically, and the colors—pink and white, purple and white—were like a big Christmas cake. Then I realized the scheme of Western life. Western people take everything from nature and boil it down to their *human* nature. This is entirely different from the oriental attitude. Mind is chopped up into the human idea of arrangement, which has nothing to do with nature's natural beauty.

A Japanese artist made an alcove, intending to place a statue in it. In the end, he picked up a little pebble and looked at it all day. To him, it expressed the mystery of the world in a way that no man-made statue could match. The pebble speaks the entire history of the world; no human being can engrave anything on it that would improve it. Beautiful scenery is a work of genius; the artist cannot change anything because it is perfect. A Japanese garden will make you realize the beauty that is not arranged. When you see a volcano, vomiting smoke like one long stroke of the brush, endlessly, uninterruptedly, you can get an idea of this flowing without intermission.

When I was beginning to make poems, sometimes it took me three months to make one poem. Later, it would flow from me in perfect form. I would just take a pencil and write it all at once. If I had to change one word, it would have to be done over from the start, for it would not be in perfect uninterrupted thought. If I changed one corner, I would have to make a new poem.

A poor businessman regulates the actions of his workmen according to his own mind, not of those working for him. A good businessman studies the nature of his workmen and uses them kindly to bring out the best in their natures. It is like getting a new dog; you must use him kindly according to his nature.

"When you train yourself to be one with your own nature, this is merit; and when you discipline yourself, you are possessed of virtue." By this training you will understand how to find your original nature. A snake or a tiger does not need to do this. You must understand the time, the place and condition, and act accordingly. That is good behavior.

For instance, perhaps you are invited to a party on a hot day, and you must go in formal clothes with a swallow's tail hanging behind you. You don't wipe your face using your handkerchief like a bath-towel! This would not be good behavior. Of course, no one will make such a formal invitation to me in New York—only the Japanese Embassy in Washington.

When you train yourself to be one with your original nature, first you must discover what it is. And when you train yourself in good conduct, you must discover what that is. For instance, what is good conduct on the battlefield? To kill the enemy or to save him?

When I was drafted and went to Manchuria, I was 23 years old. I was a monk, but according to the law I had to go. So I had to decide how to behave on the battlefield. As a monk, how do I behave? I had to create a new morality and a new rule of behavior, and I had to bear it.

"Good friends, merit must be attained though introspection of your original nature; it is not to be sought from almsgiving and offerings. So, good fortune and merit are different. It was not that Bodhidharma was wrong, but that Emperor Wu didn't grasp the truth." According to the Sixth Patriarch, finding your original nature was merit. How do you find it? By giving one thousand dollars to China? Emperor Wu Ti's idea was of this kind.

In this country, you do not talk so much about merit, but in our country it is very important. If a lady drops her hairpin in a Japanese street, it is picked up by a boy who may be trying to accumulate merit for his next incarnation. Funny, isn't it? Everyone tries to pile up merit so they will be born in a better house in their next incarnation.

Merit and reincarnation have been connected for a long, long time in China and Japan. Everything that happens is explained by this accumulation of merit. For instance, my friend and I both came from the same temple, but now one is an abbot and the other is begging bread. Of course, from the Buddhist standpoint, reincarnation is just a hypothesis. From the human standpoint, it looks as if it must be so. The human being creates such ideas and then explains everything from them. From the standpoint of Reality, this hypothesis may or may not be true. You can make all kinds of hypotheses in this life. For instance, I am walking on the street, and a beautiful woman smiles. I think she is smiling at me, but she is really smiling at her dog. If I approach her and say, "How do you do?" she will probably slap me. In this way I would find out that my hypothesis was wrong. To explain reincarnation we have a different hypotheses from the usual one. Some day I will explain this.

The Prefect Wei questioned the Master again: "Your disciple always saw that the monks and the laymen invoke Amitabha Buddha because of their wish to be born in the Western Heaven. I implore your Reverence to explain for me whether this is possible or not, and resolve my doubts."

The Master said: "Your Lordship, listen carefully, and I, Hui-neng, will explain it for you."

"When the Buddha was sojourning in Shravasti, he expounded the converting of the mind toward the Pure Land in the West. It is clearly stated in the sutra that the Pure Land is not very far from here. It is 108,000 miles away. Metaphorically, this means the ten evils and the eight errors[10] that are in ourselves estrange us from the Pure Land so that it seems to be at a great distance. The Buddha spoke of the Pure Land as 'far' for those of inferior endowment but as 'near' for those of superior capacity. There are two sorts of humans but not two sorts of Dharma. Enlightenment and delusion differ; awakening takes more or less time on account of differing human capacities. The deluded one repeats the Buddha's name, seeking to be born in the Pure Land. The awakened one purifies his own mind, for, as the Buddha said, 'When the mind is pure, the Buddha land is simultaneously pure.'"

SOKEI-AN SAYS:

In this part, the Prefect Wei Chu is asking the Sixth Patriarch a question about the Pure Land religion. He had seen many monks and laymen muttering words—the name of Amitabha—with the desire to be reborn in the Pure Land of the Western Heaven. This made him doubtful. The inspector general was not convinced by this religion of the Western Heaven, so he questioned the Sixth Patriarch about it.

The Pure Land religion is very interesting when observed from the Zen standpoint; and if you observe any other religion that takes heaven as its faith, it can be criticized as the Sixth Patriarch criticized it.

The Prefect Wei questioned the Master again: "Your disciple always saw that the monks and the laymen invoke Amitabha Buddha because of their wish to be born in the Western Heaven. I implore your Reverence to explain for me whether this is possible or not, and resolve my doubts." The Master said: "Your Lordship, listen carefully, and I, Hui-neng, will explain it for you." Amitabha, or "Amida" in Japanese, means "boundless life" and "boundless light." Amida is the Buddha of the Western Heaven.

In Buddhism there are many heavens. This heaven refers to the beliefs of the so-called Pure Land sect.If you go to Tibet, you will hear the same chant. I am told that recently the Tibetans use electric power to recite it.

In Japan when an old grandmother is dying, she will have this chanted and the children will say: "Please don't die now. We haven't recited the chant a thousand times yet, so you can't go to heaven!" And the grandmother will hold with her teeth to the edge of the bed until they have finished the chanting. Queer isn't it? If you just call the name of Amitabha, you can go to heaven. Amitabha is the sun, the god of the Western Heaven. Preceding this Amitabha, light-worship was probably star-worship. Amitabha was a "looking-down lord." I don't know how to translate this exactly, but it means "looking down on the world from a high heaven."

The Western idea of religion from the beginning was sun-worship, as in Egypt and in Greece. Then it came into Shinto worship. They all worshipped the sun. Sunshine came into the world, into fish, into monks, into everything. The sun is the Son of the Empty Sky, the Father, and it falls to the ground to arise once more in the morning. In Shinto, the sun is considered the Daughter of Heaven and the Mother of the World because it produces and creates. Of course, in the beginning, it was the image of the sun. We think that Avalokiteshrvara worship was brought from the Western world. In Persia it was very important before it came into Buddhism. In Buddhism you will find almost all the elements of all religions in the world, and they can be explained without any superstition. So Amitabha originated in sun-worship. Now it is the Pure Land Sect.

My Zen sect has nothing to do with the Pure Land sect. However, to promulgate Buddhism through this Pure Land idea is not so bad.

"When the Buddha was sojourning in Shravasti, he expounded the converting of the mind toward the Pure Land in the West. It is clearly stated in the sutra": Today we have investigated the old scriptures, especially the *Agamas*, and we find no teaching of this type. Of course, some say there was some sutra that contained this teaching, but it no longer exists. We do not believe that there was any Pure Land teaching spoken of by any contemporary of the Buddha. However, we take this statement as true for the purpose of noting the Sixth Patriarch's view about the Pure Land teaching as a statement made by the Buddha.

". . . That the Pure Land is not very far from here. It is 108,000 miles away. Metaphorically, this means the ten evils and the eight errors that are in ourselves estrange us from the Pure Land so that it seems to be at a great distance. The Buddha spoke of the Pure Land as 'far' for those of inferior endowment, but as 'near' for those of superior capacity." Some people think that the Pure Land, the land in the Western sky, is very far away. It is like heaven. No one can reach there with his flesh, but after death his spirit will go there. The Sixth Patriarch said it isn't very far from here. So 108,000 miles was not intended as an actual number of miles. In ancient days, a thousand miles was an endless distance. The mind of man at that time conceived the infinite in terms of the finite. Therefore, 108,000 miles was an infinite number. So the Sixth Patriarch is saying, according to the text, that it is our notions, ideas, words, and mind-stuff that estrange us from purity.

The Pure Land conception is a round-about way of arriving at a conclusion. In Zen, there is no such lengthy way of traveling. We take a direct way, as in the koan: "Without using an inch of rope, save the one in the bottomless well." And if anyone asks me what the primary substance is, I will slap his face—"Oh, that is it!"

However, the West takes a microscope and analyzes electrons and protons, then gathers the elements analyzed together, builds up concepts, and says, "Well, this is the primary substance." But we in the Orient mediate and meditate and keep our minds like crystal. Then we say: "The mind that we are using now and the primary substance of mind are one and the same mind." This is how we think about the question. The waves and the ocean are substantially the same existence.

From the Zen standpoint, the mind of human beings is a very queer and awkward thing. It doesn't choose a shortcut or even a direct route, but goes around and around. Our attitude, our thinking, is like someone who, wanting to get from this house on West 70th street to South Ferry, goes north to the Harlem River, then to the East River, and finally to South Ferry. For instance, when you start to make a poem, you think you have to use all the adjectives you know. When you want to describe a mountain, you think you must say: "It's soaring into the sky—green, rich, high, and shining in the rain." Why don't you just say, "The green mountain"? So too, when you want to describe original nature, you think you have to use all those technical terms to say one thing. Of course, you make that thing very far away! By expounding it, you estrange yourself from the pure mind. Deeming it far away, you make it so. To think that we cannot reach heaven now, but that after death we go there, is just a notion. In contradiction to this notion, it is said, "Let the heavenly kingdom come to earth." How can one pull the heavenly kingdom down to earth? With what rope?

At any moment, if you lose your notions, you can build heaven on earth. Anyone who supplicates God to make the heavenly kingdom come to earth should know that heaven is on earth and not in the sky. It was the prayer of Christ: "Thy kingdom come." But today, people try to make this heavenly kingdom on earth with charity institutions, shaking tambourines on the street corners, or beating drums. The Buddhist attitude is different: "Go back home and meditate and the kingdom comes immediately. Don't give away food or stop eating for one day. Don't beg for the kingdom to come; just meditate."

To save people *en masse* is not the Oriental way. There is no mass production of salvation. The Oriental tries to convert one by one. We do not want a machinery religion. And to us, the nearness of it is evident. When you prove to yourself what you were before father and mother, you prove IT. The Pure Land is immediately upon the tip of your nose, your lip, your eye. You are standing face to face with the Pure Land. What is in you before father and mother is the Pure land, the pure Dharma.

"There are two sorts of humans but not two sorts of Dharma. Enlightenment and delusion differ. Awakening takes more or less time on account of differing human capacities. The deluded one repeats the Buddha's name, seeking to be born in the Pure Land." One may take a long, long time to pass a koan. Another will pass it at once and chatter, chatter, chatter, and forget it. Which is better? One is like an ox that drags a stone very slowly with a long breath and a strong pull; step by step he gains a foothold. The other is like a prancing pony—gallop, gallop, gallop. This koan business is like washing your hands with soap. Koans destroy all erroneous notions and clean up your mind. Then with that original quality of mind, something flashes through your mind, and you are awake—*bodhi*, satori!

These words are very important, as is the wisdom that awakens, *prajna*. Awakening is the most amazing experience in human life. But there are many different kinds of awakening. It is the same with the awakening to sex which comes to all. When we scientifically awaken to sex, this is to awake only in one direction; we may still be sleeping in many other directions. Awaken in all directions. Awakening also comes at different times, for there is the slow nature, the quick, the shallow, and the profound nature.

"The awakened one purifies his own mind, for, as the Buddha said, 'When the mind is pure, the Buddha land is simultaneously pure.'" When I started to study Buddhism and was studying koans, Zen and Buddhism seemed from my height the size of the whole universe. Today, I must confess Buddhism and Zen are just some old furniture in the corner of my mind. I, today, a man at the age of fifty-five, really

enjoy my own mind more than Zen and Buddhism. But this was a gift from Buddhism, so I appreciate the kindness of Buddhism. This, our heart, is important. We must have something that is original, that is not Buddhism or Zen, science or religion, or philosophy. I did not find it for a long, long time—and Buddhism and Zen were a hard burden. Now I speak about Buddhism and Zen in lectures; but when I am alone I do not speak or think of Buddhism. I enjoy something that has no name but is quite natural. Perhaps you call it the Pure Land. It is wonderful, the Pure Land. Someone asked me to go for a vacation to Nyack for one month, but I refused. I just stay here and live in my own pure mind.

[The Master continued:] "Even a man of the East, if his mind is pure, will be free of sin. And even a man of the West, if he has an impure mind, is sinful. If the man of the East commits a sin, he repeats the name of the Buddha that he may be born in the Western Heaven; but if the man of the West commits a sin, in what heaven will he be born by calling upon the Buddha? Ordinary fools do not know their own nature, so they do not know the Pure land within themselves and pray for rebirth in the East or West. But for the enlightened, wherever they are is the same. As the Buddha said, 'Wherever you are is always serene.'

"Your Lordship, if you do not keep evil thoughts in your mind, the Western Heaven will not be far away. If you harbor an evil thought in your mind, repeating the Buddha's name will not cause you to be reborn in the Pure Land. I advise you now, worthy scholars, first remove the ten evils, and you will cover the one hundred thousand miles. After that, removing the eight errors, you will pass through the eight thousand miles. If you see your own nature at every instant in your own mind and live every day in the even, plain, and straight mind, you will reach heaven and see Amitabha in the time it takes to snap your fingers."

SOKEI-AN SAYS:

To go to the Western Heaven, it is said, you must cover 108,000 miles. Of course, such notions are not scientific but so-called "religious" concepts. It is like the stories of heaven told in Christian Sunday schools. Taken literally, if you think that after death you will be alive in heaven and that you will meet your husband there, you would have to think very carefully before taking a second husband! They were talking about different things in those ancient days. We do not know how to interpret their ideas for today. So we must always observe the wonderful gift of common sense. Common sense is natural; it's better than philosophy or science. We must make our common sense bigger, but our common sense is so small, and *this* is so big.

"Even a man of the East, if his mind is pure, will be free of sin. And even a man of the West, if he has an impure mind, is sinful. If the man of the East commits a sin, he repeats the name of the Buddha that he may be born in the Western Heaven; but if the man of the West commits a sin, in what heaven will he be born by calling upon the Buddha?" This "man of the East" doesn't mean a man of Eastern China. The Sixth Patriarch was talking about the Western Heaven, the Pure Land, so he speaks of the East as of his own sect, the Zen sect.

The word "impure" does not mean the usual purity or impurity. The usual impurity in Buddhism is often taken to mean eating fish or flesh, or walking the street with a lady. I have a friend in California who put out a sign that said, "No ladies admitted here." What is this view? That women are filthy? To me women are very important—mother of my Buddhist child, and mother also of earth. This does not signify that type of impurity.

All mind containing mind-stuff is impure. But if you look at the light and conceive nothing but the light, that is pure mind according to the ancient idea. For instance, when I am burning incense, as I do now, and some thoughts come into my mind—"Oyster, awfully good!"—then my mind is impure. But when I am burning incense with nothing else in my mind, that is purity of mind. This is the original idea of purity and impurity. It is as a baby looks at its mother's face without any other thought. This was the ancient Buddhist idea of purity.

Today we have a different idea of purity. We know more about the mind. When I am doing this (burning incense), through the subconscious state one million different minds pass through every action. So the impure idea cannot be accepted logically because psychologically we no longer accept this idea of purity. The idea of impurity today may be a man drunk at a bar, doubts, entanglements, and unfaithfulness.

The Sixth Patriarch's idea of purity was that the mind must be like a mirror—if there is any cloud, you are sinful. This "sinful" is not in the moral but in the philosophical sense. For instance, if a lady has two gentlemen who are pursuing her for marriage, if she does not think carefully from a sincere heart, then from the Oriental view, she is committing a sin. To cherish a doubt in your mind and not get rid of it, this is sinful.

"Ordinary fools do not know their own nature, so they do not know the Pure land within themselves and pray for rebirth in the East or West. "East" and "West" don't mean anything here. If the man belongs to the East and commits a sin, they think he will perhaps change his flesh and be born in the Western Heaven.

Your primary intrinsic nature is like the clear sky, a clear mirror or clear water. It is not so easy to find your original nature. You are affected, you try to be something—a wise man, a smart fellow, a good or bad man. You are putting something over your original nature. When you have inborn beauty, you do not need to put something over it. Finding your own real heart, you do not need to put anything over it. Good professors are harder to find than a good farmers, for they are more likely to be affected. A Buddhist monk from Tokyo will tell you all kinds of things about everything, but in a mountain temple you can more easily find someone with real heart.

"But for the enlightened, wherever they are is the same, as the Buddha said, 'Wherever you are is always serene.'" The enlightened dwell in their own houses. This means that you do not try to find anything on the outside or inside. If you use your mind to find it, it is too late, and if you use your eye to look at it, it is too late.

Where is your original home? It is not your mother's or your father's house. It is not your apartment. You came from your own home, but you have forgotten, and you cannot find your way back. You search everywhere for the door to your original nature.

You will find it in meditation, a wonderful device. Sit down and rest. In a moment you are in the Pure Land. You don't need to practice meditation for even half an hour. When you come home from business, sit down for a moment on the sofa. One moment is enough to think, "In this moment I am in my original home," and you are there. But if you cannot find it in *this* moment, you can never find it. Your original home is your original nature, and your original nature is enlightenment. You do not need to go to the Catskill Mountains for a vacation.

"Your Lordship, if you do not keep evil thoughts in your mind, the Western Heaven will not be far away. If you harbor an evil thought in your mind, repeating the Buddha's name will not cause you to be reborn in the Pure Land. I advise you now, worthy scholars, first remove the ten evils, and you will cover the one

hundred thousand miles. After that, removing the eight errors, you will pass through the eight thousand miles." The Sixth Patriarch states very clearly, "If you do not keep evil thoughts in your mind, the Western Heaven will not be far away."

You must keep that feeling of rest. Even though you are on the battlefield, the place of your mind must be in that place on the sofa. When you come back home from your office, take a bath, put on your slippers and pajamas and go to your sofa—you have nothing to think about. You think of nothing, for the work of the day is done, and the work of tomorrow is not yet begun. In that moment, when you need think nothing, the Western Heaven is not far away. *This is heaven.*

When I was in Japan, I was a sculptor, but when I came to America, I realized I had to give it up. I changed my art and became a poet. As an artist, I needed many things: a studio for painting, paints, canvas, brushes, and for carving—clay, wood, and knives. But as a poet, all I needed was a pencil and a piece of paper and the corner of my bed. Finally, I could not even be sure of keeping my bed, nor my trunk, nor even my suitcase. So my pen became my standing point; or perhaps it was the paper at the bottom of the pen under the sky that was the wholeness I had to have. But most often I found it on a corner of my bed.

When the Sixth Patriarch advises removing the ten evils he is giving a lecture about Buddhism, and it is not important. He is speaking about the 108,000 miles that separate you from heaven. The ten evils means not being in accordance with the ten commandments. Of course, one of the most important ones is: You must not disdain the Buddha's Law, which is the law of the universe. You must not speak despisingly of the universe. When you truly come to understand the universal law, there is nothing to despise and nothing to be denied. You will find a wonderful world, a real heaven. You will have great freedom and a peaceful heart. If you are a statesman or a president, you must have this understanding or else you cannot bring peace to the world around you. You must look at everything according to its own nature, accepting everything, the ugly bedbug as well as the beautiful nightingale. You shall not let the Buddha's Law disappear. If you really observe this commandment, you don't need to pay attention to any of the others. Just this one is enough. It is the true law of Buddhism.

The eight errors correspond to the Eightfold Golden Path. If you have followed this path, you have covered the 108,000 miles and have already gone to heaven. This was the idea of the Sixth Patriarch as he explained it to Prefect Wei.

"*If you see your own nature at every instant in your own mind and live every day in the even, plain, and straight mind, you will reach heaven and see Amitabha in the time it takes to snap your fingers.*" The "snap of the fingers" is the Indian view of a short moment.

If you have really passed the first koan, you will know the "even, plain, and straight mind." But few students can penetrate so deeply at first. So, passing through many koans, gradually disburdening yourself of the many heavy cargoes you bear in your mind, eradicating your many afflictions and your ego, at last you will find this even mind and will live every day in it. Finally, you will become aware of *this* moment. Your mind will be clear and mellow. Your physical body will be as big as the universe, and you will realize that without this awareness, you cannot enter Buddhism, though you meditate for a hundred years. Your soul pervades the universe, and you become one with it. You don't feel that your skin sets any boundary to your body—"Oh, this is it!" In Sanskrit, this is called *bodhi*. Without it, there is no Buddhism. It is as when Mahakashyapa called Ananda, and Ananda answered, "Yes!" In that moment all wisdom burst into his mind. Wonderful moment!

When you attain to *this* moment, you will attain to that even, plain, and straight mind. Sit down upon your cushion and sooner or later you will attain awareness, and you will enter Buddhism. Therefore this *bodhi* as taught by the Sixth Patriarch is important. You will reach heaven in the snap of your fingers.

[The Master continued:] "Your Lordship, if you simply practice the ten virtues, what need is there to pray for rebirth? And without extirpating the ten evil minds, what Buddha will descend from heaven to receive you? If you are enlightened to the unborn by the teachings of sudden awakening, you will see the Western Heaven in a moment. Without enlightenment, even though you pray to the Buddha to be born there, heaven will remain far off.

"How can you ever arrive there? I, Hui-neng, with all of you, will move into the Western Heaven in this very moment. Behold it before your eyes! Do you all want to see it or not?"

Bowing, the multitude said: "If we could see it right here, what further need would we have to pray to the Buddha for rebirth there? Oh, Master, we entreat you, in your benevolence, to reveal to us the Western Heaven, that we may all be able to see it!"

SOKEI-AN SAYS:

The Sixth Patriarch is giving a commentary on the Pure Land faith from the standpoint of Zen, his Zen. To think heaven is far away is the usual conception of all kinds of religious people. But the Zen school teaches that heaven is not in the Western sky, nor in the East, but within your own mind. If you find heaven within your own mind, you will realize the heaven of Zen on the face of the earth.

"Your Lordship, if you simply practice the ten virtues, what need is there to pray for rebirth? And without extirpating the ten evil minds, what Buddha will descend from heaven to receive you?" From the Christian standpoint, we cannot meet God without the intercession of Christ. In the Pure Land sect of Buddhism, your prayer will be heard by chanting the name of Amitabha. But from the Zen standpoint, it comes through awakening. Though you meditate for a hundred years, if awareness does not come, you cannot see God. This awareness is the Son of God. So, from our standpoint, Christianity is very easy to understand. (I wonder how they would understand this. Perhaps they would say that it profanes the sacred teachings!) You must awaken as a Christian just as Shakyamuni Buddha awoke. Through Buddha we reach the East and the West. If one speaks straight, all religions are one.

The Pure Land people believed that after their death, they would be received in the Western Heaven and would have a new birth in the Lotus Land. So, accordingly, the name of Amitabha Buddha was invoked. Offering their supplication, they believed they would be received by Amitabha. But the Sixth Patriarch said: "If you simply practice the ten virtues, what need is there to pray for rebirth?"

The ten virtues can be boiled down into one. To express this, I would say it is an even mind: natural as a tree, as the clouds of the sky, natural as rising smoke, without attachment or any particular view. This is according to the law of nature. The human mind must be like this. Then you know how to react, how to fight a good fight. That is the result of practicing the ten virtues. But when you see somebody walking on your green grass, you throw a stone at him. With such an ill temper, you may kill a man. An elder sister gets a beautiful kimono; the younger sister goes with the scissors and cuts it to pieces. Or someone marries a beautiful woman: "She is too good for him. I will kill him!" These are examples of the ten evil ways of thinking.

"If you are enlightened to the unborn by the teachings of sudden awakening, you will see the Western Heaven in a moment." This "unborn" is an important term in Buddhism. In Japanese it is just one word, *musho*, no-life. Because it was not born, there is no mortal life that will die. Curious! In other words,

nothing is created because the life of elements has no beginning and no end. When we are sitting on chairs, twenty or thirty people looking at each other, everyone seems to have his own soul. But if we think, "There is just one soul," then our individual souls are as if stretched and woven together to make the world, the universe. Perhaps, you will be washing your face and all of a sudden—"Oh, this is not a small soul,"—it will come to you. In that moment, you have sudden enlightenment. Those of you who take *sanzen* will see the heaven of the Western world.

"Without enlightenment, even though you pray to the Buddha to be born there, heaven will remain far off." Amitabha will not come, even with all your relatives surrounding your bed reciting the name of Buddha.

In this country there is no Amitabha, but there is: "Oh, good grandmother, do not die until you have signed your last will to me!" And grandmother, trying to live one moment longer, holding pen in hand, breathes her last.

As a ceremony, the dying moment is of great significance. Confucius said: "When a bird is dying, it cries; it is beautiful. And when a man is dying, he speaks; and it is beautiful." Observing the dying moment in both bird and man, Confucius saw beauty. The great man does this, but the small man pays no attention. He does not take off his hat, even if his friend dies on the battlefield.

"How can you ever arrive there? I, Hui-neng, with all of you, will move into the Western Heaven in this very moment." The Sixth Patriarch was speaking to everyone, to the whole world, when he made this statement. This was many centuries ago. As soon as they heard this, they knelt down, joined hands and realized that heaven is right here. Such a simple religion! It will be easily accepted by the even mind. Do not think that Zen is complicated. It is a plain road.

"Behold it before your eyes. Do you see it, or not?" Now, in this very moment, said the Sixth Patriarch, if you wish to move into the Western Heaven, watch your step! We shall move right now. Behold it now before your eyes. Look at it *here*. Don't look for it in the sky or on the earth. Look at it in front of you! It's as when Lin-chi said to his followers: "Do you want to meet the patriarch, the Buddha? He is none other than you who stand before me listening to my talk." Here, the Sixth Patriarch called it the Western Heaven.

If you try to see *this*, it is not in any name, whether you call it heaven or hell. Neither is it God or Buddha, man or demon. If you try to look at *this*, to the right or left, in front or in back, you cannot find it. And if you try to find *this* inside or outside, you will also fail to find it. To find it is as hard as for a sharp sword to cut itself. It can cut something else, but not itself. It's as if a candle flame were to try to burn itself: it can burn something—my finger, this handkerchief—but it cannot burn itself. A mirror reflects all of existence, but it cannot mirror itself. So when the human mind tries to find something outside itself, it also fails to find itself. Therefore, the Sixth Patriarch said: "Look at it immediately before your eyes, and you can see it."

Failing to find it outside yourself, you try to find it in a name, and you fail again. The true teacher is not outside of you. Nor can you find it inside youself, for there is no inside. What do you mean when you say "inside"? Inside your stomach? Inside your brain? The inside of a brain is just like the inside of a radio. Perhaps the sound comes from the inside of a radio, but the waves, the cause of the sound, are not there, the vibration is not there. So, too, the cause of yourself is not inside you. Fire is not always in the candle flame. Something comes from the outside to feed the flame, and it appears here.

Do not think that consciousness is like a telephone operator always sitting on a chair in your brain. If you seek it inside or outside, you may find the waves of consciousness; but you will not find any function of consciousness. It's like trying to catch a fish in the water. If you try to catch it in front of you, it appears in back of you, and vice versa. It is very hard to catch. In an airplane, you can see in almost all directions, but there is one blind spot: you cannot see the tail of the plane. When you try to find your own being, you cannot find it because it is your blind spot. Do you wish to see it?

Ananda was a disciple of the Buddha, an attendant. After the Buddha's death, Mahakashyapa transmitted the Buddha's sacred message to Ananda. Until that time, Ananda hadn't awakened to the Buddha's enlightenment. Ananda questioned Mahakashyapa: "The Buddha transmitted to you his robe and bowl, and beside these there was something else. What was this esoteric teaching?" The Buddha transmitted all of the written teaching to Ananda and the esoteric teaching to Mahakashyapa. So when Ananda questioned Mahakashyapa, "What was it that was transmitted?" Mahakashyapa called his name, "Ananda! Ananda!" And Ananda answered, "Yes!" "Pull down the flagpole in front of the gate." In that precise moment, as Ananda stood there, all of a sudden enlightenment burst into his mind—"Ah! *This is It!*"

What is *this*? It is no secret. *This* is Zen—so plain, so apparent. There is no mystery in it, but everyone calls it esoteric. When you come into Zen, there is nothing esoteric. Everything is as clear as your own palm before your eyes.

In India, there was the sect of the Jains, an esoteric sect. Their doctrine is not so different from Buddhism, but it has one creed that keeps all things in their naked shape—they will not speak a word or express anything. Zen is like this; it handles everything in its naked shape. It transmits naked soul to naked soul without a word. This is the esoteric teaching. This is the foundation of daily life.

From the day when you see this, you will not wear a mind made in a factory. You may wear clothes made in a factory, but you will make some changes before you put them on. It is the same with your mind. The mind that you wear is made by somebody else. All your thoughts are made by someone else, and you are squeezed into this factory-made mind and these factory-made thoughts, living there from morning to evening. You live and perform in mob thoughts, mob consciousness, and mob psychology. From birth to death you never see your naked soul, which is always covered with its factory-made clothing. In the end of life, in the moment before death, you will regret that you have never seen your own naked mind. You had better wake up, see your naked mind, and make your own clothes. In the restaurant, you can see them all wearing the same clothes. Look on the rack and you will see that all the men's hats are alike. Not only do people look alike, but they manifest their emotions alike. In this way, they live and die. That is human life. What a shame! What use is there in bearing such agony to perform such foolishness? You must see your naked soul once in your lifetime, find its beauty. Then you will find your Western Heaven with the Buddha sitting in it.

Bowing, the multitude said: "If we could see it immediately here, why should we supplicate the Buddha for our birth in Heaven?" This direct religion is different from indirect religion. Indirect religion leads you through the sky, where you find yourself behind some cloud. But direct religion destroys the clouds of the sky in your mind, as you kill an annoying fly in the palm of your hand. When the clouds are destroyed, heaven immediately appears. So do not supplicate: "O God in heaven, please let me have five dollars in the evening to buy a new hat!" Or, "O Father, all humans are in agony; out of your mercy please stop the revolution in Spain!" Of course, indirect religion is not bad; it has meaning for sleeping minds. But it doesn't to my mind.

I was the child of a Shinto priest, and from the age of seven, I saw that it was foolish to supplicate. I wished to see who God was, so I went, in my father's absence, into the sanctuary of the shrine. There I found a mirror, and in that moment, I understood what God was. So I always tried to find the God that is not in form and not in the sky, on the earth or anywhere. God was very near to me always.

When my father died, I was told by another Shinto priest to go to the shrine and bring back holy water to sprinkle on my father's face and dead body. But when I opened the shrine, I immediately felt a great wall between that God and myself. I realized that my mind did not penetrate to that God, and I came back empty-handed. The priest said to me, "Why didn't you bring back the holy water?" I answered, "No use."

Queer! As a child, when I really needed God, I found a wall between him and me that I could not penetrate. It filled me with a deep question. At that time, I was fifteen years old. Though I was born in the house of a Shinto priest, and from infancty had no doubt that I was in the bosom of God, when I really needed a God, I could not reach him. He wasn't in the shrine, and he wasn't in heaven. I couldn't save my father by supplication to God. But when I came to the Zen school, I was given a koan in *sanzen*: "Before father and mother, what was your original aspect?" When I destroyed this first koan and got into this original aspect, I met God, and I destroyed this question that had bothered me for years. That was a very long time ago. It was the first step, the entrance into true Buddhism. So I never supplicate the Buddha for my birth in heaven because I know where heaven is.

"Oh, Master, we entreat you, out of your benevolence, to reveal to us the the Western Heaven, that we may see it!" They were good-hearted people, honest and sincere. I was a child in the modern period, but these were people of the seventh century, and they were simple and naive.

The Master said to the multitude: "Your physical body is a castle. Your eyes, ears, nose, and tongue are the gates thereof. There are five gates outside, and inside there is the gate of consciousness. Mind is the ground, nature is the king, and the king dwells upon the ground of mind. When nature is governing, the king is enthroned; when nature fades, the king is no more. When nature is governing, body and mind exist; when nature fades, body and mind are destroyed. You will attain buddhahood in your own nature. Do not try to find it outside yourself. When your nature is deluded, you are a sentient being; when your nature is awakened, you are Buddha. Compassion is Avalokiteshvara; joyful giving is Mahasthamaprapta. That which purifies is Shakyamuni Buddha; that which is plain and straight is Amitabha Buddha. The human ego is Mount Sumeru; greed is the ocean; passions are the waves. Venomous harm is an evil dragon; falsehood is a truculent ghost; anxiety is a shark; avarice is hell; folly is a beast."

SOKEI-AN SAYS:

This nature about which the Sixth Patriarch is speaking is different from our usual understanding of nature. We might say: "Nature in the Yosemite Valley is very beautiful." Nor is it as we might say of someone: "His nature is sweet." If the mind is an ocean of fire, this nature, as used here, expresses an idea that is like the fire vibrating in a candle flame. You remember when Prometheus went to heaven and brought down fire to the earth? This fire is nature, in English, animus. It is like our alaya-consciousness, the foundation of manas consciousness.

The Master said to the multitude: "Your physical body is a castle. Your eyes, ears, nose, and tongue are the gates thereof. There are five gates outside, and inside there is the gate of consciousness." This "gate of consciousness" is important. Everyone's gate is called "I." Temporarily, I call this the "I-gate." If you awaken, this I-gate becomes *prajna*.

Whenever my Aunt came, when I was a child, she would give me some kind of candy, so I was always eagerly awaiting her coming. One time, she arrived very late. It seemed to me that I woke up and ate that candy, for in the morning I found some squashed on my pillow, and my mouth was smeared, but I could not remember eating it. Why didn't I taste that candy in my sleeping mind? I couldn't remember because I didn't taste it with my waking mind. Sleeping mind is different from awakened mind. It's as though you were sleeping in broad daylight under the sun. You look at the sun with your eyes, but you are snoring. That is life.

A *sanzen* student once asked his master: "What is the difference between the sleeping life and the waking life?" The Zen master said: "Can you make a distinction if you put frost on snow?" Your I-gate must awake so that you can see both sides at once.

"Mind is the ground. Nature is the king. And the king dwells upon the ground of mind." This "mind," or "soul," is *hsin*; and "nature" is "orginal nature."

This mind or soul is not like the English soul, which is like a jack-o'-lantern, a fire which, after death, will go away somewhere. What a childish idea! Nor do we mean the soul asleep under a rock or stone in some corner of the earth, which hides away until the Last Day when the angel blows the golden trumpet and awakens the dead to be judged. There is no such soul in existence! This soul is like the ocean, the great empty ocean. Buddhists are always talking about this empty, bottomless, boundless ocean. This ocean is the ocean of soul. In English, you might call it the "chaos of the infinite." Really, you cannot say anything about it, yet it is the foundation of the Buddhist "conception."

In the Buddha's enlightenment, there is nothing that is taken as the center, such as the sun, the moon, a star, or a spark in your mind. The Buddha's enlightenment is the chaos of the infinite, the ocean of soul. If you gather it many, many times in your palm, you will see it is a moonprint from the bottomless and endless ocean of timelessness and spacelessness. The moon is the nature, original nature or Self you gathered from the ocean of soul. But if you gather it only once or twice, you will never realize it. When you have gathered that moon many times, you will finally realize that this is the moon that is floating in the empty ocean of soul and that you have gathered it. This is the soul of all life, sentient and insentient. This nature, this moon, is the mind of all sentient beings, the empty soul of man, woman, trees, and weeds. All that grows and perishes has this nature within it. When you see this nature within yourself, it is beautiful, and it is the king. It dwells upon the earth of soul, and it shines in the empty, eternal ocean.

If you observe all the universe in such a way, you will realize that heaven in your own mind. Do not think that it is outside, at the end of the universe. Know that it is immediately here. Gather it from the empty ocean like a child that finds its own birth in the empty ocean of soul.

"When nature is governing, the king is enthroned; when nature fades, the king is no more. When nature is governing, body and mind exist; when nature fades, body and mind are destroyed." Then everything becomes disordered and you die. If you say that the brain is first, the mind is second, and the heart is third, then nature is fourth and soul is fifth. That is all that governs you, but they are one family. Soul is the father-consciousness, and nature is the mother-consciousnsss; then there are heart, mind, and brain.

I don't think Westerners make such an order, but to understand mind activities, it is better. The nature of which the Sixth Patriarch is speaking here is the mother-consciousness. So it would be better to say: "When the queen is governing, the king is enthroned; when the queen fades, the king is no more."

When nature fades, the body will die. Thus, the whole world disappears from you, and you yourself will disappear from your own consciousness. Then your consciousness disappears and returns to the ocean of nirvana. All the beautiful things, the ugly and the good things end there. From my own view of my own life, I realize that in my youth I was using my brain. Later, I used my mind and heart. These days I am trying to use my own nature. Where you place the center of your activity determines your attitude toward your own life. You must understand this.

When Japanese children study, they have to draw Chinese characters with a brush. They cannot make very big characters because at first they use their fingertips. Then, when they study character writing from a teacher, the teacher says: "Don't touch your hand to the table. Hold your arm in the air." The child says: "How can I make small characters this way?" His hand shakes. The teacher says: "Put your strength in your shoulder, don't move your hand or elbow. Let your hand relax and draw the character from your shoulder." You can do the smallest character in this way. The student can then write either small or large. Sometimes, at first, the child will hold the brush too tightly. If using a pencil, he can break the point. Then the teacher will try to take the pencil from his hand until he is holding it so lightly that it can be easily slipped out of his fingers. Finally there will be rhythm in the movement of the pencil-work, and it will be free and easy. If a big character is to be painted, even the hip is used to give greater force to the flow of the lines. Then it is the whole body that is used and not only the shoulder. I am not an expert in golf, but in looking at how it is played, I observe that there is also this movement from the hip. If the player strikes from the shoulder, the ball does not drive straight. In boxing also, I observe that the boxers give the successful blows with the body. All art has this same knack. When I was studying wood carving, I was afraid that I would hit my hand with the heavy hammer, which I struck from my elbow. Then my teacher showed me a big arm angle and said: "Swing it from the shoulder." It is always said, you must use your head. But when you use your own brain, you make many mistakes. I say, use your father-and-mother consciousness. Keep your mind and brain and heart relaxed—free.

When I was studying oil painting, my teacher said: "Don't hold the brush so tightly. Hold the far end lightly." In such a way, you can hold your brain, mind, and heart very easily. Keep your strength in your nature and soul. Do you know how to do this? I am quite sure that you have not yet found your soul and nature. You must find them. When you do, you will hold the upper structure of consciousness lightly, so that it can relax, so it can vibrate—taking action and reaction easily. If you hold it tightly, the tension kills the function. You use your brain and not your own nature. You must draw yourself down to the level of nature. Hold the drawing-pen lightly!

Great generals who command armies must understand nature's movement, which takes action in the farthest sphere and in the human heart. It is like the ebb and flow of the tide. To land an army from the sea at low tide would be foolish. Wait until high tide to reach the shore, then energy and time is conserved. In time of flood-tide, you push the boat into the sea; you don't struggle with it in ebb-tide.

The nature of the human being is in company with the nature of nature. When you really feel your feet touch the ground and come to the father-consciousness, then you feel that the sky is shining on your back, and standing upon the earth, you feel yourself become divine.

In book-reading or in movie-going, you cannot get this. To get it, you must sit down on the floor and throw yourself into nature. Breathe in the rhythm of nature, then you will find nature within and without yourself. Then the brain becomes easy, vibrating in accordance with communication and function. Otherwise, tension fills the brain and it becomes fixed, squeezed like a lemon.

Sometimes you see people like those in the subway with their faces all puckered and screwed up. They are too tight to function. However, when you see the picture of a bodhisattva, you see a face that has a tranquil expression. Sitting upon a rock, motionless, its expression is one of serenity and will power. Its brain is cool and its heart calm. It has a pliant attitude, as pliant as the smoke of incense. Like the branches of a weeping willow, it moves at the mercy of the wind, but deeply rooted. This is the feminine attitude. Pliant of mind with a deep root in nature, like the weeds in the marsh, nothing can break it. If one takes the attitude of the willow bending to the wind, one will never be uprooted. But if one takes the attitude of a straight pine tree, one clap of wind can snap the trunk and one will fall.

You will attain buddhahood in your own nature. Do not try to find it outside yourself." When you find your nature—Hmm!

You won't find buddha in the brain but in your true nature. You won't find it in the church, temple, or library, or in lectures. You will find it immediately in your own nature. Then you will attain buddhahood. When you give up clenching your brain and kneading your heart like a piece of dough, and just sit down upon your own Christian light, you will find your nature there. Of course, sitting down is not the point. Finding your nature is the point. And by sitting down quietly, this consciousness becomes like a bolt of electricity from the brain to the soul. So you will find *prajna*. It gives you enlightenment.

This is *not* the structure of the backbone of the body, even though you concentrate on each joint of the spinal column and call each by name, painting them in different colors. I don't give a fig for that kind of thing. When the ancient sutras speak of "backbone," the backbone of the skeleton is not meant. It has been falsely interpreted by some Indian teachers. What is meant here is the backbone of consciousness, the structure of consciousness, from the soul to the brain. Half-baked yoga is very dangerous. It makes people into worms. Such teaching is erroneous.

"When your nature is deluded, you are a sentient being; when your nature is awakened, you are Buddha." If you cannot find your own nature, you cannot find your own brain, nor your own soul. You are like the child that goes to a formal party wearing his father's high silk hat—you are not living your own life. You are living in somebody else's thoughts and ideas.

"Compassion is Avalokiteshvara": Compassion is love, and Avalokiteshvara is the image of this compassion. He will enter all the vessels of the human heart, into every part of one's being. Bodhisattvas associate with others in compassion. That is love, a wonderful thing. But here is one more thing that is as important as love.

"Joyful renunciation is Mahasthamaprapta." Renunciation is "to throw away." It is represented as a bodhisattva or a sage with a two-edged sword in hand. He is very calm. Renunciation means that you give up all worry—*all* worry. When you worry, squeezing your face like a lemon, you must give it up. Go to the washroom and scrub your face, then brush it with talcum. But giving up is not so easy!

When I was thinking about coming to America, trying to make a decision to become a monk, I hesitated many times. I had no business with which to support myself. Where would I get donations? How would I live? I thought I might starve to death. So I worried and couldn't decide to take the vow of a monk. It's easy deciding on a job, but it's hard to give up. Renunciation is the hard way. Well, if I go to the river bank, sit there and starve, perhaps death will visit me. My relatives will think me crazy, my wife will run away, and my children will abuse me. So in my own mind, I had to make a vow, as Shakyamuni decided to sit under the Bodhi Tree: "I will not give up until I come to the conclusion of my philosophy, my thoughts."

I had decided, like the Buddha, that I would not give up before I had attained enlightenment. After Shakyamuni's enlightenment, he took a bath and accepted milk from a little cowgirl. The Buddha was a true prince, but he had renounced everything. To rid himself of the agony of his mind, he left home. So when he gave up the practice of asceticism, this was his conclusion: he accepted milk from a cow-maid. Of course, this is to be taken symbolically: she is nature, the mother-consciousness.

The power of renunciation, personified, is a sage, a bodhisattva. This renunciation and compassion make a balance. If you love someone, you must have renunciation on the other side, or else your love is attachment. In human life, the most noble thing is renunciation, and the sweetest thing is love.

"That which purifies is Shakyamuni Buddha; that which is plain and straight is Amitabha Buddha." That which purifies is personified by Shakyamuni Buddha. He sweeps your unimportant mind away.

Amitabha Buddha, as you know, is the god of the Western Heaven. His name means "boundless light"; he personifies peace. Amitabha worship came from India. It was not originally from China.

While the people of India are worshipping the setting sun, the Japanese are worshipping the rising sun; and in the Tibetan hills, where the evenings are very beautiful, the temple gongs vibrate their tones in the desert, and all kneel down. Man naturally knows how to make his mind pure in the deep moment of worship. Bowing to the setting sun can be a wonderful moment. These days, you come back from work, take off your clothes, bathe, lie down, and smoke a cigarette. This, too, can be a wonderful moment.

"The human ego is Mount Sumeru; greed is the ocean; passions are the waves": "Mount Sumeru" is the great mountain which fills the whole inside of you, all made by yourself. You put your brain on top of this mountainous ego, and observe the world so. Do you like that type of observation?

"Venomous harm is an evil dragon": "Venomous harm" is when you try, by contrivance, to ensnare your enemies and kill them, not knowing why. The one who was killed didn't know why, and the one who killed didn't know it was for revenge. This is "an evil dragon."

"Falsehood is a truculent ghost": This is contriving to tell lies without showing your face to your enemy. You are like a ghost, hiding yourself as you try to harm another.

"Anxiety is a shark": Anxiety is like a fish that comes slowly to your feet without making any noise, and all of a sudden takes over your life.

"Avarice is hell; folly is a beast." You are devoured by your own desire.

All consciousness is your own mind activity. When you make gingerbread, it is your own cooking. And you try to live in the world you have made. How can you live comfortably? You must try to live in Great Nature. I shall try to explain this later.

[The Master continued:] "Good friends, if you always practice the ten virtues, heaven will come to you. If you annihilate your ego, Mount Sumeru will crumble, turning a somersault. Then the sea of desire will dry up; the waves of suffering will vanish; the fish and dragons of danger will be no more. The Buddha of self-awakening who dwells upon the ground of your mind will radiate his effulgence through the six outer gateways, and the force of his purity will conquer the six heavens of the world of desire. When your original nature turns its light within, the three kinds of poison will be driven out and all sin deserving of hell torture will be instantaneously wiped away. Thus your mind within and without will become bright and penetrating, no different from the Western Heaven. Without performing this practice, how can you reach there?"

Having heard this, the multitude were fully awakened in their original nature, and all made a bow, declaring in one breath: "How wonderful! May all sentient beings who hear this awaken at once."

SOKEI-AN SAYS:

This part of the record shows the naivete of men's minds at that time. The Sixth Patriarch, using metaphors, destroyed their superstitions, but they still believed they would go to the Western Heaven after death, that they would be accepted as children by the hand of Amitabha, and that they would live in peace and happiness forever on the lotus flowers blooming in the pond of pure, heavenly water.

This type of faith is comparable today to the Christian faith. Its adherents believe there is a heaven in the sky and that the child who died will be waiting for them at the Golden Gates, surrounded by a golden cloud. A professor once told me that animals do not think, but they dream, and when they dream, they dream in images—trees, water, cats, cows. People in the cave age, since they didn't have many words to express their thoughts, composed their thoughts in images like those in dreams. The golden gates of heaven, lotus flowers, and crystalline ponds, surrounded by clouds like rainbows, are cavemen's thoughts. Civilized beings do not cherish such childlike illustrations in their minds. The Sixth Patriarch was attempting to destroy all those picturesque religious thoughts, so he spoke in metaphor.

"Good friends, if you always practice the ten virtues, heaven will come to you." If we are to draw up to the table of human life, we must have some sort of commandments in order to live with others without disturbing them. We must have commandments such as not to kill, steal, lie, etc. But this human world is too complicated to be divided into two parts, good and bad; the measure is too small. The study of the commandments is very difficult in Buddhism, and the ten virtues are but a minor scheme within them. But you must start with them as you would learn to play the piano with scales. Then heaven will spread itself like a carpet at your feet.

"If you annihilate your ego, Mount Sumeru will crumble, turning a somersault. Then the sea of desire will dry up; the waves of suffering will vanish; the fish and dragons of danger will be no more." Mount Sumeru means the whole world. The Sixth Patriarch says if you annihilate your ego, "Mount Sumeru will crumble . . ." All this material, this manifestation of physical existence and imagination, which created heaven in the empty sky, will vanish. It will vanish like a bad child and turn a somersault. It will jump out of the universe. Heaven, the earth, and hell will crumble, and even *you* will turn a somersault. I faithfully believe this.

I abominate the idea of ascending higher and higher to the top. It is this ego that must be destroyed, wiped from the human mind. You may have the notion of going higher and higher, but if someone were to give you a black eye in your mediation, you would drop down to earth quickly enough! You are not going to heaven. You are only thinking of it in your mind. When all such thoughts are destroyed, heaven spreads out like a carpet underfoot. This idea of turning a somersault in the sky is a very interesting Chinese idiom. There is no such idea in the West.

Meditation has nothing to do with the Sixth Patriarch's Zen. You must change your attitude and become yourself. You must prove this no-ego. How do you prove it? Wisdom will prove it in one moment.

"The Buddha of self-awakening who dwells upon the ground of your mind will radiate his effulgence through the six outer gateways, and the force of his purity will conquer the six heavens of the world of desire." The Buddha of awakening is *this* Buddha of ours. In *sanzen*, you are practicing this Buddha of awakening. It is the one who dwells on the soil of your mind. Buddha is not in the Western Heaven, but dwells upon the soil of your own mind.

The six outer gateways, of course, are the senses—eye, ear, nose, tongue, and so on.

The "force of his purity" is the attitude of your mind, which takes all these paddings of the mind away from you and makes your mind pure. All these paddings, everything that is thrown into your mind like ashes thrown into water, become like a sewer. All of this must be taken away in order to make your mind pure.

About this purity: Everyone has an idea of purity, thinking that it means: "Don't smoke cigarettes"; "Don't drink wine"; "Don't be seen with ladies—go to church." The best thing is not to believe your mind, even when it comes and whispers to you. Just don't believe. Say, "Hello!" and let it go. We say, "Don't entertain it." Then your mind will become clear, and you will find the purity of your mind. Then you will return to the original condition of your nature, which is not influenced by your surroundings. This is the newborn mind, yet it is not stupid. Keep this clear mind which is not the padded brain. It is bright with the force of wisdom.

The "six heavens of the world of desire" are not evil, but people think of them as evil. The world of desire, the Kama Heaven, is the lowest demon heaven. The desire that belongs to earth is eating, the desire to support the physical body. The desire that belongs to heaven is generating, to preserve your generation. To eat and generate are the two desires, and these angels are guardians of the functions of human beings. People call them evil. Some Methodism crept into Buddhism here.

"When your original nature turns its light within, the three kinds of poison will be driven out and all sin deserving of hell torture will be instantaneously wiped away." The three kinds of poison are avarice, anger, and ignorance.

"Thus your mind within and without will become bright and penetrating, no different from the Western Heaven. Without performing this practice, how can you reach there?" When you realize the original substance that is your original self, original body and mind—the original of all things—there will be no torture, and no anxiety. Then all guilt and all sin will be wiped away. When you pass the first koan, you will prove this. The first gate is very difficult to go through. If you come to me in the clothes you wear in ordinary life, I will throw you out.

Having heard this, the multitude were fully awakened in their original nature, and all made a bow, declaring in one breath: "How wonderful! May all sentient beings who hear this awaken at once." I am quite sure that all those disciples were not enlightened.

Many philosophers have seen Reality, but they could not bring it into actuality. In Zen, you must prove that actuality and Reality are not two different existences, but one. Then you will be a sage, and you will prove it in *sanzen.*

The key is in the hand of the Zen master. We are proud to hold this key and to give it to those who will open the door of Reality. Then, when you come back from this door, your usual human life is not the same as it was before you entered the gate. All human life, all that you see, has a different significance. And from that moment, the true life begins. Before this time, though you breathe, you are sleeping. Many complain of those who are awakened, saying that they disturb those who are still asleep.

The Master said: "Good friends, if you wish to practice this, you can do so living at home. It is not dependent upon monastic life. If you are able to practice this while living in your home, you will be the same as he whose heart is good even though he lives in the East. If you do not practice this while living in the temple, you will be the same as he whose heart is bad even though he lives in the West. If only your mind is pure, that is the West within your own nature."

The Prefect Wei again questioned the Master: "How can a layman practice this? I pray you to teach us."

The Master said: "I will recite for you a gatha *on formlessness. Conduct your practice relying upon this only, and you will always be with me. If you do otherwise, then so far as enlightenment, there will be no use in shaving your head and living away from home."*

SOKEI-AN SAYS:

We are coming to the end of this chapter on the subject of the Pure Land. In the fourth chapter the Sixth Patriarch will talk about wisdom and tranquillity, *samadhi* and *prajna*.

The Master said: "Good friends, if you wish to practice this, you can do so living at home. It is not dependent upon monastic life. The Sixth Patriarch has said that the lay person can also attain enlightenment. It is not dependent upon monastic life. Even though you become a monk or nun and live in a temple, if you do not care about the practice of daily life, you are worse than those living in a lay family.

There are many lay people who have a profound knowledge, who are truly enlightened. In the Buddha's time, he called them bodhisattvas. Later, bodhisattvas came to be looked upon as demigods. "Sattva" means being, the being who has an enlightened mind, the awakened being. So the Buddha called those lay brothers "bodhisattvas."

I give the name "*koji*" [layman] to my students. When the Zen master gives this name to anyone, that one must have entered and is no longer outside the gate. In my group, those who have been given Zen names are inside of Buddhism.

Those of the Pure Land sect thought that all those who had entered were in the Western Heaven. Making a distinction from the Western Heaven, they deduced that the heaven of the others must be in the East.

If you are able to practice this while living in your home, you will be the same as he whose heart is good even though he lives in the East. If you do not practice this while living in the temple, you will be the same as he whose heart is bad even though he lives in the West. If only your mind is pure, that is the West within your own nature." Pureness of mind *is* the Western Heaven. It is very simple, but very hard to attain. Buddhists say, "Pureness of the abdomen, pureness of the mind; pureness of wisdom, pureness of speech."

The abdomen is the base, but we do not mean the physical abdomen. When we are sitting upon the line of life and death, we say we are sitting on the abdomen. It is like a great general sitting in his tent receiving messages from every side of the battle. He is sitting on the earth. When he is asked for his decision, his decision is spoken from his abdomen, as I say "No!" to a student's answer to a koan. No teacher will give you the answer to a koan. You have to break through by yourself, with your own power. That is Zen. To talk about the mind being pure, the abdomen and the heart must be pure. Remember that your abdomen is the line between life and death. You must sit upon this line every day and at every moment.

The Prefect Wei again questioned the Master: "How can a layman practice this? I pray you to teach us." The Master said: "I will recite for you a gatha *on formlessness. Conduct your practice relying upon this only, and you will always be with me. If you do otherwise, then so far as enlightenment, there will be no use in shaving your head and living away from home."* The Sixth Patriarch has a commandment, and that commandment is the formula of no-formula of mind-formlessness.

I think I have told you of this before. Our mind must be in this kind of moldless form. A sock has a formula, or mold. But our mind should have no-mold. However, our mother made a mold for us, the whole world made a formula for us, and we have to put our self into these molds because of circumstances. But when we get out, it is ridiculous to remain within these molds, to hold on to them. This is the theory of the Sixth Patriarch's commandment. You cannot carry out the intrinsic formula because you have made an extrinsic formula. You must break this and enter Natural Being. The only difference between the enlightened one and the deluded one is in sitting on the abdomen, not hanging onto life and death.

"*This is the [Master's]* gatha:

> *"If your mind is plain, why should you strive to keep the commandments?*
> *If your conduct is straight, why should you struggle to practice meditation?*
>
> *If you know your debt to your parents, you know how to be dutiful to them*
> *If every one of you knows your duty, those of lower and higher station will open their hearts to one*
> *another in compassion*
>
> *If you know modesty, the humble and exalted will be reconciled*
> *If you know patience, all evil wranglings will cease*
>
> *If by rubbing two pieces of wood together, you can make fire*
> *Surely, red lotuses will grow from the mud*
>
> *Good medicine will be bitter to the taste*
> *And good advice will sound harsh to the ear*
>
> *Mending your faults, you will surely give rise to wisdom*
> *Clinging to your defects, you will lack wisdom*
> *Every day you should practice that which benefits others*
> *Your attainment of enlightenment, however, will not be due to the money that you give away*
>
> *Seek enlightenment by introspecting your own mind*
> *Do not seek it outside*
>
> *When you practice as I have told you*
> *You will see the Western Heaven before your eyes"*

The Master continued: "*Good friends, if you all practice* bodhi *by according with this verse, you will realize your own true nature and directly attain the truth of Buddhism. Time will not wait for you! Everyone had better go now. I shall return to Ts'ao-ch'i. If you have doubts, come and ask your questions.*"

Thus the governor and his staff and the men and women who were in the assembly all were enlightened and accepted the Master's teachings to uphold.

SOKEI-AN SAYS:

This is the Sixth Patriarch's song:

"*If your mind is plain, why should you strive to keep the commandments?*" This is the first line of the chant. These commandments are the commandments given to you by the Buddha. You do not touch mind-itself when you are in some mold received through circumstance. You must find your own commandment, which is written in your heart and mind.

"If your conduct is straight, why should you struggle to practice meditation?" If one has a naturally deep heart, a clear abdomen, a bright mind, that one does not need to practice meditation.

If you know your debt to your parents, you know how to be dutiful to them." This is the usual Chinese virtue of filial piety. The Chinese placed more emphasis upon this than on any other virtue. They thought it was the foundation of all virtue because the Golden Age was in the past and not in the future. The Chinese believed they came from a wonderful civilization which was not of men but of gods. So the father is always superior and the child is inferior, devoluting from generation to generation. Their religious consciousness points to the past, a looking back to their source. Naturally, they pay great respect to their parents.

According to the teaching of Buddhism, you should not kill anyone, so how can you forsake your father and mother? If you get servants for the sake of the children, why not for the sake of the parents? In the Orient, no one must sacrifice more for his children than for his parents. We do not like to see a woman attached to her children and looking scornfully at her old mother.

The Sixth Patriarch was Oriental, so his record takes an Oriental view.

"If every one of you knows your duty, those of lower and higher station will open their hearts to one another in compassion." In the Orient, when a servant dies proudly in front of his lord's horse, the lord cries: "Brave warrior! I will take care of your children!" This is not cold capitalism. Capitalism is as a whip in a galley-ship. Men are not chained with iron but with dollar bills. There was no such capitalism in the Orient. There was a relation between lower and higher minds by compassion.

"If you know modesty, the humble and exalted will be reconciled." Modesty! When I came to this country as a wood-carver, the studio boss said, "Are you good?" "No," I said, "I am poor. But if you use me you will find what I can do." "But this is not a school of carving!" I did not get the job and I was discouraged. But my friend said to me: "This is America. You must say, 'I am the best artist in the world—seventy-five dollars a week!'" So I went back another time and said, "I am the best artist in the world!" and the boss took me at once. Everything is bluff.

Modesty is very important, as well as a good brain and good speech. This is the law. Usually we are upside down. We have wonderful speech, clever minds, but bad hearts. In other words, we have no guts. We are no good.

"If you know patience, all evil wranglings will cease." Today, we are no longer patient. In the factory, the boss says, "Work faster!" and the next day it's the same—there's no end. Patience does not serve us today. We must have a new commandment. I have a good commandment that I produced myself. Someday I will tell you, for patience is no longer expedient.

"If by rubbing two pieces of wood together, you can make fire/ Surely, red lotuses will grow from the mud./ Good medicine will be bitter to the taste/ And good advice will sound harsh to the ear." Also, there was a commandment not to abuse others for their faults nor to boast of your own ability.

"Mending your fault, will surely give rise to wisdom/ Clinging to your defects, you will lack wisdom/ Every day you should practice that which benefits others." This commandment is also no good today. There is no altruism. Today one has to be a strong egoist to win the fierce struggle of life.

"Your attainment of enlightenment, however, will not be due to the money that you give away." By giving money to the temple, you cannot attain enlightenment, but people still think so today.

Seek enlightenment by introspecting your own mind/ Do not seek it outside/ When you practice as I have told you/ You will see the Western Heaven before your eyes." Here, right here, is the end of the chapter. It is not so important to talk about, but the chant is made on the tenfold commandments of Mahayana Buddhism: "You shall not kill," "You shall not steal," and so on. These are heavy commandments. "You shall not lie." "You shall not be angry." "You shall keep your treasure." "You shall not despise the Buddha's threefold treasures"—Buddha, Dharma, Sangha. This last one was very important to the Sixth Patriarch. It is important that you know this. The rest is not so important.

The Master continued: "Good friends, if you all practice bodhi *by according with this verse, you will realize your own true nature and directly attain the truth of Buddhism. Time will not wait for you! Everyone had better go now. I shall return to Ts'ao-ch'i."* "Ts'ao-ch'i," the place of his temple, is my name in Japanese, Sokei. The Sixth Patriarch went south as I came east. This is another analogous relation!

"If you have doubts, come and ask your questions." Then the Sixth Patriarch retired.

Thus the governor and his staff and the men and women who were in the assembly all were enlightened and accepted the Master's teachings to uphold. I wish that all *here* would be enlightened as soon as I finish this lecture.

CHAPTER IV

SAMADHI AND PRAJNA

"Good friends, my Dharma is based upon samadhi *and* prajna. *All of you, do not say in delusion that* samadhi *and wisdom are different. They are one entity and are not two.* Samadhi *is the body of wisdom, and wisdom (*prajna*) is the function of* samadhi. *Wisdom appears in* samadhi. Samadhi *appears in wisdom. If you understand this, you will study samadhi and wisdom equally. You who study the way, do not say that* samadhi *precedes wisdom, or that the two are separate and distinct. If anyone has this view, his Dharma is based on dualism. Though his words are good, his mind is not good. His* samadhi *and wisdom exist in vain since they are not equal. But if speech and mind are both good, inside and outside are one, and* samadhi *and wisdom will be equal."*

SOKEI-AN SAYS:

This is a famous chapter in the record of the Sixth Patriarch. In this chapter, the Sixth Patriarch speaks about his foundation of Zen. You will not find a more simplified and direct speech about Zen and meditation throughout the scriptures of Buddhism.

I think the Sixth Patriarch never dreamed that his record, and especially this chapter, would be explained to Westerners in New York. Reading this chapter, I feel that I am in a valley between huge mountains, and that the ancient simple-minded woodcutters, fishermen, monks, and nuns who are living in the mountains have come to the place where they always make their gatherings, and that I am one of them now reading this chapter. From my own standpoint, as a Zen monk, I seldom meet human beings; few come to see me. Perhaps my pupils living in this mountain, are waterfalls, shadows, rainbows, and twigs. There are lions and tigers and the wind howling around us. We are now gathering to read this scripture and to enrich our souls.

I translate the Sanskrit word *samadhi* into English as "tranquil meditation," or you could call it "absorption into Reality."

Habitually, you think of this and that with names and forms. This mind activity is quite natural, but it is a nuisance. When your brain has nothing to do, it takes a vacation and makes this mind-stuff, which has little to do with the real life you are confronting, and it is very, very annoying. When I was in Manchuria, in a truck that might be blown up at any time so that the next moment I might be dead, there was not much time to think, but there was still this mind-stuff. In tranquil meditation, we annihilate this mind-stuff, not by force but by practice.

I was eighteen years old when I first introspected my mind and realized for the first time that my mind was always flowing. It was like looking into a dirty pond. I realized that something was moving inside, but I couldn't see the bottom.

I am quite sure that many people, mature people—forty, fifty years old—have never introspected their minds, have never known what is going on there. When I was very young, I made an attempt to keep a record of my mind activity from morning to evening, seeking to find out what I was thinking. I wrote ten pages a day. After a time, I gave up; there was too much. Of course, my mother found out and laughed at me.

At the age of twenty, when I came to Zen, I realized the value of introspection. In tranquil meditation you can see everything, all the activites of your mind, from top to bottom. Naturally, the activities of your mind that are useless will cease to exist. You have to practice this until your mind becomes clear as crystal. One hour, two hours, and you become independent of that mind activity, and mind activity does not bother you at all. You can objectify that activity as if it were the mind activity of someone else. Finally it comes to an end. In that moment, you realize that you are absorbed in Great Consciousness. This is *samadhi*.

In the regular rule of the Zen school, the Zen master will give a koan to the student who has experienced this *samadhi*. With the first koan—"Before father and mother, what is your original aspect?"—the student comes into absorption and then into real existence. This is not mind-stuff or philosophy in your head. So it is wrong to give a koan to one who has no experience of *samadhi*. Though you pass the 1700 koans, if you have no experience of *samadhi*, your experience is not very deep. So you must practice *samadhi*.

When I was young, I used to practice *samadhi* before I went to bed, or in the early morning sitting on the edge of my bed. Crossing my legs, I would practice for fifteen minutes to a half hour every morning, every evening, too. This is necessary for a Zen student. In that meditation, you forget the agony of the struggle of life; you lose that horrible, insecure feeling. You are like the honest Christian who depends upon God and is not afraid of what will happen to him in the next moment. A real Zen student will find tranquillity of mind in *samadhi*. He relies on something very deep and infinite. He has realized that life is just an air bubble that may vanish in a moment. He is not disturbed, and he does not have regrets. Why should he be afraid of this and that? We say he has a strong abdomen (guts). But it is not only guts, it is faith.

In the Sixth Patriarch's Zen, the emphasis is on wisdom, the awareness of intrinsic wisdom. It is the flash that comes across your mind that recognizes a situation or phase of your mind. *Samadhi* is like entire darkness, and wisdom is like a light that elucidates that darkness.

In the Zen before the Sixth Patriarch, there were two schools—the Northern and the Southern. The Northern School did not place their emphasis on wisdom. Their type of meditation was endless absorption in *samadhi* with no activity. To them, the practice of meditation was Buddhism. But the Sixth Patriarch placed his emphasis on awareness. Without this awareness, though you practice meditation for seven years, there is no enlightenment. This awareness, this wisdom is enlightenment. When you realize it, you see. It is like an electric light discovering that it itself is shining. When you take *sanzen* and toil on a koan—"Before father and mother . . ."—in deep concentration, you will recognize this wisdom—"Oh, that's it!" In that moment, you are enlightened. This is called wisdom, the awareness that is intrinsic. This awareness discovers itself. So, without wisdom, there is no Buddhism.

The Sixth Patriarch's school advocated the teaching of sudden enlightenment. The Northern School advocated the teaching of gradual enlightenment. When you become aware of your intrinsic wisdom, *in that moment* you are enlightened. In koan study, when you come to the Sixth Patriarch's answer to the disputing monks—"It is not the wind nor the banner that is moving; your souls are moving"—you will realize *samadhi*, that great tranquility. This koan will bring you to the tranquillity of the *alaya*-consciousness. Then there is Joshu's Pink Infant koan: "Has the pink infant six consciousnesses or not?" "Pink infant" means a baby just arrived in the world. He cannot hear, smell, or taste—he has no consciousness of his surroundings. You cannot say he hasn't six consciousnesses, for they are latent; and you cannot say he has them because there is no scale. When you realize this koan in your mind, you attain the awareness of intrinsic wisdom. I cannot explain this in words, but in your koan practice you will find it yourself. There are many koans that point to this awareness of intrinsic wisdom, and there are many that point to *samadhi*. Another that points to wisdom is: "Buddha's *samyaksambodhi* came from this sutra. What is this sutra?"

"Good friends, my Dharma is based upon samadhi"—tranquil meditation—*"and* prajna*"*—wisdom.

"All of you, do not say in delusion that samadhi *and wisdom are different. They are one entity and are not two."* Now we do not need to explain anything. If we have the experience of *samadhi*, wisdom is there, and if we have the experience of wisdom, *samadhi* is there. Each is within the other. Take the diagram of a cube. The top is wisdom, and the base is *samadhi*. In real practice, we cannot separate these two; base and top are one.

There are four periods in Zen study: In the beginning, you realize *samadhi*; second, you realize wisdom; third, you realize emptiness; and fourth, you affirm everything. There is nothing in the world that you can deny. You will affirm from God to the bedbug. But before you come to this conclusion, the first three stages must be passed.

"Samadhi is the body"—the substantial part—*"of wisdom, and wisdom is the function of samadhi. Wisdom appears in* samadhi*. Samadhi appears in wisdom."* From the angle of each, the other appears. To say that fire is the body of light and that light is the function of fire is the same thing.

This is not very easy. It sounds simple, but we have to practice it for a long time. I went through all the koans and when my teacher gave me final acknowledgment, I came to America and was living in downtown New York. During those years, I was living in emptiness—nothingness. One day I stumbled on a question: "If everything is emptiness, why does consciousness exist?" A simple question, but very deep. Where does this awareness come from? In nothingness, awareness and nothingness were two different existences—separate to me—and I could not make them one. I looked up at the ceiling and this wisdom was like a needle eye, and from the hole in the ceiling, I saw endless vistas, the entire universe. I laughed to myself. This is what the Sixth Patriarch meant when he said that *samadhi* and wisdom are one. From that day, I really grasped the Sixth Patriarch's mind. But it was not so easy.

"If you understand this, you will study samadhi *and wisdom equally. You who study the way, do not say that* samadhi *precedes wisdom, or that the two are separate and distinct."* Yet, in my experience, *samadhi* came first, emptiness second, and wisdom third. Again I entered emptiness, after which *samadhi* and wisdom became one. There is not only one way, but many different ways, according to the person; and there is some difference in time. Now, I would say that *samadhi* and wisdom came at the same time.

All the 1700 koans can be reduced to *samadhi* and wisdom. The realization of wisdom is the conclusion of Zen.

"If anyone has this view, his Dharma is based on dualism. Though his words are good, his mind is not good. His samadhi *and wisdom exist in vain since they are not equal."* Because his *samadhi* and wisdom are just knowledge, just information in his brain. So, borne in the air of experience, they hang there as a picture hangs on the wall.

"But if speech and mind are both good, inside and outside are one, and samadhi *and wisdom will be equal."* Wisdom is not your own. It is the activity of the universe. And *samadhi* is the endless *samadhi* of the universe—your own little ego will be forgotten. When you realize that *samadhi* and wisdom are not different, you will become a great sentient being. We call such beings bodhisattvas.

This is the first part of the Sixth Patriarch's discourse on *samadhi* and wisdom. It will take more time, so I shall translate it line by line. Do not swallow this as an easy-looking task. This is the real principle of Zen. You will realize it in your later Zen study.

"When you attain enlightenment by your own efforts, your practice does not depend upon debate. If you debate the sequence of samadhi *and wisdom, you are the same as any deluded being. By endlessly disputing with others, you increase your ego and cannot free yourself from the four conceptions.*

"Good friends, what do samadhi and wisdom resemble? They resemble a candle's flame and its light. When there is a flame, there will be light. If there is no flame, there will be darkness. The flame is the body of light, and light is the function of the flame. These names are two, but the substance is originally one. The relation of samadhi *to wisdom is like this as well."*

SOKEI-AN SAYS:

In the last lecture, I explained to you the meaning of *samadhi* and wisdom, but I shall explain it once more because many were missing at the last meeting. These lectures are very important. I am sorry that those who are absent are not hearing what I say only once in a lifetime. This lecture tonight, if you miss it, you may never hear again in so complete an expression. So you should not miss my lectures—not for my sake, but for your own. Please do not make excuses. I spend all day translating this to speak about forty-five minutes before a few people because you cannot depend upon a poor translation. All must ask, "What is *samadhi*? What is wisdom?" for they know nothing about it. Perhaps it is absurd, in this age, to translate such a sutra. But I hope you will remember my words and try to attain the foundation of life, to realize my teaching, and to get this profound wisdom.

Samadhi, intense meditation, means to be absorbed in the depths of Reality. It is different from the abandonment of your mind in sleep, when you are absorbed in the chaos of darkness. In *samadhi*, you are absorbed in Reality. When you are in the sleeping state or in *avidya* (darkness), intrinsic wisdom is latent, dormant. When you come forth into this world, you are using this intrinsic wisdom unconsciously, as, in the deep sea, the fish do not know that they have a wonderful lantern, but use it unconsciously. When you recognize this wisdom, you use it consciously. This conscious, awakened wisdom is called *prajna*. With this *prajna*, you will observe Reality in profound absorption once more. This is nirvana, when our wisdom becomes our own. When you die without the attainment of nirvana, you will go into chaos, the darkness of the infinite, with your sleeping wisdom. We call this "endless hell" and "eternal darkness."

When you abandon all conceptions in profound meditation, you will come to it, be one with it, and you will realize that intrinsic wisdom is there. It is just as when a pond is very quiet and from the center a little ripple appears without any stone having been thrown. It is a very quiet motion. When this intrinsic wisdom upheaves and all of a sudden—"Ah! *This is That!*"—it is eternal. It is like standing under a crystal bell in a tower—without any breeze one hears it. It's as if angels were singing sutras in the distance, though they are near to you.

The Sixth Patriarch is talking about this: *samadhi* and wisdom appear at the same time; there is no sequence of time between them. *Samadhi* is in wisdom, and wisdom is in *samadhi*.

"When you attain enlightenment by your own efforts, your practice does not *depend upon debate."* All of a sudden you realize your intrinsic wisdom.

Almost all religions depend upon debate. They talk and argue like drunkards, and they call it religion. In the Zen school, we do not talk about anything—and there is no debate! Enlightenment does not come from debating. Each individual will take his own seat, and upon this seat, he will enlighten himself.

In the Northern school, they placed emphasis upon intense meditation—sitting all day. When eating and working, they are in Zen. But in the Sixth Patriarch's school, the emphasis was placed on intrinsic wisdom. In one second, realize and become aware—Ah! That is the end of it. So in any place, any circumstance—Ah!—and it is over. At any second, while you are working at your desk, in a factory, or depositing a coin in the subway turnstile, you get a glimpse—Ah!—and it is all over.

In China, a monk was sweeping in the garden. A pebble struck a bamboo root and—Ah! Do not think this is a marvel. It is Reality. It is not like a flash in the eye, making the world look different. It is not so foolish. It is the diamond of the mind, the source from which spring all the laws of the universe.

This is the Sixth Patriarch's school of Zen. But, as a foundation, we must practice meditation, the foundation of Zen. If you haven't much meditation, you may pass koans, and you may attain wisdom, but it will shine dimly. But when you find IT, the whole universe shines, and you are its master. Only such meditation practice will enable you to discover intrinsic wisdom.

When you study painting, you are not given paints, canvas, and brush for a long time. For many years you have only charcoal and a piece of paper in your hand. You make light and shadow, light and shadow, until light and shadow are swallowed in your mind. Later, when your eye is developed, you will see light and shadow in color. When you look at a nude, you will not see this light and shadow, but only the outline of the body. So in Zen, one must be in *dharmakaya*, the first stage. This foundation must be made first. Some of my students have been here for five or six years, and they are still in the same stage. In this omnipresent stage, when you are free, no words bother you. No matter from what angle the teacher comes to you, you say, "Ah!" Then there is a second stage: you are seeing my light and shade, and you will answer yes or no. In the second stage, you are like a man standing before a cliff. But there are three stages . . .

In Zen, there is no speech and no debate: "Which comes first, *samadhi* or wisdom?"—talking like a drunken person. You don't need anyone's help to get Zen. You realize this Reality with your intrinsic wisdom.

"If you debate upon the sequence of samadhi *and wisdom, you are the same as any deluded being. By endlessly disputing with others, you increase your ego and cannot free yourself from the four conceptions."* You will never succeed in getting religion through argument. In fact, argument is of no use. It is like the diplomat: his "Yes" is not true, and his "No" is not true. Sometimes his "Yes" is "No," and sometimes his "No" is "Yes." It is like an eel that you cannot catch. Buddhist argument is also like an eel. When you try to catch the head, it slips out at the tail and vice versa.

The four conceptions are very interesting. They are: yes, no, yes and no, not-yes-and-no. In argument, whatever you may say in any catagory, the final answer comes to these.

"Good friends, what do samadhi *and wisdom resemble? They resemble a candle's flame and its light. When there is a flame, there will be light. If there is no flame, there will be darkness. The flame is the body of light, and light is the function of the flame. These names are two, but the substance is originally one. The relation of* samadhi *to wisdom is like this as well."* They are the same thing. Profound meditation is the candle, and intrinsic wisdom is light. The body means substance. With this physical body and stuffed mind, you think you are deluded, and you look around for your original nature. But original nature is intrinsic wisdom. When you come into the world at birth, you have this wisdom, and also in death. You are *originally* enlightened, but you do not realize it. In truth, you don't need to worry about it, you have

nothing to fear from this physical body or the sawdust in your mind. You only have to find the center. The Sixth Patriarch kindly explains this, but we do not need it. I repeat that *samadhi* and wisdom are the foundation of Zen. It is very easy to speak about but hard to attain, especially wisdom.

The Master addressed the multitude: "Good friends, samadhi *of one practice means that whether going, standing, sitting, or lying—in whatever place or time—you always practice singleness and straightness of mind. Vimalakirti said: 'Straightness of mind is the place of Dharma practice; it is the Pure Land.' Do not let your mind be crooked while your mouth only talks of straightness; do not talk about* samadhi *of one practice while never practicing straightness of mind. Just practice straightness of mind and do not attach to anything.*

"The deluded adhere to the form of things and attach to their notion of samadhi *of one practice, insisting that sitting down continually without motion and never fluttering the mind uselessly is what is called* samadhi *of one practice. Anyone who practices with such a view is the same as an inanimate object. It becomes a causal obstacle to the way of Buddhism.*

"Good friends, the stream of the Way must be flowing. Why, then, restrain it? If your mind is not restricted by things, the Way will flow. If your mind is restricted by some teaching, you are binding yourself with your own hand. If you insist that sitting down continually without motion is commendable, your view is like that of Shariputra, who was censured by Vimalakirti when he was meditating silently in the woods."

SOKEI-AN SAYS:

Speaking thus, the Sixth Patriarch violently objected to the meditation of the Northern School of Zen as blind meditation in a cave. The Northern School believed in keeping the eyes closed and in keeping oneself motionless. This is like going into a cave and trying to hibernate! Even *arhats* do not practice such a blind meditation. Why do people make such an error? Because their view does not go beyond duality: "is and is not," "dark and light," "yes and no," "good and bad," "inside and outside." It is always one or the other. He closes his eyes; he opens his eyes; so his view is never the complete view.

They practiced upon the earth from the human aspect. Suppose we leave the surface of the earth and go up into interstellar space, which is entirely dark. From the darkness of interstellar space, we see shadow and light, before and after. *Dharmakaya* is like interstellar space. *Sambhogakaya* is like light in the air. *Nirmanakaya* is like color, all the many different shades of color. Light and color are two phases of *Sambhogakaya*. *Nirmanakaya* is the transformable body of light. *Dharmakaya* is the eternal darkness which is not shadow in contrast to light.

Now, when we enter this *dharmakaya*, it is not dead. It is filled with the vibrations of the sun's rays. From that standpoint, that aspect, we look into the center—shadow and light. You do not enter into this darkness by closing your eyes. When you meditate with closed eyes, you are still in shadow. If you think that by closing your eyes you will find *dharmakaya*, it is an error; you will not find Reality. It is not *dharmakaya*. The sun's rays penetrating through the air change into light. The quality of *dharmakaya* is the same as that of shadow: it does not change its quality but is transmuted into light. Light and darkness are not in the closing or opening of the eyes. Shadow and light are two relative aspects. When you think of darkness, closing your eyes, then think of light with open eyes, it is not absolute. Truth will not be realized in such a way. When you meditate, pay no attention to the eyes—open or closed—and don't think "is" or "is not." Reality is not a logical conclusion. Reality is a *becoming*.

The Sixth Patriarch opposed the method and understanding of the Northern School of Zen. From the Buddha's time there were monks who practiced half-baked Buddhism, never realizing the *samadhi* of one practice.

"The Master addressed the multitude: "Good friends, samadhi of one practice means that whether going, standing, sitting, or lying—in whatever place or time—you always practice singleness and straightness of mind." This means that you act with just one thing in mind. "Going, standing, sitting, or lying" are the four postures, the Four Dignities, and that is all we can do, after all.

Samadhi is one of the important terms of Buddhism. It is this: in intrinsic meditation, you become one with the object. Now, when you try to think of your grandmother who is in another country, you cannot see her in the flesh, but you concentrate, and then all of a sudden she appears in your mind, and you can see her as if she were standing before you. At such times you are one with her; you feel as though you had become grandmother herself. This is called *samadhi*. It is more profound than concentration. When you think of the koan, "Before father and mother, what were you?" at first you think of it outside yourself. Then, concentrated, you will enter into it.

In the moment when intrinsic wisdom penetrates throughout the universe, your enlightenment is there. It is like a cat watching a rat—intrinsic concentration. Both cat and rat are in *samadhi*. When the rat moves, the cat moves too. When the cat's concentration becomes weak, the rat runs away, the *samadhi* is lost. *Samadhi* is a wonderful moment. You can observe it in the swordsman. But the *samadhi* of the Sixth Patriarch must not have any weak moment. It must be like an artist at work. When you watch a Japanese artist drawing a plum branch, he does it in just one stroke from top to bottom, and he shows the exact motion of the branch. The plum tree is living.

The *samadhi* of one practice, in modern parlance, is like monism. But from the Buddhist standpoint, monism is not just "one"; it is a different type of dualism. Monism is the conclusion of dualism, because without conceiving dualism, we cannot arrive at monism. Dualism is the cause, and monism is the result. The attitude of the Buddhist is that he does not care about monism or dualism, the "two" or the "one." Nor does he care about "shadow" or "light," "is" or "is not." "Yes" or "no" have nothing to do with the truth. Reality is neither yes nor no. Before the human being could speak or think of anything, Reality was existing. When you grasp that Reality, you grasp straightness, and you are practicing straightness of mind.

In Sanskrit, the *samadhi* of one practice is *ekavyuha-samadhi*, meaning the "*samadhi* which adorns Reality with oneness." (*Eka* is one; *vyuha* is to adorn.) To affirm and to deny is dualism. To think of something or to refuse the thought is the same. The true Buddhist attitude is very difficult. When you observe the koan, "Without depending upon anything, manifest your own mind," you will get the answer to the *samadhi* of one practice. This does not mean harping upon one word. It is the *attitude* of practice, not the practice itself.

The Sixth Patriarch practiced nothing but this: Do not adhere to any existence—sitting, standing, lying or walking. In your answer, you must be natural.

"Vimalakirti said: 'Straightness of mind is the place of Dharma practice; it is the Pure Land.' Do not let your mind be crooked while your mouth only talks of straightness; do not talk about samadhi *of one practice while never practicing straightness of mind."* Straightness of mind is an attitude, not a practice. The practice of Zen is like lightning in the sky. It does not stay in one place, as the American Indians never traced the same road. And it will not be caught in any one thing. But the human mind is not like this. To be "free as a bird in the sky" has the smell of Buddhism in it.

"Just practice straightness of mind and do not attach to anything." You do not need to be frightened or affected, you need not dramatize yourself or try to make yourself attractive. Just be yourself!

"The deluded adhere to the form of things and attach to their notion of samadhi *of one practice":* "Form" means a "certain position." To stick to form is not important. The deluded restrain the mind. You must keep your mind free and not pursue it. When you read a book, you let your mind flow, but you do not pursue it.

". . . Insisting that sitting down continually without motion and never fluttering the mind uselessly is what is called samadhi *of one practice. Anyone who practices with such a view is the same as an inanimate object."* Like stone. Many monks fall into this pit and think that they are true Buddhists.

"It becomes a causal obstacle to the way of Buddhism." This kind of Buddhism was practiced at the end of Buddhism in India, when the Buddhist monks were wiped out by the Moslems. Bodhidharma never practiced such a Buddhism. It is not authentic Buddhism. Sitting on a rock for ten years is just a game for beggars. Buddhism is not a dead fish.

"Good friends, the stream of the Way must be flowing. Why, then, restrain it? If your mind is restricted by some teaching, you are binding yourself with your own hand." When you invent nonsense, you arrest your own mind. Then you cannot flow with nature.

We read the records of the old patriarchs to understand our own times. Ripples of sand are left by water after the water is gone. It is the idea of human beings to stick to the old, old laws though time though conditions have changed. Nature flows. The law is living. All law is living and flowing. You have to keep your eyes open and react at every moment to what is new. To be restricted by your own ideas is like keeping yourself in jail.

"If your mind is not restricted by things, the Way will flow. If you insist that sitting down continually without motion is commendable, your view is like that of Shariputra, who was censured by Vimalakirti when he was meditating silently in the woods." Without practicing the *samadhi* of annihilation, you can reveal all the dignity of Buddhism. And without annihilating your mind, you can get into a pure state. Without throwing away the Buddhistic attitude, you can live as a pure layman. Your mind will not be restrained inside or outside—you can realize all phenomena. Without annihilating your afflictions, you can enter nirvana. Vimalakirti said this, but I tell you that the Sixth Patriarch's record is the conclusion of this practice.

"Good friends, people will urge you to practice sitting down to introspect your mind, absorbed in tranquillity without moving or standing up. But the deluded do not understand this, and adhering to it become insane. There are many who have such a view and teach it to others. For this reason, you must know that this is a serious error.

"Good friends, the true teaching originally does not have [two types of teachings,] sudden and gradual. To be keen or dull is in the nature of man. The deluded will practice gradually, and the enlightened come to it immediately. When you yourself know your original mind and see your original nature, no [such] differences exist. But, temporarily, those names, sudden and gradual, were devised.

"Good friends, in my teachings, no-thought is the first principle. Formlessness is the body. Standing upon nowhere is the foundation.

SOKEI-AN SAYS:

In the previous lectures, the Sixth Patriarch spoke on *samadhi* and *prajna*. That is, tranquil meditation and intrinsic wisdom.

The Northern School placed its emphasis upon tranquil and intense meditation as the way of attainment, while the Southern School placed its emphasis upon intrinsic wisdom. In terms of Buddhism, this wisdom which is innately possessed by the mind of man is called *prajna*. It is not only in the mind of man, but in the tactual sense of a tree, or in the nature of balancing weight in any material object, or in the reaction to surroundings in inanimate objects. The elemental forces in all entities of the universe can be called intrinsic wisdom. So the Northern School placed its emphasis upon the negative force, and the Southern School placed its emphasis upon the active force. We are descendents of the Sixth Patriarch, so we belong to the Southern School. The Northern School has expired. No torch was handed down.

"Good friends, people will urge you to practice sitting down to introspect your mind, absorbed in tranquillity without moving or standing up." The Sixth Patriarch is talking about the Northern School and, perhaps, its head, Shen-hsiu, a contemporary of the Sixth Patriarch. He, too, was a disciple of the Fifth Patriarch, a scholar, an educated man, an eminent figure in Chinese Buddhism.

These "people" always practiced the "fathomless tranquillity" type of meditation. That this was the way to attain results is being questioned by the Sixth Patriarch. However, the Northern School's statement is really wonderful. There is nothing wrong with it. Anyone could accept it. I don't think there is any error here. The "moving" means not just the moving of the body, but also that of the mind. The "sitting" is one of the Four Dignities: sitting, standing, walking, lying down. With the human body, we cannot do anything other than these four movements. So sitting is to sit down upon the ground in accordance with the formula of meditating tranquilly, and by doing this, to apprehend the original nature of the sentient being.

While Western schools were trying to prove Reality by demonstrating, reasoning or analyzing, the Chinese and Hindus were meditating upon their own consciousnesses—a shortcut. While the West puts on more and more eyeglasses with which to see, we give up our physical eyesight to gaze inward. Which is the right way? We plunge into the ocean of consciousness. We do not have to know what it is. We plunge, then feel. No one believes this way is effective and so easy.

"But the deluded do not understand this and adhering to it become insane." The deluded one thinks, "Isn't it wonderful!"

In the Buddha's time, the monks begged in the morning, then returned and rested. Because their lying down would have been disgraceful before the students, they sat, and the students imitated them. Then they became attached to the formula of "sitting," though this had nothing to do with anything. They thought that if they kept their bodies in a certain shape, they would be enlightened, even though their minds were absent.

No one thing—not your brain, not a broom, not your hipbone, nor any attitude of body—can bring you to enlightenment. It is intrinsic wisdom, your own mind, that enlightens you and rights your inverted view. There are many who have such an upside-down view.

"There are many who have such a view, and teach it to others. For this reason, you must know that this is a serious error!" The Master of the Northern School said to sit and meditate until a result is obtained. But his disciples were not doing it for the result but for the sake of the formula. They thought that sitting on a quilt was Buddhism. If this were so, then a cat sitting on a quilt would be a Buddhist, too—or an American Indian. Use your head, not notions. Use your common sense.

"Good friends, the true teaching originally does not have [two types of teachings,] sudden and gradual." From the Sixth Patriarch's time, there were these two types of teaching. True Zen, however, is that which was handed down from the Buddha.

"To be keen or dull is in the nature of man. The deluded will practice gradually, and the enlightened come to it immediately. When you yourself know your original mind and see your original nature, no [such] differences exist. But, temporarily, those names, sudden and gradual, were devised."—Made for the deluded ones.

For Zen students, the conclusion of Zen is daily life, and it is not so easy to come to this. Then there is one more stage—art, the art of life. Christians do not seem to have this. Once I said to a Christian: "I am going to a moving picture." "Oh, are you? A Japanese monk going to a moving picture?" Do you think a Japanese monk must not eat meat or see a moving picture? A painting of a dancing figure on the wall is different from living flesh, and the life depicted on the stage is different from the similar scenes in real life that it portrays. So though we say that everyday life is the conclusion of Zen, there are many degrees in everyday life. Zen students must observe this.

"Good friends, in my teachings, no-thought is the first principle. Formlessness is the body. Standing upon nowhere is the foundation." You cannot come to this by words.

"No-thought"—mindlessness—means that your mind is not your own. This is not stupidity. Mindlessness means that you do not own your mind; it is not the mind of a particular human being.

"Formlessness" means to have *no particular* form in your mind—not a triangle or a square. It is like water that will shape itself according to circumstances.

"Standing upon nowhere" means not to stand upon *any particular* place—on silence or on speech. Do not stand upon God or upon Buddha. Stand upon everywhere. We stand upon *dharmakaya*. This is the foundation.

"Formlessness means though you are within form, you yourself are free from form. No-thought means though you utilize thought, you yourself have no thought. Standing upon nowhere is the true nature of man. It means that in the world, whether you meet good or evil, love or hatred, enmity or affection, or stinging and deceitful speech, you recognize them all to be empty, not thinking of revenge, but letting each moment of thought follow the next without any thought of what is past. If [due to attachment to particular thoughts,] the past thought, the present thought, and the future thought follow one another uninterrupted, this is called being in bondage. But if from one moment of thought to the next, you do not stand upon any circumstance, this is called freedom from bondage. For this reason, I say that standing upon nowhere is the foundation."

SOKEI-AN SAYS:

In these lines, the Sixth Patriarch confessed his experience of meditation, and he indicated for us the true attitude of meditation in his own school. Of course, there are many attitudes of meditation, but this was the Sixth Patriarch's attitude, and we as his disciples should follow the method he laid down. Thus, he explained these three principles: Formlessness is the foundation of the Buddhist commandments. Mindlessness is the foundation of the Buddhist's daily life. Standing upon nowhere is the foundation of Buddhism itself.

These are the foundations of Buddhism. So now you have your three foundations, for living, for your philosophy, and for your faith.

"Formlessness means though you are within form, you yourself are free from form." "Form" means a triangle, a square, an octagon, point, or line. There are all kinds of forms: male, female, form of air, of liquid and of solid. Also our language has its own grammatical form. When we study English, we have to study its form—subject, object, attributes, etc. In our commandments, our morality, there is the form of law—you shall not kill, steal, lie, etc. The Buddhist commandments also include: "You shall not become intoxicated, nor make another intoxicated." The 285 commandments for monks, which are all "forms," are established upon a foundation which is formlessness.

How do you think about this? What is the basic form of water? Is it liquid, solid, or vapor? You cannot answer, for water is amorphous; it has no form. And though you have a female body, you yourself are not female; you are beyond sex distinction. Though I am in a male body, my soul is free from my male form. Reality has no form, but it will take all kinds of forms.

"No-thought means though you utilize thought, you yourself have no thought." From morning to evening, through all your days, you utilize your minds one after another, but you yourself will not lean upon a *particular* mind. If your mind is in a morbid condition, you will then cling to a particular mind, like an insane man who calls out one name from morning to evening and does not realize that he is insane. If you observe the world from a particular angle, which is a fixed idea, Buddhists think you are insane. Some obnoxious Freudians and their followers, for instance, observe all the universe from one gate so that, to them, the whole world is nothing but sex, and all will become satyrs or nymphomaniacs. They are certainly not free from form! They are attached to the forms of this physical body. We believe the mind is not male or female, that the mind has no sex. But in the world of desire, *kamadhatu*, the eye has sex, being the eye of a woman or a man. Even the dimples have sex. The beings above the world of desire, in the world of form, *rupadhatu*, though their bodies have sex, their "I" is neither male nor female and has no element of sex. In *arupadhatu*, the world of formlessness, there are about thirteen stages. (I think I will repeat this lecture sometime for new students, so that they will realize there is no sex in *arupadhatu* as well.) Those in *arupadhatu* are quite free from sexual distinction. So, though you utilize your mind from morning to evening, you have no particular mind. You yourself are not mind.

Mind and mind-motion must be separated. Mind is in movement. It carries the mind-stuff as waves carry debris: old shoes, dead cats, weeds, sawdust. But the waves remain pure. If you can clean up the debris in your mind, you will have pure mind-movement. Immediately, you will make contact with the universe. However, this movement is not yourself. You have all kinds of mind-stuff that come from the outside and eat your soul like parasites, but they are not yourself. In the moment when you have no particular mind, you can peep into the mystery of the universe.

"Standing upon nowhere is the true nature of man." Your nature, which reincarnates through many kalpas, does not stand upon any one place. It does not stand upon this earth, Mars, Venus, or on the solar system, or on the empty sky. Sometimes it takes the form of a cat or a cow. Sometimes it embodies in a cockroach. But it has no particular abode. Now, if you know this, you will easily understand this line:

"It means that in the world, whether you meet good or evil, love or hatred, enmity or affection, or stinging and deceitful speech, you recognize them all to be empty, not thinking of revenge, but letting each moment of thought follow the next without any thought of what is past." All these things are like waves biting the rocks. Some waves seem to be giggling and making ripples; some are angry and swallowing huge steamboats; and some are playing with babies on the warm sea beach. But all are like water evaporating into steam. When the kalpa fire comes, all will be annihilated. You can dispute indefinitely, or pull up your

eyebrow as in a Japanese print, or pull down your lip like the Bodhidharma drawn by Mr. Miya. But the true attitude of mind is to let mind go.

"If [due to attachment to particular thoughts,] the past thought, the present thought, and the future thought follow one another uninterrupted, this is called being in bondage. But if from one moment of thought to the next, you do not stand upon any circumstance, this is called freedom from bondage." This is the important principle. In your meditation, your mind will lie and play with your mind-stuff. When you look out of the window, do you make conversation with the policeman, iceman, cat, dog? No. But you do this when your mind meets mind stuff, it changes a million times a day; you even talk to yourself when you are alone. It is not necessary to stop that mind activity; just let the mind go. This is the true idea of meditation. Don't try to stop the mind; let it go.

You know that this is true about writing. Writing must flow like water with natural rhythm. When you start, do not stop until the end of the line. Don't change the words, and don't think about what to say first. Just write it at once, as it comes to your mind, and amend it later if necessary. This applies to all the arts and to religion, as well.

"For this reason, I say that standing upon nowhere is the foundation." If you want to be master of strategy on the battlefield, you must not have a fixed idea. You, however, do not follow this teaching; you have a fixed idea—it doesn't come from the heart. You build a restaurant on some corner, open for business, and no one comes. In the Orient, we know the enemy does not always come from the same place. So when you begin anything, do not keep any fixed idea. Let it grow of itself.

When I began business, I took the attitude of the Sixth Patriarch. The house was the important thing. So I had a house, a chair, an altar, and a pebble stone. At first, I worshipped that. So I began. I just came here, took off my hat, sat down on a chair, and began to speak of Buddhism. That is all.

A sage was meditating on a mountain for some days. Now and then he went down to bring up food. One day a friend obstructed his way, and he went aside from the path. There he saw many ascetics sitting along the rocks. "Who are you?" he asked. "We are your followers," they said. "We hid ourselves so as not to disturb your meditation."

A teacher must have food in his own bowl to feed himself before he can teach anyone else. Then it flows out. This is the rule for all religious teachers.

"Good friends, to be free from all form is called formlessness. Free yourself from form, and the dharma body will manifest its intrinsic purity. For this reason, I say that formlessness is the body.

"Good friends, when your mind remains unstained in all circumstances, that is no-thought. Relying upon your own mind, you are always free from circumstances and do not give rise to mind in response to circumstances. But if you just think nothing whatsoever and completely annihilate your thoughts, when the flow of thoughts ceases and you die, you will only be reborn someplace else. This is a great error! I want you who are studying Buddhism to consider this. It is pardonable that you yourself commit an error, not knowing the principle of the teachings; but how can you mislead others? In your own delusion, you do not see this and slander the Buddhist scriptures. For this reason, I make no-thought the fundamental principle of my teaching."

SOKEI-AN SAYS:

The Sixth Patriarch, Hui-neng, has here defined the fundamental principle of his sect as "no-thought." Perhaps "mindlessness" is nearer to English usage. This gives you a clear idea of the attitude of mind in Zen meditation.

When you see an autumn pool with red maple leaves in it, it may seem as though the water is stained red. But if you scoop up the water, you will see that the water is as pure as it ever was. The red or pink of all those colored leaves cannot tint the water, which always remains unstained. Our mind must be the same as that autumn pool with all that stuff in it. It must be kept unstained. This is the natural condition of the mind. If you see a donkey, you think of it, but when the donkey goes away, you think nothing. This is no-thought, mindlessness.

I shall explain this a little more carefully. Our mind is separated into mind activity and mind-stuff. It is like water and the dirt in the water. All the debris, like dead cats and so forth, is mind-stuff. But the waves that carry it away are mind activity. If you practice meditation, you will observe a pandemonium of things. They will amaze you and make it difficult to keep yourself quiet. You must go deep, to the bottom of the mind. There you will find something always moving, like gossamer in a New Jersey spring, or like steam from a kettle spout. In the distance you can see it, but nearby you do not. This is *manas*-consciousness, the marvelous vibration of the mind that creates the seeds of thought. Gradually the seeds grow and create mind stuff—you see the faces of demons or dragons. Mind activity without waves is as pure as universal consciousness. Mindlessness is this: waves are always fluctuating, but the nature of the water remains unchanged. In high surf or in a whirlpool, it is calm, like a mirror with no mark of any sort.

Our mind is just like water. Sometimes it becomes disturbed and creates a commotion; but when it is calm, it is like a mirror, keeping no marks or impressions of any activity. This is the original nature of the mind. You must keep your mind like this always. Do not put it into a mold. Do not make a gelatin pudding of your mind. When you see your mind forming a mold, bring it back to a liquid. After you use it, always bring it back to liquid form. Almost everyone's mind is either like pudding in a mold or so hard that it must be crushed with a hammer. You must break these molds, they must be crushed. Do not accept molds from other minds and think that they are yours. In any mold, it is not your mind activity; it is somebody else's mind created with words. I do not accept this mind. You must sculpture your own mind, create it, use your pure mind activity without the mind-stuff. That is Zen. You can call it by any name. Call it dog or call it noumena, but the substance of mind is always the same. It doesn't change from the original condition.

"Good friends, to be free from all form is called formlessness. Free yourself from form, and the dharma body will manifest its intrinsic purity. For this reason, I say that formlessness is the body." When you understand *dharmakaya*, the "dharma body," you can emancipate yourself and be free from all names. You must train yourself well for several years, then you can step up into the second stage of Zen. In this stage, your mind will be emancipated at every moment. You are smiling, crying, buying, selling, but in every act from morning to evening your mind will be emancipated from it all. You will not go home with a frown between your brows, like all those people in the subway who keep the troubles of the day. When you step out of your office, you forget about it.

Good friends, when your mind remains unstained in all circumstances, that is no-thought. Relying upon your own mind, you are always free from circumstances, and do not give rise to mind in response to circumstances." Standing upon your mind activity, you will think of "dog," "cat," "horse," "donkey" as merely mind-stuff. But standing upon your own mind, you can emancipate yourself. You can bring the whole mind into one pocket. You can swallow the whole ocean. You can bring one million things into one, and create one million things from one.

"But if you just think nothing whatsoever and completely annihilate your thoughts, when the flow of thoughts ceases and you die, you will only be reborn someplace else. This is a great error! I want you who are studying Buddhism to consider this." The author is speaking about the school that thinks stopping the mind's activity is Buddhism.

You try to think nothing, but the mind cannot do this for very long. I have experienced this. In meditation, all of a sudden I am thinking: "The cat will jump into my pickles!" Some people think this is Zen. But while you are embodied in thoughts, from one thing to another, from spider to tiger to liver, all is transmigrating, and you have no chance to become a Buddha. Some think this will be after death, but it can happen at any moment. Karma and reincarnation are explained in mind activity.

The Buddha said that the really enlightened one will not reincarnate again. He will go just once and will not return. When you really find mindlessness, you will not come back anymore. After "annihilating the last mind," you will never return. You will attain nirvana. The *anagamin* will go away and not come back anymore. The *arhat* comes and goes at will. He is supported by everything—the sun, the moon, the stars, the whole universe. He accepts all mind-stuff and mind-activity, but he does not go with it. He speaks to the pedestrian from the window, but he does not follow him.

"It is pardonable that you yourself commit an error, not knowing the principle of the teachings; but how can you mislead others?" When you look at the moon, do not think it is moving. Moving is not yourself, but the four elements and mind-stuff. Moving is the sky. Sailing is not the moon, it is the cloud. Flowing is not the body, it is the water, but not the water that composes your physical body. When you look down from a bridge, you feel that the bridge is flowing but you are not moving yourself. You yourself are not moving, because it is the water that is flowing. You think that you are getting old, but this "old" is not yourself. Your self is always young. And moving is not your self because your self is always quiet. You don't know this, so you commit errors. With such a wrong attitude, you think it is the Buddhist Dharma, and you will tell another that you are enlightened. When you say that you are enlightened, you are not enlightened. This is a commandment in Buddhism. If you violate this, you are not a Buddhist.

At one time, there was a group of monks stricken by famine. No one could get anything to eat, for no one had anything to give. The Buddha ordered the monks to scatter all over India, to seek families who had something to give. When at a little village someone said, "No one has ever come here, so perhaps we can say we are *anagamin* or *arhats*, and they will support us." The families believed them and gave them food and beds. Twice a year, Buddhist monks have an assembly, so in the rainy season they went back to the Buddha's place. The monks there were all skin and bones, all were emaciated. They sympathized with one another for undergoing that hard year. Then the monks with greasy faces and big bellies came in, and the Buddha asked them: "Where have you been?" They replied: "Oh, we had no trouble begging for food. We fared well." The Buddha said: "You are not enlightened, but you told people that you were. Therefore I make this commandment: No one who is not enlightened shall call himself enlightened."

In Western terms, this is called "bearing false witness." No one who is a Buddhist would do this. If he does, he is not a Buddhist and is never considered one.

The last part is not so important, but I shall read it again.

"In your own delusion, you do not see this and slander the Buddhist scriptures. For this reason, I make no-thought the fundamental principle of my teaching."

"Good friends, why do I make no-thought the fundamental principle of my teaching? Because you merely talk about the realization of your intrinsic nature with your mouths, so that the deluded entertain notions in all circumstances, and give free rein to the evil views in their minds, from which spring all sorts of afflictions and imaginings. There is not a single thing that you can conceive in your original nature. If you conceive of anything, you will speak blindly about fortune and disaster, and this is what I call afflictions and wayward imaginings. For this reason, I make no-thought the fundamental principle of my teaching."

SOKEI-AN SAYS:

This part will cover almost all the structure of the Zen sect. It is a very important part, and the Sixth Patriarch explained it openly. He did not conceal anything. If you have the Eye of Zen, this part will be very clear to you.

"Good friends, why do I make no-thought the fundamental principle of my teaching? Because you merely talk about the realization of your intrinsic nature with your mouths": Not only you, but many Buddhists and many kinds of religious teachers are merely talking about "God," the "Buddha," the "Infinite," the "Absolute," "Atman," "Oversoul," "Universal Consciousness," and what not. They give all those names to your intrinsic nature. But this "your" of the Sixth Patriarch is not such a small "your." Before father and mother, what were you? This "you" is not Mr. or Mrs. So-and-So. It is your original nature.

The word "you" or "I" in Buddhism is just something to denote the subject. But when I say, "this I" or "you," "this I" or "you" covers the whole universe. And when you realize this, *you* pervade the universe, and the whole world will come under *your* wings. God or Brahma is nothing but a synonym of this *you*. But you are speaking about the realization of your intrinsic nature by mouth from morning to evening, and you never know what you are speaking about.

If your teacher is this kind of person, his disciples are also. They are doing nothing but speaking from their names and conceptions. It's as though you were in a drugstore or on a street corner talking about the names of medicines and never taking a dose of them. Or you are at a restaurant window reading the menu; you know the names, but like poor hungry people who have never tasted the food, you never eat.

"So that the deluded entertain notions in all circumstances": When I was young, I went to the ocean outside Tokyo where there was a little island in the sea, about like Staten Island. A couple of American missionary women were living there—Christians—I forget their names. They were barely supporting themselves. In the morning, they went fishing. In the evening, they would teach. These women would kneel down on the shore, clasp their hands, and with tears, offer prayers to God. The neighborhood boys lined up to see them. These women must have been very lonesome, like exiles on a faraway island, never meeting anyone of their own kind. They were about thirty-five years old. No islander could understand their language. They picked up some of our language from the fishermen and tried, with this, to teach the Gospel of Christ. They would kneel and pray. It was a miserable sight. Finally, they sent two Japanese boys to America. I met them in Berkeley, and we talked over the old days. They told me that they had been sent to study Christianity by the missionary women. I thought: "Well, some fruit was gathered on that lonesome island, nursed by the hearts of those two old maids." The two boys were educated and went back to Japan. They had become eminent Christian teachers.

Zen students do not wipe tears from their eyes, or join hands offering prayers to heaven. I do not blame anyone for doing this, but such people have a crude conception of religion. This picturesque old-style religion was the result of sentimentalism. But one who has a cool brain cannot accept that type of religion. Of course, there are many Oriental religions of this type. But I am sure that the Sixth Patriarch, for one, would not, in any circumstances, have cried aloud the name of God or of Buddha. He thought that all such petition and tears was just mind-stuff, not the true, essential nature of the human soul.

"And give free rein to the evil views in their minds": They do not penetrate to their own view of religion, so they cling to different names and even kill each other over these names. So there is religious persecution in even what we call "the flower of civilization." One sect drives out the other because they do not know their own teaching and cannot grasp the other's. The people of different religions won't intermarry. Though their hearts love one another, the differences in their religions prevent them from marriage.

". . . From which spring all sorts of afflictions and imaginings."—"My God is omnipresent! Your God is personified!"

"There is not a single thing that you can conceive in your original nature." Because conceptions are nothing but conceptions, they never bring you to the gate of true religion. When you enter that gate, you cannot think of spirit nor can you think of the physical body. You cannot speak of good and bad, present or future, time or space. There is neither past, present, nor future, neither spiritual nor physical, creation or destruction. It exists from the beginningless beginning to the endless end.

Here, Hui-neng intimately states the aspect of your original nature. At these words, your mind attains enlightenment. As the Buddha said when he had attained enlightenment under the Bodhi tree: "When one Buddha attains enlightenment, the whole world, the great earth, trees and weeds, all attain buddhahood." Why trees and weeds? That was an aspect of his attainment. After six years of meditation from early morning to evening, he found the truth—"Ah!" In that great tranquillity, there was not a trace of human thought. His soul melted into the soul of the universe. Through the night, he remained in this tranquillity, and in the early morning, he saw one star twinkle in the eastern sky. He then became aware of his boundless existence. He was tree and weed, heaven and earth. He was everything. It was then that he said: "When a Buddha attains enlightenment, the whole world, the great earth, trees and weeds, all attain Buddhahood!" This is described in a sutra that was translated into Chinese. When you read the Agama Sutras, you will come upon these lines about the enlightenment of the Buddha.

Upon this, the Buddha founded his religion. If you cannot understand this, you don't understand religion. If you do not go through this gate, you cannot enter Buddhism. It is the one and only gate. There is no other way to enter. Today, thousands of teachers speak about Buddhism, but none of them truly knows it.

"If you conceive of anything, you will speak blindly about fortune and disaster": Perhaps you have the idea that the *alaya*-consciousness holds the seeds, that the seeds carry karma and that you will receive reward and punishment.

Conceptions such as these about karma are from the human standpoint. But when you really grasp *dharmakaya*, who carries the seeds of the universe? I carry. You carry. But who receives the karma? Whose karma did I receive and carry now? You come to the gate, and your ego will be destroyed. You will realize that there is no single individual soul existing in the universe bearing a separate karma. All souls are interrelated. So in the conclusion, we must have compassion for others because we do not know whose karma we are bearing, whose karma we are paying off.

In the Orient, in the evening, a fire moth will come and hover in the circle of a flame. The children will try to kill it, but the grandfather stops them saying, "Perhaps it is the spirit of your grandmother who comes to see you." A foolish idea, but it catches the child's fancy. Or a spider will come—"It may be the spirit of your cousin!" You can eat meat, but you cannot help feeling compassion when you are consuming the flesh of animals. Japanese children wail after their pig has been taken away. They will run half a mile calling the name of their pig. It's hard on the Japanese father to become a pig-man. In Japan, people will ask why they are making such fierce faces. And they will say, "Because I am eating meat!"

Evil and suffering arise from conceptions. From these conceptions, people speak about fortune and disaster. They are always in fear, suffering physically and mentally.

"And this is what I call afflictions and wayward imaginings. For this reason, I make no-thought the fundamental principle of my teaching" Mindlessness! It is not *human-mind*, you know. The mind of mindlessness is not human. Wonderful mind!

An old Japanese story talks marvelously about this mindlessness: An old man cutting bamboo in a wood found a little girl. Every day this little one grew. However, in four years she became a daughter of twenty! She was so beautiful that all the people in the city honored her. Finally, the Emperor and all his court heard of her. Some months later, in May, she became melancholy, and the old couple asked her what had happened. "I felt something that I did not understand." In June, she stayed in her room in fear of going anywhere. In July, she started weeping: "I have to go back home, and I cannot tell you why!" The old couple didn't understand. August came, and she went outside, looked at the moon, and cried. In September, she said: "My home is the moon. On the fifteenth, I must return." The Emperor, who loved her, heard of this and sent soldiers who put her into a cupboard, shut the door and stood with their arrows watching the moon. After a while, the soldiers fell down on their faces. A white cloud full of queer figures had come down from the moon. The cupboard opened, and the girl came out, saying: "Before I put on the winged robe of mindlessness, I realize that I love you, O Emperor." Then she put on the robe and rose into the sky.

But we, from universal mindlessness, will enter into the human heart, human suffering, and human compassion.

"Good friends, 'no' means 'no' what? 'Thought' means 'thinking' what? 'No' means no dualistic conceptions, no afflictions of mind. 'Thought' means that one keeps the essential nature of bhutatathata *in mind. Bhutatathata is the substance of thought. Thought is the activity of* bhutatathata. *Bhutatathata in its original nature gives rise to thoughts. Eyes, ears, nose, tongue are all incapable of thinking. Bhutatathata, however, innately possesses the faculty of animating thought. If* bhutatathata *did not exist, forms and sounds would instantly vanish.*

"Good friends, bhutatathata *in its original nature manifests as mind, and so possesses the six roots: seeing, hearing, smelling, tasting, touching and knowing. But because it remains unstained by things, true nature is always free. The [Vimalakirti] sutra says: 'It [i.e. true nature] can readily distinguish the myriad forms of things, while never departing from the original principle.'"*

SOKEI-AN SAYS:

This is the famous part in which the Sixth Patriarch explains the relation between *bhutatathata* and its activity. *Bhutatathata* is very important in Buddhism. Dr. Suzuki translated it in the early days of his work as "Suchness." But we came to understand that there was no such word in English. But there is "Isness" or "Existence-Itself"—that which exists as it is. Bhutatathata means "*This* Exists."

Many people ask this question of Buddhists: "How can the two aspects, *bhutatatathata* and the human being's activity, be combined? One is transcendental existence and the other is secular and profane. How can they meet? It's as if God and man would shake hands."

To a Buddhist, the answer is very plain. The *shastra* written by Asvaghosha on *The Awakening of Faith in the Mahayana* explains it very carefully. This was translated long ago by Dr. Suzuki, but it is now out of print.

The Sixth Patriarch explains it here in a few words spoken to his students from the platform made of earth. "No-thought," mindlessness—in Sanskrit, *asmrti*—combines *bhutatathata* and the activities of the *alaya*-consciousness. Buddhist theory always has these two aspects: nirvana (absolute existence) and samsara (transmigrating existence). The *alaya*-consciousness transmigrates through many phases of consciousness, but *bhutatathata* never changes its face throughout time and space.

How, then, does the changeless *bhutatathata* become the changing *alaya*-consciousness? This has been a very great question since ancient days. Many Zen students experience it but have difficulty in expressing their understanding. There is a koan that makes it clear how the absolute becomes phenomenal activity: "A sutra describes a bell tower in the Jetavana Vihara. At the four corners of the eaves are hung silver bells that murmur with the breeze. If there is no breeze, they are silent. But there is a crystal bell in the center that always murmurs, with or without a breeze." How? Why? That is the question. When you grasp the point of this koan, you will understand how *bhutatathata* becomes *alaya*-consciousness, how the absolute changes into the relative.

It is like zero. Zero is always zero; it never becomes one because you cannot add anything to zero. However, in the *I Ching,* to make zero into one is quite easy: when you recognize zero and point it out—"This is zero"—at that point, zero becomes one. Then, there must be something existing before zero (now one). So they postulate an absolute zero. Now we have the absolute zero, the relative zero, and one, making three. But the zero and the three are the same in their way of thinking.

"Good friends, 'no' means 'no what?' 'Thought' means 'thinking what'?" No-thought is made up of two characters, *mu* and *nen.*

'No' means no dualistic conceptions, no afflictions of mind." "No," *mu,* means that two different entities—duality—do not exist in the world. Hence these afflictions of mind have no essential existence. Observed from the essential standpoint, there is no duality, no two different existences, so there is no reason to feel agony. But those who cannot transcend the idea of these two opposites will suffer.

There is just *mu,* absolute nothingness. There is no matter, whatsoever in the world, not only in the world, but in the whole universe. However, if you conceive of "nothingness," it is not true nothingness. You must destroy that conception, and then the real *mu,* real nothingness, will appear to you.

"'Thought' means that one keeps the essential nature of bhutatathata *in mind."* In your essential nature, you feel every moment as an indicator of your condition. In such a way we are created. Without *nen,* without "stuff," the substance of thoughts would not be constituted. Your mind is always flowing like a stream, changing phase from moment to moment. Thoughts are a very important indicator of your condition—the circumstances of your being. If your mind is not quite free, if you attach to any one thing, conceive an idea or a superstition, the indicator does not indicate the "circumstance" of your being with any clarity. Accordingly, as you think this and that, your thoughts, flowing from morning to evening, encounter and register circumstances in your mind. When your circumstances become narrow

and bound, your stream of thought becomes rapid and the waves are high. When your circumstances broaden, your thoughts become more broad and plain, the stream of thought moves more freely, easily and more quietly. So, from morning to evening, from moment to moment, your thoughts change. Following your different feelings and emotions, you think this and that. This changing feeling is the barometer of your condition. The flowing thoughts are an indicator of your changing feelings and emotions—your reaction to circumstances is translated into thoughts. For instance, the end of the month is coming, and you know you have to pay the rent. Your heart is ringing an alarm bell, but you pay no attention, for your thoughts are not natural. So when the circumstances of the first of the month come, you are in trouble. To a deluded one, thoughts are merely irritating demons. To an enlightened one, thoughts are important.

"Bhutatathata is the substance of thought. Thought is the activity of bhutatathata. Bhutatathata *in its original nature gives rise to thoughts." Nen* (acting mind) must have substance, just as the waves of the ocean have substance. As the substance of the waves is water, so the substance of the waves of mind is bhutatathata, and *nen* is the activity of *bhutatathata* as waves are the activity of water. So the original ability of *bhutatathata* and its activity, our daily lives, are one, not two. *Bhutatathata* is quietude, and *nen* is activity. Why should it be difficult to make clear that these are not two different things, but aspects that are one and inseparable? They are one in your own experience.

"Eyes, ears, nose, tongue are all incapable of thinking". Each has its function.

"Bhutatathata, however, innately possesses the faculty of animating thought. If bhutatathata *did not exist, forms and sounds would instantly vanish."* "Animating thought" means thinking. But this thinking doesn't come from the eyes, nose, ears, or tongue. From morning to evening, this thinking that goes on is not your activity. It is the activity of *bhutatathata*. So you are, in reality, a wonderful being.

When you come to this conclusion, your universe suddenly expands, your circumstances broaden, and your mind shines in a limitless universe. Your mind activities are no longer afflictions, and you will have a clear and shining face. This is my prediction.

"Good friends, bhutatathata *in its original nature manifests as mind, and so possesses the six roots: seeing, hearing, smelling, tasting, touching, and knowing." Bhutatathata* is like God or a human being; it possesses six roots—five senses plus one mind. From the Buddha's standpoint, we are a universe. This is a microcosm, and a universe is contained in it. But, from the Christian standpoint, man is like God and God is like man. However, this is just using words. The essential thought can be the same, just a different standpoint.

When I hold up a glass filled with water, this is water. But when a human being looks at it, it is not true existence because the human being blends his looking with the five senses. If you take color, form, taste, smell, and touch from this object, then it exists as it is. What is it?

In the first koan—"Before father and mother, what were you?"—the original aspect is that which is not blended with your five senses. We have never seen the original aspect except through notion, emotion, reason, and philosophy, which are to us identified with the thing itself. When you do this, it is not the thing itself. But if you stand within it, all your five senses are included in it. Then it is not abstract but concrete. Later, I will explain how to get the answer to your first koan in your practice of meditation.

A philosophical conclusion is not identification with the real answer. The real answer does not need any symbol or word. It is the thing itself. I was told a story of an artist who tried to make the sound of a drop of water falling on a board with a drum and a piano, but he couldn't make a sound that could be identified as a drop of water. So he asked the janitor's boy, Johnny, to do it. The janitor's boy came, looked and said: "Where is the board?" He ran out, for there was no board, brought one and dropped water on it.

149

The artist had tried to make a sound that could be identified as a drop of water, but Johnny went back to the real sound. The only way to do it is to make the sound itself.

"But because it remains unstained by things" When one's eye sees the color red, the eye is not stained. When one hears a loud sound, the ear is not made noisy, nor do obnoxious odors stain the nose. These impressions pass away like a moonprint in water. It shines beautifully, but we cannot catch it—*there is no moon in the water.* The five senses are like water that retains the images of the outside but cannot be stained by them, so they always remain pure. All our anxieties and worries are like waves, like shadows that pass over the clear water and fade away, mirrored but not held. It is like the gong that produces a sound that fades as we listen. If you know this, you need not suffer so much, for you can change your way of life and adapt yourself to your environment. Then you will find freedom of mind.

When I sent my wife and children back to Japan, I was very sad. Behind every bush-top I kept seeing the face of my little boy. Everywhere I turned, he was there. It was very hard. I thought I couldn't stand it, couldn't stay here, but I got out of it.

"True nature is always free." You carry all your furniture to the roof when a flood comes into the house. But when the flood goes away, you do not leave the furniture on the housetop, you carry it down. We do not need to make any fixed law. Time changes everything. Therefore, we make laws according to time, place and condition. There are no longer hoopskirts or short skirts that show the knees like round faces.

"The sutra says: It [i.e. true nature] can readily distinguish the myriad forms of things, while never departing from the original principle." There is no need to talk about the original principle because if we find anything to say about it, it is not the original principle. This first law you must understand is *dharmakaya.* The second law, *sambhogakaya,* is the law of our own consciousness. It is experienced as if it were in the sky, like heat, light, or sound carried in all directions. It is space and time, north and south, east and west, top and bottom at once. I strike the gong, and it sounds all over—every moment in each place. In the second law, consciousness is proven to one's self by one's own exertion and proven to another that sees all this as ourselves. Consciousness proven to one's self sees *dharmakaya*; consciousness proven to another sees the outside.

The third law, *nirmanakaya,* is like a New York street—one-way. You cannot go in all directions. When *bhutatathata* enters into the third law, enters into a woman's body, a man's body, a rooster's body, it is limited in its form and function.

Although we cannot talk about the first law, our consciousness knows what it is and calls it intuition. It is intellectual intuition, of which there are two kinds: sensuous intuition and intellectual intuition. Sensuous intuition is seeing, hearing, and so on, without any previous experience of eye or ear. Seeing and hearing, receiving impressions from the outside, are intrinsic to human beings. Intellectual intuition, however, is intuition that we cannot perceive through our five senses. Intellectual intuition knows noumenon; sensuous intuition knows phenomena. When intuition knows about the first law, it does not make any mental motion. If there is any motion, a word in your brain in meditation, it is no longer the first law. Intuition is the intrinsic faculty of our consciousness, not *feeling* that your husband is a bad man. So this falls into the German idea of intuition, but we are not following German philosophy. The Buddha taught this 2400 years ago. I wonder if the Germans ever heard about this or had some Hindu teacher, just as Dr. Carus expressed his knowledge of Buddhism, but suppressed the name of young Dr. Suzuki who helped him very much.

We have all these laws in our consciousness but we do not use them.

Well, this is the end of the Sixth Patriarch's discourse on *samadhi* and *prajna.*

CHAPTER V

SITTING IN MEDITATION

The Master preached to the multitude: "This gate of meditation adheres neither to mind nor to purity nor to motionlessness. If you say you adhere to mind, mind is originally a delusion; so knowing that mind is a phantom, there is nothing there to adhere to. If you say you adhere to purity, the nature of man is originally pure; but due to your deluded thoughts, bhutatathata *is veiled by delusion. When delusion is gone, your intrinsic nature reveals its own purity. When you stir your mind to adhere to purity, you only give birth to a deluded purity. Delusion has no place to exist except within your adhesive mind. Purity has no particular aspect, but you construct its particular form. This is called artificial practice. If anyone takes this view, he obstructs the flow of his original nature and will find himself, instead, bound by purity."*

SOKEI-AN SAYS:

The first chapter of this . . . begins with his own biography—how and where and when. The second chapter is on *prajna*, so-called intuitive transcendental wisdom—but from the tree's sense. Do not use this "intuition" in the modern mystical sense. It is the intrinsic faculty of our consciousness. The third chapter is on the Pure Land sect from the Zen standpoint. The fourth chapter is on *samadhi* and *prajna*, tranquil meditation and wisdom.

Now, in the fifth chapter, the Sixth Patriarch is going to talk about *zazen*. *Za*, in Japanese, means to sit down; *zen* is to think quietly. So in *zazen* you sit down and think quietly. That's the literal meaning. In the English sense, you meditate upon something. Now let us think of Buddhist meditation.

The Master preached to the multitude: "This gate of meditation adheres neither to mind nor to purity nor to motionlessness." When you are meditating and you close your eyes and adhere to your mind, you are keeping your mind in darkness, just as if you were a hibernating frog or snake in a cave. And when you are adhering to purity in your meditation, you do not want to think about money or women, earthquakes or thunderstorms or fire. And then, of course, you adhere to motionlessness, but then you must go to New Jersey! The human being cannot do such a thing.

Well, this is how we usually meditate. But now the Sixth Patriarch is going to explain *zazen*.

In theosophy, they have veils and overcoats that put out the light. Why? They don't want to see an ugly world, so they fly to the sky, to Tibet. We cannot have such lunatics, you know.

"If you say you adhere to mind": This means to adhere to your inmost mind in meditation. Many Oriental teachers tell their disciples: "Don't look at the outside. Don't look anywhere! Adhere to your mind." So, in your meditation, you bite your lower lip, close your eyes, and adhere to your mind.

"Mind is originally a delusion": From the Sixth Patriarch's standpoint, there is no such thing as mind. If you find such a thing in meditation, it is a delusion. You close your eyes and think you are adhering to mind, but there is no inside. You think that you are in darkness, but it is not true, you are not in darkness. And it is neither deep nor shallow; it is just your thoughts. The Theosophist thinks he will ascend higher

and higher. There is no higher, or lower; he is just sitting on a chair. There is no high or low place in the universe. Everything is the same.

"*So knowing that mind is a phantom . . .*": Just a mirage. You are just thinking about it.

"*There is nothing there to adhere to.*" You are adhering to the mind in vain because there is nothing to which you can adhere. This is the foundation of the Sixth Patriarch's Zen. He throws out all that meaningless meditation and comes back to the original, ordinary human consciousness.

Everybody despises *this* place, but there is no other place in which to stay. One day I found *this* place, and here I stay. I threw away all the affected attitudes I had acted out. And there are many affected attitudes in Buddhism. Some people worship them. To them, such attitudes appear wonderful. To me, it looks like a crocodile! I have no tail on my end and no horns on my head. I am a human being on two legs. Finally, I decided to live in my present consciousness. And, after thirty-four years, I opened my eyes and accepted the outside—this human world. I did not imitate the monks, but settled down on my human heart. So some will say that Sokei-an says he is a Zen monk, but he is just like an ordinary man. To this, I make no reply, for I know why they think this. Many people go to Japan, see the Zen monks, then come back to New York and find me in my apartment, sometimes telling a bad story. But I stay in this present consciousness.

"*If you say you adhere to purity, the nature of man is originally pure*": This "originally pure" is synonomous with *dharmakaya*.

It is told that, in ancient days, some enlightened monks came to the Buddha and manifested their *dharmakaya*. They disappeared from the center of the universe and appeared at the border, then disappeared from the border and reappeared in the center. They emerged from the earth and submerged into water. They flew through the sky and passed through keyholes. Everyone thinks this is a miracle like those performed at Coney Island where the ladies exclaim, "How wonderful!" But if you know *dharmakaya*, you will understand how those great arhats demonstrated before the Buddha.

Your original nature is *dharmakaya*. *This* is without color, sound, space, time, or motion. It exists as it is.

The question of purity is most difficult to solve, especially in Hinayana, but the adherents of all religions have problems with fictitious purity. Listening to the Sixth Patriarch's Record, you must emancipate yourself from your deluded concept of purity.

"*But due to your deluded thoughts*, bhutatathata *is veiled by delusion.*" What is the meaning of "veiled"? Minds, theories, imaginings, are veils shrouding us from *bhutatathata* so that we cannot find it. We are shrouded by turns of cloth, as you would wrap a beautiful crystal bowl in cheesecloth. So, seeing this, would you go to a cheesecloth store for a crystal bowl? Limited by rigid words and ideas, you have entirely forgotten that it is within you. How can there be enlightenment? All this wrapping is done by pedantic scholars, a remnant of medieval scholastic life.

"*When delusion is gone, your intrinsic nature reveals its own purity.*" If you can exterminate your delusion, then you will find your original nature.

"*When you stir your mind to adhere to purity, you only give birth to a deluded purity.*" That is, when you make a special effort to adhere to purity. If you go to Ceylon, you will see monks gazing at the tips of their noses or at their navels. In order to adhere to purity, they never look into the powdered or rouged face of a woman.

What do *you* mean by purity—to close your eyes and fold your hands? Do you think this is purity within you? Most religious teachers take such an attitude and teach in that way. Because they close all their sense organs, they think they are pure. But closing the sense organs does not create purity because *your nature is originally pure*, therefore your five consciousnesses, are originally pure. So you do not need to do anything at all. *Just as you are is purity.* Delusion is a phantom and does not really exist.

"Delusion has no place to exist except within your adhesive mind. Purity has no particular aspect, but you construct its particular form." When you go to Japan, you will find the Shintoist washing his hands at the shrine trying to keep himself pure. So a hundred thousand others wash their hands in the same polluted water! Others, following a leader, go up a mountain to become pure. In trying to be pure, people make many formulas of purity. You see these formulas in all religions from ancient days. Funny, isn't it?

"This is called artificial practice. If anyone takes this view, he obstructs the flow of his original nature and will find himself, instead, bound by purity." He is in a jail of purity that he built himself.

This kind of purity makes many difficulties. When you ask why monks keep themselves aloof and do not marry or imitate that attitude even though they are not really doing it—this is a big question for everyone. Many monks do not know the answer.

After you have graduated from grammar school and high school, then go on to the university and get a diploma, you do not use grammar-school ways any more. But when you teach, you must begin all over again. You must come down from the "university way" to the "way of grammar school" and speak the language that these students can understand. In Buddhist study, the first-grade student goes up to the mountain top. He gives up his fiancee, takes his last drink of wine and renounces the world. Many do go to the mountain top. Naturally, they cannot take a soft attitude. Pure or not pure means nothing to them. All the husky *arhat*-type monks are really grammar school teachers of Buddhism. But ours is a high grade study of Buddhism. So do not take a grammar-school attitude.

The Sixth Patriarch's record is the conclusion of Buddhism, the father and mother of a long lineage. You are living in this conclusion, but you do not know it. When you come to a teacher to straighten your mind, your teacher will take you to the top of the mountain, not to straighten your mind, *but to take your mind away.*

Zen teaches satori—awakening. You will realize that the tip of your toe and the tip of your finger are pure. But first, you must realize original purity.

Koans destroy all delusions, all mind-stuff. In the beginning, you will accept the Buddhist teachings. In Zen, you will accept a new ideology, and then the teacher will destroy that ideology, leaving you with nothing to say, nothing to express. At first, you will try all kinds of answers and expressions, but finally, *there is nothing to do.* You will vomit out your struggle with agony, and at last realize—*That is it!* The Buddha called this nirvana. Then, slowly, you will come down to the tip of your finger and the tip of your toe, and you will go back to your wife, to your husband, to your home. How do you do this? This is the reason that the Buddhist monk takes the *arhat* attitude. If you climb the Alps, you must hire a man who knows the mountains inch by inch. He does not want to go there. But if someone comes to him and says, "Take me to the top of the mountain," he will remove his polished shoes and white collar, and put on mountain-climbing clothes for the ascent. It is the same with a monk. He may be living a layman's life, but if a novice asks him to lead him to the mountain top, he says, "All right!" Then he shaves his head and leaves home to teach. Many people cannot understand the frank attitude of an enlightened teacher who lives as a layman.

"Good friends, if you practice motionlessness [of mind], when you meet someone, you pay no attention to whether he is good or evil, right or wrong, or has various faults. This is the intrinsically motionless nature of mind.

"Good friends, the deluded keep their bodies *motionless, but no sooner do they open their mouths than they chatter about others' right and wrong, strong or weak points, likes and dislikes, obstructing the Way. If you adhere to your mind or to purity, that adherence obstructs the Way.*

"Good friends, what is meant by 'sitting in meditation'? In this gate of Dharma, there is neither obstruction nor hindrance. If your mind does not give rise to thoughts without, in any circumstance, whether virtuous or evil, that is called 'sitting'. And when you behold the motionlessness of your intrinsic nature within, that is called 'meditation.'"

SOKEI-AN SAYS:

Quiescence of mind is just sitting quietly, tranquilly connecting to the Great Mind, the mind of the universe. It is motionless mind, the mind of the great ox, the great cow, the great elephant—not the mind of a little dog or a chattering human being.

In meditation, make the mind as motionless as a mountain. To practice this, you must have faith that you are going back to the original mind of the great universe, original nature. You must know that you are one with the universe. This term handled mentally prevents you from entering the mind of the universe. Do not make the mistake of trying to grasp it with your brain. Grasp it with integral existence, with your whole nature. Do not *think* using this mind.

"Good friends, if you practice motionlessness [of mind], when you meet someone, you pay no attention to whether he is good or evil, right or wrong, or has various faults. This is the intrinsically motionless nature of mind." Your attitude toward a saint will be the same as that toward a criminal. When you meet a saint, you will not smile, and when you meet a criminal, you will not frown. You will communicate with everyone as yourself. You need not take any special attitude toward anyone whom you confront. This is the usual attitude of a Zen student. Do not feel that you must maintain your dignity or impress your greatness upon anyone. Just meet everyone as you would meet the soul of the universe. If you have become one with the universe, you do not need to flatter the powerful or scorn the weak. With your own quiescence, you will meet the other's quiescence. This is the real meaning of democracy. It was the attitude of Lincoln. It is being the same with a steel worker as with a great man.

"Good friends, the deluded keep their bodies *motionless"*: Many students think that quiescence is motionlessness of the physical body. Perhaps this is why the Sixth Patriarch, here, calls some of his students "deluded."

What is the position of meditation? People pay fifty dollars for railroad fare to come here and ask me how to hold the spine; how to close the eyes; how to breathe; how to count the breaths; how to take the air in through the nostrils. Physical posture is important, of course, but the mental attitude of meditation is more important. They do not ask questions about that, but they ask how to breathe from the nose, as though it were something mysterious!

"But no sooner do they open their mouths than they chatter about others' right and wrong, strong or weak points, likes and dislikes, obstructing the Way." Such an attitude shows that your mental attitude is not right. The Zen student meets others as an ox meets a chicken. Of course, when you practice meditation for a long time, you will find this out naturally. When you cultivate your own position of mind, you will find out how to adapt yourself to each person you meet, according to his nature and state of mind.

Practice meditation and mind your own business. If you talk about whether others are right or wrong, you are violating the law of your intrinsic nature. Your mind should be as big as the sky, not as small as the water in a glass. It should be as deep as the ocean, with only the waves on the surface fluctuating. The water at the bottom of the sea is eternally quiet. You will talk and smile, but the bottom of your mind will be empty and still, reaching to the empty universe.

In ancient days, a Chinese novelist said: "No one can understand a woman's mind because it is empty." But I think that man's mind is also empty, empty as the sky. If there is anything in your mind, it is ego. When you are man made by man and not made by God, you are violating the law of intrinsic nature.

"If you adhere to your mind or to purity, that adherence obstructs the Way." If you adhere to purity of mind, you are practicing what we call "fox meditation." The dilettante, like the fox in a cave, meditates in darkness. Many people make such a mistake. I saw a man cover his face with his cap. "Why?" I asked him. "Because I don't want to see the dark world," he said.

Keep your eyes open. What is wrong with the outside world, the world of the four elements—earth, water, fire, and air? That which is wrong in the world is in man's mind. So do not close your eyes; keep them half-open. At the beginning, perhaps it is easier to keep the eyes closed, but this is not permitted for more than a half year to ten months. Try to keep your eyes as those in the statue of the Buddha, not looking straight in front, for that makes the eyes cross. Direct the eyeballs to the left or right. This is the true attitude of meditation. Do not think anything about purity of mind. When you try to keep your mind empty, you think this is so-called purity of mind, but it is dilettante meditation. The real meditator takes no such attitude. His mind is like a calm moon in an empty sky. The clouds, the stars and seasons come and go, but the quiet moon in the sky does not move. What moves are the driven clouds.

All will go through your brain and heart, will be reflected, but your mind will not go with it. You must practice meditation for a long time to realize this. If you adhere to each phenomenon that comes to your mind, that adherence becomes an obstruction to Dharma. Do not let the activity of mind, the whirlpools, waves, and so forth, obstruct the flowing of the stream. Do not take hold of all the circumstances that come close to your mind. If you adhere to a circumstance and try to keep it forever, it becomes an obstruction to Dharma. Dharma here means the Law of the Universe.

"Good friends, what is meant by 'sitting in meditation'?" The Sixth Patriarch is talking about his attitude of mind in the practice of seated meditation or zazen—meditating in a sitting posture.

"In this gate of Dharma . . .": "Dharma" here means "universal law." "Gate" means "religion," or a particular school. One could say that he is in that gate as one would say, "the gate of Columbia" or "the gate of Harvard."

"There is neither obstruction nor hindrance." In meditation, the mind extends endlessly to east, west, north, and south. The center pervades throughout the universe. The spatial, three-dimensional mind is molded in such a way. But in meditation the mind is also molded in duration, which is a wonderful thing. This duration is not a straight line, but is expanding. Perhaps you could call it the fourth dimension. The Oriental does not use that word, but certainly in meditation we can experience that fourth-dimensional space.

"If your mind does not give rise to thoughts without, in any circumstance, whether virtuous or evil, that is called 'sitting.' And when you behold the motionlessness of your intrinsic nature within, that is called 'meditation.'" Not rousing your mind in all circumstances outside yourself, so that there is no hindrance, is *za*—sitting. You are the master in all circumstances. You are not sitting upon your chair, but on top of the universe. You are sitting upon the Universal Sun, the Absolute, the Vairochana Buddha. This earth,

not the universe, has day and night. The universe of zazen has neither day nor night. When the Hindu says you are "sitting upon the Universal Sun," he has a wonderful imagination, but do not take this literally, and do not dramatize yourself. Just sit calmly.

When you finally behold the quiescence of your original mind, or nature, within yourself, it is not so easy to understand. But when you have passed the first koan, "Before father and mother, what were you?" and you reach your original nature, there is neither inside nor outside, neither time nor space, neither spirit nor matter. Then there is no word to think, no silence to keep, no sound to refuse to hear. You lose the bottom of your mind and go back to universal nature. From the top of your head to the tip of your toe, you will realize your original nature. And when you behold IT—not thinking or talking about it—this is Zen. The English word "meditation" is so small that it does not cover the true attitude called Zen.

"Good friends, what is that called 'ch'an meditation'? When your mind leaves the forms of external existence, it is called 'ch'an.' And when your mind is kept undisturbed within, it is called 'meditation.' When your mind adheres to form without, it will be disturbed within; but when your mind takes leave of form without, it will not be disturbed. Your original nature is intrinsically pure and peaceful; but because of your seeing the outside and having thoughts about it, your mind becomes disturbed. When you see all outside circumstances, yet your mind is not disturbed, you are in true meditation.

"Good friends, outwardly when your mind takes leave of form, it is none other than 'ch'an'; inwardly when your mind is not disturbed, it is none other than 'meditation.' Outwardly 'ch'an,' inwardly 'meditation'—this is what constitutes 'ch'an meditation.' It is said in the Sutra of the Bodhisattva Commandments: *'Your own nature is originally pure.'*

"Good friends, see for yourselves in every instant of thought that your nature is originally pure, and by your own practice, attain buddhahood yourselves."

SOKEI-AN SAYS:

This is the last part of the chapter on *zazen*. Now, the Sixth Patriarch was talking about his concept of *zazen*, "*ch'an* meditation," to the multitude and to his disciples. From the next lecture on, he speaks about an entirely different thing.

"Good friends, what is that called 'ch'an *meditation'?"* In this paragraph, Hui-neng explains *ch'an* and *ch'an* meditation almost completely. In Japanese, "Zen" is the name by which we call our sect. It is here, in this sense, that quiet meditation and the result of such meditation is *samadhi*. By quiet meditation, you will attain quiescence. This does not mean an absence of intellect. Instead, you will attain the source of intellect. *Samadhi* is not mere tranquillity; it is the realization of original wisdom and the universal principle. With a deluded mind, in quietude, you will attain only deluded dreams. Only the awakened mind will attain the wisdom that innately exists in your own mind.

Many people ask: "If you keep yourself quiet and don't reason, will you not return to the original stupidity of a dog or a cat sleeping in the daylight? How will you then attain enlightenment? In the Western world we use reason to attain. How is the Oriental going to attain enlightenment by closing his eyes and crossing his legs?" Our answer is this: Please practice *zazen* according to our method. Not until you do this can we explain anything about it. It would be like teaching you how to swim without your going into the water.

"When your mind leaves the forms of external existence, it is called 'ch'an.'" This is one of the great lines of this sutra. Leaving the forms of external existence is the practice that you are exercising in Zen. Go through the keyhole. Go through the stone wall. Take Mount Fuji out of your pillbox. Stop the faraway sailing boat and the gong of the temple. Take Manhattan out of your pocketbook. Without using your hand, make me stand up. Without wetting your sleeves, remove a stone from the bottomless sea. All these koans make you destroy the forms or conceptions of external existence—you get rid of those forms. Consequently, you attain *dharmakaya*, the omnipresent body of essential existence.

"And when your mind is kept undisturbed within, it is called 'meditation.'" Your mind naturally attains tranquillity. When you see the sun and moon, the stars, flowers, mountains and rivers, they are pure to your consciousness, pure as the blue sky. You are not fooled by those existences, and you attain meditation, which is the state of *sambhogakaya*. But, without first having attained *dharmakaya*, without knowing *samadhi*, you cannot prove this *sambhogakaya*.

"When your mind adheres to form without, it will be disturbed within": "Neither wind nor banner is moving; your minds are moving." This was the Sixth Patriarch's answer to the monks who were disputing over the banner flying in the breeze. "The wind is moving." "No, the banner is moving." There was no end to the argument until the Sixth Patriarch, sweeping the garden with his broom, heard the discussion and said: "Neither wind nor banner is moving; your minds are moving." This is one of the great koans in the Zen School.

When you answer this koan, in that moment you attain *sambhogakaya*, the *sambhogakaya* that has two faces: the negative aspect that is the quiet part facing Reality, and the positive aspect that faces actuality. Like intuition, *sambhogakaya* attains absolute existence without reason. The part facing actuality is the intuition that accepts sensual existence as it appears to our senses—the sensual side of experience, immediate knowledge. It is through the Sixth Patriarch's "Wind and Banner" koan that you will attain the intuition to see *nirmanakaya*. The Buddha said that was the wisdom provided by yourself, while the other was the wisdom provided by others. So in the *Trikaya*, there is:

> *Dharmakaya*
> *Sambhogakaya* facing *Dharmakaya*
> *Sambhogakaya* facing *Nirmanakaya*
> *Nirmanakaya*.

Your original nature is *Dharmakaya*.

You must know these four stages of the *Trikaya*, especially the two faces of *sambhogakaya*—one facing *dharmakaya*, the other *nirmanakaya*.

"But when your mind takes leave of form without, it will not be disturbed. Your original nature is intrinsically pure and peaceful": Your original nature is *dharmakaya* nature. "Pure and peaceful" is the Zen mind.

"But because of your seeing the outside and having thoughts about it, your mind becomes disturbed." We try to arrange the laws of the universe by our experience. This is impossible. It is like a child looking at a mechanical toy's outside, not understanding the inside, and asking you why it runs. You must find the law of *alaya*-consciousness, and then you will understand why we accept all outside form, shape, and color. Then you will understand the trick of the universe and the cause of seeing the outside. And when

you understand how to accept the outside, the whole world and sky will be in your hand. Until then, even though you have eyes, you won't see anything at all.

"When you see all outside circumstances, yet your mind is not disturbed, you are in true meditation." This can be done when you pass through Zen. When you see everything at once, you see both phenomena and noumena at the same moment. With all senses outside and all the reality of the universe inside, you are seeing it at once, and you are not a bit disturbed. You attain this when you pass the first koan. It's not a small thing passing the first koan. So don't be discouraged when you come into Zen and your wisdom is limited, so limited you cannot see it. Even passing one koan can help you a great deal. Just as you can seed a fire in kindling wood, blow and make a flame that grows into a conflagration that annihilates everything, you can attain nirvana. Don't be discouraged! When you attain the first koan and then listen to my lecture, you will say, "But I didn't realize so much!"

All students have that same feeling.

"Good friends, outwardly when your mind takes leave of form, it is none other than 'ch'an,' and when inwardly your mind is not disturbed, it is none other than 'meditation.' Outwardly 'ch'an,' inwardly 'meditation'—this is what constitutes 'ch'an meditation.'" I think this much is very important, but I am not sure about the rest. They may be the words of the Sixth Patriarch, but what follows may have been inserted by some disciple.

"It is said in the Sutra of the Bodhisattva Commandments:*"* The *Sutra of the Bodhisattva Commandments* is the end of Zen study. You will pass through the ten essential commandments or rather one commandment that includes the ten—each commandment is also the other nine. These commandments are like Indra's net, one law interlaces with the others, all are contained in each, netted together like a net of jade.

"'Your own nature is originally pure.'" This is the basis of the commandments. So without this study, you cannot really understand human life. These commandments are the criterion for the Buddhist life and are really not commandments. They are a guide in daily life. But if you attach to *even one thing*, you violate this commandment. The true universe has no idea of attachment.

"Good friends, see for yourselves in every instant of thought that your nature is originally pure, and by your own practice attain buddhahood yourselves."

CHAPTER VI

CONFESSION

When the Great Master saw the multitude that had gathered at the temple from Kuang-chou, Shao-chou and every corner of the land in order to hear his sermon, he ascended the high seat and addressed them, saying:

*"Good friends, this must be born from your own nature. At all times, in every moment of thought, you must purify your mind. By your own effort and your own practice, you must see your own dharma body (*dharmakaya*) and the Buddha within your own mind. Reform and discipline yourselves and observe the commandments (*shila*).*

"In truth, you do not need to come here. But as you have already come here from afar and assembled together like this, we must all have previous affinities with one another.

"Every one of you should now kneel. I will first transmit to you the incense of dharmakaya, which consists of the five elements of your own nature; and then I will teach you the formless confession."

*Everyone knelt down. The Master said: "The first is the incense of commandment (*shila*). When you possess neither falsehood nor evil, neither jealousy, greed, anger, nor malice within your mind, it is called the incense of commandment.*

*"The second is the incense of tranquillity (*samadhi*). When your mind is not agitated by observing all outside appearances, good or bad, it is called the incense of tranquillity.*

*"The third is the incense of wisdom (*prajna*). When your mind is without obstruction and you constantly observe your original nature with wisdom so that you do no evil, and when your mind remains without attachment, though performing virtuous deeds, so that you have respect for your superiors and compassion for your inferiors and sympathy for the poor and for the friendless, it is called the incense of wisdom.*

*"The fourth is the incense of emancipation (*vimukti*). When your mind no longer attaches to the outside, not judging things in terms of good and bad, but remaining free and unobstructed, it is called the incense of liberation.*

*"The fifth is the incense of the knowledge of emancipation (*vimukti-jnana*). Though your mind no longer attaches to the outside, you must not hold to quiescence or submerge yourself in emptiness, but must realize your own intrinsic mind by broadening your learning and acquiring further knowledge. To attain the enlightenment of all the buddhas, meeting things peacefully with the light [of wisdom], making no distinction between self and others, and coming directly to enlightenment, the true unchanging nature of things—this is called the incense of the wisdom of emancipation.*

"Good friends, these incenses perfume your mind within. Do not seek them without!"

SOKEI-AN SAYS:

In the last chapter, the Sixth Patriarch preached his sermon on meditation, which is the main practice of the Zen School. Now he is about to speak about confession. Confession in the Buddhist sense is different from that of Christianity. Today, in Buddhism, the *sanzen* that you are exercising is confession. But in ancient days, it was the confession of the monks. In the Buddha's time, the monks went one by one to see the Buddha, who was meditating in the deep woods. They went to him to confess their thoughts as "erroneous-mind." Mahakashyapa and Shariputra all went thus and confessed, but the monks had nothing to confess—no sins committed. They were afraid of erroneous thoughts. They wanted to purify their minds, from the foundation of their consciousness to the top. This was the origin of confession in Buddhism, and now our confession has changed its form to *sanzen*. We come to the master one by one and join our hands to the bodhisattva who holds the wisdom of Buddha. Then we confess our conceptions, and the master judges the right or wrong of it. Your *sanzen* is a form of confession. Of course, when laymen went to see the Buddha, they confessed their erroneous deeds: "I killed six oxen. What will happen in my next incarnation?" And the Buddha would say: "You will go through six hells. Go, and do not kill again." This was the formula for laymen.

When the Great Master saw the multitude that had gathered at the temple from Kuang-chou, Shao-chou and every corner of the land in order to hear his sermon, he ascended the high seat and addressed them, saying: The high seat was an altar or platform made of earth, and the temple was on a hill on the southern prairie of China. Today, it is not prepossessing. Perhaps it was a beautiful place then. Now it is a nest of bandits.

"Good friends, this must be born from your own nature. At all times, in every moment of thought, you must purify your mind. By your own effort and your own practice, you must see your own dharma body (dharmakaya) and the Buddha within your own mind." This faith is clear, and you do not wait for anyone to give it to you. It does not come from the hand of an angel or a god. You will conceive this faith in your own mind, out of your own soul, which is your own intrinsic nature.

Now, as you try to meditate, this is how your mind works: "Today, I'll go downtown, and tomorrow I'll have lunch with John." On a little lower shelf of consciousness, as you are thinking this, there are all the noises of the street—the horns and the elevated train. On a still lower shelf, there are jealousies and angers; and on a still lower shelf, nature is supporting your life—your heart is pumping blood, your stomach is digesting food. Below all this, Great Universal Consciousness spreads out like the ocean, and you are in midair meditating in this ocean.

Stop those conscious shelves of existence. Destroy those superstitions—purify! Wash off your erroneous notions, and come to your own consciousness that is universal to every mortal being. Do not try to find that universal consciousness within yourself. That consciousness is everywhere; you are sitting in it. And do not think it is deep. What do you mean by deep? Do not use the words "higher" or "deeper." It is better to use "boundless" or "limitless" when you speak of this consciousness. When you sit upon your seat, you are permeating in manifold directions. IT has no limit. IT is boundless and endless time.

According to Buddhism, this is *dharmakaya*, the body of omnipresence, the "Buddha within your own mind." It has no time or space. It existed before time and space, and it will continue to exist after time and space. It is non-created and non-destroyed. So when you are washing dishes, scrubbing floors, *you* are Buddha. But you think you are a human being. If you destroy this idea of individual being, you become Universal Self. Then you are Buddha. Siddhartha Buddha was a man who lived 2,500 years ago, but *this* is your own Buddha. You yourself are Buddha.

"Reform and discipline yourselves and observe the commandments (shila)." Philosophy is not the only element of religion. Conscience, the intrinsic measure of religion as morality and commandments, is also an important element of religion. In Sanskrit, conscience is *shila*, the innate measure of our morality. *Vinaya* is the written law that regulates our daily life. So *shila* is intrinsic in all sentient beings, and *vinaya*

is made by man. *Shila* is not only existing in man, but in all sentient beings. It is manifested in various ways according to circumstances of their lives.

The commandments of Buddhism are based upon *shila*. In a Christian theory of morality, it is said that fear is the origin of morality, that morality is derived from fear—the first knowledge of human beings and the cause of all their agonies. Man found this first knowledge when Adam accepted the apple from Eve. Until that time, man lived in the wisdom of God, but from the moment man discovered his own knowledge, he had to support himself by his own toil. Therefore, God drove him out of the Garden of Eden. This was taught to us at school by a teacher of Western philosophy. It was quite interesting, but from the Buddhist viewpoint, fear is not the cause of morality. Fear is the result of human life, and morality is also. From head to tail, all morality is the result of human existence. It is common to all who are living in a social order.

The origin of morality is easily explained. Man's mind must have something by which to innately measure human life. This is conscience. Conscience is like a mirror or scale. It is like a compass that always points to the North Pole. This conscience is not only in the human being, it is in everything. It is like the law of magnetics. It was upon this base that the Buddhist commandments were established.

To "reform and discipline" yourself means to get into a new life. The commandments are given by the teacher: "Do not kill or steal"; "you must not please yourself"; "you must not blame others for offenses"; "you must not keep your treasure (withhold your knowledge) when others need it." But these are not the real commandments. These you will find by yourself in your own heart. Until then, we give you no formal commandments. So you must reach to the very bottom of your heart and touch the real body of commandment—*you will meet your own conscience*. IT, with its green eyes, watches you day and night, and you cannot escape it. Finally, when you accept yourself, I can pronounce, "I sanction you," and you are free. You knew no ease before you came here, but now you will understand the last great commandment of Buddhism, which is "all that you do from morning to evening."

It seems to me the audience gathered about the earthen platform was not very enlightened, so this lecture is not very deep. When you come to study commandments, you will hear some very surprising stories.

"In truth, you do not need to come here." That is, you can find it in your own heart.

"But as you have already come here from afar and assembled together like this, we must all have previous affinities with one another." We must all have these affinities with each other because we are taking shelter under the same tree and touching sleeves in passing. We are together because the previous relation is proved—the theory of reincarnation.

"Every one of you should now kneel. I will first transmit to you the incense of dharmakaya, *which consists of the five elements of your own nature":* A long time ago when I was giving you lectures on the technical terms of Buddhism, I explained the meaning of the five skandhas, the five shadows of unenlightened mind. But *these* shadows, the "elements of your own nature," are like the shadows of *enlightened* mind. They are the incense of the enlightened one, the Buddha, the five elements of your own nature.

These elements or shadows are piled up like the colors of a flame burning on a candle—from the bottom blue to the center yellow to the top white. In such a way, these shadows are one's mind. They are gradually exposed from the inmost consciousness to the outermost consciousness. Speaking picturesquely, it is like an egg—the yellow center, the white, and then the shell. So our minds from the center to the surface are different shadows; but these shadows are the shadows of the enlightened one, and *shila* is at the center.

The five elements are: 1) Commandments (*shila*): You do not wish to kill, to steal, etc., because it is innate within you. 2) Tranquillity (*samadhi*): You do not wish a bustling life or to make money. 3) Wisdom (*prajna*): You do not wish to live in delusion. 4) Emancipation (*vimukti*): You do not wish to suffer the pangs of conscience, but wish to live a life of sanction. When you come near to one who is emancipated, you feel no pang of conscience, you feel at ease, you sense the fragrance of incense. With others, you feel strange. They do not emit this fragrance. 5) Knowledge of Emancipation (*vimukti-jnana*): Teaching. You know how you were emancipated, so you will teach it. This is the hardest of all.

The Sixth Patriarch said to his multitude that he would give to them the incence of *dharmakaya*. The five elements are *here*. They are not just the words of Hui-neng. He said they are the elements of your nature.

"And then I will teach you the formless confession." If your mind is not empty, you cannot understand formless confession. I will translate this confession later.

Of course, I do not believe these are the words of the Sixth Patriarch because he would not have given such details, as he was a great master of the Southern School. I imagine that all these details were written by his disciples and later included in the main lines of the record. They are included by scholars, but for my part, I do not include them as important. However, to give you the full translation, I must include them and give you my commentary on these not-so-important lines.

The Master had asked everyone to kneel down; then he said:

*"The first is the incense of commandment (*shila*)."* *Shila* means present conscience, like incense that perfumes your character. Intrinsically you possess it. It is not given to you by a teacher, or by Buddha. As a human being, you have it innately. Even animals have their own conscience. All have it. The hungry tiger will not kill another tiger, but the mother will kill one cub to save the others. Only then are the others permitted to eat it. Before this, even in the greatest hunger, they will not eat one another.

There is a story in Buddhism: A prince, who was a bodhisattva, was looking down from a cliff and saw a mother tiger about to kill one of her starving cubs. Seeing this, the prince went down the cliff and offered himself to the mother tiger, but the mother tiger would not kill him. Even in her grief, about to kill her offspring, she could not kill a human being. Realizing this, the prince went back and threw himself from the cliff. The mother tiger saw him dead, stained in his own blood. Only then would she eat him. You will see this story often, carved on stones or told in bronze.

So *shila* is innate conscience, and it is difficult to violate. It is like the incense of your nature, which perfumes your character and permeates your house; if anyone comes in, you smell him. And if you meet anyone who violates his own conscience, run from him.

"When you possess neither falsehood nor evil, neither jealousy, greed, anger, nor malice within your mind, it is called the incense of commandment." It is hard *not* to possess any of these qualities within your mind. But if your soul does not fall into egoism, your nature is not your own, it is the bodhisattva's. It is universal.

"The second is the incense of tranquillity (samadhi)." This *samadhi* dwells in quietude and tranquillity like the beautiful aquamarine that forms a shining blue crystallization at the bottom of the sea. If your mind is always fluctuating, you will not find this *samadhi* at the bottom of your mind.

"When your mind is not agitated by observing all outside appearances, good or bad; it is called the incense of tranquillity." When you see something good, particularly for you, it carries your own desire but may be bad for someone else. Why do you have to call a thing good or bad?

"The third is the incense of wisdom (prajna)." This wisdom is intrinsic wisdom, diamond wisdom. If you do not have it, how can you keep your mind quiet? When a child is left alone by its parents, it will

cry because it is annoyed by the outside. It sees the shadow of the tiger in the woods. The outside of self is uncertain, so how can you conquer such disturbance? Only with your own transcendental wisdom. So *prajna* is the shadow of that wisdom.

"When your mind is without obstruction and you constantly observe your original nature with wisdom so that you do no evil, and when your mind remains without attachment, though performing virtuous deeds, so that you have respect for your superiors and compassion for your inferiors and sympathy for the poor and for the friendless, it is called the incense of wisdom." Original mind is your *alaya*-consciousness. You will observe it with your *prajna*, your transcendental wisdom. Then you will understand the bottom of your own mind, which connects you to universal consciousness, the Great Universe. You are originally connected, but you are isolated from it by your attitude, your own ignorance. So by your own wisdom, you must recognize this original state. Only religion gives you the key to make you one with the universe.

The "virtuous deeds" are the six *paramitas*. There is no time to explain this now, but I think you know about the *paramitas*. These are the deeds of a bodhisattva who will take no reward.

*"The fourth is the incense of emancipation (*vimukti*)."* If you are not emancipated from all superstitions and delusions, you cannot attain transcendental wisdom. Emancipation is like a robe you are wearing. It will keep this diamond wisdom in your bosom.

"When your mind no longer attaches to the outside, not judging things in terms of good and bad, but remaining free and unobstructed, it is called the incense of emancipation." For instance, your horoscope says that it is a clear day, but you see that it is raining. Or a friend says that there is a job for you, and says, "Go get it!" But the horoscope says "No, go north today." So you do not go for the job on Seventh Avenue. You go to the Bronx!

You must free yourself from all these things, and not only these things, but from philosophies and sciences that are expressed in terms. You must find that which is not interpreted by the human being, for you cannot interpret enough from the human standpoint. When you are thinking and trying to understand by reasoning, it is a terrible way. The wisteria vine that climbs upward finds its way naturally.

"The fifth is the incense of the knowledge of emancipation (vimukti-jnana*).* You can emancipate yourself by your own attainment; but if you do not have the knowledge of your own emancipation, you cannot emancipate another.

The Buddha told how he found his own emancipation by his own method, so he knew how to help others, and we are still using his way.

"Though your mind no longer attaches to the outside, you must not hold to quiescence or submerge yourself in emptiness": When you attain unity with the universe, you will fear this breaking off. You think you are one with the great quietude of the universe. But you are not; you have fallen into the trap of emptiness, the *term* emptiness.

It's like stopping a bottle—nothing comes out. You must throw the stopper away and realize that things cannot manifest themselves by their own knowledge. Then you will really touch something intangible and ungraspable, and you will understand. To take the stopper off and get into real emptiness, this is the secret of Buddhism.

"But must realize your own intrinsic mind by broadening your learning and acquiring further knowledge. To attain the enlightenment of all the buddhas, meeting things peacefully with the light [of wisdom], making no distinction between self and others, and coming directly to enlightenment, the true unchanging nature of things—this is called the incense of the wisdom of emancipation." "Self and others" here means all relative existences—yes and no, zero and one, night and day. You must give all this away.

You must give up this dualistic attitude and attain to the one-view, the single eye. Finally, you will also have to relinquish this "oneness of the universe."

When I was young, I asked my teacher: "Is it true that the most truthful moment of mind is when I am asleep?" "Yes, it is," he answered. "But it seems to me that when I go home and talk to my mother, that is the true time." So I realized that from morning to evening, I am true. There is no false time. The koan "Depending upon nothing, manifest your own mind" is a trick to cut through to quick realization; then every moment is a true moment. Zen is not really difficult. You must touch the magnetism of the *dharmakaya* and then—AH!—you will realize your self.

Good friends, these incenses perfume your mind within. Do not seek them without!" These incenses, the pure shadows of enlightened mind, perfume your mind within. When you do something, it always perfumes, or fumigates your mind, just as smoke fumigates your sleeves. It permeates your inmost mind, perfumes the seeds of your consciousness, and carries your karma to your next incarnation. Do not seek these incenses on the outside.

"Now I shall teach you how to make formless confession. By this confession, the sins that you have committed through past incarnations will be expiated, and the three karmas, which you are creating, shall become pure.

"Good friends, all of you together repeat after me:

We, your disciples, have realized that our minds from one moment of thought to the next, throughout the past, present and future, are not stained by the delusions that result from ignorance.

We confess our sins, all deeds and delusions that result from ignorance. May they cease at once and never arise again!

We, your disciples, have realized that our minds from one moment of thought to the next throughout the past, present and future, are not stained by the delusions that result from pride and arrogance.

We confess our sins, all our evil acts, our pride and arrogance. May they cease at once and never arise again!

We, your disciples, have realized that our minds from one moment of thought to the next throughout the past, present and future, are not stained by the delusions that result from feelings of jealousy.

We confess our sins, all our evil deeds and our feelings of jealousy. May they cease at once and never arise again!

"Good friends, this is what I call formless confession [ch'an-hui].

"What is meant by 'ch'an,' and what is meant by 'hui'? 'Ch'an' is that you confess your previous errors. You confess from the bottom of your mind all the previous evil karmas you created and the sins you committed as the result of your delusion, arrogance, jealousy and the like, never letting them arise again. This is called 'ch'an.' 'Hui' is that you repent of wrongs [you may commit] in the future. You realize the evil karmas that you may commit in the future, and the sins you may commit as the result of your delusion, arrogance, jealousy and the like, abjuring them all forever and repeating them no more. This is called 'hui.' Therefore, this expression, 'ch'an-hui,' means confession.

"The common-minded man in his ignorance knows only how to confess his previous errors but does not know how to repent his future wrongs. By failing to repent his future wrongs, his previous errors do not

cease. If previous errors do not cease and wrongs continue to be committed in the future, how can you call it confession?"

SOKEI-AN SAYS:

In the last lecture, the Sixth Patriarch was speaking to his disciples about the five incenses that perfume your mind.

"Now," the Patriarch says, *"I shall teach you how to make formless confession. By this confession, the sins that you have committed through past incarnations will be expiated":* This is where he speaks about the formless confession of non-existence.

We have realized that everything we see on the outside, phenomena, can be reduced to original essence. Of course, we each speak about it differently and from different angles, and we can name it in our own terms; but after all, it is essential oneness.

In that state of existence, all discriminations cease to exist, but really our minds came from that state originally. So if you go back to that state of realization, the sins that you have committed in some period, or some country, or in some situation will be reduced to nothingness. The sins that were committed by you will be forgotten when you attain oneness, and those who have not realized original oneness by their own wisdom will suffer for what they have committed.

Of course, real confession is not just confessing whatever sins you have committed, but attaining original oneness in your own mind. It is easy to speak about original oneness philosophically, but it is difficult to realize. Until that day, you really cannot accept yourself, you must criticize yourself from morning to evening. You will stop on the day that you are born into original oneness. Those born into original oneness are pure and can accept themselves. This is a religious mystery!

You must struggle hard many, many years for this oneness, which is not really "one," either. For absolute oneness is not one. It cannot be compared with anything. If it can be compared with something else, it is not absolute. It is not real nothingness.

"And the three karmas, which you are creating, shall become pure." Old karmas will be expiated. This expiation is absolute salvation in Buddhism. When you realize it once, from that day you are not yourself, you are part of the Great Universe. You are not performing your life according to your own ideas. From that day, life will be bestowed upon you. You will be emancipated. Pain and agony will no longer be yours. From that moment, all your deeds will be pure deeds. They will be just the same as before, but your consciousness will accept them differently.

This world is nothing but your mind, you know. So if your mind permits your deeds, they are pure—it is absolute permission. But your mind cannot do this before it is one with absolute oneness. This state cannot be spoken of in words, so temporarily, I use the term "absolute oneness."

"Good friends, all of you together repeat after me:

We, your disciples, have realized that our minds from one moment of thought to the next, throughout the past, present and future, are not stained by the delusions that result from ignorance.

We confess our sins, all deeds and delusions that result from ignorance. May they cease at once and never arise again!"

We, your disciples, have realized that our minds from one moment of thought to the next throughout the past, present and future, are not stained by the delusions that result from pride and arrogance.

We confess our sins, all our evil acts, our pride and arrogance. May they cease at once and never arise again!

We, your disciples, have realized that our minds from one moment of thought to the next throughout the past, present and future, are not stained by the delusions that result from feelings of jealousy.

We confess our sins, all our evil deeds and our feelings of jealousy. May they cease at once and never arise again!

Good friends, this is what I call formless confession. When in the autumn we go to the woods and see a pool of water, the water seems stained by red and yellow leaves. But when we take the water in our hands, it is pure. Defiled mind is your delusion. The pool is your mind, and when you return to original consciousness, you know that your mind is not stained. There is no more reward and no more punishment, for it is complete emancipation. You as an individual cease to exist; you go back to the bosom of Great Consciousness. You are ignorant because you do not know this *dharmakaya*.

You ask: "How, if the individual ego ceases to exist can the Buddhist maintain the idea of reincarnation?" Well, reincarnation to the Buddhist means no particular body and no particular soul. It is original oneness with the universe. When you go back to the body of the universe, this discreet ego ceases to exist. When you realize this, you know that your delusion came from your own ignorance, your own arrogance and pride, your own feelings of jealousy. These are really obstacles to coming into religion. You cannot enter the gate of religion through philosophy or science. There is just one avenue.

When I was young, about nineteen, and studying art, I studied sculpture from Egyptian to Greek, to Roman, to modern French. Then I went back to Oriental art and finally came to modern art with living models. I was sketching outside, carrying my canvas under my arm. How I adored nature! I surrendered absolutely. The farmers thought I was crazy to join my hands and kneel down before a brook or tree or a little flower. I came into religion through art. But there is another way, through daily life. From that humility before nature, I came to the gate of Buddhism. If you have no pride or arrogance in your mind, to enter the gate is quite simple.

"What is meant by 'ch'an'? *What is meant by* 'hui'? 'Ch'an' *is that you confess your previous errors. You confess from the bottom of your mind all the previous evil karmas you created and the sins you committed as the result of your delusion, arrogance, jealousy and the like, never letting them arise again. This is called* 'ch'an.' 'Hui' *is that you repent of wrongs [you may commit] in the future. You realize the evil karmas that you may commit in the future, and the sins you may commit as the result of your delusion, arrogance, jealousy and the like, abjuring them all forever and repeating them no more. This is called* 'hui.' *Therefore, this expression,* 'ch'an-hui,' *means confession."* Confession is based upon non-existence, not objective existence. Law, for instance, is objective existence, if you do such and such, you will go to jail. It's like writing on a clean slate. But *intrinsic* law is not written anywhere, and it is not objective; this law is like a white sheet of paper on which no particular law is written.

Human conscience is like that clean slate, so it is called formless confession, the form of non-existence. If anything happens outside of this, it makes an immediate reaction. From this clean slate, we make confession, not from any ulterior motives, but from the bottom of our mind. Confession might be from your erroneous reasoning—what you have picked up from the past, from personal experience that is not quite adapted to the present. But when you make a real confession, you will find the base of human knowledge that is common to all, and you will find that it is a clean sheet of white paper. Take the sheet of paper away and, in Buddhist terms, it is empty.

No particular explanation is necessary on the lines of the text, but I will say a few words on karma: The Buddhist believes that this life is the karma of a previous existence. Evil karma you must repay with your own agony. For instance, an Oriental religious teacher comes to a place like New York City and tries to get pupils. The people from China or Japan who know him whisper, whisper, whisper. The Buddhist attitude is to accept this in silence, not object, and say, "I'm glad you have given me an opportunity to pay back my old karma." If you were not pure in the past and people talk about you, it's no use becoming excited. Later, when you have paid all your debts, you can create something. But if you become frightened when you put on your pure robe and run away to another town because all are standing up and making a fuss over you, you will repeat this same experience again and again until you realize it is all just human nature.

Today, a queer cult is coming from Germany—Freudianism—which is based on a deluded view. Man's mind always adheres to the deluded view and to his private desires. I do not have much time, so I cannot explain this in detail.

"The common-minded man in his ignorance knows only how to confess his previous errors but does not know how to repent his future wrongs. By failing to repent his future wrongs, his previous errors do not cease. If previous errors do not cease and wrongs continue to be committed in the future, how can you call it confession?" A husband may take a drink in the evening and slap his wife's face. The next morning, he apologizes, but that noon he drinks again and slaps her face again. If you do not clean up your deluded view, you will always repeat your faults.

In the early periods of human life, fathers married daughters and mothers married sons. The father would be jealous of the son and the mother would hide him. When the son was twenty-one, she sometimes led him to the place where the father was sleeping and bade him kill the father. Men also married their sisters. Such turmoil! Then the first commandment was written: "Fathers shall not marry daughters, nor mothers marry sons."

I had some mice here who had babies. At first each mouse had wished to make her own nest and have her own babies, but it was very hard to sort out all the babies and take them to their own nests—no mouse knew which baby was her own. So all the mothers came together, and all the babies were adopted in common. It must have been terribly confusing! Human beings, I am sure, experienced this a long time ago and slowly evolved the morality we have today. When you look back, you realize the value of today's morality.

A mysterious law is written in the human heart, which it cannot explain: No man wishes to permit his wife to be taken by someone else. This is in the bottom of his heart. He will hear a whisper—"No, love and sex are not the same thing!"

"Good friends, now that you have finished your confession, let me repeat for you the Four Great Vows. All of you listen carefully and pay close attention.

Sentient beings, which abide within my own mind, are numberless; I vow to enlighten[11] them all.

Worldly desires within my own mind are endless; I vow to bring them to an end.

The gates of Dharma within my own nature are manifold; I vow to enter them all.

The Buddha Way within my own nature is ever beyond; I vow to attain it."

SOKEI-AN SAYS:

Now the Sixth Patriarch is is going to talk about the Four Great Vows of Buddhism.

"Good friends, now that you have finished your confession, let me repeat for you the Four Great Vows. All of you listen carefully and pay close attention." The Sixth Patriarch is going to recite the Four Great Vows with the multitude. We always recite these vows at the end of the evening lectures. You will find these vows in the old scriptures of Buddhism. Translated from the original Sanskrit, they are in the Shingon school, the Zen school, the Tendai school—all schools of Buddhism have the Four Great Vows. The Sixth Patriarch expressed these vows as his own. Using his own terms, he inserted more words between the lines; for instance: "those which abide within my mind" and "within my own nature." Each vow corresponds to a part of the foundation of Buddhist commandments. I shall give you this knowledge.

"Sentient beings, those which abide within my own mind, are numberless; I vow to enlighten them all." "Sentient beings" are those beings that live from morning to evening to accomplish their desire. In Buddhism, there is no particular ego within you. You yourself are an aggregation of the elements of beings within you—the elements of insects, fish, pigeons, and all varieties of animals. They are the sentient beings. Each individual possesses a city of sentient beings within himself.

"Worldly desires within my own mind are endless; I vow to bring them to an end." How do we bring these disturbing qualities in our minds to an end? The Buddhist thinks it can be done by meditation. In this meditation, your aim is the cessation of all desires so that pure knowledge appears in your mind, *but the outside is still with you.* The commandments that are established on the soil of desire are called paramitas.

The monks, while in their training, will refuse to be disturbed by visits from their families. This vow was established upon this mind. You must not see women, must not marry, and so on. It was quite natural for the monks to observe this.

When you come back to your own consciousness, your original state, the law is written on this original consciousness. If anyone tries to kill it, you must realize that you cannot kill *atman.* This is so-called natural morality.

"'The gates of Dharma within my own nature are manifold; I vow to enter them all." This third vow was established on the ground of everyday life and activity, which is not natural but determined by conditions. For instance, when you swim, you must put on a bathing suit, but you cannot go into a church wearing a bathing suit. (I am not quite sure about this last, but in New York I am sure you cannot.) And here, the Japanese do not like to see a Japanese walk in the street with an American woman. This is taboo.

You must understand these laws (Dharma) of morality, which really belong to the nature of man, and the laws which belong to the king.

In some factories, no one is permitted to smoke, for example; they are ruled by the king of that factory. In the early days of Buddhism, all the weak worked in the fields as farmers and the strong went to battle, while the brainy ones sat in their caves thinking and did not produce anything. So their fathers did not give them anything to eat. (Of course, the mothers would go in the evening and bring them food.) And they were not permitted to marry, either, because they couldn't even support themselves. They were just thinking and thinking about spiritual power. Today, this brain work is more important than manual labor, so we cannot apply the 2,500-year-old laws to such people.

It is through the gates of Dharma that you will enter the world of formlessness.

"The Buddha Way, within my own nature, is ever beyond; I vow to attain it." With this as the conclusion, you will attain Buddhahood, and no commandment is needed in this state. Standing upon this state, you will make the commandments yourself. However, if you have the notion that the whole universe is really nothing, that there is no law of causation, that the result is not the consequence of the cause, and that you have no need to fear the whip of karma, since there is no law, no morality, and neither good nor evil exists—if this is your hypothetical conclusion, you are violating the commandments of the Buddha. You must understand that these are the laws of morality, which really belong to the nature of man and to the present, as if by order of a king.

"Good friends, do you realize what you have said: 'Sentient beings are numberless; I vow to enlighten them all'? It is not I, Hui-neng, who makes them enlightened, but you, good friends, [who must enlighten] those sentient beings that abide within the mind. These minds are the minds of delusion, deceit, evil, jealousy, and malice. All of these are sentient beings. Each of you must yourselves convert [these sentient beings], which are within your own nature, to enlightenment. This is called true conversion.

"What is meant by 'convert [these sentient beings], which are your own nature, to enlightenment'? It is that you convert sentient beings—the false views, the afflictions and the ignorance within your mind—by your true view. When you attain the true view, you convert each of these sentient beings—ignorance, delusion—by destroying them with your prajna wisdom—the false is converted to the true, delusion to enlightenment, ignorance to wisdom, and evil to virtue. This is what is called true conversion."

"'Worldly desires are endless; I vow to bring them to an end' is that you eliminate your erroneous thoughts and useless imagination with your innate prajna.

"'The Gates of Dharma are manifold; I vow to enter them all' is that you must recognize your own original nature and always perform your deeds in accordance with the law of true Dharma. This is called true learning.

"'The Buddha Way is ever beyond; I vow to attain it' is that, always humble, you perform your deeds in accordance with truth, free from both delusion and awakening, and that you find prajna always growing within you.

"Abandoning both truth and falsehood, you will at once find your Buddha-nature, and upon reciting these words, instantly realize the teaching of Buddhism. The ceaseless desire of your heart to perform this practice is the force of your prayer."

SOKEI-AN SAYS:

Through these Four Great Vows, you can enter into Buddhism, just as the Zen monk, practicing meditation, enters Buddhism.

In the early period of Zen, Zen monks lived in the Vinaya school, the school of commandments. The monks were practicing meditation, observing the commandments and discoursing philosophically.

All these approaches to Buddhism were existing at the same time. Later, monks practiced one part in particular, either the commandments or meditation. So while Lin-chi and Huang-po did not speak much about the commandments, the Sixth Patriarch spoke about them very carefully.

"Good friends, do you realize what you have said: 'Sentient beings are numberless; I vow to enlighten them all'? It is not I, Hui-neng, who makes them enlightened, but you, good friends, [who must enlighten] those sentient beings that abide within the mind. These minds are the minds of delusion, deceit, evil, jealousy, and malice. All of these are sentient beings. Each of you must yourselves convert [these sentient beings], which are within your own nature, to enlightenment. This is called true conversion." If you observe these commandments, you can annihilate all delusions, and so on. But if, observing the conditional commandment, you have to keep your pride, there will be difficulties. It was established as a law.

"What is meant by 'convert [these sentient beings], which are your own nature, to enlightenment'? It is that you convert sentient beings—the false views, the afflictions and the ignorance within your mind—by your true view." The "true view" is part of the Eightfold Noble Path: 1) true view; 2) true goal; 3) true speech; 4) true action; 5) true living; 6) true effort; 7) true mindfulness; 8) true contemplation.

True view is the most important. By *sanzen* you are trying to attain the true view of Buddhism. If you try to make a view with some term, your view is not true. If you say that the universe was created by God, you are not taking a true view. For a true Buddhist, this is not the true view. From the original standpoint, which is not the human standpoint, there is no universe, no creation, no becoming, and no God—no such existence, because there is no consciousness in the *original* view. Then why do we call this a view? Because there is nothing to talk about, and "nothing to talk about" is a view, as I explained in one of my lectures last week.

When there is nothing to talk about and nothing to think about, it is the true view. Funny, isn't it? Then how do you express it? Lin-chi expressed it with a shout, Te-shan expressed it with a stick, Ma-tsu expressed it in a few words, and Chu-chih expressed it with a finger. I think that in *sanzen*, day by day, the true view becomes deeper and broader. It is useless if you try to grasp this true view by discourse, by reading or by thinking—it cannot be attained. This is particularly Buddhist. If you wish to grasp the true view, you had better try immediately in this moment. Otherwise, you must practice *zazen* for a long time.

The "false view" is not only one but many—each word is a false view and an affliction. From morning to evening your mind is not easy; there is always something affecting your consciousness, and you cannot get out of it. Your "ignorance" is the ignorance of the law of the universe. There is a good koan for this: "If you meet a giant dragon that catches you and flings you around the universe, throwing you into hellfire, at that moment how do you observe the commandments?" Through this koan, you will really grasp the true foundation of the commandments.

I realized this when I joined the army in the Russo-Japanese War. We were marching under a shower of fire. My comrades on the left and right were falling down. There was no hope left and it was a piercing moment! I thought, "How can I observe my commandment at this moment?" At such a moment, affliction is nothing at all. Hatred, anxiety, anger, love, joy mean nothing. If you come to the true foundation of the commandments, the battlefield is a good experience for everyone. To the conscientious one, the experience of war can be a great teaching. To the depraved one, it means nothing. It is only horrible.

Had I been taught this in my youth, perhaps I could have escaped the horsewhip of karma. But no one taught me the real law. Later, I learned about the commandments of the universe and sentient beings—life, natural consciousness, and the agreements between human beings. For instance: you shall not go to church on Sunday morning in your bathing suit, and you shall not eat garlic before entering the temple. This law is not quite natural to human beings, but it was made. For with that odor of garlic, both men and devas will turn their backs on you and run away.

When I was ignorant, I felt many times that men and devas were against me. I did not know what I was doing. It was not clear and seemed to be imposed—you must do this, and you cannot do that! For thirty years I was making that karma. I asked my teacher, who said: "Find out by your own exertion. If I told you, you would not believe."

"When you attain the true view, you convert each of these sentient beings—ignorance, delusion—by destroying them with your prajna-*wisdom": Prajna-*wisdom is Manjushri, the god of intrinsic wisdom. He holds a diamond sword in his hand to destroy all false views, afflictions, and ignorance. Manjushri really means *dharmakaya* wisdom.

When you come in for *sanzen* and have answered 203 koans, you will think that you have attained *dharmakaya*. I thought so, too! The first time I went back to Japan and met my teacher after years of separation, I said: "Perhaps I can teach my students *dharmakaya*." My teacher said nothing, but smiled, and I suddenly realized that I did not know anything about *dharmakaya* and must go all over it again. Hopeless moment! Each time you pass that gate, your knowledge becomes deeper, and your wisdom becomes clearer. I am within the door of *dharmakaya* thirty-five years now.

It is said in the *Prajnaparamita* sutras: "If you try to see Buddha with your eyes, or try to hear Buddha with your ears, you cannot find Buddha." Truly, Buddha can only be found with *prajna*. *Prajna* is diamond wisdom, the supreme wisdom. With it you can see *dharmakaya*.

Occasionally, people ask me: "When you step out of the mirror that reflects nothing, and there is no reflection, how can you see anything?" This is a good question that only Zen students will understand.

"The false is converted to the true, delusion to enlightenment, ignorance to wisdom, and evil to virtue. This is what is called true conversion." I do not accept such conversion. When you go to a Shingon temple, the priest will drop water on the head of an infant seven days after its birth and shout—"Yaaah!" Then he will say: "You are converted." Such religion is like opium. It is good for nothing.

I was born the son of a Shinto priest, and I saw enough of such religion. I did not believe in it from the first day. I knew that human prayer through the human throat cannot be heard by God, but that the prayer which *can* be heard is daily life. I knew this when I was five years old, a true child. When I was fifteen, my father was dying, and my mother sent for some sacred water. Until that day, I had believed it was sacred; but that day, no: it was old water, stale and with dust in it. From being surrounded by God, the gate was now closed to me. Perhaps it was because of this, that when I was twenty, I came to Zen. In Zen, I found God again.

"'Worldly desires are endless; I vow to bring them to an end' is that you eliminate your erroneous thoughts and useless imagination with your innate prajna." We are reciting this every night at the close of the lecture, but these worldly desires come and come. You cannot entirely destroy them. But when you reach *anasrava*, the state of non-leakage, that is the true end.

I read in a book that a traveller came to a monastery and asked: "Is this the end of the road?" A monk said, "No, go over the mountain." So he followed a narrow way over the mountain. "Is this the end of the road?" Again he was told, "No." Then he came to the edge of a cliff—nothing there but the sky! It was the true end.

To the little woodworm eating wood inside a tree, the tree is the universe. He eats the wood and makes dung of the wood, and when he comes out into the sun, that is the end of him. It is the same with us. You who are taking *sanzen*, I will tell you when you come to the end. Then, whatever comes, don't worry.

Without this joy, this enlightenment, human life is ashes. It does not mean anything at all.

"'The Gates of Dharma are manifold'": "Gates" means divisions. "Dharma" means Buddha's teachings, the law of the universe—all the laws of the universe. It was originally limited, but in Mahayana the meaning becomes quite broad. Today, there are many divisions to study in the scientific and metaphysical fields that were not studied by the monks of that day. No one can fully accomplish even one of them in a lifetime.

"'I vow to enter them all' is that you must recognize your own original nature and always perform your deeds in accordance with the law of true Dharma. This is called true learning." If I cannot do it in this life, I will do it in the next life. This is the Buddhist view.

From the Zen standpoint, this entrance to all gates is simple, you must recognize your own original nature. This is the first step in understanding the mystery of the world.

Before father and mother, what were you? By this gate, you will enter the gate of your primal being. But to enter a gate does not mean to step forward. It means to retreat back into your own consciousness. By meditation, you will break through the dam of original nature—of all being—and always perform your deeds in accordance with the law of "true Dharma"—true learning. Return to this field, and you will perform your daily life from the true Dharma standpoint.

Buddhism does not take a symbolic or mythological view of this world. Buddhism takes a radical view. So the Buddhist thinks his daily life from morning to evening is in service to God, and his joys and his tears, his sighs and his songs are an offered hymn. But the Buddhist does not speak in such terms. He says: "I put on my vesture"; "I eat my food"; "I carry water"; "I plow the field."

Weeping, laughing, eating is a hymn. Your house is a church, and your physical body is a shrine. Your consciousness is a priest, and your Buddha nature is God. So to feed your physical body is a festival, to nourish your mental body is a sermon, and to meditate is the ritual of your consciousness. There is no other religion that teaches this. To teach this, they have to build a temple and set up symbols. The true meaning is not there. They disdain daily life and desecrate the temple.

Thus, we have to teach according to the Dharma, through strength, bodily strength. Every joy is true joy, and every tear is a true tear in accordance with the law of true Dharma. True gentlemen will follow this way. This attitude is religion.

When I went to hear my teacher speak about this, I did not understand because I was in the 33rd heaven. I am not there now. I am on the ground.

"'The Buddha Way is ever beyond'": This is the wisdom of Buddha, Buddha knowledge—Buddhism. When you are living in Buddhism, it is mysterious.

When I bow down to the candle, it is the result of a chain of karma that began when I received this body. I am here a little while, a rainbow. Life, a lotus flower, blooms when the chords of consciousness interplay. If you say the world is everlasting and that you will conquer it with your power and your wisdom, if you think you will live forever, have love forever, wealth forever—you will not see this dream. If you understand your ego and think, "I AM," and keep these words ever active, you will notice this dream. From the eternal view, there is nothing to keep permanently. A moment—I and you, this life—and then back to infinite chaos, like a silhouette reflected in lightning. We see this world as a silhouette, and this makes life religious. But when your friend dies, and you say: "Go back to eternity, my friend, you did not pay me the five dollars you owe me," is that religion? A little of the Oriental view helps.

New York is very mysterious. It is not necessary to go to Miami. Each moment gives you a wonderful poem of joy and sorrow that is endless.

"'I vow to attain it' is that, always humble, you perform your deeds in accordance with truth, free from both delusion and awakening": On the true stage of daily life, you shall not be somebody, you must be nobody. You must be humble—a great soul. Then you can perform great deeds. Free yourself from awakening. Awake in this life. In true life, there is no such contradiction, nor is there one in the eternal view.

"And that you find prajna *always growing within you."* You can see something with *prajna* that your five senses cannot see. With *prajna*, you will see it. We cannot see eternal time and eternal space with our eye. Our eye cannot see it, but with *prajna* intuition—not your common intuition, you will see that which does not relate to your five senses.

Do you see it now?

"Abandoning both truth and falsehood, you will at once find your Buddha-nature, and upon reciting these words, instantly realize the teaching of Buddhism. The ceaseless desire of your heart to perform this practice is the force of your prayer." When you abandon and give up what is true and what is false and take the attitude of meditation, the performance of your deeds from morning to evening is the *real* prayer.

When I was living in Seattle, Washington, there was a big slope up Washington Street. It was a shortcut to my home, but it was very steep. When I came back home from work I would take this shortcut. On a very hot day I would think about this very hard. I would think: "This is my prayer. I am going up with my own power. With all my strength, I go up this slope." And I would have another thought as I reached the top: "This world turns very fast and very hard by its own power. This is the world's prayer. Every day as it turns from east to west, it is the prayer of the universe."

You must offer something, some strength, for a prayer. The whole world is moving in its orbit as a star moves. That is its prayer. Your whole life is a prayer; prayer is your daily life from morning to evening. When you understand this, your prayer is heard.

"Good friends, now we have made our Four Great Vows. In addition to this, I will give you the formless commandments of the three refuges.

"Good friends, we take refuge in awakening, [in the Buddha] supremely revered among men; we take refuge in the truth, [in the Dharma,] which frees us from desire; we take refuge in purity, [in the Sangha,] whose members are honored above all sentient beings. From this day, we shall call the Buddha our teacher, shall never take refuge in demons or heretics, and shall ever testify to our enlightenment with the three treasures of our own nature.

"Good friends, I urge you to take refuge in the three treasures of your own nature. These are: the Buddha of awakening, the Dharma of truth, and the Sangha *of purity.*

"When you take refuge in the awakening of your mind, deluded thoughts will not arise. Having few desires, you will be content and renounce wealth and lust. Then you may call yourself Buddha, 'he who is revered among men'.

SOKEI-AN SAYS:

The Sixth Patriach said: *"Good friends, now we have made our Four Great Vows."* When you have a true heart as a man or a woman, and once in your life have made a vow to do something, you cannot abandon it or violate it so easily, for religion is the foundation of your heart and soul. When you make a vow, you should not throw it away for some trifling reason, for hatred or for ego—"Well, I quit"—and let it go and forget all about it. If you do, then I do not call it making a vow. If you have really made a vow with all your heart and soul, you are not going to give up because there is someone you do not want to meet at the temple. When you really make a vow, it is your decision, and you will uphold it all your life. To be sure, it is very easy to make a vow for big things, as a soldier, for instance, makes a vow to sacrifice himself for his country. But it is not so easy to keep a vow when it is a trifling thing—such as making a vow not to borrow from your friends, and the next morning you call up and say, "Will you lend me five dollars for a couple of days? I need it." If you are going to give up a vow so easily, why make it at all if you are going to throw it away like this?

You did not make your decision to study Zen in a couple of days, yet you come for one or two years, make a vow, and then throw it away like an old slipper. If you make a vow, if you make a decision, you should uphold it all your life. In such a way, Buddhists have handed down, from the Buddha's time, the vow to enter the *sangha* of Buddhism. When you entered the Sangha, you made this vow, and you were admitted.

In addition to this, I will give you the formless commandments of the three refuges. Good friends, we take refuge in awakening, [in the Buddha], supremely revered among men; we take refuge in the truth, [in the Dharma,] which frees us from desire; we take refuge in purity, [in the Sangha,*] whose members are honored above all sentient beings."* These three refuges are that Buddha exists, not individual existence; that Dharma exists in our hearts; and that *sangha* exists for Buddha's disciples. These are the three refuges for us to be converted, the three refuges which we must remember, and upon which we must find a foundation if we are to exist.

Now, there is just one substantial body in the world. With this substantial body, the wooden man sings and the stone woman dances. With this substantial body, you will stop the sailing boat on the faraway ocean. Something you cannot do, you will ask someone else to do. Your body is in San Francisco, Chicago, New York, Japan—your body is everywhere. I can ask my *dharmakaya* to carry my message to Japan, and it will carry my letter to Japan. If you do not take this *dharmakaya* attitude, what will you do? You will mail the letter yourself, not trusting anyone, and it will take five cents and a two-month voyage to get there. This you understand, but when you open your own book, you do not understand. If you do not see this, you are still in the old physical body, still eating your food for yourself and not for anyone else, saving your money for yourself and not for anyone else. Your physical body is very limited, and your mind is narrow, too.

So to "take refuge in Buddha" means to take refuge in *dharmakaya*. At the end of the day, I close my eyes and peace comes because I know my *dharmakaya* does not die.

Dharmakaya means something to the Buddhist. You realize this when you are taking *sanzen* and you can go through the keyhole or sail over the Great Water—all those old transcendental things.

You must not pass a koan, then put it on the shelf. If you do not realize this, you are still in the same old physical body; you do not realize the value of your Buddhism. You are still in the old physical world, and you will not become a bodhisattva.

"From this day, we will call the Buddha our teacher": "The Buddha" is Shakyamuni Buddha, Buddha in the shape of a man. We worship his footprint because he found his *dharmakaya*. He renounced the men of the world and the life in the world of these men.

When you find your *dharmakaya* and really understand its meaning, you cannot help renouncing the life of the man of the world. If you keep your ego and desire to satisfy your ego's wishes, you are still living in your old physical body and not in *dharmakaya*. To live in *dharmakaya* is the true meaning of taking refuge in Buddha. Buddha was the most honorable among the group of those who have realized their own *dharmakaya*.

"And will never take refuge in demons or heretics": This is a very old teaching. When the Buddha was in India, there were many heretics who worshipped their own gods, so when they entered the *sangha*, they made this vow. But you say, "Throughout my life, I . . .," and in three days you throw it away in the garbage can. What kind of vow is that?

"And shall ever testify to our enlightenment with the three treasures of our own nature. In Buddhism, you do not listen to anyone else's enlightenment. It is your own enlightenment that you are endeavoring to attain. Standing before the Buddha of your own nature, before the Dharma of your own nature, and before the Sangha of your own nature, you bear witness to whether your enlightenment is true or false.

In *sanzen* you testify as to the truth or falsity of your own enlightenment within the three treasures. My mind and your mind is the same mind. My Dharma and Buddha's Dharma is the same Dharma. When you come into the Zen room, you join your hands and bow to your own and Buddha's enlightenment.

There was once a student here who said he could not bow to me. How foolish! He thought I was a demigod. You do not bow to Sokei-an; there is no Sokei-an in the Zen room. You bow before the Three Treasures. But *you* bow before the Three Treasures and say: "Oh, Reverend gave me such a terrible koan! I quit!" There is no such terrible koan. It is your mind that is impure.

Good friends, I urge you to take refuge in the three treasures of your own nature. These are: the Buddha of awakening, the Dharma of truth, and the Sangha of purity." The Three Treasures are those answers which you attain through *zazen*.

"When you take refuge in the awakening of your mind, deluded thoughts will not arise. Having few desires, you will be content and renounce wealth and lust. Then you may call yourself Buddha, 'he who is revered among men.'" When you really understand the true meaning of the law of causation, you will accept the result of past karma, and you will not complain. You will not swim against the stream.

A gentleman from Japan said to me: "Why don't you act forcefully and advertise more?" I am Japanese, and I came to this country where the diplomatic condition between the white man and the yellow man is not quite fifty-fifty. We are poor economically, so our children will not go up, and Western culture will not come down. The whole situation of the world will not permit a Japanese man to do something in the field of religion in America. But if you open your eyes to all the waves of *dharmakaya*, you will know that you are one of them. You will understand your position, wherever you are. Then you will abjure thirst and lust, anger and selfishness, which is the real source of your agony. Then you will attain Buddhahood.

"If you take refuge in the truth of your own mind, you will not, from one moment of thought to the next, entertain erroneous views. Since there are no erroneous views, there is no "self" and no "other," no arrogance, greed or attachment. Then you may call yourself Buddha, 'he who has renounced desire.'

"If you take refuge in the purity of your own mind, you may deliver yourself from the world of afflictions and desires because your original nature is unstained. Then you may call yourself Buddha, 'he who is most honored of the order (sangha*).'*

"If you can perform this practice, you will take refuge in yourself. The common-minded man does not understand this. Though he takes the three refuges from morning to evening, if he says, 'I take refuge in the

Buddha,' where is the Buddha? If he cannot see the Buddha, in what does he take refuge? His words are simply false.

Good friends, each of you, examine this matter carefully for yourselves, and do not allow your mind to commit errors!"

SOKEI-AN SAYS:

According to the Sixth Patriarch, if you take refuge in the true law of your own mind, you will not, from one moment of thought to the next, entertain erroneous views. When you sit down, make a sit-down strike against all notions, all this outside, and contemplate your own consciousness. Then your erroneous views will cease. This is taking refuge in the construction of your own mind, the consciousness of your own existence.

According to modern psychological theory, there are three stages of consciousness: unconsciousness, subconsciousness, and "present" consciousness; and in the Buddhist theory there are eight. But in Zen, we are not studying these consciousnesses as a theory. In our meditation, we realize these eight consciousnesses one by one, from top to bottom and from bottom to top. To popularize the Buddhist theory, they gave it an elaborate philosophy in order to explain it. But all this philosophy is not important because Buddhism is really a very primitive religion. In this sense, Buddhism is very peculiar. You do not need to read anything or go to church. All you need to do to understand Buddhism is to sit down on your cushion and meditate upon your original consciousness. It is the only way to understand Buddhism because it is the true law of your own mind. Buddhism is a religion based upon the consciousness of sentient beings, not only human beings but all beings.

"Since there are no erroneous views, there is no "self" and no "other," no arrogance, greed or attachment. Then you may call yourself Buddha, "he who has renounced desire." Buddhism is the religion of non-ego. We do not believe in individual souls. We do not believe that souls are created by God one by one, some made favorably and some not, some made for Fifth Avenue and some to be sold on Second Avenue.

An Indian questioner asked Nagarjuna: "You say that all souls are the same. Is my soul the same as that of the worm on top of the dung heap?" Nargarjuna answered: "That worm that is eaten by the sparrow has a soul that is the same as yours." This is the Buddhist viewpoint.

The Buddha said to his disciples: "There are no castes in sentient beings; all are the same." Buddhists do not believe that white men are created by God and that yellow men come from the devil. Ego makes this arrogance. This kind of ego takes an attitude of attachment.

"If you take refuge in the purity of your own mind . . .": And all mind is originally pure in the state of original consciousness.

"You may deliver yourself from the world of afflictions and desires because your original nature is unstained. Then you may call yourself Buddha, 'he who is most honored of the order (sangha*).'"* Mental afflictions or physical difficulties are really nothing but waves fluctuating on the surface of the ocean. If you do not take an egoistic attitude, it is not *you* that suffers. It is your karma following the law of causation and giving you the circumstances that carry you into difficulties and laziness. If you do not let go of your ego, you will not understand this law, or succeed in understanding Buddhism. But until that time, you will say: "Oh, I don't want to go there because everyone gives me the cold shoulder," or "I won't go there because the air is so icy." If you do not change such an attitude, you will suffer. You cannot take this attitude and live happily.

"If you can perform this practice, you will take refuge in yourself. When we say, "Take refuge in Buddha—in *dharmakaya,*" this means that you are taking refuge in your *own* consciousness. This is your *own* shrine of Buddha, and Buddha is in this shrine.

"The common-minded man does not understand this. Though he takes the three refuges from morning to evening": As you do when you come here and recite the refuges.

"If he says, 'I take refuge in the Buddha,' where is the Buddha?" This is the same as asking, "Where is God?" to the Japanese Christian kneeling on the sand by the sea, praying, "Oh God!"

So, where is God? Somewhere in the sky? In Heaven? Is there any Pure God in Heaven? You do not know. But the Buddhist takes refuge in the Three Treasures! So where is this Buddha? Dead? If not, what is it?

"If he cannot see the Buddha, in what does he take refuge? The Buddhist is quite particular and very exact about this. When the Buddhist says, "I saw Buddha with my eye," he means his physical eye. So when you take *sanzen,* I will say: "Show it to me. I have listened to your words, and I understand your abstract theory. But I come from Missouri, you've got to show it to me!"

"His words are simply false." When you join hands to God in heaven, are you quite sure God is in heaven? At night, the heaven above is the heaven below. In what part of heaven does God exist? Where? If you do not know, the idea becomes false.

"Good friends, each of you examine this matter carefully for yourselves, and do not allow your mind to commit errors! From morning to evening you do not know that all these refuges are in your consciousness. See if you cannot see the Buddha.

"It is said clearly in the [Avatamsaka] Sutra that you take refuge in the Buddha of your own nature. It does not say that you take refuge in the Buddha that is not your own nature. If you do not take refuge within yourself, in what do you take refuge? Now, if you have already enlightened yourself, you ought each to take refuge in the three treasures of your own mind. If you regulate your mind within and respect others without, you are taking refuge in your own nature."

SOKEI-AN SAYS:

This is the explanation of your first koan. The secret is disclosed. The koan, "Before your father and mother, what were you?" was given to a monk by the Sixth Patriarch as a mysterious word, but the secret significance of this koan was given by him here. He explains it as clearly as if he were showing you an apple on his palm. He caught it as he said:

"It is said clearly in the [Avantamsaka] Sutra that you take refuge in the Buddha of your own nature. It does not say that you take refuge in the Buddha that is not your own nature." From the Zen standpoint, there is no Buddha but your own self. Everyone is Buddha. Everyone is God. There is no soul created by God because every soul is God. Every soul is Buddha. There is no "special" water created for every individual vessel. The water in each is the same water.

From the Buddhist view, our soul is one of the waves on the Ocean of Soul. When we die, the waves cease and go back to the waveless ocean. The surface of the sea is fluctuating and dashing waves toward the sky, but at the bottom there is eternal calm. The soul that emerges and submerges is the shadow of the fluctuating soul that is called, in modern terms, the unconscious. But if you go back deeper than the unconscious, you will not come back anymore because you have returned to the Ocean of Soul—the Womb of Buddha. All enlightened souls come from that Womb, the *Tathagatagarbha*.

You do not need to do anything to realize that you are buddha. Your original nature is buddha. You are IT. It is only your notion that separates you. It is your ignorance that separates you from your original nature that is buddha. The enlightened one sees everything in the state of original force. There is no woman or man, neither money nor diamonds. They are nothing but forms of the original force.

Someone may come and spit in your face, but that does not harm the original force, so you need not notice it. When you see everything as this original force, all is simple and clear. But to reach this original force, you must deprive yourself of all your notions. If someone with a sword in his hand comes to see you, you will probably view him with your own notion. You must see him as a force, and then it is clear. Look at everything without any interpretation by the notions in your mind. Original force is Soul. It is Mind; not the human mind, but MIND.

So, Zen has nothing to do with notions. Notions are ailments and amusements, and you are always answering them. Meditation is a method to get away from them. (I do not like to translate the word "Zen" as "meditation," because Zen and meditation are not the same.)

When you are sitting on your bed and taking off your shoes, some gossip you heard at the temple tumbles out of your mind. So you put your shoes on again, and you reach for the telephone and chatter, chatter, chatter. Your friend says, "Come over!" and you take a taxi even if it is eleven o'clock at night. These are all notions, and when you meditate they all come out. Chug, chug, chug!—always in the brain. You cannot help it.

You cannot escape these notions growing out of the unconscious like mushrooms. You cannot keep those birds of notion from coming into your brain and chattering, but you need not answer them. Living under the elevated train, if you entertain the noise, you will die in half a day, so you forget about it. But you are like the man who went to the country and couldn't bear the noise of the country, so he came back to the city at once.

Therefore, we have nothing to do with notions, and we do not entertain them. We sit on them. And if you do train yourself in meditation for many years, you will grow strong. You will read another's mind directly. You will become physically calm and mentally powerful because you will not waste your brain power on notions. To have a strong personality, meditation is the best practice. Zen students are always calm and healthy-looking because of *zazen*.

When you see a beautiful woman, she is just beautiful. Entertaining notions is the first step to disaster. If you do not entertain notions, your Buddha is immediate. When you go home, watch your mind for five minutes, and you will see a pandemoniac parade. I was eighteen when I realized that I was thinking something all the time. I said to my mother: "I think someone is living in my attic." "Then you are insane," she answered.

"If you do not take refuge within yourself, in what do you take refuge?" Buddha is yourself, and the law is written in your body.

"Now, if you have already enlightened yourself, you ought each to take refuge in the three treasures of your own mind." The Three Treasures of Buddha, Buddha's Teaching (Dharma), and Buddha's Community (Sangha).

"Of your own mind" does not mean this mind [pointing to his head]. This skull is your radio. You gather thoughts from the Universe of Mind, which is not in your skull. With the radio in your skull, you gather notions from the Infinite Mind, and anyone who is in your same vibration catches your vibrations. So when we gather here, we get vibrations or broadcasts of two thousand years ago. All of these minds are the Community of Buddha.

"If you regulate your mind within and respect others without, you are taking refuge in your own nature." But your mind is like an uncultivated forest filled with skunks and snakes. Clean it out! Make of it a beautiful garden. If you regulate your mind within, you will respect yourself, and then you will respect others.

"Good friends, now that you have sincerely taken refuge in the three treasures of your own nature. I shall explain to you the one-body Trikaya Buddha of your own nature so that you may see the three bodies and clearly realize for yourselves your own self-nature. All of you, repeat after me:

"With my very body, I take refuge in the pure Dharmakaya *Buddha.*
With my very body, I take refuge in the perfect Sambhogakaya *Buddha.*
With my very body, I take refuge in the numberless Nirmanakaya *Buddhas."*

"Good friends, the physical body is an abode; you cannot say that you take refuge in it. The Trikaya *Buddha is in your own nature. Everyone in the world has this within. [But] because your mind is deluded, you cannot see your inner nature. Because you seek the* Trikaya *Buddha without, you cannot see the* Trikaya *Buddha within. Give heed to my sermon! I shall disclose the* Trikaya *Buddha of your own nature within. This* Trikaya *Buddha is born from your own nature. You will not find it outside."*

SOKEI-AN SAYS:

I do not know if every one of you can understand these lines without any explanation, but I shall read them once more, and give you some remarks on these important lines.

"Good friends, now that you have sincerely taken refuge in the three treasures of your own nature. I shall explain to you the one-body Trikaya Buddha of your own nature so that you may see the three bodies and clearly realize for yourselves your own self-nature. All of you, repeat after me:

"With my very body, I take refuge in the pure Dharmakaya *Buddha.*
With my very body, I take refuge in the perfect Sambhogakaya *Buddha.*
With my very body, I take refuge in the numberless Nirmanakaya *Buddhas."*

The Trikaya Buddha is:

1) The Pure *Dharmakaya* Buddha—the omnipresent, elemental and original body; but it is not shadow, and it is not invisible.
2) The Perfect *Sambhogakaya* Buddha—consciousnesss, fire-consciousness.
3) The Numberless *Nirmanakaya* Buddhas that pervades the universe. You prove it with your physical body.

Thus there are three bodies in one body—one body observed from three standpoints or phases.

"Good friends, the physical body is an abode; you cannot say that you take refuge in it. This "abode" can be translated as "shrine," the shrine of Buddha. When you close your hands on your breast and stand before Buddha, you will realize that the physical body is an abode of Buddha. To say that you cannot take refuge in the physical body is really taking the view of a common-minded person because to him the physical body does not mean anything. But to the enlightened person, there is no physical body. His own body is really the *Trikaya* Buddha. IT is the physical body.

It's funny, isn't it? You cannot separate yourself from your body and stand before it. It's as if I were to take myself out of this wooden image and bow before it.

"The Trikaya Buddha is in your own nature." That is, in our own nature. When we join our hands on our breast and look upon ourselves from outside this physical body, stand before it and look into original nature, we find that this is the *Trikaya* Buddha within us. Those who worship God from the outside cannot realize this. They cannot free themselves and stand before their bodies, join hands and look into the *Trikaya* Buddha and find themselves within it. This state of being is permitted only to enlightened human beings, only to Zen students.

This means, of course, that the *Trikaya* Buddha is yourself. You realize this when you enter the first gate into Buddhism. So, really, the *Trikaya* Buddha is the initiation into Buddhism. It is a revelation—the whole mysterious world is manifested. You have seen the *Saddharma-pundarika*, the Pure White Lotus of the True Dharma. It is realization.

You will hear many words from the lips of Christian teachers about revelation. But *this* is revelation—God reveals Himself to us. You have your own teacher! But you come to this revelation, and you have no realization of its value.

If you are in a desert with no water, eating grass, and suddenly you see that you yourself are pervading heaven and earth, how wonderful! But in ancient days, it was rare for anyone to come to this realization. So the Buddha with his compassion devised this method. Now one can come into it quite easily.

Anyone who crossed this continent 150 years ago from east to west traveled in a covered wagon. It was a wonderful continent, a revelation! But today, everyone pays $150 and goes by train, and they do not see the wonder of it. In olden days, they fought Indians and starvation. Wagons broke and horses died. They knew what it meant. It was a real adventure.

The Buddha found it so meditating under a tree for six years, and the hermits found it under the desert sun. They appreciated the value of revelation. Today, you will find it in the *sanzen* room under the koan, "Before father and mother, what were you?" or the koan of the hand.

It is easy now, but it is the same revelation. If your master is broad and humble and you are really earnest, when you prove the first koan, you will appreciate revelation.

When I passed the first koan, I felt for seven days as if I were swinging in the air. It was so wonderful! You must cast away all notions, all convictions. When the old monk Kyogen was sweeping pebble stones in his garden—"OH!"—all the universe appeared in his mind. Hakuin, who had been meditating many days, entered it in sound with the midnight gong, but his *Trikaya* was still in the state of a dream. The next morning, he went out to beg still thinking nothing but revelation. An old woman refused to give him anything, saying, "Go away!" He did not hear her words, and the woman became impatient. With her bamboo broom, she knocked him into a rice swamp (his own mind). When he came out, he suddenly realized—*This is IT!*—and he rushed to his teacher's room. Immediately, his teacher said: "That is right. You have passed it."

Please do not think that *Oshô* is losing his temper if he shouts at you when you do not pass your koan in three or six months. Do not take a personal view of *sanzen*. There is no person present.

"Everyone in the world has this within. [But] because your mind is deluded, you cannot see your inner nature. Because you seek the Trikaya *Buddha without, you cannot see the* Trikaya *Buddha within. Give heed to my sermon! I shall disclose the Trikaya Buddha of your own nature within. This Trikaya Buddha is born from your own nature. You will not find it outside."* Trikaya Buddha means *Dharmakaya* Buddha, *Sambhogakaya* Buddha, *Nirmanakaya* Buddha.

Nirmanakaya Buddha means a man, a woman, a mouse, a cat, a postman, a policeman. In *Sambhogakaya* Buddha there is something common to all—consciousness. *Nirmanakaya* has beginning and end, but *Dharmakaya* Buddha is eternal. It is not born, and it will not die. How could you find the *Trikaya* Buddha outside? It is really foolish to kneel down and say, "Oh God!" and cry. It's nothing; you look like a child.

Well, I am quite sure that John Wesley, the originator of Methodism, and other Christian masters realized the true *Trikaya* Buddha within themselves—Father, Son, and Holy Ghost. But common-minded men and women do not understand, so they make a picture of heaven and hell. It's impossible to save their souls. I met such a woman. She drank very strong alcohol and was deluded all of her life.

"What is that which is called the pure Dharmakaya *Buddha? The nature of man in the world is originally pure. All things arise from his own nature. Think of bad things, and you do something bad. Think of good things, and you do something good. Thus all things exist within your own nature, like the sun and moon that are always bright, and the sky that is always clear. But when the sky is covered by clouds, the world, while still bright above, is dark below until a blast of wind sweeps away the clouds, disclosing all the phenomena in the sky and upon the earth. So is the nature of man, ever flowing like those clouds in the sky.*

"Good friends, knowledge is like the sun, and wisdom is like the moon. Knowledge and wisdom should always be bright. But when your mind cleaves to the outside and the clouds of delusion cover your original nature, they cannot remain bright, as they should be. But if you meet one who is enlightened and hear the true Dharma, you will then abandon delusion by your own exertion of mind. Thus, inside and outside will become as clear as crystal, and all things will be revealed within you. One who sees his own intrinsic nature will be like this. This is called your pure Dharmakaya *Buddha.*

SOKEI-AN SAYS:

I will read these lines again and give you my commentary.

"What is that which is called the pure Dharmakaya *Buddha?"* A monk asked Yun-men: "What is Buddha?" Yun-men answered: "A dung-scraper." I cannot give such an answer to young American ladies! If I did give such an answer, they would just perish and disappear from the group. Of course, this proves impure meditation—no *dharmakaya* in it.

"The nature of man in the world is originally pure. All things arise from his own nature." Not his own notion or his own idea, but his own *nature*, which is not ego and is originally pure. As long as you keep your ego, you cannot see your own nature.

It seems to me that in order to understand daily life, you must really solve the first koan that is given to you. From my own experience, you must find your answer and analyze it very carefully. Then you can apply it to daily life.

Pure *dharmakaya* is a dung-scraper, all right. But does that mean I can do any abominable thing? Well, I cannot accept that as Zen teaching.

Dharmakaya is all. There is no woman and no man included in it. It is not something to apply to daily life. *Dharmakaya* is the foundation. You do not root out the root and apply it to the ceiling—it is the root!

Do not criticize Zen teaching after a few months of study. It takes years to realize the value of it.

"Think of bad things, and you do something bad. Think of good things, and you do something good." I do not think you need an explanation of this.

"Thus all things exist within your own nature as the sun and moon that are always bright, and the sky that is always clear." "Things" here means those semi-phenomenal existences, the material of the mind—your own thoughts that come from the outside and stay in your mind as seeds. You see everything on the outside through those colored conceptions, as if you were looking through colored glass. But you do not truly see the outside, you do not see its true existence. When you think of something as good or bad, it is your own habit of thought.

People's minds are always influenced by topography. Topographical conditions can possess pessimistic thoughts, like those in India. When you go to India, all your ideas change. There the bamboo grows in a day and perishes in a day. In such a climate, you realize that wealth, beauty, youth, and so forth will perish like mushrooms after rain. It's like a dream. So religions are always influenced by topography. In Tibet, the practice of meditation is hard because they must sit quietly all winter as there is no production. In that high climate, there is not much wood for fire, so they put on all their blankets and eat very little, perhaps once in three days. They take this mode of life into their religion.

In an an old sutra, there is a story about a very beautiful woman. Her body was as slender as a bow. But she had decided to become a nun, so she cut her beautiful hair and gave up her beautiful clothes. One day, she came to a garden in a temple where the Buddha was staying. She looked at herself in the garden pool and saw that she was beautiful, like the Greek Narcissus who admired his own beauty. As she was admiring her reflection in the water, she saw the full moon reflecting back at her. But it was not the moon, it was a beautiful woman more beautiful than herself. "Who are you?" she asked the stranger. "My young sister, I understand you wish to become a nun. Why? You are young and your skin is so beautiful. Why are you abandoning your life in the world? Why not stay in the world, and enjoy it?"—etc. She, who was so young and so beautiful, suddenly became enlightened and awoke to a new life. She had realized that the phenomenal world is like a dream. She embraced the older woman and wept on her lap, and as she wept, the older woman died and changed into a white star.

This is not a true story, of course. But 2,500 years ago, in India, it was quite a natural thing for a young woman to give up the worldly life and become a nun.

"But when the sky is covered by clouds, the world, while still bright above, is dark below until a blast of wind sweeps away the clouds, disclosing all the phenomena in the sky and upon the earth. So is the nature of man, ever flowing like those clouds in the sky." We do not see such quick changes in the weather in this country, but in Japan at about sunset, the black clouds often cover your head. Tornado-like winds suck the fish up from the water and throw them about. When I was living on top of a mountain, and thunder, lightning, and rain were at my feet, the sky would clear in about ten minutes, and I could see the setting sun. Just so the mind thinks of this and that. The mind cries, then laughs, thinks of jewels, then of cigarettes, endlessly thinking of something. But it never pays attention to that which makes us think like clouds flowing in the sky.

"Good friends, your knowledge is like the sun, and wisdom is like the moon." Your first training as a lay novice in Buddhism is to control your mind by looking into it. You must look at the activity of your mind with effort. When you look into your mind, you will get a surprise—you will see flowing clouds.

You must meditate and not think "consciousness" or "subconsciousness," but just look into your mind and not allow yourself to be carried away by these thoughts that flow in your brain.

For example, you are reading a book, and you suddenly think of your friend, and you go to the telephone and call—"Hello!"—and put on your hat and go. You have been carried away by your thoughts.

This training is to put a rope on your thoughts and hold tight so the thoughts do not disturb your mind—your real mind. This is the first thing a beginner must practice in Buddhism.

I think I must explain this "knowledge" that is like the sun and the moon. This knowledge is almost synonymous with intellect. It is the mental function that makes you aware of what is happening in your mind or outside your mind. Buddha, which means awakened one, is the one who has awakened to the intellect within himself.

The Buddha thought the whole world was born from this intellect, which is a universal force—the cosmic dynamo of God. If I say "God," it sounds like religion, and if I say "cosmic dynamo," it means something scientific. I could also say, "Oversoul" or "Superman" or "Transcendentalism." Words always mislead. We say "Buddha," and you think of one who is always in meditation, but it is really one who has awakened this intellect in himself. Shakyamuni realized this within himself, and he completed this realization within himself.

"Knowledge and wisdom should always be bright, but when your mind cleaves to the outside and the clouds of delusion cover your original nature, they cannot remain bright as they should be." When your mind cleaves to the outside, you think that red is the color of this wooden fish, and that green or blue is the color of water. You think that water is cold and fire is hot. When you cut your hand with a knife, you think the pain belongs to the knife. All this is not a quality belonging to the outside; it is the subjective sense-perception.

People's view of the whole world is topsy-turvy, upside-down. Naturally they cannot observe anything exactly as it is exists. This cloud of delusion covers their original nature.

"But if you meet one who is enlightened and hear the true Dharma . . .": Like the Sixth Patriarch who heard an old man reciting a sutra on a street corner—"Depending upon nothing, realize your own mind"—

"You will then abandon delusion by your own exertion of mind." But you never think your own thoughts. You depend on this religion or that ism. So you only think thoughts that have been thought by someone else. So I say, depend only on yourself, your own intrinsic nature.

This is awkward Buddhism. For three drops of water, a lady paid a Hindu $25 for enlightenment. But the true Buddhist does not do this.

What is the true way to enlighten yourself? Just slip into meditation and control your flowing mind. But the mind is very difficult to control. When you are meditating, you hear something; you think of a man who owes you $25; or you are saying "Hello!" on a telephone. Then you are back again, meditating. Then you think of a cigarette, and it is very difficult. You become weary. From your little corner, you count your grains of poppy seed like a cat watching a mouse as it comes out of its hole.

You must begin this way when you are young. Then you will go back to the soul of the universe, and you will realize you are part of it—the barrier is removed. And from that day, you will understand all religions and all teachings. And you will know there is only one way to get into enlightenment, and that is through one's own nature. There is no enlightenment in books.

Mind . . . Cat . . . Thoughts . . . Mice . . . Snap them up one by one!

"Thus, inside and outside will become as clear as crystal, and all things will be revealed within you." The outside and the inside! The visible and the invisible! This is seeing your own nature—in Japanese, *kensho.*

One who sees his own intrinsic nature will be like this. This is called your pure Dharmakaya *Buddha."* Through the koan "Before father and mother," you will get into it. You will truly see your own original nature. With this first koan, you come into the first gate of your soul. Call it by any name.

"Good friends, when you take refuge in your own nature, you will have taken refuge in the true Buddha. By taking refuge in oneself, one can remove the evils within—envy, crookedness, egoism, deceit, contemptuousness, arrogance, heresy, pride, and all other evils arising at any time. If you see your own errors and do not discuss the good and the bad of others, you have taken refuge in yourself. If you practice modesty of mind, are always respectful to others, and see your own original nature penetrating everywhere without obstruction, you have taken refuge in yourself.

"What is that which is called perfect sambhogakya? *It is this: just as a candle flame dispels a thousand years of darkness, so the light of wisdom annihilates 10,000 years of ignorance."*

SOKEI-AN SAYS:

From the next chapter on, the *Record of the Sixth Patriarch* will become very interesting. It is on the affinity between the Master and his disciples. One by one, they came to have interviews with him, and there were many questions and answers. This chapter on confession, however, has really been quite tiresome. It will be over very soon.

In the previous lecture, the Sixth Patriarch spoke about *dharmakaya,* the base of buddha-consciousness. Now he is speaking about *sambhogakaya,* the conscious mind of Buddha. In the following lectures, he will speak more about *sambogakaya* and about *nirmanakaya.*

"Good friends, when you take refuge in your own nature, you will have taken refuge in the true Buddha." The true Buddhist attitude is not to take refuge in anything but yourself. So to take refuge in yourself is to take refuge in the true Buddha. One's own nature is, of course, original nature.

"By taking refuge in oneself, one can remove the evils within—envy, crookedness, egoism, deceit, contemptuousness, arrogance, heresy, pride, and all other evils arising at any time." Of course, taking refuge does not mean taking refuge in your good or bad nature. It means taking refuge in original nature, that which will not be created or destroyed.

Naturally, if you root out and remove all those evil minds, you can find your own original nature, just as a muddy pool becomes pure when you take out all the dirt. So to see original nature, it is not necessary to read any books or to listen to any lectures. Can you hear the sound of the hand? So many things are in your mind that you cannot hear the sound. But when you take all those "evils" away, you will hear it immediately.

"If you see your own errors and do not discuss the good and the bad of others, you have taken refuge in yourself. If you practice modesty of mind, are always respectful to others, and see your own original nature penetrating everywhere without obstruction, you have taken refuge in yourself." Not to discuss the good and the bad of others is one of the "ten Commandments" of Buddhism. To protect oneself by censuring

another is an offence. In the course of his public life, a teacher must censure others; but in his private life, he does not. Of course, not talking about other's likes or dislikes is also a commandment we observe in private life.

I am bringing Buddhism to America. As yet, it has no value. But America will slowly realize its value and say that Buddhism gives us something we can use as a base or foundation for our mind. Buddhism can help you in all aspects of your private life. Suppose you are standing in a corner of your office waiting for your boss to fire you. You are shaking with fright. Someone comes to you and says, "The boss wants to see you." Your friend tells you: "Don't be discouraged. Be brave." You go to the boss's office, and he keeps you waiting. You are more frightened. Such agony! Then the boss says, "Starting next week your wages will be raised," and you say, "Oh, thank you, thank you!" And you think the raise will be five dollars—you can make a first payment on an auto or a radio. When you find that the raise is only one dollar, you do not have the courage to ask for more. But if your mind is firm in Buddhism, at each step you will know what to do. Buddhism will help you in every crisis.

Now, I am here as your Osho. If I go to a night club—of course, I have no money to go, but if I had the money to go, and went there to sing and dance, I would not be paying respect to you for your respect to me. For my life has a public nature as well as a private one. If I were to flatter the many young ladies who come here, I would be mocking you, as I am accepting your respect as your teacher. This is the public aspect of my life. So our public life must be lived in a true way.

It is like a highway, and our private houses are standing on both sides of this highway. The highway is the public way. To reach your porch, by a little road off to the side, is your private way. Now, if your private way comes to be a public way, and you still behave as if it were your private way, your private way will be annihilated. If you say, "I will fight for my rights!" it is only your right if it is a private right. We do not censure the private way, but the public way punishes with annihilation. In the army, we accept orders from the officer—"Yes, Sir!"—and do it. We are not slaves, and he is not "The Master." But there is a public force. And if a boss squeezes his employees' wages to buy his daughter something—sit down!

My Buddhism is not altogether public yet, but I am certainly working for it.

"What is that which is called the perfect sambhogakaya?" First it was asked, "What is the pure *dharmakaya*?" Now it is asked, "What is the perfect *sambhogakaya*?"

Dharmakaya is like the air or etheric atmosphere. *Sambhogakaya* is like light. *Dharmakaya* is the consciousness of the universe, not your own consciousness. *Sambhogakaya* is the consciousness of the existence of *dharmakaya*. So *dharmakaya* does not know its own nature. That which knows *dharmakaya* is *sambogakaya*. *Sambhogakaya* is consciousnes. Consciousness is the innate nature of *dharmakaya*.

Once while the Sixth Patriarch was meditating, he saw a fire burning at the bottom of some clear, deep water. This means that *dharmakaya* suddenly realized its own existence. That which "recognizes" is really *sambhogakaya*. We call it wisdom. The Sixth Patriarch called it *prajna* and *samadhi*. Everyone will understand *dharmakaya* and *nirmanakaya*, but *sambhogakaya* is hard to understand.

"It is this: just as a candle flame dispels a thousand years of darkness, so the light of wisdom annihilates ten-thousand years of ignorance." You certainly do not yet realize your own original nature. But when you come to Zen and toil over your koan—then, without speaking a word, without entertaining any thought or trying to express it in any form—all of a sudden, sitting on your chair, you know *This is That!* If that just comes but once in your lifetime, a million years of darkness will be dispelled.

In the beginning, your enlightenment is so weak that I must guard it as I would a windowpane—I wipe it every day. If you are not here for three or four days, your mind becomes so smeared that I must wash it all over again, as a mother washes her child. After another three or four days, you are all dirty again when you should be as clean as glass.

I will wipe you until you find out that filth is not the real attitude of mind. But some day you will find that clear mirror, and you will come into my room with it. I will look at you with respect, and you will know who this Sokei-an is. To find this mirror is not so hard. Just wipe it all off and come in shining. You will look at me, and I will look at you. Then you will understand what Buddhism is.

"Do not think of what is past, for it is over and cannot be grasped, nor think of what lies ahead. If your mind is clear from one moment of thought to the next, you will see your original nature.[12]

"Evil and virtue differ, but original nature is non-dual, and this non-dual nature is called reality. That in your original nature which is not stained by evil or virtue is called the Buddha of Perfect Sambhogakaya. *If you harbor a single evil thought in your original nature, you will destroy the cause of 10,000 years' virtue. But if you harbor a single good thought in your original nature, all evils, countless in number as the grains of sand of the Ganges, will cease, and you will directly attain the highest enlightenment. When you see [the nature of your mind] from one moment of thought to the next, never losing sight of your original mind, that is called* sambhogakaya."

SOKEI-AN SAYS:

The Sixth Patriarch has been speaking about the Triune Body, the *Trikaya* Buddha, and taking refuge in the Three Treasures—Buddha, Dharma, and *Sangha*—Buddha as *dharmakaya*, Dharma as *sambhogakaya*, and *Sangha* as *nirmanakaya*. These three are the foundation of Buddhist confession.

Shila, conscience, has two elements: the body of conscience (the body of commandment) and the written law, (the *vinaya*). So the body of conscience is *this* [touching his body]. The body of conscience is that which appears in this living body, in this living mind as realization. To burn a finger is this realization.

When you find the cornerstone of the written law, you will have a clue to the attainment of the whole body of conscience. When you contact something with both body *and* mind, you will understand clearly. To such a one, the written commandment is not necessary, while to one who has not found *this body*, the written commandment is very important.

The written law is nothing but a photograph of the body of conscience. We are entirely deaf to our still, small voice, the voice of the *daemon*. If we do not recover the ear to hear it, how will we ever recover or discover the body of Buddha, which is our true conscience?

In Buddhism, we are taught to empty the mind completely and to hear our conscience. It is the only way. Your looking glass is covered with filth, so clean it up. You must demolish all images, all previous conceptions. Your imagination must be cleaned up, too. Finally, you will be one plain mind, which is the body of conscience, and it will become very clear and simple.

This is the talk of a Buddhist monk. The commandment "you must not kill" is naturally written in your soul, on anyone's conscience. But when you are compelled to become a soldier and to work hard on the battlefield, you must kill. There is no contradiction here—if you understand the body of commandment. But when your conscience is as if painted over with white paint, you lose the body of commandment. So the Sixth Patriarch here comes to the same conclusion as in Zen. They are alike, and his *shila* and Zen are alike. His Zen is to find your own original nature.

"Do not think of what is past, for it is over and cannot be grasped, nor think of what lies ahead. If your mind is clear from one moment of thought to the next, you will see your original nature." Sometimes you cannot apply the law of commandment that worked in some past experience to the present moment. You are correct because the written law is not always applicable. You must mind the *present* body of commandment and what *it* says. From the Zen standpoint, mind and body are the same, and when the expected future is at hand, its circumstances may be entirely different from what was expected.

There is an ancient commandment that monks may not tell the commandments to women who wear high-heeled shoes, for, as they are women of the world, monks are not permitted to speak Buddhism to them. If your mind is not blurred, painted over, or in the custody of the old tradition, you can see your original nature right now.

"Evil and virtue differ, but original nature is non-dual": The Sixth Patriarch does not mean good and bad. To him, "evil" means all the external and extraneous attitudes of Buddhism. "Virtue" means experience, the intimate experience of Buddhism through the heart and soul. They are two sides of one thing, like a sheet of paper.

"And this non-dual nature is called reality. That in your original nature which is not stained by evil or virtue is called the Buddha of Perfect Sambhogakaya." Here, the "Buddha of Perfect *Sambhogakaya*" means light, awareness, the force of a potential power.

Dharmakaya is also potential force, but not focused. It is like the ocean. When a cyclone moves over the ocean, making the waves circle and twist like a top, the top of the wave is *sambhogakaya*. When a newborn baby cries, "Wa-a-ah!" at that moment *sambhogakaya* is born.

When the baby Buddha was born, he is quoted as saying, "Between heaven and earth, I am the only one to be revered!" Tradition is a queer thing, isn't it? Of course, what the infant Buddha said was, "Wa-a-ah!" So this infant's wail was canonized. When Christ was born the Son of God, he also said, "Wa-a-ah!"

Well [looking at his watch], the time has come, so I will brush up quickly.

"If you harbor a single evil thought in your original nature, you will destroy the cause of ten-thousand years' virtue. But if you harbor a single good thought in your original nature, all evils, countless in number as the grains of sand of the Ganges will cease, and you will directly attain the highest enlightenment." The grains of sand of the Ganges is the usual Buddhist illustration. When you come into my Zen room and answer the koan "Before father and mother," and find the answer without a word, this is the plain ground of religion.

Now, think of it: just having one thought! Or maybe you are thinking about a shephard with a staff in his hand appearing on Broadway. Too much!

Try to find something that is true in your daily life and settle down upon it. That is our religion. Nature is our shrine, and all human life is our *sangha*. Daily life is our retreat, and that is all.

When you see [the nature of your mind] from one moment of thought to the next, never losing sight of your original mind, that is called sambhogakaya." When you find it, you will never forget it!

When I teach Buddhism to a student one or two years, and I say, "But surely you understand Buddhism!" If he says, "I have no recollection at all," it is a good answer, and I will accept it—if it is a true one. This is what a monk said after studying Buddhism for thirty years. But the answer can just as well be dumb, and that is all there is to it.

Sambhogakaya is something common to all. It is the "body of awareness common to all." This word is sometimes translated as "body of enjoyment," but that is not quite right. It can be "intellect common to all." You realize this intellect as your physical body and living soul.

The activity of *sambhogakaya* arises from *dharmakaya* and appears in accordance with place, time, and condition, which is then called *nirmanakaya*. You see it everywhere. You see it on the street corner shining shoes, selling peanuts, selling newspapers. All these are performances of *nirmanakaya*—the shoemaker in his shop, the butcher chopping meat, the fisherman cutting off the fishes' heads, the monks in their temples praying. The one who understands all this will swallow it all as ONENESS, and he will not reject anything, but gather it all to his stomach, his big heart—like Wallace Beery!

I like America. It is something America has naturally—a great heart!

"What is that which is called the hundred decillion nirmanakayas? *If you do not entertain thoughts of anything, your nature is originally like the empty sky. But if the mind entertains one moment of discriminative thought, it is called transformation. If you think of evil, you will be changed into a hell-dweller. If you think of good, you will be changed into a heavenly being. The venomous becomes a serpent and the compassionate becomes a bodhisattva. Transformed by wisdom, you will ascend; transformed by ignorance, you will descend. Thus, you will undergo many changes in your own nature. The deluded one will be unaware of this, and from one moment of thought to the next, he will think of evil and practice it. Yet, if he brings his mind back to virtue for even one moment of thought, wisdom will be born. This is called* Nirmanakaya *Buddha within your own nature.*

SOKEI-AN SAYS:

Nirmanakaya is one of the three bodies of Buddha, the materialized body of Buddha. Buddha in human form. In personified Buddhism—Avalokiteshvara.

"What is that which is called the hundred decillion nirmanakayas?*"* The "decillion *nirmanakayas*" are shadowy, semi-incarnated beings, all the different kinds of minds. In Christianity, thay are beings of purgatory; in Buddhism, they are the shadows between soul and matter. Magicians use these shadows to blind men's souls. They send their mind shadow into your mind. True Dharma is different. It takes your shadowy being away from your mind and annihilates it.

Each mind is a different being in Buddhism, so there is a new mind being born and a mind dying at every moment. Buddhism does not take this physical body as a single unit. A multitude of beings are living in this physical body, just as the box of a radio is not the entire unit; you hear thousands of singers through it. So through this physical body, you will hear thousands of beings.

"If you do not entertain thoughts of anything, your nature is originally like the empty sky":—Empty.

True Dharma tears down the sky and keeps tearing it down until you see the bottom of your existence. Unless you do this, you cannot see the empty sky.

"But if the mind entertains one moment of discriminative thought, it is called transformation." Transformation is the way of *nirmanakaya*, a transformation of one's body in accordance with one's mind—from hell, to hungry ghost, to beast, to angry spirit, to human being, to angel or *deva*. There are six evil transformations. The original idea was five; then angry spirit, *ashura*, was added. *Ashuras* are angels who fell down to hell and became demons.

"If you think of evil, you will be changed into a hell-dweller. If you think of good, you will be changed into a heavenly being. The venomous becomes a serpent and the compassionate becomes a bodhisattva. "Hell" is *naraka*, a place for dead or disembodied spirits who are in eternal agony. "Heaven" is nirvana, eternal peace and rest. "Bodhisattva" means "non-ego Buddha," an awakened one. So if there are twenty bodhisattvas, they are just like one. And if there is one bodhisattva, he is just like twenty.

This is the nature of the bodhisattva. He observes Buddha's six paramitas. Buddha is the completely Enlightened One who has attained the highest enlightenment—*samyaksambodhi.*

Transformed by wisdom, you will ascend; transformed by ignorance, you will descend. Thus, you will undergo many changes in your own nature. The deluded one will be unaware of this, and from one moment of thought to the next, he will think of evil and practice it." "Transformed by wisdom" means *bodhi*, the power of awakening within us. To be awakened with this power is Wisdom. To "ascend" means to go from hell to buddha. To "descend" means to go from buddha to hell.

"Yet, if he brings his mind back to virtue for even one moment of thought, wisdom will be born. This is called Nirmanakaya *Buddha within your own nature."* All that you think is mind-stuff, but without it, you cannot think. Mind-stuff is semi-material, semi-spiritual. It has place, but it does not take up space.

It is a queer being, this mind-stuff, and you cannot deny its existence. If when you are meditating, you have one thought like a small black cloud, a storm begins to brew in your mind. Then you go from heaven to hell, from Buddha to hell.

The Zen student knows when this mind-stuff is at work and puts strength into his abdomen and controls it. Ignorance is like a washerwoman's mind: you do not know anything. Every moment you undergo change, you are ascending and descending. You do not know how to struggle with it. So you go, perhaps, to an analyst. Why don't you analyze yourself, and cure your own sickness?

Gather your thoughts and see the bottom of your mind. From that base, intrinsic wisdom will be born, which is enlightenment. Do not allow yourself to be used by the transformations of *nirmanakaya*. You must *use* it.

"Good friends, dharmakaya *has the intrinsic faculty of self-awareness at every moment. This is* Sambhogakaya *Buddha. When* sambhogakaya *discriminates, it is* Nirmanakaya *Buddha. When you realize and manifest for yourselves the power of your own meritorious nature, that is taking true refuge. Skin and flesh make up your physical body, which is a temporary dwelling, so you cannot say you are taking refuge in it. When you realize your own threefold body, you will acknowledge the buddha of your own nature.*

SOKEI-AN SAYS:

After this comes the Sixth Patriarch's song or *gatha*, which I will translate next week.

First, I will give you an explanation of Zen, then I will give my commentary.

In Sanskrit, Zen is *dhyana*. In China, it is pronounced *ch'an*. Dhyana is the usual contemplation, as you can see everywhere in the statues of Buddha. He sits cross-legged with his hands in his lap and his eyes half-closed. He is in contemplation.

There are many sects of Buddhism, but the Zen sect especially emphasizes *dhyana*. Those of this sect are not permitted in their first years of study to read the scriptures. They hate words like poison. Without books, they try to find true wisdom in their own mind by themselves. Later, the student will want to know what others think, so he will go to the library in any large temple, pull out the books, and read them. Then he will realize that the experience of others is not different from his own. When we realize how small is our own conceptual achievement compared to the experience of those wonderful men of the past, we learn to value those old masters. Of course, in ancient times, there were teachers who were models for their students. After many weeks or months of study, a student will go to a teacher and express his attainment. The teacher will measure him and give an answer in one of two words—yes or no. But first the student has to open the eye of Buddhism, and Zen is the eye of Buddhism, the real core.

"Good friends, dharmakaya *has the intrinsic faculty of self-awareness at every moment." Dharmakaya* is the first word you may question.

Buddha has three bodies in one body—*dharmakaya, sambhogakaya,* and *nirmanakaya*—which are very important terms in Buddhism. *Dharmakaya* is the omnipresent body through space and time or beyond space and time, beyond the five senses. This is very easy to understand in Zen.

Buddha does not mean Shakyamuni Buddha who lived about 2,500 years ago. This buddha is the Knower, the one who has wisdom. The one who has awakened to his own wisdom is the Buddha of human flesh. But the buddha that is the omniscient wisdom of the universe exists forever, from the beginningless beginning to the endless end. In one word, it is your God.

The Shakyas had their God, and the Moslems have Allah. So if your religion is Zen, Buddha means Wisdom, and this Wisdom has three different names—*dharmakaya, sambogakaya, nirmanakaya.* That is all. The idea is expressed in different languages according to your race, but all refer to the same thing.

In this passage, *dharmakaya* is equivalent to Reality, existence itself. What we call existence is not existence itself. It is external to us through our five senses—the sky is blue, the water is green, the fire is red, man speaks, and the birds sing. Sounds and colors are subjective visions, illusions. This is not existence itself, it is the experience of our five senses, the experience of phenomena which appears optically or vibrates in our eardrums. Whatever tinpan alley you go into will not have the sound; it is the eardrum which makes the sound. It is an illusion; it is not a real form of existence. We cannot see the real form of existence with our five senses. But our intellect *directly* knows it. Science will help Buddhism in this as a friend.

According to Immanuel Kant, our "intellectual intuition" knows existence "all at once." This intuition is *prajna.* The transcendental school of New England called it "transcendental wisdom"—direct knowledge.

In *Dharmakaya,* this intuitional faculty is latent and unknown, but it appears in itself. It is in the "Father," and it will enter his child, the "Son," as existence. *Dharmakaya* is awareness itself. Knowledge comes by association.

Religion is quite clear, you know, and as you come closer, you will meet it as you would go through a small gate.

"This is Sambhogakaya *Buddha. Sambhogakaya* is the consciousness that is common to all, not as the separate souls of fish, let us say, but as the one soul common to all fish, one consciousness, from beginning to end. And this one consciousness was given to all of us as this body of water, was given to us drop by drop to be transformed into different forms of development. But it is all from one. The consciousness of the inside and the consciousness of the outside meet each other and realize they are one existence. If you stand in absolute Emptiness with your eye open to the infinite, you will not realize your own ego. Your consciousness of this will come by contact, which is yoga.

When sambhogakaya discriminates, it is Nirmanakaya Buddha." Sambhogakaya is awareness; one *knows* existence. A baby does not know he exists in his mother's body, but you know your own existence with your awakened intellect. So the *Nirmanakaya* Buddha is the performance of this knowledge of self-knowing, the transformation body. You transform your state of mind from heaven to hell according to your wisdom and mind. Transformation itself is *nirmanakaya*.

Nirmanakaya Buddha means that, according to the construction of one's body, one takes one's part—as a cat, "Meow!" or as a dog, "Bow-wow!"

"*When you realize and manifest for yourselves the power of your own meritorious nature, that is taking true refuge.*" Or be converted to. In the beginning of my lectures, I always recite: "I take refuge in Buddha. I take refuge in Dharma. I take refuge in Sangha." Well, I take refuge in my three bodies—my Buddha, my Dharma, my Sangha. As the Quakers say, "Take refuge within."

"*Skin and flesh make up your physical body, which is a temporary dwelling, so you cannot say you are taking refuge in it. When you realize your own threefold body, you will acknowledge the buddha of your own nature.*" I must say two or three words about "your own meritorious nature."

This consciousness produces many things. The fertility of the earth is symbolized by woman—for instance, the statue of the Greek Artemis with one thousand breasts. This material form is just matter. This "dwelling" is a shrine, a storehouse, and you take refuge in it. Why did Hui-neng not say that you take refuge in your physical body? Because there are three phases to your physical body which is God—*dharmakaya, sambogakaya, nirmanakaya*.

The only way to gain access to Buddha is to contemplate within yourself without words. Make contact with your own soul. It is not even necessary to make contact with IT. Realize that *you are IT*. You must take off all that mind-stuff from your soul.

We have come to the end of the Sixth Patriarch's lecture on the Three Treasures and the Three Bodies. Take refuge in *Dharmakaya, Sambhogakaya*, and in *Nirmanakaya*.

"I have made a song of formlessness. The moment you recite it, the sins caused by your delusions through kalpas of time will instantly be erased. The song says:

"The deluded one cultivates good fortune but does not cultivate the Way
He insists that cultivating good fortune is the Way

He says that giving alms and making offerings are the way to secure unlimited good fortune
But the three evils continue to be produced in his mind

He may desire to atone for his sins by his good fortune,
But even if he obtains good fortune in his next life, his sins will still remain

You must eradicate the cause of the sins within your own mind
This is called true confession within your own nature

When you understand the true confession of the Mahayana,
You will eradicate falsehood and practice truth; thus you will be without sin

Students of the Way, always contemplate your nature
Then you will be the same as all the buddhas

The patriarchs who came before me handed down only this teaching of sudden enlightenment
I pray that living beings everywhere become one in the realization of original nature

If you wish to find dharmakaya
You must cleanse your mind, discarding all forms

Endeavor to see your own essential nature; do not be indolent!
Your life comes to an end with your last moment of thought

If you wish to awaken to the Mahayana and see your original nature
You must strive singe-mindedly, reverently placing your palms together"

The Master said: "Good friends, all of you should recite this song. If you practice in accordance with it, you will instantly see your own nature. Then, even though you are a thousand miles away from me, you are always at my side. But if you do not see it instantly, though you are here at my side, it is as if you were a thousand miles away. Why do you need to go to the trouble of coming all this distance? Take care of yourselves!"

There was no one among the multitude who heard this sermon who was not enlightened and overjoyed. They all put it into practice, and all were delighted, upholding the teaching.

SOKEI-AN SAYS:

It is very seldom that you find this kind of confession in a Zen record. From the standpoint of the Zen sect, the Sixth Patriarch accepted the old formulas and digested them with his wisdom and assimilated them into his own Zen attitude. So from this, you will understand that confession, in the true sense, is very different from the popularized form of confession.

"I have made a song of formlessness." Formlessness is like a stream or a river between mountains.

"The moment you recite it, the sins caused by your delusions through kalpas of time will instantly be erased." We do not often use the word sin. It is borrowed from Christianity.

A commandment is in a particular form for a time. In modern times, the old commandments do not suit us anymore. But if you say the Buddhist must not eat meat, all right. In Japan there are many vegetables, but if you are here, there are only potatoes and cabbages. There are very few vegetables compared to Japan. In Seattle, one potato cost ten cents. That's more than meat. You must not say one must go hungry, that the Buddhist cannot eat meat. I said a while ago that here in New York, no young girl may go into a church in a bathing suit. But I now hear that two or three weeks ago one did.

The song says: "The deluded one cultivates good fortune but does not cultivate the Way/ He insists that cultivating good fortune is the Way/ He says that giving alms and making offerings are the way to secure unlimited good fortune/ But the three evils continue to be produced in his mind/ He may desire to atone for his sins by his good fortune,/ But even if he obtains good fortune in his next life, his sins will still remain." This fortune is very different from your idea of fortune as good or bad. What the Buddhist thinks of as fortune is that one seizes the opportunity to accumulate good karma—"I am very fortunate that I have assisted somebody today in his difficulty." So that by charity, principally, one can gather good karma. This is a very popular idea in Buddhism. To make good karma is to have good fortune. To make evil karma is bad fortune, sin.

When one knows the Law of Mind, the Law of Nature, and the Law of Man, then one is enlightened. Certainly, the enlightened one knows and realizes all spheres of consciousness. The Buddhist thinks that consciousness has many degrees of evolution. When one has realized all the degrees of the evolution of his consciousness, he realizes the Law of Mind, of Nature, and of Man, and we call him an Enlightened One.

The three evils or poisons are passion, anger, and ignorance—"original suffering." Sin—evil karma—is what came from the original suffering of passion, anger, and ignorance. These are erroneous states, and the Christian thinks that they are sin.

Passion is controlled by *shila*—conscience (morality). Anger is controlled by meditation. Ignorance is enlightened by wisdom. They are originally the same in nature and are in the primitive stage. Conscience, meditation, and wisdom are in the developed stage.

"You must eradicate the cause of the sins within your own mind/ This is called true confession within your own nature/ When you understand the true confession of the Mahayana,/ You will eradicate falsehood and practice truth; thus you will be without sin." "True confession" is meditation. We in the Orient do not confess our sins to the reverend in the monastery as people do here. Here one confesses and then goes home and commits another sin. Conscience applies to the moral side of conduct. When it takes its activity from intellect first, you call it wisdom. To find out the real cause of suffering is real salvation.

To "practice truth" in Buddhism is to practice non-ego—no sinful desire, no artificiality. That is, be natural with no particular establishment of law. This last is very hard to understand. Suppose the water that runs between two mountains has a particular law, to go two miles here and then turn and go on two miles there? Water flows naturally, it will change its course at any time. It makes no mistake.

"Students of the Way, always contemplate your nature/ Then you will be the same as all the buddhas." Your pure nature is your original nature, which is intrinsic nature. In one word, it is buddha-nature or God-nature. It is common to all sentient beings. Original nature has a tendency to find good even in evil, as the ivy plant instinctively turns to light even in darkness.

The deluded one's soul is buried under imagination and superstition. He has no time to find his own true nature; his mind is stuffed with sawdust. The direct way is through contemplation.

"The patriarchs who came before me handed down only this teaching of sudden enlightenment/ I pray that living beings everywhere become one in the realization of original nature." Learning how to open your eye for the first time is difficult. I am fifty-five years old, and everyone thinks I could live perhaps twenty-eight or thirty more years. Perhaps I could live to be one hundred twenty-five years, but this would sit heavily upon me!

"If you wish to find dharmakaya/*You must cleanse your mind, discarding all forms."* This is the best way to find buddha. There is no other way.

"Endeavor to see your own essential nature; do not be indolent!" "Essential nature" may seem peculiar to your ear. It is just original or intrinsic nature. We say of nature that it is "good or bad," "sweet or malicious," but essential nature is different from this sort of human nature. In a word, essential nature is Soul, the Universal Nature that is within man. But this nature is really deeper and higher than the mere nature of man. It is original, universal nature that enshrines in man. Therefore, it is the link between man and the universe.

Theoretically speaking, something that stands between man and God is always very important in all types of religion. However, the Buddhist does not think there is any particular one who stands between God and man. This linkage is within man's nature. So if I were to use your terms, I would say that Christ is within man's nature and that through Him, man will know God. In Buddhism, we awaken to our own essential nature. Thus, by this enlightened wisdom, we directly know God—Buddha.

"Your life comes to an end with your last moment of thought." Nirmanakaya is the body that lives on earth and eats. *Sambhogakaya* is the Soul that is common to all sentient beings, and this Soul, which is the Ocean, is in *dharmakaya*. *Sambhogakaya* is in the body of man, of every man. *Nirmanakaya* is the body of all sentient beings, and it is neither sacred nor profane.

"If you wish to awaken to the Mahayana and see your original nature . . ." In this Western hemisphere, Mahayana and Hinayana are misunderstood. In this country, it is believed that Hinayana is some kind of religion from Ceylon, Burma or Siam, and that Mahayana is dominant in Japan. "Hinayana is southern, and Mahayana is northern"—it came from the Gobi Desert! Some European scholar said that Mahayana literature is neglible and that it is not authentic. They have made, therefore, their own notions about all of this. But in the East, Hinayana and Mahayana are like two wheels of a cart or the two wings of a bird, and he who struggles between Mahayana and Hinayana will have no time to come down to his own village and find his own home.

And the Mahayanaists! To popularize the essence of Buddhism, they made a new school—Amida Buddhism. Call out the name Amida incessantly, and you will be saved. It's not for the person who studies with his brain, this kind of Mahayana. So please do not mix up these terms with those invented by European scholars.

The meaning of Mahayana is not necessarily original nature, but it is a link. The Buddha was a Mahayanaist, but the disciples who were unenlightened were Hinayanaists. However, these terms do not really mean anything here because in the Buddha's day there were no sects, no Hinayana or Mahayana. It was after about two hundred years that sects developed. So Mahayana means "awaking to the true teachings of Buddhism."

You must strive singe-mindedly, reverently placing your palms together." When I was in the monastery, an elder monk who taught me how to meditate was always beating his abdomen, so all of us young monks made faces, and grunted, too! It was not necessary to do this at all. I'm quite fat, so I can make a good sound beating my abdomen, but younger monks do not have much of an abdomen. The elders would carve six foot sticks of oak, strike the floor, and hit their abdomens.

The ideas of meditation are difficult for you. You think about something like the moon, and you meditate very softly and sweetly, but your notions come from the outside. Or there is nothing in your mind; then some notion comes in, and you watch it very carefully, like a cat, but then you think, "I am thinking nothing!" It's not so easy.

To find your original nature, you must make the decision to annihilate all words. We call the monk who meditates thus a fish-minded monk. He does not think about anything, but has a large eye like a Zen monk. Unfortunately, I do not have the large eye, but I can imagine it. So forget to think! What you get without thinking is true, like the monk who was sweeping the courtyard without any thoughts. When his broom struck a pebble, the pebble hit a tree—"Oh, *That's It!"*

Now, if you are always thinking something—a nice night, a blue moon and radio songs—you will get tired. But Buddhist meditation is easy, easier than any other because we do not meditate on the substance of our brains. So I hope you try it once. It is very difficult to eliminate the mind.

The Master said: "Good friends, all of you should recite this song. If you practice in accordance with it, you will instantly see your own nature. Then, even though you are a thousand miles away from me, you are always at my side. But if you do not see it instantly, though you are here at my side, it is as if you were a thousand miles away. Why do you need to go to the trouble of coming all this distance? Take care of yourselves!" In Buddhism, we meditate upon all the shadows of consciousness—the body, sense-perceptions, mind stuff, dreams, visions of heaven and of hell, pure force or mind activity without matter (pure mind force without mind-stuff), and consciousness itself. We *look* at all these shadows of consciousness in meditation, but we do not meditate upon words. We are taught to stay in one position for about three months—up and down, up and down—and then to take up our koan, "Before father and mother."

We call this the true practice of Zen. But the practice of Zen and Zen itself are two entirely different things.

I hope those who have some spare time between their activities will practice Zen. It will help your religious honesty.

There was no one among the multitude who heard this sermon who was not enlightened and overjoyed. They all put it into practice, and all were delighted, upholding the teaching." From the Buddha's day, meditation and the result of meditation have been handed down, but not in speech and not in writing. The actual experience of essential nature is handed down face to face. When the disciple comes to that state—"I realize it!"—it is proven: *This is That!*

The answer is the same for everyone. It is not my answer or your answer. It is the universal answer. You will realize it, when you embody it, like the moth that dives into a flame. There is no more moth and no more flame.

CHAPTER VII

AFFINITY

After the Dharma was transmitted to the Master at Huang-mei, he returned to Ts'ao Hou village in Shao-chou, but no one observed it. A Confucian scholar, Liu Chih-lueh, received him with great reverence. Liu had an aunt who was a nun named Wu-chin-ts'ang. She was always reciting the Nirvana Sutra.

The Master, having listened to her recitation for a while, apprehended the sutra's profound meaning and expounded it to her. The nun took one of the sutra scrolls and questioned him about certain characters.

The Master said: "I cannot read the characters, but nevertheless you may ask me the meaning."

The nun said: "How can you understand the meaning if you cannot even read the characters?"

The Master answered: "The profound principle of all the Buddhas has nothing to do with the written characters of the scriptures."

The nun was astonished and told the virtuous elders in the neighboring villages: "He is someone who has wisdom. We should entreat him to accept our support."

There was a man named Ts'a Shu-liang, who was a descendent of Duke Wu of the Wei dynasty (220-265). He came with the villagers to pay their homage to the Master. At that time the old temple, Pao-lin, was still in ruins from a battle-fire at the end of the Sui dynasty (689-618). So they rebuilt the temple upon the old foundation and asked the Master to abide there. Overnight it became a splendid temple.

The Master lived there for a little more than nine months. In order to avoid the wicked parties that were searching for him, he fled to a mountain in front of the temple. The pursuers set fire to the grasses and trees, but the Master made a narrow escape, hiding himself among some rocks. The impressions of the creases in his robe and of his crossed legs are still visible on one of the rocks. This is the reason it is called the "Refuge Rock."

Recalling the instructions of the Fifth Patriarch, "When you come to Huai and Hui, stay and hide yourself," the Master left the temple, covering his traces in these two villages.

SOKEI-AN SAYS:

I am translating the record of Hui-neng, the great Chinese Zen Master, who lived in the T'ang dynasty, about the eighth century. The T'ang dynasty was China's highest period of civilization.

I have now come almost to the center of the record, which I have been translating for two years. Each evening, after reading the translation, little by little I give you my commentary on it. This chapter is on the affinity between the Master, Hui-neng, and his disciples.

After the Dharma was transmitted to the Master at Huang-mei, he returned to Ts'ao Hou village in Shao-chou, but no one observed it. "Ts'ao-chi"—"Sôkei", my name in the Japanese way of saying it—was a hermitage in the canyon of Hou. This canyon was not like the Grand Canyon, but was like a flat valley. The Sixth Patriarch was living in this Hou country. Sokei-an is the name given to me by my teacher.

A Confucian scholar, Liu Chih-lueh, received him with great reverence. Liu had an aunt who was a nun named Wu-chin-ts'ang. She was always reciting the Nirvana Sutra*. A very famous sutra. Liu may have seen the Sixth Patriarch once at the temple in Huang-mei.*

The Master, having listened to her recitation for a while, apprehended the sutra's profound meaning and expounded it to her. The nun took one of the sutra scrolls and questioned him about certain characters. The Master said: "I cannot read the characters, but nevertheless you may ask me the meaning." The nun said: "How can you understand the meaning if you cannot even read the characters?" The Master answered: "The profound principal of all the Buddhas has nothing to do with the written characters of the scriptures." The nun was astonished and told the virtuous elders in the neighboring villages: "He is someone who has wisdom. We should entreat him to accept our support." This was was the sentiment in those times. Even in my own time, I did not strive to be supported when I first came to America.

There was a man named Ts'ao Shu-liang, who was a descendent of Duke Wu of the Wei dynasty. He came with the villagers to pay their homage to the Master. And then all the farmers realized: "Oh, he must be the guest at the Confucian scholar's house!"

At that time the old temple, Pao-lin, was still in ruins from a battle-fire at the end of the Sui dynasty. So they rebuilt the temple upon the old foundation and asked the Master to abide there. Overnight it became a splendid temple. This temple still exists. About fifteen years ago, the Japanese made a donation to help rebuild it. In Buddhism, there is no discrimination between Chinese and Japanese.

The Master lived there for a little more than nine months. In order to avoid the wicked parties that were searching for him, he fled to a mountain in front of the temple. The pursuers set fire to the grasses and trees, but the Master made a narrow escape, hiding himself among some rocks. All this happened before the Sixth Patriarch had really begun to preach his wisdom to the multitude. The parties who were searching for him were unenlightened monks, disciples of the Fifth Patriarch. Among these men, who had renounced the world, envy and jealousy still existed. They wished to find and to kill the Sixth Patriarch. But it was not only out of envy and jealousy. Behind this there were two great currents of Buddhism struggling against each other. One side of Buddhism was quite pedantic. It tried to keep the forms and formulas exactly as they had come from India, and, in trying to keep these forms, paid no attention to the Buddhist life, or to enlightenment. The other side of Buddhism tried to keep the Buddhist spirit, the real core of Buddhism. The monks were trying to enlighten themselves, to express Buddhism in their own terms, to adapt the terms of Buddhism in accordance with their own climate and customs because "antique" Buddhism could easily fall into an "image."

When I observe the knowledge of European scholars who have studied Buddhism, I notice they want to keep the antique forms as long as possible. They like rules: the Buddhist monk will only take one meal of vegetables, will not shake hands with a lady, and so on. If a Buddhist monk comes from Ceylon to New York, and you go to shake hands with him, he will withdraw his hand. One came here at the same time I did. I was shaking hands with everyone, and he said of me, "That monk is shaking hands and is breaking the commandments." That he keeps these commandments has a very deep significance. It is not merely to follow forms. I do not say that monks, in these modern times, should violate the commandments. But I say they should know the real significance of the commandments. The monk's commandment is the intuitive reaction to daily life.

Well, there were these two schools in China, each trying to annihilate the other. Therefore, the Sixth Patriarch was in danger after the Fifth Patriarch transmitted the Dharma to him.

The impressions of the creases in his robe and of his crossed legs are still visible on one of the rocks. This is the reason it is called the "Refuge Rock." This is just description.

Recalling the instructions of the Fifth Patriarch, "When you come to Huai and Hui, stay and hide yourself," the Master left the temple, covering his traces in these two villages. Today, we do not know what these two names signify.

The monk Fa-hai, a native of Ch'u-chiang in Shao-chou, came to pay homage to the Master for the first time and asked this question: "It is said, 'This very Mind is buddha.' I beg your instruction on this."

The Master answered: "When the preceding thought does not arise, that is Mind. When the succeeding thought does not cease, that is buddha. When you manifest all the forms of the world, that is Mind; and when you abandon all the forms of the world, that is buddha. If I were to explain it in detail, I would never finish, even in kalpas. Listen to me recite my gatha:

"Mind itself is wisdom
Buddha itself is samadhi

When wisdom and samadhi *are equally maintained*
The mind will be pure

Awakening to this Dharma
Results from cultivating your nature

Using that which is originally uncreated
Practice to attain both wisdom and samadhi
This is the right practice"

At the Master's words, Fa-hai attained great enlightenment, extolling the Master with this gatha:

"Mind itself is buddha!
Not realizing this, I submitted myself to ignorance

Now I understand that by practicing both wisdom and samadhi
One can renounce all things"

SOKEI-AN SAYS:

From here, this text becomes very important.

The monk Fa-hai, a native of Ch'u-chiang in Shao-chou, came to pay homage to the Master for the first time and asked this question: Fa-hai was not the best, but he was the first disciple of the Sixth Patriarch. He was not a man of letters.

"It is said, 'This very Mind is buddha.' I beg your instruction on this." "This very mind is buddha"—very plain, very simple, and it's true.

The Chinese have many words that express mind: *hsin*, *nien*, etc., and each has many shades of meaning. From the Buddhist standpoint, it is not so easy to describe the mind because of its many states. English expressions include "soul," "heart," and "brain." Localizing the mind is very difficult and makes for philosophical confusion. Some Oriental teachers localize the mind somewhere two inches above your head and relate it to the spine and hip bones.

The mind, in Mahayana Buddhism, is quite difficult to study. But in Hinayana (primitive) Buddhism, it is simple. It is the five shadows of mind—form, sensation, thought, mental formations, and consciousness. And it is "mind," also. The "outside" is an extension of mind—we see our "inside" on the "outside." The mind you see on the outside is the activity of your own mind, but if you say it is the "extension of *my* mind," you do not understand very well. Outside *is* your mind. Outside is I-NESS. Someone observes *this*, but we do not know who.

When you dream, you are not dreaming; someone is dreaming you because you are not in it. Consciousness dreams you. So it is not yourself at all, but the consciousness of nature. In Buddhism, there is no isolated consciousness. The Buddhist soul covers the endless space of the universe. *This* that hears, thinks, sees is not yours. *This* that sleeps, eats, dreams is not you, and you have nothing to do with it. The One is in a puppy, pussycat, fly, or man. In Indian art, the One has six feet, six hands, and six heads; and in the palm of each hand and in the sole of each foot, there is an eye. In each end of hair, there is an eye; and in each pore of the skin, there is an eye. The Buddhist God is not good-looking at all compared to the Christian God! In Buddhism, six symbolizes omnipotence.

From this gate [Sokei-an touched his heart], we can see All-Mind. When a Buddhist gets into his own mind, he is in the avenue of all minds. Through this mind, you can go anywhere. So the Buddhist practices getting into all states of mind through meditation. To embody your own mind is the first practice.

The Master answered: "When the preceding thought does not arise, that is Mind. When the succeeding thought does not cease, that is buddha. When you manifest all the forms of the world, that is Mind; and when you abandon all the forms of the world, that is buddha." Before your mind was born, it was in its original state; and after your mind realizes that it will never cease, it will become buddha itself. As a rule, however, you are living outside your mind, living beside yourself.

Before this mind was born, before you want to eat, sleep, buy, go to Japan, and so forth, it is in its original state. When you abandon the active mind and meditate, it is there. When you break the ice, the water is there at once. So when you break this mind, the original mind is there. When you realize that all these minds will never cease, you will be Buddha. And when you die, you will leave your body as ash, your blood as water, your breath as wind, and your consciousness will go back to the Ocean of Consciousness. And where will all the thoughts go? They will be kept in everyone's brain. All those thoughts are from the outside. "But I created those thoughts!" No, they have always existed everywhere. They are the common property of all human beings. All your thoughts will return to the Ocean of Consciousness. When we are in the bath, hot water is common to all. We are all moving in one bathtub, so nothing will cease to exist after your death. "So when I come back I can use those thoughts?" Never mind about coming back. Nothing will cease to exist after your death.

To the Buddhist, it is difficult to be born as a human being—the sun is in your right hand, the moon is in your left hand, the stars are in your fingertips. When you abandon all forms of nature, you will discover buddha-nature in yourself. You will go back and be fused with Universal Consciousness—to the Christian, God is a "Person." But to the Buddhist, "He" is the "Universe."

Really, there is no "body" in the universe. "Universal body" is Buddha, and Buddha's body is myself. In prayer we say: "I embody in you, and you embody in me. I embody Buddha, and Buddha embodies me. I embody the Universe, and the Universe embodies me." So the Universe will amalgamate with you, and you will prove buddha-nature in yourself. You and Buddha are one.

If I were to explain it in detail, I would never finish, even in kalpas. *"Kalpas"* is a Sanskrit word used for the English expression "eons of time." Somewhere in India, in ancient days, there was a huge stone. Every hundred years an angel descended from heaven and swept this huge stone with her gossamer-like sleeve. Finally, the angel swept the stone away. To do this, it took about one *kalpa*. This is a long time! In Buddhist literature, you will often find this expression. It is an idiom, an emphasis with no special meaning.

Listen to me recite my gatha: The word *"gatha"* has a long "a." It means a four-line poem. But the Sixth Patriarch's *gathas* are more than four lines. The Buddha often ended a sermon with a *gatha*. He spoke conversationally with his disciples, and then, to finish his speech, recited a *gatha* extemporaneously.

"Mind itself is wisdom/ Buddha itself is samadhi." Wisdom and *samadhi* are the principal Buddhist terms in this translation. *Samadhi* is absorption. Wisdom—*prajna*—is intrinsic wisdom, not acquired wisdom. The diamond is intrinsically a beautiful stone, but when you find one in a mine, it is not beautiful at all. When you cut and polish it, you will see the value of it. Gold is intrinsically beautiful, but you would not recognize it if you were to take it from a river bed. Only when you refine it will you see its value. If you go to Alaska for gold, and you wash the river all day long in a pan, all you get is one or two glitters. But have a barrel of gold—then you will see the beauty!

All sentient beings have intrinsic wisdom in common. But until you find it, you do not realize the value of it. It always whispers in your mind, but you have doubts and do not know what to do. This wisdom is whispering to you, but you do not listen, so you cannot attain.

Samadhi, absorption, is sometimes positive and sometimes passive. I use it here in the passive sense. We are absorbed in Great Buddha-Nature, a bottomless ocean. You yourself are not absorbing, you are absorbed. One European scholar translated *samadhi* as "ecstasy," like a dream. I do not agree. There is no ecstasy in this absorption, nor is it sleep. Such absorption is very hard to explain; it is an experience.

Many Buddhists misunderstand absorption, so they meditate day and night, close their eyes in mountain caves, and think they have realized absorption. Meditation is only a means to attain this absorption. One who does not have a teacher often falls into this erroneous absorption. Really, true absorption is a Buddhist secret and difficult to explain. You do not close your eyes or take an aloof attitude or keep yourself in a mountain cave. When you realize that *there is no ego*, no particular soul that is under your control, you will attain it.

Buddhists do not believe that particular souls are created, unlike Christians. We do not believe that a particular soul is created for you or me. To speak dualistically, dividing all into spirit and matter, every being has its own particular existence. The soul, according to circumstances, performs its own life: in a woman, the woman's life; in a cat, the cat's life; in a dog, the dog's life; in a sparrow, the sparrow's life. According to the law of causation, our physical body, our organic system, will go through many phases, will become many things. From the view of karma, we have to take this dualistic attitude for a while. Then we take the empty view.

When you realize non-ego, that the soul is not created or acquired, and not only realize it, but demonstrate it with your own mind, then, in one meditation, in five minutes, you will realize this great absorption. But with your egotistical view, entertaining your individual soul as a superstition, and cherishing this superstition, you can hardly attain *samadhi*.

"*When wisdom and* samadhi *are equally maintained/ The mind will be pure/ Awakening to this Dharma/ Results from cultivating your nature*" Attaining wisdom and realizing *samadhi* always follows after your attainment of non-ego. Realization of non-ego is the result of humility. When you surrender to the universe, all is well. Through modesty and humility, you will realize this non-ego.

"*Using that which is originally uncreated . . .*" When you find a man worshipping a young mother, this is nature from the true standpoint—all is empty. Then there will come a change. Buddhists will go over the mountains and face any danger to find enlightenment.

"*Practice to attain both wisdom and* samadhi/ *This is the right practice.*" I was seven years in that helpless humility, practicing meditation very hard. When I wrote to my teacher, he answered: "You have attained wisdom, but your absorption is not quite real. I must see you once more." I went seven thousand miles and manifested my absorption and got my teacher's full recognition. It was not easy. It was a lifetime! You must meet someone who has the experience, and you must see eye to eye with him. It took me many months to experience this.

Thus, from the Buddha's time, this has been handed down from soul to soul, eye to eye, living together and talking together. For this you must have a true teacher, one who has attained. Of course, when you attain this by yourself—*This is That!* That is all.

From that day, you can call yourself a torch holder of Buddhism. It does not come in two or three years; it may take twenty. It is not easy, but one who has really attained knows this absorption.

At the Master's words, Fa-hai attained great enlightenment, extolling the Master with this gatha: "*Mind itself is Buddha! Not realizing this, I submitted myself to ignorance/ Now I understand that by practicing both wisdom and* samadhi/ *One can renounce all things.*"

The monk Fa-ta was a native of Hung-chou. When he was seven years old, he became a Buddhist monk. He was always reciting the Lotus Sutra. *When he came to bow to the Master, his head did not touch the ground. The Master said to him reprovingly: "If your head does not touch the ground, you might just as well not bow. You have something in your mind. What is it you are hiding?"*

The monk answered: "I recite the Lotus Sutra. *I have repeated it over three thousand times."*

The Master said: "Even if you have recited it ten thousand times and understood its significance, if you do not think you have done anything superior, then you will be walking with me. Failing in your practice, you are completely unaware of your error. Listen to me as I recite this gatha:

"The purpose of your obeisance is to lower the banner of pride
Why does your head not touch the ground?

If you cherish your ego
You commit an error

If you forget your own merits
You will enjoy blessings beyond compare"

The Master said: "What is your name?" The monk answered: "Fa-ta ('To attain the Dharma.')" The Master said: "Well, if that is your name, have you attained the Dharma?"
Again the Master recited a gatha:

"Your name is 'To Attain the Dharma'
You have never ceased in your efforts to recite the sutra

[Yet] mere recitation is but the vain repetition of your voice
Only enlighten your mind, and you become a bodhisattva

There must be some past affinity between us
So I am speaking to you about this now

Just have faith that Buddha is without words
Then lotus petals will fall from your lips"

SOKEI-AN SAYS:

Today, there are about one hundred Zen masters living in Japan, so this Zen teaching is something like a candle light flickering in the wind. In Japan, the lineage of Zen has almost expired. And in the next hundred years, if we do not guard this flame, it will vanish, and the Buddha's true Dharma will end in the human world. The end is quite predictable. There are many erroneous teachers, and no one knows who is right and who is wrong.

Here in America, we are thirty or forty years in Buddhism. In Japan, we have had Buddhism for 1,300 years. The Japanese Emperor invited Chinese Buddhists to come to Japan. Of course, here in America, I do not pay much attention to etiquette, but I was asked to come here by those who were trying to find a mind and a soul.

The monk Fa-ta was a native of Hung-chou. When he was seven years old, he became a Buddhist monk. To become a Buddhist monk at the age of seven is quite early in the Buddhist order. It was permitted from the age of twelve. But this child entered the sangha when he was only seven, just as our children today go to grammar school at that age. From the sound of his talk, at the time of his coming to pay homage to the Sixth Patriarch, he was about nineteen. But he was a bright child. When these boys come into the sangha, they are not fully ordained monks. Fully ordained monks must be at least twenty years old.

Hung-chou was in Central China, and the Sixth Patriarch was living in Southern China, so Fa-ta came some distance.

He was always reciting the Lotus Sutra. This is a very long sutra. To recite it from beginning to end takes a long time. Following their teacher in chanting the sutras, the monks think that reciting something of which they do not know the meaning will gain them merit, just as one blind cow will lead other blind cows to the edge of a cliff and fall into a dale.

When he came to bow to the Master, his head did not touch the ground. When Fa-ta paid homage, though he bowed low, his head did not touch the ground. When a man's heart is not true to his religion, he cannot bow to the ground. He is uncomfortable and tries to slide away.

The Master said to him reprovingly: "If your head does not touch the ground, you might just as well not bow. You have something in your mind. What is it you are hiding?" Confess it! In regards to the true Dharma, he must speak to the young monk from his position as master.

In Japan, many people think: "Well, the Zen monks are quite nice to us. If we enter the temple, how nice they will be!" But when they shave their heads and enter, the very next day they are beaten! Only a boy who has a true heart can maintain himself in a Zen temple. To beat young students is to find their true heart. The Oriental father's method of finding the true heart is different from the Western mother's attitude of guarding her baby. Of course, the Western mother's attitude of guarding her baby is very beautiful, but you must not forget the Eastern father's effort.

It is not easy to maintain oneself under the master's staff. When anyone comes here, I do not ask, "What is your favorite practice?" If I did, they would go—perhaps into psychoanalysis, Christian Science, or Theosophy. But the Sixth Patriarch asked this question of the young monk.

The monk answered: "I recite the Lotus Sutra*. I have repeated it over three thousand times."* He said this very proudly.

The Master said: "Even if you have recited it ten thousand times and understood its significance, if you do not think you have done anything superior, then you will be walking with me. Failing in your practice, you are completely unaware of your error." Though the Master's words were severe, there was great sympathy in his voice. There was a very young boy standing before him, and we can suppose that the Master was about my own age.

The Sixth Patriarch is saying, "Even if you understand it, better follow me. You may be educated in the sutras and understand religion, but you are *not* enlightened!"

The Sixth Patriarch had confidence in his own teaching, and he spoke with power. When I read the Bible, I realized that Jesus also spoke with power and authority. If someone reads a book about Paris and knows the names of all the streets and so on, perhaps he can fool people who were never there into thinking he had been there. But he would not fool anyone who had been there, even for one day.

Please do not misunderstand my words about enlightenment. There is an entrance, a true conception to real Dharma. There is just one gate, and all men who have attained passed through that gate and came back.

"Listen to me as I recite this gatha: *"The purpose of your obeisance is to lower the banner of pride/ Why does your head not touch the ground? / If you cherish your ego/ You commit an error/ If you forget your own merits/ You will enjoy blessings beyond compare."* The Sixth Patriarch's *gatha* is not beautiful, for the Master was not a poet. I should translate this into rhyme, but my ignorance of the English language makes it impossible. But someone versed in verses may do so.

This "banner of pride" is the first sign that you enter my kind of religion, and that you "lower" your banner of pride is to humble your proud heart. Without this, you can never see the true law of nature, never see the true heart of the human being. Your nature must be humble and true to yourself. The man who is uncomfortable and cannot rest until he solves his problems, that kind of man I love. I do not like to associate with a man who does not solve his problems or his questions. I feel quite uncomfortable with him. So you must lower your banner of pride. Crush it, and throw it away.

When I was young, I was an art student before entering the monastery. I made copies of plaster of paris statues. Then I came into nature, and I saw that nature is the best artist in the world. I bowed down and made my obeisance to nature. I sketched out-of-doors with tears in my eyes. Of course, I was a fanatic. But when I came to the temple, I had no difficulty in paying homage to my teacher. I will bow down to the truth though it is a man of flesh. I paid obeisance from my true heart. It made it easy for me to get into Buddhism, for I really threw myself down before Buddha.

The Master said: "What is your name?" The monk answered: "Fa-ta ('To attain the Dharma.')" The Master said: "Well, if that is your name, have you attained the Dharma?" Poor child! Then the Master made his answer, composing it in a song.

Again the Master recited a gatha*:* "Gatha," as you know, is a poem. They still do this in Japan. After a lecture, they put it into a concise form and sing it. Hui-neng wasn't a very good poet, but the ideas expressed in this *gatha* are profound.

"Your name is 'To Attain the Dharma'"/ You have never ceased in your efforts to recite the sutra." Dharma is an important word. It has twenty-four different meanings. It can mean "entity," and it can mean "Reality." To attain the Dharma is a most important thing because we must do this by our own exertion. So, to enter Buddhism, we make a question that is the deepest and largest and most important. Usually the teacher will ask: "Why do you wish to solve your problem?"

[Yet] mere recitation is but the vain repetition of your voice/ Only enlighten your mind, and you become a bodhisattva." "Bodhisattva" means "enlightened gentleman." About eight hundred years after the Buddha's death, the dominant meaning was demigod or saint. But in my school of Zen, bodhisattva still keeps its original meaning—enlightened gentleman or lady. Those who are enlightened are called bodhisattvas.

"There must be some past affinity between us/ So I am speaking to you about this now." "Affinity" is Buddhist talk, and quite sentimental. The Sixth Patriarch was a man of compassion, different from the monks of today who would not speak in such a way.

"Just have faith that Buddha is without words/ Then lotus petals will fall from your lips." Much like your Christianity isn't it? The gate must be opened humbly, and when the door is open, we must enter in silence.

After listening to the gatha, Fa-ta repented and declared: "From now on, I shall humble myself before everyone. Though I, your disciple, practice reciting the Lotus Sutra, *I do not yet understand its significance, and doubts about it constantly fill my mind. With your vast wisdom, I implore your Reverence to briefly expound for me the essential meaning of the sutra."*

The Master said: "Fa-ta, when it comes to Dharma, you have attained well, but not when it comes to your own mind. There is nothing to doubt in the sutra itself; the doubts are in your mind. When you recite the sutra, what do you take to be its essential teaching?"

Fa-ta replied. "I am stupid. I have been reciting the sutra only following the characters. How can I know its essential teaching?"

The Master said: "I cannot read characters, so you had better recite it. Then I will expound its meaning for you."

Thereupon Fa-ta recited the sutra aloud until he came to the "Parables" chapter.

The Master said: "Stop! The purpose of the Buddha's appearance in the world is the essential teaching of this sutra. The many parables in this sutra are simply illustrations of this. What is this 'purpose?' The sutra says: 'All the Buddhas' incarnations in the world are for only one great purpose.' This 'one great purpose' is to awaken to the knowledge of Buddha."

SOKEI-AN SAYS:

There are no important techincal terms here, so I will immediately make my commentary.

Zen was originally Buddha's Buddhism. It was not the Buddhism of Buddha's disciples. In India, this torch of the true teaching, which was not in a form to be popularized, was held through twenty-seven generations. In the twenty-eighth generation it was held by Bodhidharma. Then Bodhidharma brought the torch into China and handed it down to his disciples, who were Chinese. But in the Zen School, this torch is not bestowed by the teacher upon the disciple. The disciple by his own mental power or by his own power of enlightenment takes the torch from the hand of the teacher. Thus the torch has escaped expiring from the world.

It is easy to hand something down when you are dying—"Hold this, and when you are dying, hand it to *your* child." That is easy. But in Zen, the master hides the secret very subtly. The disciple, with great effort, exertion, wisdom, and mental power, attains this in his mind without the aid of the teacher. And when he attains it, he then expresses or reveals it. His teacher, who from his own experience had attained it and proved it to his own teacher, judges his disciple's attainment. He has no favoritism, but judges in one answer—yes or no.

When a student has stepped up to the highest knowledge attained by Buddha, the teacher acknowledges him as one who has attained true Buddhist wisdom. Then he goes away, and according to his nature may enter the world for his own experience or go into a cave. Later, he will come back, and the teacher will ordain him as one of the torch holders. When the master dies, the best disciple will succeed him. The others will also be torch holders, but they will go all over the world and help in the propagation of the Dharma. So there is no torch transmission without looking at each other, no other medium—physical or metaphysical. It can only be done face to face, eye to eye. This way, which is the highest reached by Buddha, is not very easy.

Buddha transmitted this to Mahakashyapa, and he to Ananda, the Buddha's personal attendant. During Buddha's life, Ananda did not attain, so Buddha could not prove this to him. So Mahakashyapa, as Buddha's representative, proved Ananda's attainment, and Ananda transmitted this to Sanavasa, and so on, through to Bodhidharma, the Twenty-Eighth Patriarch. Bodhidharma handed it down to the Chinese, and then after twenty-seven generations, it was transmitted to the Japanese.

In Japan, this torch has almost gone out. Through twenty-five hundred years of Buddhist history, this is the first time we have confronted this most dangerous and critical period. Can the torch survive? If not, it will expire and be lost until another advent of Buddha. I have explained, particularly here, the relation between the teacher and the disciple of Zen.

This young monk came to the Sixth Patriarch and did not touch his head to the ground, and the Sixth Patriarch said, "You have something in your mind. Tell me!" The young student said that he had recited the *Lotus Sutra* three thousand times. The Sixth Patriarch said, "Your reciting of the sutra three-thousand times means nothing if you do not attain the principal teaching of the sutra."

Many monks choose sutras to recite from the vast collection in the so-called "three baskets" of Buddhist literature, consisting of five thousand forty-eight volumes. They may choose the *Lotus, Nirvana, Mahaprajnaparamita, Avatamsaka, Lankavatara,* or *Diamond Sutras.* Sometimes they recite their teacher's particular choice. In the large temples, five or six who are reading the same sutra will recite it together with the usual drumming. After a monk has repeated it about one hundred times, an elder monk will teach a younger monk its meaning. When he is well-versed in this, he begins to practice each line in meditation, after which he goes to the master and tries to realize from his own consciousness that which was written in the sutra. This is not easy. If one honestly follows the way of the Buddhist monk, it will take about forty years. I was one of those crazy ones, and now I am almost in my coffin. One foot is already there!

There is only one way to enter Buddhism: that is to enter your original mind, your original nature. Everyone tries to attain by learning something, by putting more coats and dresses on. But the true way of learning Buddhism is not to learn but to unlearn. You strip away your bits of knowledge, one by one, until you come to your naked mind; and through this gate, you enter the Ocean of Consciousness.

Original Mind is simple, but you use images when you begin to think about something—using words to reason about it. You are using symbols of the external world—images such as "lamp," "incense," "electricity," etc. Then you reason and make words for that which is not even existing outside—abstract nouns, for instance. Without these words, you cannot think at all. But these images and words are not mind itself. We call them mind-stuff. You dream of a cat, but where is it? It has form and space, but no weight. It is not a three—or four-pound cat, and its space is not geometrical, not triangular, round, or square. It does not exist outside, and when you wake up, it does not exist at all. Dreams are queer things. They are semi-embodied existences, or semi-material embodiments—a space that has no place. Our mind is of this semi-material world. Our bodies belong to the animal world. So a human being is a semi-embodied being. The mental being is not this physical body. We use words and vision as our body, and live in it, but it is like debris in a river, or sawdust flowing in a stream. If you take all this stuff out, then you see pure water, pure mind.

Mind is pure mind activity, the subjective; and pure mind-stuff is the objective. So when you try to grasp *real* mind activity, you must give up mind-stuff. In order to reach the mind of Buddha, you must annihilate it. Without thinking a word, or seeing a figure, you are in pure mind activity. It is not your mind. It is Universal, Original Mind—Buddha Mind.

Buddha is not the human being who lived two or three thousand years ago. Buddha awoke from his embodied state to his unembodied state. How can you reach that state while your mind is filled with dead rats and drowned cats?

You must annihilate mind-stuff, purify mind activity, and immediately reach the Ocean of Universal Mind. It is infinite, boundless space with all potential power. From ancient days, the Buddha tried to attain this through silence and meditation.

Attaining this state, we realize the power that sustains this physical life. You will know that which is digesting your food without paying any attention to it. When you enter this stream, you are carried along with it. You will flow in that stream, and you will not be uncomfortable anymore. Your mind will have a foundation, and your thoughts will have substance. You will be calm. Your eye will shine, and you will look different than you did yesterday. Those who have experienced this, and wish to talk about it, will invent some metaphor, and you will swallow it. They will say: "In that state, there is no high or low, no space or time." These are just words, just illustrations, an invention of names like a fireman's ladder—each step leading to nothing.

In the *Lotus Sutra*, there are many parables. One that I remember is about a king who lost his child on the way to wage war with his neighbors. After the war, he ordered a search to be made all over the country, but in vain. Fifteen years later, a subject said to the king: "I am sure a young man I found among the gutter cleaners is your son." In India, at that time, dung-scraping was terrible work. The subject said to the king: "You had better go yourself, look at him, and prove to yourself whether he is your son or not." The king went and watched him scrape dung, and saw that the dung-scraper was his own child.

He ordered the police to take him, but the boy fled in fear. The child did not know that his father was trying to save him. He did not know that he was the son of a king. Finally, the king realized that he alone, through love, could save his child. So he disguised himself as a dung-scraper in order to meet him. Later, he was able to approach him and make friends, but he could not yet reveal himself. Slowly he told his story, and bit by bit the boy came to trust him. Sometimes they would eat together. But one day, the boy said: "I cannot go to eat with you. I have no money." So the king said, "Come with me, I have saved some money." Then he helped the boy to get some clothes, and taught him proper speech. At last, he got the boy a new job as a policeman, and gradually, he made a gentleman out of him. Then he told him: "You are my own child." "No!" said the boy, "I am the child of a dung-scraper!" Then the king said, "But *I* am your true father," and later the boy became his father's successor.

This story is an illustration of how Buddha came down to this filthy world, started from the beginning with a deluded mind, and gradually attained to the highest state.

Cease reading! Metaphors are of no use if you do not grasp their meaning. Grasping the real core of the metaphor, you will attain enlightenment.

[The Master continued:] "People in the world, in their delusion, attach to forms without and to emptiness within. If you can be free from form, while in the realm of form, if you can be free from emptiness, while in the realm of emptiness, you will not be deluded within or without. If you attain this Dharma, in an instant of thought your mind will open. This is 'opening to the knowledge of Buddha.' Buddha is to awaken.

"[The Lotus Sutra *says that] there are four stages of awakening: 1) Initiation[13] to the knowledge of awakening; 2) Demonstration of the knowledge of awakening; 3) Realization of the knowledge of awakening; 4) Actualization of the knowledge of awakening. When you hear of the initiation and the demonstration [of the teaching], you will be able to realize and actualize it. Thus you will attain the knowledge of awakening, and your intrinsic nature will be revealed.*

"Be careful not to misunderstand the meaning of the sutra! When you hear about the initiation, demonstration, realization and actualization, do not think: 'This is the wisdom of the Buddha; it has nothing to do with me.' If you think so, you are slandering the sutra and the Buddha. He [who has attained this] is already a buddha, he is already endowed with knowledge, so why does he need any initiation? You should now have faith in the fact that buddha-knowledge is your own mind, and that there is no other buddha."

SOKEI-AN SAYS:

To transmit Zen there is no procedure. We place emphasis on the transmission from teacher to student, face to face and heart to heart. The stories of these transmissions, such as this record, are not Zen itself, but they talk about Zen.

Of course, Oriental religion is now a type of antique, but there is a living core in this religion, and it always teaches something new. When I came to this country, people would say, "Buddhism is quite old, and Christianity is new," and I would say, "Yes, but Buddhism is only five hundred years older than Christianity." "Oh, I thought Buddhism was some kind of Nestorian Christianity." There is no more reason that Buddhism would be Nestorian Christianity than that Christianity should come and steal Buddhism and bring it back to Rome! From the Buddha's time, nothing new has been discovered about the human mind.

"People in the world, in their delusion, attach to forms without and to emptiness within. If you can be free from form, while in the realm of form, if you can be free from emptiness, while in the realm of emptiness, you will not be deluded within or without." When we talk about this universe, which is absolute oneness, we must use two terms: form and emptiness. Form is outside, and emptiness is the result of our meditation, or the consummation of meditation. Through this meditation, we realize that our consciousness is empty and that there is no God sitting in the shrine of consciousness. Consciousness is submerged in emptiness. This emptiness is empty as matter, but as spirit, it exists throughout time and space.

Many people think that emptiness is the summit of Buddhism. Many Buddhists also believe this. But logically speaking, it cannot be the summit because we discover it through meditation—our internal emptiness corresponding to external form. And if there is no external form, there is no emptiness. So this emptiness is not emptiness itself; it is the term "emptiness," the notion of emptiness, a representation of the real emptiness. So please do not think that your conception is true emptiness. It is just a notion. A Buddhist who studies under a true teacher knows this. You think that emptiness is subjective, but the emptiness of your notion is only some form of the objective.

When I was reading the *Critique of Pure Reason*, the famous book written by Immanuel Kant, I realized that he was criticizing those mountain dwellers in almost the same terms as the Buddhist. It is a good way to attack those who think that God is somewhere inside or outside. You must not think that Buddhism is a treasure only of the East. It is also the treasure of the West. Buddhism is Buddhism in whatever country it exists. But you must not accept your own notion of it.

"Attachment to external forms" means that you think red is there, sound is there, and taste comes from food. But all this is neither here nor there, as I have told you many times. Attachment to external forms is illustrated in an old story:

A young monk and an old monk traveling on foot came to a flooded river bank. There stood a young girl who was bitterly weeping. "Perhaps we could help her," said the old monk. So he asked the girl what was wrong. "My mother is dying, and I cannot cross this river to reach her. She will die while I'm waiting to cross!" The old monk tucked up his robes and said, "Stop crying, I will carry you across the river." The young monk was shocked. "Remember the commandment," he said. "You shall not touch a woman to take her in your arms." "Be quiet!" said the old monk. "You are blindly following the commandment." So the old monk carried her across the river in his arms and put her down on the other shore. "Run," he said. "Perhaps you will get to your mother before she dies." Then he and the young monk went on silently. That evening, they came to an inn. While they were washing their feet, the young monk groaned aloud. "What is the matter?" asked the old monk. "I am thinking of your great sin," answered the young monk. "We have the commandment not to touch a woman, and you carried that young girl in your arms across the river." "I followed that commandment very carefully," said the old monk. "You, however, have been carrying that girl in your arms all day, while I dropped her long ago."

In the practice of Buddhism under a teacher, this is a very important gate. Almost all other religions are attached to the outside or to the inside or to both. Or else, they do not know anything about either one of them. If you cling to the outside form or to internal emptiness, your mind will be deluded. If God exists inside, he must also exist outside. And if he exists outside, he exists inside as well. When we talk of Reality itself, we avoid the terms "inside" and "outside." Reality, absolute existence, is not knowledge.

"If you attain this Dharma, in an instant of thought your mind will open. This is 'opening to the knowledge of Buddha.' Buddha is to awaken." Buddha means the "one who has awakened." At the base of Buddhism there is nothing but attaining Reality itself.

"[The Lotus Sutra *says that] there are four stages of awakening: 1) Initiation to the knowledge of awakening; 2) Demonstration of the knowledge of awakening; 3) Realization of the knowledge of awakening; 4) Actualization of the knowledge of awakening. When you hear of the initiation and the demonstration [of the teaching], you will be able to realize and actualize it. Thus you will attain the knowledge of awakening, and your intrinsic nature will be revealed.* These four stages are very important:

1) Initiation: This that I am giving you now, and to which you are listening, following that stream. It is the explanation of the theory and doctrine of Buddhism, to give you the canonized idea of Buddhism, handed down from generation to generation. All the 5,048 sutras are nothing but a description of the initiation to Buddhism.

2) Demonstration: After your initiation through the scriptures, you come to the actual teachers who instruct you in meditation. These masters will demonstrate Buddhism. One will teach you how to meditate on fire and to concentrate into it. Your mind will be exalted by the fire, and you will enter *samadhi*. Through this, you will make an approach to Reality. Then you accept a question from your teacher and meditate upon it. For instance, "Before father and mother—before Adam and Eve—what were you?" (The five senses are the Mother, Eve. Consciousness is the Father, Adam. But Eve is *Maya*, who is the creator of the universe, the dream maker. So "Before Adam and Eve" means before the creation of the universe.)

In Buddhism, there is no creator working to create. No one was creating anything then or working hard. No God creating another God. Nothing was created. Everything is always originally and endlessly existing. *This One* is existing from beginningless beginning to endless end. In this meditation, you begin real practice with your teacher. "Before consciousness emerged from this unconscious dynamo, what was it?" When you accept such a question, you will demonstrate your awakening to Buddhism.

3) Realization: When you pass a koan and cannot say a word, or think anything, you feel that your body covers the whole universe. You will not come back any more because you have realized this absolute Emptiness with your heart, mind, emotions, and physical body. When your wisdom attains this state, the material world will cease to exist because mind is detached from the five senses.

4) Actualization: You are an arhat, one who is supported. Your consciousness is supported by all of the outside, and you accept this consciousness as the food of your own reality. There is nothing to attach to on the outside, but everything is supporting you.

The Zen master teaches meditation and actualization. Meditation is the power of converging and the power of diverging actualization. The two combine to give you the whole picture of Reality. When you realize actuality and Reality at once, you are enlightened. Then you live in everyday life and observe it. You change your point of view completely and are born again in this lifetime.

These are the four stages in the attainment of Buddhism as described by the Sixth Patriarch. He was a very queer teacher. He was no scholar and never heard a lecture. He pounded rice for eight months, and then he met the master eye to eye. I think he must have attained through these four stages. In all things, he speaks like the Buddha.

"Be careful not to misunderstand the meaning of the sutra! When you hear about the initiation, demonstration, realization and actualization, do not think: 'This is the wisdom of the Buddha; it has

nothing to do with me.' If you think so, you are slandering the sutra and the Buddha. He [who has attained this] is already a buddha, he is already endowed with knowledge, so why does he need any initiation? The Sixth Patriarch is saying: "I have nothing to do with your attaining buddha-knowledge. This is not my pie, it is yours. I do not put my finger in it."

It is true. My teacher never taught me a thing. No Zen master teaches anything. I discovered it for myself, as each one must do. Then it is authorized by the master. So the scriptural record is used merely to compare with one's own experience.

Initiation, demonstration, realization, and actualization have great significance in Buddhism. These four words speak almost the whole of Buddhism. This is the knowledge of Buddha. By reading about Buddhism, you do not become a Buddhist. But when you pass the four stages, you will have the knowledge of Buddha—the ultimate of the Buddha's six years of meditation under the Bodhi Tree.

At first, the Buddha fasted until he lost his mental power, and then he realized that this was the wrong way to enlightenment. Then he bathed, ate, and returned to meditation for twenty-one days. Watching the morning star in his conscious and subconscious mind, he attained the highest enlightenment. At that moment, the whole universe became enlightened—people, trees, stones, and so forth. It was the universe, not himself, that had this attainment. It was not his own consciousness. It was intrinsic and universal consciousness. There was no barrier between the man and the universe.

You should now have faith in the fact that buddha-knowledge is your own mind, and that there is no other Buddha." It is difficult to have faith in that which you do not yet know. In Zen, you enter religion with doubt and with questions. When your doubt is conquered, then you can have faith.

[The Master continued:] "All sentient beings conceal their intrinsic brightness, clinging to objects and disturbing their minds in response to external change, fondly chasing after things. This is why the Buddha rose from his deep meditation to give them kind advice in order that they may find rest, instructing them: 'Do not seek in the external world, for you and Buddha are one and the same!' Therefore we speak of the discovery of buddha-knowledge. I, too, exhort everyone to continually discover buddha-knowledge within his own mind. The mind of man in the world is wicked; he creates evil karma in his delusion; he talks well but possesses an evil mind, [filled with] greed, anger, jealousy, sycophancy and arrogance; he encroaches upon others and causes harm, and so naturally develops the mind of a sentient being. If you can keep your mind upright, always giving rise to wisdom and introspecting your mind, you will put a stop to evil notions and practice good. This is to discover buddha-knowledge yourself.

"Always be intent upon discovering buddha-knowledge, not the knowledge of sentient beings. If you discover (initiate) the knowledge of Buddha, you will deliver yourself from the world; if you develop the knowledge of sentient beings, you will remain always in the world. If you cling slavishly to your recitation [of the sutra] and fancy that you render some meritorious service to your fellow beings, you are not one whit different from the yak that cherishes its own tail."

SOKEI-AN SAYS:

Zen is to think without words. This Zen way was prevalent all over Asia and China at the time of Bodhidharma and after. When we think with words, we are in dualism. But when we think without words, the mind works like lightning, question and answer come at the same moment. When the question becomes distinct and clear, the answer is there.

"All sentient beings conceal their intrinsic brightness, clinging to objects and disturbing their minds in response to external change, fondly chasing after things." The outside is always changing, and when you lean upon it, you are always in turmoil. Intrinsic ignorance and darkness are the first cause of existence. You are born out of that, and it obscures your wisdom.

"This is why the Buddha rose from his deep meditation to give them kind advice in order that they may find rest": Buddha rising is not Shakyamuni Buddha; it is your own buddha rising to your aid. In your agony, you search for the true foundation of life. Your intrinsic wisdom will be born from your consciousness, and with that light, the darkness will be dispelled.

"Instructing them: 'Do not seek in the external world, for you and Buddha are one and the same!'" In modern science, the electron and proton are believed to hold the secret of the universe. The astronomical law is also there. Scientists have realized that all laws are ruled by one law, that the law of gravity in the electron is the law of gravity in the entire solar system. But the Buddhist has known this for a long time. The Buddha discovered nearly three thousand years ago that the law that rules our mind is the law that rules the universe.

Scientists are approaching Reality through analysis. Other types are making access to Reality by meditation, without using apparatus made of matter. We use the apparatus of mind itself—mind discipline. We use this consciousness and make contact with our own mind, with Reality, through our own consciousness.

Therefore we speak of the discovery of buddha-knowledge." Awakened or enlightened knowledge. This is really a description of our own nature. Beyond this material existence, we discover the reality of things, of ourselves, of our own nature. Then, awakened, we come back to the stage of actual life, and we recognize this stage again with the knowledge attained in the state of Reality. We observe this world once more and correct our former distortion and make upright our former upside-down view.

Naturally, we will be emancipated from all superstition, erroneous views, and all the names and convictions in which we were formerly enmeshed. We will gain freedom of mind even though our physical bodies are subject to the restrictions and impediments of physical law. It no longer has the power to torture our minds. When we die, we will smile as if we were going into a pleasant sleep.

"I, too, exhort everyone to continually discover buddha-knowledge within his own mind. The mind of man in the world is wicked; he creates evil karma in his delusion; he talks well but possesses an evil mind, [filled with] greed, anger, jealousy, sycophancy and arrogance; he encroaches upon others and causes harm, and so naturally develops the mind of a sentient being." Sentient being is an important technical term in Buddhism. Sentient beings, in their mental state, are living in consecutive stages of evolution. In the Western world, this is the theory of evolution. The Buddha discovered evolution in the mental state of being.

In Buddhism, the lowest state is called *naraka*, hell, the state of disembodied spirits. These spirits have desire but cannot find their path because they have lost their physical bodies. It is a state of death. There is no lower state in mental evolution.

The next stage is that of the semi-embodied *preta*. Pretas take possession of physical bodies as instruments to carry out their evil designs. One who is possessed by a preta is called a hungry ghost. A preta appears in the world when he possesses anything physical. The human mind unconsciously does things under the spell of such beings.

Then come *ashsura* (angry demon), animal (beast), human being, and *deva*, which is an angel. The human being is living in an animal body and possesses it, but the human being is mind also, and the deva is the king of the mind. Deva is higher than human but is semi-embodied.

"If you can keep your mind upright, always giving rise to wisdom and introspecting your mind, you will put a stop to evil notions and practice good. This is to discover buddha-knowledge yourself." Reality is not attained through sense-perception, but through intuition. Reverse the process, and you attain the actuality of the phenomenal world. The difference between religion and philosophy is that the conclusion of philosophy is not religious, but the realization of the conclusion is. So the Sixth Patriarch said:

"Always be intent upon discovering buddha-knowledge, not the knowledge of sentient beings. If you discover (initiate) the knowledge of Buddha, you will deliver yourself from the world": All external existence is an illusion of the sense-perceptions, so we cannot find Buddha there. All significance is in a subjective condition. In the pure objective world, there is no human mind. It is the pure reality of matter.

If you develop the knowledge of sentient beings, you will remain always in *the world. If you cling slavishly to your recitation [of the sutra] and fancy that you render some meritorious service to your fellow beings, you are not one whit different from the yak that cherishes its own tail."* Man's mind has been deluded a long time by "personified" religion. One who has buddha-knowledge observes everything in the state of Reality. Therefore he is not disturbed by the changing existence outside.

Reality is this daily life. Take, for instance, money. What is money to you? When you have money in your hand, you are happy. And when you put it in the bank, you are afraid of losing it. When you see it in gold, you are pleased; but when someone gives you a check, you do not feel so pleased. The reality of money is wealth, the result of the actual force that you have created. Wealth assumes many forms. In the future, it may be indicated by electric symbols. But the deluded one will attach to the shape of Reality and not to Reality itself.

People's minds are so shallow. They are always observing Reality in form, in emotion, but not Reality itself. So they remain in this old world of wars, famine, earthquakes, and so forth. In a small economic circle, we realize the benefit of money to all—whoever may have it. But in a large group, this truth is lost sight of. The whole world must be awakened to see everything in the form of Reality.

When we observe physical existence from the state of Reality, the physical is Reality carried into physical manifestations. The law that governs steam will not govern ice. The law that governs ice will not govern water, even though they are both the same material. The law must be applied differently in different circumstances.

Moral law cannot be applied to objective Reality (science, molecular substance, etc.) Is red pure? Is white pure? Color has nothing to do with the Reality of purity or impurity. Objective existence has nothing to do with good or bad. Nothing is good, and nothing is bad. Goodness and badness exist only in the mind of man.

The attributes of God are the attributes of your own mind. Buddha personified in the form of a man is your own notion. It is not the reality of your mind, not yourself, and not the universe. Reality cannot be put into the shape of a person or beast. Reality itself possesses infinite power. So a personalized God is not a pure form of religion; it is a secondary form. But since the human mind is childish, the religious teacher uses allegory and personification to convey his meaning. Our mind receives impressions of motion, beauty, ideas, and so forth. We throw them forth from our mind upon our environment, and we observe the world through the veil and shadow we cast upon it. Thus we learn to distrust our sense impressions, our mind, and even our consciousness until we break through to universal consciousness. This can be done only by meditation. It takes a long time. It is difficult for a person to do something that he has not done in a past life, such as to speak English.

Fa-ta said: "If what you say is true, then so long as I grasp the meaning of the sutra, I needn't bother to recite it. Is that correct?"

The Master said: "The sutra does you no harm and will not obstruct your mind. Whether a person is enlightened or not, is harmed or benefited, depends only upon him.

"When you recite the sutra with your mouth and practice it in your mind, you are revolving the sutra; but when you recite it with your mouth without practicing it in your mind, the sutra is revolving you. Listen while I recite a gatha.

> *When your mind is deluded, you are revolved by the law of the* Lotus Sutra
> *When your mind is enlightened, you revolve the* Lotus Sutra
>
> *You were reciting the sutra for a long time, without understanding*
> *You, therefore, became an enemy of its real meaning*
>
> *Your empty-minded mind is straight mind*
> *Errors are committed by the mind that is stuffed[14]*
>
> *Forget the mind, emptied or stuffed*
> *And you will always find yourself driving the White Oxcart"*

Having heard the gatha, *Fa-ta sobbed from his heart. Suddenly enlightened, he said to the Master: "Till now, I never truly revolved the* Lotus Sutra; *I have been revolved* by the sutra."

SOKEI-AN SAYS:

There are many types of religion in the world, but Zen is a peculiar type of religion. Zen reveals itself by showing Reality, while other religions reveal their reality through terms or symbols or images to the people who cannot grasp Reality itself.

When you render Reality in an image—the iconographic type of religion—you find a religion whose adherents worship idols. An image may be mental, harbored in the mind rather than definitely rendered in a physical form. It may be personified. If Reality is rendered in terms that are explained by terms, then that religion falls into a philosophical or theoretical type of belief. The theoretical type canonizes Reality into philosophical form so that one can think about it logically; and if you try to express this type of reality, this type of religion, through symbols, you will not use personified gods but symbols such as dragons, lotus flowers, triangles, or squares. These symbols will constitute the idea of Reality, which will then take on the appearance of ritual.

Pure Buddhism, which is like Zen, does not use any of these, but reveals Reality directly to its followers—the Buddha shows the lotus to Mahakashyapa; the master shows the hand, slaps the student, or shouts, thus revealing Reality itself. But the disciple is oftentimes blind and not ready to see Reality—he sees nothing but phenomena. He thinks that Reality is something else and somewhere else rather than right here. He is deluded in his upside-down view. The Zen master always shows you Reality, but the deluded disciple cannot see it.

Ananda asked Mahakashyapa what else besides the robe and bowl the Buddha had transmitted to him. Mahakashyapa called, "Ananda!" and Ananda answered, "Yes." Mahakashyapa said, "Thus have I transmitted the secret of the Buddha's esoteric teachings to you." Some people think this is just conversation—"Mr. Brown!" "Yes!" In this conversation, Zen is dancing so vividly that there is nothing else but Reality in the exchange. The deluded ones cannot grasp this, so an iconographic, theoretic, or symbolic religion is made to open their eyes. But this Zen is the pure Buddhism taught by the Buddha.

Other schools of Buddhism are the Buddhism of the Buddha's disciples. They made a religion to approach immature minds. But today, men's minds are more developed, and we do not need these halfway religions. We must make immediate contact with man's mind.

Fa-ta said: "If what you say is true, then so long as I grasp the meaning of the sutra, I needn't bother to recite it. Is that correct? The Master said: "The sutra does you no harm and will not obstruct your mind. Whether a person is enlightened or not, is harmed or benefited, depends only upon him." The sutra in the book is just a shadow of it. You must realize the the Law of the Sacred White Lotus, the consciousness of Buddha that is in your own consciousness.

"When you recite the sutra with your mouth and practice it in your mind, you are revolving the sutra; but when you recite it with your mouth without *practicing it in your mind, the sutra is revolving you.* Revolving the sutra is done by the empty mind. Empty mind does not mean the mind of an idiot. But you must meet a real teacher to understand this empty mind.

Take this glass of water. It is not empty, and yet, it is as clear and transparent as the empty sky. It looks empty, but it is full of everything. The sky is the mother that begets everything.

Thirty years ago, there was a student whom I met who said, "How do you do?" in a faded, weak voice. Thirty years later, I met him again, and he said, "Hello!" I asked, "Have you found the empty mind?" "No," he answered, "There is no such thing." We looked at each other and smiled.

There is an esoteric secret here.

Listen while I recite a gatha.

"When your mind is deluded, you are revolved by the law of the Lotus Sutra/ *When your mind is enlightened, you revolve the* Lotus Sutra." Buddhist monks observed some queer commandments, such as not eating meat. But when they went to Kashmir, where it is very cold, there were no vegetables. The people were eating veal, pig, and birds, so the monks almost starved. But remembering the Buddha's saying that the commandments can be altered according to time and place, they, too, began to eat meat. Today, in my sect in Japan, the secular novices can marry, but when they take the full vow, they cannot.

Laws exist in some form, then are altered according to time and place.

"You were reciting the sutra for a long time, without understanding/ You, therefore, became an enemy of its real meaning." The Sixth Patriarch told this young monk that reciting the sutra for such a long time, without knowing the law, turned the sutra into venom and an enemy. I have heard that some American Christians wish to bring back the old "dry law" once more. I do not drink wine because my body does not care for it, so I personally do not care whether there is a dry law or not. But I think that was a bad law for this country, that it was venom.

"Your empty-minded mind is straight mind/ Errors are committed by the mind that is stuffed." Christians call it a pure mind, but what they call a pure mind is really a stuffed mind. When I try to

talk to someone whose mind is stuffed, whatever I say, he twists and distorts the meaning. When I say to a mother, "I asked your daughter to meet my friends from Japan," the mother replies, "Why are you insulting me! When you have an eighty-year-old friend, please invite me!" This is very awkward for me. I know there is something in her mind. Her age is like a thorn stuck into her skin.

The empty mind is the daily mind, the ordinary mind. You must not dramatize it or keep an affected attitude toward it.

"Forget the mind, emptied or stuffed/ And you will always find yourself driving the White Oxcart." In the *Lotus Sutra* there is the famous allegory of a burning house. In this allegory, the metaphor of the White Ox is used.[15] This White Ox means universal law. It is also a symbol of this present consciousness in the human being. The house that is burning is the world—not this world but the world of your own conception, a purely subjective world. There is no human life in the absolute objective world.

The Buddha taught the Universal Law, the sacred law of sentient beings, the natural law of all sentient beings, and the law of both sentient and insentient beings.

When you forget the stuffed mind, you realize you are always driving the vehicle of the White Ox.

Having heard the gatha, Fa-ta sobbed from his heart. Those sentimental young monks always do this—go off in a corner and sob. The old monk says, "Stop dramatizing yourself! Get out!"

Suddenly enlightened—I hope so!—*He said to the Master: "Till now, I never truly revolved the* Lotus Sutra; *I have been revolved* by *the sutra."* I doubt the Sixth Patriarch said this bit, but it is sound. "Revolve" means the whole potential power of mind. Sometimes when you come to the Buddhist faith, you reach a place where there is nothing on which to depend—no God, no matter or consciousness. So where were you when you were in Reality?

There is no Buddhism in Buddha's mind. His mind is himself, and he does not speak himself. The true religious teacher does not speak and does not try to convert.

Fa-ta continued: *"It is said in the sutra that even if all the great disciples of the Buddha, from shravakas to bodhisattvas, utterly exhausted their powers of reasoning, they would be unable to fathom the depths of buddha-knowledge. Now, you have said that a common-minded man, by simply realizing his own mind, attains buddha-wisdom. However, apart from those of the highest ability, [such a teaching] will surely invite skepticism and slander. It is also said in the sutra that there are three kinds of vehicles: the goat vehicle, the deer vehicle, and the ox vehicle. How do they differ from the vehicle of the White Ox? I beg you to explain this."*

The Master said: *"The meaning of the sutra is clear, but because of your delusion, you misunderstand it. Those who are of the three vehicles cannot fathom the depth of buddha-knowledge because they erroneously rely on reasoning. The more you think, exhausting your mental powers, the further away you are. The Buddha originally expounded this law for the common-minded man; he did not expound it for himself. Those unable to put their faith in this principle may withdraw from the assembly. Such a one does not understand that he is already seated upon the White Ox cart, and is still looking for the three vehicles outside.*

"The sutra tells you clearly: 'There is only the one Buddha vehicle; no other vehicles exist.' Hence, all those countless theories, fictions and proverbs are only expedients for you [to discover] this one Buddha vehicle. Why don't you understand? The three kinds of vehicles are fictitious, invented for the men of yesterday; but this one vehicle is real, [disclosed] to the man of today. I teach that you must abandon the fictitious and come back to Reality.

"When you have come back to Reality, this Reality does not need to be called by any name. Know that all treasures belong to you and are yours to use. To have no notion of a 'father' or a 'child' or of 'using [anything]' is what it means to observe the Lotus Sutra. *From kalpa to kalpa, the sutra will never leave your hands; from morning to evening, no moment will pass without reciting the sutra."*

SOKEI-AN SAYS:

"Fa-ta continued: "It is said in the sutra that even if all the great disciples of the Buddha, from shravakas *to bodhisattvas utterly exhausted their powers of reasoning, they would be unable to fathom the depths of buddha-knowledge."* In Buddhism there are three classes of disciples: *shravakas, pratyekabuddhas,* and bodhisattvas. *Shravakas* are ascetics—monks living in caves who have heard the voice of the Buddha's teachings. *Pratyekabuddhas* are naturally enlightened ones—those who, for example, while looking at a flower in spring, realize emergence and submergence. They have attained fortunately, casually, or accidentally, but they cannot speak about their attainment to others. Bodhisattvas are those who can teach their enlightened brothers.

The words "utterly exhausted their powers of reasoning" are really the center of this part. "Reasoning" means our daily exercise of reasoning that is common to all human beings, and "powers of reasoning" is so-called philosophizing. But to reason with words and to philosophize with your knowledge will not lead you into true religion. It will only lead you into philosophy. Philosophy takes you to the gate of religion, and from that gate, you must enter into the religious experience itself. In Christianity, it is faith in God, but in Buddhism it is the experience of Reality. We experience Reality without taking any measure, by reason or philosophy.

We cannot talk about this experience. It is not a physical experience like sickness, being spanked by father, being in prison, or being in a hospital because you have some trouble with your nerves. There are many experiences, as when you elope to Rio de Janeiro and an American policeman brings you back. But they are not religious experiences. A religious experience is not physical; it is mental. To say "experience" is awkward. It means revelation, a revelation that takes place through one's own endeavor of meditation, or some other practice.

It is easy to have this revelation of Reality through your meditation, but Buddhist meditation is different from other forms of meditation. The Buddhist meditates purely upon his own consciousness, his own mind, not on the world of thoughts. He does this for a long time. You had better start for half an hour, and if you find you cannot do it, then try for ten minutes. You will realize the storm of thoughts that will attack your mind.

I started this meditation when I was seventeen years old, and I could not concentrate because of my thoughts. I realized that what suffers is not myself. It is some other being that occupies my mind and makes this suffering. I hated it. Then I started to take notes on everything I was thinking each day. The first day—one page. The second day—two pages. By the fourth day, it was four pages. It was endless, and I gave it up.

If you do not exercise this meditation, your mind will be like the wild woods—no path, no road, and infested with many insects and venomous animals. You must arrange your mind beautifully, and make a natural garden with nothing artificial in it but it must remain wild woods. You should start young about 22, 23, or 24. Some start late. One started at six and attained at eighty. Another started at eighty, and in three months he had the secret. I say the "secret," but there is no secret. All you have to do is to abandon all words and assumptions for Reality itself. Everything is a symbol, but symbols are not Reality.

"Now, you have said that a common-minded man, by simply realizing his own mind, attains buddha-wisdom. However, apart from those of the highest ability, [such a teaching] will surely invite skepticism and slander." Simple minds attain wisdom first. Educated minds take longer. They have to get rid of all their mind-stuff.

Buddha-knowledge is deep. In the beginning, you think this buddha-knowledge is quite remote. But when you attain it, it is quite clear—it is yourself!

"It is also said in the sutra that there are three kinds of vehicles: the goat vehicle, the deer vehicle, and the ox vehicle. How do they differ from the vehicle of the White Ox? I beg you to explain this." Fa-ta is asking about the significance of the vehicles in the *Lotus Sutra*, which are, of course, fictitious. There is only one vehicle: the true vehicle of the White Ox, the *buddhayana*.

Those of the goat vehicle mentally suppress their desire for the world. Those of the deer vehicle understand the existence of the world through the twelve stages of causation. The students standing on these lower stages begin their practice at the stage of *kamadhatu*, the world of desire, and move to *arupadhatu*, the world of formlessness. The ox-vehicle bodhisattvas pass through these two types of religion and attain a higher type of religion. The bodhisattva does not take the upside-down view. He starts from *arupadhatu* and limits the experience of *kamadhatu*. The lower ones say, "Leave your physical body and keep away from the world." The bodhisattva, however, embodies the physical body from the disembodied state and observes the six *paramitas*:

1) To give.
2) To observe the commandments. By virtuous influence the bodhisattva takes away fear, thus giving fearlessness to the pupil by speaking to him. This is the highest gift. *Shravakas, pratyekabuddhas* and bodhisattvas observe the same commandments, but their motives are different.
3) Forebearance, or patience.
4) To endeavor. The pupil courageously labors from morning to evening to attain the true dharma. The monk works harder still to gather invisible treasures.
5) Practice—attainment through meditation.
6) Enlightened wisdom—*prajna* power.

A bodhisattva observes these six *paramitas*. The first three *paramitas* are *the dana-paramitas*. The last three are *the prajna-paramitas*. The six are really two.

To know that you yourself are Buddha is the White Ox vehicle, the one vehicle in the world and the only truth. To help you to understand this, the Buddha spoke about the three types of vehicles.

The Master said: "The meaning of the sutra is clear, but because of your delusion, you misunderstand it. Those who are of the three vehicles cannot fathom the depth of buddha-knowledge because they erroneously rely on reasoning." Buddha-knowledge is like the empty sky possessing omnipotence. But everyone must first go through all the different states of consciousness. Then he can rest upon his present consciousness.

Kamadhatu, we say, is the world of desire in which we are living. *Kamadhatu* implies to see, to hear, the element of purpose in our subjective mind. But there is no purpose in the objective world. A man can look at beautiful garments impersonally, with no desire to own or buy them, while a woman cannot separate the clothes from her purpose and desire. The subjective world is involved with our desires. The objective world is purely aesthetic, but the common-minded man has no alternative, he always lives in *kamadhatu.*

To enter Buddhism you must abandon *kamadhatu* and enter *rupadhatu*, then abandon *rupadhatu* and enter *arupadhatu.* Finally you must abandon arupadhatu and enter the world of neither thoughts nor no-thoughts. This is not a transcendental world. We can live in these three worlds at once, possessing them but not being possessed by them.

"The more you think, exhausting your mental powers, the further away you are. The Buddha originally expounded this law for the common-minded man; he did not expound it for himself. Those unable to put their faith in this principle may withdraw from the assembly. Such a one does not understand that he is already seated upon the White Ox cart, and is still looking for the three vehicles outside." Sitting upon the White Ox vehicle means you have made a final decision to accept yourself. And when you accept yourself, you must accept the whole world—you must affirm. And how can you affirm without denying? This is the problem of human life. You do not need the three inferior vehicles. From the first day, seat yourself upon the White Ox, which is present consciousness.

When I came to this country the last time, I was teaching American young ladies to meditate for half an hour. In three days no one came into my place. So I taught them to meditate for five minutes, and that was very long. So I reduced it to one minute, and one young lady fainted.

"The sutra tells you clearly: 'There is only the one Buddha vehicle; no other vehicles exist.' Hence, all those countless theories, fictions and proverbs are only expedients for you [to discover] this one Buddha vehicle. Why don't you understand? The three kinds of vehicles are fictitious, invented for the men of yesterday; but this one vehicle is real, [disclosed] to the man of today. I teach that you must abandon the fictitious and come back to Reality." The Buddha invented a fiction, an ink picture explaining and dramatizing the attributes of Reality allegorically. This fictitious dramatization is fraudulent and not a fact.

"When you have come back to Reality, this Reality does not need to be called by any name." Bodhidharma, in the religion begun by him, did not speak a word, nor did he point out a thing with his finger-tip. What he did was to point out souls and make them see the fact that is Reality.

"Know that all treasures belong to you and are yours to use. To have no notion of a 'father' or a 'child' or of 'using [anything]' is what it means to observe the Lotus Sutra. *From kalpa to kalpa the sutra will never leave your hands; from morning to evening, no moment will pass without reciting the sutra."* The Sixth Patriarch said to Fa-ta that he must leave those fictions and come back to fact. If the Master who points out your soul says, "This is the Buddha that you are seeking," you will not believe it. So the Master makes many contrivances to lead you to accept yourself as a buddha.

Buddhism is the type of religion that teaches you to find emancipation with your enlightened wisdom. It is not an emotional religion; it is intellectual. In Buddhism, there is no present, past or future, just this present consciousness, right here and now. *This* is the conclusion of Buddhism. If you accept this, or do not accept it, remain or go, no one will hinder you. But first, you must understand your present condition, the *buddhayana*, the true vehicle. You need not try to be an *arhat* or a bodhisattva. Just settle down and be a human being.

The allegory in the *Lotus Sutra* that had been recited three thousand times teaches that you must objectify yourself. Think of yourself as two persons. Walk behind yourself. Observe yourself listening to my talk and to your own thoughts. This is a trick to find your true self. So the self existing now is not the true self. It is the representative of the true self.

Thus you attain the Ocean of Consciousness, the Law of the White Lotus. This is the meaning of the *Lotus Sutra*.

Having received this enlightened instruction, Fa-ta danced with joy and extolled the Master in the following gatha:

"The recitation of the sutra, repeated three thousand times
Was annihilated with a single word from the stream of Ts'ao-ch'i

So long as you do not understand the meaning of transcending the world
How can you put an end to the delusions of accumulated former lives?

The vehicles of goat, deer, and ox are invented fictions
Carefully expounded for the beginner, the intermediate, and the mature

Does anyone know that in the burning house
Dwells the Dharma King himself?"

The Master said: "From now on you can call yourself a sutra-reciting monk."
Thereafter, Fa-ta, having realized the innermost mystery of Dharma, continued to recite the sutra.

SOKEI-AN SAYS:

This is the end of the dialogue between the Master and the monk Fa-ta.

Having received this enlightened instruction, Fa-ta danced with joy and extolled the Master in the following gatha: *"The recitation of the sutra, repeated three thousand times/ Was annihilated with a single word from the stream of Ts'ao-ch'i."* In the previous lectures, the Master said to Fa-ta that he must return to the fact of Reality, which is not called by any name, and that from kalpa to kalpa, morning to evening, and in every moment, he is always reciting the sutra. Then Fa-ta said that his three thousand recitations of the sutra had been annihilated by a single line from the sutra of Ts'ao-ch'i.

This was the Buddha's experience as described by his disciples. The best way to realize the Buddha's experience is to find it out by yourself and to follow in his footsteps by your own practice. Then you will find Buddha written within yourself. The written sutra means nothing if you just recite it three thousand times like a parrot. Hui-neng, the Master, said stop repeating the sutra and observe what is written in your own mind.

"So long as you do not understand the meaning of transcending the world/ How can you put an end to the delusions of accumulated former lives?" There are two meanings to this "transcending the world," which, in a general sense, means taking an attitude of aloofness to this human world. The first is to keep away physically—one does not go home but stays on the mountaintop. The second is to keep away mentally by remaining aloof though in the city. Both of these, however, are not the true meaning of the words "transcending the world."

How to transcend the world is the principle of Zen. One thinks but is not thinking thoughts. One uses thoughts as the instruments of thinking. In other words, one is using money; one is not used by money. This is transcending.

In learning how to transcend the world, you will of course commit many errors. In your old age you will look back to see how far you have come. You may find that you have made many enemies, or have not cultivated virtue.

"The vehicles of goat, deer, and ox are invented fictions/ Carefully expounded for the beginner, the intermediate, and the mature." I think you know about these vehicles and that they are fictitious.

Think of the story of Maya and the birth of the Buddha. Here, the god Brahma handed the infant to the god Indra, who laid him on the earth. Then the child walked seven times around the earth, saying, "I am the only one to be venerated in heaven and on earth." This is a lovely story, but do not swallow this invented fiction. You must grasp what is in the Master's mind. Do not grasp a fiction. The form of religion must not be confused with its reality.

These three vehicles, the goat, deer, and ox, are the same as sophomore, junior, and senior in the university. Then there is post-graduate. So it is foolish to pick up one corner and think that it is the whole of religion. You do not pick up some Hinayana, and think it is the whole of Buddhism, nor do you pick up some Mahayana and think it is the highest, despising Hinayana.

"Does anyone know that in the burning house/ Dwells the Dharma King himself?" This "burning house" is allegorical. This world is that house on fire. Children are playing in the house, and there are many treasures and toys in this house.

In the story, the father tried to take the children out of the burning house. First, he brought the goat vehicle into the yard to attract the children of the *shravaka* stage, showing them how much better it is than the burning house. The mature ones did not like the goat vehicle, so the deer (*pratyekabuddha*) vehicle was made for them. Then the father invented other vehicles to entice the children out of the burning house—the bodhisattva, etc.

In the goat vehicle, your agony comes from your desire—"Suppress desire!" In the deer vehicle, your agony comes from your ignorance of the law of the universe and of man. These devices were invented to emancipate you from the agony of life. There are many types of salvation.

In conclusion, man is the master of the universe. He is always the Dharma King. There is no house on fire when you really discover that this place is the highest of all places among the existences in the universe. There is no mystery in religion. It seems so only from the outside.

The Master said: "From now on you can call yourself a sutra-reciting monk." All the laws are written in his mind.

Thereafter, Fa-ta, having realized the innermost mystery of the Dharma, continued to recite the Sutra.

Chih-t'ung was a native of An-feng, of Sho-chou. He was studying the Lankavatara Sutra. *Although he had read the sutra over a thousand times, he did not understand the three bodies (trikaya) and the four wisdoms [of Buddha.] He bowed to the Master and entreated him to expound their significance.*

The Master said: "As to the three bodies: the pure dharmakaya *is your essential nature; the perfect* sambhogakaya *is your intrinsic wisdom; the million* nirmanakayas *are your activity. If you speak about the three bodies as apart from your original nature, they are bodies without wisdom. If you realize that the three bodies have no self-nature, you will reveal the four wisdoms of awakening."*

SOKEI-AN SAYS:

Chih-t'ung was a native of An-feng, of Sho-chou. He was studying the Lankavatara Sutra. *Although he had read the sutra over a thousand times, he did not understand the three bodies* (trikaya) *and the four wisdoms [of Buddha.] He bowed to the Master and entreated him to expound their significance.* These three bodies and four wisdoms are very important in Buddhism, as is the importance of the Triune Body of Christ (Father, Son, and Holy Ghost) in Christianity. The Triune Body of Buddha is called the "*Trikaya.*" These three bodies and four wisdoms are the backbone of the theory of the *Lankavatara Sutra,* and though this monk had recited the sutra one thousand times, he did not grasp the meaning of the three bodies or the four wisdoms.

The four intuitions, or wisdoms, of Buddha are:

1) Great Mirror Wisdom (*adarshana-jnana*): The mirror-like consciousness of enlightenment. The Great Mirror of the Sky. Space itself has consciousness.

2) Universal Wisdom (*samata-jnana*): It means to know that which is alike, the human side of alaya-consciousness. *Samata* is "sameness." My consciousness, your consciousness, everyone's consciousness are all the same. The dew drops are the same on the rose, the violet, and the tulip—pure and apart from the flowers. It is identical consciousness throughout all forms and natures of beings.

3) Profound Observing Wisdom (*pratyaveksana-jnana*): It means to know one's own mind by introspection. Human beings have this, but animals do not. Their consciousness is centered on objective existence and never comes back to self-consciousness. So they are not aware of their own existence. But human beings have this power. They have the ability to look into their own minds.

When I was a novice, my name was Shigetsu, meaning "to point out the moon with one's finger." The novice doesn't look at the moon, but at the pointer (as a cat might). The sutra is the finger that points out something, yet most people look at the words and go no further.

4) Perfecting Wisdom (*krityannusthana-jnana*): It means the intuition to perform that which should be done. To practice this you must abandon your position. If you have some preconceived notion or conviction, you cannot act freely or see another's point of view.

In ancient days, if a monk wished to ask a question of the master, he bowed. No one would stand at the door and say: "Hello! Oh, hello!" Nor would he say: "Oh, by the way, I wish to know something. Can you tell me?" Sometimes such a one will come to my door.

When I officiate at a ritual and bow as my teacher did, some say to me: "I don't care about the ritual. I want reality!" This is like going to a restaurant and saying to the waiter: "I don't care for all of this silver and linen. Take it away and just bring me the meat." And the waiter saying, "If you want meat, go to a butcher!"

The beautiful part of life is the ritualistic part. When the family comes and eats their dinner together, you would not snatch your food from the pot. You should put it on a plate, garnish it with greens and put beautiful silver and linen on the table with flowers in the center. This is a ritual. A wedding is a ritual. A man and a woman do not marry on a street corner, but go to a church to be wed. Dogs and cats have no ritual, but human beings without ritual are savages. They do not know the beauty of human life.

The Master said: "As to the three bodies . . . :"—Dharmakaya, *sambhogakaya*, and *nirmanakaya*. The three laws through time and space.

"The pure dharmakaya *is your essential nature"*: Dharmakaya is the Body of Law, the Dharma body. In this sense, the body itself is law, the first law of the universe, and it is immaculate. Why do I say it is immaculate? Because we cannot express this law by form, by word, or by all the existences in the world. The law exists without being perceived by the human mind, and it exists absolutely alone without being conceived by the human mind. So it is the immaculate law, the *dharmakaya*.

When the ancient Christians said that God exists outside the universe, they could not conceive of God existing within. The human mind cannot measure the immaculate existence of God. We can only measure outside, so we put God outside. Today, science says that there is no outside. But today, philosophy says that what we cannot perceive is outside the universe, and we cannot deny that things do exist outside of human knowledge.

The first law is *dharmakaya*, pure *dharmakaya*. Why is it pure? Because it is not blended with the human mind.

"The perfect sambhogakaya *is your intrinsic wisdom; the million* nirmanakayas *are your activity."* The second law is intrinsic wisdom, the human mind itself. It pervades and penetrates all directions at once, vibrating throughout the universe like a radio. Now it is *here*, then *there* all at once. In modern terms, it exists fourth-dimensionally. So the human mind is the second law, mind itself.

The second law is the radio. The first law is the telegram over the wire. As to the third law, take a young baby. When it is born, it does not know the first law, but it knows the second law—"A-a-ah!" It tries to rule the mother by the second law, but the mother asks him to obey the third law. As he grows up, he realizes that he must live by the third law. The third law makes harmony, it has direction. It goes to the east, but cannot go west, like the "one-way" street here in New York City. When a stranger visits New York, sometimes a policeman says, "A New York horse knows the traffic rules better than you do!"

To sum up: The first law is essential nature—immaculate, pure, omnipresent, omnipotent *dharmakaya*, the Father, God.

The second law is perfect *sambhogakaya*, your intrinsic wisdom, the Son. Through this second law, you will understand the first law. You will say, "Oh God, how can my prayer be accepted through this representative of God?" The answer is *sambhogakaya*, your own intrinsic wisdom, which cannot be created by your own effort. This was in God (the first law), and now it is in me (the second law). I follow this.

Sambhogakaya consciousness stands between *dharmakaya* and *nirmanakaya*. You pray for something through Jesus Christ, the Son—*sambogakaya*. This intrinsic wisdom is from God, the Master. I follow him.

Nirmanakaya, the third law, is the body that transforms itself, the Holy Ghost. The transformation comes from the inside of each person. The Bodhisattva Avalokiteshvara transforms himself into thousands of different bodies to work his salvation. He transforms himself into the body of a woman to save the woman. He transforms himself into the body of the king to save the king. He transforms himself into the body of a beggar to save the beggar. Avalokiteshvara throws himself into the gutter and transforms himself into the one who is lying in the gutter to save that one and to hold him up. All these manifest his way of deliverance.

Many misunderstand these words. They think saving a beggar means becoming a beggar, or saving a street woman means becoming a prostitute. The transformation of Avalokiteshvara means that he does not ask a Buddhist teacher or a Christian priest to do it for him. He does it himself.

So this means that to be saved, one becomes Avalokiteshvara and awakens. This physical human being (yourself) is changed from impure to pure. That is the transformation. You must not misunderstand this, or you will fall into a terrible pit and will not be able to come out. Each human being is Avalokiteshvara, or in your terms, the Holy Ghost, the messenger of God.

"If you speak about the three bodies as apart from your original nature, they are bodies without wisdom." That is, they are only bodies carved in stone. Avalokiteshvara or Christ is unrelated to you.

"If you realize that the three bodies have no self-nature, you will reveal the four wisdoms of awakening." When you understand the existence of the three bodies, you will not find yourself any more. Your self will have gone elsewhere.

Religion is not yet dead; it is living. But it takes a real teacher to speak the real gospel.

[The Master continued:] "Listen as I recite this gatha*:*

> *"Your own nature intrinsically possesses the three bodies*
> *And when you are enlightened, it becomes the four wisdoms*
>
> *Without leaving the realm of seeing and hearing*
> *You ascend to the state of buddhahood*
>
> *Now that I have expounded this for you*
> *Believe my words and never be deluded again*
>
> *Do not follow those who are always searching outside*
> *Who talk about enlightenment all day long"*

Again Chih-t'ung questioned the Master: "May I hear your exposition of the meaning of the four wisdoms?"
The Master answered: "If you have understood the three bodies, the four wisdoms should be clear. Why question me again?"

SOKEI-AN SAYS:

I have been translating this Zen scripture, *The Record of the Sixth Patriarch*, for about two years now. First I read my translation to you, then I give you my commentary.

Starting from Bodhidharma, who went to China from India in the sixth century, the Sixth Patriarch, Hui-neng, was the sixth generation in the Zen lineage. He lived during the T'ang dynasty. In his lifetime he answered many questions asked by many monks.

This part is a dialogue between the Sixth Patriarch and a young monk called Chih-t'ung. Chih-t'ung had recited the *Lankavatara Sutra* about a thousand times, yet he did not understand the significance of the three bodies and the four wisdoms of Buddha.

The Sixth Patriarch said: *"Listen as I recite this* gatha: *"Your own nature intrinsically possesses the three bodies."* The three bodies are *dharmakaya*, *sambhogakaya*, and *nirmanakaya*. *Dharmakaya* is essential nature. *Sambhogakaya* is present consciousness, intrinsic wisdom. *Nirmanakaya* is performance.

Dharmakaya is the body that is omnipresent; it pervades endless space. Or you can say that it has no space and no time; it is beyond space and time. However, do not think that "omnipresent" is like the omnipresence of a cat. When I first came to New York and would go to the restaurants and delicatessens in the neighborhood where I was living, there was always a black cat. Even when I would go home at night, the black cat would be at my door—an omnipresent cat!

Here, omnipresent means the timeless, spaceless state, a state that we cannot experience with our five senses, but which our intuition apprehends. According to Western philosophy, the spaceless and timeless state cannot be understood with empirical knowledge. Only with transcendental knowledge can it be understood immediately. If you have not proved this yet, you should do so.

Sambhogakaya is *this* consciousness. It is a secret state. You do not need to use any apparatus to apprehend it; your consciousness knows it immediately. To know and to be conscious of this state is called "the state of Buddha." *Sambhogakaya* is the consciousness that is the center of all unity.

When I was young, I worked hard to find my own consciousness. Everyone said, "You have it, so why ask so much about it?" I tried hard to understand the nature of this consciousness, thinking that it was somewhere very deep, so big and so remote that it was not even consciousness. But consciousness is very clear when you truly find it, not remote at all.

Nirmanakaya is the body of transformation. According with your thoughts, you transform yourself from devil to angel every moment. You transform from demon to *preta*, from *preta* to animal, from animal to *deva*—from heaven to hell in a moment. Watch your mind and you will realize (in accordance with your karma) these transformations. You must understand that your mental body is reincarnating every moment. If you want to find the law of the universe, find it through the activity of your mind.

Modern science tells us of the proton, electron, and so on. But the Buddha discovered 2,500 years ago that this body is a microcosm of the macrocosm. And now modern science tells us that in every atom there is a solar system.

This body is an extension of the mind. When you change your facial expressions and body postures and the gestures of your hands, you are in transformation every moment.

This is my commentary on the three bodies. The three bodies are in the mind of everyone. It is not necessary to acquire the Buddha's three bodies because you already possess them.

". . . And when you are enlightened, it becomes the four wisdoms." This wisdom is *jnana*. In English you could translate it as "intuition." Jnana is so direct and so instantaneous that you do not need to have experience; it works immediately.

The four wisdoms of your enlightened nature are:

l) The Great Mirror Wisdom (*adarshana-jnana*)—the Great Empty Mirror suspended in the sky, timeless and boundless like *dharmakaya*. Everything is stored in this empty mirror. The word "mirror" is a very expressive word for the first state of consciousness. This consciousness exists alone, single and immaculate. It cannot conceive of its own existence. Nothing can be compared with it; you cannot say a word. One moment or one million years is exactly the same in the empty mirror. It sees everything at once. If you keep awake, in a flash you will see it and find it out for yourself. But if you think something, you will never realize original consciousness. It is not in the mind busy from morning to evening that you see it. Christ said in the Garden of Gethsemane: "Watch and pray lest ye enter into temptation." I think many of those sayings of the Christ come from his own experience. Those who have it will smile. Only so will you find your own mind. You do not need to practice meditation for three or four years, but you must keep awake.

2) Universal Wisdom (*samata-jnana*)—this wisdom is to realize the sameness of things. This fire, that fire, any fire are all the same. The magnitude of the fire is different, but the fire itself is the same in quality and nature, no matter what the size. And so it is with the second consciousness. This, that, and every consciousness is the same. The magnitude differs, but the consciousness is the same.

3) Profound Observing Wisdom (*pratyaveksana-jnana*)—this third consciousness is to know one's own mind by introspection. This is meditation. But meditation does not mean going to sleep or sitting with closed eyes. To meditate is not to snore.

4) Perfecting Wisdom (*krityannusthana-jnana*)—this fourth consciousness is the intuition to do that which should be done. It performs the straight reaction to everything. In the human being, you could say it is the reaction, as when your face is slapped, you either step back or you think about it and wait. In nature, one can say that it will be a hard winter because the musk melon is making a hard shell. In the animal, it is instinct.

"Without leaving the realm of seeing and hearing/ You ascend to the state of buddhahood." In Japan, when children go for walks in the country, sometimes they find small dark holes on the sides of mountains. When they crawl inside, sometimes they find monks sitting in the darkness, so they run out in fright. These monks are trying to attain *dharmakaya*, but actually, they are in their imaginations. They meditate for years in darkness, like a fox. But you can grasp it, the state of buddha, in this realm of seeing and hearing.

"Now that I have expounded this for you/Believe my words and never be deluded again/ Do not follow those who are always searching outside/ Who talk about enlightenment all day long." There is nothing to believe in Buddhism. It is self-evident. Once you have experienced it, you will never forget it. There is no doubt, it is always with you. Do not go to libraries as I did. I found the most important sutras and spent twelve years of my young life reading them. You must find Buddha in your own shrine, not in churches, books, or anything else.

Buddhism emphasizes meditation. If, in meditation, you keep your mind to one point, suddenly, like a flash, it will come to you, as it came to the monk who was sweeping the garden. A pebble hit a bamboo root and suddenly—"Oh!" Or as it came to Hakuin when he heard the temple gong and realized that the whole world was in his own mind.

To attain *dharmakaya* is the first step of all religions. Religion begins from this gate. When you realize the three bodies and the four wisdoms, every act is a sermon. Every moment, in every action, you are preaching true religion. It is different from just singing in church on Sunday.

Again Chih-t'ung questioned the Master: "May I hear your exposition of the meaning of the four wisdoms?" Of course, the Sixth Patriarch did not explain as I explain to you.

The Master answered: "If you have understood the three bodies, the four wisdoms should be clear. Why question me again?" "What, you haven't attained it yet?" The monk had to surrender in silence. It was a terrible moment for the monk when he was discovered.

[The master continued:] "If you speak about the four wisdoms as apart from the three bodies, they are wisdoms without bodies. Therefore even one who innately possesses this wisdom will find [himself] lacking it."

The Master recited another gatha:

"The great and perfect mirror wisdom is pure by nature
Equally innate [in all sentient beings], so that the mind is free from illness

The profound observing wisdom that perceives [all things]
is not a faculty that can be acquired
The perfecting wisdom that performs the activities [of sentient life]
is the same as the perfect mirror
The fifth and the eighth, the sixth and the seventh [consciousnesses]
When they ripen are transformed

They are only names
They are not real entitities

If you do not attach to those transformation
You can forever remain in supreme samadhi*"*

SOKEI-AN SAYS:

Zen, being one of the many sects of Buddhism, claims that it is the eye of Buddhism. If you study Buddhism historically, you will find that the Buddha's Buddhism was Zen. Zen does not worship deities. The student of Zen does not worship an outside God. Buddha never invoked any prayer or offered supplication to deities, so his adherents never utter any word of prayer with their lips. Our meditation takes the place of prayer in the other religions.

"If you speak about the four wisdoms as apart from the three bodies, they are wisdoms without bodies." This wisdom is intuition, intellectual intuition—*prajna.*

The Buddhist attitude to this wisdom is different from other religions. The Buddhist thinks that this physical body itself is consciousness, as when you pinch your hand and you feel pain. We do not make any distinction between the physical body and mental wisdom. It is all one and the same thing. The whole universe to the Buddhist is consciousness. As a German philosopher said, "Nature is our mental state." So when we observe nature and see the Hudson River, we think this scene is the extension of our own consciousness. The Buddhist thinks all this phenomena is nothing but objectified consciousness.

A goddess in Greek mythology thought a monster was pursuing her, so she ran through the mountains, until she fainted on the beach and lost consciousness. She had fallen into a deep sleep. When the tide washed her body, she awoke and looked around and saw the monster watching her from behind the waves. She started to run and the monster followed her. She stopped; it stopped. Finally, she realized that the monster was not another being. It was part of herself, her own tail. She had been transformed by

Jupiter while she was sleeping. So objectified consciousness is the universe. Subjective consciousness is our own mind. But when we conceive this as two things, we are speaking of wisdom as unrelated to the body. This type of wisdom has no place to exist, no place to dwell.

Everyone talks about God and consciousness, but the words are always abstract. They cannot find a concrete God with their naked eye, so they despise the naked eye. If you despise the naked eye, you despise everything in the universe. In Buddhism, the physical eye has a very important place. It is a link between so-called spirit and so-called matter. This is the consciousness that you are speaking about when, in your idiom, you say, "Seeing is believing." In Zen there is also seeing is believing. The Zen master will say: "Stop talking to me about Reality. Show me!"

Buddha said this eye is the eye of communication, or the highest eye among the physical eyes. This eye, which I am talking about, is a very important part of Buddhism. This eye is the physical eye, the *deva* eye, the eye of wisdom, the eye of Dharma, and the eye of Buddha. In Buddhism, all the theories take this hairpin turn—the physical eye and the Buddha eye are the same.

"Therefore even one who innately possesses this wisdom will find [himself] lacking it." This is because his knowledge is abstract. He has an eye, but it is the same as having no eye.

In meditation people close their eyes. This is the usual habit of the amateur meditator. He is dreaming and snoring. His mind is very dark. Foreign professors and scholars who go to Kyoto and say they know all about meditation meditate with the monks and fall asleep in five minutes. Do not close your eyes when you meditate. See all at once, and think all at once. Can you do this? Unfortunately not!

Do not engage your thoughts. When a thought comes, let it go. When another comes, let it go. That is the way of meditation. So watch your thoughts very carefully; not the thoughts from the outside, but the thoughts that haunt your brain. Finally, you will not be one with your thoughts, you will not attach to them. You will hear your heart beat with a big sound, and your tongue will feel thick and heavy. You will have disveiled yourself. You will have found your true self, and you will not be a human being any more.

The Theosophists say that Isis was disveiled. It is not necessary for Isis to be disveiled. Disveil yourself. Believe my word and try it. It is analogous to the experience of passing through an endless desert—there is nothing to compare it with. Disveiling yourself and finding your true self is exactly the same.

It is not necessary to pick a quiet or mountainous place. You can meditate under the elevated train, where you can find the body of wisdom before your eyes. We cannot force people to believe without seeing.

The Master recited another gatha: *"The great and perfect mirror wisdom is pure by nature."* This is the first wisdom, great and perfect as the sky, a great mirror that accepts all reflections. The Buddhist always uses the sky as analogous to this first consciousness. There is nothing bigger than the sky. I strike this gong and the sky "feels" it and keeps it forever. When the Buddha said this to his disciples, they asked how a sound so small could be heard so far. Today, the radio proves that a sound can be felt anywhere.

The sky is consciousness. The sky is the universe. The sky is not in a bosom or womb of any kind. The sky is immaculate and exists immaculately.

"Equally innate [in all sentient beings], so that the mind is free from illness." The second wisdom Buddha's wisdom, is enlightenment. It cannot be burned in fire or drowned in water. It cannot be destroyed.

Our consciousness and the consciousness of the saint are the same throughout all *kalpas*. Consciousness will never die in sufferings.

"The profound observing wisdom that perceives [all things] is not a faculty that can be acquired." It is not a mysterious power, nor is it the clairvoyance of the woman who acts as a medium. Everyone's consciousness is this medium.

When you find your own consciousness, you can look at the other and observe the mind of the other. You can see the human mind, the tiger mind, the elephant mind, the elk mind, and the mouse mind. It is wonderful to have this perfect mind, this perfect mirror.

"*The perfecting wisdom that performs the activities [of sentient life] is the same as the perfect mirror.*" This is the fourth wisdom. Its activity is the same as the first.

"*The fifth and the eighth, the sixth and the seventh [consciousnesses]/ When they ripen are transformed// They are only names/ They are not real entitites/ If you do not attach to those transformations/ You can forever remain in supreme* samadh." There is no more time. As this is very important, I shall speak about it in the next lecture.[16]

Chih-t'ung was suddenly enlightened to the wisdom in his original nature. He then offered a gatha:

"*The three bodies originally are my own body*
The four wisdoms originally manifest in my mind

Not obstructing one another
The bodies and wisdoms form a unity responding to everything
and accommodating all forms

To 'practice' is only deluded activity
To keep oneself inactive is unnatural
Thanks to your Reverence, I have realized the mysterious principle
All names that have stained [my mind] are utterly destroyed"

SOKEI-AN SAYS:

Regarding the three bodies of Buddha: You must not think that Shakyamuni Buddha had three different bodies. The three bodies mean three different stages in one body, three-in-one, like that little bottle of oil called "Three-In-One Oil." Perhaps this expression comes from the Christian idea of the Trinity. The three bodies are *dharmakaya, sambhogakaya*, and *nirmanakaya*.

Dharmakaya is spatially boundless, limitless and endless—the first law. If we observe this omnipresent body as Reality, which does not correspond to our five senses, it is spaceless and timeless. So we can say that it exists outside of the universe, outside of our experience, and this means Reality. Inside of our universe means that which we can experience with our five senses, but outside—no.

Sambhogakaya is consciousness, awakened consciousness. You are aware of your own existence with your own consciousness. It is very plain. You can prove it directly by yourself. Yet it is not dogma. You do not need to have anyone prove it to you. It is the second law.

Then there is *nirmanakaya*, the body of transformation, the third law. When you enter fire, you are transformed into fire. When you enter water, you are transformed into water. When you enter earth, you are transformed into earth, and when you enter air, you are transformed into air. When you eat an onion, you are transformed by the onion, or you transform the onion into yourself. When you meet an enemy in battle, you are transformed into an *ashura*, fighting demon. You transform yourself according to the circumstances that you undergo.

These three bodies or phases are one—just like steam, water and ice, vapor, liquid, and solid. The four wisdoms are:

1) Great Mirror Wisdom—the wisdom of *dharmakaya* that is like a mirror in the sky. But this mirror cannot prove its own existence because there is nothing to be reflected upon it.

2) Universal Wisdom—the wisdom of *sambhogakaya* that is consciousness common to all sentient beings. This consciousness stands face-to-face with *dharmakaya*. They are both mirrors. One mirror reflects the other with nothing in between, as Christ saw God, there being no difference between them.

3) Profound Observing Wisdom—the wisdom of *sambhogakaya* that is the introspection into one's own nature, one's own thoughts, and one's own consciousness. This wisdom faces *nirmanakya*, the outside, and observes and knows the law of phenomena. So *sambhogakaya* is like a mirror with two sides, one facing *dharmakaya* and the other facing *nirmanakaya*—one to God and one to man. Every human being has this, but he knows only one side—the outside. *Dharmakaya* is always casting a reflection upon your mirror, on the back of it, but you do not see it. When you do not think anything, you will see it. The Christian teacher says: "Don't reason, only believe." Well, I hope he knows what he is saying! To unveil that mystery, don't reason about it. All religions say this, but sometimes the teachers do not realize it themselves. You must realize it through meditation.

4) Perfecting Wisdom—the wisdom of *nirmanakaya* that watches daily conduct.

In the center, the wisdom of *sambhogakaya* is two: to see inside and to see outside. *Dharmakaya* wisdom is inside, and *nirmanakaya* wisdom is outside. Everyone should realize this.

It seems to me that the three bodies theory is common to all religions, but the theory of the four wisdoms is particularly Buddhistic. I have never heard another religion speak about it.

Chih-t'ung was suddenly enlightened to the wisdom in his original nature. He then offered a gatha: Consciousness is the second law. The first law is original nature, so-called. Chih-t'ung saw and he was enlightened. His enlightenment was not so sudden, but it was delightful. Enlightenment will come only when you are very careful with your own mind.

"What is consciousness?" is always the question. This eye is consciousness, but all other consciousnesses must help the eye, which is not consciousness itself. Don't look at my eye! Look at your own eye!

I show you this *hossu*—what is it? The monks in India and China use this to drive insects away from their faces. You understand this. Consciousness helps the child who picks up a hot coal and cries, "Wa-a-ah!" to understand it. You have your finger, but you do not know how to use it on the piano keys because you are not aware of the faculty of your five fingers. You must be aware of your own existence. This is the main point in entering the religion of Buddhism. How do you do this?

"*The three bodies originally are my own body/ The four wisdoms originally manifest in my mind/ Not obstructing one another / The bodies and wisdoms form a unity responding to everything and accommodating all forms.*" This is Buddhism. There is no obstruction, for the bodies are the same, and they are one. Without the physical body, you cannot prove the spiritual. These clear mirrors will reflect each other, but there will be no figure between them; nothing exists between them. Then they turn out, according to your five senses, to physical existence. Consciousness comes into the body, and it acts like a human being.

All things have this consciousness—cat, dog, earth, water, fire, and air. It conforms to their shapes because it has no ego. The Buddhist believes we have an amorphous consciousness that takes different shapes. We do not believe that God made the spirit of each creation differently, that each consciousness is specially created. We are like foam, like bubbles in the Ocean of Consciousness. For a little while we have this spark, this body, and we reflect everything. The law of causality will create this once more. This is the law of incarnation. So why all of a sudden do you abominate this?

There is no reason. A Buddhist does not draw any distinction between the physical and the spiritual. When you talk about immorality, it has nothing to do with this. Morality is the rule between human beings. This is a different standpoint. It has no relation to human law. Of course, human beings as members of the social body, must observe moral laws in order to exist. We have no value otherwise. It is natural to observe these laws.

"To 'practice' is only deluded activity/ To keep oneself inactive is unnatural/ Thanks to your Reverence, I have realized the mysterious principle/ All names that have stained [my mind] are utterly destroyed." You will find the law of nature, and then you can do what you want. The "mysterious principle" is *dharmakaya*, the first wisdom. When you know Reality, you do not need names anymore.

This is the end of the dialogue between the Sixth Patriarch and Chih-t'ung. The next monk is Chih-ch'ang. He was from Kuei-ch'i in Hsin-chou. I have not so far located it on the map I have. I have a very old map.

The monk Chih-ch'ang was a native of Kuei-ch'i in Hsin-chou. He became a monk when he was a boy, determined to find his original nature. One day, he came to pay his homage to the Master, who questioned him, saying: "Where do you come from, and what do you seek?"

Chih-ch'ang said: "Recently, I visited Pai Feng Mountain. I paid homage to Master Ta-t'ung who elucidated for me the meaning of 'seeing one's original nature and attaining buddhahood.' Still harboring some doubt about the matter, I have come a great distance to prostrate myself before you. I beg you, Master, to kindly instruct me."

The Master said: "What were [Ta-t'ung's] words? Try to tell me."

Chih-ch'ang answered: "I stayed about three months [in the temple], but found no opportunity to receive [Ta-t'ung's] instruction. Intent on realizing the Dharma one evening, I ventured to visit [Ta-t'ung] alone in his room. I asked him: 'What are my original mind and my original nature?'"

"Ta-t'ung answered, 'Do you see the sky?' I said, 'Yes.' He told me: 'When you see the sky, has it any form?' I replied, 'The sky has no shape; how can it have any form?' [Ta-t'ung] said: 'Your original nature is just like the sky; nothing in it is to be seen. This is the true view. There is nothing to be known. This is true wisdom. There is neither green nor yellow, long nor short. Simply realize the essence that is the knower itself, pure and perfect. This is what is meant by seeing one's original nature and attaining buddhahood, or the knowledge of the Tathagata.'"

SOKEI-AN SAYS:

Every Wednesday evening I talk about Zen. Zen is a queer sect in Buddhism. It does not use the written scriptures, and it has no canon. From the beginning, the students of this sect take this physical body as the law of Buddhism, this mental state or mental body as a scripture or canon, and this consciousness or cognizance as Buddha. That is all. By meditation, they observe mental phenomena as the canon, and in every deed, every action, they find the law that is written on their bodies. Then, returning to their own consciousness, they find Buddha within themselves.

In Buddhism, Buddha is the Knower, or Wisdom. Wisdom is our God. Buddhism is the religion that depends upon the power of wisdom, so it is the religion of wisdom. Of course, Buddhism teaches compassion and sympathy, but it does not begin from this. It teaches love, but primarily it teaches wisdom. So this Knower, who knows the law within and without, is Buddha and God.

The Zen student has three methods by which to realize this wisdom: The first is action with the physical body. The second is speech, that is heard or read with the mind. The third is silence. Silence immediately approximates the goal of wisdom.

So the farmers who could not read came to Zen because Zen does not need the knowledge of reading. The warriors who fought on the battlefield came to Zen and asked their questions of their masters before going off to their death. Later, artists and writers came to Zen. Today, in Japan, Zen is the religion of the intelligentsia. In China, it is said, Zen has decayed and there is no truly enlightened school. But do they know? Perhaps some Zen master is a farmer in the deep country. Others say a few enlightened men are now in Tibet, but in India there are none.

Hui-neng, the Sixth Patriarch, is now conversing with a young monk, who came from a great distance. He was trying to find the answer that would enlighten him.

The monk Chih-ch'ang was a native of Kuei-ch'i in Hsin-chou. He became a monk when he was a boy, determined to find his original nature." That is, *dharmakaya, sambhogakaya, nirmanakaya.*

Chih-ch'ang was a little boy with a shaved head and probably had a little bunch of hair his elder brothers could pull.

One day, he came to pay his homage to the Master, who questioned him, saying: "Where do you come from, and what do you seek?" A very big question! Where do you come from? How far is your country from your original nature? In this life, what do you seek?

If I were to ask you where you come from, how would you answer? I came from San Francisco? From Japan? I was born from my mother? From the Virgin Mary? I came from heaven? From God? I came from—I don't know, but God knows! It is very hard to make an accurate answer.

In the Zen school, this is difficult to answer—"I came from where there is no time and space." It is not so easy to trace back in your human knowledge to where you came from. Chih-ch'ang did not take this question literally—"Where have you been?" "Oh, I was at 125th street!"

The Zen master always asks this question. It sounds like everyday talk, but it has a deep meaning. Occasionally a young monk will answer differently—"I come like the wind!" I hit him, for I don't want to hear such talk. I want the real state, the state you can see through Buddha's eye.

Chih-ch'ang said: "Recently, I visited Pai Feng Mountain. I paid homage to Master Ta-t'ung who elucidated for me the meaning of 'seeing one's original nature and attaining buddhahood.'" "Seeing one's own original nature" is a famous phrase in Zen. It is almost like a motto. They don't say to "know" your original nature." They say to "see," to "manifest," or to "reveal" your original nature.

You have an ugly nature, a superior, or inferior nature, a dog-like or a cat-like nature, but it is always your second nature. You have adopted that nature from your circumstances or environment, your mother, father, or family, just as you have inherited your nature from your country and period. This nature is not original but acquired. The nature that is intrinsic, old as the universe, and remote as your God, is original nature. You must find it. To "find" it usually signifies searching in the dark with your fingertips. But the Zen student finds it with his naked eye.

Seeing is believing. If you talk of God or Buddha, you have never seen them. So how can you talk! We do not care about the Buddha carved in wood or in stone, or the Buddha who lived in India 2,500 years ago. He has nothing to do with us. We pay our homage to him as our ancestor, but we do not worship him as a personal God. The personal God, which is existing, is not the image or the icon. It is *this* [pointing to his heart]. I am not talking about myself. It is you, I, they. You must see Reality with your own eyes.

In Buddhism, the eye has a very important place because it is the key point between the inside and the outside. The eye is aided and supplemented by the other senses, which are the instruments of the eye. The human being adopts this in his law courts. The evidence must be proved. So in the Zen school, we always say "see," "manifest," or "reveal."

"Still harboring some doubt about the matter, I have come a great distance to prostrate myself before you. I beg you, Master, to kindly instruct me." This ancient etiquette was different than today.

Living here alone, in the morning, while sweeping the floor, sometimes there is a knock on the door. Sometimes the visitors take off their hats, sometimes they have cigars in their mouths—"Hi! I want to know something about Buddhism!" With my broom in hand, I am ready to strike. But of course I do not.

The Master said: "What were [Ta-t'ung's] words? Try to tell me." Chih-ch'ang answered: "I stayed about three months [in the temple], but found no opportunity to receive [Ta-t'ung's] instruction." In the temples of China and Japan, the monks who had enlightened themselves—their task done—became ascetics and paid no attention to the younger monks. The younger monks had to work hard in the gardens and paddy-fields and had no time to ask questions. If they did venture to ask a question, they were told: "Attain it yourself!" That was the usual answer.

Some crazy minister came to my door and asked: "Is war good or bad?" I was sweeping my floor, and I said: "Tell me, is this broom good or bad?"

Usually, in Japan, when one says: "I have a doubt about this," the answer is "Get out of here and don't bother me!" It is different with Christianity. They come to your door at breakfast time, open your mouth, put Christianity in it, shake it down, and you either vomit or manage to digest it!

"Intent on realizing the Dharma one evening, I ventured to visit [Ta-t'ung] alone in his room. I asked him: 'What are my original mind and my original nature?'" "What is the reality of my original mind and my original nature?"

"Reality" is always a very important word in Buddhism. From the beginning to the end of Buddhist theory, you keep coming across this word. What is reality? This is the great question. When you understand its meaning, your study of Buddhism is over.

What we see with our five senses is not Reality. This color, sound, smell, taste, and touch is the phenomenon of Reality, not Reality itself. When we come across Reality itself with our five senses, this Reality will be visualized as phenomena corresponding to our five senses. So what Reality is in itself is an abstract question because you cannot see it with your eyes, hear it with your ears, touch, smell, or taste it. You cannot experience Reality itself with your five senses. However, it is intelligible to your mind, and it can be seen with your inner eye, your mind's eye—intuition, intellectual intuition. In Buddhism, this realization is your own mental experience. No Buddha can explain it to you. You must realize it through your own intuition.

The Zen sect emphasizes practice to attain this Reality by your own exertion. The student who has realized Reality itself will become a teacher. He will be your guide post, and he will acknowledge whether you have already attained or not. It is very easy to talk about Reality, but to experience it and to understand it is not so easy.

So Chih-ch'ang asked his question. There is no escape if someone asks you, "What is your Reality?" You may say, "Reality is God." And if they question, "What is God?" "God knows—that is enough!"

Well, how can you stand upon such an uncertain foundation? How can you build your life upon such a foundation? We must have something that is fundamental, solid, and concrete. In Zen we would not call it "God," and we would not call it "Buddha." We would say that Reality is our own nature or soul. Then what is soul? Children believe it is a green light, like a jack-o'-lantern. We are fooled for a long time by such fictitious ideas.

In ancient days, men's minds were so immature, they could not think of anything that was not in human shape. They thought that the hurricane was the work of the god of the wind, a huge bag of wind. And when the god of the wind was asked by a higher god to push the wind in, he pushed and the whole world was swept up. The same with thunder and with lightning. In Japan, when children are bad, they believe that a god will come down and take out their navel, so when thunder comes, they hold their stomachs and run down to the cellar.

Well, superstitions still exist in this century, but the twentieth century has come—we must awake! In the Zen school, this Reality is your own nature, so you must discover this original nature. Your own nature today is so vitiated, so distorted that it is not your real nature. It is your second nature, your third, your fourth, and fifth nature. The direct way to find Reality itself is through nature itself and not through any scientific method. If you seek to find Reality in matter, you will understand the reality of matter, but it is still matter and not yourself. If you find it through yourself, by your own wisdom, it is direct knowledge, while the scientific method is the indirect way.

It seems to me that in this Western hemisphere direct knowledge was never emphasized. The West has followed the objective method of the Greeks, trying to arrive at truth through the phenomenal world, while in India, the monks tried to find their original nature as described in the six hundred scrolls and the twelve hundred years of the *prajnaparamita* sutras. They did not build anything, but they unlearned, peeled off the first skin, the second, and the third, as a monkey opens a coconut, or as you would peel an onion. In the end, there is nothing. To reach the nothingness they speak about took about twelve hundred years.

In this Western world, men piled up and piled up. They made all these skyscrapers. Eastern civilization went diametrically opposite. While one civilization was piling up, the other was digging into itself. They failed to find the bottom, but they found nothingness, and by this the Hindus built the theory of non-ego. The Western theory was built on ego. So what shall we do in this situation today? We must understand both theories—East and West. We are living on one earth. Space has been conquered by speed. There is no more East or West, so we must understand both points of view and both theories, or we are not human beings.

Chih-ch'ang was asking his own question of someone else. You must find out yourself. What is the taste of water? Taste it and find out.

In Zen study, you are asked: "Before father and mother, what were you?" This is exactly the same question. You must discover it for yourself.

Then Ta-t'ung answered:

"'*Do you see the sky?' I said, 'Yes.' He told me: 'When you see the sky, has it any form?' I replied, 'The sky has no shape; how can it have any form?'[Ta-t'ung] said: 'Your original nature is just like the sky; nothing in it is to be seen. This is the true view.*'" Ta-t'ung asked Chih-ch'ang if he could see the sky. Then: "When you see the sky, do you know whether it has any shape or not?" Chih-ch'ang looked at the sky and could see no shape. It was neither flat nor triangular. The sky had no shape. In meditation, when you find yourself, Reality has no shape. It is not round, square, smooth, or rough. It is like the sky, the empty sky. Your original nature is like that.

This was the ancient way of proving emptiness. In the modern way, you get a triangle, use higher mathematics, electrons and protons. You calculate speed—ten thousand miles in one moment—and finally you conclude that the ether is empty. The same answer but a different way of coming to it. The ancients had two naked eyes and the moderns have many apparatuses, so there is not much human progress.

This emptiness is a very important word in Buddhism. When you arrive at emptiness, your knowledge is of no use and there is nothing to think about. In that moment something will flash through your mind, and you will enter Reality.

In Christianity, it is said that God lives outside of the universe. But there is no outside of the universe; you live in your own mind. Another way is just to have faith and not think about anything. When there is nothing to think about, that is the gate opening into Reality. But many people, when they come to this point of nothing to think about, never enter the gate.

Some English philosopher criticized Kant's philosophy, saying: "If it is not knowable, why do we have to bother about it?" And he gave up.

Standing upon this emptiness, we can cast our eye over the whole phenomenal world. If there is nothing in our eye, we can observe all at once. So we must stand upon Nothingness to have a true view.

"There is nothing to be known. This is true wisdom. There is neither green, nor yellow, long nor short." Funny, isn't it? These people lived in the fifth century, and Immanuel Kant in the nineteenth century, yet their views correspond. And if we go back to the Buddha, who lived 2,500 years ago, we find that his Buddhism was exactly like this. While the Brahmins were saying "atman" (ego), he was saying "anatman" (no-ego).

Ego is the expression of one truth, and no-ego is the expression of another. Whether you call your own nature "ego" or "no-ego" is immaterial as long as you understand what your nature is.

"Simply realize the essence that is the knower itself, pure and perfect." The knower is Buddha.

A long time ago in Seattle, Washington, I was standing on a wooden bridge on some little island between Seattle and Tacoma. I was resting my arm on the the bridge, and in that moment I forgot my own eye, ear, all my sense perceptions. There was just immense consciousness, which is like a mirror, and I was resting upon it. I felt that my mind was so large and so old in time that all the sounds were heard by IT and not by my own ear. My soul contained the whole universe. IT knows the Knower itself.

"This is what is meant by seeing one's original nature and attaining buddhahood, or the knowledge of the Tathagata." There is significance in this Tathagata, which I shall explain at some other time.

Chih-ch'ang said: "Though I listened to his instruction, I still have not fully understood. Please teach me."
The Master said: "Ta-t'ung's words still retain some trace of the theoretical view, and that is why you have not yet understood. Now let me instruct you with a gatha:

"Though you do not see a thing, if you still cherish the 'empty' view
It is like a floating cloud that covers the face of the sun

Though you do not know a thing, if you cherish this knowledge of 'emptiness,'
It is as though a clear sky were to produce a flash of lightning

At any moment
This kind of seeing and knowing may arise

If you mistakenly attach to them
How can you find the means [to dispel them]?

You must know, in each instant of thought, that this is wrong
Then your own mysterious light will always be manifesting"

SOKEI-AN SAYS:

I shall give a little commentary on these lines.

Buddhism has existed in the Orient for 2,500 years. The real future of Buddhism today looks like some chimera or demon, and not all of it is living. Many parts are already dead. But in this corpse of a great religion there is some living spot, which is really the essential part of Buddhism itself. This Zen sect is the living spot. Buddhism died a long time ago in India, but is still living, though half decayed, in China and Japan. In Japan, these last thirty years, Buddhism almost died from corruption. But then it swallowed European science and found its own vital spot, and started to live again. The Buddhism of ancient days met a young European science and began to revive. I am speaking very plainly, and I may be criticized by the Japanese who are still keeping the ancient rites.

I am commenting on a conversation between the Zen Master Hui-neng and a young monk who came and asked him a question. He had been to another master and had accepted his instruction, but he did not understand the words spoken by his teacher, Master Ta-t'ung. The Sixth Patriarch said, "What was the word that he gave you?" So the young monk repeated the words spoken by Ta-t'ung that were given in the previous lecture. The Sixth Patriarch understood the words of Ta-t'ung.

Chih-ch'ang said: "Though I listened to his instruction, I still have not fully understood. Please teach me." This was the young monk's confession. Ta-t'ung's instruction was: "Do you see the sky?" Chih-ch'ang said, "Yes." Ta-t'ung asked: "When you see the sky, has it any form?" The monk replied, "The sky has no shape; how can it have any form?" Ta-t'ung said: "Your original nature is just like the sky; nothing in it is to be seen."

These words were spoken by Ta-t'ung. He was not a monk of the Zen sect, but of the Hua-yen sect.

The Master said: "Ta-t'ung's words still retain some trace of the theoretical view, and that is why you have not yet understood." From the Buddhist standpoint, these words are not in error. Ta-t'ung was trying to explain the essential nature of man in a metaphor such as the sky.

These days, scientists of the Western world attempt to find the essential state of an entity through the microscope. They analyze objective matter, divide it, and then call that indivisible thing a molecule. But then that indivisible thing is divided and is called an atom. The atom is divided thinner and thinner, until finally reaching the electron and proton. We have not—as of yet—invented a finer apparatus to divide the electron and proton. Perhaps in the future someone will divide all the four or five different elements.

In philosophy, they would say that Reality is something that is infinite and always leads people into the chaos of nothingness. I am quoting the words used by Eddington.[17]

In the Orient, the analysis of the entity developed by means of introspection. This means, as you know, to look within yourself. Your scientists look outside of themselves.into matter. By looking into matter, they invented many things. Today, through the science of optics, the study of light, scientists have come to doubt color, which relates to our five senses and the essential state of matter, noumena. They clearly divide noumenon and phenomenon, that which is real and that which is unreal.

In the Orient, while this outer development was being made, men developed their own consciousness through meditation, reaching to the bottomless state, which is called *shunyata*—emptiness, nothingness, the state of annihilation. But this does not mean a state of "no-entity"; annihilation is the state of *no-division.* This is a state of undivided purity we call Emptiness. It is like an omnipotent empty ocean, and this empty ocean produces everything.

Ta-t'ung invented a fiction, borrowing from the empty sky—"Your essential nature is like the sky." Everyone will fall into the same error, as I did myself. "Well, there is nothing you can do with essential nature; anything I do will be wrong." So for six years I was like a floating cloud. A policeman would have to carry me out of the street.

Religion is a dangerous thing. It does queer things to people. As in my own case, I was not in true emptiness; I was in the notion of emptiness. I was repeating this word for six years. I was in a solid lump of sugar made of this word "emptiness." This same error is also in the word "God." One paints the word in the brain, G-O-D, like the God painted by Michelangelo in the Sistine Chapel, a notion of God. The notion of emptiness must be destroyed. What will happen then?

When one is young, one meditates all the time. In the monastery, I was a very busy novice. I meditated with my back against the wall by day, and in the evening out in the fields. It is an old custom, the posture of meditation. You put your strength in your belly and you keep your eyes partly open. Otherwise, you will be carried out of meditation and begin to dream. If you go to sleep, it is better to go to bed. If you daydream, better go to a movie. Do not become a movie producer in your meditation—"It's a beautiful world! Beautiful woman, beautiful beefsteak and onions!" This is not meditation; it is just delusion.

In meditation, I always feel my heart beating in the time of four. My hand becomes very heavy, and my tongue becomes heavy. In this state, you sink under the control of nature. You are keeping every view within your mind, every sound, every vibration. Then you suddenly stand up in fear. You dare not go any deeper. This is the usual dividing line. From here you will go into *samadhi.* For a long time, I asked, "Am I alive or dead?" I was existing in a pure state. Suddenly I came up again and saw a new world. It was the old world, and I had separated from it.

Meditation is a device, not Buddhism itself. And emptiness is the result of this device; it is not a true state. But the student may fall into a trap here and live in a mountain cave like a wolf or a fox, eating weeds. He may die like a fox, calling it the highest religion.

If this is religion, it must be annihilation. It is a device and a fake, not religion itself. The Buddha warned his disciples many times not to fall into this error. So some today are not emphasizing meditation. Without meditation, they say, you can find it. Well, it's safe, but without meditation, you cannot find it, and Ta-t'ung's metaphor of the empty sky will lead to error.

To discover what this watch is [holds up watch], you will take it apart and put it together again, screwing it tight. So an analogy is a device to get a synthetic view. Do you think you can build a house by just destroying the one that is there? No. So you must understand your own present state and your own actions in detail.

"Now let me instruct you with a gatha: *Though you do not see a thing, if you still cherish the 'empty' view/ It is like a floating cloud that covers the face of the sun."* That is, you are still in an erroneous state.

A child of four or five years is really in an empty state, but this child does not keep this emptiness in his mind. A child's mind is free, divine, not nailed down or nailed up on the wall, not crucified. It is free, living, and walking on the earth, not killed by the two ideas of good and bad, time and space, not crushed between two robbers. But our mind must be killed once, so that we can get into Emptiness.

"Though you do not know a thing, if you cherish this knowledge of 'emptiness'/ It is as though a clear sky were to produce a flash of lightning." This is the emptiness of nature itself. It is empty, but in this dynamic silence, the thunder roars. This is the true state of mind. It is the mind of a child—pure, free, and empty. Like an angel.

You must scrape off the dust, analyze and become fine. You will see the wrinkles fall away from your face. However, I am not advertising a beauty parlor!

"At any moment/ This kind of seeing and knowing may arise/ If you mistakenly attach to them/ How can you find the means [to dispel them]?" This device is the teachings of the Buddha. Though the Zen sect uses the device of meditation, there are many other devices in Buddhism. I am not a narrow sectarian. I stick to my own sect, but I understand the others.

"You must know, in each instant of thought, that this is wrong/ Then your own mysterious light will always be manifesting." I know that I am existing now. What part of myself knows this? Myself? No, there is no "myself." This immediate knowledge is quite mysterious. It is the knowledge that is manifesting through you and through me.

I am not making *this* manifestation. *This* is not myself. Then who is *this*? It is the Self everlasting, acting through me.

The mystery of religion is very near to you. Do not seek it far away. Find it in yourself. If I talk too much, I will spoil your finding it. Keep it in silence.

Upon hearing the gatha, *Chih-ch'ang's mind suddenly awakened. He then composed the following* gatha:

> *"Rashly giving rise to conceptions*
> *I was seeking enlightenment in attachment to forms*
>
> *If one cherishes a single thought of being enlightened*
> *How can one transcend one's past delusions?*
>
> *My original nature is the source of enlightenment*
> *But I was diverted by the wandering stream of samsara*
>
> *If I had not entered the room of the patriarch*
> *I might have found myself astray, lost in the realm of dualism"*

One day, Chih-ch'ang questioned the Master: "The Buddha preached the three vehicles and then preached the highest vehicle. I fail to understand [how there can be a highest vehicle besides the three.] Please elucidate this for me."

The Master said: "Do not attach to the external form of things. The four vehicles do not exist in the Dharma; such distinctions only exist in people's minds.

"Seeing and hearing, or reciting sutras are inferior vehicles; realizing the Dharma and understanding its meaning are intermediate vehicles; practicing according to the Dharma is a higher vehicle. When, however, you penetrate all the Dharmas and all the Dharmas are complete within you, when you remain unstained by [any belief] and leave all formulas behind with nothing to cling to, this is the highest vehicle. 'Vehicle' signifies 'action' or 'practice'; it has nothing to do with mere argument. You must practice this yourself. Do not question me. At all times, your self-nature is naturally complete."

Chih-ch'ang bowed in gratitude. He served as the Master's attendant until the end of the Master's life.

SOKEI-AN SAYS:

Zen was called by many names in India, sometimes it was called the Yoga School. Yoga is unity. To unite with the universal spirit is Yoga. The Zen student does this through meditation, which was called *dhyana*. In China it is called, *chan*; in Japan, *zen*.

A young monk paying homage to the Sixth Patriarch asked him a question. The Master gave him his answer. This is like a catechism. Instead of answering in prose, the master, or the Zen student, answers in an extemporaneous poem.

Upon hearing the gatha, Chih-ch'ang's mind suddenly awakened. He then composed the following gatha: In the West, enlightenment is something like inspiration. You are enlightened when God reveals to you the mystery of the universe. All of a sudden you become a sage. In Oriental thought, enlightenment is awakening. When one realizes the Reality of this existence, it is not in any passive sense; he enlightens himself and then observes the law of nature and of man.

"Rashly giving rise to conceptions/ I was seeking enlightenment in attachment to forms." That is, I made or created a theoretical view.

In Buddhism, when you see Reality, you do not need an explanation; it will be manifested. *There* is a board, and *here* is a stick. When the stick strikes the board, the board vibrates, the vibration strikes the ear, and consciousness recognizes it. Do you need an explanation? No. You hear the sound of the stick striking the board. Do not ask what or why. It is like bringing back the menu from the Ritz or from Longchamps and reading it but not eating.

"If one cherishes a single thought of being enlightened/ How can one transcend one's past delusions?" Enlightenment is true knowledge, or awakening. Poetical expressions like "light of enlightenment," "to flash through," "to transcend" mean to take an aloof attitude from the dream of delusion.

There was once a lady here who went to a Hindu teacher to get enlightenment. He pinched her nose and asked if there was a green light in her mind. She said, "Yes," and he said, "Then you are enlightened! Twenty-five dollars please!"

When you do not awaken, you sleep through a long incarnation, like a woodworm eating his life away inside a tree trunk. He makes his dreams and eats his dreams and fertilizes them with their dung. When he comes out to transcend these phenomena, he dies. When you wake from a dream—"Oh, I saw the face of a tiger!"—you know it was only a dream. If you dream, you must know that it is a dream. The Buddha always refers to the "long night." The long night was, perhaps, the Buddha's own teaching from his own experience.

There is a story of a blind turtle endlessly swimming in the dark ocean. Hearing there was a sky, and dreaming about it through many generations, he never had the opportunity of seeing it. An ancestor had given him an eye on the underside of his body, which he guarded very carefully. One day he comes upon a piece of floating wood and climbs up on it, and for the first time he knows the rest foretold by an ancestor. Remembering another story about the sky, he tries to turn over, but falls again into the ocean. He catches hold of the wood with his feet and hangs upside down underneath. The floating piece of wood has a knothole in it, the hole and the eye meet . . . Finally he sees the sky.

This is an illustration of the long night and the rare opportunity of coming upon a real teacher.

"My original nature is the source of enlightenment/ But I was diverted by the wandering stream of samsara/ If I had not entered the room of the patriarch/ I might have found myself astray, lost in the realm of dualism." "Room" means "Buddhism," the school of Buddha, the Zen sect. These two ways (i.e., the realm of dualism), always puzzle the student. I once said to my mother: "If I go to the monastery, I cannot marry!" "No, child." "If I marry, I cannot go to the monastery!" "No, child." "What shall I do?" My mother said, "Make your own decision."

The science of enlightenment is very important. The Buddha came upon it by introspecting his own mind. Western science found its own way of enlightenment through the analysis of outer matter, struggling to arrive at the foundation of the universe. In the West, analytical psychoanalysts or psychologists are always trying to analyze others' minds, never their own. I was once associating with a psychologist who asked me, "What dreams did you have last night?" I said, "Well, it is very seldom I entertain a dream, but in any case, I had no dream last night." "Oh, you are hiding something." "No, I never hide anything."

Pandemoniac mind is merely shadow mind. True mind is light at the center. It is not your mind, but the mind created by nature. Nature in the Orient has a great meaning; it is buddha-nature. You must find the light at the center. The entrance to all religions is through the gate of not entertaining your own mind. The sage finds that subject and object are one.

While meditating, the monk Hakuin, a famous Zen master, heard a temple gong that was about five miles away. This gong rang within the *garbha*, the Womb of Mind. *Garbha* is the sacred word for womb. In that moment, he felt that all the universe was in this Mind. "This must be the entrance!" he thought. But in the morning, it had faded. Begging food from door to door, bowl in hand, "Ho . . . ! Ho . . . ! Ho . . . !" he came to the door of an old woman who had fed him every morning. She observed that he was different, that he was in a trance. She was an old woman, but she was a Zen student, had the Zen spirit. "Oh, he is asleep!" she said, and she took the broom and smacked him. Hakuin fell over backwards into a rice paddy. When he came to, he emerged like a drowned rat. And suddenly, no longer in a trance, he realized Reality. Then he went back to his temple, saw his teacher, and expressed his experience.

One day, Chih-ch'ang questioned the Master: "The Buddha preached the three vehicles and then preached the highest vehicle. I fail to understand [how there can be a highest vehicle besides the three.] Please elucidate this for me." The Master said: "Do not attach to the external form of things. The four vehicles to do not exist in the Dharma; such distinctions only exist in people's minds." Mmmmmm. I only have five minutes more.

These three vehicles (*yana*) today would be called the Hinayana, *shravakayana*, *pratyekabuddhayana*, and *bodhisattvayana*; or Hinayana, quasi-Mahayana, and Mahayana.

"Seeing and hearing, or reciting sutras are inferior vehicles; realizing the Dharma and understanding its meaning are intermediate vehicles; practicing according to the Dharma is a higher vehicle." The *shravakayana* is the monks's way. The *pratyekabuddhayana* is the scholar's way; through the law of causation, he will find salvation. The *bodhisattvayana* is the way of enlightenment with sympathy and understanding.

These three comprise all religions, but there is a fourth *yana*.

When, however, you penetrate all the Dharmas and all the Dharmas are complete within you, when you remain unstained by [any belief] and leave all formulas behind with nothing to cling to, this is the highest vehicle." This is the *buddhayana.* One who observes the supreme vehicle is like Buddha himself, and anyone observing him from a distance feels he is a sage. But when one nears him, he is like his own father. He has human feeling. Confucius said about his visit to Lao-tzu that from a distance, Lao-tzu seemed to be a saint, but when he was close to him, he seemed to be nothing but a man.

"'Vehicle' signifies 'action' or 'practice'; it has nothing to do with mere argument. You must practice this yourself. Do not question me. At all times, your self-nature is naturally complete." Yana means teaching. Today we call it "religion." In the West, religion is limited in meaning; one must have some deity to worship, a person or some personal attribute. But in the Orient, *yana* has a very broad meaning. It includes everything. Science is a *yana.* Philosophy is a *yana.* Religion is also a *yana.* So *yana* includes all cultures of man.

Today, the religious teacher deals in religion only. In ancient days, those observing higher vehicles found a way to express their enlightenment by conduct, by silence, and by speech. These were bodhisattvas.

Chih-ch'ang bowed in gratitude. He served as the Master's attendant until the end of the Master's life. In Buddhism, there are no slaves. If one serves the master, he serves from his heart. We serve him because he is a torch. We have to understand true service to the world and to man. But to understand, you must understand non-ego. I have spoken many times of non-ego, but you do not understand. Love is different from beauty or agony; it is non-ego.

So we have the Buddhist's non-ego and the Christian's love—the same thing, different words.

The monk Chih-tao was a native of Nan-hai, in Kuang-chou. Seeking the Master's instruction, he asked: "For more than ten years, ever since I left home to become a monk, I have been reading the Nirvana Sutra, *but its essential meaning is not yet clear to me. I entreat you, Master, to elucidate it."*

The Master said, "What part of the sutra is not yet clear to you?"

The monk answered: "I have doubts about the lines: 'All samskaras *are mutable, subject to birth and death; when birth and death cease, in nirvana there is peace.'"* [18]

SOKEI-AN SAYS:

Buddhism developed in India about five hundred years after the Buddha's death. In China, it was officially adopted in the first century A.D. About five hundred years later, the Chinese digested Indian Buddhism theoretically, then they simplified it. They created Zen. The Chinese did not accept the mythology and the theology of Buddhism, but did accept the Reality of Buddhism, explaining it in their own terms. Of course, there wasn't much to explain because Reality is true existence, which cannot be explained by any philosophical term.

The Indian monk Bodhidharma went to Southern China by sea and landed in Yang-chow, Canton of today. The Emperor Wu Ti requested an interview with him, but he failed to understand Bodhidharma's Buddhism. Bodhidharma's view was that Reality, without reasoning, could be grasped immediately, within one's heart.

The monk Chih-tao was a native of Nan-hai, in Kwang-tung. Nan-hai, meaning Southern Sea, is a little town still in Kwang-tung. Kwang-tung is near Canton.

Seeking the Master's instruction, he asked: "For more than ten years, ever since I left home to become a monk..." In the Orient, monks and women are considered "homeless." The woman's parents' home is not hers, nor is the home of her husband. And when she goes to live with her daughter, her daughter's home is not hers. It's the same with monks. They have no home because they live under trees or in temples. The temples belong to the laymen. An American gentleman tried to form a little monastery in Santa Barbara by making young American gentlemen into homeless monks. One young man arrived with his wife! The man who tried to establish this monastery was an idealist. Finally, he returned to his native Vermont and became homeless himself.

"I have been reading the Nirvana Sutra, *but its essential meaning is not yet clear to me. I entreat you, Master, to elucidate it."* The Master said, *"What part of the sutra is not yet clear to you?"* The monk answered: *"I have doubts about the lines: 'All* samskaras *are mutable, subject to birth and death; when birth and death cease, in nirvana there is peace.'"* These lines of the *Nirvana Sutra* are very famous in Buddhism. Many European scholars have translated them in their own way. One English translation of *samskara* has been "confection." I opened the dictionary and found "confection," and I did not understand. Then, one day, a Ceylonese friend told me that in Ceylonese, *samskara* means "confection," or cakes made with seeds. Then I understood. This is a famous mistranslation, and it should be changed. When I went back to Japan, I spoke to the young monks about it, and they laughed. If I live to be eighty, I shall make a book of famous mistranslations of Buddhism. I have already picked out about one hundred whose meaning I cannot make out!

Samskara is the seed-holder that holds the molecules, the seeds of objective existence. Subjectively, it is your subconscious mind that retains everything, an element of your present mind. When you go to your psychoanalyst, he questions and examines you. He asks: "What do you fear?" You say: "I fear a lion." Such an answer has many elements, which you can find by analyzing yourself, even without a psychoanalyst. There are many elements in the mind, and each one is *samskara*. The mind consists of many *samskaras*.

"All *samakaras*" here means all we can see on the outside—in English, phenomena. In Buddhism, *samskara* is used in a broad sense. How would you like it if I translated it this way: "All these confections and cakes are mutable"?

All phenomena are mutable. While you are looking at it, everything changes its face like the clouds in the sky or the waves on the sea. Mutability, in Sanskrit *anitya*, is one of the great principles of Buddhism. In this existing world, nothing exists that is eternal. Once there was a wonderful country called Greece. Now where is that country? Once there was a wonderful country called Egypt. Where is that country now?

Upon this mutability, the Buddha founded his doctrine. The human being must find something eternal—but *how* in this mortal life? So the Buddha said, "By giving up, by relinquishing, you attain eternity." To find the true foundation of life, you must find a place that is true, clear, and simple. Buddhism appears quite pessimistic, but at the root of this pessimism, there is joy and peace. Now, for instance, you are dancing and singing in a roadhouse with your friends. Your butler comes and gives you a slip of paper saying that all your money is gone. Are you happy now? This mutability is one of the great elements of Buddhism.

"Subject to birth and death": Birth and death is usual in our mortal life. Samskara undergoes birth and death, mentally and physically. It emerges from universal consciousness into human consciousness and submerges itself from human consciousness into universal consciousness in death.

"When birth and death cease, in nirvana there is peace": This is the Buddhist faith. I have questioned many friends in America about this, and I have found that they do not like this wipe-out of death. Someone said, "I have found some peace here." I said, "There is no peace in this physical realm." Here is hope and fear. I accept both, and I enjoy myself with this. But I say, "In nirvana there is peace."

You must understand what nirvana is while you are living. Then you will not doubt in the moment of death. You will not cling to the bed or the hand of anyone. You will say, "When I die, I shall enter nirvana." Are you sure? You will not go to nirvana if you do not know nirvana while you are living. You must let go, or you will be born again in *samsara*, transmigrating through the three worlds, reincarnating in agony after agony.

In Japan when a monk speaks in this way, the young monks say, "This is a monk's plot, trying to scare us to death." It is true; it is not fiction. From the monk's philosophy, we can accept this plausible hypothesis.

In the Buddha's desire to save human beings from agony, he decided to find a way out. He meditated for many years, and no one ever spoke a word of enlightenment to him. The birds sang to him, the water sang to him, and the mountain echoed, but these were insentient. One day, a beautiful demon approached, a *raksha*—a Hindu demon is not always ugly to see—and sang to the Buddha half of this gatha in a loud voice: "All *samskaras* are mutable, subject to birth and death; when birth and death cease, in nirvana there is peace." Then the *raksha* disappeared, completing the rest of the *gatha* inaudibly while an invisible *gandharva* played it. No words were heard in the air. The Buddha repeated the words he had heard and said, "This is the truth, and I wish to hear the rest." The invisible demon said, "If you wish to hear the rest of the *gatha*, sacrifice yourself to the god of the ashuras and leap from the cliff, down to the valley." The Buddha answered, "If I throw myself off the cliff, I will be dead," thereby depriving humanity of truth. So the *raksha* wrote the other half of the *gatha* on each leaf of every tree and on every blade of grass and on each and every entity on the earth so that all might know the truth. Then the Buddha went to the edge of the cliff and jumped. As he was falling, the demon loudly sang the rest of the *gatha*: "When birth and death cease, in nirvana there is peace." Just before the Buddha hit the bottom, the demon caught his two feet and gave him life, telling him to preach this truth to man. This is a beautiful story about mutability.

The Master said, "Why do you doubt these lines?"

Chih-tao said: "All beings have two bodies called rupakaya *and* dharmakaya. Rupakaya *[the physical body] is mutable and undergoes birth and death. Dharmakaya is eternal; it has neither knowledge nor sensation. It is said in the sutra: 'When birth and death cease, in nirvana there is peace.' But which of the two bodies ceases and which finds peace? When* rupakaya *dies, the four elements separate. This is agony; agony cannot be called peace. If* dharmakaya *were to cease, it would be like a plant or a piece of stone or tile. Who then enjoys peace? Moreover, dharma-nature is the body of birth and death; and the five shadows are the function of birth and death. One body performs five functions. Birth and death are perpetual. When birth occurs, the function comes forth from the body. When death occurs, the function returns to the body. If one accepts that rebirth exists, then sentient beings never die. If one does not accept that rebirth exists, then sentient beings permanently return to a state of annihilation and become no different from inanimate objects. In that case, all things would be extinguished by nirvana, never to arise again. How, then, could there be any peace?"*

SOKEI-AN SAYS:

During the T'ang and Sung dynasties in China, Buddhism entered its golden age. It was a period of scholastic Buddhism. But the Sixth Patriarch established a different school. He established the school of sudden enlightenment. According to him, Buddhism does not need scholastic knowledge. Enlightenment can be obtained all of a sudden. He did not emphasize meditation either.

The Sixth Patriarch became quite famous in that time, and many young monks came and paid him homage. They came to the great master to question him about their doubts, which he destroyed for their sakes.

The Master said, "Why do you doubt these lines?" The lines were: "All *samskaras* are mutable, subject to birth and death; when birth and death cease, in nirvana there is peace."

Chih-tao said: "All beings have two bodies called rupakaya and dharmakaya. *Rupakaya [the physical body] is mutable and undergoes birth and death.* Dharmakaya *is eternal; it has neither knowledge nor sensation."* The monk is saying that *dharmakaya* is the pure spiritual body, which is eternal and nescient, devoid of self-awareness.

Rupakaya is appearance, physical being. It is the spirit that enters the eye and the ear, just like your feet slipping into your slippers. This spirit drops into the skin of your five senses and becomes a human being.

"It is said in the sutra: 'When birth and death cease, in nirvana there is peace' But which of the two bodies ceases and which finds peace? When rupakaya *dies the four elements"*—earth, water, fire, and air—*"separate." This is agony; agony cannot be called peace. If* dharmakaya *were to cease, it would be like a plant or a piece of stone or tile."* Like a piece of glass, or like the sun. Well, we can see the sun, but the sun does not know its own existence. So with the earth, it, too, is insentient. But plants, which grow out of the earth, have life, and all the men who are born on the earth have life. The earth gives life and the sun gives life, for they are the foundation of life. Therefore, they *are* living and sentient. They are part of the Ocean of Consciousness, like our own consciousness, but from the monk's standpoint, they seem unconscious.

A young boy went to a Shinto priest and asked a question: "Is water a sentient being?" The Shinto priest said, "No." The child said: "I don't understand. You have always said the sun is a sentient being, the mother goddess of the world. Why aren't fire and water sentient beings?" The priest said, "Bring me some water." The child brought him water in a cup. The priest asked, "Is it living?" The child said, "No, but it is not dead. It is living in some way." The priest said (this is a famous answer in Shinto): "When you pick up a piece of earth and ask about it, it is dead. When you return it to the earth, it is living. With fire and water, it is the same."

When we are analyzing, we are killing living things. It is by synthesis that we give life to the dead. By mind, we kill things. So to say that *dharmakaya* "has neither knowledge nor sensation" is, from the human point of view, an abstract view taken from human life.

"Who then enjoys peace?" If you wish to know the link between consciousness and unconsciousness, practice meditation, and you will find that marvellous link. From our standpoint, nirvana *appears* as an annihilated state. I cannot express this secret of Buddhism by words. You must attain it from your own meditation.

"Moreover, dharma-nature is the body of birth and death; and the five shadows are the function of birth and death. One body performs five functions. Birth and death are perpetual. When birth occurs, the function comes forth from the body. When death occurs, the function returns to the body." It is hard to translate *dharmata*, dharma-nature, into English. It means all this elemental, essential existence. It is the essential body, and has no physical form. But as a whole, it is a body, and it is infinite. There is no end to it in time or space. This essence creates the human body—or any form. It undergoes birth and death, emergence and submergence, like the waves of the ocean that emerge and swallow ships, or become calm and smooth like a mirror after a storm. The body of the ocean undergoes birth and death.

Scientists say there are molecules, atoms, electrons, protons, and ether. The electricity you see is embodied. But Orientals did not analyze outer existence. They introspected their mind activity. Throwing an apple into the field, mind observes mind itself. The law is written in the mind, so through introspection, mind finds the law, the universal mind that is the foundation of the universe.

The five shadows are *rupa, vedana, samjna, samskara,* and *vijnana. Rupa* is the world of forms. *Vedana* is the world of the senses. *Samjna* is the world dealing with thoughts. *Samskara* is the essential mind, the power of doing. *Samjna* is limited to the human mind, but *samskara* is boundless. Food is digested, spring turns to autumn. It is creative nature, instinct. The mother sleeps and in the spring she comes to life. *Vijnana* is the consciousness that is everlasting, deeper than *samskara.* It is the eternal Father that gives everlasting life, the Ocean of Consciousness, of which *samskara* is the Mother. Birth and death are nothing but the proper performance of this dharma-nature.

"If one accepts that rebirth exists, then sentient beings never die. If one does not accept that rebirth exists, then sentient beings permanently return to a state of annihilation and become no different from inanimate objects. In that case, all things would be extinguished by nirvana, never to arise again." The popular view is that all sentient beings will die and fall into nirvana, the state of annihilation, which means that whatever acts are committed, there is no punishment and no merit. If you conceive such a view, you will become a real nihilist and will not care what you do in your lifetime. The Buddha denied such a view.

"How, then, could there be any peace?" The Sixth Patriarch says you find peace in *awakened* consciousness. In the awareness of nirvana, no human body exists, so there is no one to enjoy peace and no one to suffer agony. In other religions they might say this body goes to heaven and enjoys peace.

When religion is rendered mythologically, it creates a notion like heaven. The priest commits a pious fraud by giving you this notion of heaven, as well, because he believes theology cannot be understood by the popular mind and will not be accepted. The theologian, however, does not believe this.

The Sixth Patriarch was not a religionist or a mythologist. He was a realist. He *demonstrated* the state of Reality itself and did not render this religion in terms of mythology or theology. He said there is no human consciousness in nirvana, so there is neither peace nor no-peace.

These ideas have been popularly debated for 2,500 years. Such analytical discussions are for philosophers or scientists, not for Buddhists. Blind meditation does not bring enlightenment. What merit could there be in such meditation? Buddhism always relates itself to your own intellect, to your own *awakened* mind. Without this relationship, there can be no true state of awakening.

To observe the world by analysis, you must observe existence in two ways: being and non-being. If you do not fall into the eternal view, you fall into the view of annihilation. Your knowledge is not complete. You will make an analysis, but must again gather those fragments to make a synthetic view and must observe everything at once, not one by one.

Analysis is the way of the philosopher and the scientist. The religious way is to make a synthesis, to put it all together, and then look at it all at once. You must find truth in both ways, and when the ends meet, you will have the key to the mysterious wisdom that is eternal. Analysis and synthesis must meet to form the true conclusion.

Avalokiteshvara observes everything at once. He transforms himself into a thousand hands, holding a thousand instruments, and he holds these instruments all at once. This is a representation of the synthetic view. When one forgets this view, he forgets the feeling of religion. At this time, among clergymen, there is only discussion. They have forgotten their own standpoint.

The Master said: "You are a follower of Shakya. Why do you discuss the law of the supreme vehicle, following the heretical views of immutability and annihilation? According to your view, dharmakaya *exists apart from* rupakaya. *You seek the state of annihilation outside of birth and death. You talk about the eternal peace of nirvana, declaring there to be a body that experiences this. You cling to life and death, immersed in worldly delights.*

"You should now know that all deluded men take the combination of the five shadows to be their own selves. Discriminating all phenomena, they take them to be the external forms of the world. They love life and hate death. As they transmigrate, drifting from one moment of thought to the next, they do not know that [existence] is empty and fleeting, like a dream or a mirage. They mistake the eternal peace of nirvana for suffering and constantly chase after [what they desire]. Because of this, the Buddha had compassion on mankind and revealed the true peace of nirvana."

"In this moment there is neither birth nor death, nor the need to annihilate birth and death. This is the revelation of the state of [absolute] annihilation. When it is revealed without any notion that it is revealed, this is the eternal peace of nirvana. There is no one who enjoys this peace and no one who does not enjoy it. How then can there be the five functions of the one body? Furthermore, how can anyone say that all things will be extinguished by nirvana, never to arise again? This is disparaging the Buddha and reviling the Dharma."

SOKEI-AN SAYS:

This passage is part of a catechism between the young monk Chih-tao, a student of the Northern School, and the Sixth Patriarch.

What I have been lecturing upon lately is the problem of nirvana, which can be translated into English as the "state of annihilation." The word annihilation somehow misleads and puzzles people's minds. The Sixth Patriarch is now explaining this to the young monk.

The Master said: "You are a follower of Shakya." The tribe of Buddha, a disciple of the Buddha. If you come from Oklahoma, we will call you an Oklahoman.

"Why do you discuss the law of the supreme vehicle, following the heretical views of immutability and annihilation?" There were ninety-six kinds of heretics in India, and in the Buddha's time, there were six kinds of heretical sects. One of these heretical sects believed that existence is empty-nature and that nothing has moral nature. In the end, everything ceases to exists in absolute annihilation. If this is so, as I have told you, man can do anything. There is no need to observe any moral code or convention—a son can kill his father, a mother can marry her child. Whatever conventions exist are just convenient regulations among human beings, but, essentially, there are no rules. Well, there are men living among us who observe the universe from extreme angles—analytically. They have lost their balance of mind.

Kaluda, one of these heretics, was a materialist. To him, all exists eternally as matter. The human being is simply an organism consisting of the four great elements: fire, water, earth and air—nothing but a body of chemicals. These elements decompose, but exist forever as the "essence of matter." This is also a one-sided view. Heretics fall onto one side of a dilemma, never observing both sides at once. About life and death, one says, "You are growing every day," and another says, "You are dying every day." Which is true? Growing is the same as dying. You must not observe from one side only, nor from a corner.

"According to your view, dharmakaya *exists apart from* rupakaya. *You seek the state of annihilation outside of birth and death. You talk about the eternal peace of nirvana, declaring there to be a body that experiences this."* There are some sects that dislike this existence and hope to be born after death in some kind of heaven. Their hope is always in the future. If you think that *rupakaya* is different from *dharmakaya*, then you belong to those sects. This is a very pessimistic view of life. Every day is empty because you think life is not worth anything. You seek a spiritual life outside your physical body and talk about peace in nirvana. The psychological view is that peace is not in the future, in that annihilated and nescient state, where there is no time or space. Peace is in the present, and you must take care of the present or you will have no future.

True peace is within your own wisdom. Those who accept the physical body as the reality of existence have a one-sided view. This physical body is a phenomenon existing in accordance with your five senses, and they are not Reality. Each group of sentient beings lives in a different world having different types of sense organs. None see exactly the same phenomena.

When I was at the University of Tokyo, a professor showed us how insects see. I put on the lens of a fly and saw my friend in seven colors, repeated in thirty-two spectral lenses, and all the universe was a rainbow and manifold. How can you say this physical body is real? If you believe in the reality of the physical body, you will believe it to be sinful, and you might enter a cave and meditate like a fox. The Sixth Patriarch rejected this view. He said the Buddhist lives in the world of pure force, not in no-force. Pure force and no-force are different.

"You cling to life and death, immersed in worldly delights." If you think that life and death is the true reality, you cling to worldly life and the chaos of the infinite after death. We are not balanced if we are one-sided and forget the synthetic attitude.

"You should now know that all deluded men take the combination of the five shadows to be their own selves. Discriminating all phenomena, they take them to be the external forms of the world. They love life and hate death." If you take the dualistic attitude, meaning your physical existence is repulsive and an abstract spiritual existence is spiritualizing and peaceful, you will not be able to stick to your view. You will have to accept this physical existence in spite of rejecting it. Thinking you can "reject" or "affirm" your physical existence, you imagine a spiritual life outside of your physical life. As a consequence, you indulge your physical pleasure or you torture your physical body, like those who practice mortification. And you always place emphasis on life after death, forgetting this present life. Or you do not accept life after death but cling to this life only, saying, "The past is not existing, and the future has not come. The only truth in life is the moment and getting the best out of this world!"

This erroneous view of life is caused by a dualistic attitude that conceives the world in words such as "good or bad," "yes or no," "sooner or later," "to or fro," "life or death." There is no word that means "yes and no" at once, and no word that means "good and bad" at once. So man thinks of existence as physical and spiritual. The spiritual is first and good, the physical is next and bad. How awkward!

The human mind basically uses four types of dualistic discrimination in observing something: 1) good and not bad; 2) bad and not good; 3) good and bad; 4) not good and bad. In Buddhism we call these the "Four Bases of Reasoning."

One must find a view that does not fall into these four types of discrimination. The Zen that I am teaching you is the practice of grasping the absolute view, and when you grasp it absolutely, then you can talk about it.

"As they transmigrate, drifting from one moment of thought to the next, they do not know that [existence] is empty and fleeting, like a dream or a mirage." They not only entertain this dream but become a "member" of that dream. That is the world they know. It is like a merry-go-round. Everyone is raving and screaming and killing each other, using their weapons and declaring self-defense. The pandemoniac procession of your dream is the same. You must control it. The statesmen and the military cannot. Only your own Buddha can control it. If everyone were to control his own mind, this merry-go-round, this pandemonium and war would stop.

Everyone suffers from a flowing, haunting mind, a mind like an old man shaking with palsy. It must be exterminated like a bad habit. If you introspect your mind, minute by minute, it is like running water. You think of a cigarette, a postcard, giving a gift to the postman, not getting a letter from your sweetheart, and you go to bed in tears. That is the human mind.

I was annoyed with my mother after my father's death because she cried at night. Why did she have to have that agony? After I went into the temple, I practiced introspection. Then I understood my mother's morbid dreaming—and not only hers. I also understood the morbid, flowing mind that is like a man sitting in a chair, insanely tapping on the table.

To educate people, we create universities and schools, running everyone into a mold like a pattern in a shoe factory. They wear the same clothes and eat the same food. They put on the same hat, and the hat is restless. It moves up and down because it covers the same muscles of the same mind. But in the ancient schools, this was not so. Unfortunately, we have forgotten their method.

Without enlightenment, education means nothing; it only creates more and more mind-stuff. It does not teach one how to control the mind—and you do have a controlling power, a conscious center. You can live sanely, but if you lose control of that center, you will become insane.

If you entertain your mind, you will fall into a bad habit. To cure your mind, practice meditation. Just look into it. Look into that pandemoniac parade of thoughts. Look carefully, hard, and boldly. Then in time, it will be cured, and you will see the bottom of your mind. When it is cleaned up, you will see the mirror of your consciousness. You will really become a child of God, instead of living in a mirage.

"They mistake the eternal peace of nirvana for suffering, and constantly chase after [what they desire]." Man erroneously thinks that nirvana comes through time. But we can reach nirvana immediately, at this moment. Do not think horizontally, but perpendicularly. Penetrate with your five senses and find IT. If you do not realize it in this moment, you will not realize it at the moment of death.

The *arhat* took a long time to prepare and be ready for the end of his life. His way of practicing meditation was wrong—*he stopped all activities instead of observing them.* To put a bird in a cage, cutting its feathers and stopping its song, is not the way to keep a bird.

"Because of this, the Buddha had compassion on mankind and revealed the true peace of nirvana." When men's minds become bright and wise, Buddhism moves into that country. When their minds become dark and inert, Buddhism leaves that country. Like a plant, Buddhism blooms in warmth and dies in a chill climate. When it dies, it leaves behind dead bodies such as stone and wooden images, paintings and music, monks and nuns. The true Dharma is gone, and no one knows the meaning of it. Monks recite the sutras, but they do not understand. Perhaps some of them have the awakened eye, but they have forgotten the secret, the mystery of Buddhism. True understanding has nothing to do with Buddhism, but it has much to do with man's power of mind and with his ability. The Sixth Patriarch always placed emphasis upon the power of the intellect. This is the standpoint of Hui-neng, which is different from the other Buddhists of that time, such as this monk.

"In this moment there is neither birth nor death, nor the need to annihilate birth and death." Is there any moment? No. it immediately transcends time and space. There is no birth and death that must cease; there is no birth or death existing. Of course, this was the Buddha's conception of nirvana, though the wording is T'ang-dynasty Chinese. Such words would never have been spoken in India.

So, what is this moment?

In the Buddha's time, many schools of Buddhism and many disciples were speaking about the reality of existence. One type of argument said that the past does not exist and the future has not yet come. Between the past and the future is the present, but the present never exists because the past and the future are not existing. So what is it?

Another type of argument said that the present exists as past, present, and future in a moment that exists only by virtue of our sense-perceptions. They tried to prove that the present is not existing, that there is neither birth nor death in this moment.

The Sixth Patriarch hated this type of philosophical argument. It does not help men's minds at all. If a mind tries to find this moment too many times, it may become insane.

People usually think that annihilation means that all existence must be wiped out and that then nirvana will be revealed. But men's minds are analytical, not synthetic. They tend to see only one part at a time. They see life and suppress death, and vice versa. Birth and death are two extremes, like black and white, good and bad, man and beast, pure and impure. All these dualities are included in birth and death. Birth and death do not prevent one from attaining nirvana.

Look at a mirror. It is clear and pure. To prove its clarity and purity, we need not wipe out the figures that are reflected in it. If the mirror were not originally pure and clear, the figures would not reflect. So nirvana is like a mirror, and birth and death are the reflected figures in it. Therefore, to attain nirvana, you do not need to take the reflections away. There is a moon in the heavens and cherry blossoms on earth, and under the blossoms there are young men and women dancing in the moonlight. All these figures in the mirror of the universe are accepted in the pure state of nirvana.

If you accept your life with the understanding that this is a perfect and pure life, all your agonies and afflictions will be wiped away. Nirvana will be in your daily life from morning to evening. You will not need to change anything. Each one—soldier, monk, or king—will observe his own life. Our daily life itself is nirvana. This is the conclusion. But people do not understand this, so they struggle. These were the thoughts of the Sixth Patriarch.

The Buddha said as much when he was passing the burning woods. Trees were blazing, and wisteria were curling like women in agony. A disciple said, "All human life is like that—on fire." Another disciple asked the Buddha, "How does one escape?" The Buddha said: "One who is burning with desire will understand how to get out of the agony of desire. Do not refrain from burning. Go into the fire and find nirvana." These were his words.

It is remarkable that these early records are still in our hands. The Buddha did not refuse life. He accepted and affirmed it, but not in its deluded aspect of affliction and desire. "All is Reality" does not mean physical existence, but essential existence. You cannot materialize Emptiness—take it away and hide it somewhere else. There is nowhere else to hide it. All existing energy is merely changing its face. Look at *this* with the eye, and you see phenomena. Look at *this* from the inside, and you see only essential existence. Look at *this* through green glass, red glass. Change the glass, and you change the outside. See it with your eye, and it is phenomena. See it with your consciousness, and you see nirvana—the eternal peace of nirvana. You do not need to destroy anything. When you come to the conclusion that life is pure, you have eternal peace. When you realize that everything is in the state of nirvana, you don't have to enjoy it.

People think that in nirvana all existence will be annihilated and that there will be no incarnation. The Buddha never said that all things must be kept in annihilation. Birth and death is a viewpoint. From the real standpoint, nothing appears and nothing disappears. Birth and death is a subjective conception. Objectively, there is nothing to worry about. There is no birth and death that must cease.

"This is the revelation of the state of [absolute] annihilation. When it is revealed without any notion that it is revealed, this is the eternal peace of nirvana. There is no one who enjoys this peace and no one who does not enjoy it. How then can there be the five functions of the one body?" Do not close your eyes. Keep your eyes open and observe. Cast your eyes into the whole structure of consciousness at once, from top to bottom, and then everything is in front of your face. That is the aspect of absolute annihilation. You do not need to brush away the waves of the ocean to observe the ocean. Simply observe—look at the waves and see the ocean. To destroy and burn up all relative existence is not absolute annihilation at all. This is the key to open all the mysteries of religion.

Now I have explained the way to practice. When you have time, practice this through all the stages of the five shadows. Without practice there is no Buddhism. When I was a boy, I read pamphlets about how to swim. They came regularly, for months. Then I went to practice and sank down very quickly.

Objectify your mind and observe it. Objectify and observe the shadows. It is hard work. Your mind is subjective, and you are steeped in it. When I was young, I practiced observing these shadows consecutively every three months—three months on *rupa*, three months on *vedana*, and so on. But now, every morning I just wash my dishes, clean my house, study, and walk in the street.

"Furthermore, how can anyone say that all things will be extinguished by nirvana, never to arise again?" You increase your mental agony by refusing this life, talking about sin and so forth, thinking you will find heaven after death. You must find it while you are living. The cat, the dog, the flower—all of nature accepts its life and lives it happily. To accept this life, you must work hard in your mind to gain understanding. Life and death is just subjective. You must know it is your own delusion.

"This is disparaging the Buddha and reviling the Dharma." There are many religions on earth, many of fear and many of power. Buddhism is the religion of peace and inner joy. Buddha is Universal Wisdom, the awakened mind. You must not confuse Buddha with Shakyamuni Buddha, who attained enlightenment. Buddha is the wisdom that is common to all sentient beings in the Ocean of Consciousness. Shakyamuni was the human being who awakened to this. His mind was not different from ours, only we are still sleeping. The Sixth Patriarch is hinting to us about this.

Observe the activities of your mind and do not entertain thoughts. You need not wait until the end of your life to find nirvana at the bottom of your mind. As a matter of fact, at the bottom of the mind is the real place where man's mind lives.

The Buddha found this method 2,500 years ago. Before that, people believed that nirvana was reached only after death. The Buddha found this shortcut, and now we can reach there at once. I began at the age of twenty-three and found it at forty-seven. But anyway, it can be within a lifetime.

[The Master said:] "Listen to my gatha:

The highest mahanirvana
Is perfect, transparent, and everlastingly tranquil

The fool thinks it is the state of death
The heretic clings to it as the state of annihilation

He who seeks Hinayana attainment
Calls it 'purposelessness'

All these are in the realm of speculation based on delusion
And are the causes of the sixty-two heretical views

Such people rashly invent hypothetical names
How can names embody the truth?

Only the extraordinary man
Can penetrate [Reality] without either attachment or detachment

Through understanding the five shadows of mind
And the ego within them

He finds that every image manifesting externally
And every sound

Are all like dreams and phantoms
And so holds no views of 'sacred' or 'profane'

Nor does he entertain the notion of nirvana
But annihilates the twofold view [of affirmation and negation] and the three-fold view [of past,
present and future]

He always responds to the functioning of his senses
Without being conscious of responding

He recognizes the distinctions between all things
Without being conscious of recognizing them

Even when the kalpa *fire burns the bottom of the sea*
And the wind knocks the mountains together
The true eternal peace of extinction
And the manifestation of nirvana remain just as they are

I have been speaking forcefully
To make you abandon your erroneous views

Do not form some notion from my words
Then I shall admit that you have a little knowledge"

Hearing the gatha, *Chih-tao received great enlightenment. Dancing with joy, he bowed and withdrew.*

SOKEI-AN SAYS:

This is the song given to the young monk Chih-tao by the Sixth Patriarch. In this song, which was originally in rhyme, he is explaining the meaning of true nirvana. Nirvana is one of the important terms of Buddhism. But in ancient times no one really grasped the true meaning of nirvana as Shakyamuni Buddha himself had attained it.

[The Master said:] "Listen to my gatha: The highest mahanirvana/ *Is perfect, transparent, and everlastingly tranquil."* Not even the Sixth Patriarch can render the true meaning of nirvana in words. The true attainment of Buddhism is impossible to translate or convey through speech. You must experience it yourself, so that you can understand the taste of it, just as you do when you swallow water.

Mahanirvana, the Great Mirror, is perfect, transparent, and, like the universe, without limit. It is transparent because it is Absolute Reality. There is no form or color within this Absolute Reality. It is everlastingly tranquil because there is no space, time, or movement whatsoever. This is a picturesque explanation, but if you really attain nirvana, these words mean nothing.

"The fool thinks it is the state of death." Everyone thinks that nirvana is the state of death. In the Buddha's time, the monks were explaining nirvana to students as if there were two types of nirvana: nirvana-with-remainder and nirvana-without-remainder.

When you attain nirvana through meditation, nirvana-with-remainder means your mind is merged into universal consciousness. Your physical body still remains, but you are not annihilated. Though your mind goes back, your physical body remains and is no longer yours; it belongs to the earth. The "matter" itself is existing, so it is called nirvana-with-remainder.

Nirvana-without-remainder is when your consciousness is blown out like a candle flame, and your physical existence decomposes. Then you enter nirvana. All that you knew will be forgotten. The ashes of your cremated body will become earth, and you will be annihilated absolutely. This is the common understanding, but it is erroneous.

When I was a novice practicing meditation, we meditated for long periods of time every night and day. Once a monk remained in the state of nirvana for several days. He was so deep in meditation, he did not go to supper. At noon, some days later, the monks went back and found that his body had begun to rot and worms had appeared. The odor of death was present. The monks thought: "Poor monk! He went so deep, he couldn't come back. He must have died in meditation. What shall we do?" The abbot said: "Oh, he's alright. He'll come back tonight." That night the monk's consciousness returned to his body. When the abbot stood before him, the monk struck him down. The teacher said, "You have attained!" The monk said, "From now on, I don't care for all those scraps of paper."[19] The teacher said, "Very good, from now on you can walk the Buddha path."

Many idiots practice this. The monk came back, but he did not attain anything. He had a one-in-a-million chance. "Oh, I was hibernating for a while!"—like a snake or a frog in the mud sleeping under the earth—"Nirvana is like death!" Not everyone who goes into nirvana attains it. One must have the wisdom that corresponds to its Reality.

"The heretic clings to it as the state of annihilation." They think that this is the goal of attainment, so they fall into nihilism. They think that life is valueless and not worth living. They lose God, Reality, and Love. They also lose their religion. This is also an erroneous conviction.

"He who seeks Hinayana attainment/ Calls it 'purposelessness.'" Like the one who comes back and says: "Nirvana is purposelessness. To have an idea of intention in this life is erroneous." So he sits down.

This is not a joke! I was in that state for six years when I first came to New York. I sat in the street, abandoned, without resistance, and a policeman came and picked me up. This type of purposelessness is not the real type that was spoken of by the Buddha. One can fall into it and become a loafer, a tramp, or a hobo, and think it is a wonderful religion. Now I know it was an error, but I enjoyed it. I was wrong. At that time, my teacher just looked at me, said nothing, and gave me no advice. While I was sleeping, my friends kept their hands off and let me sleep as long as I could. They were very kind. These errors are test periods for Buddhists.

"All these are in the realm of speculation based on delusion/ And are the causes of the sixty-two heretical views/ Such people rashly invent hypothetical names/ How can names embody the truth?" These convictions are erroneous. They are our minds' notions. We live our lives according to erroneous understandings. We give them names like "Socialism," "Anarchism," "Realism," "Naturalism," "Egoism," "Nihilism," and "Marxism." They are only notions, conclusions of erroneous reasonings. Entertaining these erroneous notions, we perform our daily life according to these attitudes—"My conviction is Communism!"

A boy came to my house for a while. One day I looked into his eyes and said: "You have some notion. What is this all about?" His expression was harsh and dry. I said, "Get out!" He came back because he could not do business with Communism—not true Communism, of course. There are many like him.

The Sixth Patriarch was criticizing the erroneous view of nirvana supposedly conceived by Shakyamuni. But it was not his true idea. Perhaps, they translated his idea in their own fashion, so the Sixth Patriarch criticized it. Now he speaks his true conviction.

"Only the extraordinary man/ Can penetrate [Reality] without either attachment or detachment." Why only the extraordinary man? One must drop all and plunge into nirvana—penetrate the real state of nirvana. Philosophy leads only to the gate. One must go further.

When the candle-moth flies into the flame, there is no more moth and no more flame. Philosophy carries you near nirvana. When one really embodies into nirvana, one forgets the reasons that were made based on our sense experiences.

The term "nirvana" is akin to your philosophical term "reality." It means extinction by which you attain Reality. There is no way to demonstrate or to measure the true state of Reality. This physical existence is a dream. The monk who stays in a cave has a notion of nirvana. It is impossible to understand nirvana by logic or the conclusions of logic. They have nothing to do with Reality. If Reality were a man, he would laugh. Wipe away all those reasonings, which have nothing to do with the real state, and you will then stand on the threshold of nirvana. Logic is convenient to explain things to others, but it is awkward when speaking to one's own mind. Speak to yourself without words. To attain nirvana, you do not need any measure.

"Through understanding the five shadows of mind/ And the ego within them / He finds that every image manifesting externally/ And every sound/ Are all like dreams and phantoms/ And so holds no views of 'sacred' or 'profane.'" Forms are phenomena, not Reality. All these images and their voices are merely a dream. Men who talk of sacred and secular have not attained Reality. You do not need to have a notion of nirvana. I do not take any view. Sometimes I use terms like "monism," "pluralism," or "dualism" to explain something, but I do not contradict myself. You must attain freedom of mind.

Nor does he entertain the notion of nirvana/ But annihilates the twofold view [of affirmation and negation] and the three-fold view [of past, present and future]." You are always in nirvana, but you do not know it. With the device of meditation you will. When you attain nirvana, you will not need the device any more.

Your father gives you a million dollars. You begin to count it bit by bit so that you know you have it. Three months later, you find it was a million dollars and two cents. So with meditation, you go over your nirvana bit by bit and attain it in its entirety. It was always there anyway.

If you detach from nirvana, you will be an agnostic: you will despise friendship, loyalty and sincerity. The Hinayanist, however, attaches to nirvana. True attainment neither attaches nor detaches.

There is only one eternal consciousness, and you are in it from morning to evening, in life and death. When we come back from nirvana, we see white clouds, seven colors, and forms. We realize that the world is the result of consciousness, a conscious act. And all the world has the same consciousness.

"He always responds to the functioning of his senses/ Without being conscious of responding." With this "He," the idea of Buddha, has changed. Previously, "He" was Buddha himself. Here, "He" is almost like our natural, divine self—the Buddha within.

Using these words can become so ridiculous! I drink water, and I know it is cold. It is the function of the sense faculty to respond without being conscious of responding. It is not that the mind says, "This is cold," and the tongue says, "Yes, it is." There is no conversation between the mind and the tongue. The mind manifests through the tongue. I drink this water without being conscious that it is cold. When we do not think about it, then it is not mysterious at all; but when we think about this profoundly, then it becomes really mysterious.

[Sokei-an picked up an object from the table.]

This is not red, and it is not green. As Reality, everything is transparent; only our sense organs render it opaque. Colors do not exist in reality. They are vibrations in our eyes. Red is a slow vibration, and blue is a quick vibration. So the absolute object, the objective reality, has no color, sound, taste, smell, or feeling. But when we were born, we believed that all phenomena were existing.

How does the sentient being have this faculty? When we meet a long electric wavelength, we see boiling red. When we meet a quick wavelength, we see purple. If the wavelength is very fast, we cannot see it; it is an X ray. And so with sound. Distant thunder is slow, mysterious, and beautiful, but nearby thunder can cause death. We think we can measure these realities, but we are only creating the whole objective world. We are Maya itself. It proves that we are a common consciousness, that we are one being. Animals and insects have their own consciousness of the world. This is a very important point.

"He recognizes the distinctions between all things/ Without being conscious of recognizing them." When I was a baby, I had many aunts, so I was passed from lap to lap. I did not recognize their faces at first, for I always saw my mother. But later, I recognized the distinction between them. This function is always given to us, and it is very mysterious, but it is erroneous to think this is the way to find nirvana. This is also important.

Some Buddhists believe that to attain nirvana, you must unravel everything, and others believe you do not need to unravel everything to attain nirvana. So there are two schools. The first school, which says to level all complications, is called Hinayana. The second school, which says one can immediately attain nirvana without leveling complications, is Mahayana.

A monk climbed a mountain and cut bamboo and tree branches to make a hut. A friend visited him on the mountain and asked to see the mountain. The monk said, "Well, to show you the mountain itself, I would have to destroy my hut." "Very well," the friend said, "destroy it." So the monk took apart the ceiling and the floor, and said, "Now you can see the mountain." "Yes, beautiful, isn't it?"

This friend of his visited another monk, on another mountain top, living in a little hut of scraps. He said to the monk, "Show me the mountain." The monk answered: "I could destroy the hut, but why should I? You already see the mountain."

Hinayana takes an analytical attitude in finding nirvana. The Mahayana takes the synthetic way. These two types of view certainly make two types of religion.

The true view, in reality, is that visible and invisible, real and illusory, analytical and synthetic are non-existent.

"Even when the kalpa *fire burns the bottom of the sea/ And the wind knocks the mountains together/ The true eternal peace of extinction/ And the manifestation of nirvana remain just as they are."* This is Buddhist mythology. You know the *kalpa* story: An angel, once a year, sweeps a huge stone with her gossamer sleeve, and when the stone is entirely swept away, one *kalpa* will have passed. As you see, a *kalpa* is a long, long time. At the end of a kalpa we will have seen ten suns circle the earth and everything reduced to *akasha*, etheric-space—the state of nirvana. A cool wind will rise and create a rain that will fall endlessly through this space, contracting the hot etheric fire, creating a new world and the beginning of human life.

It is very hard to accept this kind of story. The story of the Garden of Eden is easier. Adam was made from earth, and Eve was made from his rib. However, the Eastern story is more beautiful.

"I have been speaking forcefully / To make you abandon your erroneous views." The Sixth Patriarch was from South China, and the central Chinese thought the southern Chinese were barbarous. The Sixth Patriarch did not speak in a polished tone of voice or in beautiful Chinese.

"Do not form some notion from my words." If you do, you will not grasp the real nirvana.

"Then I shall admit that you have a little knowledge." Goodness gracious, a little knowledge! The Sixth Patriarch spoke very directly.

Hearing the gatha, Chih-tao received great enlightenment. I hope so. The record always says so of those who interview the Master. Chinese literature is very exaggerative—"Suddenly, enlightenment burst in his mind!"

Dancing with joy, he bowed and withdrew. In Chinese, "He danced and leaped, and then retired." This is a little too much. I think he just quietly retired.

Ch'an Master Hsing-ssu was a native of An-ch'eng in Chi-chou. His family name was Liu. Having heard of the fame of the teaching of Ts'ao-ch'i, he came directly to pay homage to the Master. He asked: "What shall I practice to avoid falling into the conventional stages of Buddhism?"

The Master said, "What is it that you have been practicing?"

He replied: "I have never cared for any practice, even that which leads to the highest wisdom."

The Master said: "Then into what conventional stages have you fallen?"

He replied: "Since I have never followed any practice, even that which leads to the highest wisdom, into what stage could I fall?"

The Master profoundly acknowledged [Hsing-ssu's] attainment and appointed him head of the assembly of monks.

One day the Master said to him: "Go now and convert people. Do not let the teaching expire."

Having attained the Dharma, Hsing-ssu returned to Chi-chou and stayed on Ch'ing-yuan Mountain, carrying out his mission.

SOKEI-AN SAYS:

Just reading these Chinese names, I think you will be annoyed. But to have a record for your notebooks, I must explain them carefully. I shall not give this type of lecture again in my lifetime.

Ch'an Master Hsing-ssu was a native of An-ch'eng in Chi-chou. Chi-chou is a mountain district that borders Southern China on the south part of the Yangtse River. In ancient days, this was a very civilized part of China.

His family name was Liu. He was Mr. Liu before he became a monk. He must have studied Buddhism for a long time.

Having heard of the fame of the teaching of Ts'ao-ch'i: Ts'ao-ch'i is the territory in which the Sixth Patriarch had his temple. The prairie mountains of Ts'ao-ch'i are washed with rivers and streams. In the summertime the region is very hot. In Japanese, Ts'ao-ch'i is Sokei. This is my name given to me by my teacher. But I am not he, so do not make a mistake!

He came directly: At that time, there were no street cars or trains. The monks traveled on foot from one corner of that vast country to the other, sometimes walking three or four years. Without money, begging for food and sleeping under trees by the roadside, they searched for masters. Buddhism was the highest culture, and the temples were its universities. Today, a young man wanting to study at Yale comes from the West by train. But a young man in China wanting culture had to travel far. From Chi-chou to Ts'ao-ch'i is about two hundred miles. This is not so far if you drive your automobile, but if you walk, it is some distance.

To pay homage to the Master. Chinese students still follow this style of homage. With incense in their hands, they salute, as I salute the Buddha. Here in America, the minister offers his hand—"How do you do?"

When I saw Ruth St. Denis[20] teaching her students the profound Buddhist salute, I asked her why she bent her hands to her forehead. She said, "Because it's so beautiful!" I did not tell her it means to embrace the feet of the Buddha. And the Buddha did not wear stockings. I'm sure they smelled like cheese!

In those days, there was no sense of time. People came from a distance, put on their robes, washed their hands and feet, spread their *nishidanas* (mats), and saluted.

He finally put a question to the Master: No monk would immediately ask a question. He would retire for two or three months; then, if he saw an opportunity, he would ask the master something.

"What shall I practice to avoid falling into the conventional stages of Buddhism?" From the Buddha's time to that of the Sixth Patriarch, Buddhist monks practiced many contrivances. Later, these contrivances multiplied to the point that there was produced a pedantic form of Buddhism. Students were reading volumes of sutras—an enormous task and too much for any one lifetime. These days, they are printed in small type, so they can be put into one bookcase. I have them here in my house and have not read even half of them!

The Buddha had no books to read. He was meditating, as were his disciples. Occasionally, the Buddha gave them a talk, and once a month, at full moon, the monks would confess their faults. Then the Buddha would give them instruction. The old style of Buddhism came back again, untangled by philosophy. It is now called the Zen School.

The Master said, "What is it that you have been practicing?" The Master examined the young monk: "Do you practice commandments, or do you observe a metaphysical type of Buddhism, or do you practice symbolic Buddhism? What kind of Buddhism have you been studying?"

In symbolic Buddhism, everything in the world is a symbol, and all sentient beings have a meaning. For example, the sun in the sky, the center of the solar system, is the center of production. Therefore it is of the female gender and is called Tathagatagarbha, the Holy Womb. The male element, the invisible moon, then covers the female—a wonderful system, wonderful! Your mind extends to the outer world and does not return to your own experience, your own consciousness. This is the Buddhism of the extrovert.

The Metaphysical School uses the technical terms of philosophy. The Zen School, however, does not use symbols or terms of philosophy; we attain Reality immediately. The Sixth Patriarch tested Hsing-ssu to see if he had the nature of a real Zen monk. Perhaps he had tried some kind of practice.

He replied, "I have never cared for any practice, even that which leads to the highest wisdom." According to Buddhism, there are ten stages to the highest enlightenment, from first to last. But this monk said he never cared for the highest enlightenment. Well, if you were the child of a millionaire, you would probably say you never cared for money.

Hsing-ssu had attained the real state of nirvana, so there was no Buddhism left for him. He did not want to speak of it in philosophical terms. What was his attitude?—"I don't give a fig for the highest wisdom." His words sound as if he never cared for Buddhism. He had passed through all the conventional stages and did not care for conventional Buddhism anymore. He had his own wisdom, his own religion. But he was a monk, he had already shaved his head, joined his hands and burned incense. So he paid homage to the Patriarch and stayed for a few months before asking his question. He cared so much for Buddhism that he passed through all those measures. Anyone who wishes to be religious must attain this stage. A true man never cares for religion. You must pass this stage once, otherwise you will fall into agnosticism and not attain true religion.

The Master said: "Then into what conventional stages have you fallen?" He replied: "Since I have never followed any practice, even that which leads to the highest wisdom, into what stage could I fall?"—"If there is no stage, I wonder how I could fall into a stage." The words are very simple, but the meaning is very deep.

When I was seriously observing 250 commandments in my youth—you must not kill, steal, drink wine, etc.—I looked into nature and found that there were no commandments. Now I know there are. If you walk through Central Park on a cold night with nothing on, you will have pneumonia by the next morning. If you walk into a fire, you will burn. If you are in the ocean, hanging on to a piece of wood, do you think you can hang on forever? You will finally fall asleep and sink, and you will not come back again.

Experience is a wonderful thing. It is how we understand the law of nature. Nature has wonderful laws, but no commandments. If you violate the law, the punishment comes immediately. In society, we must have laws to preserve social order. Laws are necessary. It is the same in the monastery. In your labor unions, the men drop the work from their hands at six o'clock and go home. It's the union law.

I observed the commandments carefully in the monastery because if I had not, I would have been thrown out. I thought there must be some other way to understand the truth of the commandments, so

I turned to nature and did not fall into conventional stages, but I understood them. I worked hard for a long, long time.

Today, I do not blame anyone for anything. I came to the ocean, to the ground of real freedom. This is not the ground of so-called "abandonment." It is understanding the nature of human life. So I can sympathize with those men and women who are violating conventional stages without knowing what they are doing. This is a profound problem.

One must attain freedom through Buddhism. Through this old master one can come to this field of freedom without violating the conventional law.

The Master profoundly acknowledged [Hsing-ssu's] attainment: When the Zen master grants his acknowledgment to the student, he doesn't say yes or no. It is in silence. It's his decision, and he doesn't say, "Fine, very good, one hundred percent, here's your diploma." No!

And appointed him head of the assembly of monks. After about a year he made him superintendent of the monks.

One day the Master said to him: "Go now and convert people."—"Now your studies are over. Thank you very much."

It is very hard when the Zen master says this. The master will not pay the disciple any salary to teach in school. The disciple will go somewhere and strive. If he cannot make converts, he will not eat. Sometimes he gives up being a monk and goes into the fields, and nature gives him a grant. But if his nature is not to accept anything, he will lose his robe. To be ordained is not from the teacher, it is from Buddha, or, as we say, from nature. It is not good to pay a monk one penny.

"Do not let the teaching expire." Altogether it has been 128 generations. We still hold the torch, but it is very dangerous now. It is like a single candle before a storm.

Having attained the dharma, Hsing-ssu returned to Chi-chou and stayed on Ch'ing-yuan Mountain, carrying out his mission. He and another teacher, Nan-yueh Huai-jang, became the main figures of the Zen School.

Ch'an Master Huai-jan was a child of the Tu family in Ching-chou. He first met National Teacher Hui-an of Mt. Sung. Hui-an sent him to Ts'ao-ch'i to interview the Master. When Huai-jang arrived, he went to the Master and bowed.

The Master asked him, "Where do you come from?"

Huai-jang answered, "From Mt. Sung."

The Master asked, "What is that which has come thus?"

Huai-jang answered, "If it could be defined as a thing, it would not be what you have asked of me."

The Master asked, "Can it be practiced and attained?"

Huai-jang answered, "It is not that it cannot be practiced and attained, but that it cannot be defiled."

The Master said: "It is precisely this not being defiled which is cherished by all the buddhas. You know it already; I know it also. In India, Prajnatara predicted that from your feet would come a horse that would trample to death everyone on earth. You know this in your mind, but do not begin too soon to give your teaching."

Huai-jang instantly understood. He served the Master as his attendant for fifteen years, each day penetrating more deeply. Later, he went to Nan Yo and widely promulgated the Ch'an teaching. The Emperor bestowed upon him the posthumous name Ta-hui (Great Wisdom).

SOKEI-AN SAYS:

Serving under the Sixth Patriarch were two eminent Zen masters: Ch'ing-yuan Hsing-ssu of Ch'ing-yuan Mountain and Nan-yueh Huai-jang of Nan-yueh Mountain. After Bodhidharma, they are in the seventh generation of Zen masters. There were others, less eminent, who also attained Zen masterhood.

Ch'an Master Huai-jang was a child of the Tu family in Chin-chou. He first met National Teacher Hui-an of Mt. Sung. Tu is a family name, like the poet Tu Fu. When a Zen master is called National Teacher, it means he is the Zen master of the Emperor.

Hui-an was a contemporary of the Fifth Patriarch, Hung-jen. He was an old man at the time. He died in 709 A.D. a famous Zen master. Huai-jang went to see him.

Hui-an sent him to Ts'ao-ch'i to interview the Master. When Huai-jang arrived, he went to the Master and bowed. The Master asked him, "Where do you come from?" This is a very simple question, but when the Master asked it, it sounded very deep. If he were to come to my house, I would ask him the same question. By his answer, I would immediately discover whether he has some attainment or is just a blank-minded man without any penetration—any insight into his mind.

Huai-jang answered, "From Mt. Sung." He parried lightly like a fencer. He realized the depth of the question.

The Master asked, "What is that which has come thus?" The first thrust of the Sixth Patriarch's sword was not so forceful, but the second was fierce. Huai-jang could not evade the question. The Sixth Patriarch did not say, "*Who* is he that has come thus?" He said, "*What* is that which has come thus?" Translating this, one might make a mistake and translate it as, "Who is this?" Such a translation would throw off the deepest meaning. "What" does not mean man, nor does it mean God, neither does it mean beast or devil. This "what" expressed by the Sixth Patriarch is most profound.

What is it that has come thus? The one appearing before the Sixth Patriarch is not a man or a god. What would you say to such a question? Electron?—you would be hit by the Sixth Patriarch. How would you express it? If you do not understand "What is that which has come thus?" then you do not know the foundation of human life or of universal activity. Such a simple question is very difficult to grasp.

Huai-jang answered, "If it could be defined as a thing, it would not be what you have asked of me."—"If I could explain it by an example or define it in a word, it would not be what you have asked of me."

This is how Huai-jang answered. If you handle this koan in the Zen room, you must present your own answer. You should not imitate Huai-jang or call it the Triune Body. It is a mysterious power. It is fundamental being.

The Master asked, "Can it be practiced and attained?" That is: "I understand your thoughts, but can it be attained by making an effort?"

Huai-jang answered, "It is not that it cannot be practiced and attained": Yes, by struggle and meditation one can attain, and when one attains, it will be the end of effort. He cannot change it or make it better. He cannot subdue it or cut it, cook it or eat it.

In Zen, we show the hand. Show me the sound of your hand. Can you cut it and fry it like bacon and bring it to me? And if your hand slaps my face, I will ask it, "What is that which comes thus?"

Hakuin's famous koan, "Can you hear the sound of one hand?" is the same as the Sixth Patriarch's question. An American doctor answered by saying, "Two hands produce the sound." Such a cheap answer desecrates the koan. Any monologist can give you that answer on a street corner. Hakuin did not mean this hand.

When you go to the Metropolitan Museum, you will see Rodin's sculpture of the hand. He did not portray man's hand; he had more sense than that. When you attain it, it will be the end.

"*. . . But that it cannot be defiled.*" The Master said: "*It is precisely this not being defiled which is cherished by all the buddhas.*" This undefilable foundation of esoteric Buddhism was cherished by the buddhas and bodhisattvas. When a Buddhist teaches, he says something like "Cherish your pure and perfect jewel-soul." This is symbolism. This jewel is in your mind. You must discover this million-year-old jewel yourself. It was that which stood before the Sixth Patriarch. But do not think it has a shape or is transparent or opaque. It is your task to find out what it is. Buddha's advent was to discover the jewel in the heart, and our work is to find it in our own, to satisfy ourselves in our lifetime.

You know it already; I know it also. In India, Prajnatara predicted that from your feet would come a horse that would trample to death everyone on earth. The twenty-seventh patriarch after the Buddha was living in Southern India. He presaged that in the future a disciple of Huai-jang, Ma-tsu Tao-i, would come forth from him and tread upon everyone in the world. There is no historical value in this prediction. Perhaps one of Ma-tsu's disciples inserted this.

"*You know this in your mind, but do not begin too soon to give your teaching.*" This will be suggested by every teacher. We were told: "Do not begin too soon to give your teaching. Wait twenty years!" But we were too impatient. The ancients stayed in the mountains and waited until someone came and dug them up. No Zen master says, "I am a Zen master!" announcing it on the street corner.

Huai-jang instantly understood. He served the Master as his attendant for fifteen years, each day penetrating more deeply. As always, apprentices who wish to study painting or sculpture go to the master's house and study for many years, face to face, soul to soul. I like this face-to-face apprenticeship. It is better than the way of education today that is without personal contact.

Later, he went to Nan Yo and widely promulgated the Ch'an teaching. The Emperor bestowed upon him the posthumous name Ta-hui (Great Wisdom). He died in 744 A.D.

The next monk to visit the Sixth Patriarch was another famous student. He attained enlightenment in just one night, saying, "I do not need to stay another night." There were many types of visitors.

Ch'an Master Hsuan-chueh of Yung-chia was of the Tai family in Wen province. In his youth he studied the sutra teachings and commentaries, and was accomplished in the meditation practice of the T'ien-t'ai school. He found enlightenment through reading the Vimalakirti Sutra.

The Master's disciple Hsuan-t'se paid him an unexpected visit. They had a discussion, and finding that Hsuan-chueh's words were in agreement with those of the patriarchs, Hsuan-t'se asked him: "From whom did you receive the Dharma?"

Hsuan-chueh replied: "While studying the sutras and commentaries, I received instruction in each from a particular master. Subsequently, through the Vimalakirti Sutra, *I realized the principle of the buddha-mind. But as yet there has been no one able to prove the genuineness of my attainment."*

Hsuan-t'se said: "Before the appearance of the Wei-yin-wang Buddha, realizing enlightenment on one's own without a master was acceptable; but after the Wei-yin-wang Buddha, all such attainment belongs to the heresy of spontaneous existence."

Hsuan-chueh said: "I entreat you to prove the genuineness of my attainment."

Hsuan-t'se replied: "My own word carries no weight. However, at Ts'ao-ch'i is the Sixth Patriarch. Students are assembling there from every quarter like gathering clouds in order to receive the Dharma. If you wish to go, I will accompany you."

SOKEI-AN SAYS:

Then they went to pay their homage to the Sixth Patriarch.

Ch'an Master Hsuan-chueh of Yung-chia was of the Tai family in Wen province. In his youth he studied the sutra teachings and commentaries, and was accomplished in the meditation practice of the T'ien-t'ai school. The Tai family lived in Yung-chia, an old town in Wen province between Canton and Shanghai in the eastern part of China. About seventy miles from Yung-chia is a famous mountain called T'ien-t'ai. This mountain is covered with Buddhist temples.

Preceding the period of the Sixth Patriarch, a famous scholar founded the T'ien-t'ai School of Buddhism. T'ien-t'ai was, at that time, the most famous center of Buddhism in Southern China. Always covered in mist, Mt. T'ien-t'ai lay beside the seashore, where the beaches were washed by evening tides. In the distance was a silvery river. This mountain was a favorite subject of Chinese paintings. Today, it is surrounded by munition factories, slaughter houses, and white men's villas that smell of beefsteak. Modern civilization has almost vitiated this sacred mountain. Fortunately, not all the temples have been destroyed by war.

He found enlightenment through reading the Vimalakirti Sutra. The Indian Vimalkirti was a contemporary of Shakyamuni Buddha. He was a layman who had enlightened knowledge. As there is no proof of his historical existence, he is a rather mythical figure. He is a symbol of layman's Buddhism.

The *Vimalakirti Sutra* describes his life and the events surrounding his sickness: The Buddha's monastic order was so perfect that Vimalakirti expressed his antagonism toward the perfect law by becoming sick. This means no one can observe commandments without the physical body. So he expressed his idea by the attitude of illness. The Buddha worried and asked his disciples to go to his sick-bed. All the disciples refused to go because all who met with him in discussion were out-argued. Finally, the Buddha asked Manjushri to go and pay homage to him. Only Manjushri could talk with Vimalakirti fifty-fifty.

Manjushri went with five thousand disciples, and Vimalakirti seated them all in his room with space to spare. This is a mysterious story. How could Vimalakirti seat five thousand people in his room?—a question which is a very interesting koan.

This sutra is very important in Mahayana Buddhism. Many monks believe they must keep away from home and daily tasks to attain enlightenment. Without leaving home, they believe, they cannot attain. Vimalakirti said this type of enlightenment is of no use; at home, we can attain enlightenment. Through this sutra, we understand that we can attain enlightenment while performing our daily tasks without practicing Buddhist commandments or meditations. It is natural that this sutra would have a very important place in the history of Buddhism.

While Hsuan-chueh was reading the *Vimalakirti Sutra*, he found enlightenment: "Oh, I see! This is the true view. I wonder if there is anyone else who has attained as I have attained?"

The Master's disciple Hsuan-t'se paid him an unexpected visit. Hsuan-t'se was a native of Wu province. Perhaps he had been visiting his home, and on the way back to the Sixth Patriarch's temple, he dropped in on Hsuan-chueh, having heard of his enlightenment.

They had a discussion, and finding that Hsuan-chueh's words were in agreement with those of the patriarchs, Hsuan-t'se asked him: "From whom did you receive the Dharma?"—"You speak like a patriarch. Who is your teacher?"

It's queer, isn't it? The Sixth Patriarch, for instance, was not a philosopher, and he was not learned. He was a farmer and the child of a farmer in Hsin-chou. To attain enlightenment, you do not need to be learned; you can be a child of a farmer or a mechanic. And if you do attain, you will also speak as if you had read all the sutras. So Hsuan-chueh's expression and words naturally resembled that of preceding masters.

Hsuan-chueh replied: "While studying the sutras and commentaries, I received instruction in each from a particular master." As a monk, of course, he was instructed in the sutras, *vinaya* (commandments) and the *abhidharma* (philosophy); and in Japan, there is a master for each. Hsuan-chueh said he had followed many teachers in his studies.

"Subsequently, through the Vimalakirti Sutra, *I realized the principle of the buddha-mind."* "Buddha-mind" is Zen. Without a teacher, he attained Zen.

"But as yet there has been no one able to prove the genuineness of my attainment."—"Is there anyone in the world who can judge whether my enlightenment is true or false?"

Hsuan-t'se said: "Before the appearance of the Wei-yin-wang Buddha, realizing enlightenment on one's own without a master was acceptable; but after the Wei-yin-wang Buddha, all such attainment belongs to the heresy of spontaneous existence." Wei-yin-wang Buddha in Sanskrit is a long name (*Bhisma-garjita-ghosa-svara-raja*). Before this first Buddha, there was no enlightenment in Buddhism.

"Before Wei-yin-wang Buddha" means before human knowledge, before anyone knew the law of man. After this buddha, enlightenment was proved without discussion or argument.

Shakyamuni's enlightenment and Mahakashyapa's enlightenment are the same enlightenment. If you are a sophist and say, "Well, I'm not sure the Buddha's enlightenment was perfect," you are not a Buddhist. We believe the Buddha was truly enlightened.

My teacher acknowledged my enlightenment, his teacher acknowledged his enlightenment, and so on back to the Buddha. If there is any room left for argument, it is not Reality. When someone says, "I am enlightened," and another says, "No," that is not Reality.

An old man once came here and asked about me: "Do you think Sokei-an is truly enlightened? Who knows what he really attained?" He never asked me a question or tried to prove anything because he didn't want to hear. He wanted to keep his glass diamonds.

Hsuan-chueh said: "I entreat you to prove the genuineness of my attainment." A true man, wasn't he? But, then, Hsuan-t'se was a true monk.

Hsuan-t'se replied: "My own word carries no weight. However, at Ts'ao-ch'i is the Sixth Patriarch." Sokei is Japanese for Ts'ao-ch'i. Ts'ao-ch'i was the district where the Sixth Patriarch had his temple. My teacher gave me the name Sokei-an, but I am not as good as the Sixth Patriarch. He attained his enlightenment and went to T'ao-ch'i. I attained, and I came to America.

"Students are assembling there from every quarter like gathering clouds in order to receive the Dharma." Those who had attained enlightenment went and compared: "I have a ruby, and you have a ruby. I think mine is genuine. How about yours? Please, no pink glass from Second Avenue!"

"If you wish to go, I will accompany you." Then they departed.

Hsuan-chueh was not a novice. He went with a long cane with six brass rings clanging on top. In this way, he walked the road to Ts'ao-ch'i. When he arrived, he entered the Master's room. Without salutation, he circled the Master three times and then stood looking at him. He was a brave monk. Then the Sixth Patriarch asked a question.

A long time ago, someone came to my house with a manuscript and said, "I came from So-and-so." I asked, "What is your name?" He said, "Roshi." Then I asked, "What are you?" He said, "A Zen master."

"How do you teach Zen?" He did not think this question was very important. "Oh," he said, "by lectures and so forth." If you can teach Zen by lectures, you can pick fish out of tree-tops, or teach boxing by correspondence! I said, "Can you speak Chinese?" "No," he said, "I'm not Chinese." He was Hindu.

It is not easy finding a Zen master. If you wish to study Zen, come to me. I will look into your eye and find out whether you know Zen or not.

Hsuan-chueh went with Hsuan-t'se to pay homage to the Master. He circled the Master three times, then stood before him holding his staff.

The Master said: "The bearing of a monk should have three thousand dignities and eighty thousand civilities. Where do you come from, honored one, that you are so overbearing?"

Hsuan-chueh answered: "Birth and death are the greatest problems, and the death of a mortal comes quickly."

The Master said: "Why not realize that which is not born, and attain that which is not quick?"

Hsuan-chueh answered: "If I realized it, it would not be born; if I attained it, it would not be quick."

The Master said: "True, true!"

Thereupon Hsuan-chueh bowed in the proper manner and promptly began to leave.

The Master said: "Are you not leaving too quickly?"

Hsuan-chueh replied: "Originally, there is no motion, so how can anything be quick?"

The Master said: "Who is he who knows there is no motion?"

Hsuan-chueh answered: "Master, you yourself are creating discrimination."

The Master said: "You have truly realized the mind of the unborn."

Hsuan-chueh said: "If it is not born, how can it have any mind?"

The Master replied: "If it has no mind, who knows it?"

Hsuan-chueh said: "Knowing also has no mind."

The Master said: "Very good. At least remain one night."

People therefore named him "One-night Chieh ('Overnight Enlightenment')." Later, he wrote "The Song of Attaining the Way," which became very popular.

SOKEI-AN SAYS:

I shall give a brief commentary on these lines.

Hsuan-chueh went with Hsuan-t'se to pay homage to the Master. He circled the Master three times, then stood before him holding his staff. As soon as he came in, without saluting, he circled the Master three times. This is an old custom in India. When the monks went to see the Master, or when they left, they would circle him three times. The Sixth Patriarch looked at Hsuan-chueh and realized his attainment, so he tested him.

The Master said: "The bearing of a monk should have three thousand dignities and eighty thousand civilities. Where do you come from, honored one, that you are so overbearing?" From the time of Shakyamuni, monks have been observing many commandments. The etiquette of the "three thousand dignities and eighty thousand civilities" is a little exaggerated, but they did place emphasis on daily proprieties.

When I go to Japan, I go into my Master's room with Western-style trousers on and bow before him. I cannot ask him to allow me to stretch my legs. In half an hour I cannot walk! It is not like here in America—"How do you do?" and shake hands. In Japan, we bow low. In the temples the monks keep a traditional etiquette.

The Sixth Patriarch asked: "Where do you come from honored one?"—a deep question. "And why are you so overbearing?"—why are you so arrogant?

Hsuan-chueh answered: "Birth and death are the greatest problems, and the death of a mortal comes quickly. The Master said: "Why not realize that which is not born, and attain that which is not quick?"—"You have said that life is mutable, so why not attain the state that is neither in time nor in space?"

Hsuan-chueh answered: "If I realized it, it would not be born; if I attained it, it would not be quick." That is—"If I attain it, there is nothing to speak about."

The Master said: "True, true!" Thereupon Hsuan-chueh bowed in the proper manner": This is our daily etiquette. The traditional bow to the master has been handed down from generation to generation, and we continue to do so. The monk spreads his mat, kneels on his left knee, takes the foot of the master, and presses it to his brow. This is not worship. It's like shaking hands or kissing your mother. So don't think I bow down here to worship; it's just etiquette.

"And promptly began to leave." Hsuan-chueh thought: "Our interview is over, and in our conversation, he acknowledged my enlightenment, so there is nothing more to be said. My enlightenment is the same as his." But the Sixth Patriarch did not quite agree. Something more needed to be dug out of Hsuan-chueh's mind. So the Master said:

"Are you not leaving too quickly?" Hsuan-chueh replied: "Originally, there is no motion, so how can anything be quick?"—"I said goodbye as soon as I came in. From the original standpoint, all of this is motionless. To stay a million years or one moment is the same. I am not in the state of motion."

The Master said: "Who is he who knows there is no motion?" The Master drove a nail into the main point—"Who is he?" God? Man? You? I? The Universe? Or is it Universal Consciousness?

Hsuan-chueh answered: "Master, you yourself are creating discrimination."—"Don't ask me! Better ask yourself! You know it, so why ask me?" In the Zen school, this is "seizing the other's weapon and thrusting it back at him."

The Master said: "You have truly realized the mind of the unborn." The unborn is not God, man, *atman*, or consciousness. Many think this one is a state. If you conceive a center in the mind, you must conceive an *atman*, ego, or separate consciousness, but the Buddha's religion of non-ego does not accept such a viewpoint. We have consciousness, but we must destroy the idea that it is the conclusion.

Hsuan-chueh said: "If it is not born, how can it have any mind?" The Master replied: "If it has no mind, who knows it?"—"Is there anyone who is able to know it?"

This is a very deep pit. The Sixth Patriarch dug it for Hsuan-chueh, and then tried to push him into it. There is no consciousness or God in this pit, only nothingness and annihilation. If anyone swallows this, he will fall into the pit. Hsuan-chueh was certainly a monk who had attained.

Hsuan-chueh said: "Knowing also has no mind." This consciousness is also not consciousness. This is an extremely important point in Buddhism. It is the so-called "hairpin-turn recognition of Buddha." To go to Fishkill, you have to go on such-and-such a road. If you miss the hairpin turn, you will not get there. Without this hairpin turn, we cannot attain.

This is the subjective view. The annihilated state is subjective, and the subjective state ends there. Then everything turns into the objective view. If you attain the state of annihilation, you must annihilate that state also, and then you will see clearly.

The Master said: "Very good. At least remain one night." This is very nice, but such conversation is not really necessary in Zen. In the morning we say, "Good morning," and in the evening we say, "Good night." It is very significant—if we know what we mean. In the morning, you come from darkness, and now it is light. In the evening, you come from light, and now there is darkness. You must annihilate both darkness and light.

People therefore named him "One-night Chieh ('Overnight Enlightenment')." Chieh means "Profound Enlightenment."

Later, he wrote "The Song of Attaining the Way," which became very popular. The song is very popular among Zen people. Sometime I will translate it. The poem is not very long, and there would be nothing to comment upon. It is all written out.

The Ch'an monk Chih-huang first studied under the Fifth Patriarch. He thought he had attained true samadhi. *He lived in a hut and had practiced meditation a full twenty years.*

Hsuan-t'se, a disciple of the Patriarch, reached Ho-pei during a pilgrimage, and having heard of the fame of Chih-huang, visited him in his hut and questioned him: "What is it you do here?"

Chih-huang said, "I go into samadhi."

Hsuan-t'se asked: "You say you go into samadhi. *Do you go into it with or without your mind? If you go into samadhi without your mind, all insentient things, even trees and plants and stones, must attain* samadhi. *If you go into* samadhi *with your mind, all sentient beings, all that has consciousness, must attain* samadhi."

Chih-huang said, "When I go into samadhi, *I am not aware whether I have any mind or not."*

Hsuan-t'se said: "Not being aware whether you have any mind or not is eternal samadhi. *How can there be any 'going into' or 'coming out?' If there is any going into or coming out, it is not complete* samadhi."

Chih-huang had no reply. For a while he remained silent.

SOKEI-AN SAYS:

Zen is a sect of Buddhism. In India, it was a type of yoga school called Dhyana, meaning meditation or contemplation. This sect in India placed emphasis upon meditation, while other Buddhist sects placed emphasis on commandments, philosophical discourses, and rituals.

The Ch'an monk Chih-huang first studied under the Fifth Patriarch. Chih-huang visited the Fifth Patriarch, who was then living in Huang-mei, on the northern shore of the Yangtse River opposite Nanking. There was a mountain called East Mountain, and the Fifth Patriarch was living there. Chih-huang went to pay homage to the Fifth Patriarch and stayed there awhile, but he did not become a disciple.

He thought he had attained true samadhi. *Samadhi* appears many times in the sutras of Buddhism. European scholars usually translate the word as "concentration," but this is not accurate. *Samadhi* is the *climax* to concentration on an object or a thought—a subjective object. But Buddhists think that mind or thought is also objective. Drawing a line between the objective and subjective in Buddhism is impossible.

To a Buddhist, everything that exists inside or outside is objective. The subjective is purely the state of nothingness—potential nothingness. And all potentialities are in this nothingness—like your ether.

You stand there as a being—not necessarily a human being—and concentrate on a thought, an object, mind, or outer phenomena. When the outer and the inner become fused, that state is called *samadhi*. When the moth jumps into the flame, this brings an end to moth and flame. This is the realization of samadhi—complete contact and complete unity.

In some sutras there are about 500 different types of samadhi. There is the samadhi of the lion, of the snake, etc. When a man concentrates into the lion thought, he himself, with his mind, completely becomes a lion. There was a Japanese artist named Sosen who painted nothing but monkeys. He lived with them and lived like them, until he finally understood their thought. Then he took his brush in hand and painted them as they stood behind him and criticized his work. He was always in monkey-samadhi.

There are many kinds and degrees of samadhi. When Chih-huang thought he had attained true samadhi, he meant the highest fundamental samadhi.

He lived in a hut and had practiced meditation a full twenty years. Many monks, even in this civilized twentieth century, practice meditation for twenty or twenty-five years. It is the usual thing in Buddhism.

When Dr. Goddard of Vermont went to China to promulgate Christianity, he saw a little monk sitting in meditation on a cliff, and noticed the rotting food beside him that had been offered to him by the farmers. Ten years later, he passed the same place again and saw the monk meditating on the same corner of the same cliff. I think he was impressed. His Christian faith became very shaky after that.

Hsuan-t'se, a disciple of the Patriarch, reached Ho-pei during a pilgrimage": Ho-pei was north of the Yellow River. *Ho* means Yellow River and *pei* means northern. Hsuan-t'se, the Sixth Patriarch's disciple, traveled all over China as a pilgrim, as monks are still doing today. Japanese monks are going to China, and Tibetan monks are going to Japan.

At the mouth of the Yangtse River is an island covered with many temples filled with Japanese and Chinese monks. When the Japanese invaded this spot, they found many Japanese monks there. The Abbot said: "Oh, you're soldiers. What side? Oh, Japanese! Come in!" No enemy there.

And having heard of the fame of Chih-huang, visited him in his hut. He questioned Chih-huang: "What is it you do here?" Not a very polite question!

There were two different schools of Zen in China at that time, the Northern School and the Southern School. The Northern School placed emphasis on meditation. They annihilated all states of consciousness and kept themselves in an unconscious state. They thought they were one with all the universe in this *samadhi*. The Sixth Patriarch, the originator of the Southern School of Zen, was different. He thought that long meditation was useless, that it was like an insect or an animal hibernating through the winter.

Our center of consciousness is this intellect, the power of knowing. Without it, we cannot do anything, so we need to know it. Though you are in nirvana, if you do not know it, it is of no value. But if you are in the state of nirvana for one moment and know it, it is the highest attainment. The Sixth Patriarch placed emphasis on the power of knowing.

This is very important to you.

Chih-huang said, "I go into samadhi." *Hsuan-t'se asked: "You say you go into* samadhi. *Do you go into it with or without your mind?"*—"Do you go into *samadhi* with your awareness?"

When you were in your mother's bosom, you were in *samadhi* without awareness. But awareness, which is consciousness, was already there in that latent state. All this earth is insentient, isn't it? Earth, fire, water, and air are nothing but insentient objects, but the sentient soul is within them.

There was a long-running discussion in England about whether or not the seed of life came from another star. When I was in Tokyo, this question was debated for two or three years in an English magazine. It is a deep question.

"If you go into samadhi *without your mind, all insentient things, even trees and plants, and stones must attain samadhi."* This is why samadhi is so wonderful. Even pebbles, bricks and rubbish attain samadhi.

"If you go into samadhi with your mind, all sentient things, all that has consciousness, must attain samadhi." Attaining samadhi means nothing without knowing it. That is the point.

Chih-huang said, "When I go into samadhi, *I am not aware whether I have any mind or not."* Good answer, too!

When I go into and come out of *samadhi*, I do not pay any attention to whether I have consciousness or not. Why do I have to pay attention to it, or introspect it? It is always with me. It is like having a nose, isn't it? Whether you pay attention to it or not, it will not go away. A good answer.

Hsuan-t'se said: "Not being aware whether you have any mind or not is eternal samadhi. *How can there be any 'going into' or 'coming out?'"* The eternal samadhi is the usual, everyday samadhi—get up, eat, put your shoes on, and scratch your back. This everyday samadhi is good; it is the *samadhi* of the human being.

When you eat breakfast, do you think you are going into the *"samadhi* of eating breakfast?" And when you are through eating, do you think you are coming out of *samadhi*? Hsuan-t'se's statement is very important.

"If there is any going into or coming out, it is not complete samadhi." Where is there to go? There is no place to go—or come out of. There is no space or time in *samadhi*. If we talk about it, horizontally or otherwise, it is just picturesque. There is no way to describe it in pictures or words.

Chih-huang had no reply. For a while he remained silent. Without a word, Chih-huang thought he could convey his idea to Hsuan-t'se. This type of silence is not deep meditation or high attainment. When you say "d-e-e-p" or "h-i-g-h-e-s-t" meditation, it is just speech. His was just a real *samadhi*. Chih-huang realized that Hsuan-t'se was not a mere monk, that he had certainly attained something.

When you live in a little village in a corner of the world, with two or three acres of land, you think it means nothing. But when you give it up and go to the city, after a while you think: "Yes, I had a little corner of land and a little bungalow. I can't make a living here, so I will return." After wandering for a time, you return home and find *samadhi*. You settle down and say "Good morning" and "Good evening." Someone might say: "Why practice meditation? Why believe in Buddhism or any other religion? We should wipe out all superstitions, monks, and relics. Then we can just eat, sleep, and work."

Is this the highest *samadhi*? This will be answered in the next commentary.

Then Chih-huang questioned Hsuan-t'se: "Whose successor are you?"
Hsuan-t'se said, "My teacher is the Sixth Patriarch of Ts'ao-ch'i."
Chih-huang said, "How does the Sixth Patriarch regard Ch'an samadhi?"
Hsuan-t'se replied: "My Master teaches that Ch'an samadhi *is marvelously transparent and perfectly tranquil. In it, body and function are one; the five shadows of mind are originally empty; the six dusts of sensation have no real existence; there is neither going into nor coming out, neither being disturbed nor being tranquil. The nature of Ch'an* samadhi *is non-abiding, even beyond abiding in Ch'an* samadhi. Ch'an

samadhi is non-arising and beyond even giving rise to the notion of Ch'an samadhi. *Mind is like the empty sky, but not limited by the notion of the empty sky."*

Hearing this, Chih-huang immediately went to see the Master.

SOKEI-AN SAYS:

Hsuan-t'se, a disciple of the Sixth Patriarch, traveled all over China visiting many famous Buddhists. When he arrived in Northern China, he met Chih-huang. Chih-huang had been practicing meditation for twenty years. The conversation between Chih-huang and Hsuan-t'se was translated and explained in the last lecture. For the sake of visitors tonight, I shall read a passage from that translation:

Chih-huang said, "When I go into samadhi, *I am not aware whether I have any mind or not." Hsuan-t'se said: "Not being aware whether you have any mind or not is eternal* samadhi. *How can there be any 'going into' or 'coming out?' If there is any going into or coming out, it is not complete* samadhi." I shall speak of this.

Samadhi can be a synonym for the word "yoga," meaning to make complete contact. So in meditation, your inside and outside will be a complete unity, and you then grasp *samadhi*. After this, it will be explained by positive and negative.

With explanations like these, there will be misunderstandings. Many reject the physical body because they erroneously consider it sinful and unclean. But there is no truth in that conception. You accept your spiritual self because you think it is Reality—True Being. Then you try to grasp it, but you fail to grasp it because there is nothing you can grasp. You find yourself a failure because you divided one thing into two hypothetical existences. You observe Reality through analysis. You must take a synthetic view, and observe the whole thing at once without cutting it in two.

In meditation, the outside and the inside completely merge, and you grasp Reality. So you must wipe out all words. You must not borrow any symbol from the outside. You must practice meditation with what you have, the physical body and its extension: 1) The six dusts of sensation—the five senses and the mind, with the addition of inner phenomena such as dreams and thoughts. 2) The five shadows of mind—*rupa, vedana, samskara, samjna,* and *vijnana.* And 3) the four great elements—earth, water, fire and air, with an added fifth, ether.

This is your property, and it is enough for meditation. So before you practice meditation, you must agree with me that you do not need any other property in your brain. Abandon all words and you will return to the true entity.

When you meditate on that which is your own, you will grasp *samadhi*, and your inside and the outside will merge, and you will be in complete unity with the universe. Then you can return to words and symbols if you want to talk about it.

Before *samadhi*, if you try to explain it by a human word, you do not know what you are talking about. It's as if you were to talk of New York City: "Oh yes! Fifth Avenue, Sixth Avenue, Eleventh Avenue—Broadway crosses at Eleventh Avenue!" It sounds foolish.[21]

Then Chih-huang questioned Hsuan-t'se: "Whose successor are you?" Hsuan-t'se said, "My teacher is the Sixth Patriarch of Ts'ao-ch'i." In Zen, the transmission of attainment is very important. We do not attain our enlightenment from written scriptures or from teachers; it is from our own experience—*This is That!* Then you must make sure your experience is true.

To test your enlightenment, you must meet someone who has already experienced enlightenment. When you go to him and talk of your experience, you will probably explain it to him philosophically. Then he will just say: "Hush! If you have attained, what is this . . . ?"

You answer to prove whether your attainment is true or not. So you must meet someone who has already experienced and who will give you his acknowledgment: "I agree with you. I have experienced the same, and my teacher has experienced the same, and his teacher before him, and so on back to Bodhidharma and the Buddha." You cannot describe it in words, for there is nothing to talk about. The transmission is from eye to eye, heart to heart, and soul to soul. That is enough to really meet each other.

Hsuan-t'se said he was the disciple of Ts'ao-ch'i, the name of the territory in which the Sixth Patriarch was living. Ancient students traveled thousands of miles in search of masters. Today, in our materialistically convenient world, our minds have become like feathers—very light. This modern mind is spoiled and unable to engage in anything profound.

Chih-huang said, "How does the Sixth Patriarch regard Ch'an samadhi?*"* He does not understand the true Zen way, but it cannot be helped because he had not yet met any true Zen master.

Hsuan-t'se replied: "My Master teaches that Ch'an samadhi *is marvelously transparent and perfectly tranquil."* Like a crystal ball? If so, you can go to New Jersey and pay five dollars to a Hindu who puts a towel on his head and tells you: "In your last incarnation, you stole three chickens, and now you have three moles on your lips. To get rid of these moles, give me three chickens." Good idea!

In it, body and function are one; the five shadows of mind are originally empty": The reality of *samadhi* is exactly the same as this actual existence. The five shadows of mind are:

1) Rupa—material existence or phenomena.
2) Vedana—sense perceptions: seeing, hearing, etc.
3) Samjna—inner phenomena such as thoughts, dreams, memory, all that haunts the mind.
4) *Samskara*—a creative faculty that penetrates the subconscious with the seeds of *samjna* and moves with the movement of the subconscious. *Samskara* does not belong to you. It belongs to nature. Nature gives you seeds, which you in turn give to your children.
5) *Vijnana*—universal consciousness, so-called "vibrations"—"Oh, I went there and felt his vibrations!" You may think you have a consciousness, but this is not so. This profound, immediate consciousness is not yours. As consciousness, all is one mind. The other four shadows are differentiated, so we think we are made differently. This is the egoistic view. Each person views it through his own window and thinks it is exclusively his, but it is all one and belongs to no one. Everyone is essentially the same. We see it through the four shadows, so it appears to be different. In meditation, we must go through *vijnana* to the bottom. Originally, all are non-ego. We must meditate on each of these aspects of consciousness. When one attains Reality, there are no shadows.

". . . And the six dusts of sensation have no real existence": The six dusts are color, sound, etc. They, all the dusts of your mind, are not real. They are like a dream in which you find a one-hundred-dollar bill on the street corner, look around, put it in your pocket, and spend it. Then you wake up.

"There is neither going into nor coming out, neither being disturbed nor being tranquil." You are disturbed because you are in a dream.

"The nature of Ch'an samadhi *is non-abiding, even beyond abiding in Ch'an samadhi. Ch'an samadhi is non-arising and beyond even giving rise to the notion of Ch'an* samadhi."* You think that you attain Zen *samadhi* or that you can beget Zen *samadhi.* No, it is intrinsic. Your nature is Zen *samadhi* from the beginningless beginning. Before father and mother, your aspect was the *state* of not being born, not the concept of not being born.

"Mind is like the empty sky, but not limited by the notion of the empty sky." He does not mean that you must be stupid, but that you must be like the empty sky. All of the Orient is following this conception. Keep your mind clean. It is not necessary to say "sinless" or "sinful." Desire is a natural function. When I say keep your mind clean, what do you do? You act like this [imitates], and you fall into the view of emptiness.

Hearing this, Chih-huang immediately went to see the Master. From Ho-pei to Ts'ao-ch'i is about the distance from New York to Seattle—three thousand miles. And he didn't hitchhike, he walked!

The Master asked Chih-huang, "Where have you come from, honorable one?"

Chih-huang explained the reason for his coming.

The Master said: "It is as you have said. If you keep your mind as empty as the sky, but do not attach to the empty view, functioning freely and losing all consciousness of self both in activity and in quietude, forgetting distinctions of sacred or secular so that both objective appearance and subjective contents cease to exist, nature and form will be one, and there will be no time you are not in samadhi.*"*

Whereupon Chih-huang experienced great enlightenment, and of the mind he had attained during his twenty years [practice], no trace remained.

That night the people of Ho-pei heard a voice in the sky saying, "Today Ch'an Master Chih-huang has attained enlightenment." Later, Chih-huang took leave of the Master and returned to Ho-pei, where he instructed monks, nuns, and male and female followers.

SOKEI-AN SAYS:

This is the end of the dialogue between the Sixth Patriarch and the monk Chih-huang.

The Master asked Chih-huang, "Where have you come from, honorable one?" The Sixth Patriarch was a humble man.

Chih-huang explained the reason for his coming.—"I met your disciple, Hsuan-t'se, and we fell into discussion. He told me the definition you give to *samadhi*. I have been meditating for twenty years, and my view is so-and-so."

The Master said: "It is as you have said. If you keep your mind as empty as the sky, but do not attach to the empty view": You should keep your mind as pure and empty as the sky, and unattached to your notions. This is the usual attitude of the Buddhist. Your mind is like a well-balanced garden—many blossoms of thought will bloom. But at that moment, you can only entertain one blossom; all the other blossoms are of no use in that moment. So do not entertain those notions which grow in your mind, and do not attach to the empty view. As long as you entertain this notion, your mind is not empty yet. So do not fall into the term "emptiness." A real Buddhist will not force himself to be empty—he will not keep an empty attitude, but he is always empty as the sky.

It is like a harp string that is tense, neither fixed nor loose. Only then can the string vibrate so as to make sound. The harp is empty when the strings are tense and ready to play. When your finger plucks the string, it sounds. But if you hold the string, it will never sound. If you fix in your mind the notion of emptiness, the strings of your heart are not free. So, in Buddhism, you must be careful not to be a dilettante.

"Functioning freely and losing all consciousness of self both in activity and in quietude": It is very important to practice this everyday with a Zen attitude.

When your mind is kept empty, you naturally use yourself freely like a child, without self-consciousness or acting. When you grow up, you are not natural. You are always acting and always self-conscious. If you are tense, you cannot catch a ball, but if you keep your mind empty, you will catch it.

Be naive and simple like a child. Do not act all the time. But in meditation, you think of a million things—your skin itches!—and you cannot be quiet. You must lose the consciousness of self, both in activity and quietude.

"Forgetting distinctions of sacred or secular": A black stone never thinks it is black, or a white stone that it is white. Sacred man, secular man, they are man. That is all. Do not bother thinking with these words.

"So that both objective appearance and subjective contents cease to exist, nature and form will be one": When I was seventeen years old, a student who was studying law taught me four words: subjective, objective, abstract, and concrete. I fell into sickness when I heard those words, so I entered the monastery at the age of twenty.

Objective appearance and subjective contents do not exist. They are merely two notions for the same thing. As long as you entertain these two notions—these two philosophical terms—you will never see Reality. These notions will cease in your empty mind. In that moment, you will realize that mind and body are one and the same thing.

"And there will be no time you are not in samadhi." You go to a mountain retreat and continually meditate within your own consciousness. You think you are in a high place—in the transcendental world—only you are not in the transcendental world. These notions are a fiction; it is a novel written in your own mind. And in your novel, you are sacred, but you are not sacred. These notions are forgotten in true *samadhi*. When you realize that, there is no need to call yourself either sacred or profane. You will transcend these notions and become a real man. If you are a monk, you will observe the law of the monk. If you are a secular man, you will observe the law of the secular man.

It is not necessary to meditate from morning to evening—*you are always in* samadhi. It is not necessary to keep the posture of meditation. When you walk or when you sit, you are always in *samadhi*. This is true samadhi.

Whereupon Chih-huang experienced great enlightenment, and of the mind he had attained during his twenty years [practice], no trace remained. He had closed his eyes and meditated twenty years like a snake under the winter ground. Many think this is the highest attainment. But if it is the highest attainment, why should we seek the highest attainment? The Sixth Patriarch's viewpoint here was different from that of the Buddha.

That night the people of Ho-pei heard a voice in the sky saying, "Today Ch'an Master Chih-huang has attained enlightenment." Later, Chih-huang took leave of the Master and returned to Ho-pei, where he instructed monks, nuns, and male and female followers. Chih-huang was in Canton, and people on the bank of the Yellow River heard it from the sky. Not today!

The description is very mysterious. It is just a description of *dharmakaya*, a description of omnipresence. Just the type of description you will understand.

A monk questioned the Master: "Who is he who has attained the mystery of Huang-mei's teaching?"

The Master said, "One who knows Buddhism would attain it."

The monk said, "Has your Reverence attained it?"

The Master said, "I do not know Buddhism."

SOKEI-AN SAYS:

This monk could have heard that Chih-huang had attained enlightenment when he paid a visit to the Sixth Patriarch, so he asked the Master a question.

"Who is he who has attained the mystery of Huang-mei's teaching?" The Master said, "One who knows Buddhism would attain it." If you read all the sutras, can you attain it? If you meditate twenty years, can you attain it? If you know true Buddhism, can you attain it?

The monk said, "Has your Reverence attained it?" He asked a very foolish question, but he was not an entirely blind monk. He knew that the Sixth Patriarch had attained.

The Master said, "I do not know Buddhism." He had meditated a long time, and he did not know Buddhism. To those who have attained, there is no Buddhism, there is no religion. Religion has ceased to exist. From morning to evening, we wake up, stretch, pat the cat's head, put our feet in our slippers, and work hard all day. From morning to evening, we are always in the religious life. So there is only this life. There is no other.

You may ask: "Then why do you wear those robes?" Why does a soldier wear his uniform on the battlefield? The uniform does not fight the battle.

When I put these robes on, I reach to that religion which is like the empty sky. That is true salvation. I offer you such a religion, to save your mind and give you comfort so that you will find your own salvation.

One day the Master wanted to wash the robe that had been handed down to him [by Hung-jen], but he failed to find a clear stream nearby. About five li from the back of the temple, he found a dense woodland, with cool and balmy air. The Master thrust his staff into the ground, and where he touched it, water sprang out, forming a pond. He then knelt and washed his robe.

All of a sudden, a monk appeared upon a rock and bowed to the Master.

The monk said: "I am Fang-pien, a native of Szechwan. Yesterday, I met Bodhidharma in the southern part of India. He urged me: 'Return quickly to China. Both the Eye of the True Dharma and the sanghati robe, handed down to me from Mahakashyapa, I have now transmitted to the Sixth Patriarch at Ts'ao-ch'i in Shao-chou. Go there and pay homage.' I have come a great distance. I beg you, show me the robe and bowl that my master handed down to you."

The Master showed the robe and bowl to Fang-pien. Then he asked him a question: "What is your profession?"

Fang-pien said, "I am skilled at making images in clay."

Assuming a serious expression, the Master said, "Show me your work."

Fang-pien was at a loss.

Several days later, Fang-pien made a clay image of the Master that was about seven inches high. Fang-pien had exhausted his skill upon it.

Laughing, the Master declared: "You only know how to model clay images; you do not know how to model buddha-nature." The Master stretched out his hand, patted Fang-pien's head and said: "Be forever a field of blessings for mankind."

SOKEI-AN SAYS:

Buddhism was officially accepted by the Chinese about the middle of the first century. They studied Buddhism and translated it into Chinese from the Sanskrit. That took time. Then it took about 500 years to digest it. So it was in the fifth century that Buddhism was actually transmitted to China by Indian monks.

The Chinese, through their own hearts, had faith in Buddhism, and in their own terms they talked about it; and it was so-called Ch'an—Zen. So the dominant note in Zen is the particular expression of the Chinese, which they expressed in three ways: in gesture, in silence, and in poetic terms. They did not follow the terms that were written in the scriptures. Those who made this new movement in Buddhism underwent much opposition, but after a few hundred years they established the Zen sect.

The originator of this new movement in China was Bodhidharma, a monk from India. The monks who followed him were mostly followers of the Vinaya sect. They did not belong to the philosophical school of Buddhism. They followed the commandments instead of theory. From the Vinaya sect, there is an avenue that leads very near Zen, but there is no avenue from the philosophical school. You must take a long road to come from there to Zen!

Tonight, I am translating the story of a monk who was a native of a region on the border of Western China near Tibet. He came to the temple of the Sixth Patriarch and had an interview with him. Then the Sixth Patriarch asked him a question, and he answered.

One day the Master wanted to wash the robe that had been handed down to him by [Hung-jen]. The Sixth Patriarch was attempting to wash the golden robe. This robe does not exist anymore. It was handed down from the Buddha to Mahakashyapa, from Mahakashyapa to Ananda, and so forth through twenty-seven generations to Bodhidharma, who brought it into China. Bodhidharma handed it down through six generations to the Sixth Patriarch. The Sixth Patriarch did not hand it down to anyone. It was in his temple for a long time. Today, we will not see any remnant of it.

But he failed to find a clear spring nearby. Anyone can expect to fail in finding a clear spring in that country—there is no clear water! The land is without trees, a desert. It is hard to find an oasis because there is nothing but dry land, yellow earth, and muddy water. However, it is not like the deserts of Arabia or America.

About five li from the back of the temple, he found a dense woodland, with cool and balmy air. Ten years ago, we collected some money and sent it to China to repair the Sixth Patriarch's temple. The reports that came back said the money had been used, so we did something for the Sixth Patriarch. However, a gentleman who had lived in China promised me six years ago he would visit the temple. I thought it was dangerous to go without a guard. The temple was a nest of bandits, but he went anyway.

The Master thrust his staff into the ground, and where he touched it, water sprang out, forming a pond. In China and Japan, the Buddhist monk was always the one who found the well. The Sixth Patriarch realized there was subterranean water in the woodland, so he stuck his staff in.

He then knelt and washed his robe. All of a sudden, a monk appeared upon a rock and bowed to the Master. Perhaps he came down from the sky or sprang out of the earth. All of a sudden he appeared on a huge rock and bowed to the Sixth Patriarch while the Patriarch was drying his robe.

The monk said: "I am Fang-pien, a native of Szechwan." Szechwan, as I said, is near Tibet in Western China. I think you have heard the name. To go to Tibet from China is very difficult, but this monk came from Szechwan to see the Sixth Patriarch.

In Szechwan, you see the skylit teeth of wild animals, and high cliffs near a blue sky, and there they disappear.

"Yesterday, I met Bodhidharma in the southern part of India." This part of the story is very mysterious. Bodhidharma went to China and returned to India in the fifth century. The *Record of the Sixth Patriarch* takes place in the seventh century. "Yesterday, I met him." This is quite mystifying.

There are two versions of the Bodhidharma story: One is that he died in China, and the other is that he went back to India. In the first version, some monks who hated him tried to poison him four times. The fifth time he said, "They wish to kill me, so I will amuse them." He took the poison and died, and he was buried in the mountains of Honan. In the second version, a monk who was passing through the Pamir Karakorum Pass on his way to China met Bodhidharma. The patriarch was in his bare feet. In one hand he carried a sutra, and in the other he carried a shoe. The monk asked him if he was the Patriarch Bodhidharma. He said: "Yes. I have done my part, and now I am going back to India." On his arrival in China, the monk told his story. When the Chinese heard this, they opened Bodhidharma's tomb and found only one shoe.

When I was a child, I did not sleep for several nights after I heard this. I asked my teacher about it, and he said, "You are too young." The next time I asked a teacher, I was forty, and he said, "You are too young." Today, I think I understand.

It was two hundred years after the death of Bodhidharma that Fang-pien said, "I saw him!" Was it a monk's trick or was it someone else? Perhaps there were many Bodhidharmas—like the famous white horse that never died! Every time a horse died, they would substitute an identical white horse.

"He urged me: 'Return quickly to China. Both the Eye of the True Dharma and the sanghati robe handed down to me from Mahakashyapa I have now transmitted to the Sixth Patriarch at Ts'ao-ch'i in Shao-chou. Go there and pay homage.'" The Buddha transmitted to his disciple Mahakashyapa three times. First, he divided his Golden Lion's Throne and made Mahakashyapa sit next to him. Mahakashyapa was an ascetic, a very strict ascetic. Everyone laughed at him when he entered the *sangha*, but the Buddha divided his seat with him. This throne was not made of gold, nor was it in the form of a lion. It was just the name of the place where the Buddha sat. Wherever it was, it was called the Golden Lion's Throne.

The second time was when the Buddha twirled the blue lotus flower and remained silent for a time. No one understood, but Mahakashyapa smiled. The Buddha said: "I have transmitted the Dharma. Uphold it. Do not let it be lost to posterity." It was upheld in India for twenty-eight generations, in China for twenty-nine generations, and in Japan for twenty-six generations. The mystery of the esoteric teaching handed down from the Buddha, generation after generation, is still in existence. It is not written in books or spoken in words. Therefore, it is called the mystery of the esoteric teachings.

And thirdly, when the Buddha died, the Buddha's coffin was put on top of a pile of wood, but the wood would not catch fire. Mahakashyapa, living at a distance, ran five days and nights to be by the Buddha's side. When he arrived, the fire burst from the Buddha's heart.

"I have come a great distance. I beg you, show me the robe and bowl that my master handed down to you." The Buddha—I mean here Shakyamuni—handed down to his great disciple, Mahakashyapa, three things: the mystery of the esoteric teachings, the sanghati robe, and the bowl. The bowl was taken to China, and then to Japan. I saw this bowl. I doubt it was the same one. Of course, the Buddha handed down two or three robes.

As for the esoteric teachings: When Mahakashyapa was dying, he went to the top of Rooster Peak Mountain—it was one of two rocks that looked just like the feet of a rooster—and in a cave, he entered the *samadhi* of annihilation. He annihilated his mind and entered nirvana. His flesh and bones were reduced to ashes and scattered to the winds. In his meditation, he held the golden robe handed to him by the Buddha. This golden robe exists and can be seen, if you have the eye to see it. If you meet the Buddha in the deep *samadhi* of annihilation, you will understand what this golden robe is.

The Master showed the robe and bowl to Fang-pien. Then he asked him a question: "What is your profession?" Fang-pien said, "I am skilled at making images in clay." You may think Buddhist monks only meditate in temples and do nothing, but this is only your imagination. We do many things. Each monk has his own profession. If there is among us a monk who is a good cook or has a beautiful voice, he is invited from temple to temple. Some of us play instruments, others may study some particular part of Buddhism, such as radical Buddhism. We have famous poets, painters, judges, and actors. I studied primitive Buddhism, Zen, and sculpture. Fang-pien made clay images.

Zen is a large ocean, so I studied koans. In sculpture, I began by studying Buddhist, Egyptian, and Greek images, then nature and nudes, till I returned to carving Buddha.

Assuming a serious expression the Master said, "Show me your work." Fang-pien was at a loss. He did not understand the true meaning of the Sixth Patriarch's words.

When I was young, my teacher asked me: "How many years have you been studying sculpture?" I said, "About six years." He said, "Carve me a buddha." It took me about fifteen days to carve the buddha. When I showed it to him, he said, "What is this?" and he threw it out the window and into the pond. It seemed unkind, but it was not meant to be. He meant for me to carve the Buddha in myself. So the Sixth Patriarch said to Fang-pien, "Show me your work!"

If he worships the image carved in wood, that is idol worship—not this real self. You must find the real self first. That was in the Sixth Patriarch's mind when he said, "Show me your work!" And that is also why Fang-pien was at a loss.

Several days later, Fang-pien made a clay image of the Master that was about seven inches high. Fang-pien had exhausted his skill upon it. The Chinese are marvelous clay modelers. When I went to Northern China, I saw many clay buddhas here and there, especially in the temples of Lamaism. In these temples, the clay images are very big and are usually painted. The old ones give the temples very beautiful atmospheres—the colors have come off, beaten by rain drops.

In China, many places produce this clay, but in Japan, there is no clay to be used; it is a country of misty weather, and clay does not keep a long time. If you find any clay image from the T'ang dynasty today, it would be very dear. A clay image seven inches high would bring about $50,000 in American money, easily. I saw one painted in soft pale colors from the Sung dynasty at the Yamanaka Company. It was very beautiful.

It is said the Buddha had thirty-three holy signs throughout his body. His eyebrows were small and round like crescent moons. His eyes were calm and moved like lotus leaves, and on the surface of each fingertip and toe was a whirlpool of rings. Those disciples who were enlightened could see all thirty-three holy signs, but those who were unenlightened only saw thirty-two. This last sign, which was the symbol of Buddha, was hidden from the eyes of the unenlightened.

This is a famous story. Perhaps Fang-pien knew of it and realized the Sixth Patriarch's question had a profound meaning. This story, of course, is nothing but legendary talk. The true meaning is that Reality is intangible. With the physical eye we see phenomena, but we cannot see Reality. The Buddha's highest holy sign is invisible. This is the philosophy told of in the legend.

The Sixth Patriarch said to Fang-pien, "Make my image!" Fang-pien did not know how to answer. He wasn't an entirely bright monk.

Laughing, the Master declared: "You only know how to model clay images, you do not know how to model buddha-nature." Fang-pien succeeded in making the image of the Sixth Patriarch, but he failed to portray his buddha-nature. When you practice *sanzen*, you are carving out the buddha-nature in yourself. The ancient monks said: "When you practice meditation one minute, you are a one-minute Buddha; and when you practice meditation one hour, you are a one-hour Buddha." This Buddha is, of course, a conclusion. You should not just swallow this conclusion. If you do, you will not be able to digest it. Go to the bottom first, and find out what those ancient Zen masters meant.

The Master stretched out his hand, patted Fang-pien's head and said: "Be forever a field of blessings for mankind." In the margin of this part of the text, several lines are printed:

"The Master then rewarded him with his robe"—not the robe handed down to him from the foregoing teacher, but the one he was wearing—"which Fang-pien divided into three pieces. The first, he used to wrap the clay image; the second, he kept for himself; the third, he wrapped in palm leaves and buried, vowing: 'Later, when this robe is found, I shall appear in the world as abbot of this temple, which I shall then rebuild.'"

Then it adds that about 350 years afterwards, a monk found the buried robe, and it was as new as it was 350 years before.

There was a monk who recited for the Master a gatha *of Ch'an Master Wo-lun:*

> *"Wo-lun has a gift*
> *He can make a hundred thoughts cease at once*
> *When he faces the outer world, no mind arises*
> *His enlightened wisdom grows day by day"*

Having heard this, the Master said: "This gatha still does not illuminate the bottom of the mind. If one practiced meditation according to this gatha*, he would only be binding himself with more ropes."*
The Master thereupon presented a gatha *of his own:*

> *"Hui-neng has no such gift*
> *He does not make a hundred thoughts cease at once*
> *When he faces the outer world, many minds arise in him*
> *How is his enlightened wisdom to grow?"*

SOKEI-AN SAYS:

Zen, in the ocean of Buddhism, is a school or sect that expresses Buddhism's essential principles. Zen, having developed in China, took on the element of Taoism, a fact no one would deny. These two songs express the front and back of Buddhism, like the two sides of a cloth.

There was a monk who recited for the Master a gatha of Ch'an Master Wo-lun: After Bodhidharma, there were about three kinds of Buddhism: T'ien-tai, Shingon, and Zen. The monk was reciting the song made by Wo-lun.

"Wo-lun has a gift/ He can make a hundred thoughts cease at once/ When he faces the outer world, no mind arises/ His enlightened wisdom grows day by day." When he meditates, all his thoughts disappear. Then he can see his intrinsic consciousness as a mirror. When you have a mirror, you must wash it with Bon-ami and scrub it clean. But here, you run around, go to the library, go to the university, and put more things into your mind. In the end, you go to the insane asylum, like those Siberian peasants with so many clothes on that the clothes stick to their skins—the clothing cannot be removed without the skin coming off as well.

The sages of the past did not do this. First, they cleaned up their minds. Some say to me, "But Sokei-an, this will make me stupid!" Better be stupid than wise.

This song is a song of another school of Zen, a "Hinayanistic" school. There is no Mahayana in it. To suppress all thought and present "no-mind" to the world is only one side of Buddhism. Buddhism is a two-fold religion, like a handkerchief. One side cannot be separated from the other. The Buddha explained one side and transmitted the other to Mahakashyapa. When we study his teachings, we see that the Buddha had concealed another side, like the father who tells his children not to eat candy, but in his mind he says, "You can have a little." Someone asked the Buddha why he had not taught the other side, and he said, "It does not bring merit." Just as there is no merit in showing a child candy.

Having heard this, the Master said: "This gatha still does not illuminate the bottom of the mind. If one practiced meditation according to this gatha, he would only be binding himself with more ropes." The Sixth Patriarch is saying Wo-lun's song is half the truth, not all of it.

When Buddhism was carried into the Western world, the Pali scriptures from Ceylon were carried into this hemisphere. They were Hinayana Buddhism. So Buddhist scholars thought that Buddhism was entirely negative. This was their error. Before King Kanishka (an Indian king of the first century A.D.), there were no Mahayana commentaries. The commentaries that came out of King Kanishka's great assembly of five hundred leading monks were not exactly complete. They stressed that part of Buddha's Buddhism that emphasized negative aspects, suppressing other parts of the teaching.

To eradicate one's disturbed view of the world, eradicate notions, then a new and natural life will arise. When you have an ache in your stomach, you must clean it out, then you can eat again. So you must clean up your mind to correct your distorted view of the world. The positive aspect will then come naturally. It is not necessary to teach it.

But if I *were* a teacher, I would teach my students one thing: What I stand upon, I must know very clearly. If today I try this, and tomorrow I try the other, I, as a teacher, am not teaching my children the true way. If I were a general of an army, I would be clear as to the outcome. Otherwise I would not be able to command and ask this army to enter the fire of battle. In ordinary life, teachers do not see children dying. But in war we see that and the death of soldiers.

Politicians must also have a substantial realization in their minds. If the politician has no philosophy, no straight view, and his mind is in a dream, everyone will suffer terribly.

The Sixth Patriarch did not close his eye or his mind. He kept them open. His wisdom grew day by day, but he did not tell you everything.

The Master thereupon presented a gatha *of his own: "Hui-neng has no such gift/ He does not make a hundred thoughts cease at once/ When he faces the outer world, many minds arise in him/ How is his enlightened wisdom to grow?"* This completes the front and back of Buddhism. Hinayana and Mahayana are just its two names. You could say the Buddha's Buddhism is Hinayana, and the Buddhism of the bodhisattva is Mahayana, and as a layman you must study both sides. You must go to the top of the mountain, and then come down again. So do not think that Buddhism is just negative without the positive aspect.

There is an interesting koan: A monk said to a Zen master, "When I and you and you and I are enlightened, what shall we do?" The Zen master said, "We shall like skylarks descend from the zenith of the world to the earth." The monk said, "Where shall we go then?" The Zen master said: "I will go into the bush. You had better go to the village."

When we have studied Buddhism and meditated to find enlightenment and the Reality of the entire world, and we have been from the top to the bottom, then what shall we do? One will go to the village, and the other will go to the mountaintop.

So enlightenment is not only for monks, but for everyone. And you will choose, according to your nature, whether you will be a farmer, butcher, merchant, fisherman, or monk. So do not think that the monk's life is the highest position and the layman's the lowest position. That is erroneous. We must discover Reality first. Then we, in the actuality of the world, can choose. I will carry people from the foot of the mountain to the top, and from the top to the foot. You will carry people from the foot of the mountain to the ocean.

To understand human life—if you wish to live substantially and honestly—you must understand the two sides of the world: the actual side and the real side. On the actual side, you have black, gold, and vermillion. But this is not the real world we are living in. We are living in a world where there is no color at all. It is the world of Reality. From this world you are carried back into this actual temporal state. Then you know what it is, and it will not disturb you.

Nothingness must be attained once, thoroughly and truly in your own experience. How to attain it is the problem. There is no one particular way. There are many ways, but you must attain it once.

CHAPTER VIII

SUDDEN AND GRADUAL

At that time, the Patriarch was in Ts'ao-ch'i at the Pao-lin monastery, and the great Master Shen-hsiu was in Ching-nan at the Yu-ch'uan temple. Both schools were flourishing, spreading their teachings. People called them Southern Neng and Northern Hsiu. Consequently, [the Ch'an sect] split into two schools, the Southern and the Northern, the schools of Sudden Enlightenment and Gradual Enlightenment. Students, however, failed to grasp the essential principle.

The Master told the monks of the assembly: "Although man is either southern or northern, the Dharma is originally one. Although the Dharma is one, realization is sudden or gradual. What is meant by sudden and gradual? In the Dharma there is no sudden or gradual; man is simply swift or slow [in attaining it]. Hence, we speak of 'sudden' and 'gradual.'"

The followers of Shen-hsiu, however, despised the patriarch of the Southern school. "He can't read even a single character," they said, "what is there to admire?"

Shen-hsiu told them: "He attained wisdom without a teacher and has a profound realization of the highest vehicle. I am not to be compared with him. My master, the Fifth Patriarch, personally transmitted to him the robe and the Dharma. How could he have done so without good reason? I regret that I am so far away that I cannot go personally to receive his instruction. I am undeserving of the emperor's patronage. All of you, do not tarry here. Go to Ts'ao-ch'i and solve your problems!"

SOKEI-AN SAYS:

The Fifth Patriarch had two eminent disciples: one was Shen-hsiu and the other was Hui-neng. Shen-hsiu was a learned man and a philosopher, but Hui-neng was a manual laborer and an illiterate. He sold kindling wood in the town of Hsin-chou in Southern China. Enlightenment, therefore, does not always reveal itself in the mind of a scholar. In fact, one who has a simple and pure mind can attain enlightenment more easily than one who always reasons about everything and is always gathering knowledge. To say it another way: one who is near nature attains enlightenment with more ease than one who has an artificial mind.

In Buddhism, we use the term "enlightenment"; but you in Christianity say, "God will reveal Himself." If you think of God as invented by human knowledge or as having such attributes as hands, arms and legs, a tail, or as vomiting fire, and dancing in midair, you will never attain enlightenment.

When your mind is pure and simple, when you are not sleeping or dreaming, when your mind is tense while thinking of nothing, all of a sudden you will come close to enlightenment. It may happen that while sitting on a bench on Riverside Drive, looking out over the Hudson River shining like silver on a rainy evening, your mind becomes one with the universe, and you are aware of it. In that moment of awareness, you touch the universal vibration, and you understand the meaning of God. If you are always sleeping, you will never have this opportunity, so you must strive to attain it. If you strive every day and think about it every day, in a few years, at some psychological moment, you will be thrown into it. Then, to make sure of your experience, you must go to someone who has had this experience. After that, you must live in it always.

At that time, the Patriarch was in Ts'ao-ch'i at the Pao-lin monastery, and the great Master Shen-hsiu was in Ching-nan at the Yu-ch'uan temple. Both schools were flourishing, spreading their teachings. People called them Southern Neng and Northern Hsiu. Consequently, [the Ch'an sect] split into two schools, the Southern and the Northern, the schools of Sudden Enlightenment and Gradual Enlightenment. Students, however, failed to grasp the essential principle. Hui-neng attained suddenly, so his sect is called the School of Sudden Enlightenment. Shen-hsiu attained enlightenment later, so they called his school the School of Gradual Enlightenment. He became the head of Yu-ch'uan Temple and was protected by the Emperor. Everyone thought he was the Sixth Patriarch, but Hung-jen, the fifth patriarch, had transmitted his Dharma and robe to the illiterate Hui-neng.

The Master told the monks of the assembly: "Although man is either southern or northern, the Dharma is originally one. Although the Dharma is one, realization is sudden or gradual. What is meant by sudden and gradual? In the Dharma there is no sudden or gradual; man is simply swift or slow [in attaining it]. Hence, we speak of 'sudden' and 'gradual.'" There are many ways of attaining enlightenment. When you attain, there is the objective state and the daily life that you are living. You return to this active life with enlightenment. Many people attain something, but it is only a delusive enlightenment. It must be tested by one who has true attainment.

Enlightenment does not always belong to those who have beautiful whiskers or wear beautiful gowns. The scholar may not always be enlightened. Sometimes an illiterate, who may not be able to write his name, is enlightened. One monk may come for two weeks and break into enlightenment; another may hold a koan for twenty years with nothing, but sooner or later he will attain. The slow one, according to his nature, attains it slowly. We do not put engines into bulls to make them swift. He may walk slowly, but someday he will arrive at the goal.

The followers of Shen-hsiu, however, despised the patriarch of the Southern school. "He can't read even a single character," they said, "what is there to admire?" The monks would say: "He's illiterate! He can't read. He's nothing but a common layman. Shen-hsiu, our teacher, is a great scholar. Perhaps the teacher of the Southern School has some enlightenment, but he can't talk about it."

This was the war between the two Zen schools. After the Sixth Patriarch's death, Shen-hui, a disciple of Hui-neng, went to the Northern School and made a great demonstration of sudden enlightenment. According to Professor Hu-shih, who is now the Chinese Ambassador to the United States, this record of the Sixth Patriarch was written by Shen-hui. He also wrote a record of his own. It was discovered about six years ago in an excavation in Tun-huang, China. Shen-hui later became the seventh patriarch, but his sect was of no importance until now.

It happens today that philosophical students of the Northern, or Gradual School, say of the Southern Zen students: "Oh, they have something, all right, but they cannot talk about it! When they come before a Zen monk, there is just one question: 'What is Buddha?' If the monk cannot answer, they knock him into the middle of next week!"

Yes, Zen must be used in every moment.

Once you have attained enlightenment, it is always with you, as Christ is always with you. When you find enlightenment once, you have it always. It does not come and go. When you see Christ, you know God. When you see Reality, you are enlightened. It is the same thing as this hand. It may have a front and a back, but it is the same hand. So when you enter into true understanding, you will always have it.

In Christianity, life after enlightenment is transubstantiation. After you attain, water is the blood of Christ, the earth is the body of Christ, and the air is the breath of Christ. You are going to live in this transubstantiated universe. From our standpoint, Christianity is essentially the same as Buddhism. If we see Christianity as different, we are not enlightened.

Shen-hsiu told them: "He attained wisdom without a teacher and has a profound realization of the highest vehicle. I am not to be compared with him." Shen-hsiu was a humble monk. Some say a disciple of Hui-neng wrote this.

"My master, the Fifth Patriarch, personally transmitted to him the robe and the Dharma." I have translated this part already in Chapter I, as you will find out when this translation is over, from the book that will be printed by my students.

"How could he have done so without good reason?" When the Fifth Patriarch, Hung-jen, called Hui-neng in the night and transmitted the robe, the bowl, and the Dharma—something unwritten—this was no common thing. When we transmit, we give a little memorandum. If we do not find a disciple, we burn up the little bit of paper. That is so-called transmission. Today, transmission is given as a receipt for your donation in building a temple!

"I regret that I am so far away that I cannot go to personally receive his instruction. I am undeserving of the emperor's patronage." The emperor was Chung-yueh. It is said the empress summoned Shen-hsiu to the palace at Ch'ang-an, and he went. When he arrived, the empress invited him into the bathing garden and attended him with a hundred beautiful maidens of the court. The bathing garden was surrounded by green trees and flowers and looked like an Arabian or Turkish bath—many nude beauties could be seen. But this is not strange today, we see it everywhere. Look at Coney Island! But then, the view was strange.

From behind a screen the empress observed him, to see how he would deport himself among the girls. Of course, you know, Shen-hsiu would not have gone there, but it is said that he did, and that he acted as if there were nobody there. The master washed his hands and toes and acted as if he was in his own monastery, surrounded by his own monks. The empress realized he was a great master. Had he said: "Terrible, terrible! Naked women!" The Empress would have said, "Put him out!" Perhaps she was the first flapper in China.

Then Shen-hsiu said:

"All of you, do not tarry here. Go to Ts'ao-ch'i and solve your problems!"

One day [Shen-hsiu] told his disciple Chih-ch'eng: "You are wise and learned. Go to Ts'ao-ch'i on my behalf and listen to the Dharma. If you should hear [Hui-neng's] teachings, do your utmost to remember them and repeat them to me when you return."

Obeying, Chih-ch'eng went to Ts'ao-ch'i and paid homage to the Master with the other monks, but he did not reveal where he had come from.

At that time, the Master addressed the multitude saying: "There is a Dharma thief here now, concealing himself among this assembly."

Chih-ch'eng came forward, bowed low, and confessed in detail why he had come.

The Master said: "You have come from Yu-ch'uan. You must be a spy!"

Chih-ch'eng answered: "I am not!"

The Master said: "How can you deny it?"

Chih-ch'eng replied: "Before I heard you preach, it was so; but having heard you now, it is so no longer."
The Master said: "What does your master teach his disciples?"

Chih-ch'eng answered: "He always teaches his disciples that they should concentrate their minds to contemplate stillness, sitting continually in meditation without lying down."

The Master said: "Concentrating one's mind to contemplate stillness is a sickness. It is not Ch'an. Sitting continually in meditation and keeping one's physical body restrained—how does this help you to [realize] the truth?"

The Master said: "Listen as I recite a gatha.

> *Though you sit in mediation, without lying down, from the time you are born*
> *Or lie down without sitting up, after you die*
> *How could you produce any merit*
> *With this bunch of stinking bones?"*

SOKEI-AN SAYS:

The Fifth Patriarch's disciple, Shen-hsiu, now master of the Northern School of Zen in China, commanded his disciple Chih-ch'eng to go south and pay homage to the Sixth Patriarch to learn the mystery of the Southern School.

One day [Shen-hsiu] told his disciple Chih-ch'eng: "You are wise and learned. Go to Ts'ao-ch'i on my behalf and listen to the Dharma. The distance from Ching-nan to Ts'ao-ch'i was about the distance from St. Louis to New York.

If you should hear [Hui-neng's] teachings, do your utmost to remember them and repeat them to me when you return." Obeying, Chih-ch'eng went to Ts'ao-ch'i and paid homage to the Master with the other monks: He entered with the multitude. Every day ten to fifteen monks would want to pay homage to the Patriarch. They came from many parts of China. From among these monks, Chih-ch'eng approached the Sixth Patriarch and paid him homage.

"But he did not reveal where he had come from." I think he was bashful and did not want to say that he was a disciple of Shen-hsiu and that he had come from Yu-ch'uan temple.

At that time, the Master addressed the multitude saying: "There is a Dharma thief here now, concealing himself among this assembly." Perhaps it was afternoon. The Patriarch took his seat to give his lecture and looked over the multitude and found him—"A stranger!" He could feel him. Where did he come from? If Shen-hsiu were insignificant, the Patriarch would not have spoken a word, he would have ignored him. Perhaps Chih-ch'eng had something in his eye or in his features that indicated that he was a thief attempting to steal his teachings.

Chih-ch'eng came forward, bowed low, and confessed in detail why he had come. The Master said: "You have come from Yu-ch'uan. You must be a spy!" Chih-ch'eng answered: "I am not!" The Master said: "How can you deny it?" Chih-ch'eng replied: "Before I heard you preach, it was so; but having heard you now, it is so no longer." Once, when I went to see a friend of mine, I said, "I came from Ryomo,"[22] and he said, "How is Ryomo today?" He tried to understand me by such questions. It's the usual thing in Buddhism.

In the Buddha's time, monks and nuns went before the Buddha and demonstrated their attainment. Once a nun stood before the Buddha and appeared in multifold directions and then disappeared in multifold directions. Then she stood before the Buddha, and her upper body disappeared into the sky, and her lower body turned to water! She went through a keyhole and walked on water—the usual thing.

Today in the Zen school, we say: "Oh, you're a Zen monk! Go into the next room without opening the door!" If he is not a Zen monk, he will be frightened, but if he is a Zen monk . . .

Or we might say—"Without using your hand, make me stand up." When I had this koan, I had a friend who went into the Zen room first, and he shouted, "Fire, fire!" He was thrown out. In Zen, this is considered making a detailed demonstration.

In Japan, a monk was once asked by a master: "Stop the train that is coming!" The monk went to the railroad track and stopped a train—he was thrown out. Another was: "Stop the sailing boat on the faraway ocean." It is pretty hard to make a demonstration. You cannot use theory.

What about—"Cut off your hand, cook it, put it on a plate, and bring it to me"?

In the Zen room, your check or paper money is of no use. You have to pay in real cash. You must grasp Reality itself. You have to use *dharmakaya* cash! Mysterious, isn't it?

When we have attained this, we do not need to do anything more. A mountain is a mountain and water is water. We do not have to meditate to say that water is water, or to pass through the keyhole. These are mere contrivances to attain Reality. After attainment, you do not need to pass through the keyhole any more.

Chih-ch'eng was not meek, as he dared to say such words before the Sixth Patriarch. When we examine the Soto School to find out whether they know anything about Zen, we find that they have swallowed everything in one gulp and have not digested it—like having an inheritance without using it.

The Master said: "What does your Master teach his disciples?" Chih-ch'eng answered: "He always teaches his disciples that they should concentrate their minds to contemplate stillness, sitting continually in meditation without lying down." This is the Northern type of Zen, and we find such contrivances today. Many monks practice this kind of meditation because they know of no other. They just sit, and sitting is all, the beginning and the end. Sitting is the entrance, and sitting is the exit. When you sit for one moment, you are Buddha for one moment. When you sit for one hour, you are Buddha for one hour. And when you realize that you are a buddha, you stand up and walk. When walking, eating—from morning to evening, buddha. Buddha is always with you after your realization. As Christ said: "Lo, I am always with you, even unto the end of the world." If they can attain in this way, it is good. But the trouble is that they just sit.

In the Southern School of Zen, when we meditate, we concentrate ourselves upon that focus, but meditation is not the main point. To *strike that focus* is the main point. So we can stand and meditate; we can meditate anywhere. We meditate working in the garden, in the kitchen.

The Northern School is negative, and the Southern School is positive. The Northern School is gradual, and the Southern School is sudden—like a bursting balloon! This was especially true of the Sixth Patriarch's Zen. Today, you are practicing the method of these two schools. Every Wednesday and Saturday you come here early before the lecture and meditate for a half hour. Good! It will become a habit unconsciously.

The Master said: "Concentrating one's mind to contemplate stillness is a sickness."—A Zen sickness. There are many Zen sicknesses. Some Zen students think that when they have become very active, very deep or smart, Zen caused the change. But it's only a sickness, an unsound conviction. If it's a sickness, it's not Zen.

True Zen is different. When an outsider looks at us, he never finds out we are Zen students. All he sees are plain, ordinary people. Some Zen teachers, with their fingertips touching, draw their lips down tight, as if tying a balloon. There is something affected in this, something unnatural. Another shortcoming of the Zen student appears when he becomes humorous. But we think this attitude is better than walking the street with a staff!

"It is not Ch'an."—Zen.

"Sitting continually in meditation and keeping one's physical body restrained—how does this help you to [realize] the truth?" There are many schools of sitting—"Breathe from the right corner of the nose, then from the other." This is a type of exercise that fools people. I do not waste my time exercising in such ways.

The Master said: "Listen as I recite a gatha.

Though you sit in mediation, without lying down, from the time you are born/ Or lie down without sitting up, after you die/ How could you produce any merit/ With this bunch of stinking bones?" The Buddha taught his disciples that one should observe two important practices to attain wisdom: the first is to observe commandments; the second is to practice meditation. The third, of course, was to attain enlightenment. By observing the commandments, one will attain quietude: one's physical and mental bodies will not run amuck. Secondly, in this quiet mind, one can concentrate upon the great question: What is soul? And, awakening into this soul, attain enlightenment.

When I was young, I met an old monk from a small village in the northern country of Japan. He was the abbot of the village temple and had no fame; yet, his teaching helped me very much. Once he said to me: "You must meditate symbolically. Your physical body is a symbol of the earth; keep it quiet. Do not create an earthquake with your physical body. Second, your mind is a symbol of water; keep it smooth. Do not make a storm out of it. Third, your emotion is a symbol of fire; control it. Do not make a conflagration out of it. Fourth, your will power, which corresponds to samskara, is a symbol of air; keep it tense, but do not make a tornado out of it. Fifth, your alaya-consciousness is a symbol of ether, which is like interstellar space; it must be transcended. You will attain enlightenment when these five great elements are in one *samadhi*."

This is a true yoga. Keeping your physical body quiet, without the cessation of mental disturbance, you will not attain enlightenment. Of course, if someone attains enlightenment in the middle of a battlefield or on a stormy ocean or in a fire, it is because he has been practicing this true concentration, and it burst out in that moment of intense activity.

Bowing again, Chih-ch'eng said: "For nine years I studied under Master Shen-hsiu, but did not attain enlightenment. Now, hearing your words only once, I have instantly realized original mind. For me, life and death is the most profound question. In your great compassion, please instruct me further."

The Master said: "I have heard that your master instructs his disciples in shila, samadhi, *and* prajna. *I wonder what form the practice of* shila, samadhi, *and* prajna *takes according to your teacher. Explain it to me."*

Chih-ch'eng said: "The great master Shen-hsiu says: 'To commit no evil is shila. *To practice all virtue is* prajna. *To purify your mind is* samadhi.' *This is what he teaches. I wonder, how do you teach?"*

The Master replied: "If I claimed I had a teaching to give people, I would be deceiving you. I simply free people from their bonds, according to their circumstances, and provisionally designate this as samadhi. *Your master's* shila, samadhi, *and* prajna *are truly unthinkable. My* shila, samadhi, *and* prajna *are different."*

Chih-ch'eng said: "There is only one kind of shila, samadhi *and* prajna. *How is it possible for [yours] to be different?"*

SOKEI-AN SAYS:

In the previous part, Chih-ch'eng, the disciple of Shen-hsiu, the master of the Northern School, told the Sixth Patriarch that his teacher always instructed his disciples to meditate for long periods of time. The Sixth Patriarch criticized this, saying that meditation without rest is an ailment and not a sound teaching. After this, he recited a *gatha*.

Bowing again, Chih-ch'eng said: "For nine years I studied under Master Shen-hsiu, but did not attain enlightenment." He is talking very badly of Shen-hsiu. If you read the Northern sect's record, you will see that Shen-hsiu was not a bad master.

"Now, hearing your words only once, I have instantly realized original mind." Hui-neng said that meditation is not needed; you can attain enlightenment in a moment. This is true, but you must concentrate on your own personal question.

When I was a boy, I was looking at a lotus pond in autumn. All the petals of the lotus were brown and the leaves and stems were dying. The whole scene was really very beautiful. I would not have put in or taken out a single stem. I bowed down to nature and tried to understand. I thought if I could solve that, I would know something. This question haunted my mind for a long time. One day, I went out to sketch with my easel and palette. I made the colors, looked, and tried, but I simply could not work. That was when I gave up art and entered a Zen monastery. There I found the answer to the question that opened the gate. I did not care for art anymore. When I understood, art no longer lured me. Art did not matter.

"For me, life and death is the most profound question. In your great compassion, please instruct me further." One should know what death is and what life is, and one should be enlightened. Enlightenment is important.

In this Western country, people say, "If only I knew the will of God, I would not commit this offense." Then why not strive to understand God's will? If one knew, one would be a soothsayer, a messenger of the oracle, a sage!

The Master said: "I have heard that your master instructs his disciples in shila, samadhi, *and* prajna. *I wonder what form the practice of* shila, samadhi, *and* prajna *takes according to your teacher. Explain it to me."* Chih-ch'eng said: "The great master Shen-hsiu says: 'To commit no evil is shila. To practice all virtue is prajna. To purify your mind is samadhi.' This is what he teaches. I wonder, how do you teach?" There was a Zen master whose name was Niao-k'e. People called him Bird's Nest because he lived in a tree. He went about the village begging for food and returned to the tree to eat, to drink, and to meditate. In the evenings, he slept there. It was his home. The governor at that time was a famous poet by the name of Pai Le-t'ien. He was also a Zen student. Having heard of the famous Zen Master Bird's Nest, he went to visit him with his subjects. Being a Chinese gentleman, he never went anywhere without his followers holding his paraphernalia. When Governor Pai Le-t'ien arrived, Bird's Nest was sitting in the tree. He had made a roof over his head with foliage and had fastened branches into a seat. Leaves were his cushion. Old utensils were hung here and there. This was all of his property. Pai Le-t'ien looked up at him and said, "Your position is very dangerous." Niao-k'e opened his eye, looked down upon him and said, "Who are you?" Pai Le-t'ien replied: "I am the governor of this territory. My name is Pai Le-t'ien." Bird's Nest looked down and said, "Your position is rather dangerous!" The governor was embarrassed. He said to Bird's Nest: "I came here to beg from you a word of enlightenment. Please bestow your teaching upon me." Out of the treetop, Bird's Nest said, "Do not commit any evil, and practice all the virtues." Pai Le-t'ien said, "Even three-year-old children know that." Bird's Nest said, "Three-year-old children know it, yet the eighty-year-old man cannot practice it."

"Do not commit any evil and practice all the virtues," appears in the *Agama Sutras* as the Buddha's words. "To purify your mind is *samadhi*" covers Buddhism entirely.

Chih-ch'eng thought the words of his master words precious and wonderful.

The Master replied: "If I claimed I had a teaching to give people, I would be deceiving you. I simply free people from their bonds, according to their circumstances, and provisionally designate this as samadhi." In the Western world, there was a philosophical school called nominalism. Nominalists explain all existence as simply concepts of the human world—names. The reality that is individual has no name—something like Zen! So Hui-neng was a sort of nominalist in China.

For example, we might say we have a name for each shade of color in the rainbow, and if we were to invent more names, people would probably perceive more colors. In the beginning, there were only three colors. Later, the intermediate colors were named. Actually, there is no particular shade of color in the rainbow because all the colors blur one into the other. So the seven different colors are really only seven different names.

Take this hand for instance: why do we call it a hand and not a foot? A Zen master asked, "Why do you call a hand a hand?" There is no reason. You see the hand, you do not see reality. I call it a hand and you think it is a hand. So I say, "Cook your hand and bring it to me," and you say: "But it will hurt! How can I?" You see how names bind you? You must be freed from names to grasp Reality.

If I say to you, "Stop the sailing boat a thousand miles away," you will not be able to. There is a famous story about a feudal lord who was stuck with this koan for three years. One evening, his Zen master said, "Of course, of course, my lord, but can you stop the boat?" And the feudal lord was puzzled again. So the Zen master jumped up and threw a bowl of soup at him while the boat sailed on. He did not know Reality. You think you are meditating, but you are rotating.

My student, the Baroness, was stuck two years with her sailing boat. After the two years, her sailing boat began to sail, so I gave her the name "Jeweled Sailing Boat." It certainly was a big boat! And when she finds Reality, she will find it valuable.

The Sixth Patriarch said he gave deliverance to everyone according to their circumstances. But everyone hides the mind in invisible words, and then cannot find it. They argue and dispute over words, mere words, in a scholastic and pedantic way. No one cares for the *reality* of those words. If I wish to do something, everyone tells me I have no moral right, so I cannot do it. These things are in men's minds.

Hui-neng says he designates everything provisionally, therefore all names are provisional. I call IT *dharmakaya*, and occasionally I call it *sambhogakaya* or *nirmanakaya*. Call it by any name, it is just an empty name.

"Your master's shila, samadhi, *and* prajna *are truly unthinkable. My* shila, samadhi, *and* prajna *are different."* In the Zen school for example, *shila* is a great study. Your first commandment is: "You shall not kill." What does this mean? In a sutra it is written that agnosticism kills everything that is living. Reality is a living being. Can you conceive of killing everything? The Zen student's understanding of this is the result of his own effort. So if you think you can kill, you will fall into agnosticism.

"You shall not steal": Nothing belongs to anyone; everything belongs to everyone. The idea of possession is stealing. So, if you wish to have something, you are stealing.

"You shall not commit adultery": This is a famous koan, and everyone would like to hear the meaning of this. It is selflessness. You may believe you love when you see a beautiful woman, but love does not belong to the human being. Christianity says this. You may be an ugly boy, but if you fall in love, you may not be able to get out. So love is not in your power. If you love for an ulterior motive, for money, success, or power, if there is a because about it, it is adultery. And there is also another deeper meaning, and that is attachment. The husband that says to his wife, "Stay in the house and don't go out!" is also committing adultery. Even this is just written, it is not a true definition. How can one give a complete definition of *shila*? When Shen-hsiu said, "Do not commit any evil," it was superficial.

As for *samadhi*, when you go to the theater, you forget your own existence, your mind unites with that of the actor. You become one with the actor, and you become one with the drama. When you leave the theater, you realize you were somewhere else, and all of a sudden your daily life seems uninteresting. While you were in the theater, you were in *samadhi*—absorption, concentration, or trance (according to European scholars). Christians experience this in prayer and in the singing of hymns.

And *prajna*? Through *prajna*, wisdom, you exercise your intellect. It is a natural form of meditation. When you sit before an artist who is painting your portrait, and he asks you to place your chin on your arm and look up—well, it may be very beautiful, but it is not meditation. When we want to meditate on anything, we sit down in the natural attitude for thinking.

Samadhi is not attained by the excitement of emotion but by its control. *Shila* is attained through will power. *Prajna* is the attainment of wisdom.

The Sixth Patriarch's criticism was harsh.

Chih-ch'eng said: "There is only one kind of shila, samadhi *and* prajna. *How is it possible for [yours] to be different?"* Funny isn't it?

The Sixth Patriarch will give his definitions in the next lecture.

The Master said: "Your teacher's shila, samadhi, *and* prajna *are for teaching people of the Great Vehicle (the Mahayana); but my* shila, samadhi, *and* prajna *are for teaching people of the highest vehicle. Your teacher's view of enlightenment differs from mine: his is a slow approach to enlightenment, whereas mine is a sudden approach. Listen to my teaching and observe whether it is the same as his.*

"I teach nothing that is incompatible with the reality of my own nature. If anyone teaches some truth that departs from the body, it is an abstract theory, and you will always remain deluded about your original nature. You must know that all things come forth from your original nature. To make use of this is the true teaching of shila, samadhi, *and* prajna.*"

SOKEI-AN SAYS:

Shen-hsiu sent his disciple Chih-ch'eng to the Southern School of the Sixth Patriarch to find out what kind of teaching was being promulgated. The Sixth Patriarch asked Chih-ch'eng what his master was teaching. Chih-ch'eng said, "*Shila, samadhi,* and *prajna.*" The Sixth Patriarch asked Chih-ch'eng how his master defined them. Chih-ch'eng said: "To commit no evil is *shila*. To practice all virtue is *prajna*. To purify your mind is *samadhi*. This is what he teaches." To this the Sixth Patriarch replied that his definitions were different.

Then the Master said: "*Your teacher's* shila, samadhi, *and* prajna *are for teaching people of the Great Vehicle (the Mahayana). But my* shila, samadhi, *and* prajna *are for teaching people of the highest vehicle.*" Today, people think that if a monk eats meat, he is Mahayana, and if he refuses meat, he is Hinayana. You cannot come to a true conclusion from this. Hinayana approaches wisdom through the cessation of desire. The Mahayana attitude is that after you attain wisdom, you descend to daily life. There is no higher vehicle. This so-called "highest vehicle" *is* the realization of everyday life. From morning to evening is the demonstration of Reality.

"Your teacher's view of enlightenment differs from mine, his is a slow approach to enlightenment, whereas mine is a sudden approach." One who practices cessation of desire and concentrates his thoughts, moving from *rupa* to *vedana*, to *samjna*, to *samskara*, to *vijnana*—where he flashes the mirror and realizes Reality—practices the so-called slow approach to enlightenment. Mahayanists do not necessarily practice this.

If *vijnana* is the mirror, you need only realize you are back of it. This is sudden enlightenment. Hinayana is like little Alice in Wonderland trying to enter the mirror from this side. Mahayana says, Why try to enter the mirror as if it were outside of us? We ourselves are the mirror. The back and the front are within us all of the time. Through the back we see the front, just like the man who operates a magic lantern. The man stands behind the lantern and projects pictures before him onto the screen. So how do you realize that you are behind the mirror at this very moment? It is sudden enlightenment if you do.

"Listen to my teaching and observe whether it is the same as his. I teach nothing that is incompatible with the reality of my own nature." That is, Reality itself. Reality is our own nature. What is Reality? Go home and open your encyclopedia or your Webster's dictionary. There you will find a definition of Reality!

The existing phenomenal world is not Reality. Time and space belong to our five senses, and we are in our five senses. We cannot see anything that is in the state outside of these five senses. We can only think that there is the outside of consciousness. Our intelligence tells us that there is this state. The condition outside of time and space is not anything we can see or talk about. There is no color, no smell, no taste, no sound, no contact. It is so-called Reality. To attain this Reality is *prajna*, and everyone's nature is this Reality.

The Sixth Patriarch experienced it, and out of his experience he spoke. The Zen monk reaches *alaya*-consciousness through meditation on the five *skandhas*. When we practice this, many times back and forth, and we understand the law of existence, we can talk about it. That is why the Sixth Patriarch said he preached "nothing that is incompatible with the reality of my own nature." Really, I am a Hinayanist!

"If anyone teaches some truth that departs from the body, it is an abstract theory, and you will always remain deluded about your original nature." When I talk about Paris, my talk is only an abstract theory because I have never been there.

This "body" is *dharmakaya*. The true meaning is difficult to say. *Dharmakaya* does not mean physical body, and it is not abstract. It is like saying "body of water." Occasionally, in Sanskrit, you find the phrase "body of emptiness," for emptiness also has a body. *Dharmakaya* is the body that covers the universe from corner to corner. There is no corner, so it covers infinite space. There is no infinite space in *dharmakaya*, so *dharmakaya* does not cover anything. So if you preach something that departs from the *reality* of *dharmakaya*, your preaching is an abstract theory. If you stand up with your robes on and talk about God and you have never met God, you do not know anything about God.

"You must know that all things come forth from your original nature." When we say "your" original nature, who is this "you?" You say "I." But what is this "I?"

"To make use of this is the true teaching of shila, samadhi, *and* prajna." This is the Sixth Patriarch's definition. Everything flows out of the mind of God, so there is nothing in the world that is evil or impure or vile. In his moment of death, the criminal, if he could understand, would find emancipation. This is the law of God.

Human law is different. The manifestation of *dharmakaya* is from top to bottom. The law of the human being is from bottom to top. Of course, you shall not kill, shall not commit adultery. If there were no one but yourself, you could do anything you wanted; but you are living with your brothers and sisters in this world. You must then know these laws. If you know them, you will really be emancipated.

The Master said: Listen to my gatha:

> *Your mind is without [the attitude of] censure*
> *This is the* shila *of original nature*

> *Your mind is without igorance*
> *This is the* prajna *of original nature*

> *Your mind is without disturbance*
> *This is the* samadhi *of original nature*

> *That which can be neither increased nor decreased*
> *Is your own diamond nature*

> *Whether the body comes or goes*
> *Originally there is only* samadhi

Hearing this, Chih-ch'eng asked the Master's forgiveness and offered a gatha:

> *"In the body of illusion [formed by] the five shadows of mind*
> *How can illusion ever cease?*

> *If you attempt to find* bhutatathata
> *The truth [you find] will only be impure"*

The Master acknowledged the correctness of Chih-ch'eng's words.

SOKEI-AN SAYS:

I shall give you a commentary on these lines.

In the period of the T'ang dynasty, Chinese Buddhism developed according to an entirely different conception of Buddhism, called *dhyana*. Today we call it Zen. Zen developed into two schools, the Northern School and the Southern School. The Northern School, the School of Gradual Enlightenment, placed its emphasis on meditation. It was through meditation that one reached original nature, which is Buddha. The Southern School, the School of Sudden Enlightenment, placed its emphasis on realization. Its practice was not meditation but the attainment of enlightenment—in any moment. A master of the Southern School said, "One can attain enlightenment at any moment, awake or asleep, in doing anything."

The master of the Northern School, Shen-hsiu, had sent one of his disciples, Chih-ch'eng, a young monk, to the Southern School. The monk questioned the Sixth Patriarch about *shila*, *samadhi*, and *prajna*.

The Master said: Listen to my gatha: *Your mind is without [the attitude of] censure/ This is the* shila *of original nature."* *Shila* is the subjective principle by which we make the laws of daily behavior. The reality of existence has no form or any particular appearance—the outside is always changing. If you try to formulate, in your mind, a law on this reality, to blame others for their faults or to praise them for their merits, you will not be able to do so because you cannot formulate a particular law out of *shila*. *Shila* is behind the law. The law is really only your particular idea in your mind. Original nature is the principle of *shila* itself, so we do not need to create an additional principle.

"Your mind is without igorance/ This is the prajna *of original nature."* I saw a European translation of *prajna*, wisdom, as "transcendental light"; but I do not agree with this translation, though there is some transcendentalism in it. Of course, no one wishes to keep their mind in a state of ignorance. Original nature is the ability that brings us from darkness to light, from ignorance to wisdom, from sickness to health, and from disturbance to quietude.

"Your mind is without disturbance/ This is the samadhi *of original nature."* *Samadhi* is another word that is difficult to translate into English. When you go to the cinema, you are absorbed in the scene, and you become one with the actors on the screen. In the theater, if tragedy is on the stage, you weep and are terribly disturbed. And when you leave the theater and face a banal world, you realize you became completely identified with the play, the barrier between you and the universe was broken. You woke up from that dream, you were in *samadhi*. So, in meditation, if you keep your mind quiet, you will become one with the universe, as you did in the theater.

When we are in meditation, we are keeping ourselves quiet. We are regulating our breath and keeping our minds pure. We feel our hearts pumping. We feel heavy, and we cannot lift our hands. And if we feel fear, we just experience this *samadhi*. Then, after a while, there is no *prajna* and no Zen. It is a very tedious and important moment. But in that moment your brain is bothered, and you cannot attain. In the Northern School, they practice for this type of *samadhi*, but they realize nothing. So the Sixth Patriarch criticized the Northern School.

"That which can be neither increased nor decreased/ is your own diamond nature." It is called "diamond" because it cannot be destroyed. The things we see, we can destroy, and we can destroy consciousness, too. But the *reality* of consciousness we cannot destroy. It is the diamond nature of our intrinsic self.

Consciousness is like a mirror, reflecting everything as it is but remaining untouched and unchanged itself. The mirror reflects everything instantly as it appears on its surface: round things reflect as round, square things as square, a lion as a lion. Only the mirror itself is not reflected. Your mind must be like this mirror.

"Whether the body comes or goes/ Originally there is only samadhi."* The body that "comes or goes" is Tathagata. Tathagata means "THAT" or "IT." Tathagata is the *samadhi* of your original nature. If you realize Tathagata, then every moment you are in Zen.

This is the end of the Sixth Patriarch's spontaneous poem given to Chih-ch'eng. He was not a poet. You might say he was a Zen master who was a poor poet of China.

Hearing this, Chih-ch'eng asked the Master's forgiveness and offered a gatha: *"In the body of illusion [formed by] the five shadows of mind/ How can illusion ever cease?"* We must annihilate our illusions. Philosophically we invent annihilation because we have these eyes, ears and mind. But actually we are in this place by keeping this reality, not by destroying it.

Why do we have to worry about this existence? Delusion is not existence. Delusion is our mind, our thoughts. So how are we to accept this existence? Buddha said, "Everything which exists is a dream." Well, this is not a dream; this is Reality. You cannot see it with your consciousness. So you think *this* is material and *that* is spiritual and each must be somewhere, and you divide it into two parts. But there is another side, another view, the inverted view of existence.

Our mind is deluded, but objective phenomena is pure existence—Reality. It is only our thoughts about it that are deluded. If you see the world in analysis, you know the analytic view only. You must know it synthetically also.

"*If you attempt to find* bhutatathata/ *The truth [you find] will only be impure.*" This bowl does not exist as it is. You are deluded by your conceptions and the seven colors of your eye. It is not a real understanding of the world. It is erroneous, and it is impure.

Dr. Suzuki translates *bhutatathatha* as "suchness," but I never use this. There is also the word "isness," but we do not call it by any name. You can, however, call it Reality. Buddha came from THIS, so we can say we came from THAT.

The Master acknowledged the correctnes of Chih-ch'eng's words. There is more here; you must be very careful in reading this line. The Sixth Patriarch just gave the acknowledgment—he did not say anything. If any one of you had made this poem and given it to me, I would not have said anything. This monk is very young.

[*The Master*] *said: "Your teacher's* shila, *samadhi, and* prajna *can be recommended for those who have a limited capacity for wisdom; but my* shila, samadhi, *and* prajna *are for those of unbounded wisdom. If you realize your original nature, you will not need to devise notions of enlightenment or nirvana, or to invent any [idea of] liberation and the knowledge of liberation.*

"Only when there is not a single law that can be grasped is it possible to lay down ten thousand different laws. If you apprehend the meaning of this, that is the body of Buddha. It is also enlightenment and nirvana and the knowledge of liberation.

"One who has realized original nature is free to devise [any law] and is also free not to devise [any law]. To come or to go is at his discretion. Nothing can deter or obstruct him. He acts according to events; he answers according to the problem. He manifests his transformation body (nirmanakaya) *everywhere, but does not deviate from original nature. He has attained the freedom of supernatural power and the* samadhi *of leisurely play. This is 'realizing original nature.'"*

SOKEI-AN SAYS:

In the previous lectures, the Sixth Patriarch has been answering Chih-ch'eng's questions about *shila, samadhi, prajna.* This part covers some of the essential teachings of Buddhism, such as original nature.

Original nature should be translated as "Reality," that stiff technical term of philosophy. In Zen terms, the reality of *yourself* is original nature. You are composed of a physical body and a mental body. The physical body consists of the four great elements—earth, fire, water and air. The mental body consists of five shadows—the physical body, the activity of the sense organs, thoughts, the creative activities such as will power (positive and negative), and consciousness. What we perceive is a rainbow of four great elements and five shadows. But what is the *reality* of these mental and physical phenomena? The reality of these phenomena is original nature.

In Zen, emphasis is placed on emancipation from all mental and physical structures. Today, in Japanese, we call it *kensho*—seeing into one's own original nature. "Before your father and mother, what were you?" In the Zen room, I ask you this question, and you give me an answer. But having no karma of merit, the flash of light in that moment goes, and you fall into the usual human state. It should not be so. You should remain there and see everything from that state. It is like a mother and her baby. The mother takes hold of her baby's hand to walk, and then releases it; but the baby falls and cannot walk. When you have this flash, you must not lose it, you must cultivate it. I do not blame you, but you must work. I realize that to attain enlightenment is not an easy affair.

[The Master] said: "Your teacher's shila, samadhi, *and* prajna *can be recommended for those who have a limited capacity for wisdom; but my* shila, samadhi, *and* prajna *are for those of unbounded wisdom."* The Sixth Patriarch is saying *shila, samadhi,* and *prajna* are the original nature of all human beings. So when you attain original nature, you attain these, the Buddha's mind, at the same time.

The Sixth Patriarch's record has been criticized because many parts were written by his disciple Shen-hui, the real center pole of the Sixth Patriarch's teaching. In the record, Shen-hui changed some lines and created others. Dr. Suzuki agrees and I agree. The Sixth Patriarch would not have disparaged the Northern School so much.

"If you realize your original nature, you will not need to devise notions of enlightenment or nirvana, or to invent any [idea of] liberation and the knowledge of liberation." Liberation is really the mind operating *naturally* to clear away delusion and sickness for enlightenment. Knowledge of liberation is the awareness of emancipation when we see the world once more. "Enlightenment," "nirvana," and "liberation" are only devices to help us realize original nature.

"Only when there is not a single law that can be grasped is it possible to lay down ten thousand different laws." In the state of your original nature, like the Sahara Desert, there are no laws. You can travel in any direction. In the physical state, you cannot. There is the law between *earth, air, fire,* and *water,* between time and space, good and bad, white and black, man and woman. The standpoint of one who has attained original nature is that there are no laws, but at the same time there are many laws. If you are the mayor of New York City, you can make many laws and you can abolish laws, but you cannot do this if you cannot grasp one essential thing—Reality.

In Christianity, God has all laws in his hands. But in Buddhism, you must have all laws in *your* hand. Socially, we must make laws. Laws exists for historical and moral reasons.

Human society has many laws, but the Buddhist has five: 1) You shall not kill—the elemental law. 2) You shall not steal—the elemental law of economy. 3) You shall not commit adultery—the elemental law of morality. 4) You shall not lie—the elemental law of politics. 5) You shall not become intoxicated—the elemental law of delusion—so called education.

These are the elemental functions of human minds. You must observe the world from this standpoint. Then you can be ladies and gentlemen. But you follow blindly.

"If you apprehend the meaning of this, that is the body of Buddha." When you attain the body of Buddha—*dharmakaya,* the omnipresent and omnipotent body—you can act on your potential knowledge. You open your eye to your own wisdom, to the state of nirvana, and to the state where you will be emancipated from this human world. When you are emancipated and standing on your own two feet, you will observe this human physical world once more.

"It is also enlightenment and nirvana and the knowledge of liberation." Enlightenment is active; nirvana is passive. Enlightenment is emergence; nirvana is submergence. Enlightenment and nirvana are phenomena that appear in our own mind. In reality, there is no such thing. Enlightenment and nirvana are different words that are the same in significance. Both of them were invented by the mind. So we do not need to devise a "liberated" wisdom. People invented this idea of liberation. No one has been trapped in a physical body or deluded by a mental body. Souls have been and will be free from the first day of creation to the last day of destruction. Ideas of emancipation are delusions. The one who attains this can be called an *arhat*.

"One who has realized original nature is free to devise [any law] and is also free not to devise [any law]. To come or to go is at his discretion. Nothing can deter or obstruct him. He acts according to events; he answers according to the problem." If you go to the Sahara Desert, there are no laws. When you come back, you are free to make more—if you wish. But if you are blind, you go to the Sahara Desert or Salt Lake and still observe traffic regulations! On the battlefield, it is the same. So one who invents a law can really follow a law. This law can be translated as "Dharma," but I prefer to translate it as "law."

Open your eye to your original nature. Then from that enlightened state, you will see human life.

"He manifests his transformation body (nirmanakaya) *everywhere, but does not deviate from original nature. He has attained the freedom of supernatural power and the samadhi of leisurely play. This is 'realizing original nature.'"* He has a penetrating mind. When he buys *from* a farmer, his money is transformed into grain, but he is not involved.

There are six supernatural wisdoms, but I do not have time to explain them to you now. Buddha's mind and the six supernatural wisdoms must be attained at the same time to see the transformation of all bodies.

We must realize, and we must emphasize the necessity of realization. We must have what Buddha had under the Bodhi tree. Without it, there is no Buddhism.

Next Saturday is Buddha's birthday. I was invited to lunch somewhere—an Indian restaurant—by Das Gupta, and then I have been invited at night to speak at the peace dinner of the Indo-American Association at the Ceylon India Inn. These circulars tell where this dinner is.

Das Gupta's luncheon is 75¢, and the Ceylon Indian dinner is $1.00. I will curtail my lecture next Saturday night at ten o'clock, and if any of you come with me, it will be wonderful business for them—about $20.00. It is not my way! No such law is written in my mind. But it is the Buddha's birthday, and we will go.

Again Chih-ch'eng questioned the Master: "What is meant by 'not devising [any law]?'"

The Master said: "Original nature is without censure, without ignorance, without disturbance. At every moment it perceives with prajna *wisdom, always detached from formulas or laws, free to do anything and go anywhere. Why should it devise anything? Original nature is naturally enlightened. Realization is sudden, and practice is sudden. There are no gradual stages. That is why we speak of devising no laws. All things naturally abide in perfect quiescence. What 'stages' could there be?"*

Chih-ch'eng bowed low and entreated the Master to let him be his attendant, serving him diligently day and night.

SOKEI-AN SAYS:

This is a conversation between the Sixth Patriarch and the young monk Chih-ch'eng.

Again Chih-ch'eng questioned the Master: "What is meant by 'not devising [any law]?'" "Not devising any law" does not mean here not to devise any social law, but rather that Buddhism does not need to devise any particular canonical or theological law.

The Master said: "Original nature is without censure, without ignorance, without disturbance." What is original nature? This is a deep question. The mind that we possess is not the original mind. This is the mind we have *created*. Behind this mind there is another, the intrinsic mind. The intrinsic mind is our original nature, and our original nature is an existence beyond the state of being human. To us, it is God. In Zen, there is no God on the outside. The original nature of a human being *is* God, and it is not human. And there is no original nature that is mine or yours. When we find the original nature in us, the original nature is one and the same. This point of view is a little different from Christianity. We have no separate soul. Our souls are originally one and the same.

The Sixth Patriarch is explaining the attributes of original nature. Original nature does not criticize, nor does it blame others for their offences, or praise others for their merits. There are no particular rules for the punishment or praise of others. There is no particular person who should be punished. Your error is not *your* error. In Buddhism, it is the error of karma.

What I am speaking about is quite a distinctive view. It is something like relativity. For example, this bowl is here because I am supporting it in my hand, and I am here because this chair is supporting me. This chair is here because the house is supporting it. This house, my home, is here because New York City is here supporting it. In Sanskrit, this is called *pratyaya*—relative existence. Napoleon was a famous general because he was born in that condition and with that nature. So time, place, and condition created Napoleon. He was not Napoleon solely by his own power.

"At every moment it perceives with prajna *wisdom, always detached from formulas or laws, free to do anything and go anywhere. Why should it devise anything?* You think you do not have *prajna*, but you always have it. You just cannot find it.

Original nature does not remain in any shape, formula, or condition, like artificial flowers. It grows. It alters its nature. It changes. It is like driving an automobile in the Gobi Desert. It is different from driving in New York. This is the law of original nature. When the law of original nature comes to New York, it takes on the nature of New York. When it enters London, it takes on the nature of London. You must not think that original nature destroys laws. It enters water and fire, and observes the law of water and of fire and of New York. When it enters the human being and the cat and dog, it observes the law of the human being and the cat and dog. When it enters the cat, the cat does not use chopsticks—dishes are used with chopsticks. When it enters the Japanese, the Japanese uses the chopsticks. In an American, it will use a knife and fork. Why should there be a fixed law?

It is in man's nature to keep everything in the best order. It is in man's nature to bring us into a quiet place. The force of original nature is to awaken. This is the intrinsic nature of man.

Original nature is naturally enlightened." This is the first step in Buddhism. There is an old Buddhist poem that says:

When you go near the sea
You hear the sound of waves

When you go near the mountain
You hear the sound of wind
When you go near your original nature
You hear no sound
You are Silence

In your SILENCE, you are aware of yourself. That is the first gate in entering Reality. You may attain the realization of it at any moment. Reality is entirely different from being informed or just knowing about it. To realize *This is That!* is to realize Reality.

"Realization is sudden, and practice is sudden. There are no gradual stages." When you sit on a bench on the bank of the Hudson River and you become aware of your own mind, and there is nothing to speak of in your mind, you and your mind become one with nature. You are absorbed in Mind. You are not keeping your eye on the cloud, and you are not keeping your eye open. But the Hudson River is there, and you are there, and you are one with the universe and the universe within you. And when there is such a moment, you will know you heard it from me. In that moment realization comes. Why should there be any method of attaining this realization graudally?

In the Northern School of Zen, the method of practice is to perform longer and longer meditations—the first day, twenty minutes, the next day, half-an-hour. And through your long meditation, you gradually attain. So we call the Northern School of Zen the Gradual School of Enlightenment. But the Sixth Patriarch said we do not need to meditate certain hours; we may attain realization at any moment. And it is true.

I have studied Zen according to the Northern School, although I am a disciple of the Southern School.

"That is why we speak of devising no laws." From the beginning, there was no law; there was a white sheet of paper. Then the first law was written. For example, the Kaiser is sacred, his words are absolutely sacred. It is a law written on a white sheet of paper. Before that, there was no law. In America—on a white sheet of paper—it is written: "We elect a president"—the first law. There is no law that says all countries must have a Kaiser. It is according to time and place. Christ devised his law, and the Buddha devised his law, but the first law was to devise no law. This came first.

"All things naturally abide in perfect quiescence. What 'stages' could there be?" Perfect quiescence is the annihilated state, a state of nothingness—*nirodha*. We do not need to reduce everything to nothingness. It is already nothingness.

Once there was a monk who lived in a hut on top of a mountain. He had gathered weeds for soft pillows and bamboo for the walls. A layman who happened to visit him one day asked: "Can you return this mountain to its original state?" The monk replied: "Can you?" The layman said: "Yes. If I were to destroy the hut, the mountain would return to its original state." The monk laughed and said: "This *is* the original state of the mountain. Everything that is this hut came from the mountain. I added nothing. So I needn't destroy the hut. Without tearing this hut down, it is the original state of the mountain."

You must understand this. We are living in nirvana and nirodha. This is no joke. While we are living, we are already dead.

Chih-ch'eng bowed low and entreated the Master to let him be his attendant, serving him diligently day and night. The monks always do this.

The conversation between Chih-ch'eng and the Master ends here.

The monk Chih-chie was a native of Kiangsi. His family name was Ch'ang; his lay surname was Hsing-ch'ang. He was a youth with a bold nature.

Following the separation [of Ch'an] into Northern and Southern teachings, though the masters of each school denied any difference existed, antagonism and hatred grew between their monks.

At that time, the disciples of the Northern sect, on their own authority, called their master, Shen-hsiu, "the Sixth Patriarch." However, resentful that people everywhere knew that the robe had been transmitted [to Hui-neng], they sent Hsing-ch'ang to assassinate him. Because of his power to penetrate others' minds, the Master knew of this in advance and had placed ten gold coins in his room. One night, Hsing-ch'ang entered the Master's room ready to assassinate him. Stretching out his neck, the Master waited for the blow of Hsing-ch'ang's sword. Three times Hsing-ch'ang struck, but the Master remained completely unharmed.

The Master said: "There will be no wrong blow from an honest sword and no straight blow from a dishonest sword. I only owe you money, not my life."

Hsing-ch'ang fell back in fear.

Finally, recovering his senses, he implored the Master to forgive him and to permit him to become a monk. The Master gave him the money and said: "You had better go now. I fear that the monks of the temple will kill you. Come another day in disguise, and I shall receive you then."

Obeying the Master's order, Hsing-ch'ang made his escape through the darkness.

Subsequently, he was admitted into a monastery and became a monk, following the commandments wholeheartedly and living the monastic life.

One day, recalling the Master's words, he returned from afar to pay homage.

The Master said: "I have often thought of you. Why are you so late in coming?"

Hsing-ch'ang said: "Before, you graciously pardoned my offense. Now, although I have renounced the world and have undertaken painful practice, I realize that I can never repay you for your benevolence, except, perhaps, by transmitting the Dharma and converting sentient beings. I am always reading the Nirvana Sutra*, but fail to understand the meaning of 'perpetuity' and 'mutability.' I beg you, in your compassion, to briefly explain these terms for me."*

SOKEI-AN SAYS:

Buddhism was transmitted to China in the first century A.D. Soldiers from China brought back sutras from Eastern Turkistan. After all the Buddhist scriptures had been studied and translated and the Chinese had become well informed on Buddhist philosophy, Bodhidharma decided to go to China to teach esoteric Buddhism. Before that time, China had already accepted exoteric Buddhism. Exoteric Buddhism can be explained by words or terms. But esoteric Buddhism cannot be explained by words or terms; it can only be transmitted from one person to another without words. I cannot transmit the taste of water to another by words, but in the esoteric way I can. If you were to ask me about the taste of water, I would say, "Please drink." Then I would say, "Have you comprehended the taste of water?" And you would say, "Yes." This is so-called esoteric Buddhism.

When Bodhidharma went to China, he did not speak one word. On Mount Sung he made a little temple, Shao-lin Monastery. There he meditated for nine years. The legend says he did not speak a word, and from morning to evening, he only practiced meditation. But in reality, he probably was making interviews with visitors or speaking of Buddhism and interviewing people about his sect, or was writing down his words to leave them for the future. He was not a monster, and he was not quiet. He did not really maintain silence for nine years. He kept himself in the attitude of meditation. This was the origin of esoteric Buddhism, called Dhyana, Ch'an, or Zen, and the beginning of the Zen School.

The monk Chih-chie was a native of Kiangsi. His family name was Ch'ang; his lay surname was Hsing-ch'ang. He was a youth with a bold nature. Following the separation [of Ch'an] into Northern and Southern teachings, though the masters of each school denied any difference existed, antagonism and hatred grew between their monks. After two hundred years, Buddhism split into two sects, the Northern and the Southern. But the masters of these two sects said, "All Zen is one, there are not two different sects." Zen masters usually agree. It is the disciples who cause trouble and hate one another.

At that time, the disciples of the Northern sect, on their own authority, called their master, Shen-hsiu, "the Sixth Patriarch." However, resentful that people everywhere knew that the robe had been transmitted [to Hui-neng], they sent Hsing-ch'ang to assassinate him. There were shave-headed monks who called themselves ascetics but did these things. Hsing-ch'ang was a young man who had a chivalrous nature, which was different from that of the European medieval knight. Oriental chivalry is like gang warfare.

Because of his power to penetrate others' minds, the Master knew of this in advance and had placed ten gold coins in his room. It was strange for any monk to keep money in his room.

One night, Hsing-ch'ang entered the Master's room ready to assassinate him. Stretching out his neck, the Master waited for the blow of Hsing-ch'ang's sword. Three times Hsing-ch'ang struck, but the Master remained completely unharmed. In another record, Hsing-ch'ang's sword broke before it reached the Master's neck. Strange, isn't it?

The Master said: "There will be no wrong blow from an honest sword and no straight blow from a dishonest sword. I only owe you money, not my life." Hsing-ch'ang fell back in fear. The Master said to Hsing-ch'ang: "Though your directions were to kill me, you came here not to take my life but for money, so I will give you your money." Then the Master looked into his eyes and Hsing-ch'ang fainted.

Finally, recovering his senses, he implored the Master to forgive him and to permit him to become a monk. His true nature appeared all of a sudden to his deluded mind. Beaten by the true force of the mind of the Sixth Patriarch, he suddenly discovered his true consciousness. Waking up from that sensitive state, he realized that he should not be wicked, but should be virtuous. In such a moment, mankind always finds the real self.

The Master gave him the money and said: "You had better go now. I fear that the monks of the temple will kill you. Come another day in disguise, and I shall receive you then." Obeying the Master's order, Hsing-ch'ang made his escape through the darkness. Subsequently, he was admitted into a monastery and became a monk, following the commandments wholeheartedly and living the monastic life. The Sixth Patriarch's temple was surrounded by bare trees and was on the shore of a river. The monk made his escape through the rushes. He did not return to his own temple but went to a small temple in the north.

Hsing-ch'ang had been an outlaw, a gambler, and a murderer. But he had suddenly found his true consciousness, so he went into the mountains and lived the life of a monk by observing the commandments.

One day, recalling the Master's words, he returned from afar to pay homage. In the original, this is not clear. The words of the Sixth Patriarch must have always been in Hsing-ch'ang's mind. He must have crossed the Yangtse River and walked over the mountain range of Kung. It was a great distance he traveled, begging for food day and night.

The Master said: "I have often thought of you. Why are you so late in coming?" Hsing-ch'ang said: "Before, you graciously pardoned my offense. Now, although I have renounced the world and have undertaken painful practice, I realize that I can never repay you for your benevolence, except, perhaps, by transmitting the Dharma and converting sentient beings." In Buddhism, the disciple repays the teacher for his teachings. He studies very hard to take what the teacher has, for the teacher does not give so easily. So this transmission in Buddhism between teacher and disciple is a real struggle. In an Oriental proverb, it is said that the mother of lion cubs throws her children three times off a cliff. If one fails to come up, the mother forsakes it. It cannot be the child of a lion.

I am not imitating the Chinese or Japanese way of handling disciples in this country because this is just the dawn before discipline begins. When I return in my next incarnation, it will be different. The teachers will demonstrate the true Oriental attitude, and in turn the disciples will repay them.

"I am always reading the Nirvana Sutra, *but fail to understand the meaning of 'perpetuity' and 'mutability.' I beg you, in your compassion, to briefly explain these terms for me."* In the Nirvana Sutra there is a famous line: "All *samskaras* are mutable." That means all phenomena are mutable like the liquid-solid-vapor phases of water. This Original Being transmigrates through the phases of animal, woman, child, and God. It transforms itself and exists forever. If you were to consider how many years I have actually been living in this world, you would have to consider my life as an amoeba, a jellyfish, a tadpole, a frog, a reptile, a bird, till this present moment—a human being, 56 years of age. This will all be wiped out to its starting point to begin again. The annihilation of the solar system will repeat itself endlessly. This process is called mutability. This is one of the great points of Buddhism. The Buddha was the first to speak of this. It is a science today.

And what is perpetuity? It is the eternal and changeless existence of the original state of Being, the original existence beyond time—immutable and perpetual. Neither water nor fire can destroy it.

We must understand these two existing conditions, which burn at both ends like a candle. The human being thinks all of this exists forever, and never knows the state of Original Being—Reality. The *Nirvana Sutra* explains it philosophically. But Hsing-ch'ang failed to understand.

In the next lecture, the Sixth Patriarch will give his commentary on *nitya* and *anitya*—mutability and perpetuity.

The Master said: "Buddha-nature is mutable, and the mind that discriminates between good and bad is perpetual."

Hsing-ch'ang said: "Your words contradict what is written in the sutra."

The Master said: "I transmit the seal of buddha-mind; how could I contradict the Buddha's sutra?"

Hsing-ch'ang replied: "The sutra says that buddha-nature is perpetual; but you say it is mutable. The sutra says that all good and bad is mutable, even the mind of enlightenment is mutable; but you say it is perpetual. The contradictions have only added to my confusion."

The Master answered: "I have heard the Nirvana Sutra *only once, a long time ago, recited by a nun named Wu-chin-ts'ang. I then expounded its meaning for her, and there was no discrepancy between my view and that of the sutra, either in word or in meaning. I hold no other view about this sutra to preach to you or to anyone."*

Hsing-ch'ang said: "I have a very superficial knowledge [of the Dharma]. I entreat you to explain it precisely to me."

SOKEI-AN SAYS:

In the last part Hsing-ch'ang said he had been repeatedly reading the *Nirvana Sutra* but was unable to grasp two terms: mutability and perpetuity. Perpetuity means the state of eternity having no phases or changes of aspect. It is the original state of existence, which is Absolute Being. Mutability is the phenomenal world, which is always changing its phases. If I were to borrow a term from your religion, "God," I would say that God is perpetual and man is mutable. God was never born and will never die, but man is born and will die. In Buddhism, *dharmakaya* is perpetual, and *nirmanakaya* is mutable. The state of absolute law, *dharmakaya*, is perpetual, and the state of transformable law, *nirmanakaya*, is mutable. But the Master said—

"Buddha-nature is mutable, and the mind that discriminates between good and bad is perpetual." This is the Sixth Patriarch's view, which is different from that written in the sutra. Buddha-nature, God—nature, is mutable, but the mind of man, which perceives all things—existence outside—and discriminates between good and bad, is perpetual. The view the Master gave Hsing-ch'ang is very queer. No wonder he found it hard to understand.

Hsing-ch'ang said: "Your words contradict what is written in the sutra." The Master said: "I transmit the seal of buddha-mind; how could I contradict the Buddha's sutra?" The Sixth Patriarch is saying: "I am the torch-holder. I possess the seal of buddha-mind, which has been transmitted from the Buddha to myself through the generations of patriarchs, so how can any words of mine be different from those written in the Buddha's sutra?" The Sixth Patriarch had confidence in his speech.

The "seal of buddha-mind" may seem strange to you. We in the East use a seal instead of a signature. The emperor signs his name and impresses his seal on the paper upon which the decree is written. When the Buddha transmitted his buddha-mind to his direct disciple Mahakashyapa, he gave his word to him, saying, "I have transmitted the mystery of esoteric Buddhism to you from my mind to your mind." This acknowledgment of the Buddha, which he gave Mahakashyapa, was like his signature—"I make this transaction to you." So when the Buddha said, "I make this transaction to you, Mahakashyapa," he stamped his seal upon Mahakashyapa's soul. So it was transmitted.

The Zen master takes the student into his Zen, and according to his judgment, gives his acknowledgment of the student's answer. This is given from his "sealed" mind. In the West, a man seals his cattle with a burning branding iron.

In the Orient, Zen transmissions are always authentic; no one imitates this. No one calls himself a Zen master when his attainment is not acknowledged by his own Zen master. There is no master not ordained by the judgment of a previous master. The monks ordained as Zen masters stayed in one temple and studied under a teacher for twenty-five to thirty-five years. Once, here in America, a man entered my home and said that he had come from the Gobi Desert, that he knew Zen, and that he was teaching it! I do not accuse him, but such things are not permitted in the Orient. There, so as not to have imitators, a monk's attainment is acknowledged by the whole group. A student should choose a real master. No one can call himself a Zen master without a previous master's authority. Otherwise, he is an imposter, a Coney Island sorcerer!

Hsing-ch'ang replied: "The sutra says that buddha-nature is perpetual; but you say it is mutable. The sutra says that all good and bad is mutable, even the mind of enlightenment is mutable; but you say it is perpetual. The contradictions have only added to my confusion." I would have said the same if I had been there. Hsing-ch'ang put his question to the Master based upon the sutra.

The Master answered: "I have heard the Nirvana Sutra *only once, a long time ago, recited by a nun named Wu-chin-ts'ang. I then expounded its meaning for her, and there was no discrepancy between my view and that of the sutra, either in word or in meaning. I hold no other view about this sutra to preach to you or to anyone."* The Sixth Patriarch was not a scholar. The record says he was illiterate, could not read or write. When he attained enlightenment, his mind was enlightened without reading sutras. Whenever he spoke, his words were always the same as the written scriptures. Everyone thought he was the living Buddha. Of course, Buddhism is not in the scriptures but in the mind.

A young man came from India and asked me a question: "How do you teach Buddhism in America, when you can neither speak nor write English? How do you teach?" My answer was, "I teach Buddhism in silence."

When I was in Japan, I was reproved by my teacher: "I hear you are speaking something. Why don't you keep your mouth shut?" But I must make *some* preparation before I can.

Hsing-ch'ang said: "I have a very superficial knowledge [of the Dharma]. I entreat you to explain it precisely to me." I have a little more time, so I will give you a brief outline of the Patriarch's answer, which will be translated next week.

The mind that is within us is buddha-mind. There is no other mind. It cannot be found in the sky or in the earth, but it can be found in man. Minds of all kinds exist in man. When man opens his mind, he finds all the minds that are sleeping in the earth and in the sky, in the trees and in invisible existences. Perhaps, you will say, electrons and protons have minds.

The Sixth Patriarch said if man's mind were perpetual, it would never attain enlightenment. Man's mind—buddha-mind—is mutable. It has periods when it is asleep and periods when it is awake. It has the capacity for development. Man's mind is buddha-mind. The mind that perceives all things and discriminates between good and bad, the mind that is sensory and perceptive, is perpetual. The Sixth Patriarch's idea that man's mind is perpetual means that perpetuity is not in man's mind, but is outside—that which is existing in relation to the mind of man. So real absolute existence is perpetual.

The Patriarch's view was that of an enlightened being, whereas the view expressed in the *Nirvana Sutra* is the usual one. Of course, the Sixth Patriarch stated his upside-down view of perpetuity and mutability to Hsing-ch'ang to awaken his mind.

Now, one more word. Buddhists, especially Zen Buddhists, emphasize first of all the fundamental law of the world and of man. Later, we explain other things. These other things are considered sciences in your schools. It is not the job of the monk to teach them; it is the job of the professor. There is only one job left for the monk: to give you, the adherents, the foundation, the knowledge of the foundation of the mind universe in meditation. Without a word or any demonstration, we point out your mind so you will become aware of possessing it as your own. We call it buddha-nature or God-nature within you. This is the only function left to monks today. In ancient days, the monks taught in all the departments of knowledge. But today, they teach only the fundamentals—*dharmakaya, sambhogakaya, nirmanakaya*. Perhaps you will study all the branches, but you must have the foundation. Many monks do not know this, so they speak about the branches on the street corner. This is not the monk's position.

The Master said: "Do you not know that if buddha-nature were perpetual, there would be no reason to discuss the question of good and evil, and there would never be a single person awakened to enlightenment? Therefore, what I teach about mutablity is the same as the Buddha's teaching of true perpetuity. Moreover, if all things were mutable, everything would have its own nature, which would be subject to life and death, and true perpetual nature would not be common to all. Therefore, what I teach about perpetuity is exactly the same as the Buddha's teaching of true mutability. The Buddha preached in order [to correct] the eight upside-down views, the mistaken ideas of perpetuity to which ordinary-minded men and heretics adhere, and the misconception of perpetuity as mutability espoused by monks and lone ascetics."

SOKEI-AN SAYS:

The Master said: "Do you not know that if buddha-nature were perpetual, there would be no reason to discuss the question of good and evil, and there would never be a single person awakened to enlightenment?": The ordinary view, as written in the *Nirvana Sutra*, is that buddha-nature is perpetual. But the Sixth Patriarch said, "Buddha-nature is mutable." Hsing-ch'ang said to the Patriarch: "Your word about buddha-nature contradicts the word in the scriptures. I beg you, please explain the true significance of perpetuity and mutability."

Buddha-nature as perpetual is the usual abstract idea that buddha-nature does not truly exist as matter. This idealism is nothing but a logical conclusion existing in one's mind, not existing as Reality. The Sixth Patriarch said that buddha-nature is not abstract but concrete. It truly exists.

Buddha-nature, in this view, is not different from the nature of man. The nature of man does not always appear as buddha-nature. Sometimes it appears as the buddha-nature of an animal or an insect. So if buddha-nature were perpetual, there would be no reason why we should discuss the question of the dharma, which is sometimes good and sometimes bad—like the six ways of sentient beings: naraka, *preta*, animal, *asura*, human being, and *deva*. In their devotion to the highest enlightenment through the kalpas, each of these beings will attain buddha-nature. It exists within them, but it is hidden. This latent buddha-nature is not a notion, a product of abstract philosophy.

If buddha-nature is perpetual, then every being must be enlightened, but many of us are not. Many of us are just blind or like Christmas decorations. It's as though you were to step into an antique shop—you wish to buy, but you are not sure what is genuine and what is not. The salesman says: "This figure is from the T'ang dynasty. Isn't it marvelous?! It's worth three thousand dollars, but it's a little damaged. So, for you—two thousand!" In China, it may only be worth five cents. It had never been dug up but was made in Shanghai. I had a friend who told me the real truth.

So the Sixth Patriarch said that buddha-nature is mutable.

"Therefore, what I teach about mutablity is the same as the Buddha's teaching of true perpetuity." Everything—this, that, man, woman, cat, dog—all have the same nature at bottom. This so-called nature exists forever. In Buddhism, it is called *alaya*-consciousness.

So all things are perpetual, though usually it is said all things are mutable because they appear and disappear.

"Moreover, if all things were mutable, everything would have its own nature, which would be subject to life and death, and true perpetual nature would not be common to all." The Sixth Patriarch insists that his own idealism is the true idea. This part of the discourse about mutability and perpetuity is very important. If you are a real student of human thought, you will not read this as though it were insignificant.

You must understand this clearly. There are those who study human beauty and human nature—sculptors, painters, dramatists, novelists and poets. Then there are those who study the value of things—economists—and those who study the destruction of conventional law by militarists. There are many departments of study. We study human thought. In this modern rush for money, we have no time to study our minds. It is the saddest period of our history. Those who study their minds will recognize that something very important is hidden in these lines of the Patriarch.

The Buddha was not always Buddha. He attained buddhahood by his own exertion after the passing of many kalpas and many incarnations. He was a sparrow, he was a snake, and he was just a man—a Buddhist who finally attained Buddhahood. But in Christianity, Christ was the child of God from the beginning to the end. He was born as the son of a carpenter, but he was not the child of the carpenter. He was the Son of God. And by the time he was twelve years old, he showed his attainment. This type of buddha-nature is perpetual, but the Sixth Patriarch's idea was that buddha-nature was mutable, so we can see the contrast.

This idea of a God who is always perfect exists in the Western mind. I always illustrate this with the plan of the Western garden, a mosaic of red, white and yellow flowers, laid out in perfect squares, circles, and triangles—perpetual. In the Orient, it is not this way. We use nature itself as the garden, and it is mutable.

Both have a truth, and we must understand them as types of thought. The Oriental, in beginning his garden, has no vision, he just begins. It grows, and it develops. Western people are different. They have a vision, have a plan, go here, go there.

I have seen this in marriage as well. Western men and women have an "idea" about marriage as home, maid, and income—one hundred and fifty dollars a week. Very well. They marry. Things go smoothly for a while. Then comes trouble—fifty dollars a week! Idealism!

We, too, have idealism in the Orient, but ours is different from yours. I do not say Oriental idealism is better, but it is different. We must study all kinds.

This discrepancy comes from thoughts, so the matter of thoughts is very important. I have a very small audience tonight, so I can talk about strategy. But I myself am not in military service!

"Therefore, what I teach about perpetuity is exactly the same as the Buddha's teaching of true mutability." Now think of those Greek Idealists and the famous Greek "ideal"—perfection is beauty, truth, and goodness, and the unity of these three is the Ideal. The "ideal" or "idea" is in everything. The sculptor carves the "idea," which is perfect, in the acanthus leaf, but no one can see it. They may make the leaf perfect, but no one can see this in nature. In nature, this "idea" is imperfect—distorted. Perfection is not *in* nature, but *behind* nature. This water container is not perfect, but the "idea" is perfect. To me, as a sculptor, your face many seem not quite arranged, but the "idea" behind it is perfect. So this world, which is nature hiding the "idea" behind it, is not perfect. We must return to the ideal of beauty, truth, and goodness, the so-called Platonic Ideal. Platonic love is not love, it is somewhere behind it. But in the Orient, even though the moon reflected on water is distorted, is pulled and pushed about and changes its shape in every moment, it is the perfect moon.

The Greek idea of nature is that it is mutable. But the Oriental idea of nature is that it is perpetual. Though it is distorted, it is perpetual, has never changed its existence. There is that incense smoke, but that incense stick has never changed its existence.

Thoughts are very queer.

"The Buddha preached in order [to correct] the eight upside-down views—the mistaken ideas of perpetuity to which ordinary-minded men and heretics adhere, and the misconception of perpetuity as mutability espoused by monks and lone ascetics." Those Hinayana monks, the *shrvakas* and *pratyekabuddas*, had these views of mutability and perpetuity.

"Heretics" here means those who believe God is in the sky or at the center of the universe, and those who say God is inside. But God is not inside—or in the stomach. You might find worms, but you will never find God. Or perhaps you think God is in your mind.

Of course, Christianity says Buddhism is heretical. We also say Christianity is heretical!

[The Master continued:] "In the Nirvana Sutra, *the Buddha destroyed these one-sided views and revealed true perpetuity, true peace, true selfhood, and true purity. By depending on the words, you violate the true meaning [of the sutra]. By denying mutability and affirming inactive perpetuity, you misunderstand the marvelous and supremely subtle words of the Buddha. Even if you read the sutra a thousand times, how will you receive any benefit?"*

Hsing-ch'ang suddenly experienced great enlightenment and recited a gatha:

"Because we cherish the mutable mind
The Buddha preached perpetual nature

If we do not realize it to be a pious fraud
We are like those who pick up pebbles from a pond [thinking them to be jewels]

Now, without making any effort
Buddha-nature has revealed itself

This is not something you gave me
Nor is it something I attained"[23]

The Master said: "You have now penetrated [Buddha-nature]. You may name yourself Chih-ch'e [Penetrating Mind Force]."

Hsing-ch'ang bowed in gratitude and retired.

SOKEI-AN SAYS:

The usual view of perpetuity and mutability is this: Our mind and all phenomena are mutable, and buddha-nature is eternal. You would say, in your terms, God is eternal, but everything existing as phenomena is mutable—changeable. The Sixth Patriarch denied this view. He said that buddha-nature is mutable and that all entities are eternal—perpetual. But Hsing-ch'ang, the young monk, was confused by the Sixth Patriarch's definitions of mutability and perpetuity.

I shall avoid repeating my commentary of the previous lectures and shall comment on the lines that I have translated for the lecture tonight.

"In the Nirvana Sutra, *the Buddha destroyed these one sided views"*: "The Buddha" means Shakyamuni Buddha, while "Buddha" without the definite article means Knowledge or Wisdom, which is God to us. So you must understand that "buddha" and "the Buddha" are not the same. The God of Buddhism is our Wisdom, the Wisdom that is common to all sentient beings. Some are still sleeping, although they intrinsically possess this Wisdom. The Buddha has awakened to this buddha, the intrinsic Wisdom

within him. Christians say that God is Love. We Buddhists say that God is Wisdom. All religions give attributes to their God.

"… And revealed true perpetuity, true peace, true selfhood, and true purity." "True perpetuity," according to the Sixth Patriarch, is this: Everything has different appearances, but original nature is common to all of them. Greek philosophy, has an entirely different explanation for the nature of things. According to Plato, this chair I sit in has, in reality, its own perfection, its own ideal form. This ideal chair exists behind the chair that appears before our eyes. Behind all phenomena is the ideal existence. What we see is the shadow of this true existence. So from the Buddhist point of view, the Platonic Ideal of existence is mutable. Platonists would say that these ideal existences are permanent. But we would not accept such permanency!

A smith may cast different bronze statues, but the bronze is the same in each. In original existence, there is no gold, no incense, no man or woman. All are amalgamated into one permanent existence. So phenomenal life is perpetual. Buddha-nature, which we have within us, enlightened or unenlightened, is mutable. If it were perpetual, how could we enlighten ourselves? The Buddha was an insect, a snake, a rabbit, a lion, a man, a woman, a criminal, and a king, finally, attaining buddhahood, Buddha. According with his own efforts, he created his own karma. Therefore, buddha-nature is mutable and not perpetual according to the Sixth Patriarch.

And "true peace?" The usual idea is that peace will come after death, that this life is agony. But peace is everywhere, if you have peace in your mind. A man in a hospital, surrounded by a hundred doctors, is not quite sure of his life, is unhappy and cannot find any peace. Yet, the soldier fighting on the battlefield finds peace in his mind.

"True selfhood" is not attained easily. You try to keep your ego, but you fail to keep it. You try to be a gentleman or a king, and you fail as well. Selfhood is not attained by pride or arrogance.

As for "true purity," you think if you put on white clothes, wash morning and evening and avoid desire, you are pure. Such purity is like keeping a white Palm Beach suit unsoiled—pure, clean, and white. But you cannot sit down or walk on a dirty street, you cannot run in the rain, and even then you can only keep it white for a couple of days. You cannot keep it white because your idea of purity is erroneous. So you brush everything away from your life and retire to a mountain to find God.

Purity is not keeping yourself clean. When you are working hard and your clothes and hands are all dirty, then your mind is pure. But when you come home, take a bath, put on perfume and lie down, then your mind is dirty and your body also.

"By depending on the words, you violate the true meaning [of the sutra]. By denying mutability and affirming inactive perpetuity, you misunderstand the marvelous and supremely subtle words of the Buddha." I have explained these marvellous words of the Buddha. When you read the sutra, you must read it very carefully.

"Even if you read the sutra a thousand times, how will you receive any benefit?" Hsing-ch'ang suddenly experienced great enlightenment and recited a gatha: Hsing-ch'ang awakened to true realization, so he made a song.

"Because we cherish the mutable mind/ The Buddha preached perpetual nature." The human being always attaches to the mutable mind, *this* mind. In the morning, you get up and you are happy, and you dance in the street. Then you become unhappy with your boss, your salary, your date for the evening. You stand waiting for hours. She never appears, and you are miserable.

"If we do not realize it to be a pious fraud/ We are like those who pick up pebbles from a pond [thinking them to be jewels]." A pious fraud is a good trick. You do something and think no one knows but God, but it is the God in you watching his creation.

"Now, without making any effort/ Buddha-nature has revealed itself/ This is not something you gave me/ Nor is it something I attained." To attain buddha-nature, those monks struggled for years, made pilgrimages and meditated. Really, if I were to say my true word, I would not say you must practice meditation to find your buddha-nature. Now, in this moment, you have it, but you do not use it. You are trying to find it.

The Master said: "You have now penetrated [Buddha-nature]. You may name yourself Chih-ch'e [Penetrating Mind Force]." Hsing-ch'ang bowed in gratitude and retired." The Zen sect is the so-called School of Sudden Enlightenment. When your mind wants to attain enlightenment, you will attain it at any moment. It is not necessary to wait for next year. In this moment, you will attain it.

There was a boy whose name was Shen-hui. He was a son of the house of Kao in Hsiang-yang. When he was thirteen years old, he came from Yu-ch'uan to pay homage to the Master.

The Master said: "Good friend, you have endured great hardship in coming such a distance, but did you bring along the original? If you have the original, you should know the master. Tell me."

Shen-hui replied: "Non-abiding is the origin. Seeing is the master."

The Master said: "How dare this little novice answer so glibly!"

Shen-hui then asked: "When you sit in meditation, Master, do you see or not?"

The Master struck Shen-hui three times with his staff and said: "When I hit you, do you feel pain or not?"

Shen-hui replied: "I feel both pain and no pain."

The Master said: "I both see and do not see."

Shen-hui questioned the Master: "What do you mean by saying that you both see and do not see?"

The Master said: "I constantly see the offenses committed in my own mind; I do not see the right and wrong, the good and bad in others. That's why I say that I both see and do not see. You said that you felt both pain and no pain. What did you mean? If you felt no pain, you would be the same as a piece of wood or a stone. But if you felt pain, you would be the same as an ordinary, unenlightened person and become angry and resentful. Your talk of seeing and not seeing is nothing but dualism. Pain and no pain belong to [the realm of] life and death. You have not even seen your original nature. How can you make fools of others like this?"

Shen-hui apologized, bowing low to the Master.

SOKEI-AN SAYS:

There was a boy whose name was Shen-hui. This boy would be the promoter of the Southern School of Zen in Northern China. He was called Ho-tse Shen-hui after the Lotus Pond Temple (Ho-tse-ssu) on the southern shore of the Yellow River. The young Shen-hui, later to become one of the famous Zen masters recognized by the emperor, called himself the Seventh Patriarch of Zen in China, but there were other parties that claimed the patriarchate. His claim was not authentic. His record was recently excavated from a cave at Tun-huang, in Kansu. For one thousand years, he existed obscurely in Zen history. But now we realize that Shen-hui, of the Ho-tse Monastery in Ch'ang-an, was one of the most active Zen masters of that period. The incident here described happened when he was thirteen years of age.

He was the son of the house of Kao in Hsiang-yang. Hsiang-yang was a mountain town on the northern shore of the Yellow River. It was the center of the Northern School of Zen.

When he was thirteen years old, he came from Yu-ch'uan to pay homage to the Master. Of course, it is the etiquette of Buddhist temples that visitors cannot immediately interview the master—"My name is such-and-such, and I have come from such-and-such a place for such-and-such a reason." Later, the master will give him an interview while the main disciples stand on both sides of him and many more monks stand against the wall. The visitor comes in and has his interview with the master, who is seated upon a chair.

No doubt the Sixth Patriarch had heard all about the child, so he gave him a kindly interview. The Sixth Patriarch was not a young man at that time; he was about sixty years of age.

The Master said: "Good friend": The Sixth Patriarch probably said, "Dear little friend."

"You have endured great hardship in coming such a distance, but did you bring along the original?" This is the usual manner of Zen questioning. The question is rather significant, and it has a deep meaning. Another question a master may give to a student is: "Before father and mother, what was your original aspect?" Meaning, in terms of your religion, before Adam and Eve, what were you?

Adam and Eve were the first human beings who recognized their own wisdom. They took themselves out of the bosom of nature, making the human being independent. But in your terms, they were the first man and the first woman. To us, this means: Before your self-realization, before the creation of the world, what were you? You may answer: "Oh, I was ether," "I was an electron," "I was a clay doll, modelled by God," or, "I was omnipotent and in the state of reality. I was one with the whole universe!" This is how students answer, but these answers are not good. So the Sixth Patriarch asked little Shen-hui if he had brought the original with him.

"If you have the original, you should know the master. Tell me." "If you have the original" does not mean your mother's and father's home. It means the original home of your soul before you were conceived by your mother. If you know that, you have a soul.

The "master" you should know is your own God. *He* is the Zen master, not the Patriarch confronting the little child. His *own* master is his God. If he knew the original, he would know his God, his master, when he met him.

We have our own master in our soul, but we have not as of yet met him, so we do not know him. Your God is always in your own mind from morning to evening, awake or asleep. Not until then can you speak or teach anything about this master to another. When you know the original, you will meet him.

Shen-hui replied: "Non-abiding is the origin. Seeing is the master." Non-abiding! Seeing! The True Soul is not living like the water in this glass. You cannot grasp the True Soul like you grasp a Halloween lantern. You cannot feel it and scream, "I found it—God!" There is no such God. With a human eye and a human mind, you will fail to find God. God is not existing in this world of phenomena, this world of seeing and hearing.

I think this sermon of mine is very familiar to you. Many Christians speak like this. I hear them on the radio. I wonder if they really know.

When I asked the man selling hot dogs on Long Island, "How's business?" he said: "I don't worry about business. I'm my own boss." All he has is a little peddling cart, but he is his own boss. Something like this was in the child's mind—"I have no place to live, but I am my own master."

If he had been just a mere child, he would have said: "My father's name is Mr. Kao, and my home is in Hsiang-yang." But this child is very smart. He is a Zen student.

The Master said: "How dare this little novice answer so glibly!" He was terribly amused. Although the Sixth Patriarch was very happy, he did not express his joy. But the child knew.

Shen-hui then asked: "When you sit in meditation, Master, do you see or not?" That is, do you see or not in your mind? As a question, by a novice thirteen years of age, this was not insignificant.

When you meditate just a couple of minutes, your mind becomes very calm, and if you keep on doing it, you will be absorbed in the mind of nature. And in that mind center, there is no self. Finding the mind center in meditation, you find the original—you find your own master.

The Master struck Shen-hui three times with his staff and said: "When I hit you, do you feel pain or not?" Zen masters always had a six-foot-long staff. They were very severe! This is the Zen style. In Zen, we do not chatter ugly things. We strike!

Shen-hui replied: "I feel both pain and no pain."—"When hit, my palm feels pain, but my mind doesn't." This is the true attitude when receiving all kinds of sicknesses. Your body is sick, but your mind is not sick, your mind is God. Your mind will never be sick. Your physical body will bear the law of causation, but you cannot change the mind.

You must understand these laws. Although one may have a straight mind, one cannot make the physical body straight at once. But when the mind is straightened, everything will be straight.

The Master said: I both see and do not see." Usually, the Patriarch's words have been explained by Zen students in this way: In meditation, one realizes one's own existence, one sees one's self. But consciousness which sees cannot see consciousness-itself like you see the outside with your eye. The eye cannot see itself, or fire burn itself. This pinching finger cannot pinch itself. The axle of a wheel does not rotate while the wheel is turning. These are not true explanations. But Hui-neng's words are usually explained in such a fashion.

Shen-hui questioned the Master: "What do you mean by saying that you both see and do not see?" Really, in the true experience of meditation—I shall give a severe criticism of the Master—the deepest principles of Zen cannot be explained in words. When Hui-neng said, "see and do not see," he was giving candy to the thirteen-year-old novice. But this novice was smart enough to ask, "What do you mean by saying that in meditation you see and do not see?" He drove the Master into a corner to catch him. The Master evaded the answer, but his own view is in his explanation.

The Master said: "I constantly see the offenses committed in my own mind; I do not see the right and wrong, the good and bad in others. That's why I say that I both see and do not see." His offences are the errors and erroneous conceptions that are conceived in his own mind. Of course, under these words are deeper meanings than appear on the surface, such as the five shadows of his own mind and all the minds created in his own brain. The Sixth Patriarch gives no heed to either the right and wrong or the good and bad in others. In such a way he explained it. This explanation can be understood as his attitude toward a thirteen-year-old mind.

When I was young, I puzzled about seeing and not-seeing myself. In meditation, I do not see myself, but in daily life, I see myself. This conception divides myself into two existences. In one, I *must* see myself. But this is foolish. These are only names! If I call IT "self," all the universe is self. And if I call IT "no-self," all the universe is no-self. I do not need to call IT either "self" or "no-self." You can call IT "self" and you can call this fellow "no-self." You can change the names but not the nature itself.

"You said that you felt both pain and no pain. What did you mean? If you felt no pain, you would be the same as a piece of wood or a stone. But if you felt pain, you would be the same as an ordinary, unenlightened person and become angry and resentful." The Sixth Patriarch scared the poor child. "If you say you do not feel pain when I strike you, you are the same as a stone or brick. If you feel pain, you are just an ordinary human being." Perhaps this ordinary man annoyed the poor child.

"Your talk of seeing and not seeing is nothing but dualism. Pain and no pain belong to [the realm of] life and death." "Pain and no pain" can be translated in many ways—"appearance and disappearance," "growth and decay," and so on. Entertaining two views is the most inconvenient way to live on the surface of the earth. Almost all people have two views: good and bad, sacred and profane, and so on. It is like having two shoes for one foot. For instance, in peaceful times you cannot kill, but on the battlefield it is permitted to kill as much as you can. I had a Christian friend who went with me to battle. He was standing sentry outside a little village when suddenly someone appeared very close to him. He shot, killing him. This bothered him for about six years. He is still living, and I hope he has made peace by this time. So two views are not very comfortable. You must hold only one view in your mind. Through this one view, you judge yourself, and you can decide your actions. One view is very convenient and comfortable. Otherwise, you must close one eye and open the other, like winking without end. You must live the broad life, in a very narrow way.

I am a Buddhist monk, and as a Buddhist monk I have many things to do. First, I must be a man, and second, I must be accepted as a man. When a monk finishes his studies, the Zen master says to him: "Now you have finished your studies. I cannot keep you any longer in my temple. I cannot feed you any longer. Go away! If you are worth anything, *nagas*, *yakshas* and *rakshas* will support you. Hide yourself. Do not call yourself a monk or a Zen master for quite a while. Do not show yourself. Wait to be found by the student."

It is true—like a diamond that is hidden. Sometimes false stones are hidden in a cave among true diamonds, and they will deceive. But the expert will know. Just once, you should put yourself into the dirt or earth. The monk or the nun will grow from that place, the plain, ordinary life. "Only yesterday he was ordained. Today, he calls himself a monk!" There is no such thing in the history of monks or nuns. You must hide, then someone will discover you. That is the way. But today you are a monk, and tomorrow you walk the street with a brass band and velvet and plumage on your hat—"I'm a monk! I'm a monk!"

"'You have not even seen your original nature." One with such a view has not yet found his original nature. The Sixth Patriarch gave a final judgment to this thirteen-year-old child.

"How can you make fools of others like this?" This was a very smart little boy. This statement of the Sixth Patriarch was very sweet—"Are you trying to impress me that you've grown big?"

Shen-hui made an apology, bowing low to the Master.

The Master continued: "If your mind is deluded, you will fail to see, and will ask a teacher to help you find the way. If your mind is enlightened, you will naturally recognize your original nature and will practice in accordance with the Dharma. But having deluded yourself, you fail to see your own mind, and instead come here and ask me whether I can see or not. I know by seeing for myself. How can I substitute [my insight for] your delusion? If you see for yourself, you will not substitute [your insight for] my delusion. Without knowing and seeing for yourself, why ask me if I see or not?"

Shen-hui bowed low again and again, over a hundred times, asking the Master's pardon for his offense. He became a faithful servant of the Master and remained with him at his beck and call.

SOKEI-AN SAYS:

The Master continued: If your mind is deluded, you will fail to see [your original nature]": In the *Surangama Sutra*, the Buddha described various deluded minds. No one can see his original nature through a deluded mind. The deluded mind is like tinted celluloid—you cannot see real colors. If the celluloid is tinted blue, the whole world will become blue as you peek through the film.

The human mind is somehow always deluded or intoxicated. If you take a little wine and say something ridiculous or something wonderful or something you never dreamed about, someone will tell you what you have said when you become sober, and you will be ashamed.

A doctor, who was a chemist, as well as a physician, went to a small village—this is not a story of America—where a student questioned him: "Doctor, tell me what creates all the phenomena on the shore, all that beauty of summer, the shades of color and those girls and boys?" The doctor said: "Hormones!" The student said: "Without hormones, what would happen to human life?" The doctor's answer was: "I never thought about it, but without hormones, there would be no human life."

The human mind is always deluded or intoxicated by some chemical element and through that chemical element its view is formed. From the religious standpoint, the human mind is always deluded by some offence, some error. The Buddha said the human mind was deluded by desires.

If you try to find your original nature through emotion, you will fail. If you try to find your original nature through reason, you will also fail. You must not be caught by the elements within your mind. When you come to take *sanzen*, the Zen master will destroy the elements within your mind. If you appear before the master wearing your emotion, he will destroy your emotion; and if you appear wearing your reasoning, he will destroy your reasoning. Thus, one by one, the master will annihilate and strip you of all those elements in your mind, as you would peel an onion, until finally, through this stripping and peeling process, your original nature is uncovered.

Once a Zen master asked a student: "Can you hear the sound of one hand?" I read an English commentary on this that said: "To make a sound, you must use both hands." When I read this, I was eating rice in my kitchen, and I blew the rice all over the table. That writer certainly observed that koan through his deluded thoughts. If a pickpocket were to observe this koan, he would be insulted! If a farmer were to observe it, he would think it impossible to do his rough work single-handed, and so on with a mother who strokes her baby with her hand. Everyone observes this koan from his own attitude, thinking he is observing it with an unbiased view.

A feudal lord had been observing this koan for a long time. He became very angry and thought he would cut down the monk who had given it to him. One day, when the lord was visiting with the monk, the monk asked him, "Can you hear the sound of one hand?" The feudal lord struck with his sword. The monk shifted his position and said, "Your answer was very good, but the sword was good, too."

When you observe this koan, you will understand my story. You must annihilate all deluded views. This is the real meaning of religion. People somehow misunderstand this. You think you must do many things or that you must not dance, smoke, or associate with ladies, and so forth. Though those Hinayana monks do not associate with ladies, never going outside the temple, they are always thinking of the world. They have the elements of the outside world in their minds. Just cutting off the outside does not help. The true Buddhist does not think in such a way.

You must understand religion. All the things that you must not do—dance, sing, smoke, touch a woman—are deluding your mind.

"*. . . And will ask a teacher to help you find the way.*"—"What? Drinking water doesn't cure your thirst? You've come to ask someone to drink it for you?" Foolish, isn't it?

"*If your mind is enlightened, you will naturally recognize your original nature, and will practice in accordance with the Dharma.*" You do not need to ask anyone any question. The law, the Dharma, is written in your own mind and body. By means of practice you understand and follow the law. You will understand what and how much you can do. Though you read a thousand books on moral ethics, if you do not practice, you do not know either.

"But having deluded yourself, you fail to see your own mind, and instead come here and ask me whether I can see or not. I know by seeing for myself." Seeing is believing. I know my original nature by seeing it. This is Zen. We do not say I know my original nature by reading about it in some book or by listening to somebody's lecture. It is not in any book, and no one can speak about it. Your original nature is yourself. But your eye is always fixed on the outside or on some notion in your mind or on psychology, psychoanalysis or sexology, and you attach to these. "How much can I eat today?" You do not ask questions of your stomach, but of the sky! "Today is Scorpio. Can I eat today?"

I am not attacking those people who believe in all of that. But from my own standpoint, I cannot believe it. The true God is *here* and not in the sky. And all those occult stories which have a meaning—Mars, Venus, Saturn, Uranus—all this is in the mind *here*. The stars which guide one's future are within one, not in the sky. All the stars are in consciousness. Some German philospher or scientist would explain these stories by symbolism—symbols of something *here*.

"How can I substitute [my insight for] your delusion? And if you see for yourself, *you will not substitute [your insight for] my delusion. Without knowing and seeing for yourself, why ask me if I see or not?"* The Sixth Patriarch very kindly explains original nature. It is very important.

In the Zen school, we say "see" original nature. Christians say, "Trust God and have faith." To have faith in God is a very clever way of speaking. They say, do not philosophize about how to conceive of His nature. Without knowing Him, without thinking of what His nature is, if you have faith in Him, you can be saved by Him. It is a Christian motto. They say that without knowing him, you must have faith in Him, and by your faith save yourself. To see your own original nature in Buddhism, you must annihilate your deluded thoughts. But in Christianity, you have faith in it without knowing what it is.

Is God true or not true? Do not think about it; just have faith in God. There is *some* connection here, but it is a different way of speaking about it. Usually, Buddhists who criticize Christianity, saying, "Foolish, how can they swallow it?" do not understand the true meaning of Christian doctrine.

On Sunday mornings, I get an intimate feeling in listening to Christian ministers on my radio. They say, "Have faith and it will save you." The words are true, though they have a hollow sound. I think the ministers do not know what they are talking about, but the words are true.

The record of the Sixth Patriarch is very precise. With his wide-awake mind, he expresses his thought very clearly to us from one thousand years ago.

Shen-hui bowed low again and again, over a hundred times, asking the Master's pardon for his offense. He became a faithful servant of the Master and remained with him at his beck and call.

One day the Master said to the monks: "I have something that has neither head nor tail, neither face nor back, nor any name to call it by. Do any of you know what it is?"

Shen-hui stepped forward and said: "It is the original state of all the buddhas and my own buddha-nature."

The Master replied: "I said that it has no name, yet right away you called it 'original state' and 'buddha-nature.' Even if you later go to live in a hut with nothing but thatch to cover your head, you will still just be a student who understands intellectually."

After the death of the Patriarch, Shen-hui went to Lo-yang and greatly promulgated the Master's teaching of sudden enlightenment. He wrote the Record of Manifesting the Teaching, *a work that has been widely read.*

SOKEI-AN SAYS:

This concludes the conversation between Shen-hui and the Sixth Patriarch. Shen-hui was only a little boy when he went to the Sixth Patriarch.

One day the Master said to the monks:" When the Master speaks like this, it is for some special occasion, such as the opening or closing of the summer training session.

"I have something that has neither head nor tail, neither face nor back, nor any name to call it by. Do any of you know what it is?" The Sixth Patriarch is talking about the first principle of his Zen, the trademark of his business: "I have something"—of course, he is talking about Reality on which everything depends—"that has neither head nor tail, neither face nor back, nor any name to call it by. Do you, any of you, know what it is?"

It's a queer thing. Ancient philosophy does not speak like the philosophies of today. They speak in an awkward fashion, like this—"which has neither head nor tail," and so forth. As usual, the mind of the human being conceives something from a name. Without a name, no one would make a conception of it. So everything that has a name exists in your brain; it does not exist in Reality.

So the Sixth Patriarch asks: "Do you, any of you, know what it is?" If it has no face or back, no head or tail, and no name. No one can conceive it. No one can know it. If you know what is high or low, wide or narrow, then it is not Reality; it is something that exists as a phenomenon. Reality is inconceivable. You cannot conceive it in your mind. Of course, when you realize what this Reality is, it will be different. It *has* a head and tail! It *has* a front and back! Usually the entrance of Zen is the climax of all other sects of Buddhism. "It has neither face nor back" is a famous description of Buddhism. It has given us some very curious stories:

Another is: A rickshaw man with an empty rickshaw enters a lonely path into a garden. He sees a woman walking very slowly. Her back was very bent. The rickshaw man calls to her: "Madame, I am going your way. Take my rickshaw!" But when she turned toward him, she had no face! And when she turned away, she had no back! She just evaporated! And the rickshaw man fainted.

Anyone who reads the Sixth Patriarch's story this way has no understanding of Zen.

Shen-hui stepped forward and said: "It is the original state of all the buddhas and my own buddha-nature." This young boy, about thirteen years of age, answered the Master's question.

Buddha's "original state" means Reality. It has no color, sound, smell, taste, or anything by which you can make a conception. It is so-called buddha-nature, which exists always, omnipresent and omniscient—one's own original nature.

In Buddhism, Reality is always spoken of in this fashion. You cannot see it, hear it, smell it, or taste it. And you cannot prove it because you would be conceiving it in your mind, and hence, it would be abstract. Everyone thinks it is Reality, but it is not. It is only your thoughts. Such people always look like this [mimics] when they talk about Reality, and like this [mimics] when they meditate. Why should anyone use such expressions to talk about Reality? Without words, Reality exists. Without thinking about it, Reality is *here.* Without knowing it, *you are in Reality.* If you realize what Reality is, then you do not need to worry about names. You do not need to make a clear expression. Just be yourself! Reality is very near.

The Master replied: "I said that it has no name, yet right away you called it 'original state' and 'buddha-nature.'" Even if you later go to live in a hut with nothing but thatch to cover your head, you will just be a student who understands intellectually." The Sixth Patriarch said: "It's gone to your head!"

Without intellectual understanding you cannot grasp it, but with intellectual understanding you stay in it. You think about God, and it always stays in your mind, in your skull. It's as though you were in the ocean and you were thinking about it—very big, very broad, full of fish and beautiful! And you dream. Finally, you come to believe that the ocean you are thinking about is the real ocean, and you never see anything more to the end of your days. But if you open your eye, the ocean is very different. It is like thinking in an abstract way or saying "O-O-M-M," and you open your eye, see it, and say, "Why should I do such a queer thing?"

I find many differences between the East and the West, some entirely different. The Western painter paints from the outside and observes closely. But about religion, he closes his eyes. The Oriental artist never paints from the outside, never copies the birds and willows. He picks up every dream in his mind and paints it. But when he comes to religion, he keeps both eyes open and tries to find Buddha or God in this human life.

Intellectual understanding! As long as you form an intellectual understanding of religion in your mind, it is after all only an intellectual understanding. It is not real religion. And what is real religion? It is very difficult to speak about.

When I was studying Zen, my teacher always watched my intellectual tendencies very carefully—"Why do that again? Why do you always . . . ?" I thought I was very stupid, but it is my way. One student who came here went away for a month and came back, and I saw his old attitude, and I corrected it. For three or four months he remained upright, and then he fell back. When I meet someone who has taken Zen for several years, and if I find he has intellectual tendencies, I know his grasp of Zen is not free or strong.

After the death of the Patriarch, Shen-hui went to Lo-yang and greatly promulgated the Master's teaching of sudden enlightenment. Shen-hui started an entirely new sect. His temple is still existing.

He wrote the Record of Manifesting the Teaching, *a work that has been widely read.* In this record, the nature of the Zen sect is explained by Shen-hui. Shen-hui also wrote the record of the Sixth Patriarch. There is no doubt about it. And we are still reading it! In this record the nature of the Zen sect is clearly explained. Anyone who truly wishes to find a foundation in daily life will find Zen a true foundation, a foundation which already exists in your mind. The foundation of life must be very solid, solid and firm like a rock. And you do not need to call it by any name.

The Master noted that a great number of monks of other schools had gathered at the temple in order to attack his teaching and stir up ill will. Having pity on them, the Master said: "Students of the Way should utterly annihilate notions, whether good or bad. That which cannot be named is named self-nature. The nature that is non-dual is named true-nature. All the [Buddha's] teachings were devised upon this true nature. You must see it instantly for yourselves."

When they heard these words, they all bowed to the Master and begged him to be their teacher.

SOKEI-AN SAYS:

This part of the record is written at the end of the conversation between Shen-hui and the Sixth Patriarch, and concludes the eighth chapter. Some scholars say the "Master" is Shen-hui himself who is speaking to his own disciples. I think this Master is the Sixth Patriarch, Master Hui-neng.

The Master noted that a great number of monks of other schools had gathered at the temple in order to attack his teaching and stir up ill will. This kind of debating of the questions and teachings of Mahayana Buddhism happened in all the Buddhist groups. All day long they were disputing about something or other. A Buddhist student should not forget that the cultivation of one's own strength in debate over someone else's theory has nothing to do with the Buddhist spirit. The Buddhist student should cultivate the strength of his guts. We do not say brain or heart. In English, "guts" carries the exact idea here. We should fight for our own existence as best we can, but to gain or to lose, we do not care about. Like the ancient warrior, we must cultivate such a spirit: to live or to die is not our prerogative; to decide how to fight is our decision. We do not need to spend our time in debating somebody's theory. If you have time to sit down, cultivate the strength of your will power. We were always told in the temple that we should not move, should not be disturbed by anything in meditation. Even a thunderbolt striking a tree outside the window should not excite us.

There is a story in ancient scripture about the Buddha's meditation: A huge thunderbolt struck and killed nine men and nine oxen. People went to the Buddha and asked him, "Did you notice the terrible thunder that killed nine men and nine oxen?" The Buddha answered: "Did it? I didn't know."

Of course, he was aware. But to describe the Buddha's calmness, the story is told as if he were unaware of the thunder. The Buddha was different. He heard the thunder, but he was not disturbed. I think such enormous strength of mind could have influential power over others. The Buddha did not meditate in order to speak or to give any theory on Buddhism. *He himself was Buddhism.* When he smiled, the whole universe smiled. When he meditated, the whole universe was shaken. This is how we are told of his tremendous influence. It did not come from debating over theories. It came from grasping emptiness. Debating the difficult questions of other sects is a very foolish thing.

Having pity on them, the Master said: "Students of the Way should utterly annihilate notions, whether good or bad." This is a very important point in Buddhism. In the causal law, there is neither good or bad. If there were no human beings living on this earth, plowing its fields and cultivating its seed, and a big flood were to wash away the surface of the earth, it would not be good or bad. But human beings were born, and they tried to accomplish their desire to live, so floods became a menace.

Good or bad always relates to one's desire. If there were no desire in the human mind, there would be no good or bad. So to think of the causal, the primal law, you do not have to think about good and bad. If you must think in words, better say, "All is good, there is no bad." Good and bad should be decided according to place, time, and condition.

"That which cannot be named is named 'self-nature.' The nature that is non-dual is named true-nature."—Neither good-nature nor bad-nature, man-nature nor God-nature.

This idea that God is good and man is bad is really very stupid. In the causal state and the primal law, there is neither God nor man, there is just Being—fire! Call it eternal fire. This fire cools, becomes gas, and crystalizes, creating all kinds of phenomena—beings which struggle to exist. Then the good and bad idea sprouts like the tips of branches. We must think of good and bad when we do business for our food and shelter, but there is no dual nature. There is just one Original Being.

The mind that cherishes no notion is the mind of *zazen*. I do not always like to use the word "meditation"—it carries with it the idea of something on which you meditate—but I am using the word meditation to take the place of *zazen* or *dhyana*. *Dhyana-yoga* is not just meditation. The Buddha didn't meditate on something that is in his brain. Such meditation creates not calmness but confusion.

Dhyana-yoga is what I always do before my lectures, but we do not need to call this by any name. The transparent and clear mind immediately leads you to your original nature, while thinking something makes you deviate from it. Notion is not original nature; notion is notion. This smoke is not original nature; it is smoke. The thoughts in your brain are smoke, too, and we do not care for this smoke. We go immediately back to the fire and become fire. The whole universe is just a mass of fire.

""All the [Buddha's] teachings were devised upon this true nature." First you must obtain true original nature in order to understand all laws; then you must devise the teachings, the entrances, and gates to that true nature. For example, "I am going to teach Buddhism to a Chinese gambler. I wonder how?" You do not need to speak so much, but you have to devise many entrances and all kinds of gates.

Without the original ground, how can you devise any gates? And if your teacher is not the original ground, how can he devise any? It's ridiculous! It's as if a five year old child were to say, "Papa, tomorrow I shall earn one million dollars, and I will give it to you as I promised!"

When you teach religion to a woman, you cannot say, "Come on!" The woman would run away. You must make a gate. And for the men students, you must make a different gate. True men shout at one another!

For the children and old people, there must be other gates through which the teaching will go out. When I was young, I was teaching the nurse of some children who came into my garden.

It is through the gate of the true ground of original mind that we gain a bodhisattva mind, which is the human mind, the animal mind, and deva mind.

"You must see it instantly for yourselves." You must not think that this is just one of the Oriental cults. All must attain original nature.

I attained this original nature by zazen, and by my own means, I give it to you. And you, by your own means, will find your answer. You will come to me and demonstrate, and I will give you my judgment. For I made my own demonstration to my teacher, as he did to his, and so on through the generations back to Japan and then to China and Bodhidharma, and from Bodhidharma to the Buddha. So this judgment goes back very far. There is no examination in writing. It is preserved eye to eye, truth to truth.

We are very grateful to the teachers who handed down this wonderful treasure to us. It should not be just for China and Japan, but for the whole world. It is not for the dreamy, vague mind. One in a thousand has this developed brain. But if you haven't the brain, you must have a strong nature. And if you haven't a strong nature, you must have will power. You must have something.

When they heard these words, they all bowed to the Master and begged him to be their teacher. Remember the story of the blind turtle? Once in a million years he saw the sky, then it was all over. Foolish!

Just annihilate all those thoughts and become a crystal bowl. Like this . . .

CHAPTER IX

THE ROYAL REQUEST

On the fifteenth day of the first month of the first year of Shen-lung, the Dowager Empress Tse-t'ien and the Emperor Chung-tsung issued the following decree:

"We have entreated the two masters [Hui-]An and [Shen-]Hsiu to accept our offerings in the palace. We shall endeavor to study their peerless vehicle whenever we can spare time from attending to the affairs of the empire. In humility, these two masters have deferred, saying: 'In the south is the Ch'an Master [Hui-]neng. To him were secectly transmitted the robe and the Dharma of the Great Master Hung-jen, who transmitted to him the seal of buddha-mind. You should summon him.'

"We hereby in haste send a royal servant, Hsieh Chien, as the bearer of our letter of invitation. We entreat you, Master, in your benevolence, to come at once to the capital."

The Master replied, declining the royal invitation on the grounds of illness and begging to live out his remaining years in the mountains.

Hsieh Chien said: "The Ch'an masters of the capital all say: 'If you wish to realize the Way, you must sit in meditation (dhyana) *and practice* samadhi. *No one has ever achieved liberation without practicing dhyana-samadhi. What sort of teaching does your Reverence advocate?"*

The Master replied: "The Way depends on the enlightenment of the mind. How could it depend on sitting? The [Diamond] Sutra says: 'If you claim that the Tathagatha either sits or lies down, you are following a false path.' For what reason? Because there is nowhere from which he comes and nowhere to which he goes. That which neither appears nor vanishes is the pure dhyana of Tathagata. [In this state], all existence, being absolutely empty, is the pure seat of the Tathagata's meditation. Ultimately, there is nothing to prove, much less any need to sit in meditation."

SOKEI-AN SAYS:

In this chapter the Sixth Patriarch clearly expresses his idea of Zen, which is entirely different from the Zen of the Northern School. In this part, he is treating meditation as if it were of no importance. Our Zen today is more or less reflects his attitude. In Buddhism, there were many teachers who denied the merit of the sitting position. In China, it was the Sixth Patriarch who did so. However, you must remember this is his particular idea.

On the fifteenth day of the first month of the first year of Shen-lung, the Dowager Empress Tse-t'ien, and the Emperor Chung-tsung issued the following decree: The fifteenth day of the first month of the New Year is usually a great festival day in China. The first year of Shen-lung was 705. *Shen* means "god," and *lung* means "dragon." The names of these periods in the dynasty were changed two or three times, upon the ascent or abdication of those on the throne.

The Dowager Empress [Wu] Tse-t'ien was a famous empress who became the mother of Buddhism in China. "Dowager Empress" sounds as if she were very old, but she was really very young. She became the empress when she was about thirty-one. The Emperor Chung-tsung, her son, was quite young when he came to the throne, so it was she who ruled the country.

Buddhism and the empress had an intimate relationship. She invited many Buddhist scholars from India to China. So when she heard that a more complete text of the *Avatamsaka Sutra* was in Khotan, in the territory of India, she sent her servants to beg for the Sanskrit text. The text was sent to China with a monk named Sikshananda. This monk traveled to Ch'ang-an and translated the sutra with Chinese scholars in A.D. 695.

"We have entreated the two masters, [Hui-]An and [Shen-]Hsiu": Both Hui-an and Shen-hsiu were disciples of the Fifth Patriarch, Hung-jen. Shen-hsiu, as you know, was master of the Northern School. It is said that Hui-an lived a long time, dying at a great age, and that Shen-hsiu was tall and handsome and had silvery hair and whiskers that looked like white cream.

"To accept our offerings in the palace." The palace was in Ch'ang-an, today's Sian, the center of the Communist army. From the descriptions we have, it was very beautiful. It doesn't mean, however, that these two monks, or any others who were invited, had always to stay there.

"We shall endeavor to study their peerless vehicle whenever we can spare time from attending to the affairs of the empire." That is, they made a study of Zen, the "peerless vehicle."

"In humility, these two masters deferred, saying, 'In the south is the Ch'an master, [Hui]-neng. To him were secectly transmitted the robe and the Dharma of the Great Master Hung-jen.'" "In humility" means the Buddhist attitude. If I were invited to America and someone had asked me who the best scholar in Japan was, I would certainly recommend him.

This robe was handed down from the Buddha to Bodhidharma and from Bodhidharma to Hui-neng. The Dharma was transmitted, but the robe became very old, and its transmission came to an end in the time of the Sixth Patriarch. This part is very carefully written in the first chapter of this record.

". . . Who transmitted to him the seal of buddha-mind. You should summon him." In Asia, we make the impression of a seal on a document, as you, here, put a signature on it. When Germany made peace with France, I heard they used a huge seal. But we in the Zen school do not use material seals. We use buddha-mind, face to face, finally reaching the same conclusion. Then the Zen master gives his acknowledgment to the disciple. This cannot be written in any book. It must be mind to mind, eye to eye, soul to soul. I repeat this many times, but there must be no error.

Once the torch holders were many. Now in all of Japan there are perhaps two hundred. It is like the shaking of a candle before a storm. Once out, no one will know what was true and what was false. No one can find out. Everything will disappear. Buddhism will be wiped out. You must understand the value of the torch holder. In this Western world, they write about it; but they do not know the existence of this line, a line with a pedigree like a dog or cat—but more important than a Pekinese!

"We hereby in haste send a royal servant, Hsieh Chien, as the bearer of our letter of invitation. Hsieh Chien was the courtier of the Emperor Chung-tsung sent to invite the Sixth Patriarch to the city. Bearing the emperor's letter, he went down south to Ts'ao-ch'i.

"We entreat you, Master, in your benevolence, to come at once to the capital." The Master replied, declining the royal invitation on the ground of illness and begging to live out his remaining years in the mountains. Refusing to live in the palace, the Sixth Patriarch stayed on the shore of Ts'ao-ch'i at the foot of a mountain, remaining there until he died.

Hsieh Chien said: "The Ch'an masters of the capital all say: 'If you wish to realize the Way, you must sit in meditation (dhyana) and practice samadhi.'" Dhyana, does not exactly convey the same meaning as the

English word translated here as "meditation." It is more than meditation. *Samadhi* can be translated into English as "absorption"—one who practices meditation is absorbed into that on which he meditates—but "absorption" is not a good translation either. There is no way to explain *samadhi* if you have had no experience of it. When you attain a real answer to a koan, at that moment you will be in *samadhi*. Absorption has a passive sense; but one realizes samadhi positively. It is true that when students just pass koans and do not get a great result it is because they are not trained to keep themselves in samadhi.

"No one has ever achieved liberation without practicing dhyana-samadhi. *What sort of teaching does your Reverence advocate?"* *Dhyana-samadhi* means *zazen.* When you practice *zazen* for many years and you attain the answer to a koan, samadhi becomes the ground of your knowledge, and you really attain enlightenment. A Zen master like the Sixth Patriarch is entirely different. He was born a bodhisattva. We cannot take his attitude. We must train ourselves in meditation and must meditate on our koans. Your experience of samadhi will testify to your knowledge of attainment. But if you are engrossed in the discussion of Buddhism and talk about it from morning to evening, you will only grow more deluded! You will never be emancipated from this deluded world.

The Master replied: "The Way depends on the enlightenment of the mind. How could it depend on sitting?" Of course, the attainment of Dharma is dependent upon enlightenment. If those who practice sitting from morning to evening attain enlightenment, then those beggars sitting on the way to the subway will attain enlightenment.

We practice the commandment to keep our mind quiet. To do this is to attain enlightenment, but we have no time for quietude. We have to attend to business and go home to fight with our wives and husbands. But the monks in the monastery had this commandment, so they meditated upon their koans with quiet mind. Then they came to enlightenment, to awakening.

To awaken is a very important point. I was very busy in the monastery. I had no time to sit and meditate, so I meditated standing! I was always concentrated—in the kitchen, in the bathroom, in the street-car, sweeping the garden, carving images for my teacher. When I came to a place where for a little while there would be no one, I stretched my mind to my koan and meditated upon it.

Some of those monks grew stupid sitting and meditating—it was nothing. You must work with your brain upon your question, must boil it down. Then the question becomes very clear. When you have any doubt about your koan, you cannot attain. To awaken is the goal.

"The Diamond Sutra *says:"* In the *Diamond Sutra*, there are three main viewpoints. We observe these viewpoints in the koans:

1) Everyone depends upon something—religious conviction, science, something heard or learned. In Christianity, it is the Bible. In Buddhism, it is the sutra. These people are like old men or women that depend upon a cane. Without a cane or notion, "depending upon nothing, manifest your mind." This is the first point.

2) All the enlightenments of the buddhas and Tathagatas come from this *Diamond Sutra*, but not from the sutra that is on paper. The second point is: "What is the *Diamond Sutra*?"

3) Those who wish to see the Tathagata with their eye, or hear him with their ear, are following a false Dharma. One cannot see the Tathagata. So the third principle of the sutra is the koan: "How do you meet the Tathagata?"

"If you claim that the Tathagatha either sits or lies down, you are following a false path.' For what reason? Because there is nowhere from which he comes and nowhere to which he goes." "Comes" and "goes," "sits" and "lies" are the so-called four dignities.

Tathagata means "as it is"—IT, the state of Reality in this phenomenal world. *This* exists as *That.* When you attain the first koan, "Before father and mother, what were you?" you realize Tathagata. This Zen koan can be explained by Christian theology, too. Christ went back to the Father without changing his physical body—z-z-z-t!—and he went up. He was Tathagata, wasn't he? But if you affirm that he who comes and goes, sits and lies—sits under the Bodhi Tree and lies under the *sala* tree—is Tathagata, you are following the false Dharma.

"That which neither appears nor vanishes is the pure dhyana *of Tathagata.* How Christ went back to his Father, from the Christian viewpoint, the popular viewpoint, indicates that he had an abode. But he who has attained true Christian knowledge has no such notion. Tathagata has no abode. He is sitting here now! Did he come from somewhere? No! Will he will go somewhere? No! He did not come, and he will not go. He did not exist from the beginning, and he will not be annihilated.

[In this state], all existence, being absolutely empty, is the pure seat of the Tathagata's meditation." In the state of Reality, existence is empty because it has never been created and will not be destroyed. It exists forever, so it cannot be destroyed. But this is just our vision. In reality, it is empty. So when you observe thus, all existence is absolutely empty, and this emptiness is then the seat on which you meditate.

"Ultimately, there is nothing to prove": This is the highest statement of Buddhism, and there can be no higher statement than this. It is the end of Zen. Zen practice comes to an end after you have attained it. The Zen master will say, "Your Zen is over." So when your knowledge becomes one with Buddha, your Zen is at an end. Knowledge of a certain kind is easy to obtain, but practice is very hard. In enlightenment, there is nothing to think about or speak about.

". . . Much less any need to sit in meditation." The Sixth Patriarch just spit it out. He was very decisive—"Cast it out!" This statement about meditation created the Southern school of Zen, but Zen students of today practice both the Southern and the Northern schools of Zen.

Your attainment must be proved, but you prove it yourself. When you get your real answer to the first koan, you will say: "It can be nothing else!" But you must go to previous masters to compare your attainment. So even though you have no answer in *sanzen,* it is better to take it. Otherwise, you will keep your old notions, and your master may die. If your hair catches fire, you don't say, "Tomorrow I will put it out." No! The Zen master will put it out immediately.

Hsieh Chien said: "When I return to the capital, the emperor is certain to ask me about your teaching. I beg you, in your benevolence, point out for me the pivot of mind. I shall present it to the emperor, the dowager empress, and the scholars in the city. It will be as though a single candle flame were to light a hundred thousand candles. Those which are unlit will be kindled, and from candle to candle, the flame will be transmitted to the endless end."

The Master said: "In the Way, there is neither light nor darkness. Light or darkness implies mutability. The light transmitted from candle to candle will be endless, but will also have an end because those names—light and darkness—are relative designations. The Vimalakirti Sutra *says: 'Dharma is beyond comparison because it exists beyond the relative state.'"*

SOKEI-AN SAYS:

Hsieh Chien said:" Hsieh Chien was the messenger to the Sixth Patriarch from the palace of the Emperor Chung-tsung.

"When I return to the capital, the emperor is certain to ask me about your teaching. I beg you, in your benevolence, point out for me the pivot of mind. I shall present it to the emperor, the dowager empress and the scholars in the city." I have used the translation "pivot of mind" for the Chinese Buddhist term *hsin-yao,* meaning "soul principle" or "principle of mind." As the eye of this fan is the pivot of the fan, so we have the pivot of mind.

Point out for me the pivot of mind. Where is it? In the brain? In the heart? In the abdomen? In the air? Where is the pivot of mind? "I beg you, O Patriarch," said Hsieh Chien, "point out for me the pivot of mind. I shall present it to the emperor and the empress and the scholars in the city." Very strange, isn't it? In ancient days, people were crazy about finding the pivot of mind, like trying to find the pivot of money today. I think, after all, the pivot of mind and the pivot of money are in the same place.

There is a famous koan about this pivot of mind, the koan of the elephant fan. A master said to his disciple: "Fetch me the elephant fan made from the bone of an elephant. I use it every day from morning to evening." The disciple said, "The fan is broken, sir." "Then bring me the elephant," said the master.

This fan is easily broken when the pivot is broken. The elephant fan is the symbol of the mind. When the pivot of the mind is broken, though we have eyes, ears, hands and feet, we are not men any more. We should be locked up somewhere as insane. But in Buddhist symbology, when the pivot of the fan we have been using is broken, it is different from insanity; it means we have attained enlightenment—the fan which we use in this deluded world, our deluded mind, has been broken; it has lost its pivot, and we have attained enlightenment. When the master said to the disciple, "Then bring me the elephant," he meant, "Bring me enlightenment." This is so-called Zen speech.

The monks said queer things—"The deluded mind has been broken!" "Oh, so your worldly mind has been broken? And you have been in heaven? Then bring me God!" It's the same thing. Then what do you do? When the pivot is broken and we attain enlightenment, what is enlightenment? Bring it to me.

This koan was produced in the later period of Zen in China. The Sixth Patriarch answers it a little later.

"It will be as though a single candle flame were to light a hundred thousand candles." When I speak about Buddhism, you go home and speak to your mother, your father, your brother and sister, like a candle lighting other candles. But it is my experience that if you speak about Buddhism to your mother, she will say, "Hush, don't speak about paganism!" One girl who came here went home and spoke to her mother about my words. Later, that young girl wrote me a very pathetic letter.

When I was young, I went to a Christian church. My uncle found out about this and became very angry. I had a hard time explaining my attitude. We are still living in medieval times and not yet free in our minds. Yet, scientifically, we are living in a modern world with electricity, protons, electrons, steam trains, etc. Mentally, however, we are still living in medieval castles surrounded by moats. Knights with long spears still stand on guard by the gates of the mind.

"Those which are unlit will be kindled, and from candle to candle, the flame will be transmitted to the endless end." In the Zen school, the fire of the candle, which is the pivot of mind, is transmitted from Shakyamuni Buddha through the generations to us.

The Master said: "In the Way, there is neither light nor darkness." The "Way" is *Tao*. As used in Chinese Buddhism, Tao signifies religion, Dharma or law, the way of knowledge, the way of morality, the way of mind—your walk in life. What is your walk? I am a physician, monk, shoemaker . . . In Chinese, these are also expressed by the word Tao. But by this Tao the Sixth Patriarch meant the highest Tao in the world. Here there is neither light nor darkness.

"Light or darkness implies mutability." Day goes and night comes; night goes and day comes. Light and dark, dark and light are endlessly changing phases. This is not the highest Tao. We have life and death, death and life, and we change accordingly. I was a student, now I am a monk. I was a soldier, now I am a physician. I was a shoemaker, now I am a grocery man. In the mind, there is life and death every day.

The goddess of the moon repeats life and death every month. On the first of the month the crescent moon appears, and on the fifteenth day, the full moon is at its zenith. On the thirtieth day the moon dies again, but the god of the sun dies every day. Our mind dies every moment, but the mind is also born every moment, is constantly mutable. The highest Tao never takes this mutable phase.

When I went to a psychoanalyst, he said, "What are you thinking now?" "A watch." "What next?" I said: "What next? Doctor, I am not thinking anything now." I despised that doctor for trying to find the system of my mind in such an artificial way.

"The light transmitted from candle to candle will be endless, but will also have an end because those names—light and darkness—are relative designations." We know heat because we know cold. We say this is red because we know green, yellow, or purple. If the whole world were red, we could not know red. When I was young, I thought all men had yellow skins because I had never seen a white man. When I was twelve years old, I went to Yokahama and saw a white man on a pier. It was so strange. It was like a fish in the sea that does not know salt water because it has never known fresh water.

We are conscious of all things because of the variety. If there were only one thing, we would not know it. If the universe is zero, when we are conscious of zero, it is already one, for zero is something. Real nothingness is neither zero nor one, so that which is the highest Dharma is neither zero nor one. It is a state that we cannot conceive with our own mind. That which we cannot see with our eye is God.

"The Vimalakirti Sutra *says: 'Dharma is beyond comparison because it exists beyond the relative state.'"* It is absolute. We observe the sun from here—we observe many things—but the sun also observes us. The whole universe is nothing but fire, and absolute. We should realize this absolute state once in our lifetime. Then from that standpoint, we will observe this world and our daily life in it. This world becomes something else—becomes a new world. You, too, become something else and have a new life.

Our life was given to us by our mother, and we came out crying "Wa-a-ah"—opened our eyes and accepted this world without question. But we have not yet created our own world. We are given this world, this big apple! We must realize it, accept it, and create our own world. When the whole world is our own, then the law is our own law.

Hsieh Chien said: "Light is the symbol of wisdom, and darkness is the symbol of suffering. If he who practices the Dharma cannot destroy his suffering by the light of wisdom, how can he emancipate himself from the beginningless [darkness] of life and death?"

The Master said: "Suffering is none other than awakening. There is no difference between them. If you destroy suffering by the light of wisdom, your view is that of a shravaka *or* pratyeka-buddha *of the [Hinayana] vehicles drawn by sheep or deer. Those endowed with superior wisdom never hold such a view."*

Hsieh Chien said: "What, then, is the Mahayana view?"

SOKEI-AN SAYS:

Hsieh Chien, the messenger from the court of the Emperor Chung-tsung and the Dowager Empress Tse-t'ien, is continuing to question the Sixth Patriarch.

"Light is the symbol of wisdom, and darkness is the symbol of suffering." "Suffering," in Sanskrit, is *klesha. Klesha* is the suffering of mind that we are entertaining from morning to evening—desire, love, hatred, all kinds of mental sufferings. *Klesha* is usually translated into English as "afflictions" or "thirst." I am using *klesha* as analogous to suffering, in its Christian usage.

As to "light" as the symbol of wisdom and "darkness" as the symbol of suffering, the Sixth Patriarch refused to take such a dualistic view. When a Christian says "love," this love is not a dualistic idea. Usually, love is one side of human emotion; the other side is hatred.

When I was young, a Christian teacher came to our country from the West and taught us that love is not the other side of hatred. Love is absolute. In the West, there is also the non-dualistic view. When Nietzsche says "energy," this energy includes *all* things—good and bad, etc. Real goodness is whole; it is called God. Hsieh Chien's statement, showed his dualistic view.

In Buddhism, there are two words that are analogous to love in English: *mahamaitri* and *mahakaruna*. Both mean love and are usually translated as "great compassion" or "great sympathy." *Mahamaitri* means to give joy, and *mahakaruna* means to take away sufferings. When the child has candy in his hand and his hands are all smeared with dust and dirt, which is also smeared on his face, the mother says, "Darling, give me that candy." But the child cries, "No!" So then father takes it from him, takes the child's suffering away. Then the mother washes the child's face and hands and gives the child another piece of candy. To give joy and to take it away is all in the name of love. There is no hatred in it. When the human being holds this attitude, there is beauty in it.

"If he who practices the Dharma cannot destroy his suffering by the light of wisdom, how can he emancipate himself from the beginningless [darkness] of birth and death?" Hsien doubted the word of the Patriarch, so he asked this question.

"The beginningless darkness of birth and death" is the transmigration of the wheel of suffering. There is nothing in the world from beginning to end but this suffering, this agony. And this agony must be annihilated. So when the light of your eyes drops to the earth, how do you emancipate yourself? This is a famous koan and Hsien Chien's question.

"When the light of your eyes drops to the earth" means that this light ceases to exist when the agony of death creeps up on you. You cannot see your daughter's face any more. Your hands still have the sense of touch, but you cannot see her. You can hear her voice faintly, but you have no power to understand her words. You cannot drink water or swallow medicine. In that last moment of life, there is a terrible agony. How do you escape this agony? This is the koan.

We recall the death of Shakyamuni Buddha when he called his attendant Ananda: "Ananda, Ananda, I am suffering. Put your hand upon my breast." In his moment of death, Shakyamuni did not say: "I am not suffering at all. I'm happy." He called Ananda. Had he not been a truly enlightened one, he would have spoken in a braggadocio manner: "I do not feel anything at all. I'm as happy as you are!" Perhaps he would have smiled as he died. All great men express their suffering at their death. It shows their greatness. But the light of wisdom cannot save one from agony. So Hsieh Chien's question was a good one: "How can he save himself? By what means?"

The Master said: "Suffering is none other than awakening. There is no difference between them." Great answer! True answer! Suffering *is* awakening. The nature of suffering is exactly the same as the nature of awakening. It is one of the great phrases of Buddhism. When the Buddha said: "Ananda, where are you? Put your hand upon my breast," that was awakening.

In Buddhism, the three poisons of greed, anger, and ignorance are *shila*, *samadhi*, and *prajna*—precepts, meditation, and wisdom (awakening). They are all of the same nature. So one nature acts in two ways—destructively and creatively.

Observing the commandments, *shila*, is the same performance with which you try to get everything into your pocket, which is greed. Practicing meditation is the same energy with which you act in the world as a passionate or angry man. Ignorance and wisdom are of the same nature as well. Ignorance is the primitive state of wisdom.

"If you destroy suffering by the light of wisdom, your view is that of a shravaka *or* pratyekabuddha *of the [Hinayana] vehicles drawn by sheep or deer."* The allegory of the vehicles is in the *Lotus Sutra*.

"Those endowed with superior wisdom never hold such a view." So why did Zen masters of the northern country of China affirm that one could emancipate oneself by the practice of meditation? They affirmed it because they thought they could attain enlightenment in meditation and destroy all *klesha*, evil, with their enlightened power. They thought they could sweep away all *klesha*, exterminate darkness from their minds, and drive away all mental sufferings by the practice of this meditation. The Sixth Patriarch opposed this view. He said suffering and awakening are of one and the same nature—there is no difference between them.

Of course, the Northern School's practice of meditation is a type of Buddhism, but the Sixth Patriarch said it was not the "highest type."

Today, in the Zen school, monks practice meditation, but they are not practicing *blind* meditation. Blind meditation means just sitting down quietly and meditating a thousand years in the cross-legged posture and breathing deeply, or breathing in with one nostril and breathing out with the other. I take this as physical exercise. It is not a Zen exercise at all.

Hsieh Chien said: "What, then, is the Mahayana view?" The Mahayana view is not dualistic. While good and bad are the two demonstrations of one nature, there can be no dualistic view. To understand this is very important in our daily life.

The Sixth Patriarch will give his answer in the next lecture.

The Master said: "The ordinary-minded man fancies that enlightenment and ignorance are two. But the wise man realizes their nature to be non-dual. The nature of non-duality is itself the nature of Reality. In the ignorant mind, the nature of Reality does not decrease, and in the wise mind, it does not increase. In the midst of contending passions, it is not disturbed, and in dhyana-samadhi, it is not calmed. It is never annihilated, nor is it everlasting. It neither comes nor goes. It is not inside, outside, or in-between. It is never born and is never extinguished. Its nature and its appearance are one. It is everlasting and unalterable. This is the Way.

SOKEI-AN SAYS:

This is a famous passage in the Sixth Patriarch's record. In it the Sixth Patriarch gives his commentary on Reality.

"The ordinary-minded man fancies that enlightenment and ignorance are two." He fancies that there are two ultimates—enlightenment and ignorance, light and darkness.

In the light of wisdom, we can see all phenomena in our mind, and by this seeing and hearing, we come to conscious awakening; we realize that someone is within us. Who is this one? All of a sudden, this one awakens to himself. He realizes who he is. This is so-called wisdom—light. To find one's self is very interesting work. Someone is in me. Who is this one? To locate him in one's self, to detect him, to find his nature, is wonderful work.

When I was young and studying wood-carving, I always realized that someone was living in my attic, carving something independently. Someone was independently thinking while I carved. Whenever I did anything—walking on the street, going to bed, working—this fellow in the attic was thinking his own thoughts. Sometimes I put my tools away and cooperated in his thinking. I became acquainted, then intimate with him. I thought he was an old man and called him a philosopher, a queer philosopher three thousand years old. Gradually, he occupied my whole house and drove out the woodcarver. Then one day, the philosopher disappeared and I discovered my self. When the philosopher snatched away all the property of the woodcarver, he disappeared and I was born! I still visit the philosopher occasionally.

When you do not find yourself, you are in darkness, as you were in your mother's womb. You are sleeping without consciousness. When you found yourself, as in a dream, you were about five years old. Then you found yourself in a storm when you were twenty. And then, everyone gave you the law: "Don't do this; don't do that; don't go to the dance or to the midnight show; go to bed!"

There are many laws to be remembered by human beings, many laws to be accepted by those who observe the law. Sometimes you accept a law three thousand years old, no longer important or necessary, but you accept it—from India, China, from anywhere. You are in custody, bound by invisible laws of nature and of society. Your mouth is fastened by towels, so you cannot speak the truth—the truth may hurt someone. You cannot use your hands. You cannot use your feet. Your whole being is completely muzzled and suppressed. You become a good man—a gentleman! But you wear eyeshades like a horse. You have accepted all those restrictions without reason. Many times you have doubted it because you do not know the origin of the law. You are too lazy to think, so you just follow. Sometimes it's safe to follow restrictions, and sometimes not. But it is your problem, and you must solve it.

Sometimes the law that fastens you offers you no aid. You are still sleeping in darkness. When you open your eye and you trace back to the original state of law and you observe the development of it and find yourself in this moment, you find your own world, your own universe. You create your own law and rule yourself. But the one who has two points—light and darkness, good and bad, etc.—puzzles between the two because he does not know the true point.

"But the wise man realizes their nature to be non-dual. The nature of non-duality is itself the nature of Reality." These are very important lines. The first appearance of a dualistic notion in the human mind is time and space. This bowl, occupying space, has three dimensions: depth, height and width. When a human being experiences endless space, all of a sudden, he realizes that space has duration. I realize I am in this space one, two, three minutes, an hour. I am in this space in which one moment is fifty-six years. It is beginningless and endless. Think about this space. The universe is in this space how many years? Time

is the quantity of space, and space is the quality of time. Some philosopher invented space-time and called it the fourth dimension. This is a very simple way of speaking about the fourth dimension, and I am not sure that there is not some error here. We call this a dualistic view.

There is space, so something is moving from *here* to *there*. But in endless space and time, nothing moves. How can you think it is moving? This "endless" idea gives us many questions. Time and space do not exist objectively because time and space belong to our consciousness, not to the object. Our consciousness is so constituted that our eyes see the outside. But space and time are subjective, and we observe them subjectively. Space is our eyes, and time is our ears. With our sense organs, we observe the outside, but that which we observe is not the thing itself. What is the thing itself? It is a great question. We call it Reality. The nature of non-duality is the nature of Reality.

"In the ignorant mind, the nature of Reality does not decrease": The ignorant man has it, but he does not know it. You have a thousand-dollar bill in your pocket, but if you do not know it, you do not have it.

When I was young, I used to hide my money in my books. One day at examination time, I put one hundred yen between the covers of a book. Later, I had to go on a journey, but I had no money. I became very angry and threw my things all about. The bill came out of the book!

"And in the wise mind, it does not increase." The wise man realizes it is Reality. From the top of his head to the tip of his toe, he realizes that nothing is increased.

"In the midst of contending passions, it is not disturbed": When the entire universe is burned by the kalpa fire, all appearances cease to exist, but Reality is not disturbed.

"And in dhyana-samadhi, *it is not calmed."* Dhyana-samadhi is the meditation of *nirodha* meditating through *kalpas* of time; all phenomena are wiped out. However, in such profound meditation, it is not calm. If you think that, it is your own imagination. You wipe everything out by that imagination. First you close your eyes and then your ears, like the little souvenir image you bought at a Japanese store. You suppress your own consciousness—"Emptiness!" A student asked: "What is buddha-nature?" The master struck him. It is not calm. The elevated train is running about, and in the harbor of New York, all the boats are moving. Even the clouds are moving.

"It is never annihilated, nor is it everlasting. It neither comes nor goes. It is not inside, outside, or in-between." Reality is always *here*. There is somebody between two things, between the outside and the inside. The outside, however, is just a dream, all exists in the inside. But when you deny the outside, where is the inside? If you deny one, you must deny both. All this phenomena is created by the mind. When the *kalpa* fire annihilates all, from that, all is again created. The *alaya*-consciousness will beget the *manas*-consciousness, which will beget the five senses.

"It is never born and is never extinguished." It does not need to appear because it never ceases.

"Its nature and its appearance are one." Its nature is the place of appearance, and its appearnce is the quality of that nature.

"It is everlasting and unalterable. This is the Way." The Sixth Patriarch is using this word Tao, "the Way," in the wide sense. Here, it means Dharma, not the usual Taoism. I know of a scholar who said that Buddhism and Taoism are combined in China because the Chinese say that they are the same. He does not know Chinese. Tao here means Dharma, the law of Reality.

Hsieh Chien said: "How do your words about the non-existence of birth and extinction differ from those of the heretics?"

The Master answered: "The heretical teachings of the non-existence of birth and extinction maintain that extinction proves the non-existence of birth, and birth proves the existence of extinction. Extinction is therefore not really extinction, and birth is not really birth. What I mean by the non-existence of birth and extinction is that, originally, there is no birth and, therefore, there is no extinction. Thus, my theory is not the same as that of the heretics.

"If you want to know the pivot of mind, just do not discrimate between good and bad. Then you will naturally attain the pure mind, fathomless, ever tranquil, limitless in its marvellous activity."

SOKEI-AN SAYS:

Heretics, of course, from the Buddhist view, were all those who were not disciples of the Buddha, like the Christian who calls the Buddhist a heretic, and vice versa.

In the Buddha's time there were nine famous heretical sects. All these sects, like the Buddha himself, spoke about the non-existence of birth and extinction. Of course, this was the Hindu's original view. This existence is not real existence, it exists only relative to our five senses. The five senses of the sentient being create this whole phenomenal world.

Hsieh Chien said: "How do your words about the non-existence of birth and extinction differ from those of the heretics?" Absolute objective existence, in Sanskrit, *utpada nirodha*, is intangible and unintelligible. *Nirodha* is death, and *utpada* is birth—the non-existence of birth and extinction.

Theoretically, life is not existing. But what can we do about the life we have now? We must accept it. We must accept this illusory existence; we cannot cling to the non-existence of life. So, the theoretical conclusion is also non-existent. If we cannot accept it, use it, grasp it, we have nothing to do with it. If it is not our own theory, does not belong to our knowledge, it does not exist within us. Extinction is also non-existence. Therefore, birth and extinction are both non-existence.

In Hindu philosophy, the theory that phenomena do not exist was held from an early philosophical period. No one would deny the world is mere illusion. All of Asia—China, Korea, Japan—adopted this non-existence theory. The people in Asia based their life upon it, and it made the Asia of today. They sniffed at life and calmly accepted it without condition. And since a man cannot literally refuse his dream—although he knows it to be a dream from beginning to end—why not enjoy it? He says: "Yes, I know the lion is a dream; but sometimes I let the lion run after me and bite at my heels. I laugh at it!" Life is a queer thing to the Orientals.

The Master answered: "The heretical teachings of the non-existence of birth and extinction maintain that extinction proves the non-existence of birth, and birth proves the existence of extinction. Extinction is, therefore, not really extinction, and birth is not really birth." Truly, the modern students of Hinduism and all the ninety-eight schools of the Upanishads do not have so simple a view as this!

The Sixth Patriarch believed all heretical views could be reduced to one thing. The non-existence view is dualistic because one is *accepting both*. Accepting both birth and extinction. We see extinction as the end of our life, when our existence will be crushed. We see extinction, therefore we know it is extinction. We see the candle flame, and we blow it out. We prove extinction—"My uncle was living yesterday. Today, he is dead."

In the beginning, there was extinction, so how can things be created? No, nothing is created, for it is created by the mind of Maya, the goddess who creates illusion. Only illusion has been created. As Reality, nothing has been created, but then we accept this illusory existence, proving we had this birth and extinction. Therefore, neither birth nor extinction are true existence. So we cannot call this "extinction" and we cannot call this "illusion." There must be some other theoretical conclusion.

Finally, we deny both and call it "the non-existence of birth and extinction." They started from two points. Their non-existence view is a dualistic conclusion deduced from two procedures—birth and extinction. If extinction is from the beginning, extinction will produce nothing. Zero produces nothing. Thus they denied both extinction and existence, calling it "the non-existence of birth and extinction." Philosophiclly, you must accept this. There is nothing wrong with it. They affirm one another and at the same time deny one another. This is a trick of thoughts.

"What I mean by the non-existence of birth and extinction is that, originally, there is no birth and, therefore, there is no extinction." Simple! Nothing is created from the beginning, and therefore, nothing will undergo destruction. You must realize that the Sixth Patriarch is not standing on either side. He is standing *somewhere else*. When he says, "Originally, there is no birth, therefore, there is no extinction," he means that in the beginning there was no one, one was not; and therefore, in the end, there will be no one.

Heretics stand *here*, then go to another point, stand *there*, then come back to the first point. But the Sixth Patriarch stands in a mysterious place. He did not say that he denied birth and death, and he did not affirm them. He was entirely outside of this. He does not think of birth and extinction in these terms. He does not say a word about them.

Here, his view is not clearly written, but the question of birth and death does not bother him at all. He accepts Reality without accepting the dualistic view of birth and extinction. He accepts Reality with an open hand, but he does not accept duality. You do not have to think about these terms. Reality is the end.

This is the so-called Zen of the Sixth Patriarch. The Zen school is really based on his attitude. If you study Zen, you will understand this.

If you say that Reality is undemonstrable, you are still standing on the dualistic attitude. The Western philosophers know what Reality is, but they speak about it from a dualistic standpoint. In Zen, we do not need to speak about it. We *sneeze*, we *yawn*, we *sleep*.

"Thus my theory is not the same as that of the heretics. If you want to know the pivot of mind . . ." This fan has a pivot. Where is the pivot of mind?

I have talked about Reality one hundred thousand times since I came to America, so I will not talk about it tonight. Go home and read about it in your encyclopedia.

"Just do not discrimate between good and bad." Do not take the Sixth Patriarch's words in the moral sense, and do not think in terms of black and white, one and zero, day and night.

"Then you will naturally attain the pure mind, fathomless, ever tranquil, limitless in its marvellous activity." This is the attitude of the Zen school. Meditate and you will naturally attain the pivot of mind. Without terms, Zen is easy to practice. But first you must fight against those one hundred thousand terms in your mind, and you must annihilate them. What is extinction? What is existence? You must annihilate these terms one by one. Then you sit down and you attain pure mind. Not your own mind, but the fathomless tranquil mind.

No human beings exist in that mind. That which exists in that mind is neither you nor God. It is the most fathomless and most tranquil mind. When you realize this original mind, you realize the nameless and original state. From there, you stand up, stretch your hand, get into your slippers and begin your daily life. The life in the world of sentient beings begins from that, the limitless, marvelous mind.

In the performances of this mind, there are many miracles, like Christ stopping the hurricane—a marvellous miracle! How did he stop the hurricane?

On receiving this instruction, Hsieh Chien suddenly experienced great enlightenment. He left Ts'ao-ch'i in deep gratitude and returned to the imperial palace to submit the Master's teachings to the emperor.

On the third day of the ninth month of the same year, the emperor issued a decree praising the Master:

"Pleading old age and illness, the Master has declined our invitation. But by practicing the Way for our benefit, he is a field of spiritual blessings for the whole country. He is like Vimalakirti who, under the pretext of illness, promulgated the Mahayana in Vaisali, transmitting the buddha-mind and enunciating the Dharma of non-duality.

"Hsieh Chien has reported to us the Master's instruction on the knowledge of Tathagata. It must be as a reward for the accumulated virtues of our forebears and for the good roots planted in our former lives that we were born as the Master's contemporaries and attained sudden enlightenment in the highest vehicle. We are deeply and eternally grateful for his benevolence. In addition, we bestow upon the Master a Mo Na Robe[24] and crystal bowl. We have commanded the Governor of Shao-chou to renovate the monastery and to convert [the Master's] birthplace to a temple to be named Kuo-en (Gratitude of the Nation) Temple."

SOKEI-AN SAYS:

On receiving this instruction, Hsieh Chien suddenly experienced great enlightenment. The words of the Sixth Patriarch were: "If you want to know the pivot of mind, just do not discrimate between good and bad." I do not know if he *was* suddenly enlightened or not. But according to this description, he was immediately enlightened upon hearing these words.

He left Ts'ao-ch'i in deep gratitude and returned to the imperial palace to submit the Master's teachings to the emperor. His report was about the Sixth Patriarch's Dharma, which was different from all the doctrines promulgated by the masters of the Northern School of Zen. They placed emphasis on the practice of meditation. Hui-neng, the master of the Southern School, placed emphasis on sudden enlightenment.

On the third day of the ninth month of the same year, the Emperor issued a decree praising the Master: The emperor gave his recognition to the Sixth Patriarch in an imperial decree. From then on he was established among the authentic Zen masters. (In the records of Chinese history, there have been many corrections to these "decrees.")

"Pleading old age and illness, the Master has declined our invitation. But by practicing the Way for our benefit, he is a field of spiritual blessings for the whole country." The emperor's words were very polite and humble. The two Zen masters of the Northern School did not refuse the emperor's invitation. They went to the city and stayed in the palace. But the Sixth Patriarch disliked the luxurious life and chose to remain in the country to promulgate his teaching in an honest monk's way. He preferred to drink from a stream and find his food in the woods. The Sixth Patriarch thought: "My teachings are so different from theirs. Let them speak about Buddhism. I shall stay in the country in silence, practicing real religion. It is useless to go to the city and associate with those luxurious and aristocratic monks."

"He is like Vimalakirti who, under the pretext of illness, promulgated the Mahayana in Vaisali, transmitting the buddha-mind and enunciating the Dharma of non-duality." Vimalakirti was a famous layman in Buddhist history, but his historical value is doubtful. We think he is a personification of layman's Buddhism in India. When my English is better, I shall translate his sutra. Vimalakirti, as a transformed Buddha, possessed knowledge of Buddha, but observed Buddhism from the layman's standpoint, not from the monk's. So this sutra became famous among the Buddhists of the Chinese Empire. The emperor clearly regarded the *Vimalakirti Sutra* as one of the principal scriptures of Buddhism.

The Buddha summoned Vimlakirti to appear before him many times, but Vimalakirti, under the pretext of illness, refused. Shariputra asked the Buddha why such a great gentleman should submit himself to illness. The Buddha answered: "Shariputra, his illness is the illness of all sentient beings. If all sentient beings were to be enlightened, Vimalakirti's illness would be removed." So Vimalakirti's view is that we have illness from the beginningless beginning to the endless end. Living with illness and attempting to cure illness is the life of sentient beings. Vimalakirti found his own place in this view and did not strive to annihilate this human life. He was the child of a Brahman and taught *madhyamika*, the non-dualistic view of Buddhism. To observe this world in terms of time and space, good or bad, pure or impure is not true Buddhism. This is the view of non-dualism promulgated by the Sixth Patriarch. And like Vimalakirti, he secluded himself.

"Hsieh Chien has reported to us the Master's instruction on the knowledge of Tathagata." I think you remember from the previous lectures how the Sixth Patriarch explained his view of Tathagata—that Tathagata never comes and never goes, and has neither appeared nor disappeared. The passage on Tathagata is very famous in the record of the Sixth Patriarch. I do not have the time to repeat it for my new audience.

"It must be as a reward for the accumulated virtues of our forebears and for the good roots planted in our former lives that we were born as the Master's contemporaries and attained sudden enlightenment in the highest vehicle. We are deeply and eternally grateful for his benevolence." These lines that were sent to Southern China follow traditional words of encouragement in Buddhism.

There is a theory of karma to be found in these lines. "Accumulated virtues" means we sowed some seed of virtue in past incarnations and are cultivating them in this life, and that we will make a harvest of our past virtues in a future life. In English, there is a word that expresses the karma theory very clearly—evolution. Darwin, who founded this theory, endorsed the theory of karma. He must have been a Buddhist in a past life. Who could believe it! But actually, the karma theory of the East is in the Western theory of evolution. It is not exactly the same, but somehow it is there. There are many books that explain the theory of karma. "My grandfather built a bridge in my old village. For a thousand years no bridge was built, but my grandfather built that bridge, and it still exists." A descendant goes to that village and someone says, "Are you a descendant of that builder?" "Yes." "Oh, we are still using it!" They take this very seriously. This is "planting a seed of merit."

To be born in the world where Buddha is, is very difficult; we incarnate through *kalpas* of time. It is very seldom that we are born as contemporaries of buddhas. When the Buddha was born and was living in the city of Rajagraha, no one knew anything about him. After his death, they regretted this, and all the cities of Magadha wailed. When the Buddha was dying, an old man tried to break in to see him. The monks asked the old man, "Why are you doing this?" He answered: "I am a very old man, and I cannot wait a day. I must see him before his death. Ananda, you must let me see him!" The Buddha overheard this and said,

"Ananda, let him in." The Buddha accepted the heretic as a disciple and gave him a robe. As the old man put it on, he was suddenly enlightened and ran into the garden. There, an angry ox, running amuck, jerked him on his horn and killed him. As he died, he said, "I am happy to enter nirvana with the Buddha."

It is very rare to be born in a country where Buddhism exists, and it is very hard to meet a true teacher, listen to that teacher, and have faith in that teacher. So they were saying, "As a reward for the past, we were born contemporaries of the Master."

"In addition, we bestow upon the Master a Mo Na Robe": The robe was probably yellow and made of very rough cloth. *Kesas* were naturally stained in a dung ditch, so they were called "dung-wiping cloths." The name is filthy, but the ascetics thought it a pure cloth. In Japan, the monks wear *kesas* made of linen stained by the flowers of trees. Sometimes they are dark green, stained by the earth; and sometimes dark grey, stained by soot. Mine is an exceptionally bright yellow. In ancient days, monks lived simply. They stained their *kesas* with earth, or with something from a ditch, or with the juice of some flowers. No one knows the origin of the name Mo Na, but it has a Korean origin. Our information about the Mo Na Robe is not very clear.

"...And crystal bowl." A bowl was offered to the Buddha, a priceless bowl that stood on the four corners of the world. In ancient mythology, there are four rajas that supported this bowl. These four maharajas are symbols of the four great elements—fire, air, water, and earth—material entities, the food of spiritual being. These four maharajas offer the bowl to Buddha. They are the four natures of God explained in symbolism. The maharajas stand in the four corners of the universe and offer food to Buddha. Of course, these are mythological explanations of Buddhism.

In the descriptions of those who went to India in the early days, the Buddha was said to have carryied that bowl. They saw the original bowl in a temple. It was purple jade. There are many beautiful stories about the Buddha's jade bowl. One of them is about a group of monkeys who wished to make an offering to the Buddha. The head monkey filled the jade bowl with honey and offered it to him. The Buddha wanted to accept the bowl, but in the honey he discovered insects and bees, so he gave it back. The monkey was sad, so he took out the bees and the ants, and offered it again. The Buddha wanted to accept it, but the bowl was so sticky that he again returned it. Then the monkey took the bowl and washed it very carefully and offered it once more. The Buddha accepted it. The monkey was so glad, he danced to the edge of a cliff and fell into the sea and died. This story sounds very sad, but it is one of the beautiful stories of Buddhism.

"Taking insects away" means to purify the mind. To "handle the sticky bowl" means to become sticky with Buddhism—it must be washed away, it smells. "Falling into the ocean" is to attain emptiness, in the Hinayana sense. So attaining emptiness, which we speak about so elaborately today, was spoken about in the Buddha's time. It is the same thing, only the expressions have changed. To read the sutras, you must keep your eye open. In these trifling stories, you will find deep meanings.

Today, we use this allegory in the monastery thus: "Clean your hand without soap!" For to find the original hand, you must take the smell of soap away. So the allegory of the ape who offered honey and the "Lifebouy soap" from America, tell of the same thing. Many other stories speak of this bowl. However, the emperor's bowl was not jade; it was crystal.

"We have commanded the Governor of Shao-chou to renovate the monastery and to convert his birthplace to a temple to be named Kuo-en (Gratitude of the Nation) Temple." These are the encouraging words the emperor sent to the Sixth Patriarch and the end of the ninth chapter of the record of the Sixth Patriarch.

CHAPTER X
FINAL INSTRUCTIONS

One day the Master summoned his disciples Fa-hai, Chih-ch'eng, Fa-ta, Shen-hui, Chih-ch'ang, Chih-t'ung, Chih-ch'e, Chih-tao, Fa-chen, Fa-ju, and so on, and said: "You are my leading disciples. After my death, each of you will become the master in a particular district.

"Now I will teach you to expound the Dharma so as not to lose the cardinal principle:

"You must first enunciate the three standpoints, the thirty-six opposite pairs of activities, and the manner in which original nature transcends the two extremes of becoming and vanishing. [But] whatever sort of teaching you expound, never depart from original nature. If anyone questions you about your teaching, answer by obliterating those relative views which contradict one another to show that, as things come and go in the law of causation, they exist only in relation to one another. In this way, you will finally annihilate the questioner's dualistic view and leave him with no place to go.

"The three standpoints are the five shadows, the twelve entrances, and the eighteen realms.

"The five shadows are: body, senses, thoughts, mind-elements, and consciousness.

"The twelve entrances consist of the six external 'dusts'—color, sound, smell, taste, touch, and mind-stuff—and the six internal 'gates'—eyes, ears, nose, tongue, body, and mind.

"The eighteen realms consist of the six dusts, the six gates, and the six consciousnesses. Original nature comprises all things and is therefore termed 'alaya-consciousness.' When discrimination arises, it is termed 'inverting-consciousness.' This, in turn, begets the six consciousnesses, producing the six gates and manifesting the six dusts. Every one of these eighteen realms derives its activity from original nature. When original nature is false, it puts forth eighteen false realms. When original nature is true, it puts forth eighteen true realms. If activity is bad, it is the activity of sentient beings. If activity is good, it is the activity of Buddha. Upon what do these activities depend? Their existence depends upon original nature."

SOKEI-AN SAYS:

The Master had now become very old, and before his death, he made a request of his disciples. He desired that his doctrine, the cardinal principle of his teaching, be preserved. Of course, this cardinal principle does not include that which was handed down in his Zen, that which is mind to mind, the unwritten seal of buddha-mind.

One day the Master summoned his disciples Fa-hai, Chih-ch'eng, Fa-ta, Shen-hui, Chih-ch'ang, Chih-t'ung, Chih-ch'e, Chih-tao, Fa-chen, Fa-ju, and so on, and said: "You are my leading disciples. After my death, each one of you will become the master in a particular district." In the previous part of this record, you have heard many of these monks' stories, so I shall not repeat them here. In the Zen records, it is not recorded that they became leaders of any centers.

"Now I will teach you to expound the Dharma so as not to lose the cardinal principle: You must first enunciate the three standpoints": The Sixth Patriarch gave three standpoints to his disciples, which were

not different from the Dharma of the Buddha. The three standpoints are the five shadows, the twelve entrances, and the eighteen realms.

The five shadows are body, senses, thoughts, mind-elements—such as motion, the unconscious motion which creates things, dreams (today, Western science is concerned with these)—and consciousness: *rupa, vedana, samjna, samskara, vijnana*. I translate the Sanskrit *skandha* as "shadow." It can also mean "neck" or "pile," as one piles up the five-tiered pagoda of the Orient. The symbol of the five shandhas or shadows is the symbol of Buddhism. When we open the pages of the Agamas, we find them immediately. Most teachers and disciples of the Orient place great emphasis on them. I have read many translations made by European scholars. None of them speak of the five shadows, none! Sometimes there is a reference, as if it were a negligible thing, but there is no study. I understood Zen through contemplation on the five shadows. I meditated on them for twelve years.

The second standpoint is the "twelve entrances"—the "six dusts" and the "six gates." They enter into the inside from the outside.

The six dusts are color, sound, odor, taste, touch, and mind-stuff. They are considered "filth" or "impurity," that which is adulterated in relation to phenomena. They are not pure, as reality is pure. They are adulterated with illusory existence. For example, a pillow has stuffing in it; but without stuffing, it would not be a pillow. Mind-stuff, the thought that haunts our brains like a ghost house, is different from our mind. To the Buddhist, this stuff is filth. Color, for example, in objective existence, separates us from the state of Reality. So we call this color filth, call this sound [rang bell] filth; taste, filth; odor, filth. This object is, as our five senses, filth, and the objects of our sixth sense are also filth.

The six gates, are the six sense organs—ear, eye, nose, tongue, skin, and mind. These are the "roots" of sentient life. Without these roots, we have no life at all. Though we have mind-stuff from the outside, without the six roots we cannot exist. The third eye, in Buddhist art, is just an invention of mind.

The "eighteen realms," the third standpoint, are the six dusts, the six gates, and the "six consciousnesses"—eye-consciousness, ear-consciousness, nose-consciousness, tongue-consciousness, skin-consciousness, and mind-consciousness. Each of these eighteen realms has its own scope, its own kingdom. We realize the nature of Reality through these realms.

Knowing the nature of our world, we know that the world is merely phenomenal existence, not true existence. But it is through this phenomenal existence that we attain true Reality, which is "real being." The Sixth Patriarch called it original nature. He said this original nature is the foundation of our activities, the foundation of all the laws of Buddhism.

Observe the reality of your mind, your original nature, through these three standpoints, and you will certainly attain enlightenment. In Buddhism, enlightenment means to "see the state of Reality." In the state of Reality, you do not have light coming out of your head or eyes, you do not have a nimbus behind you—"Oh, that man is enlightened, his eyes shine!" That man is not enlightened because his eyes shine. If that were so, a blind man could never be enlightened. You will understand the nature of our world by carefully observing these standpoints and meditating upon them.

"The thirty-six opposite pairs of activities, and the manner in which original nature transcends the two extremes of becoming and vanishing." Besides the three standpoints there are the thirty-six "faculties" of original nature, or buddha-nature. The "activities" of original nature are therefore *nirmanakaya* activities—good/bad, pure/impure, light/darkness, etc.—*sambhogakaya* manifested instrumentally. This manifestation is *nirmanakaya*.

These opposite states of activity give passage to original nature. Original nature goes through all these states but never stops in any one place, like the express train that goes from New York to San Francisco without making any stops. Original nature is like water; the opposite states are like waves. You think the waves are coming to the shore, but that is just an optical illusion, for things you throw into the water stay in one place. So what is it that comes to you in water? Scientifically, it is energy. Original nature is like this energy. It passes through many places, but it does not carry anything with it, does not carry water on its shoulders; it comes through waves.

In "becoming and vanishing," something emerges from nothing and submerges into nothing. Of course, this implies the law of causation, the twelve nidanas, the first of which is *avidya*, original darkness. It has no beginning and has not been created. It exists from the beginningless beginning in the chaos of the infinite. Within this darkness, the seeds of all things accumulate, and from these seeds everything develops. These seeds create their own world and are the elements of creative power. Consciousness is born from this unconscious state, as life is born from the earth. So consciousness is born from the womb of the unconscious world.

"[But] whatever sort of teaching you expound, never depart from original nature." The original nature of fire, of water, of air, and of man and woman is one and the same original nature. My physical body is like a wave, a wave on the ocean. But original nature is always in one place and never moves. Physical nature is "becoming and vanishing."

This is a plain theory. If you have this understanding, you will not think in terms of Western mythology or theology, of spirit and body. It is a convenient hope in the mind of man that he has a separate spirit that will hide under a rock somewhere after death and that an angel will blow a trumpet before the Last Judgment. The Oriental theory can be very uncomfortable: "If I go to the bottom of original nature, I will lose my individuality! I will not be myself!" But do not be discouraged.

"If anyone questions you about your teaching, answer by obliterating those relative views which contradict one another to show that, as things come and go in the law of causation, they exist only in relation to one another." This is the usual viewpoint of Buddhism. When you say, "Life is mutable," the teacher says, "No, life is eternal." When you say, "Life is eternal," the teacher says, "But you must not forget about mutability," and so on. If you say, "Atman exists," the teacher says, "Atman never existed without original nature."

"In this way, you will finally annihilate the questioner's dualistic view and leave him with no place to go." When you go to a Zen master, you will be driven into a corner, and you will not be able to speak a word; nor can you vanish. You cannot go through the floor or jump into the sky where you would die. But when you are driven into a corner and you are emancipated from your dualistic view, you will die there and then become Buddha's disciple.

"The three standpoints are the five shadows, the twelve entrances, and the eighteen realms. The five shadows are: body, senses, thoughts, mind-elements, and consciousness. The twelve entrances consist of the six external 'dusts'—color, sound, smell, taste, touch, and mind-stuff—and the six internal 'gates'—eyes, ears, nose, tongue, body, and mind. The eighteen realms consist of the six dusts, the six gates, and the six consciousnesses. Original nature comprises all things and is therefore termed the 'alaya-consciousness.'" European scholars translate *"alaya-*consciousness" as the "storehouse" consciousness because everything is comprised within it.

The Sixth Patriarch is saying that original nature is not different from *alaya-*consciousness and that it produces all the divisions of consciousness. In other religions, they think the root of the six consciousnesses is a huge god in the universe somewhere—atman—and that the mind of atman is *paramartha*, transcendent outside of space. This is quite queer to me, but this is how they think. In Buddhism, it is different.

You must listen to me very carefully. Atman is very clear, very tangible. We know it exists *here*. We are aware of our own consciousness, know our own consciousness. But original nature, according to the Sixth Patriarch, is not the consciousness we have *now*. It is invisible, intangible, unintelligible, and is called *anatman*, no-self. The Buddha said it was the state of nirvana. When you are conscious of this existence, then this is not the state of nirvana. This invisible, intangible, unintelligible original nature contains *all* dharmas.

"*When discrimination arises, it is termed the 'inverting consciousness.'*" It is termed the inverting consciousness, *paravrtti*, because it is "turned out." It is turned out like a potato sack is turned out.

"*This, in turn, begets the six consciousnesses, producing the six gates and manifesting the six dusts.*" We become human—"Oh, beautiful world!" We do not know it was all produced by our own sense organs. So *paravrtti* also means "to reverse." In Peekskill there is a road that sharply turns and you come back; it is a hairpin turn.

"*Every one of these eighteen realms derives its activity from original nature. When original nature is false, it puts forth eighteen false realms. When original nature is true, it puts forth eighteen true realms.*" Original nature cannot be false; it is always true. But when we observe original nature, we observe it falsely, erroneously. We think this heart is eternal consciousness. But when the end of life comes, we are frightened—"What will become of me!" Thinking this consciousness is eternal, we cannot say goodbye because our whole life is a deception.

"*If activity is bad, it is the activity of sentient beings. If activity is good, it is the activity of Buddha.*" You must control your consciousness. If you do not, you will become insane. I met many that were insane. I was talking with one about a week ago, and when she met me again—"Oh, razors everywhere!" She did not know me. She has a mind, but she lost her consciousness because she is blind.

"*Upon what do these activities depend? Their existence depends upon original nature.*" Why did the Buddha speak of such things? You have to think about it, and by thinking about it, you realize that they are not true existences.

To express original nature, he used "Tathagata." The five shadows, the twelve entrances, and the eighteen realms are not Tathagata. But if we observe them, we can realize Tathagata itself.

Sometimes I am asked why Buddhism is so analytical. The Buddhist's answer is this: "We are not merely analyzing the things that exist. It is by the analysis of all things that are existing that we understand how to observe everything synthetically. It is from this viewpoint, penetrating all states of existence, that we attain the state of Reality. Then we are satisfied with our study. Standing upon this state of Reality, we perform our daily life, which is the aim of Buddhist practice. We do not depend upon God whom we never met but are going to meet. That is the purpose of Buddhism.

This was the Sixth Patriarch's original scheme through which all Zen students can attain enlightenment.

"There are five pairs of opposites in the external world of insentient things:

1) *Heaven and Earth*
2) *Sun and Moon*
3) *Light and Darkness*
4) *Negative and Positive*
5) *Water and Fire*

"And there are twelve pairs of opposites to describe the structure of existence:

1) *Words and things*
2) *Existence and non-existence*
3) *Shape and shapelessness*
4) *Appearance and non-appearance*
5) *Leakage and non-leakage*
6) *Form and emptiness*
7) *Movement and stillness*
8) *Clarity and obscurity*
9) *Secular and sacred*
10) *Monk and layman*
11) *Old and young*
12) *Great and small*

"When original nature functions, there are nineteen pairs of opposites:

1) *Long and short*
2) *Falsehood and truth*
3) *Foolishness and wisdom*
4) *Ignorance and knowledge*
5) *Disturbance and tranquility*
6) *Compassion and malice*
7) *Right and wrong*
8) *Straight and crooked*
9) *Real and illusory*
10) *"Cross-grained" and "even-grained"*
11) *Delusion and enlightenment*
12) *Perpetuity and mutability*
13) *Sympathy and injury*
14) *Joy and anger*
15) *Generosity and greed*
16) *Progressing and regressing*
17) *Birth and death*
18) *Body of Reality (*dharmakaya*) and physical body*
19) *Body of Transformation (*nirmanakaya*) and Body of Uniformity (*sambogakaya*)*

"If you understand how to use these thirty-six pairs of opposites, [you will realize] the Way that pervades all the teachings of the sutras. Whether coming in or going out, you will avoid falling into either extreme."

SOKEI-AN SAYS:

The Sixth Patriarch is speaking about the phenomenal world as emerging from the original consciousness of man. The world that I see is mine, and the world that you see is yours. But we have the same consciousness, so we produce the same type of vision. We think we are living in one world, but this is not so. I am living in my world, and you are living in yours. This is not the world of original consciousness. The world produced by original consciousness is one and the same. We are living in a uniform world.

According to the Sixth Patriarch, the functions of our consciousness observe the outside as "good and bad," "day and night," "black and white," "red and green," "yellow and purple," all in a dualistic arrangement. The *real* outside is not dual. But we have this dualistic measure as a constituent of our consciousness, the original body of our consciousness, so all the things we see are in a dual aspect. Things stand against us in a comparative and relative sense.

All these contrasting pairs of existence do not exist individually. They are the appearances of original nature, and they are all relative appearances—a tree with two branches, one stretching to the south, the other to the north. In the spring, on the southern side, the branch blooms early. In the autumn, on the northern side, the branch's green leaves last a long time, while on the southern side there are no more green leaves. But these two existences are not *two* individual existences. They are *one* existence which takes *two* different appearances according to conditions. The Sixth Patriarch's idea was that original nature is the ground of all these appearances. This is the Buddhist view.

"There are five pairs of opposites in the external world of insentient things:1) Heaven and Earth"; 2) Sun and Moon; 3) Light and Darkness; 4) Negative and Positive; 5) Water and Fire." The Sixth Patriarch is saying that the appearances of the insentient external world are in pairs as well.

According to the Chinese, there are two elemental forces from the beginning of the world, the negative force and the positive force—in Chinese, *yin* and *yang*. Yin, the negative force, is matter and visible. Yang, the positive force, is spirit and invisible.

In this system, the sun is positive, and the moon is negative. Present-consciousness is sun-consciousness, and subconsciousness is moon-consciousness. Our subconscious mind is produced by the earth element, and heaven, which is empty, is the foundation of the universe, our state of *prajna*. Water is creative, the symbol of wisdom. Fire is destructive; it annihilates existence. It is the symbol of our passion. When these two powers combine, everything flourishes and maintains its existence. When they separate, the whole world will come to an end.

"And there are twelve pairs of opposites to describe the structure of existence:" There are more than twelve pairs. The Sixth Patriarch arranged the pairs to propound his own theory.

"1) Words and things": The word "emptiness," for instance. You should grasp the state of emptiness, not the word "emptiness." You ask me: "Well, if it is empty, how can I grasp it? If it is empty, how can we know about it?" If you do not know about emptiness, you cannot call it "emptiness." You talk about nirvana, but you do not know the state of nirvana. "Nirvana" is a word, just like the word "emptiness." You know the word but not the state, and it is the same with the word "Buddhism." You know the word but not the state. New York is a name, but the real New York is not a name. Produce a white horse out of a wine

bottle! You cannot do it, but "White Horse" is a wine. You see something, but you do not know its name. You should know both the name and the state.

"*2) Existence and non-existence*": You cannot think of non-existence, so Reality, philosophically speaking, *is* non-existence. Therefore, we do not know anything about Reality because it does not exist. Then how do we know Reality? This is mystic.

There is mystery in Buddhism because the state of Reality is beyond our five senses, but we can *realize* Reality, the main point of Buddhism. All of the 5,048 volumes of Buddhist sutras are on this practice—proving the "state without experience through the five senses," the state of Reality that exists beyond our empirical mind.

"*3) Shape and shapelessness; 4) Appearance and non-appearance; 5) Leakage and non-leakage; 6) Form and emptiness; 7) Movement and stillness*": The seven colors and seven sounds pair with non-appearance. I have spoken of this non-appearance before.

Leakage, in Sanskrit, is *ashrava*. Our consciousness is like a tub that leaks: the eye sees the outside (color, shape, perspective); the ear produces sound; the nose produces all kinds of odors; the tongue produces all taste. From morning to evening, like an old leaky tub, the water flows out continually.

Some European scholar translated this as "to discharge the fluid of the senses." Hmmm! Like perspiration, a very poor translation. I translate this, according to the Chinese, as "leakage." It moves, leaks out. It is not a state or quality, but a function of consciousness. To follow the function of the senses is *ashrava*; it pairs with *anashrava*, non-leakage, "to go against the function of the senses." So we practice from our body to the bottomless *alaya*-consciousness. We go against the flow of the sense-function, and thus annihilate all this leakage; and by this practice, we reach the state of nirvana.

I puzzled about this for a long time. I tried to do it by meditation and by the sutras, according to the method which is written in them. But following the teachings is not the real meaning. Trying to attain it is.

In order to reach this state of *anashrava*, a sage living on the shore of a lake in the Himalayas meditated every day. As he was about to enter the state of nirvana, fish raided the shore. He was so angry, he annihilated all the fish of the lake. Are you thinking you can attain the state of *anashrava* by destroying the state of *ashrava*? I thought so, too, for a long time. But why? Why not immediately reach that state? Some students looking for the root of the tree cut all the branches. But this is not the way. Leave the fruit and the flowers and find the root.

From the standpoint of Reality, nothing is moving; but from the standpoint of *ashrava*, everything is moving. Motion proves no-motion. What is the reality of it? This is a profound question for Zen students.

"*8) Clarity and obscurity; 9) Secular and sacred; 10) Monk and layman*": When all laymen attain enlightenment, the monks will disappear. When all monks are enlightened, laymen will disappear.

"*11) Old and young; 12) Great and small.*" In Reality, there is no greatness and no smallness. Size and appearance are just in our senses. When you die and get up again, there is no moment between life and death. "From this pill box, produce the Himalaya Mountains . . ." "Stop the hurricane . . ." How does one do this?

"*When original nature functions, there are nineteen pairs of opposites:*" This is not an accurate system of evolving activities. The Sixth Patriarch is just expressing his ideas spontaneously.

"*1) Long and short*": A tall man is good to clean the ceiling but bad for work down in the cellar! And when you are waiting for your love, it is a long day. But for me, it is a short day because I have so much to do.

"2) Falsehood and truth; 3) Foolishness and wisdom":—"Giving him an education will not save him!" Or: "He's sharp, very sharp! I wish he were a little dull." Or: "He is useful, but he's too fresh. He does not associate well in society."

"4) Ignorance and knowledge; 5) Disturbance and tranquility": An ignorant farmer in the country has no way to learn, but he is wise. The educated man is not wise, but he is educated; he has knowledge.

The idiot and the ignorant are always disturbed. They do not know what to do or what to think; their minds are in disorder. The wise man is always calm. He knows the present and the future. His judgment is swift and therefore calm. One man is always disturbed, the other is always tranquil, but both evolved from one nature.

"6) Compassion and malice": Compassion is friendliness; malice is poisonous. The compassionate man shakes hands from a good heart; the malicious man shakes hands, but there is some idea in his mind.

"7) Right and wrong": It is wrong to eat food any old time, but it is right to eat regularly three times a day. For me, it is bad to eat three times a day. I eat twice a day.

"8) Straight and crooked; 9) Real and illusory": He talks straight and thinks straight. He observes everything straight. He thinks and observes *penetratingly.* Crookedness does not see things straight, so the crooked man does everything in a contrived way—this way, that way, always searching for something in the darkness. He cannot go straight.

The man who sees in darkness does not need to ask questions any more. Sometimes the idiot tries to be straight, but there is too much awkwardness.

"10) "Cross-grained" and "even-grained": The dangerous man is a "cross-grained" man. You cannot easily associate with him. He is a stupid man. With the safe man, the "even-grained" man, you can easily associate.

"11) Delusion and enlightenment; 12) Perpetuity and mutability": Take the farmer, for example. Some Japanese say that Buddhism is the religion of the farmer. Of course, they are talking about mutability. The farmer sows his seed, and if the weather is bad his crop is annihilated. If it is a good winter, he will plow the ground, and in the spring, sow the seed. But mutability is always there. You sow the seed of the cabbage, and the next spring it will be incarnated. Bad seed never produces good grain, and good grain always produces good seed. The growing will start when it is right. The farmer cannot depend on the crops he gathers in the harvest because, in the future, they may be annihilated.

The Buddhist sticks to the ground, to the community. The farmer is the highest, and the merchant is the lowest. But when the merchant takes the highest position in society, the form of civilization changes. He goes all over the world exchanging knowledge and sometimes never comes back. He cannot depend upon his own ground. When the mechanic makes everything and produces everything, there must be distribution and small factories planted in different countries. The old root is ruined.

It is very interesting to observe these different classes—farmer, merchant and mechanic—with their separate civilizations. One is mutable, the other is perpetual. The farmer takes the mutable view, so he needs perpetual ground. Certainly, Buddhism is the religion of the farmer. The Buddha himself was the son of a landowner. Other tribes said they were descended from the gods, but the Shakya tribe said they were descendents of the potato!

"13) Sympathy and injury": The father takes candy from the baby; the mother, in compassion, gives him another thing—sympathy. Or take a toothache: "Oh, that's too bad, so sorry!"—compassion.

Someone comes along in sympathy: "Open your mouth, and let me see." "Yah!!" He looks and takes it out—sympathy.

Sympathy is good, but when you sympathize too much, it is bad. So, many people ask Buddhist monks: "Then what is good, and what is bad?"

The usual view, which is really the deluded view, is that you believe good and bad are existing separately. Our answer is that good and bad are the same thing, the same occurrence. They are existing relatively. Bad has no nature of its own, nor has good. Bad and good are an appearance of original nature. According to natural conditions, it occurs as good, and, according to unfortunate conditions, bad. There is no particular thing that has a bad nature or a good nature. Good and bad nature is by circumstance. A heavy overcoat is very good for winter but very bad for summer. The heavy overcoat hasn't any nature, good or bad. Things which are harmonious to circumstances are good. Things which are inharmonious to circumstances are bad. What was bad yesterday is good today. This is the Buddhist idea of good and bad. In Japan, wearing tight woolen stockings is very bad. Someone once asked me, "What has happened to your feet, some injury?"

"14) Joy and anger": Many criticize in anger. Why not accept in sympathy and give joy?

15) Generosity and greed": The true Buddhist meaning is "giving up attachment"—we *accept everything*. The doctor tells me I must die, perhaps in three months, and I accept this [shrugged shoulders]. In Japan, there is no shrug. When I came to America, I saw this queer motion—"What is this?" I asked. "It's a shrug." I looked it up in my Japanese dictionary, and it said, "to lift up the shoulders." I did not understand!

There are four great qualities in sages: compassion, sympathy, joy, and giving up attachment. All those who walk the sages' way use these four powers.

"16) Progressing and retrogressing": Progressing in the Buddhist sense is one of the Eight Noble Paths. Retrogressing is: "I am tired; I will not take *sanzen* today." And you go to the movies.

"17) Birth and death; 18) Body of Reality (dharmakaya*) and physical body"*: We have a physical body, so we can think about this Body of Reality. Theosophist philosophy has an etheric body, an astral body—we can walk out of it. But this is not the Body of Reality, *dharmakaya.*

19) Body of Transformation (nirmanakaya*) and Body of Uniformity* (sambhogakaya*)."* Your body and my body are different, but there is a body of uniformity—*sambhgakaya*. Without the transforming body, *nirmanakaya*, you cannot think of the uniform body.

In Buddhism, the symbol of the whole world, the whole universe, is the lotus. There is the white lotus, the blue lotus, the red lotus, the yellow lotus. Each has its symbolic meaning. The white lotus is the Unborn—*dharmakaya*. The seven different colors are *nirmanakaya*. The law is written on this one consciousness, this one body, which spreads out into one million consciousnesses.

There are one, two, three cherry blossoms on a tree, but they are the same. These are the evolved activities of original nature, all of them.

"If you understand how to use these thirty-six pairs of opposites, [you will realize] the Way that pervades all the teachings of the sutras": The "Way" in Chinese is "Tao," the law that pervades the universe. But here it does not carry the Chinese meaning. Here it means Dharma. The Sixth Patriarch adopted the word to express Dharma, the law of Buddhism, and not only the law of Buddhism, but the law of nature and of man.

In that bookcase are 5,048 volumes of sutras. I started to read the sutras when I was twenty years old. I am now fifty-six, and I have not covered one quarter of them yet, but the law connects us. So when you open the sutras, every one is yours, and you do not need to ask questions of any master. Of course, if you do not know the law, you will never understand, though you read the Sanskrit or Pali versions.

"*Whether coming in or going out, you will avoid falling into either extreme.* Either good *or* bad, calm *or* anger, heaven *or* earth, sun *or* moon, man *or* woman. This means *all* this existing phenomena. When I say phenomena, you think it is a ghost, but I do not mean a ghost. Phenomena is *this* objective existence, appearance itself—one thing appears as a contrasting pair. According to our philosophy, from the beginningless beginning there is no man or woman, there is only one spirit. One spirit appeared as this contrasting pair.

"*Original nature performs its activities when you are speaking with others: outside, in the world of form, but apart from form; inside, in emptiness, but apart from emptiness. If you adhere wholly to form, you will strengthen your erroneous views; if you adhere wholly to emptiness, you will increase your ignorance. Those who adhere to emptiness despise the sutras, asserting that words are useless. They maintain that words are of no avail, but are incoherent in their own speech, for their very speech itself is in the form of words. Again, they say, 'Do not use words!' But this 'do not' and 'use' themselves are words! When they hear what is taught by others, they immediately condemn them for adhering to words. You must realize that while being deluded yourself can be condoned, you must not disparage the sutras of the Buddha, for doing so you commit numberless offences. If in seeking the truth, you adhere to external forms and conceive of them as Dharma, or build temples everywhere and hold forth on the error of [affirming] either existence or non-existence, you will never, even through recurring* kalpas, *be able to find your original nature.*"

SOKEI-AN SAYS:

The Sixth Patriarch is giving his final discourse to his disciples before his death. This passage is a part of that last discourse.

"*Original nature performs its activities when you are speaking with others: outside, in the world of form, but apart from form; inside, in emptiness, but apart from emptiness.*" When we say "yes," sometimes it may mean "no." Both appear in "yes." When a diplomat says "yes," he means "perhaps" or "no." He does not say "no" from the beginning. Your original nature does not fall onto either side. Everything is in form, but nothing has form from beginning to end. At the end of the world, when everything is destroyed, there is no fixed emptiness. Original nature never stays in one absolute emptiness or in one absolute appearance; it is like the spirit that never stays in the shape of a man or a woman. The mother produces the boy, and the boy produces the girl, like a tree developing its branches. Yet, according to the Greek "idea," a chair should be a chair from beginning to end.

Plato thought there was an "ideal" chair. But the chair that exists in the phenomenal world is not an idea. It's an incomplete and insufficient one, not the complete and perfect chair that exists as an "idea." The tree in the garden that is existing now is also not perfect and complete. Pick a leaf, and look at it. It's not a perfect leaf, it's distorted. But as an "idea," it's perfect. And man now existing here is imperfect, sinful, and impure, and on this earth, degraded. But there is an "ideal" man, a pure and holy man, a perfect man and a perfect woman from the beginning. So our ambition, those of us who are existing on the surface of the earth, is to reach this perfection through evolution.

When we Oriental students dig into this in our study of Western people, we find something very different from our own thought. For example, when I went to Golden Gate State Park in San Francisco for the first time, I saw a Western garden. The flowers were arranged according to color, and the trees were planted in perfect circles with a fountain in the center. It was a perfect symmetrical design. I realized how different the idea of a garden is to us. We chop off a corner of nature and put a fence around it. To us, nature is showing her dishevelled state. But the Western idea is to conquer nature. This comes from ideation. We do not call our idea "ideation." We call it "naturalism." This natural development according to the law of appearance and its contrasting pairs is Tao. When you study Orientalism, you must understand this fundamental difference between East and West. Then open those Eastern books.

"If you adhere wholly to form, you will strengthen your erroneous views; if you adhere wholly to emptiness, you will increase your ignorance." A monk who has the wrong idea of emptiness will go to a cave, meditate, eat one grain of rice a day, and, perhaps, leave his memory in the cave. He doesn't solve his question, so he dies there, bravely practicing his meditation to the end of his life.

If you adhere to materialism—form—you think it gives you security. But you heap matter upon matter from morning to evening, heap iron upon stone and stone upon iron, until you are finally crushed. You have become a stone of materialism—the human being cannot live any more. You say you do not want to go to China because the streets are not paved, but the Chinese are walking the streets without difficulty.

If you adhere to emptiness, it is not true Buddhism. If you to attach yourself to materialism, it is also not true Buddhism.

"Those who adhere to emptiness despise the sutras, asserting that words are useless. They maintain that words are of no avail, but are incoherent in their own speech, for their very speech itself is in the form of words." A word is just a name; it cannot express Reality. However, this does not mean that words are of no avail.

The Sixth Patriarch did not accept the habitual attitude of Zen students of that period who said that we must desist from thinking and must not speak a word in our minds or with our lips. They had misunderstood the words of Bodhidharma who said: "Contrive not a word to explain Dharma. Find your original nature immediately and make yourself a buddha." They thought that silence was Dharma and that speaking "not a word" was Zen. If speaking not a word is Zen, then every deaf-mute would be a Zen student!

Bodhidharma's point is this: The sutras were written and the lectures were given to help us awaken to Reality. But these sutras and lectures are not religion. They are the ferryboat to carry us to Reality. It is by handling reality that we awaken to the state of Reality, and that is action. It is the same sort of thing that you are using in your daily life. When you are discussing something hotly with your friend, you say. "I will hit you!" and you take it out in words. But in direct action, you hit him without a word.

Bodhidharma did not employ any reasoning or give explanations for anything. To him, swallowing water was religion; eating food, sleeping, tending a shop, talking with one's neighbors was religion. Every act from morning to evening was religion. It was his means of practice, and you are in that state or you are not in that state. Of course, from this point of view, we must alter our ordinary conception of religion. When we come to this state and we are in this state from morning to evening, we do not need anyone to explain anything. That is the reason Bodhidharma said: "Contrive not a word."

So, as Zen students, contrive no explanation. It's all in your mind, in your first decision of the day: "Now I get up, and as I put my foot into my slipper this morning, I take my first step." Or take a carpenter: If two men were to stand by him, one to explain what he was doing mythologically and the other philosophically, the carpenter would just say, "I paid twenty-five cents for this hammer yesterday," and go on with his work. He has no need for their explanations. But to attain to this state, your mind must be enlightened.

Bodhidharma stood on that ground, but the monks of that day did not understand his point, so they just kept their mouths shut or stayed in the woods refusing all friends, saying, "This is religion." But you cannot use such a religion in your daily life. What are you going to do with it? Keep it in your closet? And as to reading the sutras, they say, "Oh, this is trash!"

"Again, they say, 'Do not use words!' But this 'do not' and 'use' themselves are words!" So when you go to a Zen school, and your teacher says, "Do not use words," you go back home and never read a book again, and never think again.

One day I visited a friend, and when I said, "Hello," he said nothing. Then I said, "What's the matter?" and I realized he was keeping this commandment.

Once a sage came here and did not say a word but used a slate. This was Meher Baba.[25] He has made a lot of money in America. He is speaking "a word" very loudly.

"When they hear what is taught by others, they immediately condemn them for adhering to words. You must realize that while being deluded yourself can be condoned, you must not disparage the sutras of the Buddha, for doing so you commit numberless offences." If keeping the mouth shut is Buddhism, how is it that Buddha preached for forty-nine years and left 5,048 volumes of sutras? If keeping silence is Buddhism, then the Buddha would not have spoken a word.

Your state of delusion is your own fault. You do not understand the profound method of leading people into religion. Just keeping the mouth shut and closing the eyes does not make a religion. It does not teach you anything.

"If in seeking the truth, you adhere to external forms and conceive of them as Dharma"—That is, to the mythological—*"or build temples everywhere"*—Build temples and carve images—*"and hold forth on the error of [affirming] either existence or non-existence"*—Construct theological or philosophical theories—*"you will never, even through recurring kalpas, be able to find your original nature."* The Sixth Patriarch beat the last nail into these two piles of plank: "If you are one who adheres to outer forms and conceives of them as Dharma in seeking the truth, or, if you are one who builds temples everywhere and debates the right or wrong of something or nothing, you will never, through recurring *kalpas*, be able to attain the realization of original nature." It *is* true!

"Listen, and practice according to the Dharma. Do not try to keep yourself from thinking of different things and thereby obstruct the Way. If you listen to the teaching but never practice it, you will only arouse false notions in others. If you practice according to the Dharma, that is the offering of the Dharma of not abiding in forms. If you understand how to speak, how to act, how to practice, and how to do things in this way, you will not lose the cardinal principle of my sect."

SOKEI-AN SAYS:

The Sixth Patriarch said:

"Listen, and practice according to the Dharma." "Dharma" here means not only the Eightfold Golden Path, but all those methods that were invented by the Buddha.

The first of these eight is "right view." In accordance with right view, you think correctly. Koan study in the Zen school gives you the right view, the correct view; and with this correct view, you practice your thinking, and you speak correctly in accordance with Dharma. You perform your daily life in accordance with this correct knowledge, and you live in a "right occupation." From your own devotion to the Dharma, you choose the "right expedient," the right method.

As a result, there are two religious attitudes which you must always keep in your performance of real life. They are "right attitude" of mind and "right meditation." Right view is the entrance, and "right thinking" is the way, the avenue to reach a real life. In the end, right attitude and right meditation are the conclusion of the Buddhist life. By dint of practicing it, we can call ourselves Buddhists.

Right attitude of mind is our daily attitude. It makes our life worthwhile. In Japanese, it is called *sho'nen. Sho* means right, and *nen* means mind—right mindfulness, the right attitude of mind.

In Japan, every child gets a roly-poly Bodhidharma toy sitting in the Buddhist posture. The parents purchase it from a souvenir shop. You kick it, and it rolls over, but it always comes back to the "true" posture. This is a symbol of the Zen student's posture of mind, the core of Zen. It is so important that a Zen master made a toy out of it.

Some Bodhidharma roly-poly dolls come in six different sizes. They come in a set, one within another. These represent the emergence of consciousness. Open one and there is another and another—six in all. And in the center, there is just one grain of rice, a symbol of *sho'nen.*

There is another Japanese toy invented in the Zen school to symbolize right attitude of mind: Several bamboo sticks are crossed and the ends weighted with beans to represent a scarecrow in a rice field. If you put the center on your finger, no matter which way you move your hand, it always keeps its balance. It sways and sways but never falls down.

When we have nothing to do, we come back to this *sho'nen.* When you put your physical body in the right shape, then your mind becomes the right shape, and your brain is straightened out—it doesn't play a merry-go-round tune.

Even though you pass one thousand or one million koans, know Buddhism, and have some attainment, without this right attitude of mind, you can hardly call yourself a Zen student or a Buddhist. Bodhidharma said that many attain enlightenment but few really practice right mindfulness, *sho'nen.*

The Buddhist attains Reality, and, standing in the state of Reality, performs his daily life. What makes our life different from other people's? *Sho'nen. Sho'nen* is not the ego center. It is proved in your profound meditation. Though I am very lazy and careless about it, nevertheless, I always practice it when I have time. So sit quietly, get your mind in shape and continue with *sho'nen.* It will make you a gentleman, a warrior, an artist. It will make everything straight and strong, and give you a profound nature.

This part of Zen influenced art and the daily life of the Japanese and Chinese people. When Japanese fencers meet their opponents with the sword and shout *"Kiai!"* in that moment they are creating right mindfulness, *sho'nen.* In the tea ceremony practiced by women, beautiful girls cultivate *sho'nen* as the very center of the Zen religion.

Japanese children use the term *sho'nen* in queer places. When their silk stockings become old and lose their shape, they say, "These silk stockings have lost their *sho'nen!*" And when the children cry at supper, the fathers say, "Keep your mind in shape! *Sho'nen!*" The influence of Zen in daily life is very deep.

The Zen student must always practice this when he has time. When you get into the struggle of life or you are on a battlefield, you must practice *sho'nen*. You must always keep sho'nen in mind, like the roly-poly Bodhidharma. It is not a small thing, this *sho'nen*. It made Zen a religion.

Before the lecture I come and sit here and practice *sho'nen*. When I came to America for the first time and entered a cheap hotel in Seattle, Washington, the hotel keeper was sitting in a chair, his feet up on the desk, and he said: "Waddja want?" I saw immediately that he had no *sho'nen*.

"Do not try to keep yourself from thinking of different things and thereby obstruct the Way." The people of that time said of those staying in caves meditating: "Certainly this must be heretical! When they come down to the village, they do not think!"

The words of the Sixth Patriarch's sentence marked a milestone in that period.

You have a wonderful city in your own mind, a skyscraper built of mind-stuff—visions, names, and a treasure of technical terms from philosophy. And with these philosophical terms, you are always thinking something as you build your house of stone and cement. You build your philosophical tower with this mind-stuff. Without these, you cannot think anything.

Some say Zen students are mad—"How do they think without words?" We just sit and meditate, but we do think. We find truth without words, without falling into spiritualism. From our point of view, the spiritualism that moves tables and raps out messages is not spiritual, it is a corrupted materialism. Why use knocks and rapping sounds? Why not sit still and meditate?

We can attain enlightenment; we do not need any words. But when you have attained enlightenment without words, you cannot talk about it; you are like a deaf-mute. But you say, "This is a shortcoming of the Orientals. They may be enlightened, but their streets are not paved. And they cannot conquer epidemics. They are one-sided."

To practice this, you begin from *"munen"*—no-mind, mindlessness. Mindlessness has two stages that belong to *mind-movement*: The first stage is stopping the movement of your mind with your own intention; the second stage is not stopping the movement of your mind yourself—the mind regulates itself after long practice.

"If you listen to the teaching but never practice it, you will only arouse false notions in others." Many people come here and ask me to teach them to meditate, but I never see them meditate. If you come and ask me a question and never practice, it is useless to teach you.

If you practice according to the Dharma, that is the offering of the Dharma of not abiding in forms." The "offering of the Dharma of not abiding in forms" is a quotation from the *Diamond Sutra*, the Buddha's answer to a question asked by Subhuti—"What is the offering of the Dharma of not abiding in forms? "The Buddha said: "The highest offering is an offering without color, sound, form, smell, or taste."

To practice the meditation of right attitude is the highest offering of the Dharma. You are not giving anything to the other; and it is not just that you do not use the forms, it is the attitude of giving. Christ said that when you give something to another with your right hand, do not let the left hand know about it. He was certainly talking about this "formless almsgiving."

In the *Diamond Sutra*, there are several famous koans. One of them that I give my students is: "Without depending on anything"—without residing in form; not only outer forms, but mental forms, systems of philosophy, etc.—"manifest your mind." The Sixth Patriarch, when he was a peddler selling kindling wood, heard a man recite this and was suddenly enlightened. In that moment, he dropped his kindling wood from his shoulders and attained awakening. This is a famous passage in Zen Buddhism.

"If you understand how to speak, how to act, how to practice, and how to do things in this way, you will not lose the cardinal principle of my sect." This drives everyone to the real home of Zen.

A nun was invited to a layman's house. The layman thought she might like to eat fish, so a whole fish was served—tail, fins, head, and eyes, the whole fish. Now the regulations provide: "Do not eat the meat of an animal (or fish) if you have seen its entire body." The nun was in a quandary. At that moment, one of the children put chopsticks into the fish's eye, a great delicacy, and gouged it out. The nun fainted.

When people study Buddhism, they imitate the monk's way—obey the commandments, live in caves, meditate, and so on. From our standpoint, when a fisherman studies Zen, he must be a *real* fisherman.

A Zen master came to America, and someone took him to the stockyards in Chicago. The monk cried like a baby, grew pale and left. This became a famous story. I thought it was beautiful. When I went back to Japan, I told this to my teacher. My teacher said, "He was a fool. Why did he go there, knowing about it? Buddhism will be cheapened having such a monk!"

How to speak. How to act. What is the right attitude?

When someone in Japan says to you, "I heard that you are going to America. When you return, please bring me back a souvenir that does not exist in the world," and you understand how to bring back this souvenir, you understand how to speak and how to act. It is just like Lin-chi when he visited Ta-yu, and Ta-yu said, "Your teacher is not I. It is Huang-po. Go back to him," and Lin-chi poked Ta-yu three times in the ribs.

How to act. How to create. How to create a little temple such as this one with formless almsgiving!

I began my teaching in this country by gathering some people in Central Park. The place does not matter. As the Sixth Patriarch said, "If you understand how to speak, how to act, how to practice, and how to do things in this way, you will not lose the cardinal principle of my sect."

"Whenever anyone questions you about the teaching, if he asks you about existence, answer in terms of non-existence; if he asks you about non-existence, answer in terms of existence; if he asks about the secular, answer in terms of the sacred; if he asks about the sacred, answer in terms of the secular. Since each of these extremes is dependent on its opposite, you demonstrate the principle of the Middle Way. If all answers are given in this manner, you will not lose the principle.

"For instance, if someone asks you 'What is that which is called darkness?' You will answer, 'Light is the cause; darkness is the consequence. Darkness exists when light vanishes. Darkness is revealed by light, and light is revealed by darkness. Alternately coming and going, each is the cause of the other, demonstrating the principle of the Middle Way.'

"All other questions [should be answered] like this. Hereafter, when you transmit my Dharma, you must pass down this teaching from generation to generation. Do not lose the essential principle of my sect."

SOKEI-AN SAYS:

The important part of this passage is the Middle Way. The Middle Way is the "right way" of Buddhism. The Middle Way or middle "path" or "avenue" is one of the famous terms in Buddhism, but no one knows the real meaning of it. Many scholars think the Middle Way is between two extremes such as the "good way" and the "bad way." People usually take such explanations from half-baked Buddhists.

The Buddhist term is different from that of the Confucian *chung-yung*, the Mean, which means the middle-way attitude. Its real principle is not the same as that of Buddhism. Some Confucianists, who came from Buddhist pastures or gardens, think the Confucian middle way is analogous to that of the Buddhist. Soyen Shaku's teacher, Imakita Kosen,[26] had such a conception. Kosen Roshi, who was a Confucianist before he came to the Zen school, tried to explain the Confucian middle way with the principles of Buddhism. The middle way of Confucius is like a measure—take the two extremes and find the center. It is good; it is not good. It is bad; it is not bad. There is a middle. Too kind is not real kindness, and no kindness is not kindness either. So there is a middle-way for kindness, but the Buddhist Middle Way is different.

It is like a fencer who fights two opponents—good and bad. Sometimes I smite the bad and sometimes I smite the good. Sometimes I use my weapon to attack the good, to turn it to bad. Sometimes I use my weapon to attack the bad, to turn it to good. But I am neither good nor bad. I understand both, and I use both. To pull teeth is bad, but if the teeth are bad, it is good. To kill is very bad, but driving a criminal to the electric chair and annihilating him is considered good. To kill a sentient being is bad, but killing a bedbug is good. This is called the Middle Way in Buddhism. To put on an overcoat in winter is good, but putting on an overcoat in summer, in Florida, is bad. To eat something when you are hungry is good, but eating something when you are not hungry is bad. This is the plainest explanation of the Middle Way. There is a scholastic and elaborate explanation in the *Madhyamika Shastra* written by Nagarjuna.

The Middle Way is the way of Buddhism, and it is the principle of the Sixth Patriarch and his Zen sect. He told his disciples how to demonstrate this Middle Way principle.

"Whenever anyone questions you about the teaching, if he asks you about existence, answer in terms of non-existence; if he asks you about non-existence, answer in terms of existence; if he asks about the secular, answer in terms of the sacred; if he asks about the sacred, answer in terms of the secular. Since each of these extremes is dependent on its opposite, you demonstrate the principle of the Middle Way." When Boswell was carefully discussing with Dr. Johnson Bishop Berkeley's idea that all existence is non-existent, Dr. Johnson became very angry, lost his temper, vigorously kicked a big stone in the garden, and said: "I insist that this exists! I dare you to prove that this rock is non-existent!" I think Dr. Johnson did not know Zen, but from the Zen standpoint, it was Zen.

Another example is in the *Vimalakirti Sutra*. Shariputra was listening to the sermon of Vimalakirti and a very beautiful angel, an *apsara*, sat next to him. Shariputra was a stern monk and did not like to sit next to women. Shariputra lost his temper when the *apsara* began to talk long and eloquently. He said: "How can you, a woman, come here and talk such a long time?" She said, "Haven't you heard what I said?"—meaning, if he had discriminated the voice of a woman, he was not yet a true monk. The apsara said: "I am not a woman." Shariputra replied: "If you are not a woman, transform yourself into a man."

She immediately transformed herself into a man and flew into the sky. Then Shariputra said, "Now transform yourself into a woman." The aspara returned to the shape of a woman, descended from the sky, sat next to him and said, "Can *you* change yourself into a woman?" Shariputra, by his supernatural powers, changed himself into a woman. Then she said, "Now, change back into a man." Shariputra struggled to transform himself back into a man, but he could not.

This is a very funny example, but it fits exactly this situation, for Shariputra did not understand the Middle Way. He still discriminated between man and woman. The *apsara* could change from the Middle Way, but Shariputra could not.

To observe from the Middle Way is the right view. You will get into the Middle Way as soon as you enter into Zen. You say "yes," I say "no"; you say "no," I say "yes"—but I am not yes or no.

"If all answers are given in this manner, you will not lose the principle." Hui-neng is going to answer from the Middle Way.

"For instance, if someone asks you, 'What is that which is called darkness?' You will answer, 'Light is the cause; darkness is the consequence. Darkness exists when light vanishes. Darkness is revealed by light, and light is revealed by darkness. Alternately coming and going, each is the cause of the other, demonstrating the principle of the Middle Way.'" This is the usual way of answering in the Zen school: "What is darkness?" "Darkness is the consequence of light."

Darkness is not only no-light, but it is also the darkness of the mind. The original darkness of mind, in Buddhism, is called *avidya*. When you were in your mother's bosom, you were in this beginningless darkness. When you were born, you came out of this darkness; but you were still in the darkness of mind.

We were in darkness, and now our minds are in darkness, but they were in original light. Through the *kalpas* of deluded transmigration, our mind lost its original light and fell into darkness. Therefore, when we unveil the darkness, we destroy the darkness, and light is revealed, like a blind girl who was originally not blind. When the doctor operated on her eyes and took the film away, she could see again. It is like a diamond or piece of jade concealed in rock. The jade-cutter cuts away the rock and finds the jewel within.

Your original enlightened mind is always within you. You must destroy the film of the mind, which darkens your original enlightenment, so you can finally find your original light. But your mind must be enlightened to be emancipated from this darkness.

Usually the human being is caught and in the custody of different jails, for example, spirit and matter. When you sneeze, you call this instinct, but the human being has roped his mind and put it in jail so that it has lost its own instinctive function. The mind is bound up, has lost its freedom, has fallen into hell through its own delusion. But when you take the Middle Way, or "no-way," you are not sleeping. You keep your eyes open and you keep your potentiality within yourself, full of energy. This is the Middle Way. Then you operate in a good way or a bad way, according to time and place.

When you attach yourself to the names of things, you are like an amateur painter who paints the sky using blue paint—"I brought sky-blue for the sky and Indian-red to paint an Indian"! You must use colors without names, in accordance with the light of the moment. You cannot depend on the color in a tube. A good painter always starts from the Middle Way, the aesthetic way.

From my standpoint, I say good/bad. It does not depend on an objective point of view. The pupil generally stands on one side and judges. When you stand and observe the world from the Middle Way, your standing and acting is right mindfulness. The Eightfold Noble Path is the Middle Way, but people misunderstand this. Usually they say: "He does not drink, but he smokes cigarettes. He takes the Middle Way."

You must remember my explanation and practice it carefully.

"All other questions [should be answered] like this. Hereafter, when you transmit my Dharma, you must pass down this teaching from generation to generation. Do not lose the essential principle of my sect." The essential principle is the "middle-attitude" of mind, the "no-attitude" or "no-way" of mind. It is the "infinite-attitude" of mind.

In my school, meditation is the beginning of practice, and meditation is the end of practice. We meditate upon the symmetrical mind, upon the profound mind. We meditate upon our own mind, not upon anything else—no symbol or word. Our own mind is the only object upon which we meditate.

My school, the so-called school of meditation, is not mere meditation; it reaches from the bottom of Mind to the top of the highest enlightenment, which was attained by Shakyamuni Buddha.

This is a very strange religion, a very simple religion. We worship Mind. Our mind is a little mind, but it is part of Great Mind.

In the seventh month of the year Jen Tzu (712 C.E.), the first year of the T'ai Chi and Yen Ho eras, the master commanded his disciples to go to Kuo-en Temple in Hsin-chou to erect a stupa. He urged them to hasten the construction. The pagoda was completed by the end of the following summer.

On the first day of the seventh month (713 C.E.), the Master gathered the monks and said: "Next month, I desire to depart the world. Any of you who have unsolved doubts must question me quickly. I will destroy your doubts for you so that you may annihilate your delusions. After I have gone, there will be no one to teach you."

Fa-hai and the others sobbed bitterly as they heard this. Only Shen-hui remained unmoved, not shedding any tears. The Master said: "The young monk Shen-hui is able to remain impartial towards good and evil and to be indifferent to praise and blame. He gives rise neither to joy nor sadness. You monks, however, have not attained this. While you were spending these years in the temple, what attainment were you striving for?"

SOKEI-AN SAYS:

The Sixth Patriarch's record comes slowly to the end. Perhaps, before the summer of next year, I shall finish this translation.

In the seventh month of the year Jen Tzu (712 C.E.), the first year of the T'ai Chi and Yen Ho eras, the Master commanded his disciples to go to Kuo-en Temple in Hsin-chou to erect a stupa. He urged them to hasten the construction. The pagoda was completed by the end of the following summer. Kuo-en was a small temple, originally the house of the Master's mother on the other side of the Pearl River in Hsin-chou. The Master at this time was living at Shao-chou, about two hundred miles from Canton, upstream on the Pearl River. He sent his disciples down to Hsin-chou to visit his mother's house, which was given to him by the Emperor Chung-tsung, who had made it into a temple. The Sixth Patriarch realized his life was drawing to an end.

On the first day of the seventh month (713 C.E.), the Master gathered the monks and said: "Next month, I desire to depart the world."—"From morning to evening, I depend on my disciples. I'm tired of my life. It's very difficult carrying this old body around, using this old eye, and chewing with a toothless mouth. I wish to die in August."

This is the Buddhist attitude. Those who have an egotistic mind would say, "Oh, I don't want to die! So what if I have lost my teeth and cannot eat anything and have to be carried to the bathtub? I don't want to die! I have three thousand dollars in the bank, and I don't want to give that to anyone!"

"I desire to renounce the world." This is the attitude of the monk, especially when he shaves his head and takes off the layman's robe and puts on the monk's robe. This attitude is different from just, "I want to die."

"Any of you who have unsolved doubts must question me quickly. I will destroy your doubts for you so that you may annihilate your delusions. After I have gone, there will be no one to teach you." Very kind and humane! It is a helpless time for the student when the teacher becomes old, and the student still has many koans to cover. He goes to the temple through rain, through snow, and is about to attain the knowledge of Zen in about two or three more years of *sanzen*, when all of a sudden he hears that the teacher was moved into the hospital, He doesn't know whether he will come back or not. "I'm sorry for you, my disciples. Go to some other temple and find a master." Of course, everyone likes the old Zen master. No one likes the young one just hatched out with the smell of the world, the smell of everything. Everyone loves the old Zen monk—seventy, eighty, ninety years old. "He was here this morning!" In the evening, he goes to the hospital and dies.

When I was young, I went to a teacher who was very young, so I had the opportunity of finishing my Zen study under one teacher. He is still living, and still criticizing me. I translated the *Record of Lin-chi* and asked him to write a preface. "What!" he said, "You are too young!" I was fifty then—but fifty is too young. It is very nice to have someone harshly criticize me, stick needles into me, keep me down. I appreciate the criticism.

The Buddha said: "Those unanswered questions must be answered, as you would quench a fire that is burning your hair. You cannot wait for the fire to quench itself. When a fire is burning your hair, it must be put out immediately!" The Buddha said, "Your questions must be destroyed immediately; you cannot wait."

The people of that day were very honest. Today, people are different: "Yes, I may die tomorrow. 'What is my soul?' I have twenty-five cents in my pocket. Let's go to a movie. *Sanzen* is not important."

These people take the same attitude towards everything. Really, in the Sixth Patriarch's time, there were many monks, but not many who were truly enlightened.

The relation between disciple and teacher is called *innen*, in Japanese. *Innen* is the affinity between Dharma and the affinity between persons. It is not only, according to Buddhist imagination, that we came to this place and have an affinity at this time; that affinity was *already* created in the past—"I promised to teach you, and now I have come to fulfill my promise." The doctrine of reincarnation is very beautiful. Perhaps it is just superstition, but it is imparts great richness to daily life.

The same is true of the affection between the teacher and the disciple. Once a rich rajah promised to feed the Buddha and his disciples. The following summer the Buddha remembered that promise and went to the rajah's kingdom with five hundred disciples. But the country was stricken with famine, and the rajah closed his gate. He had forgotten. The rajah gathered his own friends, and every night he made a banquet, and he gave nothing to the Buddha. The Buddha realized that the rajah had entirely forgotten. As no farmer had any food, the Buddha and his monks were starving to death. So the Buddha gave the order to scatter: "Don't stay with me." But the monks said, "No, we want to stay with you!" The Buddha then said: "No, this summer I stay here. We will meet in some other place." Ananda, realizing there was no food to offer the Buddha, took some monks and went all over the country in search of something to eat. Finally, they came to the owner of hundreds of horses. The monks asked him to give them the oats he fed to the horses, so they could sustain their teacher. The horseman heard their pleas and gave them half of the oats. The monks returned and made bread, and offered it to the Buddha. They ate the oats to support themselves through the summer. At the end of the season, the rajah remembered his promise and apologized. The monk's attitude is to accept donations but never to beg. When we read this story, we always cry at the love between the Buddha and his disciples.

Fa-hai and the others sobbed bitterly as they heard this. Only Shen-hui remained unmoved, not shedding any tears. The Master said: "The young monk Shen-hui is able to remain impartial towards good and evil and to be indifferent to praise and blame. He gives rise neither to joy nor sadness. You monks, however, have not attained this. While you were spending these years in the temple, what attainment were you striving for?—"The teacher is going to die next month!" Fa-hai, the first disciple was sobbing with everyone.

They lost themselves and returned to their old worldly attitude. But Shen-hui, the "little monk" when he went to visit the Sixth Patriarch, was different. He was just quiet, unmoved, motionless, but not empty minded. For the Zen student, this is a very important attitude. Anyone who has attained this attitude of mind has attained some degree of knowledge and understands satori.

Philosophical study—Hegel, Kant—ends very quickly, and the conclusion comes quickly, but it does not give you any satisfaction, any satori. Philosophy and satori are not in the same direction, but in entirely different and opposite directions. In philosophy, you come to a conclusion. In satori, you go to the lap of your mother. I felt so when I was meditating on my koans, as if I were going to my mother's lap. You use your mind to its utmost force, go back to your mother's lap and abandon everything. This is the real religious feeling. You worship the whole universe. You worship all of nature. You bring yourself to the bosom of nature, your mother. Then all nature's universal force supports you.

Zen is not like anything in philosophy. It is a type of art. All sincerity and worship go back to the bosom of nature. I found this knack of going back to the bosom of nature because I was an artist who worshipped nature. From that feeling, I entered Zen quickly. When you are given a koan and by philosophy get an answer, you cannot find the gate; it is a blank wall. But when you go back this way, keep your face to the phenomenal world, and step back so that the great universe embraces you, you return to its motion. There is no other way to meditate and to realize consciousness. How deep can you go back? How deep can you meditate? The way of Zen is different from all others. You cannot get it from books. You can read Dr. Suzuki and think, "Now I know! I can lecture on Zen!" But it is foolish, like a child. You must strive philosophically first, hold that rope, and then go back. If you have no philosophical conclusion, there is nothing to be realized. When you are sleeping, you go back to the bosom of nature, but you have no wisdom.

What is nature? It is not the sun and moon, mountains and stars. Nature is in your mind. When you become humble and adore everything, then you will find that soft attitude of mind that reaches to the bottom of nature. I have talked about the philosophical part of Zen so many times. Sometime I must give you a lecture on how to attain satori.

"You are weeping now, but for whom are you sorry? Are you sorry for me? If you are sorry for me because I do not know where I am going, I do know where I am going. If I did not know where I was going, I should be unable to tell you beforehand. You are weeping because you do not know where I am going. If you knew where I was going, you would not weep.

"Originally, Dharma nature is not born, nor does it perish; it neither comes nor goes. All of you, return to your seats and I will give you a gatha. I call it 'The Gatha of Truth and Falsehood, Motion and Quietude.' When you recite this gatha by heart, your minds will be identical with mine. When you practice in accordance with it, you will not lose the fundamental principle."

SOKEI-AN SAYS:

The Sixth Patriarch gathered his disciples at his knees—in your terms, near to his chair or his seat—and gave them his last discourse on his own principle of Zen. He said that he would die very soon—the next month, August—and told them, "If you have unsolved problems and doubts in your mind, ask me your questions." All the disciples sobbed because they were losing their teacher. Of course, there were more Zen masters in China, but the monks desired to stay in one place and attain enlightenment. Their teacher was going to die the next month—"What shall we do?" So they wept bitterly. The human nature of that period was very naive and very honest. Of course, they will weep when the master dies, but there is hope that they can go to another.

"You are weeping now, but for whom are you sorry? Are you sorry for me? If you are sorry for me because I do not know where I am going, I do *know where I am going."* This is a great problem. Where do you go after your death? To solve this great question, you must solve the first question: "Where are you now, and what are you at this moment?" And then the second question: "What were you and where were you before your birth?" Then you can solve the question, "Where do you go after your death?"

These are *the* great questions of sentient life.

Where are you now? Where are you *at this moment*? If your answer is "I am sitting here at 63 West 70th Street, New York," then what is 63 West 70th Street, New York? "Oh, it's an apartment house made of brick and stone." Then I would ask you, "And this brick and stone?"

It is quite a problem, a deep problem.

When I ask, "What are you?" you say: "I am a human being. I consist of the four great elements—*earth, water, fire,* and *air.*" And I ask, "So what is your mind? What does your mind consists of?" You say: "My mind? My mind is an aggregation of different elements. I can see, hear, smell, taste and feel, and I can remember my thoughts. I have a mind that reasons and dreams. In the daylight, I think, and at night I dream. And when I see myself in my dream, I think: 'Am I dreaming or is something else dreaming of me? Was I in that dream? If there is someone else, who is the one who dreams of me?'"

It is something greater than you. You are in *its* dream. You are one of the living things in its dream. You dream of a tiger, a serpent, the Hudson River, and chocolate cake all at once, and you are in the dream. *You* are not dreaming this dream; it is not you, but something deeper than you that is dreaming. We call it consciousness. Is it *your* consciousness, or is it just consciousness? What is this consciousness? You can say, "I cannot tell. Maybe it was there before I was born." If there was not a consciousness before you were born, it would be impossible for you to be born. This consciousness is something that is not yourself. It was living, is living, and will live forever. This consciousness is beginningless and endless. What do you call this consciousness? I call this consciousness "Universal Consciousness." It is all over the universe. It is omnipresent. With this consciousness, I am conscious of myself.

So when you say you are at 63 West 70th Street, New York," I will ask you, "Where you are *now*?" "Oh, I'm everywhere!" "If you are everywhere, what do you call yourself?" "I don't know."

Who are you? Where are you now? What are you now? Great questions. When you think deeply, these questions beget other questions, and these other questions beget others. There is no end.

When I came to this country, I went to Mount Rainer and sat on the corner of a stone in a little village, thinking. A farmer came along and asked: "What are you doing?" "I am thinking." "Thinking spoils your head." "Spoils my head! I've been thinking for twenty years. My head is spoiled completely!" But deep thinking does not spoil the head. It cultivates the head.

"Where are you?" is the first question.

"I'm everywhere in the universe." This is not the real answer, but temporarily I take it.

"Were you born?"

"No, I was not born. I am eternal."

"What is it that is sitting in the chair?"

"Oh . . . the eternal."

"It will die some day. It's not eternal. Where do you go after your death?"

"Nowhere. I'm eternal and boundless."

"Are you?"

Answered with the word "eternal," these questions do not have satisfactory answers. It is important to boil down all those answers and solve the question by making one answer. It is necessary to begin with the *activity* of your life. If you do not, you are just a dreamer. Without solving these questions, you are simply eating, sleeping, and dying.

"Well, I don't need to solve my questions because I'm depending on God. He solves all questions for me."

"Does He?"

"Well, God gave me this brain to use, and God will not accept my carelessness. He will say, 'Go to hell and think some more!'"

The Sixth Patriarch's disciples were weeping when he said he would die the next month.

"If I did not know where I was going, I should be unable to tell you beforehand. You are weeping because you do not know where I am going. If you knew where I was going, you would not weep." In this Zen problem we call a koan, there are many questions you must observe. When the four great elements—earth, water, fire, and air—decompose and scatter, where do you go? When your flesh returns to the earth; your blood to water; your heat to fire; your breath to air, where do you go? In the agony of death, how do you emancipate yourself from agony? You cannot drink a drop of water; you cannot swallow a pill; you cannot see faces or hear sounds; you cannot speak. You are in agony, but your mind is still bright.

At such a time, in Japan, the relatives arrive, burn incense on the altar, and everyone recites chants to invoke the Buddha to come and take grandmother away. Grandmother tries to recite, but no voice comes through her throat. Her breath does not come any more. So the grandchildren recite for her. In such a moment, how do you emancipate yourself from the agony?

Everybody and every country has different customs. Perhaps, in this country, the grandmother is told: "Grandmother, please don't die until you sign your will!" The lawyer comes and grandmother signs. In that moment, how do you escape the agony of death? In that moment, where is your soul? In your stomach? In your head? In the sky or under the earth?

All these are famous Zen problems. When you deeply think about these problems, you will not spoil your head. I promise.

"Originally, Dharma-nature is not born, nor does it perish; it neither comes nor goes." The Sixth Patriarch is further explaining the nature of Dharma, the law of the universe.

In the state of Reality, there is no life, no death, no coming and no going. All is original substance. When I say substance, it is mental substance. When you say substance, it is physical substance. You say electron and proton. We say *alaya*-consciousness.

In the substantial state of the mental world, there is no fluctuation between life and death; it is always in the same state. But it is not dark, and it is not an infinite chaos. It is wisdom itself. Your way of attaining wisdom is to study the outside. You look for wisdom on the outside. This is a good way, too. But our way is to look for wisdom within, through introspection. Then we find the original state.

"All of you, return to your seats and I will give you a gatha*. I call it 'The* Gatha *of Truth and Falsehood, Motion and Quietude.'"* "Truth" is *This*—eternal substance, the state of Reality. "Falsehood" is temporary existence, like the color of the ocean. It is sometimes blue. "Motion" covers space and takes in time; it is both time and space. But space, time, and motion are phenomena, not Reality. You think that time and space are on the outside. No. Time and space are in your body, in your mind. Immanuel Kant explained this very carefully. "Motion" is a temporary phenomenon. In Reality, there is no space, time, or motion.

"When you recite this gatha *by heart, your minds will be identical with mine. When you practice in accordance with it, you will not lose the fundamental principle."* You know, when the Christian missionaries came to my country, they said: "Buddhism has no God. It is not a religion, but a type of philosophy." Because Buddhism has no God, we children were told by the missionaries that we were pagans. We did not accept it. Our conception of God was entirely different from that of Christian missionaries. Today, I know what is the real problem and how to solve it, but at that time I did not know.

In Western science, knowledge is found by the analysis of objective existence. University professors analyze everything with microscopes. What is color? What is light? According to wave lengths, different colors appear. This is the science of optics. It proves that color is not on the outside. Waves produce color on the retina of the eye. So the reality of the outside is not color or sound. It is something entirely different. It is *nothing*. This answer meets our answer.

But Oriental philosophy is different in nature from Western science. We do not use the microscope to analyze the outside. We analyze our own mind. We analyze from consciousness to semi-consciousness to subconsciousnesss to unconsciousness, for the law of mind is common to all sentient beings. We think different things, but mind activity is the same in all. So by analyzing my mind, I know the other's mind, and I find the reality of mind at the bottom of mind. The answer is that the so-called Western "nothing" is objective, while ours is inside, but these two meet. In the Western world, there is something a little like this—psychoanalysis. But in psychoanalysis the doctor analyzes the other's mind.

When we understand each other through religion, we can really learn to understand each other once and for all.

The monks bowed, entreating the Master to recite the gatha*. The* gatha *said:*

"All things are without truth
Do not, therefore, see them as true

If you see some truth
That seeing would be completely untrue

If you were able to find some truth for yourself
It would be the truth of your own mind released from falsehood

If truth did not exist in your own mind released from falsehood
Where else would it be?

Sentient beings are able to move
Insentient things are immobile

If you train yourself to practice immobility
It is the same as the motionlessness of insentient things

But, if you see true immobility
[You realize] it exists only in relation to mobility

Immobility is just being immobile
An insentient thing lacking the seed of Buddhahood

If you are able to distinguish the forms of things
[You will attain] immobility within the highest principle

If you have this view
That is itself the activity of bhutatathata

Students of the Way
Strive hard and take care!

In the gate of the Mahayana
Do not cling to knowledge from the world of birth and death

If others accord with these words
You can discuss Buddhism together

If they do not, then, joining your hands palm to palm
Let them experience your delight

In this sect, from the beginning, there is nothing to debate
By debating, you immediately lose the principle of the Way
If you cling to opposition and debate about the teaching
You yourself will fall into the world of birth and death"

Having heard this gatha, the monks bowed in unison. Accepting the teacher's view, the mind of each disciple became one with it, and they practiced in accordance with the teaching, no longer engaging in debate. They realized that the master would not remain long in this world.

SOKEI-AN SAYS:

This is the famous *gatha* made by the Sixth Patriarch. Before his death, the Sixth Patriarch gave his final words to his disciples and left this song for them and for future disciples. It is called the *"Gatha* of

Truth and Falsehood, Motion and Quietude." If you truly understand the meaning of this gatha, you will attain the highest truth of Buddhism.

The Master recited the gatha:

"All things are without truth/ Do not, therefore, see them as true/ If you see some truth/

That seeing would be completely untrue": If you are looking for truth in objective existence or looking for truth in your mind, pursuing names, analyzing your dreams and visions—your subconscious—if you attach yourself to that mind-stuff, you will not find truth. But you say: "I have found Truth! I see the Truth!"

Some years ago, a lady came here to ask me a question about "Truth." She said when she meditated, the whole world became blue, like a blue diamond, and then it slowly changed into pink, and then became transparent, like a pink ruby: "I understand the truth, but what is the significance of this blue and pink world?" I answered, "The blue world is to see through the sky, and the pink world is blood running away." She did not understand, and went home. She did not understand light and blood because she had fallen into a type of superstition, and she called it "Truth."

"If you were *able to find some truth for yourself/ It would be the truth of your own mind released from falsehood"*: You cannot deny that you have a mind, your own mind. This mind is padded like a pillow with mind-stuff—not "true" entities, but things from outside. But if your mind is released from falsehood, you will find your original mind. So the Sixth Patriarch permitted this to be called "truth," if it is found subjectively. We can really call the Sixth Patriarch a Buddhist because his view is entirely Buddhistic.

The Buddha found his enlightenment subjectively, the Oriental attitude. Of course, many European scholars take this attitude, the subjective view. But it seems to me that they are not quite clear. They try to explain the mind by symbols, but there is nothing to explain because there is nothing in it. It is pure fire, and fire cannot burn fire. We do not need any symbolism at all, and we do not need any explanations. All things are made of fire. The whole universe is fire. We do not need to be afraid of objective existence. Objective existence is an extension of our subjective mind. So there is no objectivity; all is subjective. The whole universe is Mind.

Hegel said that what we see objectively is the extension of the subjective mind. (I did not read this in English, but in a Japanese translation. If you like, some day I will find this passage for you. It is very good.) So there is no objectivity; all is subjectivity. The whole universe is Mind. It is easy to speak about, but it is very hard to realize. When you do realize it, you are in Buddhism, you have come through the threshold of Buddhism.

"If truth did not exist in your own mind released from falsehood/ Where else would it be?": If your own mind is not pure, not distilled, it is bothered by its elements. But the elements are not impure, you know; it is you who feel them to be impure. They belong to your mind. Things that you eat are not impure, but you feel them to be sinful or impure. As I've said, objective existence is made up of pure elements: earth, water, fire and air—the four great elements.

Earth is not impure; water is not impure; neither is fire nor air impure. So your body is not impure. Nothing is impure. Why do you feel this impurity? Because your mind is impure. Your mind is still sleeping. If your mind is not pure, you really cannot see the pure world. You cannot accept this human body, and when you cannot accept this human body, you do not obey the law of the human body.

The law of the human body is this: We cannot see our back. If I am sitting here, and someone were to put dynamite in the cellar, I would not see it. So we make an agreement between ourselves and call it morality: "We shall not do anything behind one another's backs."

If you do something behind another's back, no one will trust you. This is morality. If you violate this, you are blamed and not trusted. In peaceful times, you can be a good man. But in wartime, it is very different; we do things behind the other's backs. Therefore, war is bad.

When we accept our body, we do not think we have a superior power to see through everything, everywhere. No. We accept our body as pure existence in this human world, and then we see through the human law.

Well, if everyone followed this good morality, there would be no trouble, but such a time will never come.

"Sentient beings are able to move/ Insentient things are immobile": I would like to give you a short explanation of the term "immobility."

There are two kinds of immobility: objective immobility and subjective immobility. One is materialistic immobility, the other is the immobility of the mind. This glass quietly standing here has no motion; it is insentient. It is an example of objective immobility. When we stop the activity of our mind and keep our brain without any mind activity, that is also a type of immobility, but it is also objective immobility. "But it must plainly be subjective immobility. Don't you think so, you old quack?"

If you were to ask me why, though it is "mind" immobility, it is objective immobility because *all the matter before the eyes or behind the eyes is objective matter*. We draw the line between subjectivity and objectivity in a fashion different from you.

When I was seventeen, I was puzzled by this division of subjectivity and objectivity. I ran outside and closed the door, thinking I was in objectivity. Then I ran into the house and closed the door—closed my eyes—and thought I was in subjectivity. Westerners think that what is *before the eyes* is objective and what is *behind the eyes*, subjective. But Buddhists think everything on the shelf of consciousness is objective.

Subjectivity is pure emptiness. Your memories, your thoughts, the things in your dreams that you think about in images and names are all objective entities. They are in the realm of mind, but they are not mind-by-itself, but mind-stuff. If this water were mind, the things in this water would be mind-stuff, the debris of the mind, impressions of the outside, brought into the mind by the senses. Such impressions are not pure mind-by-itself. Pure mind is mind function, mind activity, without mind-stuff. Without it, everything stops, and that is called Mind. All mind-stuff is passive.

Objective immobility and subjective immobility must be clearly distinguished. When you have matter in the mind, there is mobility; the mind moves. When the mind is without matter, there is no mobility; though the mind is moving like the waves of the ocean, it is not moving at all.

The sphere of the mind is infinite. It cannot be measured by time and space. So all motion in infinite-mind is immeasurable. We cannot measure it by any scale of the objective world. This moving mind, observed from the standpoint of mind-by-itself, is the Immobile Mind.

"If you train yourself to practice immobility/ It is the same as the motionlessness of insentient things": When I strike this gong and it vibrates, all its atoms vibrate, its elements move, but it does not know mobility. From *its* state of mind—if it has a state of mind—it is immobile.

Under the rain of bullets on the battlefield, our mind does not move at all. In American slang, we have guts—the Immobile Mind.

In the moving pictures, especially in the Wild West cowboy pictures, when the enemy has two guns, the cowboy says, "Take it easy," and he rolls his cigarette and smokes it. Wonderful!—"Take it easy!"

In Zen, try to be a cowboy—have the Immobile Mind!

"But, if you see true immobility/ [You realize] it exists only in relation to mobility": This is very important. You do not *use* the immobile mind. *You* are not immobile; your mind is, but not the stuff of mind that is moving like waves. When you truly attain this state of mind, you will see immobility *in* mobility. In the koan "Stop the far-away sailing boat from sailing," you really grasp this point.

"Immobility is just being immobile/ An insentient thing lacking the seed of Buddhahood": It's dead. Brick and stone have no buddha-nature.

If you are able to distinguish the forms of things/ [You will attain] immobility within the highest principle": The Buddha said: "When you attain the highest principle, you can change rubbish into gold." When you attain the highest principle, this objective immobility will transform itself into Mind. The Buddha said: "When one Bodhisattva attains the highest enlightenment, mountains and rivers, earth and heaven, too, will attain the highest enlightenment." As Hegel said, "The extension of nature confronting you is the extension of your consciousness." The Hegelian philosophy is very interesting.

Western philosophy tries to find reality in the objective world and in the analysis of matter. They reach objective existence and call it "reality." This is the Western method. Our method, the Eastern method, is entirely different and diametrically opposite. We analyze our own mind and separate Mind from mind-stuff. This is what the Sixth Patriarch called the "release from falsehood." We return to the pure state of mind that is bottomless, infinite, and motionless. We call it Reality.

"If you have this view/ That is itself the activity of bhutatathata*"*: Mind itself cannot see Mind without matter, as fire itself cannot burn fire, and water cannot wash water. This is "truth by its own nature"—in Sanskrit, *bhutatathata*.

Dr. D.T. Suzuki translates *bhutatathata* as "suchness"; Western philosophy says "reality-by-itself." Religiously, we call it "God," and this God exists outside of the universe because He is not *in* the world of objectivity or the world of phenomena. He is not in the realm of our mind, so we say He exists outside the universe.

Everyone misunderstands this "outside the universe"—"How can this be possible, the universe is endless. How can there be an 'outside?'" All that exists outside is not true existence; it is false existence.

If you could have this view, you would understand, not only *bhutatathata* but also the *activity* of *bhutatathata*. Then your life, from morning to evening, would be the true life.

"Students of the Way/ Strive hard, and take care!/ In the gate of the Mahayana/ Do not cling to knowledge from the world of life and death": Mahayana is the last half of Buddhism. Hinayana is analogous to your ascent to the top of a mountain. Mahayana is analogous to coming down from the top of the mountain to the foot of the mountain, from its foot to the village, from the village to the town, from the town to the city, from the city by the sea to the Great Ocean. When a monk has attained the complete knowledge of Buddha Dharma, he must teach this knowledge to the multitude. Then he takes the Mahayana attitude.

"Life and death" signifies this world. All sentient beings in this world must accept the phases of life and death, must accept this phenomenal life and death in this changeable world, this phenomenal world. In Buddhism, we accept this world as temporary existence, like a dream. We are living in this dream. My "self" is also a dream. When you dream, you dream about yourself. Your "self" is in the picture of the dream. Who dreams this picture? Are you dreaming this picture of your "self," or does somebody else dream it? This is a very important point. Think about it. My old students know this. I do not need to speak about it.

If I say this world is like a dream, you take your hat and coat and go away. You cannot accept it; you cannot penetrate this dream. Your mind is shallow, like a piece of paper. This has been so since the time of the Buddha. When he was giving his teaching, three hundred monks went away.

"If others accord with these words/ You can discuss Buddhism together": Then you can say something about Buddhism.

"If they do not, then, joining your hands palm to palm/ Let them experience your delight/ In this sect, from the beginning, there is nothing to debate/ By debating, you immediately lose the principle of the Way/ If you cling to opposition and debate about the teaching/ You yourself will fall into the world of life and death": In the Tien-t'ai schools, all those philosophical scholars are debating from morning to evening. In the Zen sect, there is no debating, no arguing. There is nothing to argue about. I ask you, "What is this?" No argument is necessary. If you do not understand, do not try to understand. If you understand, you do not need to ask me a question.

In Zen, everything is answered quickly—"What is this object?" When you think of something, you are going around the object. But when you enter it, you do not need to think about it. Before the fire moth enters the flame, it goes around it; then there is neither candle flame nor moth.

"Before father and mother, what were you?" That is the first Zen question. While you are thinking about it, you are not yet in it. When you enter it, you do not need to talk about it. It is like the taste of water. If one asks, "What is the taste of water? Is it sweet? Is it bitter?" can anyone explain? When you taste it, you will know and you will not need to talk about it any more. If you debate, you will fail to grasp the reality of it.

So if I ask you, "Where do you come from?" what do you say?

A half-baked Buddhist would answer, "There is no place to come or go because the universe is infinite." This is a very nasty answer in Buddhism. Buddhist think that it smells, that it has some purpose. We do not like such answers. Or, one could say: "Please explain your question. What do you mean by 'Where do I come from?'" Some answer this way: "I come from downtown," or, "I come from uptown." These are the usual Zen answers. They are no different from everyone's everyday answers.

A monk asked Yun-men: "Where did all the buddhas come from?" Yun-men answered: "The Great Eastern Mountain walks over the surface of the water." This koan reminds me of that mysterious story of Christ walking on the surface of the lake. When the teacher asks a question, the student understands immediately. You will observe this koan someday.

Having heard this gatha, *the monks bowed in unison. Accepting the teacher's view, the mind of each disciple became one with it—that is, in samadhi—and they practiced in accordance with the teaching, no longer engaging in debate. They realized that the master would not remain long in this world.* When I came to New York, the first three years were like a debating contest. I gave lectures and then tea. I had to speak at the top of my voice. It was a terrible time! Now I think my audience has accepted this view—no debate. We take tea, and we talk the usual things. "Where do you come from?" "The East Side." "How old are you?" One young gentleman, after turning twenty-one, did not tell his age. It's like a Zen school now.

Head Monk Fa-hai bowed once more and asked: "After your Reverence enters nirvana, who is to inherit your robe and succeed to your Dharma?"

The Master said: "Since preaching my sermon to you at Ta-fan Temple, my sermons have been recorded and promulgated widely under the title 'Sutra of the Treasure of Buddhism from the Earthen Altar.' Guard this work and hand it down from generation to generation, giving deliverance to all sentient beings. Teach only in accord with this. That is true Dharma.

SOKEI-AN SAYS:

Time is like a stream endlessly flowing, and we are now having the last gathering here for this year [1938]. In the first week of next year, we will meet here again.

The Sixth Patriarch, at the end of his life, told his disciples that there is nothing to debate in Buddhism because the Buddhist faith is faith in Reality. Of course, philosophically, there are two sides to this Reality: Reality-by-itself and Reality appearing as the true object. The true object is the Reality that is beyond time and space and includes our five senses. You do not need to talk about this phenomenal world at all. Reality-by-itself is subjective reality. It is the reality of our consciousness. But the Buddhist does not accept this philosophical definition of Reality. To the Buddhist, Reality is neither subjective nor objective. Reality is *this moment*, and it is this (struck table). Of course, I do not say that this table *is* Reality. You must understand this by meditation. There is no way to completely grasp this state of Reality in your mind, so we do not discuss it in philosophical terms. When you discuss it, you are far from the true state of Reality. When you return to yourself, you will realize it.

The Sixth Patriarch always taught in this fashion, and after generations his disciples still follow his model. If you were to ask a Zen master, "What is buddha?" (buddha here means Reality), he would lift up his *hossu* without any explanation. "Is Buddha being or non-being?" Same answer.

The Zen master Chu-chih always answered by lifting his finger: "What is nothing?" A finger. "What is everything?" A finger. "What is existence? What is non-existence?" Always one finger. One day, Chu-chih heard of a novice in the temple who mimicked him. Whenever anyone asked him a question—for example, "What is your teacher's teaching?"—the novice lifted a finger. "Is your teacher a buddha, or a mere human being?" One finger. "What are you?" "Where do you come from?" "Where do you go?" Always the same answer; he lifted one finger. So Chu-chih summoned him.

The boy presented himself before Chu-chih, and the Master showed him his finger. The novice mimicked him. Chu-chih seized the boy's finger and cut it off with his knife. Screaming, the novice ran through the halls of the temple. About to turn the corner of the temple gate, Chu-chih called to him, "Boy!" The novice turned, and the teacher lifted his finger. The novice lifted what was cut off, and suddenly he realized Reality. He had lost a finger, but he had gained the whole universe. He purchased the universe with one finger. A good bargain!

Usually American ladies do not like this story. It is not their idea of a religious attitude. They think it was bad to cut off the boy's finger. I think, it was very kind, but we shall not discuss this story. At that time, there was no debating in Buddhism. All teachings were matter-of-fact.

Head Monk Fa-hai bowed once more and asked: "After your Reverence enters nirvana, who is to inherit your robe and succeed to your Dharma?" The robe was handed down from the first patriarch, Bodhidharma, from generation to generation as proof of the genuineness of the disciple's attainment. This tradition is still kept in Zen temples. My teacher handed down to me the robe that was given to him by his teacher, Soyen Shaku. I possess it as proof of the genuineness of my attainment. Of course, you can fool unenlightened people, but you cannot fool the enlightened ones. The Buddha made a strict rule on this, and once dismissed a monk from the sangha who called himself an *arhat*. But these days, anyone who stays in a temple three days calls himself enlightened.

In the Zen school, it is different. If someone claims to be enlightened, we say, "Show me." If you do not know, you cannot show. This means to show *before my eyes*. So when you talk about enlightenment, I say, "Show me." It must be demonstrated.

Once, I met someone who, when I said, "Show me," said, "Look at my nimbus." I said, "I don't see it." He told me, "You're not enlightened." I could have said to him, "I can show you mine." If I gave him a black eye, he would see the light!

The Buddha handed down his principle to Mahakashyapa. One day, among the multitude, he lifted up a golden lotus. No one understood but Mahakashyapa, who smiled. How did he smile? What kind of a smile? We think he smiled like this—"Ha, ha, ha!"

One day I asked an old monk in Japan: "Did Mahakashyapa really smile?" "Perhaps," and he laughed.

The Buddha said: "Mahakashyapa, you have really grasped my dharma. From now on, you possess my robe. Do not lose it."

The Buddha lifted up the lotus. Chu-chih lifted his finger. Zen is always the same. So I ask: "What is Reality?"

The Master said: "Since preaching my sermon to you at Ta-fan Temple, my sermons have been recorded and promulgated widely under the title 'Sutra of the Treasure of Buddhism from the Earthen Altar.'" The Sixth Patriarch was a small man. The multitude could not see him from a distance, so the monks piled up the earth and made a platform. The Sixth Patriarch ascended this platform and preached from it.

"Guard this work and hand it down from generation to generation, giving deliverance to all sentient beings." Finally, it has been handed to this generation, and I am now translating it into English from beginning to end. In China, a monk would translate only one or two sutras in his lifetime. Today, hundreds are being translated, but these translations are no good.

Those who read this sutra will be emancipated from the bonds of the world. Human beings have roped themselves by their own minds, and in this broad universe, they are bound. They must cut this off and emancipate themselves.

"Teach only in accord with this. That is true Dharma."—"If you want to be my disciples, give your sermons in accordance with my teaching."

The Sixth Patriarch was the Zen Master who really crystallized the Zen teaching and made it the Zen school. But today, we are not entirely making an effort to follow his instructions. Our sermons approximately fall into his old model.

Many people think the Zen school is only a school of meditation, so they "talk" about Reality and "take" the attitude of meditation. But they are unable to use such an attitude in action, in active life. The old attitude of quiet meditation is good, and is still kept today in Japan in the Soto school, but the active school is Rinzai (Lin-chi) Zen. Reality is to be grasped in its most active moment. To use an analogy, the Soto school is something like a musical instrument, the strings of which are loose, so you cannot play a tune, though the sound is deep. The Rinzai school is like an instrument in which the strings are all tight. Just touch the strings, and they make a sound.

When Lin-chi asked his master, Huang-po, "What is the cardinal principle of Buddhism?" Huang-po struck him. Lin-chi asked three times and Huang-po struck him three times. After Lin-chi had been struck three times by Huang-po, he left the temple. The head monk told Lin-chi to go to Zen Master Ta-yu, "He will be very kind to you." Ta-yu was about a hundred miles away.

So Lin-chi went to Ta-yu and told him that Huang-po had hit him three times. Then he asked Ta-yu if he had made some offense. Ta-yu answered: "Huang-po was very kind to you." All of a sudden, Lin-chi understood: "Oh! Huang-po's Buddhism is not different from mine!" Ta-yu seized Lin-chi, saying, "You little monk! You just asked 'What was my offense?' and now you say, 'My Buddhism is not different from Huang-po's.'" Ta-yu took him by the throat, squeezed his neck and shook him. Lin-chi thereupon administered three blows to Ta-yu's ribs, and Ta-yu pushed him away. But Lin-chi pushed him right back. Ta-yu said: "Huang-po is your teacher! I have nothing to do with your enlightenment." It was then that Lin-chi returned to Huang-po, who again accepted him as his disciple.

Huang-po said: "What are you doing, going back and forth like this?" Lin-chi repeated Ta-yu's words, adding, "So I have come back again."

Huang-po said: "Ta-yu is a chatterer. If he were here, I would strike him."

Lin-chi answered, "You don't need to wait for him to come here. I will strike him for you!" and he struck Huang-po. Huang-po then said: "This bed wetter came back and pulled the tiger's whiskers!" Then Lin-chi shouted. Huang-po was delighted.

This is how Zen was handled in those days—no philosophical talk. All was the *conclusion* of philosophy. The Zen religion demonstrates the mighty power of the universe.

When Tung-shan, visited Yun-men, Yun-yen was an old monk and Tung-shan was a young one. Yun-men said to Tung-shan, "Where did you come from?" "I came from Ch'a-tu." "Where did you last stay?" "In Pao-tsu, in Hunan." "When did you leave there?" "August 25th." Yun-men held up his staff: "I pardon you my thirty blows. Go to the monks' quarters." Tung-shan went and the next evening went back to the Master's room again: "You said you pardoned me thirty blows. Have I committed some offense?" Yun-men said: "You rice sack! This is how you have been spending your days in Hunan?" Upon this, Tung-shan was enlightened.

Zen has its own nature. There is no description, no philosophy to talk about. The transmission of shouting and hitting was the primitive method. Today we handle Zen more delicately; it has developed. We still shout and strike, but we are not so crude. That was the beginning of Zen. All those expressions were real creations.

It was Zen Master Ma-tsu's shout that made the Rinzai school. Ma-tsu made his great shout to indicate his Zen, to show that Reality is activity. He emphasized the essence of Zen. But I do not shout here because this house would come down! If I gave Lin-chi's shout, it would fall down. When Ma-tsu shouted, his disciple Pai-chang was deaf for three days. I wish I could hear his shout, so I could be deaf for three thousand years! The Rinzai Zen school does not take a meek attitude.

"Now I have imparted to you my Dharma. [But] I will not hand down the robe. Your faith is pure and matured, and your resolve is absolute, so that you are worthy to assume the great responsibility [of promulgating the Dharma]; however, according to the meaning of the gatha *handed down by the First Patriarch, the great master Bodhidharma, the robe is not to be transmitted. The* gatha *says:*

"*I came to this land originally*
To transmit the Dharma and deliver sentient beings from delusion
A single blossom will open to reveal five petals
And the fruit will naturally appear"

SOKEI-AN SAYS:

The Sixth Patriarch conveyed the significance of Bodhidharma's *gatha* to his disciples. In ancient days, at the end of their lives, Zen masters always gave a last *gatha*. This *gatha*, a very famous one, was the *gatha* of Bodhidharma.

"Now I have imparted to you my Dharma." The Sixth Patriarch said that in his speeches he had completely imparted to his disciples the principle of Buddhism. His last sermon to his disciples has already been transmitted in previous lectures.

"[But] I will not hand down the robe." This robe was handed down from Bodhidharma through the generations to the Sixth Patriarch, but the Sixth Patriarch did not hand the robe down to his disciples because they adhered to it too much. The robe is a material object, so the Sixth Patriarch stopped the transmission.

When the Buddha died, he transmitted his robe to his disciple Mahakashyapa, asking him to transmit the robe to the next Buddha, the future Buddha, Maitreya. So Mahakashyapa, carrying the robe, entered *nirodha-samadhi*—endless absorption—to await Maitreya, to transmit the robe of Shakyamuni Buddha. This age is the interval between Shakyamuni Buddha and Maitreya Buddha.

This legend is handled as a koan in some monasteries: "Mahakashyapa entered *nirodha-samadhi* and was annihilated: his body dried up; his bones became powder; and his consciousness scattered. At this moment, where is he? And where is the golden robe of Shakyamuni Buddha which should be handed down to Maitreya, the next Buddha?"

This is a very nice koan, a nice problem. I was asked by a teacher: "What is the color of this robe? What is its size? Is it square, or is it round? Is it combustible? Is it washable?"

In the Orient, masters still hand down their own robe, or their teacher's robe, to their disciples as a diploma, to prove that they were their disciples and have studied Buddhism in their monastery, fifteen, twenty, or even thirty-five years. My teacher wrote to me: "You studied Zen in my monastery many years, but it was like one day." Only one word may be written on the back of a robe.

The monk who accepts the robe from his teacher goes around, and one by one, shows it to the brotherhood of the temple and to his relatives and friends. The monks join their hands and say, "Very well, you are the disciple of So-and-so."

In the Orient, no one can just say, "I studied Zen in such-and-such a monastery, and I was ordained a Zen master by such-and-such a teacher." There can be no bluff. The transmission of Dharma is a very important and grave matter in Oriental religion.

"Your faith is pure and matured": In Buddhism, we talk about faith. Of course, the Christian also talks about faith—faith in God. He says you must not ask questions. Without knowing anything about it, you must have faith in God. It is very hard. You must believe in God, whether you know He exists or not. Faith is first.

When you doubt, you cannot have faith in anything. When you must associate with a friend, you must first have faith—"I don't know, maybe he will kill me. Maybe he will ask me some incredible question."

I have many friends of all kinds—gamblers, gangsters, all kinds of people. When I associate with them and open my heart, they are with me. Opening their hearts, they associate with me. They say, "Reverend, if you are ever in trouble, call me up and I will send twenty men immediately." So you cannot give me a black eye!

I was a child of a Shinto priest, and I did not believe in Buddhism at first. Then a friend of mine told me that Buddhism has existed for 2,500 years and is a religion that covers half the Eastern world. He said, "There must be something in it, don't you think?" I said: "Perhaps there is." He said: "Perhaps your nature tends more to Buddhism than your father's faith. Perhaps it will give you the answer."

I was an artist and studied art from the age of fifteen. I doubted all schools of art. Finally I entered art with the faith that nature was my teacher. I was a very independent young man. I walked into a farmer's garden and set up my easel, and I knelt down and worshipped nature with tears in my eyes. The farmer said: "What is the matter, young fellow? Have you a stomach ache?" With that humbleness and faith, I entered Buddhism. Faith in art, and faith in religion is the same faith. When I had faith in nature, the street corner was a great theater to me. True drama is not performed only on the stage.

"*...And your resolve is absolute*": "Your resolve" means your determination. When you solve a question and come to a conclusion, you must have the faith to make a decision. When you take *sanzen*, when you think of an answer, you must have faith in that answer, that decision. When you go to the teacher, you accept his "Yes" or "No." For his answer is not his own creation, but has been handed down in this history of the Orient. *It* is the criterion.

Matter has three dimensions; that is a criterion. One plus one is two; that is also a criterion. No one can say no. "Where do you stand?" "I stand on my heels"—that is a criterion. You cannot stand on your head. Truth is self-proved evidence. If I throw this incense into this fire, it will be burned. That is truth, and it is "absolute."

"*. . . So that you are worthy to assume the great responsibility [of promulgating the Dharma]*": In other religions, promulgating religion is the teacher standing by the altar and making sounds. That is promulgating.

Not in our Zen school. We do not need to beat our upper and lower jaws. When we feed people, we do not call the food by name—this is such-and-such a soup, this is a lamb chop, this is a doughnut. No, we open their mouths and pour it in.

Once I invited an American friend for chop suey and gave him some. It was terrible! He asked, "What is this?" I said: "Chinese Gorganzola cheese. It's delicious! How do you like it?" It was not Gorganzola cheese, of course. China does not have Gorganzola cheese.

No need for names. We do not need to call water H_2O. Let them drink.

The true Buddhist does this work: Gives IT without a name. So when anyone talks religion to me, I say, "Stop talking religion. I come from Missouri; you've to show it to me!"

"*However, according to the meaning of the* gatha *handed down by the First Patriarch, the great master Bodhidharma, the robe is not to be transmitted." The* gatha *says:"I came to this land originally/ To transmit the Dharma and deliver sentient beings from delusion."*" There are many delusions—for example, the many young men in Japan who, when their bride dies, commit suicide. Their bride's death breaks their hearts. Or the mother who commits suicide when she loses her dear child. This is attachment and delusion.

In Japan when you marry, you carry your bride round to the neighbors, house to house. Once a bride dropped her handkerchief and was terribly ashamed. Her face became pink, and an old woman giggled. So the bride jumped into a well and died. Her husband's heart broke, so he too jumped into a well and died. Then her father and mother, with nothing more to live for, died. The old woman was terrible sorry, so she died, too. Delusion.

Destroying this kind of delusion gave me deliverance and emancipation from all cares so that I could accept this human life without question. We do not teach you to call this place a filthy place, kick your hind legs and go up to heaven. No, we do not teach this. Open your true eye, accept this as Buddha's teaching and realize it now.

The first day I came to America, I bought a one-dollar watch and destroyed it completely. Then I picked it up and enjoyed it.

"A single blossom will open to reveal five petals/ And the fruit will naturally appear." The "five petals" are the five classical schools of Zen: Ts'ao-tung, Ummon, Fa-yen, Kuei-yang, and Lin-chi. Today, in Japan, there are two schools, Soto (Ts'ao-tung) and Rinzai (Lin-chi). I belong to the Rinzai sect.

Again the Master said: "Good friends, all of you purify your minds and listen to my sermon. If you desire to realize the perfect wisdom of the buddhas, you must attain the samadhi *of one form and the* samadhi *of one practice. If, wherever you may be, you do not abide in form, if amid form you do not give rise to [notions of] like and dislike, attachment and detachment, without regard to considerations of [personal] benefit or life and death, but remain peaceful and calm, empty and disinterested, this is the samadhi of one form."*

SOKEI-AN SAYS:

This is the last sermon of Hui-neng. The principle of this sermon is the *samadhi* of "one form" and "one practice." "One form" means "one thing" or "one place," and "one practice" means "one deed" or "one action." These are technical terms the Sixth Patriarch is using.

Of course, the Sixth Patriarch did not immediately die after this sermon. He later went by boat down the river to his birthplace, Hsin-chou, Canton of today. His mother's house had been remodeled as a temple, and it was at this temple that he died. Beside the house there was a huge stone called "Farewell Rock," which still exists. It was here, across the water from Canton and near the Pearl River, that he said goodbye to his mother when he left to become a monk.

Again the Master said: "Good friends, all of you purify your minds and listen to my sermon." The usual Buddhist attitude while listening to a teacher is a pure mind. Your own opinion or your own view must be excluded from your mind. You must put aside all ideas for a while. Later, if you wish to criticize the teacher's view, it is up to you. But while you are listening, you must put aside your own view and maintain an empty, open mind. With this empty mind, you must accept the teacher's words. This is our attitude.

"If you desire to realize the perfect wisdom of the buddhas, you must attain the samadhi *of one form"*: The "perfect wisdom of the buddhas" is *sarvajna*, the "all-wisdom" attained by the Buddha, the one wisdom that is the source of all wisdoms. This first wisdom is in everyone. In English, it is *a priori* wisdom.

In meditation, when you meditate upon *this present existence*, including yourself and the universe all at once, you see the outside with your eye and you hear the outside with your ear. This awareness of existence outside and inside is one center. Of course, when I say "one center," everyone tries to find this one center in the body—in the brain, the heart, the spine. But it is *this awareness itself* that is the center. You do not need any center beyond this awareness. When you see the outside with the sense of sight, you can find the center. It is the eye. But the sense of sight is only one of the branches of your consciousness. There is a "first" consciousness. It is *here*, but do not look at me! You are sitting *there*, and you know that you are sitting *there*, and that you are aware of your *own* existence. This center of *knowing your own existence* is the awareness of you sitting there *and* here.

It is very hard to grasp this, but when you sit down and give up everything, this is the entrance. When you find your axle of wisdom, you do not need to meditate or to think of anything anymore. You just retreat from that awareness into that wisdom, deeper and deeper, and still deeper. Deep or broad does not mean anything in meditation, but still you retreat deeper and deeper. Then you enter into the state of Buddha. There is no other Buddhism. This is the only way. To explain this, the Buddha spent forty-nine years! The Buddha himself was absorbed into the immense state of existence, expanded into oneness. The Sixth Patriarch called it "one form."

Buddhism is plain. You do not need to read any book or listen to anyone. Just sit down upon your seat and realize it. Keep your eyes open and accept all the wisdom of the universe at once.

In the West, there is a philosophy of knowledge called epistemology Epistemology is nearest to the source of wisdom. It is through epistemology that Western scholars, in the Western sense, think one can reach the state of ontology. This philosophy is rather new. Of course, everything must return to your own wisdom, so what this wisdom is must be studied and investigated. Naturally, I am very interested. I think I know what this is, this wisdom explained by the wisdom of epistemology. Western philosophers are really friendly to our old Buddhism.

Of course, to attain the true state of "all-wisdom," *sarvajna*, is not so easy. The Buddha attained it in six years, but we may strive for thirty or forty years to attain it. It is not mysterious or esoteric wisdom. It is practical, plain wisdom. The Buddha's wisdom was not magic. It throws light upon the present circumstances of mankind. The stage of salvation is here. Everyone must be emancipated from the illusory notions of this earth. That was Buddhism in the early days. Later, someone invented heaven.

The heaven of Buddhism is a bottomless, endless, empty state. It is empty, but it embraces omnipotence. Through the narrow gate of the seed of wisdom, when you meditate, you can retreat into that state, enter that state. You realize your boundless body, your endless wisdom, infinite light, effulgence. This does not belong to the sky or empty space, but to the depths of your mind. So if you desire to attain the wisdom that is the source of all wisdom, you must know the samadhi of one form, which is this phenomenal world.

I can see everything here. I go out and I can see everything there. I can go beyond the sea to my own country, and I can see many things there. All these appearances, this phenomenal world, will become one. The *samadhi* of one form becomes that of only one place. This one place has no color, no sound, no taste, no smell, no touch.

Someone criticized me, saying I use too many Western philosophical terms, but these terms are very convenient. By these, the Oriental meaning can be illustrated exactly. To use a Western term, one place, means noumenon. I am an Oriental, and you are Westerners, but I think you know these terms. I must say what I think these words mean, so I speak from my own lips.

Phenomena relate to our five senses. Noumena do not relate to our five senses, energy, ether, or electricity. Noumenon, that something that exists, absolute objective being, is that "one place."

In the West, people conceive it objectively, as a real object. But in the East, people conceive it as their own mind. To us, it exists subjectively. It is subjective existence because noumenon is our own mind. In the East, our mind disappears from phenomenal existence and reappears in one form.

In poetry, this one form, this one place, is expressed by the metaphor of the countryside covered with snow.

The countryside is covered with snow
No king's palace
No beggar's hut
All is covered with silver

To me, all New York is transparent. There is just one appearance. That is, one place. You must attain this in your *samadhi*. *Samadhi* is the state you attain in your concentration.

"And the samadhi of one practice." When a farmer digs a ditch, when a clerk in a bank operates the adding machine all day long, when the teacher teaches and the painter paints, these are not many performances. From the noumenal state, there is just one performance, one "practice." You must observe the whole world from this one view. It is the entrance to the attainment of sarvajna.

A daughter was asked by her friend what her father's occupation was: "Oh, my father is just a hick farmer. I'm going to be an artist." So she went to Paris to learn to paint, despising her father who sent her the money. All this was one deed—one practice.

It is very interesting to see life in this way, to see everything from one standpoint.

"If, wherever you may be, you do not abide in form, if amid form you do not give rise to [notions of] like and dislike, attachment and detachment, without regard to considerations of [personal] benefit or life and death, but remain peaceful and calm, empty and disinterested, this is the samadhi *of one form."* Some people take this "disinterest" in a queer way. There was a Zen student who returned to his temple after a long absence. As soon as he stepped into the temple, the Abbot said: "Too bad, your teacher is dead." The Zen student laughed aloud. The Abbot then said: "Why did you laugh when you heard that your master was dead? Why don't you cry?" He then cried. This is a so-called indifferent attitude. But the true indifferent attitude is not this. This Zen student was not a true Buddhist student. He was merely imitating a disinterested attitude. "Your teacher is dead!" "Oh, is that so!" "Your teacher is alive!" "Oh, is that so!" This is not true disinterest. When you abide in one form, you do not need to take such a queer attitude. You are quite natural.

Mind itself is calm. On the surface, there are waves, but the ocean itself is calm. There are many things in the universe, but the universe itself is empty. Every day at your pleasure you attach yourself to many things. You adhere to life and dislike death. But fundamentally, you cannot discriminate between life and death. Fundamentally, you are free from life and death.

Things that are written are different from those experienced in daily life, though in principle they are the same.

"If, wherever you are, whether going, standing, sitting or lying down, your mind remains simple and direct, so that without moving from the place of enlightenment you truly realize the Pure Land, this is the samadhi *of one practice. If a person possessed these two kinds of samadhi, it would be like seeds concealed within the earth, which, if nursed, will mature into fruits. The 'one form' and the 'one practice' are just like this. The sermon I am preaching now is like the seasonable rain that gives moisture to the great earth. Your buddha-natures are like the seeds that receiving this moisture can all sprout at once.*

He who accepts my teaching is sure to attain awakening (bodhi). *He who follows my practice will surely realize the marvelous fruit.*

SOKEI-AN SAYS:

The main point of this part of the Sixth Patriarch's record is the *samadhi* of one form—"one place"—and one practice—"one deed."

We are living in many different places, and we do different work; but fundamentally, those different places are one place, and those many deeds are one deed. With such a view, we just stay in one place, from beginning to end, and we just do one thing. This view will make your life very simple, and your mind will not be so busy. One deed, one work, will give your mind a rest. You can therefore enjoy your simple and single life, though you are doing many different things and living in many different places. From "one" standpoint, you do many things and take many different roles.

The artist often takes this view. From one viewpoint, he makes a statue or paints, makes a poem, plays music, dances, and sings. But his principle of beauty is only "one," whether he is a musician, sculptor, or dancer. From the Sixth Patriarch's own viewpoint, he can be everywhere—in fire, in earth, in water, in air, or in ether. He can perform many deeds from morning to evening; it is all the same. The artist is like the mirror that reflects figures and images, but is not changed at all.

When you go to the theater and see a performance, seeing the drama, your mind becomes good or bad, beautiful or ugly in accordance with the performance. Your mind changes, and you sometimes doubt you are the same person. But when you leave the theater, you find that you are the same Mister or Miss So-and-so. It is just the attitude of your mind, and you can, in American slang, "Take it easy." In this busy, materialistic civilization, you need such a standpoint.

"If, wherever you are, whether going, standing, sitting or lying down": The four dignities—whatever you do from morning to evening.

"Your mind remains simple and direct so that without moving from the place of enlightenment, you truly realize the Pure Land, this is the samadhi *of one practice."* The original nature of mind is simple, like pure water. It is not like whisky, rum, or Benedictine.

The Chinese say a true gentlemen's friendship is like water, but a mediocre gentlemen's friendship is like honey. The true gentlemen's friendship you can enjoy for a long, long time. The mediocre gentlemen's friendship, like honey, soon gathers dust, gets sticky and draws flies. Those who have minds that are simple and direct can keep their friendships.

So your mind is your own temple in which you practice your own religion. Religion is not amusement. It is like the foundation of a house. If the foundation is simple, you do not need to change your face or think one thing in different ways. It is very hard to find a man who is direct with himself, who does not lie to his own mind. One who is not direct with himself cannot really see himself. But if you are simple and direct with yourself, you can be so with others.

It is not necessary to read the Bible or the sutras to practice the Dharma. From the Sixth Patriarch's standpoint, it could be chopping trees, gathering wood, hammering nails, writing letters, cooking, washing—all is the practice of Dharma. But you must do it with your simple and direct mind. It will become religion, your single deed in one place.

The "place of enlightenment" means any place, any street corner, office, or amusement park. Wherever one is, is the Pure Land. When Ananda preached to a queen who was in a dungeon, he gave her an analysis of the five shadows of mind and said, "You will find the Pure Land in the analysis of these five shadows of mind—wherever you are." The queen meditated in that dungeon and made it a pure land. We, too, can meditate and make a pure land. In Christian terms, the Kingdom of Heaven will appear on earth.

The Zen student attains the omnipresent body sitting on his cushion. So in your practice, while shovelling coal into the stove or washing dishes, you can in a moment change your kitchen into the Pure Land. This is a simple teaching. It is the teaching of the direct, pure mind, the Pure Land teaching.

The one practice, in Buddhist terms, is the dominion in which *dharmakaya* dwells. You must realize it in your Zen practice. Certainly, you can build the Kingdom of Heaven on earth in your daily life and in your daily mind.

"If a person possessed these two kinds of samadhi"—that is, stayed in one place and performed one deed—*"it would be like seeds concealed within the earth, which, if nursed, will mature into fruits. The 'one form' and the 'one practice' are just like this."* The seeds of these two practices make everywhere one place and every deed one deed.

In your office, though you go to this or to that room, at the end of the day, when you look back, you were standing in one place because you were doing one work. You were concentrating on one thing, and you became it. If a woman concentrates into a man, she will become that man himself; and if a man loves a woman, he will become that woman herself. This is *samadhi*. If I meditate upon *dharmakaya*, concentrate into it, I become *dharmakaya* itself. When you concentrate into music or into your voice every day, you become voice itself. So if you continually practice these two kinds of *samadhi* when you see, hear, and so forth, everything through the eighty-four thousand pores of your skin will become Buddha.

You see a friend. He is not different from yourself. Soon his mind becomes your mind. In the one principle, there is only one mind in the universe, no "I," "you," "he," "she," or "they." There is only one man in the universe. You salute him, you eat with him. You speak, you feel what all feel. Your mind becomes the mind common to all sentient beings. In such a way, you must practice. That is the seed.

A young monk who was doing the cooking in a temple was always asking his master: "Does the soup taste salty or not?" Finally, the master lost his temper and said, "Haven't you got a tongue of your own?" Only when the young monk realized that the tongue is common to all sentient beings did he become a good cook. He then advanced in his Zen study.

"The sermon I am preaching now is like the seasonable rain that gives moisture to the great earth." "Rain," as a metaphor, is very famous in Buddhism, especially in the *Lotus Sutra*.

When you go to California and the autumn rain falls, all becomes green. In summer, it is the most devastated of places. Everything is dry except for the little plants and little poppies in the sand. But when autumn comes, all is green again. I saw it in California, and it is the same in China. In Southern China, in summer, everything dries up and dies in the tropical heat. Rain falls upon the mountains, the rivers, the fields, the sea. It transforms into willow trees, leaves, and green vegetation of all kinds. It enters the water jar of the house, gets into your rouge, or in your ink, into many things. But originally, the shower that fell from heaven was just one shower, though it appears in many ways.

"Your buddha-natures are like the seeds that receiving this moisture can all sprout at once." In summer under the hot sun, the seeds are sleeping—a beautiful metaphor! But under the moistening autumn rain the seed will sprout. If you have no seeds in your mind, nothing sprouts even though it rains. The seed is this concentration in one place, in one deed, to make all deeds one deed.

The ordinary person is like a bird in a cage that has lost its freedom. He sees blue, red, and green, but he never thinks about why this is blue, red, and green. Like the child who asks his mother, "Why is this red?" and the mother answers, "Because it's red, my dear!" It doesn't bother him that his mother does not explain it. He never thinks any deeper. He never realizes that color is the vibration of ether, and that sound is the vibration of air. In meditation, you can escape from this cage of delusion; and from it, you can observe everything.

"He who accepts my teaching is sure to attain awakening (bodhi)." The Sixth Patriarch is talking about his Dharma, which was explained in the previous lectures.

There are many modes of practice or teachings in Buddhism. These modes of practice in Sanskrit are called *upayas*—expedients. For a while, you use certain specific means to accomplish your awakening, such as meditation. But do not think that this means of attaining awakening will be like an electric light in your head, that your eyes will shine, and you will be able hear sounds one thousand miles away. If you heard those sounds, you could not live. It would be too noisy! This is not awakening. You do not need to destroy the law of your physical body in Buddhist practice.

As for the Buddhist practice of not eating meat: In ancient days, and still today, Buddhists refrained from eating meat because they believed it created a fierce mind. This commandment was for Buddhists of the Buddha's time. The four laws for eating pure meat were: 1) You shall not eat meat killed for you; 2) You shall not eat meat after you have seen the whole carcass; 3) You shall not eat the meat that died fighting; 4) You shall not eat meat that is spoiled. These laws were made for the monks in Kashmir, which did not produce vegetables. Southern Buddhist monks were not eating any meat at all.

Of course, when the chicken in your backyard knows you personally, and her little chicks come up on your hand and beg for food because they have faith in you—they are small and you are big—how can you kill them and fry them in the kitchen to eat? I cannot! And the pig that knows you and follows you, how can you kill him and make him into bacon and eat him? And if you kill a man, and policemen are always after you, how can you meditate? How can you meditate if you steal something and a detective comes?

Today, I do not eat meat that I feed, but I do eat meat that I buy from the butcher, that is pure meat. As for vegetables, their consciousness is not awakened, so we can kill them and eat them.

"He who follows my practice will surely realize the marvelous fruit." The marvellous fruit is the realization of the law in nature and in the human mind. With that, we settle the questions of the moment.

Everyone knows about the Buddhism of 2,500 years ago, but we do not apply it to the life of today. Buddhism needs to be applied to the life of today, or it will be a dead religion. Archery as warfare, for example, is dead today; and Sanskrit is deadwood. These are dead customs. Once it was the custom to wear big hoopskirts, carry a fan, ride in a little carriage, and whip the horse. But not today. In New York, you do not go into the subway in a hoopskirt, and so with the Buddhism of yesterday. Like an antique vase of the Ming or Sung dynasties, it is nice to look at, but you cannot put water in it and fill it with flowers.

Religion must be a living religion. With it, you can escape from your agony and attain comfort. Even if you commit some so-called crime, and the law accuses you of being a criminal, if in jail your conscience is clear, you can escape. This comes from a deep and living religion that saves you even in the dungeon! The Sixth Patriarch calls it the "marvelous fruit of enlightenment." You must be satisfied with the law of the physical body.

Listen to my gatha:

> *"The soil of the mind harbors each seed*
> *And when rain falls everywhere, all the seeds sprout*
> *When the flower of sudden-awakening has bloomed*
> *The fruit of enlightenment will naturally appear"*

Having recited the gatha, *the Master said: "This Dharma is without duality. This mind is the same. This Way is transparent and pure, without form. Take care not to meditate on stillness or to empty your mind. This mind is originally pure; there is nothing to be acquired or gotten rid of. Every one of you, strive hard and act in accordance with circumstances."*

Thereupon the monks bowed to the Master and retired.

SOKEI-AN SAYS:

This is a most important passage. At the time the Sixth Patriarch was practicing his meditation in Southern China, there was another school of Zen called the Northern School. Their attitude in meditation was based upon tranquillity and empty mind, void mind. "Void mind" means a mind like that of an idiot, an idiot that sits on a bench along the Hudson River and thinks there is nothing to do, so he meditates on "nothing." He thinks he does not like the city, so he goes to the country, and there he also meditates on "nothing." Nothing happens in his empty meditation. While the Northern School was practicing this type of meditation, the Sixth Patriarch was emphasizing active meditation.

The usual attitude of meditation is meditation upon some problem such as geometry or the Golden Throne of Heaven. In geometry, we meditate on triangles and squares and images in the air. When we meditate on the Golden Throne of Heaven and God with a long beard surrounded by angels with the Son of God at his right hand—that is to say, on some vision—we are meditating in the usual way.

Zen meditation is quite different. In Zen meditation, we do not cast our mind towards the outside. We retreat to the inside of our mind because *this* mind is the mind of Universal Consciousness. We think the surface of water in a bottle is the surface of all water. So the surface of *this* consciousness is the surface of *all* consciousness. My consciousness is like a drop of water, and your consciousness is also like a drop of water. Each one is a drop of water, and all these drops make an ocean of water. My consciousness, your consciousness, everyone's consciousness makes an ocean of consciousness. We go back there, and we realize the force of this powerful Universal Consciousness. This is our meditation. It is not meditation in an empty, void mind, which is like sleeping. The Sixth Patriarch's active meditation produces a power from this practice. It produces a powerful, enlightened mind. The center of meditation is our own wisdom. We do not need to study wisdom from a book. It is innate in every mind—all have it. We discover this wisdom from our deluded mind.

Now, you just think about many things. You let your mind go in a circle of house repairs, life insurance, auto repairs, bills, and funeral processions. You think you have no time to discover original wisdom in your deluded mind. But you do not need time. Just come back to your own cushion and sit upon it. Give up all those mundane affairs for a while. Come back to your original consciousness. Breathe deeply and rhythmically while taking a symmetrical stance. Keep your body in balance, and abandon all unnecessary thoughts. When this quiet attitude reaches the bottom, there is an original, natural force of consciousness that will spring up. It is like diving straight down into deep water. When you touch bottom, you spring up; and when you spring up from the depths of original consciousness, your consciousness has original power. natural, universal consciousness has the power to make you spring up. Your brain becomes clear, your breathing is easy and controlled; your face is relaxed, and you have a natural, calm, healthy expression. Connect your mind to universal consciousness. The true law of nature and of man operates from the inside.

"Listen to my gatha: *The soil of the mind harbors each seed/ And when rain falls everywhere, all the seeds sprout.*" The seed of enlightenment is in your original consciousness. It is the power that springs up. In meditation, all the seeds sprout.

"When the flower of sudden awakening has bloomed/ The fruit of enlightenment will naturally appear." Sudden awakening! Suddenly you attain enlightenment. Enlightenment is always awake. When you reach the bottom, and your mind switches to universal consciousness—the whole mind—you come back up to this world, and your native wisdom bears the fruit of this awakening, *bodhi*. By this wisdom, you will settle all your troubles today.

Having recited the gatha, *the Master said: "This Dharma is without duality."* "This Dharma" is just one consciousness, the consciousness that is universal, *dharmakaya*.

"This mind is the same."—Not two.

"This Way is transparent and pure, without form." There is only one mode of practice, and all modes are pure. There is only one mind, the mind of nature. In the mind of nature, there is no human mind different from that of nature. A butcher kills animals, but in his own purpose, killing animals is pure. Soldiers are fighting across a river of blood, but in their position or circumstance, from their own standpoint, they are pure.

This purity is very hard to understand, but when you do understand the true meaning of purity, your sin is cleansed and you are pardoned. There are many who blindly follow custom. But by making religion a living thing, one can attain comfort and a certain future. One can achieve enlightenment, and after awakening, one can settle in the body again.

When you understand profound mind, you will understand your own mind, and you will gain peace. When in this moment, time, and place, you understand how to manage yourself, you will know true religion.

"Take care not to meditate on stillness or to empty your mind." Meditate upon your profound mind, the mind of nature. You know what to do, and you know purity.

"This mind is originally pure": The Sixth Patriarch did not say, "his" mind, or "God's" mind, or "that" mind. He said, *this* mind. In the Zen school, "this" is sometimes used instead of "that" or "it" because it is evident to all sentient beings. The mind is direct; it is not necessary to explain it. The mind itself is self-evident-existence; it is axiomatic. I have a mind. I know it as clearly as I see my own hand. My mind is speaking now.

Where do you find your own God? In the sky? Under the earth? The nearest avenue to the state of God is *this* mind. It is foolish to seek God's abode by looking through space, trying to find it back of some nebula or behind the Milky Way. The representative of God is standing here—*this* mind. Buddhist mind is *this* mind. This is the Buddhist faith. I am a Buddhist, and therefore I observe God from *this* standpoint.

This mind is very clear to all of us. But what is the original nature of *this* mind? Is it different in the original state from the state in which we are standing at this moment? Of course, our mind is stuffed like a pillow or like pure water that is filled with debris. If I throw incense into a glass of water, we cannot call this water pure any more. We must separate the pure quality of mind from the stuff that has accumulated in it. Every mind is always pure.

One day, when I was traveling through Idaho, I went into some woods. There I found a spring and a little pond covered with autumn leaves. The water was stained red because of the red foliage. I was very thirsty, so I knelt down and scooped some water into my hands. The water was clear. It had not been stained or tinted by the autumn leaves. Our mind, I realized, must be pure like this pond. The original nature of mind is not so far away. It can be attained immediately. Purity is the nature of this original mind.

"There is nothing to be acquired or gotten rid of." You cannot make an artificial change in it, and you cannot sift any quality from it. This is the Sixth Patriarch's view, his Buddhism. When you observe your

mind in this fashion, you will be immediately emancipated. Nothing can be subtracted from it or added to it.

The Sixth Patriarch's words are great words, but not so easily understood.

"Every one of you, strive hard and act in accordance with circumstances." "Acting in accordance with circumstances" is enlightenment. When you find that your original mind is pure mind, it is enlightened; but "awakened" is a better word.

You cannot wash a lump of clay in water, but if you keep the water quiet and calm, all the impure stuff in it will sink. You will find the water clear. When you keep your mind quiet in meditation, all impurities settle. The things that come into your mind from the outside and your original quality of mind will be clearly separated, and your mind will become clear as crystal. At that moment, this clear mind connects your individual consciousness to universal consciousness. You become a being with universal consciousness, a bodhisattva. A bodhisattva is a sentient being who has a universal, enlightened mind. Enlightened beings possess uniform minds. Your mind will become uniform with all others. Our minds have become different, but they are not originally different. Originally, they are all the same. When you realize this attainment of uniform mind, it is called awakening.

The Sixth Patriarch said, "Strive hard and act in accordance with circumstances." He is saying: "If you have a father, go back to his house. If you have a child, go to him. For many, many years you have stayed in the temple. But now, I am going to die. Each of you go back to your own home or to your original teacher."

Thereupon the multitude bowed to the Master and retired. Everyone calls Buddhists "fatalists," saying they meekly accept their fate, that they accept conditions as they are and do not try to change them. This view is entirely wrong. We know our past, and we know the present moment, and we know what will happen in the future. The reflection of the mountains is mirrored on the water upside down. If you know your past and present, you can find out your future. We are not fatalists; we know how to change conditions. You can control your future, but you cannot change your karma all of a sudden.

This present moment of mind is the result of all the past, a past of many reincarnations and many *kalpas* of transmigration. The circumstances of the present moment do not exist by accident.

On the eighth day of the seventh month, the Master suddenly addressed his disciples, saying: "I desire to return to Hsin-chou. Quickly fit out a boat."

In grief, the monks implored the Master to stay. The Master said: "Even the buddhas who appreared in this world entered nirvana. That which comes must also go. There is a place to which this physical body of mine must return."

The monks said: "Master, after you leave, when will you be back?"

The Master replied: "When the tree-leaves fall, they return to the roots. When they come [back to the branches], they speak no word."

The monks asked: "To whom have you transmitted the true eye of the Dharma?"

The Master said: "He who possesses the Way will attain it; he who possesses no-mind will apprehend it."

Again the monks inquired: "In the future, will there not be difficulties?"

The Master said: "Five or six years after my death, someone will come and take my head. Listen to my prediction:

"On a head, offerings will be made to parents
In a mouth, someone will search for food

When the disaster known as Man occurs
Yang and Liu will be officeholders"

Again the Master said: "Seventy years after my death, two bodhisattvas will come from the east. One will be a monk and the other a layman. [Working] at the same time, they will spread my teaching, establish my school, erect temples, and beget manifold Dharma heirs."

SOKEI-AN SAYS:

In the farewell assembly, the Sixth Patriarch addressed his disciples and lay followers with his last words. I have been translating this last sermon of the Sixth Patriarch for quite a while, and now it is slowly coming to an end.

On the eighth day of the seventh month, the Master suddenly addressed his disciples, saying: "I desire to return to Hsin-chou." He desired to go back to his native country. He realized his death was nearing.

"Quickly fit out a boat." The boat was not larg,e but like a sampan of today.

In grief, the monks implored the Master to stay. The Sixth Patriarch knew he would die in ten to fifteen days, but the multitude said: "We cannot believe that you will die soon. You will live forever! Please stay with us!"

The Master said: "Even the buddhas who appreared in this world entered nirvana." There were many buddhas before Shakyamuni Buddha. All appeared in this human world and showed us how to enter nirvana.

When Shakyamuni Buddha was about to die outside the city of Kushinagara in a grove of *shala* trees, he called for Ananda: "Ananda, massage my back. I feel a terrible pain!" And in agony, he died. His death was a human death, like everyone's death. This shows that he was a great teacher, a real teacher.

One monk in China asked his disciples: "Have you ever seen anyone die upside down?" A monk answered: "Yes, I saw a Zen master die upside down." So the first monk said: "Very well, I shall die making a somersault!" And he died making a somersault. Many monks have died in queer ways, but the Buddha died a great death. We must also die a great death.

"That which comes must also go." We must all die some day. We must know what death is and what will happen after death so we will not be disconcerted at that moment.

"There is a place to which this physical body of mine must return." Not only this physical body, this outward form, but this inward form, consciousness; it, too, must return somewhere.

The outward form consists of the four great elements: Its flesh is earth; its blood is water; its heat is fire; its breath is air. Flesh will return to earth; blood will return to water; heat will return to fire; and breath will return to air. You know this quite well, but where will your consciousness return? It is not very clear, is it? Where will your thoughts return? You have thought many things in your lifetime, you study so much. And you have a great deal of knowledge. But where will it all go? Will it be annihilated after your death? You must know.

You love and you hate. You have many memories. When you die, what will happen to your love and your hatred, your friendships and your memories? What will happen to this everyday life—laughing, crying, smiling, shouting? When you die, will all this come to a destructive end or will it be continued? Living forty, fifty, sixty years, you should not die like a cat or a dog. Absurd! You must know all about it.

The monks said: "Master, after you leave, when will you be back?" It must have been discouraging for the Sixth Patriarch. He had been endeavoring to promulgate his Zen for many years. Yet now, when he ordered his disciples to prepare a boat to go down the river, the monks were saying: "You cannot leave here! Certainly you will come back again!" The words sound pathetic. They have an unenlightened sound.

The Master replied: "When the tree-leaves fall, they return to the roots." The souls of the tree leaves will go back to their own roots. Not only tree leaves, but all things return to their own roots. This root is tangible. I feel the root of my mind, in myself, always. It is very near.

"When they come [back to the branches], they speak no word." When spring comes, the tree buds do not announce anything to anyone. They come in silence. When you attain enlightenment, your mind does not speak to you, does not say, "Here I am, an enlightened mind!" You cannot say a word. No one knows about it, but *you* know. It comes in silence.

The monks asked: "To whom have you transmitted the true eye of the Dharma?" The "true eye of the Dharma" is the eye of Buddhism, the true law. There were about twenty disciples living with the Sixth Patriarch, but as this description shows, there was really no one to succeed to his highest Dharma.

One day on Eagle Mountain, the Buddha showed a golden flower to his followers and disciples. He was silent, did not speak a word. Not only human beings, but even the *apsaras* and *devas* in the congregation failed to understand the significance of the Buddha's action. But Mahakashyapa, the Buddha's greatest disciple, looked into the Buddha's eyes and smiled. This was the first transmission of the Zen school. From mind to mind, from eye to eye, from soul to soul, the Dharma was transmitted without speaking a word. Then the Buddha said: "Mahakashyapa, thus have I handed down the eye of my true Dharma. Uphold it, and hand it down to your posterity from generation to generation. Do not lose it!"

Thus the eye of the true dharma was handed down in India through twenty-eight generations; in China, through twenty-seven generations; and about seven hundred years ago, it was handed down to Japan. However, the true lineage of the Zen sect has expired in India. It has been said that there are some torch-holders living in Tibet today but not in China. Perhaps, in a hundred more years, there will be none in Japan.

The Master said: "He who possesses the Way will attain it." The Zen school is very queer. We are not really teaching Zen. We are *finding* Zen in our minds, naturally. We say, "Don't you know that it is Zen you have in your mind?" We do not explain. We do not say Zen is this or Zen is that. Those with Zen minds are not limited to monks but may be businessmen, artists, military men—all kinds of people. When we meet—"Ah, that is Zen!" We shake them and make them realize it.

There is no English equivalent for what we call this in the Orient, but the nearest word is probably "opportunity." We seize an opportunity and grasp the chance of the moment. Other people do not recognize it, so they miss it. A good businessman grasps the chance to make good business in a conversation. In our tradition, to have a great opportunity, you must be prepared to grasp it. If you do not grasp it, you must complete your education through many reincarnations. Then, when you hear "a word," you will open your eye.

There are numberless men and women who meet each other, but when some particular man and woman meet, in some corner of the world, they know they belong to each other. Some particular persons have minds between which this love will be felt. This is prepared through many reincarnations. The

Buddhist teaching is the same thing. There are many people in the world; but among them, here and there, there are those who will listen to the Zen teaching and will have queer feelings, will really hear it. They will possess the Dharma in their minds, and they will attain it.

"He who possesses no-mind will apprehend it." "No-mind" does not mean that you are stupid or an idiot. You are rather like the children spoken of by Christ that were simple and naive, spontaneous and pure—their minds ready to make contact with the great teaching.

It is not easy to possess that mind. It is through generations that such noble and beautiful minds are created. They are born in certain circumstances, cultivated in such a way that they do not see everything in distortion. They see everything like a five—or six-year-old child who is pure and naive. They have empty minds. Things appear in their minds like the reflections of the moon on clear water. Their minds are ready for high beauty and for great teachings.

Again the monks inquired: "In the future, will there not be difficulties? Sometime after the Sixth Patriarch's death, a disciple, Shen-hui, called himself the Seventh Patriarch and went up to Lo-yang in Northern China. When the Sixth Patriarch died, Shen-hui was about seventeen or eighteen years old. He had come to the temple at about the age of twelve. But no one knew who Shen-hui was until 1929 when the Tun-huang excavations uncovered certain sutras in which the *Record of Shen-hui* was discovered. From these records we realize that Shen-hui was one of the eminent monks of that day. There had been some "difficulty," so his name was entirely suppressed.

The Master said: "Five or six years after my death, someone will come and take my head." "Take my head" means to possess my teaching, attain my Dharma.

"Listen to my prediction!/ On a head, offerings will be made to parents/ In a mouth, someone will search for food." These offerings are our teachings to our disciples. I came to this country, and I hand my teacher's Dharma to you. It is my compensation to my teacher for teaching me his Dharma.

In Japan and China, you will often see a mother put rice in her mouth, then put her mouth to the baby's mouth to feed the baby. The transmission of Zen is entirely like that. See each other face to face; feed each other mouth to mouth.

We do not teach a hundred percent; we teach only eighty percent. For the other twenty percent, you must work. It is like a baby learning to walk. In the beginning, I hold your hand, hold you up and make you walk, as a mother does with her child. When I let go of your hand, you fall down. It is very discouraging. Then I hold you up again. As I said, we do not teach everything. Perhaps I teach you three koans, then let you find the fourth—"In a mouth, someone will search for food." The child must be cultivated to walk by himself.

"When the disaster known as Man occurs/ Yang and Liu will be officeholders." This is a prediction. No one understands this. The one who does will become the successor to the Sixth Patriarch.

Again the Master said: "Seventy years after my death, two bodhisattvas will come from the east. One will be a monk and the other a layman. [Working] at the same time, they will spread my teaching, establish my school, erect temples, and beget manifold Dharma heirs." The Master predicted that after his death, two bodhisattvas would come who would promulgate his doctrine. They were the two Buddhist teachers Huai-jang of Nan-yueh and Hsing-ssu of Ch'ing-yuan. (Nan-yueh and Ch'ing-yuan are names of mountains. In ancient days Buddhists always lived on mountains, so we use the name of the mountain to designate the monk.) These two Zen masters became successors to his Dharma, the torch-holders of the Zen of the Sixth Patriarch. But they are not written about in some records. In the record that I am translating, however, their names are mentioned.

Huai-jang was the forefather of the Lin-chi School of Zen—in Japanese, the Rinzai School; and Hsing-ssu was the forefather of the the Ts'ao-tung School, the Soto School. These two streams of Zen are still existing in Japan.

In the Lin-chi School, Ma-tsu was the disciple of Huai-jang. Ma-tsu's disciple was Pai-chang; Pai-chang's disciple was Huang-po, and Huang-po's disciple was Lin-chi. Zen is handed down face to face. No monk may call himself a Zen master until he is ordained by his master as a teacher. In the Zen school of Buddhism, the lineage is very important. No one can say, "I am a Zen master," or write a thesis and become a Zen master. The transmission of Dharma from teacher to pupil must be proved—"Yes, we know your teacher." There is nothing to write! The Dharma is handed down from mind to mind.

Even in the Buddha's day, those who said they were teachers but were not were expelled. It was a commandment of the monks not to lie. So if anyone says he is a Zen master when he is not, he is to be expelled. This rule is strictly kept.

The monks questioned the Master: "From the advent of the buddhas and patriarchs till the present, through how many generations has the Dharma been transmitted? We entreat you to elucidate this for us."

The Master said: "The buddhas who appeared in this world in the past have been countless in number, beyond reckoning. If the seven buddhas are considered to be first: in the past Alamkaraka-kalpa, *there were the buddhas Vipasyin, Sikhin, Visvasbhu; and in the present* Bhadra-kalpa, *there have been the buddhas Krakucchanda, Kanakamuni, Kasyapa and Shakyamuni. These are the seven buddhas. Now among these seven buddhas, it was Shakyamuni who began the transmission, giving the Dharma to Mahakasyapa.*

SOKEI-AN SAYS:

The Master realized that his death was near, so he wished to die according to Chinese custom in his own hometown of Hsin-chou. Hsin-chou was on the other side of the Pearl River, downstream near the sea. The old house in which he had lived with his mother when he was young had been given to him by the emperor and remodeled into a temple called Kuo-en. At that time, he was living on the upper stream of the Pearl River, about one hundred and fifty miles from Canton, in a temple in Ts'ao-ch'i. He urged his disciples to journey with him to Hsin-chou by boat. The distance was about that from Albany to New York City. Seven disciples were to row the boat down the river to his old home and native country.

The multitude, the Prefect of Shao-chou, and the great families of Ts'ao-chi all came to see the Master off at the riverbank. So he spoke his last words to them, predicted the future and then answered the question that had been asked by the multitude: "How has the Dharma been transmitted from Shakyamuni to the Sixth Patriarch?" He then explained the matter of transmission, from the very beginning, from the remote past.

The monks questioned the Master: "From the advent of the buddhas and patriarchs till the present, through how many generations has the Dharma been transmitted? We entreat you to elucidate this for us." The ancient buddhas are all those before Shakyamuni. The forefathers are the Buddha's direct disciples, from Mahakashyapa to Bodhidharma.

The Master said: "The buddhas who appeared in this world in the past have been countless in number, beyond reckoning." This is a very interesting point. We must observe this carefully. In Christianity, there is only one Christ, but in Buddhism, the buddhas are countless in number. And Shakyamuni Buddha is one of those countless buddhas. According to legend, Shakyamuni Buddha, through many reincarnations, was a snake, a rabbit, a sparrow, a man, a woman, until he became a buddha. He was just a man who later became a buddha.

There is the story of the sparrow who hopped into the mouth of a dying tiger—the tiger had swallowed a big bone and could not get it out. The sparrow hopped into the his mouth and took out the bone and said, "Don't you feel more comfortable?" The tiger said: "If you enter my mouth once more, I will devour you!" The sparrow hopped in and was devoured—it was the tiger's nature. But the sparrow became Shakyamuni Buddha.

"*If the seven buddhas are considered to be first: in the past* Alamkaraka-kalpa, *there were the buddhas Vipasyin, Sikhin, Visvasbhu; and in the present* Bhadra-kalpa, *there have been the buddhas Krakucchanda, Kanakamuni, Kasyapa and Shakyamuni. These are the seven buddhas.*" There were countless buddhas before Shakyamuni, but we count seven buddhas only.

A *kalpa* is a long time—one million aeons of time, and many recurrences of this universe. In a legend, an angel comes down from heaven once in every hundred years and wipes the kalpa stone with his gossamer sleeve. When the *kalpa* stone has been entirely worn away, a *kalpa* has passed. A million *kalpas* is a long, long time. The *kalpa* in which we are now living is called the *Bhadra-kalpa*, the "good" *kalpa*. The *kalpa* before this *kalpa* is called *the Alamkaraka-kalpa*, or the "ornamented" *kalpa*, like the stars that ornament the sky. The first three buddhas were buddhas of the ornamented *kalpa*, and the other four buddhas appeared in this present *kalpa*.

There are many stories of these previous buddhas. One Buddha was blind, and his disciples offered him fire. It was the first fire, and by the light of this fire, this Buddha opened his blind eyes and saw the phenomenal world. So the Shakya tribe were somehow sun-worshippers like the Egyptians.

The birthplaces and teachings of these seven buddhas are written in the sutras. Perhaps they are imaginary and were created later. Then came Shakyamuni. He is the Buddha of this period. He was born about twenty-five hundred years ago, the child of the King of Kapilavastu. His name was Gautama.

"*Now among these seven buddhas, it was Shakyamuni who began the transmission, giving the Dharma to Mahakasyapa.*" Mahakashyapa was the son of a very rich man. His father was richer than the King of Magadha. Mahakashyapa threw away all his wealth and followed the Buddha. Of course, the teachings were transmitted from ancient days, but in this period, Shakyamuni commenced the transmission of the Dharma with him.

The Dharma was transmitted in three different ways. One way was mythologically. The Dharma was handed down in the form of legend. As an example: Buddha, mounted on a white elephant, descended from heaven to earth, entered the bosom of Maya, and came out of her armpit. As soon as he was born, he stood pointing with one finger to the sky and one to the earth. He walked seven steps and said: "I am the only child of God who came down to this earth." The Chinese translate this as: "Between heaven and earth, I am the only one to be revered." There are many legends, of course, legends which have symbolic meanings.

The second way of transmission was in the form of philosophy. The Dharma was explained by reason and logic, using words like a stepladder. Step by step the monks mounted slowly into Reality. The third way was handed down without words, without names. It was handed down to us as Reality-by-itself.

The first two ways are like a rich father who hands down his beautiful antique porcelain to posterity, with all its pedigree and explanations. But his grandchildren receive only the pedigree. The pottery has disappeared.

The third way, however, transmits the thing itself, directly, without any words, pedigrees, or explanations. This is the way of Zen—"Here it is! Don't lose it! Thank you very much."

The first two ways of transmission are by sutras and the *vinaya*. In the third way, there is just the scriptures that are written in the eye of Dharma. It is not on paper. In Western terms, it is the law that is written on your heart. But we do not call it "heart," we call it "eye."

The Buddha handed down to Mahakashyapa two things in one: the "pure eye of Dharma" (the soul of the universe) and the "marvelous mind in the state of nirvana." The pure eye of Dharma is one side, and the marvelous mind in the state of nirvana is the other. As our hand has two sides, back and palm, so Dharma has these two sides.

Mahakashyapa has disappeared from our sight. Where is he now? Where is the golden robe? What shape, what color is it? Can you see it? If you cannot see it, you are not Mahakashyapa's disciple.

We observe this as a koan, and the first to receive it was Mahakashyapa.

"Following Mahakasyapa in an unbroken line of succession were: 2) Ananda 3) Sanakavasa 4) Upagupta 5) Dhrtaka 6) Miccaka 7) Vasumitra. 8) Buddhanandhi 9) Buddhamitra 10) Parsva 11) Punyayasas 12) Asvaghosh13) Kapimala 14) Nagarjuna 15) Kanadeva 16) Rahulata 17) Sanghanandi 18) Gayasata 19) Kumarata 20) Jayata 21) Vasubandhu 22) Manorhita 23) Haklena 24) Simha 25) Basiasita 26) Punyamitra 27) Prajnatara 28) Bodhidharma (China) 29) Hui-k'o 30) Seng-ts'an 31) Tao-hsin 32) Hung-jen 33) Hui-neng.

"Each of those patriarchs received the Dharma from his predecessor. Hereafter, all of you must continue the transmission unbroken from generation to generation and not allow it to be misconstrued.

SOKEI-AN SAYS:

"Each of those patriarchs received the Dharma from his predecessor." That the Dharma has been handed down and transmitted from predecessor to teacher to disciple is very important in the Zen school. In other schools of Buddhism, the teacher sometimes realizes what was conceived in the mind of some previous teacher, and "all of a sudden," he says he is the disciple of such-and-such a master, and he hands down the teaching. But in Zen, the water is poured from one Zen vessel into another, lit from one candle to another. You do not invent your own Zen and all of a sudden call yourself a Zen student. You must see a teacher. Your knowledge of Zen must be acknowledged by a teacher.

If you have been meditating for a long time alone and have attained some realization and think, "This is Zen enlightenment!" go to a Zen master and ask him if your Zen attainment is exactly the same as his or not. Go and see him. Demonstrate your attainment. If he says, "Very well, your Zen is exactly the same as mine," then you are a Zen student.

Zen was transmitted alongside the literary schools of Buddhism. When you read Dr. Suzuki's Zen books or the Zen books translated by others and think that you have attained Zen, it is a great mistake. Zen is not written in any book because it cannot be expressed in words.

"Hereafter, all of you must continue the transmission unbroken from generation to generation and not allow it to be misconstrued." When I came to this country and was tramping through the Cascade Mountains, the mountains following the Columbia River, I felt that the soil of America had the essence

of Zen. The nature of the American people is like those cedar trees in the Cascade Mountains, rather coarse-grained but straight and simple. Zen is inborn in Americans. They have this precious jewel in their minds. It was given to them by nature, but this has not yet been disclosed. So they have never discovered this jewel in their nature.

Hereafter, perhaps in three hundred years, someone will come and open the box for you, and you will find the jewel for yourselves. However, Zen is very easily misunderstood because the teaching itself is a mystery—any charlatan can imitate the Zen attitude. And those who believe this attitude, imitate it and believe it is Zen. There are many such people in my own country, too. For instance, when a friend once came here and hid himself behind a screen, I said, "Come out, Mr. Oshima. Where are you?" And he answered, "Mr. Oshima is out today." And they call that Buddhism!

Or someone comes for tea, and as he pours the tea, he says, "Stop the discourse on Buddhism and have a cup of tea." He thinks this is Zen, too!

One gentleman studied Zen for a while and then went to Kyoto. The hotel manager said, "You haven't been here for years. Where have you been?" And the gentleman said, "Come near, and I will tell you." When the hotel manager came near, he slapped his face. He thinks that is Zen.

Or some painter who does not study from the foundation but imitates a master's brush, draws a very big Bodhidharma and thinks it is a Zen picture.

Everyone in Japan imitates the Zen attitude because it is simple, and there is a little humor in it, but few people really try to study Zen. They talk about koans like Hakuin's "[Sound of one] hand"—"Which hand produced the sound?" Some gentleman came to America and talked about this as a real koan! Such people are like the monologists in vaudeville. If Hakuin heard this, he would turn in his grave.

Here is another example of "monologist Zen": There was a famous Zen master who was the abbot of an old dilapidated Zen temple. He died and his disciples scattered, and only one novice was left. At that time, there was a famous Zen master named Nantembo [1839-1925]. He visited all the Zen temples and interrogated the abbots, to try them out. The novice heard that Nantembo was coming, and that he did not know the master of the temple had died. The novice went to the tofu shop and asked an old tofu man to put on the abbot's robes and sit in his chair. Nantembo came and questioned this old man, an imitation abbot. The question and answer that followed was in pantomime, the imitation of a Zen demonstration. Nantembo made a circle with thumb and forefinger. The tofu man stretched out both arms very wide. Nantembo bowed very deeply. Nantembo held up one finger, and the old man held up five. Again Nantembo bowed deeply. Then he showed three fingers, and the tofu man opened one eye. Nantembo bowed and ran out of the temple. He thought he had lost the argument.

The novice ran after him and asked the reason. Nantembo said: "I asked, 'What is a drop of water?' Your Osho answered, 'It is like the whole ocean.' Wonderful answer! Then I asked, 'What is one world?' Your teacher said, 'It is controlled by the Law of the five consciousnesses.' Wonderful view! I asked him, 'What are the three bodies of Buddha?' He answered, 'It exists under my eye.' A wonderful monk!"

The novice returned and said to the old man, "You are a wonderful man! I did not know you were so wonderful." The old tofu man said to him: "That man said that my tofu is small; I said it is big. He said he would pay one yen for it. I told him my price was five yen. He then offered three, so I looked at him and said, 'No Sale!'"

People think that this is Zen. This is the usual idea in Japan and also in America. When I speak of Zen, they think I mean such things, so few come here.

On the third day of the eighth month in the second year of Hsien-t'ien (713 C.E.), following a meal at the Kuo-en Temple, the Great Master said to his assembled disciples: "Everyone, take your seats. I must bid you farewell."

Fa-hai said: "Master, what teaching will you leave so that those who are deluded in future generations can see buddha-nature?"

The Master said: "Listen carefully. As to the deluded in future generations, one who knows sentient beings will also know buddha-nature. If you do not know sentient beings, you will never come close to finding Buddha even in a million kalpas.

Now, by letting you know the sentient being in your mind, I let you realize your buddha-nature. If you want to see buddha, just know sentient beings. Sentient beings cherish deluded notions of Buddha; Buddha does not cherish deluded notions of sentient beings. If a sentient being is aware of his own original nature, he is a buddha; if a buddha is ignorant of his own original nature, he is a sentient being. If his original nature is simple and even, a sentient being is a buddha; if his nature is uneven and distorted, a buddha is a sentient being."

SOKEI-AN SAYS:

On the third day of the eighth month in the second year of Hsien-t'ien (713 C.E.), following a meal at the Kuo-en Temple, the Great Master said to his assembled disciples: "Everyone, take your seat. I must bid you farewell." Fa-hai said: "Master, what teaching will you leave so that those who are deluded in future generations can see buddha-nature? The Master said: "Listen carefully. As to the deluded in future generations, one who knows sentient beings will also know buddha-nature." To "know sentient beings" means, according to our teaching, realizing the structure of our mind, for we have many states of consciousness: the five *skandhas*, the twelve *nidanas*, the eighteen *dhatus*, and the functions and performances of the sense organs and strata of consciousness. All sentient activities of life are the agents of the consecutive consciousnesses, or the sense organs. When your knowledge of your own being becomes complete, you will be aware of your own buddha-nature. There is no other buddha-nature beside your own sentient nature.

These days, men are generally educated and, in a sense, enlightened. But in ancient periods, men were deluded and ignorant, living like animals. When the Buddha was born twenty-four hundred years ago, he observed with his enlightened mind the barbarians and illiterate men everywhere and really thought that these deluded sentient beings must be enlightened by education. So the monasteries became cities of knowledge, knowledge of all kinds, like our universities of today. Now the monasteries are houses of ignorant men. Monks have forgotten the true meaning of enlightenment. It is the laymen who are attaining enlightenment.

Today, the monk's idea of enlightenment is some kind of superstition. They think they will attain supernatural power by attaining enlightenment. It's ridiculous! How can they attain supernatural powers when they cannot even attain natural powers? Zen students still have a deluded view of enlightenment, and charlatans talk and write about "supernatural enlightenment." They do not know true enlightenment because they have never experienced it.

When I was young, I told my teacher that I wanted to attain supernatural powers of sight, to penetrate the world right through to the other side. He laughed and said: "Your natural sight is quite perfect. When your five senses are in good order, you will not need supernatural powers."

If you do not know sentient beings, you will never come close to finding buddha even in a million kalpas." Everyone thinks that buddha is different from everyday men, from human beings. Some Buddhists believe that buddha has been living in the Western sky. We have no relation to such a buddha. We have nothing to do with the buddha living in the Western Sky. Our own buddha-nature is buddha. Of course, sentient beings are like orphans who never knew their own home.

Once there was a child who had been abandoned. He grew up and heard that his own true home was in another village. He went to the village to find his own house. Through all the streets of the village he went, visiting every house. He went into and came out of his own home but never realized it. Every man has buddha-nature within him. Going into it and coming out of it, he never realizes it is his own buddha-nature. The child finally found his home and suddenly realized that all the neighbors living there were his relatives, his cousins, uncles and aunts. Once in a long while, man realizes buddha-nature within himself. Then, suddenly, he realizes that his hand is the hand of buddha, the Lotus Hand. He realizes that he himself is buddha. There is no other buddha in the world.

"Now, by letting you know the sentient being in your mind, I let you realize your buddha-nature. If you want to see buddha, just know sentient beings." True enlightenment is clearly explained here by the Sixth Patriarch.

The buddha has three virtues in his nature: 1) the intrinsic nature for observing this present consciousness; 2) the intrinsic nature for practicing tranquility—*samadhi*; and 3) the intrinsic nature for wisdom. Sentient beings have three poisons in their natures: 1) covetousness and endless desires—lust; 2) maliciousness and cruelty—anger; and 3) idleness—no enjoyment of education, ignorance. There is an analogy between these threee poisons and the three virtues of buddha-nature: l) Controlling the intrinsic desire of man is present consciousness. These two are operated by the same factor.

2) Anger and quietude are also the performance of one particular element of mind. When it performs negatively, it is anger; when it performs positively, it is tranquillity.

3) When your wisdom is not used properly, you are ignorant; but when your wisdom is available in all circumstances, your ignorant mind will become enlightened.

So if you would like to know what buddha is, you must know what sentient life is.

"Sentient beings cherish deluded notions of buddha": The sentient mind cherishes deluded images in meditation. Sitting cross-legged with their spines straight, such people see the images of a buddha with long arms and a long tongue. Many think that is buddha, or that the Buddha of twenty-four hundred years ago is buddha. Some educated men think that buddha is awakened knowledge, the Knower, but not man particularly. Such men never come to their *own* Buddha. They think Buddha is an immortal being lying somewhere in them like a diamond hidden in a wooden statue.

Sometimes in Japan, a family will hide a diamond in a Buddha stature and hand it down from generation to generation until the last generation destroys the Buddha image and finds the diamond. They take it to a diamond dealer and find it is just glass. Someone had taken the true diamond and had put a glass one there. They never realize *the whole figure is buddha*, including this endless universe, the endless past, present, and future. How can they realize that they themselves are buddha?

"Buddha does not cherish deluded notions of sentient beings." That is, if anyone attains enlightenment, he does not cherish any deluded notions of sentient beings.

"If a sentient being is aware of his own original nature, he is a buddha": This is stated very clearly and very kindly.

"If a buddha is ignorant of his own original nature, he is a sentient being." Everyone is born a buddha, but he happens to be ignorant, so he is satisfied with his unenlightened life. When someone drops a diamond among glass beads, no one realizes it is a true diamond. The famous story in the *Lotus Sutra* illustrates this very clearly.

A child of a king became lost during a war and was carried into the enemy's country. Twenty years later, as a beggar, he returned to his own country. The king, his father, saw him on a street corner sweeping dung. (We do not see this any more in this automobile age, but in the old days the king's child was standing on a street corner sweeping dung.) The king, looking for his son, realized this dung-scraper must be of his own family. But when the king's attendant went up to him, the dung-scraper was frightened, and he ran away. It was hard to catch him. So to find him, the king himself became a dung-scraper and a beggar. Finally, they became acquainted, and they scraped the dung together. The king bought him something to wear, and little by little he then asked him to eat with him. First, because the dung-scraper had no manners, he took him to the Coffee Pot and later to Child's, and finally, to the Ritz Carlton. Then he told him he was his own true son.

If I tell you today you are a buddha, you will not believe it. Well, tomorrow I will take you to the Ritz Carlton.

"If his original nature is simple and even, a sentient being is a buddha; if his nature is uneven and distorted, a buddha is a sentient being." When you drive your automobile in the Gobi desert, you can go everywhere; there is no one-way road. The nature of your mind pervades in all directions at once, evenly, as light or heat penetrates evenly. This is buddha's nature, his even nature. The original nature of human beings is this even nature, but we are now in uneven nature, and our automobile must be driven on a one-way road. We cannot spread ourselves evenly in all directions like radio waves. We must move in one long line, like a telegraph line.

The Sixth Patriarch does not speak in philosophical terms. He speaks in ordinary terms. He did not receive his enlightenment from the sutras, so his speech is always different from others. Buddhism has become very simple in his mind.

"If your mind is uneven and disturbed, a buddha is [concealed] in a sentient being. If a single moment of thought is even and straight, a sentient being becomes a buddha. Your mind of itself possesses buddha. Your own buddha is the true buddha. If you yourself do not have buddha-mind, where are you going to look for the true buddha? Your own mind is buddha. Never doubt it! There is nothing that exists outside that can be independently established. It is original mind itself that creates all the varieties of existence. Therefore, the sutra says: 'When Mind arises, all things appear. When Mind ceases, all things cease.'"

SOKEI-AN SAYS:

The Sixth Patriarch was certainly one of the reformers of Buddhism in China. Instead of reading sutras or listening to lectures, he found the teaching in his own mind.

"If your mind is uneven and disturbed, a buddha is [concealed] in a sentient being." Of course, in English there are many words which denote the meaning of the Chinese word *"hsin,"* translated as "mind." "Mind" can mean "soul," "brain," or "consciousness"; there are many words. In this present mind, there are senses, conscious mind, and unconscious mind. In Sanskrit, there are two words that are particularly used: *hrdaya* and *citta*.

Hrdaya is the mind common to all sentient beings, including those souls that are sleeping or hibernating like vegetables or insects. This is very different from our state of mind. It is the fundamental mind. This present mind, which we experience at every moment, is not sleeping; it is awake. It can attain, according to practice, the enlightened mind. It is called *citta*. So there are two states of existence in the sentient mind. According to the Sixth Patriarch's usage of the word *hsin*, it is sometimes the basic mind, and sometimes it is the present state of mind.

The Sixth Patriarch always used "mind" as a whole: the fundamental state of universal mind, the state of mind which is common to all sentient beings.

While I am speaking here, you are listening to my speech. The mind within you is very vivid. It is the present state of mind. In our meditation, we meditate on the basic state of mind, which is called mother-consciousness, or *alaya*-consciousness. From there, we emerge to the present state of consciousness. Without philosophizing, we realize through this meditation that which is universal—what is nature, what is man, and what is the nearest way to approach this living being. It is not necessary to call it "man." It is always with you, and you will never fail to have access to it because it is an eternal, living being. When you call it "I," this sound is very narrow and small, but when you do not call it by any name and just meditate on it, you will realize that your mind will never die and can never be destroyed. Birth and death are just names, like waves coming and going on top of the great ocean. Meditation is the nearest way to attain the true state of being.

"If a single moment of thought is even and straight, a sentient being becomes buddha." The mind must always be even, simple, and plain. That is the original state of mind—calm as an ocean. The surface is fluctuating every moment, but the bottom is tranquil and eternal.

When the mind is uneven and distorted, it does not act like the mind of original nature; but when it acts according to the mind of original nature, it radiates like light waves in all directions, or like heat which permeates in manifold directions. The distorted mind acts just one way, or sometimes no way—it is confused.

Buddha is that even mind, even and calm, which radiates in multifold directions at once. The word "buddha" came from the Sanskrit root "to know." Buddha is one who knows, the knower. So this present consciousness is the buddha, the knower. We know we see, we hear, we smell, we taste, we touch. Legendarily, we say buddha, but we do not need to think buddha and "I" are different existences in the universe. There is only one universe, one universal power in all the world, and one universal intrinsic wisdom throughout all sentient beings and all insentient beings.

This power of knowing actually performing within us is buddha. This is our God. We worship this. We do not bow down to worship this buddha. We meditate upon it. We do not call its name; we do not look up to the sky or peep down into the earth to find it. It is in us. We do not know where the Buddha-mind is. It is not in the brain, or in the stomach. But we know it exists. We rest in it and meditate.

Just sit down and meditate. Don't put a little tag "I" on yourself. Peel the label off, and throw yourself into the great universe. You won't feel it at once, but do it every day, and you will feel it. On a lovely spring day, go sit on a park bench by the Hudson River and forget yourself. When your heart beats with the rhythm of the universe, there on a park bench you will find buddha.

"Your mind of itself possesses buddha." In Christianity, you say, "God is Love." In Buddhism, we say, "Your mind of itself possesses Buddha" because mind is common to all sentient beings. Mind, according to Buddhism, is not created separately. Mind is whole; it fills the universe like air, like ether. You cannot call it "my" mind, "your" mind, "their" mind. "My" mind is just like a drop of water in the ocean. How can I say "my" mind? Mind exists from beginningless beginning to endless end. It was not created. It is the creator of all appearances in the world. Very strange!

Mind is like the artist who paints scenery, or like the goldsmith who casts gold. When you think of a mind as small as yours, you wonder how it can create so much. Well, this mind is not yours. As human beings, we have human minds, so all human beings observe reality in the same way. But I do not trust the minds of other sentient beings, for they have their different worlds. Their worlds are theirs and have nothing to do with me. If you were a sentient being on another planet, you would have different senses. If you were born on some planet far from the sun, your skin would be like mist and your body like gas, you would have a different body structure. Each sentient being has, therefore, a different world. I live in my world, and you live in yours, but our consciousness is uniform. So my world and your world, though not exactly the same, are similar. "Your mind of itself possesses Buddha" is not faith or legend; it is truth.

"Your own buddha is the true buddha. If you yourself do not have buddha-mind, where are you going to look for the true buddha? Your own mind is buddha; never doubt it!" Everyone tries to find buddha in books, temples, and carved images. That is not a true way to find him. Do not think that Buddha exists outside or inside, or is carved in images, or was born in India twenty-four hundred years ago. We do not pursue such buddhas. Buddha exists as a uniform mind in all sentient beings.

"There is nothing that exists outside that can be independently established." The immediate question is: "What are they, then, the sky above, the earth below? Are they outside my mind?" We do not know what *this* really is, this thing existing *here.* Sound is created on the eardrum, not in the object, and color is created on the retina of the eye; the object has no color or shape. So what is *this* that is existing outside? We call it "reality." But what is reality? It is the world that we see in color, in shape, in our own view. The whole world is our own view. We are living in our own delusion, so all of us sentient beings are stewing in our own juice. It is called delusion because, really, there is nothing outside. True objective reality is unknown. The sky is blue, the earth is green. We are the magi. We are the creators of delusion from the basic state of consciousness.

"It is original mind itself that creates all the varieties of existence. Therefore, the sutra says: 'When Mind arises, all things appear. When Mind ceases, all things cease.'" Sometimes the Mind is very bright, and sometimes it is dark; and when it is weak, it sometimes disappears. Mind is not brain. The whole universe is Mind. The universe creates its own concentrating power as we concentrate our mind on one thing. I move because Mind is living and I am living. Mind itself concentrates itself in one place and creates heat, creates light, creates its own concentrated power. Thus *alaya*-consciousness creates this whole kaleidoscopic existence.

When my mind ceases, when your mind ceases, when all human beings cease, then all manifestations cease.

"Now I shall leave a gatha *as a parting gift. I call it 'The* Gatha *of the True Buddha of Your Own Nature.' If anyone in future generations understands its meaning, he will see for himself original mind, attain for himself the Buddha Way. The* gatha *says:*

"The bhutatathata *of your own nature is itself true buddha*
The three poisons of false views are the Demon King

When you are deluded by false views, the demon dwells in your house
When you possess the true view, buddha dwells in your house

If you allow the three poisons of false views to grow in your mind
Instantly, the Demon King will come to occupy your house
If the true view eradicates the mind of three poisons, the Demon King will be transformed into
buddha—
He who is true, not false

Dharmakaya, sambhogakaya, nirmanakaya
These three bodies are originally one body

If you are able to look into your own nature
That itself will be the cause of realizing buddhahood and awakening to enlightenment

Originally, your pure nature is born from nirmanakaya
Your pure nature is always within nirmanakaya

Your nature causes nirmanakaya *to follow the true path*
It will bring perfect [realization] that is true and infinite

Lustful nature is originally the cause of pure nature
When you rid yourself of lust, that itself is the body of pure nature

If the five kinds of sensuous desire are extirpated from your original nature
You will recognize your original nature and instantly [manifest] absolute truth

If you encounter the teaching of sudden enlightenment in this life
You will instantly realize original nature and behold the buddha

If you want to practice in order to become buddha
You must first know where the truth is to be found

If you find the truth in your own mind
That truth is itself the cause of becoming uddha

If without seeing your own original nature, you try to find buddha outside
You are an utter fool

I have now handed down to you this teaching of sudden enlightenment
To save the people of the world, you must [first] practice this yourselves

I say to you who in future will study the Way
If you do not take this view, you are simply wasting your time"

SOKEI-AN SAYS:

"Now," the Master said, *"I shall leave a* gatha *as a parting gift. I call it 'The* Gatha *of the True Buddha of Your Own Nature.' If anyone in future generations understands its meaning, he will see for himself original mind, attain for himself the Buddha Way."* If you practice meditation in accordance with this *gatha,* said the Sixth Patriarch, you will recognize your original mind.

It is not easy to recognize original mind. You can read about it, you can imagine it, but to recognize it is truly very hard work. After many years of practice the student may think he has attained original mind, but when he goes before a Zen master, the master says, "That is not original mind; you are only dreaming." Are you dreaming? What is this original mind spoken by the Sixth Patriarch?

We have this mind. It is evident that we have a mind. Is our mind not the original one? If not, what is this original mind? It is man's bad habit to think of everything as in space, time, and value. Now, I have a mind, I have this present mind. Therefore, I must have had an original mind that existed before this present mind. So we think in time. If I said, "This sky is the present sky; there must have been an original sky," it would sound ridiculous. But this sky is all the sky there is, of course, and it is a new sky.

My father had this mind. My ancestors had this mind. Adam and Eve had this mind. This is an old mind, but it is also a new mind—I have it in the present. I also say that my old mind is priceless, but that my new mind is very cheap, a depraved and degenerate mind—I would not pay one penny for this mind. Thus we put value on things. If it is old, we value it highly; if it is new, we would not pay a penny for it. A million years ago, human beings did not pay a cent for the sky, and today human beings do not pay for it. We live under the sky, and it is valueless—we do not value it in terms of money. Why then try to put a value on our mind? The sky is sometimes clouded and sometimes very bright. Our mind is the same as the sky, and it is as old as the sky. The Sixth Patriarch called it "original mind." When you meditate upon your original mind, you will find it.

When you first practice meditation, you will find a pandemoniac procession in your mind. When I was sitting in Battery Park and the Bear Mountain boat arrived, many people passed through the park—a pandemoniac procession. When you practice meditation for five minutes, you will find this pandemoniac procession. Your friend makes a funny face, the cat goes away, and so forth. I have heard that when we die, we repeat all our memories three times. In meditation, we repeat them many times. But after you have practiced for just a few months, you will not even find a mouse passing through your mind. All is quiet. You are not going anywhere, not looking into anything. You are still sitting on your chair, but you will find your original mind. This is an old mind, a timeless mind. In deep meditation, the outside vanishes from your sight, and the mind is alone in endless space, pervading in multifold directions. This is timeless mind.

Meditation is a delightful thing. We do not meditate upon some idea, symbol, or thought. We meditate upon our own mind. Our mind meditates upon Mind itself. Without using another lamp, the lamp shines.

You see this expressed in Oriental sculpture—the Hindu meditating with his eyes half-closed. In his position of repose, he calmly meditates upon his own mind. We do not meditate upon our thoughts. In Japan, I saw Rodin's "Thinker," and when I went to Columbia University, I saw it again before the Hall of Philosophy. I do not think he is thinking much! I am glad to have the opportunity to speak about our meditation.

It is easy to fall into imagination. You must meet a true Zen master who has had true experience and been tested by a previous Zen master. Your experience and your imagination must be tested by him.

Buddhadharma is Buddhism. Before you attain it, you cannot speak of Buddhism. To quench your thirst, you must drink the water yourself. No one can drink it for you.

The gatha says: "The bhutatathata *of your own nature is itself true Buddha." Alaya*-consciousness is the active mind that appears with our recognition. *Bhutatathata* is empty mind—we are not in it. When *bhutatathata* appears within our mind, we recognize it, and that is called *alaya*-consciousness. When it transcends our mind, it is *bhutatathata*. It is said that Buddhists have no God. We do not call it God, but that attribute of *bhutatathata* is the attribute of God.

The usual conception of those who entertain the mind of imagination is that *bhutatathata* is that state in which you cannot see, hear, taste, or smell, that it transcends our sense perceptions. This is a theoretical explanation. *Bhutatathata* is really different from this theory. Theoretically everyone thinks there is a state behind this phenomenal state that cannot be reached with our senses or thought of in any terms, perhaps this *bhutatathata* state. We cannot reach it with our senses, or think of it in any terms; it is only theoretical. *Bhutatathata*, exists outside the human intellect; it does not exist in the human mind. Therefore, it has no relation to us—*but this must be experienced. Bhutatathata* is not the Shakyamuni Buddha who was living twenty-five hundred years ago.

"The three poisons of false views are the Demon King." The Demon King is a famous demon, the king of them all. In Buddhist legends, when the Buddha was about to attain the highest enlightenment, the demons were afraid and said: "If the highest truth were grasped by a human mind, we would lose our existence. We should send our army and destroy Shakyamuni." So the Demon King sent his army but was defeated by the Buddha's power of mind. Then the Demon King sent his three daughters to entice the Buddha from meditation, so they danced before him; but they did not awaken him. Perhaps you have seen pictures somewhere of the three daughters of the Demon King dancing before the Buddha. The Sixth Patriarch was using this legendary story.

The "three poisons," the three venomous minds, are the three fundamental poisons of lust, anger and ignorance. Instinctively, all sentient beings endeavor to generate, to preserve their own bodies through time. Instinctively, we endeavor to find food to eat. We, human being or tiger, kill the victim, meaning food. This is so-called anger. When a person has a good position and another person comes along and takes the job away from him, this also means food. These instinctive actions are based on fundamental ignorance. They are the three venomous minds. So "false views" are the cause of the three venomous minds, the Demon King. To attack people blindly, to seize the opposite sex to generate, is a false view. This is the cause—the Demon King.

"When you are deluded by false views, the demon dwells in your house/ When you possess the true view, buddha dwells in your house." When that instinct to devour the enemy is transformed, it becomes the energy to meditate—you have the same attitude towards yourself as to your friends.

What is the true view? Many scholars talk about this. When I was a novice, this puzzled me. I had to talk, I had to see everything at once, so I looked in both ways at the same time. Ridiculous!

"If you allow the three poisons of false views to grow in your mind/ Instantly, the Demon King will come to occupy your house/ If the true view eradicates the mind of three poisons, the Demon King will be transformed into buddha/ He who is true, not false." Demon and buddha are, therefore, the same. The demon will be transformed into Buddha, as cold water is transformed into hot water. It is the same mind. But by your own practice, it will be transformed into buddha. This transformation is of great importance in Buddhism.

"Dharmakaya, sambhogakaya, nirmanakaya/ These three bodies are originally one body." In Western countries, there is a very famous theory—monism. All comes from the "One," and all is reduced to the "One." Dualism is "two"—in the beginning there was good and bad, man and woman. Pluralism is not two, but many. But from the standpoint of Reality, there is neither one, two, nor many. We do not call it "one," because one is invented by the human mind experiencing "two" or "three." The Buddha said: "If there were one, it would be none." In Reality, you need not call it one or two or three. *Bhutatathata* is Reality. Buddha is Reality. Original mind is Reality.

Dharmakaya is the omnipresent body that pervades the universe. It has no end, no center, and no beginning. *Sambhogakaya* is the intellectual center. For billions of years, it always received its own experience of existence, like the center of a nebula. Finally, it recognizes its own existence, like a human being. *Nirmanakaya* is the body of transformation. It transforms itself into many different people, millions of people, all with different bodies. But our original mind has only one body, one existence.

"One body" is the state of *bhutatathata*. When we meditate and forget our sense perceptions, this is *bhutatathata*. Then we open our eyes, and there is just one body!

We do not believe in the "astral body." *This* is etheric, astral, physical—the same body.

"If you are able to look into your own nature/ That itself will be the cause of realizing buddhahood and awakening to enlightenment." This is the attitude of Zen students. While the students of other religions look for God in the sky and for Reality in material objects, analyzing objective existence by microscope, Zen students always look deep into their own nature by tranquilizing their minds.

At first, you feel that your mind is very confused. Then you realize that your consciousness is like a deep well, a bottomless well. Later, through the practice of meditation, you feel that there is no depth in your consciousness, that consciousness is not a thing that has depth; it cannot be fathomed or measured by our imagination, nor can it be called shallow or deep. When you close your eyes to meditate, you keep yourself in "imagined" darkness and think you are in a deep state of consciousness. But this is not the darkness of deep consciousness, it is merely the darkness of the skin—your eyelid covering the retina of the eye.

I was following all the texts of Buddhism with my own knowledge. I believed there was shallow consciousness and deep consciousness, and consciousnesses called "*alaya*-consciousness," "*manas* consciousness," and "*amala*-consciousness." But such imaginings ceased to exist, one by one.

Today, I believe—of course it is my own personal view of Buddhism—that so-called *alaya*-consciousness is only a name. Consciousness itself is *this real existence*—including eye, ear, nose, tongue and the million pores of the body, the mind that perceives dreams, and the mind that perceives *samskara*. All these together are *alaya*-consciousness.

Alaya-consciousness is like the star at the head of a comet. When a comet sweeps through the sky, a long trail follows the head. This *alaya*-consciousness of mind is the head of the comet, and the tail of the comet is the whole universe—mountains and rivers, sky and oceans.

Therefore, this aspect of mountain and river, sky and ocean is my own tail, and I am looking at this tail, objectifying it. If I introspect this entire universe, the sky and the ocean, the mountains and rivers *are* my consciousness. So when I look at the sky, the beautiful clear sky, I realize it is objectified alaya-consciousness.

When you meditate, *alaya* is the deepest consciousness. When you open your eye and look at it, *alaya* is the infinite sky. When you observe the whole universe, within and without, with the eye of Zen, the entire universe, including your mind, will become very rich, very beautiful, and very great. It is a long-lived being. This is how you must observe your life. The Sixth Patriarch said, "If you are able to look into your own nature, that itself will be the cause of realizing buddhahood and awakening to enlightenment."

When you mediate upon your mind, you realize that there is neither shallow nor deep in the nature of consciousness. It is all one piece, one present existence, and it is *this moment*—this moment including the blue sky, the deep ocean, the green mountain, the shining stream of the river, and the millions of people on the surface of the earth. This appearance is the state of the dominion of Buddha. Thus, the man who perceives the whole universe is Buddha himself.

"Originally your pure nature is born from nirmanakaya." Buddha's *nirmanakayas* are covering the whole earth. When you go to Broadway you will find Buddha's *nirmanakayas* floating all over it. Every one of them is the heat of the comet. The whole world is following the one comet, and that world is common to all comets, but they are deluded.

If you were enlightened, you would see your pure nature within you. It is like the sky that you can see outside. It is boundless and bottomless. Your sense organs are just floating over that consciousness as foam floats over the waves. When this foam vanishes, you will go back to your original, pure nature. You think your mind is confused because you attach yourself too much to this mind. This mind is like air bubbles floating over the surface of the ocean. When you stand against the sky, you realize how small you are. This smallness of your existence is due to the limited experience through your five senses and the state of your existence through these senses.

"Your pure nature is always within nirmanakaya." This pure nature, which is like the ocean, is the base of your *nirmanakaya. Nirmanakaya* here means "acting body."

"Your nature causes nirmanakaya *to follow the true path."* Your pure nature does not cause it to follow. It is innate in your nature.

I do not believe the last line of this text was written by the Sixth Patriarch. From his standpoint, this line is somewhat like the words of a narrow Hinayanist. Of course, this poem was written by his disciples. Perhaps at first the Sixth Patriarch said something like this, but I do not believe he would have talked this way before his death. Someone inserted these lines as the words of the Sixth Patriarch. So I will not give a commentary on them. But I shall certainly say something about the Sixth Patriarch's viewpoint.

"It will bring perfect [realization] that is true and infinite." To practice this Dharma, you must practice the "right way." In Buddhism, the right way is the Eightfold Noble Path: right view, right contemplation, and so forth. So you must practice the Dharma, but you cannot command your *nirmanakaya* to practice. If your *nirmanakaya* finds its original nature, the Eightfold Noble Path is the original performance of your original nature.

What is right view? From my own standpoint, when you look at the sky and do not think of anything else, that is right view. When you go into the kitchen, you look at the shelf, the spoons and knives in the drawer and the garbage pail, you see the icebox.

I observe things, as they exist in my kitchen, and I do not know anything else. That is the right view. But if anyone looks at my kitchen from a moral view, then it is not right view; it is subjective view. That person is looking at my kitchen through his own concepts: "Look at those cups and glasses! They're all chipped and nicked! Someone has broken them! Look at the garbage can! It has an obnoxious odor! Somebody should wash it!" Many people observe the whole world from such a corner, but this is not the Buddha's right view.

Right view is the basis of right consideration. When you practice your meditation upon each state of your five skandhas, introspecting yourself in such a way, such practice is called right view. What is right view? The principle viewpoint of right view is, "Look once! Don't look twice." If you look at objective existence once, you look at it with your eye. If you look twice, your brain brings some subjective notion to it.

To attain this right view is very difficult. After you have passed many koans, put your mind into the fire and beat that mind and beat it again; then pull it out. You will attain right view. When you pass the first koan, without reasoning and without philosophizing, when you have eradicated all your notions and are standing in the center of the universe, at that moment you will attain right view.

"*Lustful nature is originally the cause of pure nature.*" This is like the line in the *Sutra of Perfect Awakening*: "The ore of gold is the primitive state of pure gold." The life of the caveman is the primitive state of the sacred man. This is different from Christianity, isn't it?

In Buddhism, there are many legends of the past lives of Shakyamuni Buddha. Through many incarnations he was a sparrow, a tiger, a serpent, a pigeon, and slowly he became a man. Finally, he attained buddhahood. Of course, the quality of buddhahood is in the sparrow, the serpent, the pigeon. But it is not only in sentient beings. It is in water, fire, ether—everywhere in the universe. It is in the sky, the mountain and river, in the stars, in the sun and in the moon. But when it is concentrated in this existing *alaya*-consciousness, buddha-nature awakens. It awakens to its own existence—"OH!"

In meditation, you close your eyes and meditate for three years, then you open your eyes and meditate for three years. Sometimes, as you are standing on the shore of the Hudson River, suddenly you come across your own enlightenment—"Oh-h-h! That was it!" But it will come only after long meditation. Without this long meditation, you will never come to this sudden enlightenment. Someone may come to it without any preparation, but such a one was a bodhisattva a long time.

In Christianity, the Savior was always a savior from the beginning of creation. He was created a savior. He was always perfect, from beginning to end. He was always immaculate. He was not the child of a human father. And from the first, when he appeared on this earth, he was decidedly different from other human beings. He was never a sparrow, never a rat. He was always the child of God.

But the attributes of buddha as a messiah for human beings are entirely different from those of Christ. Buddha passed through all lower sentient states and gradually ascended to the state of enlightenment by his own effort. When you compare Buddhism to Christianity, you must remember this difference. The pure nature of Christ in Christianity is deductive—there was the idea of God in the beginning. But in Buddhism, the pure nature of buddha is discovered only by our own effort. The word is "discover." Just like you discover the gold in ore, I discover buddha-nature for myself, you discover buddha-nature for yourself, and he discovers buddha-nature for himself. In Japan, this always produces an argument between Buddhists and Christians. It is a very important point.

"*When you rid yourself of lust, that itself is the body of pure nature./If the five kinds of sensuous desire are extirpated from your original nature/ You will recognize your original nature and instantly [manifest] absolute truth.*" The five kinds of sensuous desire have nothing to do with your discovering the original nature of your body. In the Chinese text, it is apparent that an illiterate monk or a Hinayana scholar inserted these lines here. I do not believe the Sixth Patriarch, who was a great Mahayanist, would have made this statement.

To attain the first gate of Buddhism, you must extricate yourself from worldly desires. Some people misunderstand Zen and look at it from a queer corner—from symbols or from a sexual view or from a psychoanalytical view. They try to find an answer to the first koan in psychoanalysis or in symbolism. One student gave me a strange answer—"A triangle is original nature." A triangle has nothing to do with original nature. Another answered, "Through the gate of mother, I can return to original nature." This is sex alright, isn't it? Terrible answer! Of course, such notions must be thrown out entirely.

If the Sixth Patriarch wrote this line from such a viewpoint, I agree.

"If you encounter the teaching of sudden enlightenment in this life . . ." Of course, the teaching of sudden enlightenment is a shortcut to attainment. The Northern School of Zen, the school of gradual enlightenment, emphasized meditation practice. Their motto was: "When you meditate you are a buddha." To the Sixth Patriarch, the founder of the Southern School of Zen, meditation was just the preparation for attaining enlightenment. The Northern School just sits without thinking. When they sit, they are buddha. When they lie down, they are not buddha. When they meditate they are buddha. When they eat, they are not buddha. The Sixth Patriarch thinks that when he eats he is enlightened buddha, when he walks he is enlightened Bbddha. Why must we attach ourselves to the form of sitting? To know buddha is the main thing. By sitting down, the Northern School thinks their minds slowly become clear, that the light of buddha, like a candle's light, slowly comes from somewhere, and that they will be enlightened.

Of course, we are of the Southern School, and we practice meditation. To concentrate the mind, you must hold the body in shape. To keep the body in balance and repose, do not gather all your face muscles to the center. Think indifferently. Do not think only in your brain, but use the whole body for thinking. That is our way. The famous sculptor Rodin made *The Thinker*. All those contorted face muscles—what is he thinking? I don't know. Perhaps he is thinking about conquering the whole earth!

While you are running around the street in a terrible confusion of mind, fighting with your friends, killing your enemies, or stealing others' property, you cannot concentrate on your problems, whose solution would awaken you to the state of Reality, the base of all existence. Therefore, you must not kill, steal, commit adultery, or tell lies—that is, in order to keep your mind quiet, keep the commandments. In quiet mind, you can meditate on the problems that must be solved and reach an answer.

". . . You will instantly realize original nature and behold the buddha." Buddha and original nature are the same in this usage.

The first problem that was very important to monks was: "What is Buddha?" This is like your first problem: "What is God?" You must find the answer, and you must realize that which is called God by name, or that which is called buddha by name. When this is realized, we say, "You are enlightened." This "enlightenment" may come any time—maybe this moment, maybe tomorrow, maybe twenty years from now. But when it comes, it comes suddenly, not gradually. When you see your image in the looking glass, it appears suddenly, not gradually. When mist clears from the sky, the moon peeps out gradually, but this gradualness is not the nature of the moon. Thus, the nature of enlightenment is not gradual, but sudden. It comes suddenly because it is always there in your mind. When the disturbance of your mind is cleared up, you find your original nature, which is called buddha.

The root of this word "buddha" is *budh*—to know, to see, to hear, to understand, to realize, to be aware of, to be conscious of. This activity of mind is buddha, and this activity of mind is intrinsic.

Before the creation of the world, there was buddha, and buddha was all. Buddha was the beginning. Therefore, we awake to the buddha-mind. All sleeping sentient beings, like trees, weeds and animals, will also awake to the state of buddha through aeons of time. Therefore, they will realize their own existence. They will become aware of their own consciousness. All sentient beings, sooner or later, will attain buddhahood, and those who attain this buddhahood will realize by themselves that they have attained buddha-knowledge, enlightenment.

Awakening does not come when you are sleeping. You must struggle to be awake. "When you are asleep and dream bad dreams, you struggle in the dream and awake from the dream." This is a famous quotation from the *Sutra of Perfect Awakening*: "If you want to practice in order to become buddha/ You must first know where the truth is to be found." Where is the buddha? In the East, we are always told from infancy, "There is no Buddha outside yourself; you, yourself, are buddha," or "The buddha is within you." And we just say, "Is that so?" and do not pay attention.

Every village builds churches; everyone goes to the House of God. But no one knows what God is; they are too busy making money, bringing in the autumn harvest, and getting married. They have no time to think about God. Then they die and never know Him. I am sure in this country, when you are naughty, your mother says, "God will punish you." But if you ask her, "What is God?" she cannot answer because she is not quite sure about it. And if you do not ask any questions, she will say nothing.

But occasionally, there is a child who is different, someone who conscientiously sits down and really, honestly starts to think about it: "Can I be a buddha? What is a buddha? How can I be a buddha?" Such a child is not often encountered. Other children think he is funny and do not associate with such a boy. They call him a "sissy," and he himself thinks perhaps he is queer and inferior. He is discouraged because people criticize him, and his sister complains: "You don't play baseball, and you're always sitting and thinking something. What are you thinking about? I don't like it." Such a boy goes to theological school with a great hope that there will be someone to tell him about God. He thinks maybe he will find out. He asks, "What is God?" No one can tell him. No one knows.

In Japan, young men go to the monasteries to find out about buddha, but no one tells them anything about it. They ask the priests and elder monks, but no one answers them. No one knows anything about it; no one can tell him. But occasionally, he will find one who knows, especially among Zen monks.

Today is a period of pragmatism and utilitarianism, of materialistic realism. This is the popular attitude today. No one cares what God is and what buddha is. If anyone speaks about it, everyone thinks he is crazy. But this is not a real, conscientious attitude for a human being.

"If you find the truth in your own mind/ That truth is itself the cause of becoming Buddha." The student starts to meditate upon the five senses. What are these eyes and ears. What is this? Why does this look red? Why does this look green? One day, he finds seventy-five cents in his pocket and runs to the bookstore to buy a book on the science of optics. He starts to learn what light is, what color is, what X rays are, what infrared and ultraviolet are, short waves of light, long waves of light. Then he understands what the eye is, how color is produced. He realizes that if he had been born on Saturn, he would have had a gaseous body. Perhaps he would have had a consciousness in this gassy body. In comparison with the body that we have, this body would be very thin and very weak. Naturally, the Saturnians would not eat what we eat. He would realize that all kinds of sentient beings are existing throughout all of space. Do not take the scientific view that sentient beings exist only on this earth. The whole universe is inhabited. Why must all bodies be like those on the planet Earth? There are many types of sentient bodies which do not appear even in the microscope of the scientist.

After the senses, he comes to *this* consciousness—"Who dreams my dream? I appear in the dream, so who is it that dreams this dream? Is it myself or not? What consciousness is this that dreams me?" Then he meditates on consciousness. In such a way, he wipes out the mist of the conscious mirror and finally finds the real mirror that is shining, that has existed from the beginningless beginning, that will exist to the endless end—"Ah, this is not I. This is my original self. It is not my ego. It is the consciousness of the world, it belongs to the universe. I-ness does not exist in the world." Then he realizes that buddha, God, is immediately *here*. Directly we know, intuitively we realize.

To clasp the hands and look up to heaven for God is silly to us. God is here within us. Why must we look up to the sky and call his name? But if your explanation is that the whole universe is an extension of our consciousness, greater than ourselves and infinite, that we can accept, that we will believe. But that there is "One" who has eyes and ears and sneezes, a God existing apart from ourselves in the sky, we do not accept. That is reading religion in terms of mythology. Find religion in terms of Reality. The sound will be entirely different.

"If without seeing your own original nature, you try to find Buddha outside/ You are an utter fool." Find buddha outside yourself? Indeed!

"I have now handed down to you this teaching of sudden enlightenment." Sudden enlightenment was not really invented by the Sixth Patriarch. It was the name he gave to the Buddhism that was brought into China by Bodhidharma. Before that, all the Buddhist teachings that were brought into China were in the form of written scriptures. Bodhidharma was the first to bring living Buddhism into China. This Buddhism was written upon his own body and mind. He opened his eye and said: "Look at my eye! This is buddha-eye! Now look at my mind. It is buddha-mind."

Without speaking a word, he handed down the buddha principle. It is clear. Buddha is not a lump of sugar. Buddha is not a candle. Buddha is not fire, is not water, but buddha-nature pervades the universe. It is everywhere.

Of course, your Christian teachers tell us God is omnipresent. We open our dictionaries and find the meaning. We know what omnipresent is. When I lived downtown, there was a black cat who always came into my house. I gave him food, and he stayed all night. In the morning, you could find him in the grocery store and in the afternoon at the butcher's. He was an omnipresent cat!

"To save the people of the world, you must [first] practice this yourselves." But you are in agony, worldly agony, the agony that comes from your discrimination. The cause of worldly agony, according to Buddha, is your idea of good and bad, life and death, beauty and ugliness, love and hate, beneficent and unbeneficent—discrimination made by you yourself, according to your own desires.

In one way, original nature has no desires, but in another way, I can say original nature is all desire at once. When it flows out like water, like air, it flows out infinitely, but it is limited. It will take the beautiful shape of a tree according to time and space. The desire to flow out from the seed will create the beautiful crystallizations of branches, leaves, and flowers. That is the symbol of our desires. When we look at our desires from the outside, we see them whole, like the growth of a tree. But when we see them from the inside, we see joy, hatred, agony, love. It is a natural phenomenon that we experience every day. But sometimes we look at it from the outside. It is a forest, a complete design. You must seek deliverance from this worldly agony, but how? When you realize your own original nature, when you observe your own portrait of desire, you will accept it, and you will understand it. You will be enlightened. But you must practice this sudden enlightenment by yourselves. I am not free to speak of everything that I know. You must practice according to your own knowledge.

"I say to you who in future will study the Way/ If you do not take this view, you are simply wasting your time." You are laggards. And this is the end of the Sixth Patriarch's last song. So at the end, you must put quotation marks.

The Sixth Patriarch's disciple Shen-hui went to Northern China and had a great debate with the Northern school students. Perhaps Shen-hui added these lines. At any rate, the Sixth Patriarch's record was later diluted by someone. Everyone who studies the Sixth Patriarch's record realizes that many lines were added for some purpose. A Chinese scholar, who is now the Chinese ambassador to America, Dr. Hu Shih, said the Sixth Patriarch's record was written by his disciple Shen-hui. To some extent, I agree with him.

I have been giving lectures on the Sixth Patriarch for about four years, and now there remain three or four more weeks. Then this long translation will come to an end. I hope that after my death someone will publish this translation in a book for future Zen students.

There are two other English translations of the Sixth Patriarch's record. One was begun by a Chinese Buddhist student, but it was never completed. The other is by Dr. D.T. Suzuki, but it is only of the first chapter.

Having recited his gatha, the Master said: "All of you, take care of yourselves! After my passing, you must not lament or weep as would people in the world. If you wear mourning or receive condolences, you are not my disciples, and [your behavior] is at variance with the True Dharma. Strive only to know your own original mind and to see your own original nature. [Your original nature] is neither moving nor still; it is not born, nor does it die; it neither comes nor goes, is neither right nor wrong, neither stays nor departs. I fear you may not understand my meaning because your minds are bewildered. Again, I ask you to strive to see your own original nature."

SOKEI-AN SAYS:

The Sixth Patriarch was dying, and by this time the famous, enlightened disciples had already left his place. But the younger unenlightened disciples were still clinging to him. Realizing he could no longer aid them, he pointed to that which they must strive to attain: enlightenment. They must see their original nature. This is the Sixth Patriarch's Zen.

Having recited his gatha, the Master said: "All of you, take care of yourselves! After my passing, you must not lament or weep as would people in the world." This was an old tradition in the Zen school. In Zen temples, when the master dies, all the disciples recite sutras before his coffin preceding the cremation. Usually, they recite three words of lament—"Ai, Ai, Ai." That is all. They do not weep or burst into tears. You must not lament emotionally in the Zen school, and your face must not be suffused with raining tears.

In Shintoism, in my own country, the wife and sisters of the deceased are not permitted to follow the coffin in the funeral procession. It is always the first son who leads. Wearing his father's costume and using a bamboo cane, he follows the coffin in his bare feet. No woman is permitted to walk in the procession.

Strange, but this is old orthodox Shinto. These days, women take part. But in my childhood, they were not permitted. Of course, in Buddhism, all follow the coffin in the funeral procession. In China, professional criers are employed—"crying men" and "crying women"—to wail and mourn. It makes for a very melancholy procession. But in the Zen sect, this wailing to the heavens is not permitted. The monks just say three words—"Ai, Ai, Ai"—and meditate. No one drops a tear. This is Zen behavior. It does not mean indifference to death. It means the monks know the meaning of death. They are emphasizing the profound, deep principle of death.

"If you wear mourning or receive condolences, you are not my disciples, and [your behavior] is at variance with the true Dharma." The disciples do not wear anything special—just their usual clothes, no special black or white.

At the time of the teacher's death, scattered disciples come to the main temple, and before their master's coffin, join their hands, burn incense three times, and meditate—no one speaks a word.

Sometimes a layman comes to the temple to offer condolences and raves about the master: "Oh, your master is dead! Such a wonderful man! What can I do?" The monks just look sarcastic and say nothing as they receive him. Then the layman asks, "Don't you feel sorry?" Well, if you have a true and honest mind, you cannot say a word. Silence is the deepest condolence.

It is a precious time. The master is dead. The man who was laughing and crying and speaking now has gone. He has left a great question for all sentient beings.

When I officiate at a funeral service, especially in America, I see the man in the casket—I look at him—and I always think: "Indeed, I strove many long years for this state of existence called death, and I know what it is." I am not ashamed to lead this dead man's spirit to the place where he has to go. A blind monk, officiating at a funeral service, comes to the dead man, but he does not know how he has lived, where he has gone, or what death is. For a blind monk is just like a beggar: he comes, conducts the service, burns incense, but he does not know anything.

There are many religious teachers who do not know the true meaning of death. Such blind teachers cannot save the soul of a cat! How can they lead the soul of a human being to death—weeping and bursting into tears and receiving the condolences of laymen? This is not the true behavior of the Buddhist.

"Strive only to know your own original mind and to see your own original nature." When you see a man who was your friend, who was eating chop suey last night and this morning is dead, do you go and look at his face and say, "I'm sorry"? If you have any sense, you have some question about death; you want to understand what death is. What will happen after death? What was I before birth? The shallow-minded man and the deep-minded man will be measured at such a moment.

There was a Zen monk who was living in a temple in a village. There was a rich man who had lost his daughter, so he asked this monk to officiate at his daughter's funeral. The monk stood before the coffin and gave a Zen shout, the Lin-chi "Ho!" In the Rinzai school, the monk shouts, that is all. Then the service is over. So at this funeral, the monk shouted at the dead daughter. The gentleman questioned him. "Where did she go when you shouted at her?" The Zen monk could not answer. The gentleman laughed: "You don't know anything about it! You shouted at the dead spirit of my daughter, and you don't know anything about it!" Then the gentleman swept his sleeves behind him and went home. Perhaps, in the American way, he would have kicked the dust, turned on his heels and gone home. The monk went home, too. That night, he ran away from the temple—he was a very conscientious monk. He went to Kyoto, to commence the real study of Zen.

"[Your original nature] is neither moving nor still; it is not born, nor does it die; it neither comes nor goes, is neither right nor wrong, neither stays nor departs." The Sixth Patriarch used these words to indicate the state of your original nature—nothing is moving, no motion. Dilettantes think this is an absolutely annihilated state.

There is no motion, but everything is moving—vividly. All elements are at work: water is flowing, fire is burning, everything is working, and it is not a contradiction. Nothing is in action in that state. The dilettante thinks it is the state of death. The Sixth Patriarch said, "Nothing is resting; everything is working from morning to evening."

When I came to America, I thought the custom of painting and rouging the dead face not a very good one. One day, I went to a funeral and saw a Japanese woman's dead face painted like a flower—her eyebrows were painted, her lips were painted. They had even kept her smiling lips! It was obnoxious and vulgar, too. I had no sympathy for the dead woman's husband who was so materialistic. How can a Buddhist monk officiate at a funeral service standing by a corpse painted like a flower? Perhaps, it is the New York style. But to me, it is a Coney Island style, showing no respect for the dead person. It is obnoxious and sacrilegious.

When you look at a dead man's face, there is no action in it, but he is not resting either. He is in eternal life. He is living. He has not gone when he dies. He has neither come nor gone. There is no beginning, no end. Therefore, there is no coming or going. And from the state of Reality, there is neither right nor wrong. Nothing is standing or walking. The shadow of the bamboo in the moonlight is sweeping the dust from the stairs all night long, but nothing has happened. No dust has been swept. No stairs have been swept. From the standpoint of Reality, nothing has happened. Not a mote of dust has been swept. We came here. We lived. We died. Nothing has happened. Originally, from the standpoint of Reality, this is the bottom of the empty sea.

"I fear you may not understand my meaning because your minds are bewildered"—"I speak profoundly, but your mind is disturbed by my death. I fear that you may not comprehend my idea."

"Again, I ask you to strive to see your own original nature." From morning to evening, you are speaking many words, and your emotions fluctuate like the waves of the ocean; but in Reality, nothing has happened. At the bottom of the empty ocean, nothing has happened. And on the surface of the sea, nothing has happened either—when you realize your original nature.

The Sixth Patriarch was pursued by enemy monks after he attained, and received his teacher's acknowledgment of enlightenment. Even religious monks can feel jealousy. Helped by the Fifth Patriarch to avoid the jealousy of his fellow monks, the Sixth Patriarch escaped to the south. As the monks were pursuing him, one of them named Ming, a tall army officer monk, caught up with him. The Sixth Patriarch left the robe and the bowl, handed down to him from his teacher, on a rock and concealed himself. Ming tried to take the robe and bowl from the rock but could not lift them, for they were as heavy as a mountain. When he failed to lift them, he became afraid—his whole body was suffused with perspiration. (This is psychology and no mystery.) But *how* the transmission was made to the Sixth Patriarch was the question that came to Ming when he could not lift the robe and the bowl.

Observing this, the Sixth Patriarch appeared and said, "Take the robe and the bowl back to the temple, but the Dharma, which was handed down from my teacher, belongs to me." Then Ming said, "Please open your honey gate so that I may understand the Dharma that you possess." The Sixth Patriarch said, "Before your father and mother, what was your original aspect?" Upon the Sixth Patriarch's words, Ming was suddenly enlightened.

Before your father and mother, what was your original aspect? Before the creation of the world, what were you? These are profound questions. If you were not there, you would never be here. If you were there, before creation, what were you?

"If after my passing, you practice this, it will be just as if I were alive. But if you violate my teaching, you will receive no benefit at all, even if I go on living."

The Master then recited the following gatha:

> *"At ease, practicing virtue*
> *Carefree, without doing evil*
> *At peace, delivered from the world of seeing and hearing*
> *Freely drifting, the mind without attachment"*

Having finished reciting the gatha, *the Master remained seated in meditation posture until midnight. Then he suddenly said to his disciples, "I am going" and immediately passed away. At that moment, the room was permeated with a strange fragrance, a white rainbow formed an arch over the earth, the trees in the forest turned white, and birds and beasts cried in despair.*

SOKEI-AN SAYS:

These are the last words of the Sixth Patriarch that were given to his disciples. There are perhaps two more weeks on which to give brief commentaries. I have spent almost four years in translating the Sixth Patriarch's record. Now it is coming to an end.

"If after my passing, you practice this, it will be just as if I were alive. But if you violate my teaching, you will receive no benefit at all, even if I go on living." "My teaching" means the teaching of sudden enlightenment. We are the distant followers of the Sixth Patriarch. Our school of Zen is the school of sudden enlightenment.

The Sixth Patriarch died in the eighth century, and we are living in the twentieth. One thousand two hundred years have passed since his death. But in comformity with his teaching, we still practice his Zen. And we are very proud of the way we have followed his teaching.

In the Orient, everyone who begins some new thing is always blamed. Everyone objects and wishes to follow the old traditional teaching. But now, everyone is proud that their faith is twenty-five hundred years old. It certainly has some value; it has existed such a long, long time on earth. This is contrary to your attitude. You have old things and like new things. You throw away old teachings and try to invent something new. Your people are like tree branches that individually spread out in all directions. But our idea is always like a tree root. Every branch must return to the root.

I came to this country to speak about this one-thousand-year-old teaching, while you are inventing new teachings every day. But the old teaching of the Sixth Patriarch, somehow, gives you a new idea.

I believe the period has come when all of you in this Western hemisphere must return to your own living axiomatic truth, which is the truth within yourself, in your own nature. From your own mind, you will discover many treasures, and from your own feeling, you will discover humanity. *To return to yourself* is the teaching of the Sixth Patriarch. He said that if you practice Zen in conformity with this teaching, it will be as though you were living with him, at that very time.

The Master then recited the following gatha: "At ease, practicing virtue"/ Carefree, without doing evil/ At peace, delivered from the world of seeing and hearing/ Freely drifting, the mind without attachment."

To the dilettante's ear, I think this sounds very strange. But from the Sixth Patriarch's standpoint, evil and virtue are secondary things. In this ideology, evil and virtue give an Oriental man an entirely different conception from yours. There is a fundamental difference in how these words are handled in the East and in the West.

Our statesmen, our diplomats, our nations blindly argue with Western people about everything because our concepts of evil and virtue are so different. Your statesmen, your diplomats, and your churchmen, without knowing how Orientals think, merely attack and blame. Their attitude is to blindly promulgate the *Western* idea of evil and virtue. When this is rejected by the Oriental man, you send your army to attack him.

From our standpoint, as men who deal with thoughts, we harbor many questions. By understanding this fundamental difference in ideology, we must prevent useless quarrels and fighting in the shower of blood and the rain of iron fire. But before we understand this fundamental difference in the concept of evil and virtue, we cannot find peace without fighting each other.

To you, virtue is the first thing. "Good" is the first attribute of God, and there is no evil in Him. God is Good, Truth, and Beauty. The Hindu god always has two sides: the creative side and the destructive side—good and bad. Perhaps this gives you a strange feeling. Why must God be bad?

Buddhists have their own way of understanding God. We do not call IT by any name. Our God is the universe, not a person and not a self. So man's nature is universal as well. If man has a nature as a person or as one separated from another person, he is not an ideal man. The characteristics of the Oriental man are derived from universal nature. You think that this man on earth is imperfect, but that behind this man there must be a perfect man, and that this perfect man appeared on earth as Christ. He is an agency of the perfect attributes of God in the form of a person.

When I studied Christianity with a Canadian missionary at the age of eighteen or nineteen, he explained what I have told you just now. I clearly remember his words. Now I understand that his ideas of God were influenced by Greek philosophy and Greek idealism. So naturally, your God is good and cannot be bad. But the missionary's word, "Good," in our conception, cannot be translated as good. I think your idea of good is some virtue which is beyond evil, which has a nature beyond the evil and virtue on earth. There is no particular word for that in your usage, so you just call it "Good." If I were to make a diagram of this, I would draw a circle with good and bad in it. Then this attribute of your God could be explained. God is Good, but good and bad are included in it. When God judges the actions of human beings, he judges them as good and bad, so God admits that there must be bad. God himself is Good. Good and bad exist on earth; but in heaven, there is only Good. If you explain it in such a way, we understand. The Oriental man can understand your idea of God.

When you never practice any virtue or any evil, you are beyond earthly evil because you are living in the state that transcends earthly virtue and evil. Of course, in Buddhism, this denotes the state of *dharmakaya*. Virtue and evil exists only in the state of *nirmanakaya*, only in the state of the third law. If you follow the traffic law of New York, you are good; if you violate the law, you are bad. If you drive your car through seventieth street from Central Park West to Columbus Avenue, you are bad; but if you drive through seventieth street from Columbus Avenue to Central Park West, you are good. If, however, you are in the Arabian desert, you can drive your car anywhere you like, and no policeman will arrest you. So, driving a car in the Arabian Desert cannot be termed good or bad. You must understand this fundamental difference.

The Sixth Patriarch spoke from this standpoint. He was a man who never practiced any virtue or practiced any evil. He came from this standpoint into the world. When I think now of what that Christian teacher taught me in my youth, I believe that, perhaps, he did not understand the true meaning of "Good." His words were from the orthodox book. It was not the fault of the theology but of the teacher. The attribute of God that is good must not be the good that exists on earth, but a heavenly virtue. Now we can agree. But God's attribute of good, in terms of human nature, we do not accept in religion. There is a fundamental difference.

No fundamental difference exists between the East and the West, but our understanding is not mutually penetrating. We are quarreling and fighting because we are ignorant, especially the statesmen and politicians, who handle the thoughts of men in their ignorant way.

You have been sending missionaries to the Orient for many years, and some of us were educated by them. Now we must explain to you how we accepted your Christianity. Your churchmen do not know anything about it. Speaking such big words on this small corner of seventieth street is not worthwhile; but my words are true. When the time comes, perhaps two hundred years from now, someone else will speak the same words I am speaking now, and you will listen. Your statesmen and also your clergymen will listen.

I do not want to speak about any national problems in my lecture, but I will say two or three more words about the relations between America and Japan in regard to the Chinese situation. America does not disagree with Japan economically about the Sino-Japanese question, but America is taking, morally, a side opposite to that of Japan. Neither understands the other. The Japanese do not understand anything about the American idea of virtue. So the two sides are just splashing each other with water for nothing. How stupid!

Having finished reciting the gatha, *the Master remained seated in meditation posture until midnight. Then he suddenly said to his disciples, "I am going" and immediately passed away."* Thus the Sixth Patriarch died.

At that moment, the room was permeated with a strange fragrance": In this country, no one would notice any strange fragrance, but those who go to Japan or China, after a sudden shower on a summer evening, will realize that the hot, wet earth has a strange fragrance. This fragrance in the air will give you a tranquil feeling. In Japan, we are living very near to the earth, while in New York, we are living on concrete. When I returned to Japan, I said, "Japan's cities seem to be in bare feet, while New York wears concrete shoes.

The strange fragrance described here evokes the wet, cold air of morning. The Sixth Patriarch died at midnight, and the cold air of the morning penetrated the room.

"A white rainbow formed an arch over the earth, the trees in the forest turned white . . ." The white rainbow appears many times in Chinese descriptions. In heroic novels and histories, before an important incident or birth of some great hero, a white rainbow is said to cover the mountains. So in any description where this white rainbow appears, you must understand that it signifies an important occasion. Therefore, when the Sixth Patriarch died, this white ribbon arched over the earth.

"And birds and beasts cried in despair." In the pictures of the Buddha's nirvana, many insects, birds and beasts felt the great loss and cried in sadness.

It seems to me that I have spoken unnecessary words here tonight, but my father was a Shinto priest. Then I followed a Christian teacher who's name was Reverend Bates of Canada. Later, I studied with a Japanese, eminent in the Japanese Christianity of that period, and then I came to Buddhism.

At my present age, I cross my arms, sit down on my cushion and think about it. I now understand the fundamental difference between the Western and Eastern teachings. This variance can be understood. There is a key to open the mystic box of two very different religions, and this key is Zen.

In the eleventh month, the officials of the three prefectures, Kwang, Shao, and Hsin, and the Master's disciples, both monks and laymen, quarreled over who should receive the Master's body, unable to agree where it was to be buried. Thereupon they burned incense and prayed: "Let the incense smoke show where the Master will be interred." The incense drifted directly to Ts'ao-ch'i. On the thirteenth day of the eleventh month, the sacred coffin, together with the robe and bowl that had been transmitted to the Master, was returned [to Ts'ao-ch'i]. In the seventh month of the following year [714 C.E.], [the body] was removed from the coffin, and the Master's disciple Fang-pien smeared it with fragrant clay.

SOKEI-AN SAYS:

I have been translating the Sixth Patriarch's Record for almost four years. Now, it has come to an end, except for one or two more lectures.

This record is the origination of the Southern School of Zen, which is the teaching of sudden enlightenment. A prince of Southern India, a rajah who became a monk, brought the meditation sect of Buddhism into China by way of the southern ocean, landing in what is today Canton. This was in the middle of the sixth century. The monk's name was Bodhidharma. He handed down this Zen school to the Buddhists of China.

Hui-neng, the Sixth Patriarch, followed in the sixth generation from Bodhidharma. He emphasized his own mind, the one mind through which one can realize one's own original nature. Original nature is the nature that we are aware of, the state that is within the five senses and is blended with the outside.

We have forgotten the state of our original nature. We are like travellers who have gone astray and forgotten the way home. Even if such a traveller returns to his own village, he cannot find his own house. Therefore, the human being who is born in this deluded state, will die in delusion unless he awakens and returns to his own original nature. This original nature is one's own Buddha. By attaining this nature, one will attain buddhahood.

This school is called "Zen" because its students do not read sutras or worship images of Buddha. As disciples of Shakyamuni Buddha, they practice meditation. That is why it is a school of meditation.

When the Sixth Patriarch died, his disciples did not cremate his body but buried it in the valley of Ts'ao-ch'i. In that place is the main temple of the Sixth Patriarch, where he lived for quite a long time. This temple is still existing today, but it has become a nest for bandits. We have seen photographs of it, and money has been donated to repair it, to rebuild the dilapidated buildings.

The Ts'ao-ch'i valley is beside one of the streams that pour into the Yellow River and Canton Bay. There are three streams that pour into the Yellow River. This one is the northern stream which leads the traveler into the territory where the Sixth Patriarch lived, Ts'ao-ch'i—in Japanese, "Sokei." My name came from this Sokei, the hermitage of the Sixth Patriarch.

In the eleventh month, the officials of the three prefectures Kuang, Shao, and Hsin and the Master's disciples, both monks and laymen, quarreled over who should receive the Master's body, unable to agree where it was to be buried. Kuang is the prefecture in which Canton exists, and Shao is on the northwest side of Canton. Hsin is on the left side of the shore of the the Pearl River, where the Sixth Patriarch was born.

So, the disciples, both monks and laymen, came scrambling to meet the body of the dead master. I am not sure that this "scrambling" is a good word, but they came in a rush because they wished to hold the Sixth Patriarch's dead body in their hands. At the time the Sixth Patriarch died, his old disciples had long before left his temple, and only the younger disciples stayed with him.

Laymen of the three prefectures also came to meet the body of the dead master. But the Sixth Patriarch did not leave any word as to where to bury his body. He was in Ts'ao-ch'i, and when he became sick, he went back to his mother's house, which had been given to him by the Emperor. (It was repaired by some rich man who made a temple out of it.) Here he died. But his body was carried into Shao by boat. Although there is no description of how the body was transported, there was no other way to carry it. As you know, the Yellow River has a tremendous mouth.

So they had no idea where to bury the Sixth Patriarch.

A Zen master's body was never cremated in China or in India because the monks believe a master never dies, but he rests in eternal meditation. The Indian fakir buries himself under the ground for about twenty days and hibernates in meditation. When his spirit returns to his body, he comes out of the ground—or out of his cave—and is massaged. Then he eats light food and drinks water. Within a week, he has recovered. He is the same as he was before he entered his long meditation. This strange custom was the reason why the monks did not cremate their Zen masters.

Where is the Zen master? They put him under the ground, without cremation, and dug holes on both sides of the tombstone. Then they put a bamboo pole into the grave, and the disciples would go every morning and call—"Hello! Hello!"—through the bamboo.

Thereupon they burned incense and prayed: "Let the incense smoke show where the Master will be interred." The incense drifted directly to Ts'ao-ch'i. The smoke indicated the way. This was also an old tradition.

The river becomes very narrow and the land is almost like a desert. On the yellow earth at Pao-lin are little forests, and there was also the temple of the Sixth Patriarch.

On the thirteenth day of the eleventh month, the sacred coffin, together with the robe and bowl that had been transmitted to the Master, was returned [to Ts'ao-ch'i]. In the seventh month of the following year [714 C.E.], [the body] was removed from the coffin and the Master's disciple Fang-pien smeared it with fragrant clay. According to this description, the Sixth Patriarch's body was preserved for a while in his temple at Pao-lin.

Usually a dead master's body is packed in vermillion earth, that is, earth mixed with some kind of quicksilver. This made a kind of cement or putty that keeps things preserved. The same material was used in Egypt. Wherever mummies are uncovered, red clay is always found clinging to the corpses and draperies. The Chinese, too, use this material to preserve dead bodies.

The sacred robe and bowl had been transmitted from Bodhidharma to Hui-k'o, to Seng-ts'an, to Tao-hsin, to Hung-jen, the Fifth Patriarch, and on to the Sixth Patriarch, Hui-neng. But the Sixth Patriarch told his disciples, "Hereafter, I will not transmit my robe and bowl to my disciples." So Fang-pien mixed the incense mud and spread it upon the corpse of the Sixth Patriarch, and then placed it back inside the sepulchre.

There are a few more lines, which I will translate for next Wednesday's lecture. After next Wednesday, I shall speak about primitive Buddhism. But if you wish some commentary on Lao-tzu, I shall be glad. I have read many translations of Lao-tzu, but I have not yet read a satisfactory one. And I have never read a commentary that does not have some Christian smell. I have often thought that, in my old age, I would do this. Perhaps I should wait five or ten more years. It is very hard to kill a Buddhist monk!

Recalling the Master's prophecy about the taking of his head, the disciples protected the base of the Master's neck by wrapping it in cloths soaked in lacquer and coating it with sheets of iron before replacing it in the stupa. Instantly a white light came forth from the stupa, reaching straight to the sky and remaining for three days. The governor of Shao province reported this to the emperor and received an imperial decree, commanding him to erect a memorial stele recording the details of the Master's religious life. The inscription states: "The Master lived for seventy-six years. When he was twenty-four, the Dharma was transmitted to him. When he was thirty-nine, he shaved his head. For thirty-seven years, he promulgated the Dharma to benefit others. His Dharma heirs numbered forty-three, and he had countless other disciples of high attainment. The robe transmitted by Bodhidharma, the Mo Na Robe and crystal bowl bestowed upon the Master by Emperor Chung-tsung, the image of the Master modeled in clay by Fang-pien, and the sacred implements the Master used are permanently preserved in Pao-lin Temple. The Sutra from the Earthen Altar remains to testify to the essential principle of the Master's teaching, to perpetuate the Three Treasures and to benefit sentient beings everywhere."

SOKEI-AN SAYS:

Recalling the Master's prophecy about the taking of his head, the disciples protected the base of the Master's neck by wrapping it in cloths soaked in lacquer and coating it with sheets of iron before replacing it in the stupa. I think you remember in the previous lecture the Master predicted that after five or six years someone would come and take his head. The disciples realized the Master's foreboding and separated his head from his body, and preserved it.

There is no description about this preservation in any other place, but his disciples remembered the prediction. Perhaps the Master was saying: "After my death, do not preserve my body, but preserve my head." According to his teaching of sudden enlightenment, he certainly placed more emphasis on his intellect than on any other part of his body. While the students in the Northern School of Zen were practicing intense meditation, the Sixth Patriarch emphasized the realization of one's original nature. Realization belongs to the intellect, not to the exercise of meditation.

The stupa is a pagoda-tower. In China, in every Zen temple, there is a stupa built of stone, tile, and clay.

Instantly a white light came forth from the stupa, reaching straight to the sky and remaining for three days. This is the usual description of a miracle when you describe the death of a wonderful man.

The governor of Shao province reported this to the emperor and received an imperial decree, commanding him to erect a memorial stele recording the details of the Master's religious life. There were three officials who came and attended the funeral service of the Sixth Patriarch. These were the officials in whose territory the Sixth Patriarch's stupa was built. Ts'ao-ch'i was a territory in the prefecture of Shao-chou. The monuments belong to each Zen temple. The objects in the temple are quite excellent and beautiful.

The inscription states: "The Master lived for seventy-six years. When he was twenty-four, the Dharma was transmitted to him. He stayed in the Fifth Patriarch's temple only eight months, pounding rice in the barn. These incidents are described in the first chapter of this record. The Fifth Patriarch called him at midnight and transmitted the Dharma which had been transmitted by Bodhidharma. The Fifth Patriarch handed down the *Diamond Sutra* and commented on it for him, and perhaps he gave him the principles of the Buddhist Ten Commandments when he transmitted the Dharma to his disciples. I never came across any description of this, but I think it is true. All descriptions of how to transmit the Dharma are still very obscure.

These days in the Zen school, we transmit the Dharma through koans. The student makes his own solution to the question, which is hidden in the koan, and the master uses this solution as a measure to prove the student's attainment. Finally, the complete Dharma is transmitted.

The Sixth Patriarch was twenty-four years old when the Dharma was transmitted to him—quite young. The Dharma was transmitted to me, from my teacher, when I was forty-seven [1928]. I began to study Zen in your America at the age of twenty. (Twenty-one in the Japanese way of counting.)

The Sixth Patriarch came from Nan-hai to the Fifth Patriarch's temple and stayed for eight months, pounding rice in the barn. There he attained the highest enlightenment. He was not an ordinary man.

I think I will give you a few remarks about Buddhism which you must not forget as long as you live. The Buddha talked about "right view." What is right view? You must first decide what your main faith is. Christians say, "Faith in God." God is in heaven, not in man. The other school of meditation thinks the principle view is in deep *samadhi*, not in *this present moment*, that one must *transcend* this present moment and enter deep samadhi, close one's eyes, close one's mind, and abandon all the world. They concentrate their minds in bottomless samadhi.

This indicates the two different faiths. The Christians have faith in God who lives outside of himself in heaven; the follower of the other school has faith within himself, in deep *samadhi*. He steps out of himself into a different faith—he refuse to be a human being. He refuses to abide in this human consciousness, which is guarded by the five senses. He refuse to *return*. Now you realize that there are these two different views.

The true Buddhist takes neither of these views. He thinks that neither of these two views are the true view, that these two views are the production of one's own thoughts.

The states of "outside" or "inside" are imaginary. They are not real; they are hypothesis. They are not proven. When you enter bottomless samadhi, you are outside of yourself. You are not conscious, you are sleeping. When you try to seek something outside in heaven, it is not demonstrated, not proven by your sight or by your intellect. It is your faith through your feeling that this must be the state of perfection and for a person who is perfect. It is inferred by your knowledge, but it is not *tested* by you.

The Buddha's right view is at this moment, in this place. The Buddha called it "the king of all *samadhis*." In this state, as a human being, guarded by these five senses and ornamented by this marvelous outside, supported by bottomless consciousness, we are now, at this moment, existing here thus. Without winking our eyes, without puzzling our minds, at this moment our spine is the pillar of our body, and as we cross our legs, they form the base of that pillar. We cross our two hands on our lap, and we see everything at once, hear every sound at once. With penetrative wisdom and a tranquil mind, we are aware of our own state. We never puzzle, though a million gods appear before us, and we are never lured or tempted though the shining, bottomless consciousness appears behind us. This is our decision at this moment, in this human body, as we are sitting here in this right view. This is the foundation of Buddhism. This is our faith. Standing on this faith, we enter all directions of human activity. If you do not know about this, you do not know Buddhism. And if anyone were to ask you, "What is your faith?" you would puzzle hard to answer. This is the Buddha's decision. It is twenty-five hundred years old.

Studying many other religions, I came to him. I took obeisance to him, saying: "You have attained the highest knowledge and from now on, you are my teacher." Thus I decided to follow his Dharma because I realized the truth of his right view. Of course, Buddhists will go through many states in meditation. Sometimes they sleep and sometimes they exalt the mind. They go through many states of mind and consciousness to find this central view, the Buddha's right view.

Before the lecture, to commemorate the Buddha's decision, we sit in meditation from one minute to five minutes. We sit in the Buddha's position before every lecture because we are his disciples. There is no other religion in the world that does this, that takes this view. If you doubt my word, study the sutras. If anyone says no, he is not a Buddhist. I assert, therefore, my authentic knowledge, and I insist that my view is true by transmitted Dharma. Transcribe this in your notebooks, and in the future, if anyone starts to argue about the Buddha's true standpoint, you must uphold this view, and with this knowledge you must teach them. If there is any biased view, mentally or materially, it is not the true view.

When you form your physical body, put your hands on your lap, fold your legs and keep your mind clear and bright. This moment is Buddha's Buddhism. Do not fancy becoming some other sentient being, or some demigod in the sky, and do not fall into the dark view of the cave dweller. Do not cherish any thought in your mind. To prove this is the right view, as the Buddha spoke it for forty-nine years, to prove this real view, the disciples of the Buddha, from generation to generation, have written the sutras—five thousand forty-eight in number. To prove this present condition of our consciousness, from the Buddha to Bodhidharma, and from Bodhidharma to us—this is Zen. It is impossible to describe in words, but it is transmitted from mind to mind. Thus the Dharma must be transmitted. Do not be disturbed by other teachings, which talk about heaven or hell. You have your position in your present moment.

When he was thirty-nine, he shaved his head. He shaved his head to take the order of the sangha when he was thirty-nine years old. After the Dharma had been transmitted to him, he went to the southern country and hid himself. One day in the temple, he was sweeping the garden while two monks were arguing about a flag that was waving above their heads. One said the banner was waving, and the other said the wind was waving. The Sixth Patriarch forgot his present position—that he was hiding himself as a common laborer—and said: "It is neither the banner nor the wind that is waving. It is your souls that are waving."

The abbot of the temple shivered when he heard this. He knew that this was no common man. He bowed to this man sweeping the garden. Then the Sixth Patriarch disclosed himself as the heir of the Fifth Patriarch. It was this abbot who shaved the head of Hui-neng and made him a monk. Until that day, he had been a lay disciple. So this Dharma is transmitted to anyone, high or low, monk or layman. To those who have the head or brain, to them, the Dharma will be transmitted. The robe or the shaved head do not make Dharma. Your enlightened mind makes Dharma, makes a true Buddhist.

For thirty-seven years, he promulgated the Dharma to benefit others. His Dharma heirs numbered forty-three, and he had countless other disciples of high attainment. The robe transmitted by Bodhidharma, the Mo Na Robe and crystal bowl bestowed upon the Master by Emperor Chung Tsung, the image of the Master modeled in clay by Fang-pien, and the sacred implements the Master used are permanently preserved in Pao-lin Temple. The Sutra from the Earthen Altar remains to testify to the essential principle of the Master's teaching, to perpetuate the Three Treasures and to benefit sentient beings everywhere." The Sixth Patriarch was a small man, and he stood on an earthen platform to give his teachings.

We are working to perpetuate these Three Treasures. I, too, am working to promulgate these teachings in this world, and to bless all sentient beings.

GLOSSARY*

(*All non-English terms are Sanskrit unless otherwise indicated. As in the foregoing text and commentary, diacritial marks are omitted)

abhidharma: early Buddhist discourses on philosophy and psychology.

Agamas: collection of treatises or sutras that comprise the basic teachings of early Buddhism.

alaya-consciousness (alayavijnana): eighth consciousness; basic or storehouse consciousness.

Amida: (J.) see *Amitabha.*

Amitabha: literally, "boundless light"; ruler of the Western Heaven or Pure Land called Sukhavati.

anagamin: a non-coming, or non-returning arhat who will not be reborn in this world.

anja: a laborer in the temple.

anasrava: state of non-leakage or discharge of afflictions and passions from the mind.

apsara: a celestial nymph, a goddes in Indra's heaven.

arhat: sage or saint who has attained release from the cycle of death and rebirth, the highest state in early Buddhism.

arupadhatu: world of formlessness; the highest realm of the *tridhatu.*

asrava: state of leakage or discharge of afflictions and passions from the mind.

Avalokiteshvara: the enlightened being (*bodhisattva*) of compassion and mercy.

Avatsamsaka sutra: the "Flower Garland Sutra," one of the key texts of Tang Buddhism.

bhutatathata: bhuta is the real, the present moment; *tatathata* is "thus always"; the eternal, impersonal, unchangeable, self-existent reality behind all phenomena.

bodhi: awakening.

Bodhidharma: (dates uncertain) was said to have arrived in China during the reign of Emperor Wu Ti of the Liang (r. 502-49), and is traditionally regarded as the twenty-eighth patriarch, or successor, in the Indian lineage to Shakyamuni Buddha, and the first patriarch and founder of Ch'an in China.

bodhisattva: enlightened being who seeks buddhahood for the benefit of others.

Brahma: Vedic god representing the absolute.

brahmacariya: to lead a chaste and holy life.

Carus, Paul. Dr. Paul Carus (1852-1919) was an editor for *The Monist* and Open Court Publishing Company in LaSalle, Illinois. His interest in comparative religion led him to invite D.T. Suzuki to the United States in 1898 to help him translate Chinese religious texts into English.

chan: (C.)(J. *zen*) Chinese word for *dhyana,* a Sanskrit word basically meaning meditation.

*ch'an-hui: : (C.)*The term "confession" consists of two Chinese characters, *ch'an*—not to be confused with the similarly pronounced character for Zen in Chinese—and *hui,* pronounced *san* and *ke* in Japanese, and read in combination as *sange.*

ch'an-ting: (C.) Ch'an meditation.

devas: angels or gods.

Chu-chih :(n.d.). a famous Tang Zen master, known for his use of the "one finger" in teaching students.

citta: seat of the intellect.

dharma: a Buddhist term that can mean law, doctrine, an element of existence, or truth.

dharmadhatu: realm of existence (*dharma*) or law; the absolute and physical universe.

dharmakaya: body of *dharma*, body of law; the essential mind of Buddha; one of the three bodies of the *trikaya*.

dharmata: the underlying nature of reality.

dhatu: world or realm

dhyana: tranquil meditation; absorption into Reality; contemplation, meditation.

Diamond Sutra: (Vajracchika-prajnaparamita-sutra) a condensation of the wisdom (*Prajnaparamita*) sutras, translated into Chinese in 400 C.E. by Kumarajiva (334-413).

Eight consciousnesses: (parijnana) 1-5) the five sense-consciousnesses: seeing, hearing, smelling, touching, tasting; 6) *manas (mano-vijnana)*, the intellectual function: knowing, judging, conceiving; 7) *klista-manas (klista-mano-vijnana)*: discriminative and calculating consciousness, the cause of egoism and individualizing, which is defiled by the germs or seeds (*bija*, data or impressions) of the eighth consciousness; 8) *alayavijnana*: the storehouse or basic consciousness that retains the seeds or germs of all phenomena.

eight errors: the delusions of 1) birth, 2) destruction, 3) oneness, 4) differentiation, 5) past, 6) future, 7) permanence, and 8) cessation.

eight upside-down views: the four deluded views of heretics and ordinary people plus the four deluded views of the adherents of the Hinayana vehicle, the *shravakas* and *pratyakabuddhas*: 1) perpetuity, 2) joy, 3) self, 4) purity, and their opposites: 5) mutability, 6) joylessness, 7) selflessness, and 8) impurity.

eighteen dhatus: the twelve *ayatana* (six sense-organs and six sense-data) and their six corresponding consciousnesses.

eightfold path: practices leading to the cessation of suffering: 1) right view (*samyag-drsthi*; 2) right thought and purpose (*samyak-samkalpa*; 3) right speech (*samyag-vac*; 4) right conduct (*samyak-karmanta*); 5) right livelihood (*samyag-ajiva*); 6) right effort (*samyag-vyayama*); 7) right mindfulness (*samyak-smrti*); 8) right concentration (*samyak-samadhi*).

ekavyuha-samadhi: one-practice *samadhi*.

field-of-merit: sphere of kindness, charity, and virtue.

five nefarious crimes: 1) parricide; 2) matricide; 3) killing an *arhat*; 4) shedding the blood of a buddha; and 5) causing disunity in the Buddhist order.

five patriarchs: The earliest patriarchs of Ch'an in China. Traditionally, they are: 1) Bodhidharma ; 2) Hui-k'o ; 3) Seng-ts'an; 4) Tao-hsin; and 5) Hung-jen.

five skandhas: the five aggregates, heaps, shadows, or scales of consciousness that comprise a human being: 1) *rupa*: the body, the five senses, and outer existence; 2) *vedana*: feelings, perception; 3) *samjna*: thoughts, conceptions; 4) *samskara*: mind-elements, mental formations; 5) *vijnana*: consciousness.

four conceptions: (avastha) the four states of all phenomena: birth, being, change, and death.

four dhyanas: the four dhyanas, or contemplations, are: 1)the attainment of bliss and joy upon the cessation of desire; 2) the attainment of bliss and joy upon the cessation of discursive thought; 3) the attainment of equanimity without joy or bliss; and 4))the attainment of equanimity and awareness alone.

four dignities: walking, standing; sitting, and lying down.

four grave prohibitions: prohibitions against killing, stealing, carnality, and lying.

four great elements: earth, water, fire, air.

four maharajhas: the four guardians of the universe.

four noble truths: 1) suffering; 2) the origin of suffering; 3) the cessation of suffering, and 4) the path towards the cessation of suffering, the *Eightfold Path.*

fourfold negation: 1) all things (*dharmas*) exist; 2) all things do not exist; 3) all things both exist and do not exist; 4) all things neither exist nor do not exist.

four wisdoms: according to Yogacara theory, when the eight consciousness are purified by enlightenment, they are said to be "turned upside down," a process called *paravritti.* Upon this upheaval, the eight consciousnesses in ignorance are transformed into the four wisdoms of enlightenment. The eighth consciousness, the fundamental storehouse consciousness (*alayavijnana*), is transformed into *adarshana-jnana,* "mirror wisdom." The seventh consciousness, the discriminating and calculating consciousness (*klista-manovijnana*), is transformed into *samata-jnana,* "non-dual wisdom." The sixth consciousness, the intellectual function (*manovijnana*), is transformed into *pratyaveksana-jnana,* "proper comprehension wisdom"; and the five senses, the five consciousnesses, are transformed into *krityannusthana-jnana,* the "perfect activity wisdom." For a detailed explanation of this process, see Roger J. Corless, *The Vision of Budddhism* (New York:Paragon House, 1989), pages 174-84.

gandharva: gods of fragrance and music, and the musicians of Indra.

gatha: a hymn or chant in metrical form.

Goddard, Dr. Dwight: (1861-1939) American Christian missionary and an early devotee of Zen and Buddhism. In 1932 he published an anthology of Buddhist scriptures, *The Buddhist Bible.*

Hakuin Ekaku: (1686-1769) famous Japanese Zen master of the Tokugawa period from whom present-day Rinzai teaching lines in Japan trace their descent.

Hinayana: small vehicle; early Buddhism.

hossu: (*J.*) a horse-hair whisk; a Buddhist ecclesiastical article.

Hotei: (C., n.d.). a wandering monk said to have lived during the tenth century, the celebrated Chinese "laughing Buddha."

hrdaya: heart, mind, or soul

Huang-po: Huang-po Hsi-yun (d.850); teacher of Lin-chi.

hungry ghost: See *preta.*

Hu-shih: Dr. Hu-shih (1891-1962) was a celebrated modern Chinese scholar, historian philosopher, and student of early Zen texts.

hui: see *ch'an-hui.*

Ikkyu Sojun: (1393-1481) celebrated and eccentric Japanese Rinzai Zen master of the late middle ages.

Indra: chief of all the Vedic gods; Emperor of Heaven and Lord of the Gods of the Sky in Hindu mythology.

indriya: the six sense-organs.

Jambudvipa: one of the four continents situated to the south of Mount Sumeru.

Jataka tales: stories detailing the previous lives of the Buddha and his followers.

Jetavana Vihara: the garden of Jetavana Monastery in Shravasti, India.

jnana: spiritual knowledge of Reality; an aspect of prajna.

Joshu: : (J.) The Tang Zen master Chao-chou Ts'ung-shen (778-897).

kalpa: incalculable period of time between the creation and recreation of the world.

kamadhatu: world of desire comprising the sensuous desire for food, sleep, and sex; the first realm of the *tridhatu.*

kensho: (J.) seeing into one's original nature.

Kepner, Audrey: one of Sokei-an's student's and transcribers.

kesa: the traditional "stole" worn by Buddhist monks.

klesha: defilement.

koan: (J., C. *kung-an*) case given to students by Zen masters for contemplation or observation.

koji: (J.) Buddhist layman.

Lankavatara Sutra: Sutra given by Buddha to the bodhisattva Mahamati (Great Wisdom) concerning the primacy of consciousness. It also propounds the Three Bodies (*dharmakaya, sambogakaya* and *nirmanakaya*) as well as the Four Wisdoms (Great Mirror Wisdom, Universal Wisdom, Profound Observing Wisdom and Perfecting Wisdom).

li: Chinese measurement roughly equivalent to l.7 miles.

Lin-chi I-Hsuan: (J: Rinzai Gigen, d.866). His record, the *Lin-chi lu,* was translated into English by Sokei-an.

Madhyamika: Madhyamika is the teaching of the Middle Way, the School said to have been founded by the Indian monk Nagarjuna around the second century.

Mahayana: great vehicle of Buddhism; later Buddhism.

manas: active, thinking, and calculating mind.

mandala: a symbolic figure, diagram, or cirle of buddhas, bodhisattvas (enlightened beings), heavens, hells, etc., used for meditation and visualization.

Manjushri: the enlightened being of Wisdom.

Ma-tsu Taoi-i: (709-788). Tang Zen master.

maya: phenomenal world of illusion, deception, and hallucination; also the mother of Shakyamuni (Queen Maya).

Miya, Mataichi: friend and patron of Sokei-an, Miya was a specialist in Chinese art who found antiques for the Yamanaka Company in New York.

munen: (J.) No-mind, mindlessness.

musho: (J.) the "Unborn," "non-arising."

nagas: serpents or dragons.

Nan-hai Eastern Ch'an Temple: located in the district of Huang-mei in Chi-chou on Yellow Plum Mountain (Huang-mei-shan) also known as East Mountain (Tung-shan). Yellow Plum Mountain also referred to the East Mountain Teaching (*Tung-shan fa-men*), the Ch'an school of the fourth and fifth patriarchs, Tao-hsin (580-651) and Hung-jen (600-674).

narakas: hell beings; one of the six states of existence.

nenbutsu: (J.) literally, "thinking of the Buddha." An invocation associated with Pure Land Buddhism.

nirmanakaya: body of transformation; one of the three bodies (*trikaya*) of Buddha.

nirodha: state of nothingness.

Nirvana Sutra: (Mahaparinirvana Sutra) Sutra of the Great Decease translated by Chu Fa-hu between 265 and 313 B.C.E.; purports to be the sermon delivered by the Buddha before his death.

Osho: (J.) a term commonly used in Japan to refer to one's priest or teacher.

paramartha: the highest and ultimate truth, reality.

paramitas: the perfections practiced by a *bodhisattva* to reach the other shore (nirvana).

prajna: highest wisdom or insight.

pratyekabuddhas: solitary enlightened ones; adherents of the Hinayana sect who gain nirvana due to their insight into the twelve *nidanas*.

pratyekabuddhayana: vehicle, or teaching, of *pratyekabuddhas*.

preta: see *six realms*.

rakshas: evil spirits.

roshi: (J.) "old teacher"; commonly used to refer to Zen masters.

rupa: the body, five senses, outer existence; one of the *five skandhas*.

rupadhatu: realm of form; the second realm of the *tridhatu*.

samadhi: state of perfect absorption into the object of contemplation; a state of non-dual consciousness.

samata: see *same-sightedness*.

sambhogakaya: body of bliss; one of the three bodies (*trikaya*) of Buddha.

same-sightedness: (*samata*) evenness, sameness, or equality.

samjna: thought, conception; one of the *five skandhas*.

samsara: eternal round (transmigration) of birth-and-death within the six realms of existence.

samskara: mind-elements and mental formations; one of the five *skandhas*.

samyaksambodhi: Absolute universal enlightenment

sanghati: a robe that is one of three regulation garments worn by a monk.

sanzen: (J.) private koan interview with the master.

saraloka: the entire world.

sarira: the remains after cremation.

sarvajna: the perfect and omniscient wisdom of the buddhas.

satori: (J.) Enlightenment or the experience of awakening.

shadows of mind: see *five skandhas*.

Shariputra: one of ten chief disciples of Shakyamuni Buddha.

shastra: a treatise.

shila: precepts followed by monks, nuns, and laymen constituting one of the *six paramitas*.

Shingon: the Japanese school of Esoteric Buddhism founded by Kukai (Kobo diashi, 774-835).

shinnyo: (J.) true thusness; ultimate reality; as-it-is-ness.

shonen: (J) right mindfulness, right attitude of mind.

shravakas: listeners; adherents of the Hinayana sect who seek enlightenment for themselves alone and can only attain nirvana by listening to the teaching.

shravakayana: vehicle or teaching of the *shravakas*.

shunyata: emptiness, nothingness, transparency.

six heavens: see *six realms*.

six paramitas: 1) generosity (*dana-paramita*); 2) discipline (*shila-paramita*); 3) patience (*kshanti-paramita*); 4) energy, or exertion (*virya-paramita*); 5) meditation (*dhyana-paramita*); 6) wisdom (*prajna-paramita*).

six realms: (*gati*) various modes of *samsaric* existence in which rebirth occurs, consisting of three lower states (*naraka*: hell beings, *preta*: hungry ghosts, and animals), and three higher states (humans, *ashuras*: angry demons or demigods, and *devas*: gods or heavenly beings).

six-supernatural wisdoms: 1) ability to transform the body; 2) ability to see anything; 3) ability to hear all sounds and understand all speech; 4) ability to mind read; 5) knowledge of all previous existences; and 6) complete knowledge of dispassion.

stupa: a tower used for the remains or relics of the dead.

Sumeru: the king of mountains in Hindu mythology; the center of the universe and the meeting place of the gods.

Surangama Sutra: a Buddhist scripture popular in East Asia.

Sutra of Perfect Awakening: (C. Yuan-chueh-ching) sutra translated into Chinese by Buddhatrata in 693 C.E.

Suzuki, D.T.: (1870-1966) Japan's preeminent interpreter of Zen in the West.

Ta-fan Temple: temple located in the district of Shao Chou.

Tathagata: thus come, so come; one of the ten titles of Buddha.

Tathagatagarbha: womb of the Buddha's teaching and the source of all truth.

T'ien-t'ai: school of Chinese Buddhism based on the *Lotus Sutra.*

Te-shan: The Zen Master Te-shan Hsuan-chien (781-867), a famous contemporary of Lin-chi. He is known for his use of the stick in teaching students.

ten commandments: the ten precepts prohibiting: 1) killing; 2) stealing; 3) unchaste behavior; 4) lying; 5) using intoxicants; 6) gossip; 7) boasting; 8) envy; 9) resentment and ill will; 10) slandering the three treasures of Buddha, Dharma, and Sangha.

ten evils: 1) killing, 2) stealing, 3) sexual misconduct, 4) lying, 5) harsh speech, 6) backbiting, 7) frivolousness, 8) covetousness, 9) malice, and 10) false views; opposite of the *ten commandments.*

Theravada: see Hinayana.

three bodies: see *trikaya.*

three karmas: (trividha-dvara) karmas of deed, word, and thought.

three poisons: afflictions of greed, anger, and ignorance.

three realms: (tridhatu) kamadhatu, rupadhatu, arupadhatu.

three treasures: three jewels of Buddha, Dharma, and Sangha.

three vehicles: (triyana) three classes of Buddhist teaching: *shrvakayana, pratyekabuddhayana,* and *bodhisattvayana.*

three worlds: the three realms or three times of past, present, and future.

transmigration: the eternal round within the *three worlds.*

tridhatu: See *three realms.*

trikaya: dharmakaya, sambhogakaya, and *nirmanakaya.*

triyana: see *three vehicles.*

true view: first of the *Eightfold Path.*

Ts'ao-ch'i: region in Kwangtung province.

tso-c'han: (J.: zazen) seated meditation.

twelve divisions of the canon: 1) sermons; 2) metrical pieces; 3) prophecies; 4) *gathas;* 5) impromptu or unsolicited addresses; 6) narratives; 7) stories of the Buddhas past lives; 8) expanded sutras; 9) miracles; 10) discourses by question and answer; 11) parables and metaphors; and 12) dogmatic treatises.

twelve nidanas: causes or links in the chain of existence: 1) old age and death; 2) rebirth; 3) existence; 4) grasping; 5) love, thirst, desire; 6) receiving, perceiving, sensation; 7) touch, contact, feeling; 8) the six senses; 9) name and form; 10) the six forms of perception, awareness or discernment; 11) action, moral conduct; and 12) ignorance.

Vaishali: city northern in India where the Second Buddhist Council was held in 386 B.C.E

vedana: feelings, perception; one of the *five skandhas.*

vijnana: consciousness; one of the *five skandhas.*

vinaya: monastic rules and regulations governing the communal life of monks and nuns.

wu-hsin: (C., J. *mu-shin*) no-mind.

wu-nien: (C., J. *mu-nen*) no-thought.

yaksha: wild demonic beings; also a clas of supernatural beings who protect the Dharm.

Yama: god of hell.

Yun-men: The famous Zen master Yun-men Wen-yen (864-949).

zazen: (J., C.: *tso-chan*) seated meditation.

FOOTNOTES

1   *The Diamond Sutra and the Sutra of Hui Neng* (Berkeley: Shambhala, 1969).

2   A number of English-language translations of the Yuan text are available. Wong Mou-lam's 1930 translation has been referred to above. More recent translations include those of Lu K'uan Yu (Charles Luk) in *Ch'an and Zen Teaching, Series Three* (Berkeley: Shambhala, 1973); Paul F. Fung and George D. Fung, *The Sutra of the Sixth Patriarch on the Pristine Orthodox Dharma* (San Francisco: Buddha's Universal Church, 1964); Heng Yin, *The Sixth Patriarch's Dharma Jewel Platform Sutra and Commentary* by Tripitaka Master Hsuan Hua (San Francisco: Sino American Buddhist Association, 1971); and John R. McRae, *The Platform Sutra of the Sixth Patriarch* (Berkeley: Numata Center, BDk English Tripitaka 73-II, 2000). *Readings of the Platform Sutra* Edited by Morten Schlutter and Steven Teiser, (Columbia University Press 2012)

3   The Tun-huang text has been translated by Wing-tsit Ch'an in *The Platform Scripture* (New York: St. Johns University Press, 1961), and Philip B. Yampolsky in The *Platform Sutra of the Sixth Patriarch* (New York: Columbia University Press, 1967).

4   See Case 3, "Gutei Raises a Finger," in *Zen Comments on the Mumonkan* by Zenkei Shibayama, translated by Sumiko Kudo (Harper & Row: New York, 1974).

5   Sokei-an is alluding to a famous story about the medieval Zen master Daitô Kokushi (1282-1337), founder of the great Kyoto temple Datiokuji.

6   Sokei-an is referring to *Nonsense*, a newspaper column he penned in Japanese in the 1930s for the Seattle *Daihoku-Nippo (Great Northern Daily News)*.

7   In concluding the formal koan interview (*sanzen*) between master and student, the Rinzai Zen master rings a small hand bell.

8   The twelve divisions of the canon are: 1) sermons; 2) scriptures—metrical pieces; 3) prophecies; 4) *gathas*; 5) impromptu or unsolicited addresses; 6) narratives; 7) stories of the Buddha's past lives; 8) expanded sutras; 9) miracles; 10) discourses by question and answer; 11) parables and metaphors; 12) dogmatic treatises.

9   Sokei-an's translation of the Chinese term *wu-nien* (*J. mu-nen*), "no-thought," is inconsistent. In this chapter he uses the Sanskrit word *asmrti*; in Chapter IV he uses "mindlessness." For the sake of consistency, "no-thought" will generally be used throughout the translation following Yampolsky in *The Platform Sutra*.

10 I.e., the precepts, or ten commandments. See glossary.

11 The Chinese character translated here by Sokei-an as "to enlighten" (C. *chih*, J. *to*) is translated by him elsewhere in this chapter as "to convert." In the Buddhist context, it has the meaning of "to save," "to convert," and, by extension, "to bring to enlightenment." Similarly, the character translated as "vow" is translated by Sokei-an elsewhere as "prayer."

12 This passage can also be translated: "Do not think of what is past, for it is over and cannot be grasped. Always think of what lies ahead. From one moment of thought to the next, your mind will be perfectly clear, and you will see your original nature."

13 In Sokei-an's original translation, the character rendered here as "initiate" also appears as "discover." For the sake of smoothness, we have retained the various translations.

14 Usually translated as: "To recite without any intention is correct / To do so with intention is false."

15 The allegory appears in Chapter III of the *Lotus Sutra*. The parable concerns a father and his children trapped in a burning house. Though the father is aware of the flames, his children are not. To persuade them to leave the

burning house, the father promises them goat, deer, and ox carts (vehicles—Sanskrit, *yanas*). Upon their exit, instead of the carts promised by their father, before them were carts drawn by great White Oxen.

[16] Sokei-an did not complete his commentary on this passage.

[17] Sir Arthur S. Eddington (1882-1944) was an English astronomer.

[18] The Chinese character *lo* (J. *raku*) indicates "bliss" or "joy." Sokei-an has translated it "peace."

[19] Presumably the monk is referring to the sutras and commentaries.

[20] Byname of Ruth Dennis (1877-1968), an American dancer and teacher of modern dance.

[21] Broadway crosses at Fifth Avenue.

[22] Sokei-an is referring to Ryomo Kyokai, where he studied Zen. Ryomo Kyokai is a laymen's society for Zen practice originally founded by the Rinzai Zen Master Kosen Imakita (1816-1892) in Tokyo in the 19th century. Sokei-an studied at the society under Sokatsu Shaku (1870-1954), heir and adopted son of Soyen Shaku (1859-1919), Kosen's student, and the first Rinzai Zen master to travel to the West. According to Sokei-an, the term "Ryomo" refers to the abandonment of the concepts of both subjectivity and objectivity. "Kyokai" means "religious society" or "church."

[23] These lines are usually translated as: "If you had not conferred this teaching upon me / I could not have had this attainment."

[24] Presumably, this was a Korean robe of high quality silk.

[25] Meher Baba (1894-1969) was an Indian spiritual master who declared himself avartar of this age. In 1925, he began to communicate by pointing to letters on an alphabet board. Later, he communicated through gestures.

Made in the USA
Monee, IL
21 December 2022

23168027R10247